PARADISE

OF THE

CHRISTIAN SOUL,

ENRICHED WITH

Choicest Delights of Varied Piety.

BY

J. M. HORST.

ADAPTED TO THE USE OF THE ENGLISH CHURCH.

Fifth Thousand.

SOLD BY JAMES PARKER & CO., OXFORD,
AND 377, STRAND, LONDON;
RIVINGTONS, WATERLOO PLACE, LONDON,
HIGH STREET, OXFORD, AND TRINITY STREET, CAMBRIDGE.
MDCCCLXIX.

ADVERTISEMENT

TO THE

PARADISE FOR THE CHRISTIAN SOUL.

BY THE EDITOR.

THREE eventful years have now passed by, since the Editor began adapting this little series of devotional works. He had a twofold object in it: first, to supply with the sort of food their souls desired, a class of minds who could not but be the objects of the deeper sympathy, because, from the circumstances of our times, they often know not where to find it; and secondly, to supply it to them in such form as he conceived the Church of England, in which GOD had vouchsafed to call him to minister to souls, would give it to them. In a word, he wished both to supply wants which he knew to exist, and to save persons from the temptation of seeking out of the Church where GOD had placed them, what might be supplied to them within her. And he hoped that the very fact of "adapting" these books "to the use of the English Church," would carry with it its own evidence that he did not wish to recommend to her children any thing but what, according to the best of his judgment, was in accordance with her principles. His standard in so doing was not his own, but that which the Homilies of the Church of England so often inculcate, and her great Divines have followed, what "was believed and taught by the old holy fathers and most ancient learned doctors, and received by the old Primitive Church, which was most uncorrupt and pure [a]." This the Church of England, who so often appeals to it in connexion with the Word of GOD, certainly did not believe to be any vague or uncertain rule. Nor, spurious passages apart, is it. Here, after the Word of God, and as its soundest expositors, has been, for these many years, his chief delight and study. Directed to Christian Antiquity by the Church in which he was admitted to minister, in her was his soul fed as in a large pasture, in her was at rest. To her, as having the pure tradition of Apostolic teaching, and, in her consentient witness, Apostolic authority, he yielded his full faith. In her he was as in his home. Her's was to him his native language. In her he sought all he wished to know, and in her found it. Her thoughts, her exposition of Holy Scripture, her faith, are his. Nothing jarred there. What she said, he wished in his measure to say; what she rejected, he rejected; where she was doubtful, he was content to be doubtful with her; what she knew not as part of the faith, he could not receive as his; where she was silent, he had no wish to pry. And when these troubled times came, in her, in another way, was his rest. Taught, himself, by the

[a] Homilies, B. ii. Serm, ii. 1, init.

Church of England, and by her directed to Christian Antiquity, and finding in her what he had been taught, (only, it is no disparagement to say, more deeply than has been common among us,) he could not think that they whom the Church acknowledged as fathers, would disown as children, those who so revered them. However, for our common sins, the Church may now be distracted, he felt that there was a real oneness of faith and Christian principle between us and those of old, as with those of other Churches now also, in all things which have been matters of faith from the first. "The hearts of the children were turned to the fathers," why not "the hearts of the fathers to the children?" Why should we think that they whom we own as "fathers," would not, if now in the flesh, and, if possible, more in their abode of love, own us as children?

Neither then did it seem any presumptuous task, as a *private* minister, to "adapt," to the use of the children of the English Church, *private* books of edification, on the same principles, and in the same way, as the Church of England had the *public* offices. Towards the English Church it did not seem undutiful to think that she was not so independent of all GOD's gifts in all other portions of the Church, that nothing might be thence transferred with advantage to her. Members of her evidently thought otherwise, since they borrowed for her, and are largely borrowing for her, from much more questionable sources, where the Sacraments are denied, and rationalism more or less gleams through.

Again, some writers as Pascal, Nicole, S. Francis de Sales, S. Charles Borromeo, a Kempis,) not to speak of

Fénélon, Massillon, and others,) have been as household names among us. The "Imitation" has been studied by devout minds, unconscious that they were not studying the produce of our own Communion.

Yet neither did it seem wrong to the Editor, to "adapt," according to a definite rule, books which had more of modern doctrine in them. For as to the authors themselves, surely we must think that in Paradise they must be glad that their writings, under any condition, short of denial of the truth, should do good to souls for whom, with them, CHRIST died. They know not, in their rest and love there, the distractions and hard judgments in the Church here below. Nor, if they here lived in a system, partly unsanctioned by Holy Scripture, and by the Primitive Church, need we think that, holy as they were, the Sight of GOD has not purged away some errors which clave to them here. Nor, need it, surely, seem either presumptuous or arbitrary, to attempt to separate, by a definite standard, that which is ancient from that which is modern; and since in all portions of the Church, (with the exception of some few great minds, as St. Bernard,) most has been learned from our common "fathers," to retain what S. Augustine, S. Chrysostom, or S. Ambrose say or what has the sanction of the whole undivided Church, and to omit what belongs to a more recent teaching.

This "definite standard" was, to the Editor, Catholic Antiquity, regard being also had to the tone of mind of the Church in which, by the mercy of GOD, he has been admitted to minister. Thus, on the doctrines of post-baptismal sin, of "works worthy of repentance," on the

Eucharistic Sacrifice, and the Real Presence, he was and is entirely persuaded that the Church of England holds all which the Ancient Church held, and so he felt that he was fully borne out, and could not do otherwise than retain any language virtually the same as that which the Ancient Fathers had used. On the other hand, he cannot but think that among the modern devotional writers of the Church of Rome, there is often language on this last great mystery, implying (to speak reverently) a local confinement and humiliation of Him Who vouchsafes to feed us with Himself, which the " fathers" would not, certainly do not, use; and this he has omitted. Again, "prayers for the departed" were retained in our first liturgy, omitted under foreign pressure, sanctioned, even while withdrawn from our public offices, and there have ever been pious and loving minds among both our Bishops and Doctors, who have openly cherished and maintained this form of Communion of Saints. Received as these prayers have been, throughout the whole Church, from the very first, and probably contained in Holy Scripture itself, (2 Tim. i. 18.) the Editor could not but retain them wherever they occured. On the other hand, He has, in every case, omitted all mention of the Invocation of Saints. For, however it may be explained by Roman Catholic controversialists, to be no more than asking the prayers of members of Christ yet in the flesh, still, in use, it is plainly more; for no one would ask those in the flesh to "protect us from the enemy," "receive us in the hour of death," " lead us to the joy of heaven," " may thy [the Blessed Virgin] abundant love cover the multitude of sins," " heal my wounds and to the mind which asketh thee, give the gifts of graces[b]," or use any of the *direct* prayers for graces which GOD Alone can bestow, which are common in Roman Catholic devotions to the Blessed Virgin. No one can look uncontroversially at such occasional addresses, as there are to martyrs in the fourth century, (and those chiefly prayers at their tombs through their intercession for miraculous aid of GOD,) and such books as " the glories of Mary," " the Month of Mary," and say that the character of the modern reliance on and invocation of Saints was that of the ancient Church. No one could (it should be thought) observe how through volumes of S. Augustine or S. Chrysostom, there is no mention of any reliance except on CHRIST Alone ; and how in modern books, S. Mary is held out as " *the* refuge of sinners," as having " the goats committed to her, as CHRIST the sheep," as " the throne of grace," to whom a sinner may have easier access than to CHRIST [c], and seriously say, that the ancient and modern teaching and practice are the same. *We* could preach whole volumes of the sermons of S. Augustine or S. Chrysostom to our people to their edification and without offence : were a Roman

---

[b] Or say, "If I walk through the midst of the shadow of death, I will fear no evil, for she is with me. If war arise against me, in this will I be confident. If my father and mother forsake me, the Mother of my Lord shall take me up."

[c] " CHRIST is not our Advocate only, but a Judge ; and since the Just is scarcely secure, how shall a sinner go to Him, as an Advocate? Therefore GOD has provided us of an advocatress, who is gentle and sweet, in whom nothing that is sharp is to be found."—Antonin. quoted by Taylor, Dissuasive, l. ii. 8.

ADVERTISEMENT.

Catholic preacher to confine himself to their preaching, he would (it has been said among themselves) be regarded as "indevout towards S. Mary," as " one whose religion was more of the head than of the heart." The Editor, then, has not ventured even upon the outskirts of so vast a system, which, even according to Roman Catholic testimony which he has had, does practically occasion many uninstructed minds to stop short in the mediation of S. Mary. When Holy Scripture is not even alleged, (as no text for the invocation of saints either is or can be quoted by Roman Catholic controversialists,) and primitive antiquity is equally silent, (now that passages as to S. Mary once attributed to S. Athanasius, S. Augustine, S. Ephrem, S. Chrysostom, under the shadow of whose great names this system grew up, are acknowledged to be spurious,) and the language of great fathers (as S. Cyril of Alexandria) has to be explained away; there was no authority to which the Editor dared to yield his faith. Taught by the Church to receive that and that alone, as matter of faith, which was part of the "good deposit," "once for all committed to the Saints," and which had been held "always, everywhere, and by all,". he did not venture to receive what was confessedly of a more recent origin, and whose tendency seemed at variance with Holy Scripture itself. While acknowledging the "authority of the Church in controversies of faith," (Art. XX.) he could not understand on what ground that vast system, as to S. Mary, could be rested, except that of a new revelation. "Developement" must surely apply to the expression, not to the substance of belief. It must be the bringing out in words of what was always inwardly held; the securing of the old, not the addition of any thing new. However the language of the Church, on the doctrine of the Holy Trinity, may have, in time, become more fixed and definite, any one would think it an impiety to imagine that S. John and S. Peter had not received, and did not deliver, all which has ever since been believed. He " who lay on Jesus' Breast," and he on whose confession of faith the Church was built, could not be ignorant of any thing belonging to that faith[d]. Neither can it be believed that they withheld any thing belonging to that faith[e]. To imagine either, was, of old, accounted to be "subjecting[f] CHRIST to reproach." Yet it seems inconceivable that S. Peter, S. John, and S. Paul should have believed what is now earnestly taught and believed upon authority *within* the Roman Church, as to the *present* Office of the Blessed Virgin, or that believing it, they could have written as (e. g.) S. Paul wrote through the HOLY GHOST, in the Epistle to the Hebrews; or that, if Almighty GOD had willed it to be believed in the Church, it should have been so excluded from Holy Scripture, and the doctrine itself not have appeared for centuries. The Editor, then, in a former work, while excluding invocations, admitted what is involved in the word θεοτόκος, as sanctioned by an Œcumenical Council, to whose authority the

[d] "For after that our Lord arose from the dead, and they were endued with the power of the Holy Spirit coming upon them from on high, they were fully filled as to all things, and had perfect knowledge." "It is unlawful to say that they preached before they had perfect knowledge." S. Iren. iii. 1. 1. "According to these," [the heretics] "Peter was imperfect; imperfect also the other Apostles. And were they to live again, they must needs become the disciples of these, that they too may become perfect. But this were absurd." Ib. 12. 7. See also in the same book, 11. ult.

[e] Ib. iii. 3. 5.   [f] Tert. de Præscr. Hær. c. 22.

English Church yields unquestioning submission. In the present, he has omitted the whole second section "Of the Worship and Veneration of Saints," and half of the seventh "On the Worship and Veneration of the Blessed Virgin Mary." And, generally, for members of the English Church, who desire the prayers of the departed, it has to him ever seemed safest to pray for them to Him, "of Whom and through Whom and to Whom are all things," our GOD and our All, Who, according to the current Roman explanation also, reveals to them the desire of those below to have their prayers.

Such instances may, perhaps, suffice to assure any who may be anxious as to such an one as the Editor, that he has had no thought of supplying, by instalments, as it were, a teaching beyond that of the Church, in which he has, by the undeserved goodness of Almighty GOD, been admitted to minister. Nor did he even wish to introduce, by his private act, whatever might, here and there, be found in Christian Antiquity, in the ages which the English Church had adopted as her pattern and guide. What were matters of faith then, can alone be matters of faith now; what were "pious opinions" then, have surely not ceased to be such now. One object alone he had before him, to furnish to minds who were yearning after deeper devotions, practical guidance, a more spiritual and inward life, aids in passing holy seasons aright, knowledge of themselves, modes of meditating on the Mysteries of the Faith and on their Redeemer's love, books which might help them, by the grace of GOD, whereby they might grow to His praise and glory, in the courts of the house of their GOD, where He had planted them. All the errors in this, as in all besides, may He forgive, Whom herein I wished to serve, expecting the dispraise of man, and seeking only the good of those for whom He shed His Blood!

And now, dear Reader, who wishest not for controversy, but for devotion, what I have written is for others, not for thee; to plead with others for what I have done for thee, not to excuse myself with thee. Here, if thou enterest, thou wilt soon forget all thy disquiets, and "the burden and heat," as "in the cool of the day," thou hearest "the Voice of the LORD GOD walking in the garden." Thou hast here a Paradise, wherein many Christian Souls have walked with great delight, and found rest, communing with their GOD. There are many voices in it, as doubtless in Paradise, there was a sweet harmony of birds soaring towards heaven, and chaunting their Maker's praise; divers flowers also as well as fruit-trees, each having its own savour and fragrance and beauty, adapted to different tastes, or to the same at different times, each supplying somewhat of its own, and all by their variety answering the manifold wants and capacities of man. Do not then despise, what thou findest good for thee, because thou mayest find near it what thou hast not yet learnt to value. Nor again, force thyself to take what is not fitted for thee, or rather, for which thou art not yet fitted; but use thankfully and devoutly what He Who Alone can teach to pray, teacheth thee. Use not what is too high for thee, such as thou now art, nor what, because new, may seem strange to thee. Take that, whereto He draws thee; use it not as something beautiful, "pleasant to the eyes, and a tree to be desired to make thee wise;' but as fruit from the tree of life, for thy refreshment and growth, and its leaves for thy healing; and as thou usest it devotionally to Him, He will instruct thee how thou mayest best become and do what He would have thee.

Glad has been the task to transplant for thee within the Church where GOD has put thee, fruits which, through His blessing and grace, have nourished many souls to life eternal. Glad is it to minister to thy contentment that thou mayest not be tempted to seek elsewhere what GOD giveth thee within her bosom, through whom He hath nourished thee, and sustained thee all thy life long hitherto. Gladder yet will it be, if thou grow thereby, to the praise and glory of His Great Name, in humility and love. And when thou hast found good for thy soul, thou wilt remember those who have laboured for thee in the Lord, out of love for Him, and for His sake, that He may be their Portion, as thine.

E. B. P.

Feast of St. Peter, 1847.

TO

. THE DEVOUT READER.

THOU hast here, dear Reader, the Paradise dressed up afresh with no less care and toil, than it was originally laid out. For as industrious gardeners are wont to be diligent in continually collecting new and rare flowers, plants, and herbs, and to remove the older when they have procured more beautiful, so hath it happened unto me. For although the former edition was received with a more kindly and indulgent favour than I hoped, I felt there was room left for second, *i. e.* better thoughts, so that I may venture to assure you, that what thou now seest is almost another and a new Paradise. But is it therefore altogether grateful and suited to all tastes? I fear not; for what single thing was ever agreeable to every person? Perhaps, they who have little or no relish for Scripture and spiritual matters, will take no delight even in the Paradise. Perhaps also its prolixity in some parts may prove a weariness.

Well; let such have their short offices, their common

little prayers, and the rites suited to their devotion. Let them use and enjoy them. Meanwhile let them allow the Paradise to those less occupied or more experienced. Some have need of milk; whilst others are more happily nourished by strong meat. I hope, however, that each will find something to refresh himself withal; only let them not bring to it a fastidious taste.

Finally, dear Reader, make such use of this, as that with its produce thou mayest strew thy path to the Paradise above; and if thou deem it worthy, offer up a prayer for the Author, even if it be but by a single aspiration to GOD.

TO THE CHRISTIAN READER.

OF THE SCOPE, PLAN, AND ORDER OF THE PARADISE.

THE present age, fertile as it is in writers, has brought forth a variety of books serviceable to Christian piety. Some furnish lessons and monitions on the spiritual life. Some suggest holy meditations and subjects for devout affections. Others again contain prayers, offices, litanies, and regularly arranged exercises of devotion. One can scarcely complain of any lack whence to draw devotion, rather, we are all-but-overwhelmed by their number and variety.

It seemed to me, therefore, no unprofitable labour to survey the gardens and plantations of other men, to cull thence plants, flowers, and shrubs of the better sorts, to lay out a new Paradise of delight, or rather of devotion; and thus to comprise in one small volume, suitable for daily use, the juice and sap of all those whose object was the cultivation of piety. This is my design and intention, which you will better understand from the plan of the book, which I now subjoin.

I. Since prayer is the longing after some good, and man has to act for an end, what, we may ask, is the end set before him that prayeth? It is GOD; the Supreme End, the Chief Good of man. Therefore, at the outset and in the first section, as is meet, the Most Holy TRINITY, the Triune GOD, is proposed as the Object of worship, in the clear vision and fruition of Whom consists the end of man. *For* GOD *Himself is the Reward of His Own service.*

III. But he that would *fear the* LORD must *depart from evil;* and we shall not depart from evil, unless from our sins we return to our senses, as it were, and exercise true repentance; and putting off the old man (with his deeds) we put on the new man; hence, therefore, the subject [here] next treated of [Part III.], is Repentance and Confession of Sins.

IV. It is not enough, however, to *depart from evil,* unless we also *learn to do well,* and pay equal regard to the practice of Christian holiness. Hence the succeeding section [IV.] will treat of a Spiritual and Religious Life, and of the virtues and means adapted to it.

V. Further, this life, that it become not weak and faint, but may be strengthened and increase more and more, needeth nourishment. And what is its food? *Bread, which strengtheneth man's heart;* even that Bread *which cometh down from heaven, and giveth life unto the world; for the Flesh of Christ is meat indeed, and His Blood is drink indeed.* This is it that repaireth and braceth the powers of the soul, that it faint not by the way. In the next Section [v.], therefore, we treat of Holy Communion and the Eucharistic Sacrifice.

VI. But since the life of man is continually exposed to many temptations and miseries, there is no more powerful inducement to endure with fortitude any labours and hardships of the present life, no greater consolation in adversity than the Example, Life, Death, and Passion of our SAVIOUR: for *as* CHRIST *hath suffered for us in the Flesh, let us arm ourselves with the same mind;* relying on this hope, *that if we suffer with Him, we shall also reign with Him.* Hence the next Section [vi.] treats of meditation upon, and imitation of, the Life and Passion of CHRIST.

VII. While we live, giving ourselves to these exercises and holy studies, we are also hastening to the goal of life. And this we shall do the more safely, if we live ever in thought of death. So, as GOD rested the seventh day from all His work that He had made, shall man also at length rest happily from all his labours, and obtain the everlasting fruition of GOD, Who is Himself the Reward of His labourers.

In this way, and by this method, I have, as it seems to me, embraced all the subjects which can be desired for the use and exercise of Christian devotion. This has been my single aim, to collect together in one small and convenient volume, the marrow and substance of all piety, with reference both to doctrine and practice; and by this labour to render a service to all, both laymen and ecclesiastics.

I would that the meditations or exercises placed at the beginning of each Section, should be read and weighed with deep attention; for in these I have given the principal instructions for a spiritual life, mostly in the words and sentences of Sacred Scripture. And I have thrown them into the form of a conference or colloquy between CHRIST and man: having found by experience, that the mind of man is the more strongly and vehemently stirred to action, the greater the authority of the teacher and adviser. Thus do words pierce the heart; being uttered not so much by man as by GOD.

"For the Word of GOD is quick, and powerful, and sharper than any two-edged sword, piercing even to the dividing asunder of soul and spirit, and of the joints and marrow, and is a discerner of the thoughts and intents of the heart." (Heb. iv. 12.)

INTRODUCTION

TO THE

PARADISE.

The Paradise which thou seest, kind Reader, is open to every one; yet I would not that any one should enter it rashly. I desire, therefore, to offer a few words of warning, at the entrance.

It is a very common error to think that devotion is to be found in books; whereas it is rather to be sought in the soul. Many think themselves devout, or are so esteemed, if, according to a certain fixed rule, they daily repeat many long prayers out of pious books, as a sort of daily task.

Be it, that this has a certain appearance of piety; and I would not utterly condemn the practice; but if such persons, meanwhile, neither alter and amend their ways, nor take any account of inward piety or solid virtue, but cling to and rest in these their forms, must not such devotion be deservedly suspected? It plainly wants that root and sap on which the whole vigour of true piety depends.

For it is a very chief praise of diligent prayer that it advances and guards holiness of life. *He hath learnt to live well*, saith S. Augustine, *who hath learnt to pray well.* Even so. Good living and good praying aid each other; neither can one exist without the other. A good life sets forth devotion; devotion preserves and promotes a good life.

Askest thou, who then may be esteemed devout? He, who with ready mind is drawn towards divine things, to prayer and offices of devotion, but who also strives to lead a life worthy of the worship of GOD. Wouldest thou then, Christian friend, be or become devout? This is wrought, not by words, how pious and holy soever, but by deeds. While, therefore, thou readest pious, holy, and devout prayers, join therewith a corresponding feeling of piety; and earnestly endeavour to work out in thyself those holy affections. Any, even an ungodly man, can readily read things devout; but to read devoutly, (to take care, that is, that the life correspond with holy words,) this belongs to the devout alone. Briefly, whatsoever thou utterest with thy lips, see thou feel it in thine heart; lest it be said to thee also, *This people honour Me with their lips, but their heart is far from Me;* or again, *Why dost thou preach My law, and takest My covenant in thy mouth, &c.?*

What is prayer but the lifting up of the mind to GOD? But how shall the mind be in the sky, if the life be in the sty?

Further, prayer is usually divided into *mental* and *vocal;* but take you heed thou understand not this as though *vocal* prayer consisted only in the use of the voice and lips; for in it, too, thought is required, if not in deliberate exercise, in habit, at least, and virtually.

For what is prayer without thought, but chaff without the grain; the bark without pith; a lamp without oil; blossoms without fruit; body without soul? Utterly deluded are they who think that GOD can be moved by fair, well-selected, or even holy words. GOD is a Spirit, and is to be worshipped in spirit.

To what end, then, are words, rites, ceremonies? may some one ask. Surely only to stir up the spirit of man. This is the only thing which GOD regards, and by which He is moved. Behold Cain and Abel, brethren. GOD seeth each of them offering; but the spirit of the offerers being different, so in the sight of GOD their offerings and acceptableness; so that He is said to have had respect solely to the sacrifice of Abel.

The threefold regard, in vocal prayer, to GOD, to the words, and to the meaning of the words, is a matter well known; and it is no part of our present design to teach at any length the doctrine of prayer. That demands a separate treatise; what is most essential the devout reader will find in the conference in the first section. But since vocal prayer is spoken of by many too disparagingly, we have thought it not beside our purpose to make a few remarks upon it at the entrance into the Paradise.

Vocal prayer, then, is of two kinds, *public* and *private*: to the former, the Psalmody of the Church, or the Canonical Hours, belong; to the latter, those voluntary prayers which any one either forms for himself, or adopts when composed by others. Of the last we are now treating; and that it may be well and profitably performed, we will presently lay down some rules needful for this; but at the same time not less suitable to the former.

There are two ways, superior to all others, in which vocal prayer may be practised.

I. When he that prayeth, attentively and accurately repeats every word he reads, so as also to understand it; but he goes on without stopping, so that the mind never dwells or ruminates upon what it reads.

This indeed is the common mode of praying; but in this way the mind of the worshipper is scarcely fed by any pious affection; for if a word or sentence should haply suggest any devout feeling or affection, this in the passing on to other parts, instantly slips away, and is lost.

Wherefore this method is like the rain or shower, falling in large quantity and with violence, which only washes the surface of the ground, without sinking into or moistening it. For before it can be drunk in, it flows off. In like manner, I say, that hasty vocal prayer affects him that useth it only sensuously; but it imbues the mind with no solid affection; the foot, as it were, being planted no where, but perpetually passing on to something else.

II. Vocal prayer is practised, when thou prayest not only with an understanding of the words, but the mind pauses awhile on single expressions, or sentences at least, which convey some definite pious meaning, weighs them, and ruminates upon them; refreshing itself as having found some grateful pasture.

Thus, for instance, in repeating the LORD's Prayer, or the Psalms, one may dwell a little on the words or sentences, and consider what heavenly spiritual honey, what taste of heaven, what consolation or instruction lies stored therein, so as from each to draw forth corresponding affections, as it may be, of faith, hope, love, and the like.

This kind of prayer is like continued rain, descending in small but numberless drops, which thus enters the earth, and sinking down into its inward parts, abundantly moistens and makes it fruitful. For such prayer has a definite end and aim, and leaves behind it definite affections impressed upon the mind, by which it is afterward refreshed, nourished, and watered more plentifully.

This method and practice of prayer we have with sufficient clearness exemplified on the LORD's Prayer, in each Part of the Paradise.

In this way F. Leonardus Lessius, a man of remarkable piety and learning, was wont to pray; as the Author of his Life tells us. [C. 10.] Take as an example, he says, his use of the LORD's Prayer, and thence judge of his other devotions : he did not go through it cursorily, as is the bad practice of many; but he repeated its several clauses twice, thrice, or oftener; nor did he pass on to the following till he had weighed every word of that which went before, and with equal care, had tasted it with devout and heartfelt affection. It is better, he said, to say the LORD's Prayer but once only, thus repeating and fully tasting its clauses, than to go through it cursorily a hundred times with slight attention.

But on this point we would offer a few

HINTS,

VERY USEFUL TO BE OBSERVED IN EVERY KIND OF PRAYER.

I. The mind must be prepared. *Before thou prayest, prepare thy soul, and be not as one that tempteth the* LORD.

Think seriously indeed what thou art about to do; for thou wilt be speaking and dealing with GOD, thy Creator, the LORD of heaven and earth; thou wilt offer praises to Him; thou wilt lay before Him thy wants and infirmities; thou wilt ask for His help and blessing. And how attentively, reverently, devoutly, piously, humbly should all this be done in the Presence of His Great Majesty!

II. Begin with an act of Contrition. For GOD *heareth not sinners;* yea, He hateth them as such, or if not penitent for their sins. And how dareth an impenitent criminal thrust himself upon the presence of an offended Judge!

III. Set before thee some good intention; yea, not one, but many; as, to make thy prayer for the glory of GOD alone; for the well-being of thyself and thy neighbour; to long to be endued with this or that virtue, or to be delivered from this or that vice, &c.

IV. Ask for grace to pray devoutly, attentively, and with profit. And meanwhile do thou resolve firmly with thyself, thou wilt not knowingly give way to any thoughts foreign to prayer, however importunately, or with whatever specious pretence of advantage they may present themselves; and, therefore, set a diligent guard over thy senses, especially thine eyes and ears. How easily doth there enter through these portals, what disturbs tranquillity of mind! Select some place best adapted to devotion, and least liable to distraction. Let the posture of the body be such as may serve to devotion.

V. During the course of thy prayer, frequently recollect your thoughts. Often renew thy remembrance of the Divine Presence. Prayer (that is, vocal prayer, especially if framed by another,) must be now and then sprinkled and seasoned, as it were, by some address of the mind's own, so that it too of itself should speak to GOD, and treat with GOD by itself, as it were, without the aid of another. And this is done by calling forth certain feelings corresponding with the words and sentences read, as of faith, hope, charity, contrition, gratitude, humility, and the like.

VI. Finally, remember to rise up from prayer reverently. Admitted by a Prince to confer with him on thine own affairs, if, forthwith, when thou hadst laid it before him, thou wert to turn thy back upon him and go away, without showing any sign of respect or gratitude, how rude and clownish were it!

Therefore ponder awhile the issue of thy prayer. Grieve for thy defects therein, and ask pardon; humbly offer and commend thy worship to God, imperfect though it be, that He may accept it through the merits of His SON JESUS CHRIST; and *that* according to the intention or object at first proposed. All this may be done briefly and readily. We will supply some forms below.

This is the way rightly and profitably to pray, or to

use the forms of prayer given in the Paradise or elsewhere; which if thou follow not, good reader, I too, freely confess that vocal prayer will be dry, void of all life, of spiritual taste and fruit; it will come to pass, as the prophet complaineth, that *ye may eat, and not have enough; ye may drink, and not be filled with drink; ye may sow much, and bring in little,* &c.

Prayers repeated from books have this disadvantage, (I deny it not, but what marvel when there lacketh that diligence in prayer whereof we have spoken?) that they often do not correspond with the special feelings or wants of the person who repeats them. Thus, the words may express compunction, the love of GOD and our neighbour, zeal for the Divine Law, detestation of covetousness, and the like, (as when one says, for example, LORD, *I am not high-minded, I have no proud looks,* or again, LORD, *what love have I unto Thy law; all the day long is my study in it. For I love Thy commandments above gold and precious stones,* &c. *Incline my heart unto Thy testimonies, and not to covetousness.*) But it may be that repeating this, he feels nothing of it in his own mind, nay, is conscious of affections opposed to those virtues, and never turns back into himself, so as even once to think of uprooting them. Therefore his prayer returneth not into his own bosom. For loading himself rapidly with food unchewed, and already, as it were, partially eaten by others, and prepared for the palate and taste of another, he is deprived of its pleasant savour, nor does he well convert it into his own blood and nourishment.

Now, what remedy is there, but with the inmost feelings of the mind to utter the pious thoughts expressed in books of prayer, as coming from himself, and in the act of reading to adapt his feelings to them ; and when he discovers in himself any workings of his rebellious nature opposed to them, to abjure them in the sight of GOD, and to endeavour, by the help of His grace, to overcome and correct them?

The prayer most safely to be relied on in this kind of devotion [vocal], is the LORD's Prayer; which, being suited to every sort and condition of men, and to the circumstances and wants of all, suggests to each appropriate and needful matter for prayer. Thou wilt not, therefore, be surprised, devout reader, to find in this new Paradise so many and such varied exercises upon the LORD's Prayer, throughout its various sections. Rather, with me, marvel that one so brief prayer should be so pregnant with devout meaning, and should supply such varied and manifold exercises of devotion.

Yet what marvel, since the Great Master Himself of all petitions in the Supreme Court, hath arranged and prepared it for us. The reader may seek its eulogies, many and beautiful are they, in the writings of S. Cyprian, S. Augustine, and others. We cannot insert them in our narrow limits.

We have moreover given several, and, indeed, new Litanies ; but let not their novelty offend any ; they consist merely of the words and sentences of Scripture. And mostly they set forth the attributes, perfections, offices, benefits, praises, and blessings, both of the Divine Nature and of the several Persons of the Most Holy Trinity ; and in fact, what are they but devout aspirations, such as any one may form from the words of Scripture taken in a sound sense?

In these, and the rest, the devout reader will, if I mistake not, find abundant matter for pious affections and holy meditations. If, perchance, prolixity in some parts should produce weariness in any, let him strive to overcome it or sweeten it with the love of GOD; if he cannot, there is no reason why the longer portions should not be divided. On the whole, as in a costly banquet, so in this Paradise, various viands are set before the guests; so that every one may select that which is most agreeable to his taste. For here too, "better is much than many words." But we will close our Introduction with the words of S. Augustine. "To be long in prayer," saith he, "is not, as some suppose, to pray with much speaking. Abundance of words is one thing, prolonged affection another. For it is written even of our LORD Himself, that He passed the whole night in prayer, and that He prayed at great length; in which, what else did He than afford us an example of praying in due season? 'In tempore Precator opportunus, cum Patre Exauditor æternus.' In time He prayed in due season, being with the FATHER, Prayer's Everlasting Hearer. Be prayer without much speaking; yet not without much praying, if we persist in fervent intention. For to speak much in prayer is to carry on an urgent business with superfluous words. But to pray much is to 'knock' unto Him to Whom we pray, with lasting and devout energy of heart. For this business is for the most part carried on with groans rather than with set speeches, with weeping rather than with words." Ep. 130. ad Probam. c. 10.

A PREPARATORY PRAYER,

WHICH MAY BE PROFITABLY USED BEFORE ANY OTHER PRAYER.

Almighty everlasting GOD, I, unworthy sinner, yet the work of Thine Own Hands, come before Thee, to praise Thee, because Thou art my GOD, LORD, Creator, Saviour, and Preserver! Who, Alone, I know, canst bestow on me and mine, gifts profitable unto salvation, for Thou art All-Mighty, and, I doubt not, that Thou willest, for Thou art All-Good. Whom all creatures in Heaven and in earth ought to praise, and never suffice to praise duly.

But, alas! how unworthy and unprepared, for my numberless sins, do I miserable approach to pray to Thee! I grieve from my inmost heart that ever I offended Thee, my GOD, Thou Chief Good, Whom I ought to have praised and loved above all things.

But make Thou me worthy through Thy Mercy, and by the Precious Blood of JESUS CHRIST Thy Son, my Saviour, cleanse me from all mine iniquities. Yea, free my heart from all vain, hurtful thoughts which are not of Thee, that in spirit and in truth I may adore and praise Thee, and obtain what I, Thy humble servant, would ask of Thy boundless Goodness; and that, according to the good pleasure of Thy most merciful Will, to which in all things I willingly submit myself. But how shall an unprofitable servant find favour in Thy Sight? Look, O FATHER, upon the Face of Thy CHRIST, in Whom Thou wert well-pleased, in Whose Name I humbly ask Thee, of Thy clemency to hear me.

Lo! His most ardent prayers, pious affections, and holy desires, His All-holy thoughts, words, and works, all the merits of His Life, Passion, and Death, I offer to Thee, that out of their perfection, and by union with them, all my defects may be supplied, and through Him, as our Mediator and Advocate, this my duty and service may be pleasing unto Thee, O FATHER Eternal.

And that, to the end that Thou wouldest take from me, whatever in me is displeasing unto Thee, especially — and —. Thine Eyes see what is imperfect in me, O Searcher of hearts. In Thy loving-kindness, bestow on me grace also, and the virtues most necessary for me, that in my vocation I may more worthily serve Thee, as — and —. Let all be to the greater glory of Thy Name, the salvation of myself and those nearest to me, particularly those to whom I am especially bound.

This one thing, O LORD, my soul vehemently desireth: namely, to serve, please, and cleave to Thee, now and for ever. For Thou art my God and mine All. Amen.

PRAYER BEFORE THE HOURS.

Open, O LORD, my mouth, to bless Thy Holy Name; for I desire with earnest attention and faithfulness to sing psalms unto Thee, and purely praise Thee, in union with that most perfect attention wherewith Thou didst beseech and praise the FATHER on earth, and especially wherewith, with the ardour of Thine Heart, and in the Bloody Sweat of Thy Brow, Thou didst pray at the Mount of Olivet.

Assist me with Thy grace, without which I can do nothing, and let the might of Thy boundless love supply every defect in me, that this my duty and service may please Thee, which I offer to the glory of Thy Name, my own and my neighbour's salvation. Amen.

Another.

Prevent, O LORD, we beseech Thee, our doings by Thy Holy Inspiration, and further them by Thy continual help, that our every prayer and work may ever begin with Thee, and being begun, may through Thee be ended. Through our LORD.

Another.

O GOD, to Whom every heart is open, and every desire speaketh, and from Whom no secret is hid, cleanse the thoughts of our heart by the inpouring of the Holy Spirit, that we may perfectly love and worthily praise Thee. Through.

A PRAYER

CLOSING THE OFFICE OR PRAYER.

Let my prayer go up as incense in Thy Sight, O King of kings, All-Good, All-Mighty, and most All-Wise. Let Thy fatherly clemency, I beseech Thee, pardon its defects and errors, and receive it in union with all the prayers of Thy Beloved SON JESUS CHRIST, and of Thine Elect in Heaven and in earth, with all love of the Church triumphant and militant. To the memory of the Passion of JESUS CHRIST my Saviour; in thanksgiving for all Thy benefits; to the salvation of all who have commended themselves to me; in satisfaction for my sins, and to obtain Thy grace, and this virtue —; and grant that I may bless Thee at all times; and as Thy praise is ever in my mouth, so also in heart and deed, I may praise Thee, that in sobriety, modesty, zeal, devotion, purity, obedience, meekness, and patience, I may please Thee: that all may love and glorify Thee, Who art blessed for ever. Amen.

Another.

Most Merciful GOD, Who out of Thine Infinite Goodness didst not disdain to admit me a sinner to stand in Thy sight, to praise Thee, pardon me, I pray, all my errors, which either from dryness, negligence, or infirmity of nature, have come upon me in my prayer; let not my prayer become sin unto me, nor mine enemy boast himself against me, that he wounds with those arms wherewith he has to be overthrown.

Look, O LORD, upon my infirmity and my misery, and forgive me all my sins, through Thine Only-Begotten SON, in Whom Thou art well pleased. Let my prayer and my work please Thee, alas! in themselves all too poor. But Thou wilt not despise them, Holy FATHER, if Thou shalt regard the Face of Thy CHRIST; for in Him Thou hast laid up all good things and treasures of graces, that out of His abundance we might be rich.

Stablish this, O GOD, that Thou hast wrought in me; for I have sworn and stedfastly purposed to keep Thy righteous judgments. Make me to love Thy commandments above gold and precious stone; may I be loved by Thee, and love Thee for ever. Amen.

Another.

Accept, most Merciful GOD, through the Merits of Thine Only-Begotten CHRIST JESUS, this my duty and service. Whatsoever has been offered aright, graciously regard; wherein I have been negligent mercifully pardon. Who in the perfect Trinity, livest and reignest, GOD for ever and ever. Amen

PARADISE FOR THE CHRISTIAN SOUL.

PART I.

LITANIES, PRAYERS, THANKSGIVINGS, VARIOUS MEDITA-
TIONS, ILLUSTRATIONS OF THE LORD'S PRAYER, AND
OTHER RELIGIOUS EXERCISES TOWARDS THE
MOST HOLY TRINITY.

The Lord's Day.

CHAPTER I.

COLLOQUY BETWEEN CHRIST AND A CHRISTIAN ON PRAYER.

§ 1. *The necessity and profitableness of prayer.*

CHRIST. Man that is born of woman hath but a short time to live, and is full of miseries; and far more miserable is he, if in the midst of that very misery he knows not that he is miserable, and poor, and naked, and weak; for then he seeks not even the remedies whereby he might be healed, and makes not GOD his helper. If thou, O man, art thus ignorant, come with Me a space apart from men; I will lead thee to solitude and there speak to thy heart, that thou mayest know thy misery and nakedness.

Call to mind then, My son, that it was I Who made thee and not thou thyself; that when as yet thou wast not, I made thee in My Image; that when thou wast lost, it was I Who redeemed thee, not with corruptible things, as silver and gold or precious stones, but with My Own Blood. And wherefore, but that thou shouldest praise My Name and serve Me in this life, and hereafter reign with Me for ever?

Consider now, that perils threaten thee in the way wherein thou walkest, before thou comest to the kingdom. Thou sittest in darkness and the shadow of death, and walkest in the midst of snares. Foes and treachery are on every side, whichsoever way thou turnest, on the right hand and on the left; without are fightings, within are fears. The devil, as a roaring lion, walketh about, seeking whom he may devour. The whole world lieth in wickedness, and enticeth that it may deceive; the flesh, thy bosom enemy, most dangerous of all, flatters to destroy. The creatures, which *should* be stepping-stones up to the CREATOR, become a trap to the feet of the unwise. Thy very senses are so many doors and windows to let death in to thy soul.

MAN. Thy words are true, O LORD, and to my sorrow how often have I felt it! O wretched man that I am, who shall deliver me from the body of this death? Whither turn amid so many dangers? How direct my feet in the way of peace and salvation, that I perish not, but come safe to Thee, my GOD, my End, my Highest Good? I am straitened on every side. Knowing not what to do, what else can I do? I will lift up mine eyes to heaven, from whence cometh my help.

CHRIST. It is this I would have thee know above all, the need of serious and frequent PRAYER. Call upon Me then in the day of trouble, so will I hear thee and thou shalt praise Me. Surely in vain is the net spread in the sight of any bird, i. e., of those who set their nest in heaven, and often wing their thoughts thitherwards from earth. For whoso dwelleth under the defence of the MOST HIGH, shall abide securely under the shadow of the ALMIGHTY. Thinkest thou thyself safe while making flesh thine arm, and leaning unto thine own understanding? Lo, man's thoughts are full of fear, and all your prudence, of uncertainty. Without Me ye can do nothing; I give the will, the power, and the deed.

Whoso without prayer have ventured on arduous deeds or striven to effect the purpose of their hearts, have been brought to nothing and confusion; they have woven spiders' webs, and been like a garden without water, and all their strength has been as the spark of tow. But for the man that gives himself to prayer, he shall be like a tree planted by the water-side, and all that he doeth shall prosper. Search the Scriptures; they testify of the marvels, passing all the power of nature, done in all ages by the virtue of prayer, by invocation of the Name of the LORD, Who only doeth wonderful things.

MAN. Have pity on me, O LORD, for I am poor and needy, like a little child that knoweth not how to go out or come in; that has hands indeed, and feet, but cannot go forth without its mother or its nurse. In vain I labour in the sweat of my brow, if I essay anything great or small without Thee, in Whom we all live, and move, and have our being, and from Whom (since of ourselves we are unable even to think anything as of ourselves) is all our sufficency.

CHRIST. If, therefore, My son, thou lack wisdom or knowledge, ask of Me and it shall be given thee. In Me are hid all the treasures of wisdom and knowledge; they will never be thine, if thou think to gain them by thine own study only and industry, without prayer. Hast thou never heard how many of My servants have frankly ascribed their progress far more to prayer than to all their reading and study? Dost thou desire honours and wealth? The whole world is Mine, and the fulness thereof: Mine is counsel, Mine is prudence, strength is Mine. By Me Kings reign, with Me are riches and glory, wealth and righteousness. I am the LORD Who raise the poor out of the dust. It is a light thing for Me, in the twinkling of an eye, to make the poor man noble, and to set the lowly with the princes of his people. Dost thou long for strength, for health, or length of days? Know that there is nothing upon earth without a cause, neither is it out of the ground that trouble springeth. It is I, Who command the sea, the winds, and all the elements, and straightway they obey Me. It is I Who slay and make alive, Who smite and make whole. In My Hands are all the ends of the earth, yea, all things submit to My Rule:

weal and woe, life and death, all that entereth into the heart of man. In vain dost thou seek these things elsewhere, if first thou seek not Me.

§ 2. *Preparation for Prayer by the affections of humility and penitence, or contrition.*

MAN. Truly every good gift, and every perfect gift is from above, even from Thee, O Most kind FATHER, Who givest to all men liberally, and art so willing and ready to give, that Thou lovest, nay, commandest us to ask of Thee.

My heart is ready, O GOD, my heart is ready, often to hold converse with Thee, and to pour forth my prayer in Thy sight.

But what is man that Thou dost so magnify him, and dost so lovingly invite him to pray, even to hold converse with Thee? Shall I, that am dust and ashes, appear in Thy sight, and speak unto my LORD? Yea, I am worse, an ungrateful and unworthy sinner, who have so often offended and done treason to Thy Majesty. Woe is me! If the just in the beginning of his speech accuseth himself and durst not approach Thee, where shall I, the ungodly and the sinner, appear? What wonder then if my spirit is vexed within me, and my heart within me is desolate, and trouble compasses me around, while I consider at once the necessity of prayer and my own unworthiness? But whither shall I go, then, from Thy Spirit, or whither shall I go, then, from Thy Presence? I am Thy servant, give me understanding, and teach me to do Thy will.

CHRIST. It is I Who invite thee to pray and to speak to me. Come, then, and fear not; yet take heed lest thou come unprepared. Consider Moses, when he is about to hold converse with Me; he is commanded to put off his shoes from off his feet. So do thou likewise. First put off thine actions and affections, which are soiled with the dust of the earth. For many, as though they thought Me, least of all, to be present with them, or least of all honourable or worthy of respect, even so, rashly and irreverently rush to hold converse with Me. Is it thus with the criminal before his judge, with the dependant before his protector, with the servant before his lord, the subject before his king, the beggar before a rich man? Do they thus plead, or is it thus, even, that one man addresses his fellow and his equal? If, then, thou wilt please Me or escape the wrath of My indignation, see that thou more diligently prepare thyself to pray. For cursed is he that doeth the work of the LORD negligently.

Prepare, therefore, thy soul before thou prayest, and be not willingly as a man that tempteth GOD. For so doeth that man, who asks for My gifts without the appointed means, or without rightly using them; who presumeth to expect from Me an answer to a prayer which he began heedlessly, and performed with a sapless soul, without relish, and without affection. These are they who honour Me with their lips, but their hearts are far from Me.

Consider now what is required of thee in this preparation.

First, grieve from thy inmost heart that thou hast so often offended Me by sinning; for praise is not comely in the mouth of a sinner. How shalt thou declare My Righteousness, and take My covenant in thy mouth, thou, who hast hated My discipline, and cast My words behind thee? To whom shall I look more readily and kindly, than to him who is of an humble spirit and contrite heart, and who trembleth at My words? I will do the will of them that fear Me, and will hear their supplication. O! how often have I called thee, and thou refusedst and despisedst all My counsel. What marvel then if I too, at times, hearken to thee more slowly; yea, if I altogether refuse to hear thee? How often hast thou shut thine ears against the cry of the poor; and dost thou wonder if, when thou criest, thy cry is not heard?

MAN. Truly, O LORD, I know, that it is even so, and that in the sight of GOD shall no man living be justified. If I would contend with Thee, I shall not be able to answer Thee one of a thousand. If I would justify myself, my own mouth will condemn me. I have sinned against Heaven and before Thee, and I am no more worthy to lift up my eyes unto Thee. O! if my heart did not reprove me, truly great confidence should I have towards GOD. If I regard iniquity in my heart, the LORD will not hear me. But who can say, "My heart is clean?" I truly am a man of polluted heart and lips; I, even I, have sinned and done evil in thy sight. Who shall make a clean thing out of that which is conceived of unclean seed;—save Thou, O LORD, Who hast washed us in Thine Own Blood? Cleanse Thou then my heart and my lips. Wash me thoroughly from my wickedness, and cleanse me from my sin. From my inmost heart I mourn, for love of Thee, that I have offended Thee, my GOD, my SAVIOUR, my Chief Good. I have sworn, and am steadfastly purposed, through Thy Grace, to keep the judgments of Thy Righteousness, specially in — and —. Despise not, O GOD, a broken and a contrite heart, neither be angry at the prayer of Thy servant.

§ 3. *Preparation for Prayer, as to the direction of our intention to the proper end.*

CHRIST. Thou acknowledgest thy sins, and I willingly know them no more. That which the blind man said, "GOD *heareth not sinners,*" is true, when spoken of the impenitent: as to him who turneth away his ear from hearing My law, even his prayer shall be abomination. Let not thy sins then make thee timorous, but humble. Verily I am well pleased with the sacrifice of a troubled spirit, a broken and a contrite heart.

Consider now diligently, with what end thou comest unto prayer. No one comes to petition his prince without some certain end; do thou also, bearing in mind thy weakness and thy needs, seriously reflect, wherefore thou wouldst hold converse with Me; what thou wouldst seek of Me; wherein thou most needest My help and My grace; what enemy most chiefly thou wouldst assail and smite with the arms of prayer; that is, for the uprooting what vice, or for the obtaining what virtue, thou dost most need heavenly succour. Fix, I say, before thee some certain end, and hither, when thou prayest, direct thy mind and thy desires. I know, indeed; for I know all the secrets of the heart, what thou needest. But I would have thee also know it, that the knowledge of thy own necessities and wants may be unto thee a goad and a spur to greater fervour and earnestness in prayer. If otherwise thou prayest, thou shalt be as one beating the air, and shooting thine arrows at random, with no fixed mark to aim at. Even so do also in all thy other addresses to Me, whether thou wouldst sing praise unto Me, or offer thanksgiving, or in whatever other way thou wouldst come before Me.

MAN. O how sweet are these Thy words unto my lips, O LORD, yea, sweeter than honey unto my mouth, with which Thou dost, with sweet condescension, teach me to pray. But alas! I will confess against myself my foolishness to the LORD, and will declare my tribulation before Him. For why should I, wretched man that I am, dissemble my misery before Thee, to Whom the secrets of my heart are open, and my sins are not hid from Thee? Lo! why I groan, for that Thy servant so seldom findeth his heart, so as to pour forth a prayer, pure and spotless in Thy Sight; so much is it carried away by the cares and anxieties of this world.

Alas! How often do I come to prayer, spiritless and without understanding, and what to pray for, I know not. My tongue prayeth, but my understanding is unfruitful. As a matter of mere sapless custom I come to pray, seldom, if ever, either mindful of the end of my prayer, that is, either of Thy glory or my own salvation; or anxious how I may duly and becomingly offer my prayer for victory over particular vices, or for obtaining more necessary virtues. Spare me, O LORD, Thou, Who alone knowest, as the true High Priest, how to feel compassion for our infirmities; for Thou knowest whereof we are made.

Thou seest, that as of old, so now, alas! the imagination of the thoughts of man's heart is prone to evil from his youth. For the body, which tendeth to corruption, weigheth down the soul, and the earthly tabernacle presseth down the imagination, which willeth to meditate, to seek and to taste those things which are above. And O the marvel! or rather, O the misery! I, unhappy that I am, feel that misery more even then, when I ought to be seeking from Thee a remedy for my woes and miseries, *at the time of prayer:* then a thousand cares assail me, and my thoughts are scattered, and my heart is wrung. O! what do I suffer within, when in my mind I have to do with heavenly things, and straightway a crowd of fleshly things mar my prayer! I long to dwell on heavenly things, but earthly things and unmortified passions press me down. Thus am I tossed in the waves of this vast sea, and am made a burthen to myself, while the spirit stretcheth upwards, and the flesh hasteth earthwards. Be not far from me, O my GOD; turn not away in anger from Thy servant; command the winds of the sea, that in my heart there may be a great calm. O LORD! all my desire is before Thee, and from Thee my groaning is not hid.

§ 4. *Fixedness of attention and reverence in Prayer. Remedy against distraction.*

CHRIST. That which a man unwillingly suffereth, shall not be imputed unto him for sin. Do thou but strive, to the utmost of thy power, to drive away those importunate flies, which defile the sacrifice of prayer. If thou canst not overcome, patiently endure. Nothing shall be taken from the merit of thy prayer; nay it shall be added to, if thou dealest manfully. I am well pleased with this agony and strife of prayer; even then am I more near, when I seem to be further absent. Be thou only careful always to have a stedfast intention of praying religiously and fixedly; specially, when thou *beginnest* to pray. And then, though thy mind, through human infirmity, may be distracted during the course of thy prayer, the strength of thy purpose at the beginning diffuseth itself throughout thy prayer, and keepeth it in value still precious, so long as no contrary will, breaking that first purpose, be admitted. What else, my son, seek I, but thy heart? If thy heart be good, all things are good.

But that thou mayest be more able to stablish thy heart when thou prayest, remember this one thing, with WHOM thou hast to do when thou prayest. For what man, did he but seriously reflect that he is standing in My sight, his Judge, his Lord and his Creator, the King of kings and Lord of lords, could do otherwise than stand amazed, in fixed attention, full of reverence and fear? Who would not be horrified at turning on Me his back, and admitting to his mind irrelevant and trifling thoughts; much more at turning his eyes to vain things, and his lips to babblings and folly? Reflect with what frame of mind, with what anxiety and awe, My well-beloved, Abraham, Moses, David, John who went before My Face, Peter, the publican, and many others, approached My Presence to hold converse with Me. Am not I, Highest and sole King of Heaven and Earth, in Whose Presence, Cherubim and Seraphim, and all the Angelic Powers stand with trembling? He that cometh to God, must believe that He is. So spake My Apostle. And thus is it plain that your unbelief and blindness, or the lukewarm faith with which you believe Me to be present, makes *you* irreverent before Me, before Whom they tremble, Who support the universe.

MAN. I am covered with shame, O LORD, when I reflect What Thou art and what I am. The vile earth-worm, the filthy frog out of its pool, ventureth to creep to the Throne of Glory of the Most High GOD, and to enter the Heavenly Court, that Court, where the King of kings sitteth on His Starry Throne, surrounded with an innumerable host of Blessed Spirits. Shall *I* enter the place of the admirable tabernacle, yea, even to the house of GOD [a]? Shall *I*, in the sight of the Angels, sing Psalms unto Thee? Shall I worship toward Thy Holy Temple and give thanks unto Thy Name? This is what holy men, Thy beloved, thought on seriously, with lively faith; and hence the devotion and the reverence wherewith they bore themselves in Thy presence, in prayer. But, woe is me! far am I from their zeal, far therefore am I from Thee; so that ofttimes I am least of all where, when I am engaged in prayer, I seem to be. And so when I would plead my cause in prayer, I make it worse, and while I wish to appease Thee, I offend Thee more.

§ 5. *Frequency and perseverance in Prayer.*

CHRIST. Is it strange that

[a] Ps. xlii. 4.

were thy treasure is, there should thy heart be also; that thy understanding should be with difficulty torn thence, where thy affection is fixed? Of earth thou art, nor dost thou enough take heed that thy conversation be in heaven; too much thou busiest thyself about earthly things, and lovest them. Hence silently spring up those thorns which so mightily rend thy heart and choke the good seed, so that it bring forth no fruit. Think now with thyself how grievously it must displease Me to see the sons of men so earnestly and so wholly taken up with the concerns of the flesh and of the world, and of the goods of this life, and so little careful of prayer, on which depends their own everlasting salvation and the glory of My Name. Behold the children of this world; they eat, they drink, they play, they spend their days in wealth[b], they waste their time in these things, and none taketh it to heart; of these are they never weary, nor count any time too long: they busy themselves about farms and yokes of oxen, they bury themselves in divers cares and employments, they engage themselves in never-ending questions, never at leisure and yet ever ill-employed, because they never find time to see—that I am GOD. Or if ever they think good to pray, they either put it off to the last moment and a less fit time, or they do it cursorily and as a task. Would any earthly prince endure to be admitted by thee to conference, only when the common herd of the dregs of the people had been admitted before him?

Not so, that man after My own heart, David My chosen; he was a king and entangled in the cares of a most vast kingdom, yet *his* eyes prevented the night-watches, that he might be occupied in My word; seven times a-day did he praise Me, yea, and at midnight did he rise to give thanks unto Me.

Not so very many other My friends, who study to please Me rather than men; to whom their soul is more than meat, or drink, or raiment; who count all things but loss, and esteem them as dung that they may win Me. Willingly they withdraw themselves from their occupations, whensoever they

---

[b] Job xxi. 13.

are able, or take care that their occupations be so arranged, that amid their outward businesses there lack not time for the one business of the soul, which outweighs all the rest; so that at stated hours they enter into their closet, and when they have shut to the door, they pray unto Me in secret, pouring out their hearts before Me; yea, early in the morning they keep watch unto Me, that the best part of the day, in which the mind is more free and pure, may be given to the noblest occupation, even prayer. And these are they who receive from Me a fuller light of understanding, by which they may be directed in their ways; these are they, who taste more fully how gracious the LORD is, and how void of wearisomeness is converse with Him[c].

Thou too, my son, consider what it shall profit thee to gain the whole world and neglect the one thing needful the care of thy soul. Set a limit, then, to thy worldly prudence; be not occupied with a multitude of things, for he that hath little business shall become wise[d]. Seek first the kingdom of GOD and His righteousness, being well assured that all other things shall be added unto you. Why art thou careful and troubled about many things? Why art thou spent with labour that profiteth not? Love thine own soul[e], pleasing GOD; to whom wilt thou be good if thou art evil to thyself[f]?

To what end art thou so intent on the success of the things which thou pursuest at the expense of prayer? Be sure of this, that good prayer will avail more towards bringing thy matters to a happy issue, than any human means. Cast thy care upon Me; for I care for thee, and so much the more as thou restest on Me with greater trust, and committest thy endeavours to My Providence. Except I build the house, their labour is but lost that build it. Believest thou this? Blessed is he that understandeth it. For many receive not this saying; they trust in their own strength, and vex themselves with manifold cares and labours, and, wretched in their imaginations, spend and waste them-

[c] Wisd. viii. 16.
[d] Ecclus. xxxviii. 24.
[e] Ecclus. xxx. 23.
[f] Ib. xiv. 5.

selves in spiders' webs out of their own substance, because they repair not with Moses to the tabernacle to ask counsel of the LORD. It is but lost labour, O ye sons of men, that ye haste to rise up early; then is the time to rise to labour, when the Sun of righteousness, invoked by prayer, shall have shone upon you.

MAN. O that Thou wouldest impress, O my LORD, these wholesome words which Thou so patiently speakest to my ears, effectually on my heart; I *understand* Thy exhortation and Thy Command; teach me also to *do* Thy Will, that I fail not to pray always; and I will always give thanks unto the LORD; His praise shall ever be in my mouth. O that my will were in Thy law, that my delight might be to meditate in it day and night. There is no moment but we enjoy Thy blessings; justly then should there be no moment without praise to Thee: and so Thy Apostle bids us pray without ceasing, and Thou Thyself, Eternal Truth, hast said, *Men ought always to pray, and not to faint.*

§ 6. *Trust and resignation in Prayer.*

CHRIST. Thou knowest these things, O man; blessed shalt thou be, if thou do them. Be not a servant that knoweth his lord's will, but doeth it not. Call to mind how I have stirred thee up, with warnings, examples, and parables, to persuade thee to perseverance, frequency, trust, and continuance in prayer. Surely He that so stirreth thee up to ask, is ready and willing to give. Remember the woman of Canaan who was so earnest in her prayer, and, though often repelled, was at last heard. Remember too him who continued at night knocking at his friend's door, till he obtained what he sought; and the unjust judge, who, though he feared not GOD nor regarded man, yet at last avenged the widow for her importunacy.

If My gifts and blessings are somewhat rarely bestowed on you, look for the reason in yourselves. The Hand of the LORD is not shortened, that He cannot show mercy upon you; it is you, who are unworthy and unable to receive, because ye ask not as is befitting so great a matter. Though at times ye approach Me, ye do it so languidly, as though ye did not desire what ye ask for; nor do ye with becoming faith implore My help. Moreover, unless I immediately grant your petition, ye despond, ye cease to pray, and speak ill, or ye have suspicions, of Me; and perverse thoughts of My Goodness arise in your hearts; as though I walked in the circuit of heaven[x], and cared not for you. Yet are not My eyes ever upon My faithful ones, and My ears ever open to their prayers? Yea, I will not fail them in the time when I may be found.

If I tarry, this too is for your good, that thy desires may grow by delay, and so thou mayest be more able to receive My gifts. There is more sweetness in gifts which have been long desired; things quickly given are held cheap. If, then, thou ask of Me, nor instantly receive, continue knocking notwithstanding, and cry unto Me; it shall at length be opened to you. Nay, if I altogether refuse, yet shalt thou equally give Me thanks, whether I give or whether I withhold, being well assured that I refuse it because I know it will not profit thee. Man often knows not what to ask for (as even the sons of Zebedee), or what is good for him in his life, in the number of the days of his pilgrimage, the time that passeth away like a shadow: but *I* know what is good for every man, and yet, by reason of the folly of men, I sometimes give in My anger, what in My favour I withhold. Know this, though I regard not thy will when thou callest upon Me, yet I will regard thy salvation. So was it with My Apostle, when he besought deliverance from the thorn in his flesh; yea, even so was I heard by My FATHER, when I prayed that the cup of Passion might pass from Me. Is the servant greater or better than his Lord? If thou wouldst pray best, let thy prayer be after the pattern of Mine own, which I poured forth in the garden, amid the utmost agonies of heart, submitting Myself wholly unto My FATHER's Will; after which pattern, too, is the form of prayer, whereby I taught My Disciples and you

[x] Job xxii. 14.

all, to pray, *Thy will be done, &c.*

§ 7. *Petition for the Divine help.*

MAN. O immeasurable love! O inexhaustible mercy! According to the riches of Thy Goodness, O LORD, Thou teachest me so fully, and exhortest me to hold converse with Thee, to Whom my goods are nothing[h]. What is this, that Thy delights are with the sons of men? O that my needy and thirsty soul longed after Thee, like as the hart desireth the water brooks, that my mouth were filled with Thy praise! O that I were as ready to receive as Thou art ready to give! The oil of thy mercy distils, yea, floweth abundantly; O let there be but empty vessels at hand to receive it! Behold the vessel of my heart; but it is full of filth and evil desires; empty it, I beseech Thee, and cleanse it, yea, enlarge it that Thou mayest fill it. I am cold, but with the fire of Thy love inflame me, that my prayer may be set forth in Thy sight as incense. O let it not creep upon the gound, pressed down by the weight of the flesh and of sin, but let it ascend quickly unto Thee, and let Thy mercy descend upon me.

[h] Ps. xvi. 2.

CHAPTER II.

VARIOUS EXPOSITIONS AND EXERCISES UPON THE LORD'S PRAYER,

The sum, the pattern, and the rule of all prayers is the LORD's *Prayer, and it is esteemed so many times the more precious, as in its claims it excels all others.*

First, in Authority and Dignity, formed by CHRIST *Himself, proceeding from His holy Mouth.*

2. It is short, also, and easy, yet full of meanings and mysteries: in a wonderful arrangement it embraces in the first perfect manner, all that can be rightly sought from GOD.

3. *It prevails with singular efficacy, in easily moving* GOD *and turning His Heart to the offerer ; for how shall not the Heavenly* FATHER *hear them who come before Him with the precepts and the words of His Beloved* SON, *our Advocate and Mediator.*

4. *Briefly, but clearly, it expresses all the parts, terms, and conditions of acceptable prayer, so that if said carefully and attentively, it mightily stirs up and promotes the spirit of devotion.*

Seeing, then, that this prayer delivered to the Apostles by the Mouth of Christ, should be specially commended to the use of Christians, and is very frequent and familiar to ecclesiastics in the Divine office, it seems good to mention some few points, with a view to its exposition, out of St. Thomas and others. If, from time to time, these be thought on, it may be that greater affection and profit will follow on the so frequent repetition of one and the same prayer.

Why is it that, as in other spiritual cases, so here we so seldom taste the sweetness of this prayer? Is it not because we are occupied with the mere rind, and rarely, if ever, penetrate within, even to the marrow?

Our FATHER *which art in heaven.*

This is the preface of the LORD's *Prayer; in it behold the good-will of* GOD *towards us, and what affections of love and awe we should feel towards Him.*

If He is a FATHER, is He not worthy of Love? Yea, and *what* love? The degree of His goodness is the measure of the love to be requited.

How great is the goodness of the Eternal FATHER! GOD is in Himself supremely blessed; Creator of Heaven and earth, King and Lord, yet He would be accounted our FATHER: and us too, vile earth-worms, yea, sinners, unworthy to be called servants, He joys in having, and in having us called His sons. O what manner of love hath the FATHER bestowed upon us, that we should be called and be the sons of GOD! O immeasurable goodness of the FATHER! Where, alas! is the equal love of the sons?

Yea, and what awe is due to the same FATHER, Who

sitteth in heaven as upon the throne of His Majesty, and yet, everywhere present, beholdeth every secret thing, and ruleth at once, all things, both in heaven and earth. Truly, great is the LORD, and marvellous, worthy to be praised; there is no end of His Power and Greatness; before Him Cherubim and Seraphim stand trembling.

Behold with what love and confidence, yea, moreover, with what lowliness and reverence, when thou prayest, thou shouldest prepare thy mind.

There now follow seven petitions, in which we pray for blessings or we deprecate evils. Since Prayer is the interpreter of our desires, those things we pray for in the LORD'S *Prayer which we desire lawfully. The first thing which falls under desire is The Chief Good, or the Final End, then those means which are proper for obtaining this, and lastly the removal of those obstacles which may hinder our attainment of it.*

Now our Chief Good, our End, is GOD, *Whose* GLORY, *first of all, in Himself, out of a simple and pure affection of love, we desire when we say,*

1. *Hallowed be Thy Name:*

i. e. Be Thy Name, which is in itself supremely holy and admirable, so accounted by all men: be It acknowledged by true faith: be It praised by constant hope: be It worshipped by sincere charity. No help of ours is needed that Thy Name be holy; but because It is holy and glorious, and so the fount and form of All Holiness, let that be by us declared by a holy life; be our life and all our actions so formed that they who see our conversation, and the works which we do, may glorify Thee, Our Father in Heaven.

Be this fixed in our heart, frequent in our mouth, pleasing to Thee in our work, HALLOWED BE THY NAME.

Here is a most easy act of purity of Intention, often to be exercised through the day.

Next after this follows a desire of the Glory of GOD, *by looking into ourselves, that* WE *may enjoy it as the chief good; this affection proceeds from that love of* GOD, *by which we love ourselves in* GOD; *hence we pray,*

2 *Thy Kingdom come:*

that is; we pray, O LORD

since we are here strangers and pilgrims from our home, and shut out from the Face of our dear Father, are pressed down by the heavy yoke of the prince of this world, we pray Thee to make us long after Thee heavenwards, with our whole heart. Let us not love the world, neither the things which are in the world, but seek and mind those things which are above. And when the end of our pilgrimage shall be come, grant us, with an even and joyful mind, to despise this kingdom of the world and all its pomps; to seek that kingdom with desire, which has been prepared for us before the foundation of the world, where Thou wilt give us the enjoyment of eternal glory with Thee, yea, of Thyself.

Now in order to enjoy that highest good, we need certain other goods as means and supports; of which the chief is Obedience to the commandments of GOD. *For neither is he fit for the kingdom of* GOD *who doeth not His will, nor doth he merit to enter eternal life who keepeth not His commandments. But who shall keep them, if He, Who commandeth, help not? Rightly then do we pray,*

3. *Thy Will be done.*

Thou knowest, O LORD, that even though our spirit be ready to do Thy Will, yet it cannot perfect it; for the flesh is weak, yet prone to evil, and fighteth against the spirit. For the body, which is liable to corruption, weigheth down the soul; so that the imagination of man's heart is inclined to evil rather than to good, even from his youth. Hence, too, how often are we ignorant, what and how we should pray, or what is expedient for us: but Thou knowest very well, Who knowest all things. Make us to know what Thou wouldest have us do: yea, with Thy constraining grace so direct our wills according to the good pleasure of Thy Will, that what Thou willest, we may will, and what Thou biddest, we may gladly perform. GIVE WHAT THOU BIDDEST AND BID WHAT THOU WILLEST.

But that man may with more joyful readiness do the bidding of GOD, *he must not be altogether destitute of the goods and provisions of this present life; for we are liable to many wants and necessities, as long as we bear about this mortal body. So we pray,*

4. *Give us this day our daily bread.*

Thou, Who openest Thy hand and fillest all things living with blessing; Who forgettest not the young ravens nor the birds of heaven, but bountifully carest for them and feedest them; wilt not Thou care for man whom Thou hast created in Thy Image, and whom, by Thy most Precious Blood, Thou hast made heir of heaven? We pray not for what may serve to luxury and pleasure, but for what may supply our need and our support, lest, perchance, the cares and anxieties of this world draw us away from Thy service. That we may serve Thee, sound in mind no less than in body, feed our souls also with the food of Thy Word, yea, strengthen us in the wilderness of this world with that heavenly and angelic BREAD, lest we faint in the way that leadeth to Thee, till we feast with Thee in Thy Kingdom.

Behold in what degree, from Whom, and to what end, goods of this world are to be prayed for.

In the following petitions we pray for the removal of those evils or obstacles, which might hinder the attainment of the END. *They are, mainly, three,*

The first is sin committed, for in many things we offend all. Hence frequently and humbly must we pray that our sins be forgiven. But in vain that man seeks mercy from the LORD, *who refuseth it, when it is in his power, to his neighbour. Bearing this in mind, we rightly use this form of prayer :*

5. *Forgive us our trespasses, as we forgive them that trespass against us.*

In many things (woe to us!) daily we offend all. LORD, we perish, unless Thou, O LORD, of Thy great goodness, save us. Yea! we know that, if man lay up wrath against man, in vain must he seek healing from Thee. From my heart, then, I forgive all my enemies, and, out of love to Thee, I am ready to do good to those who hate me, or have ever injured me. From my inmost heart I grieve that I have offended Thee; spare my sins, O LORD.

Lo, here, a very easy and useful practice for frequently exercising contrition.

The second obstacle is temptation, which solicits us to sin, and hinders us from the observance of the Divine Will. Let him, then, who is delivered from past sins, fear and fly from future ones. But who can escape without GOD? Under a sense, then, of our own weakness, and of the power of so many enemies, to whom our life is ever exposed, we pray,

6. *And lead us not into temptation.*

We confess, O LORD, that without Thee we can do nothing; all our sufficiency is of Thee; let not then Thy Grace desert us; suffer us not to fall, whenever assailed by any temptation of the world, the flesh, or the devil. Thou seest our frailty, how insidiously and how strongly tempted Thy creature is, whom Thou hast redeemed at so dear a price: we doubt not that all things are guided by the merciful counsel of Thy Providence, and that to be tempted is not an evil, but to be overcome thereby. Suffer us not, then, to be tempted above that we are able, lest peradventure we fail, but help us to overcome; easy will be the victory, if Thy Grace be with us.

Delivered from the evil of guilt, often we fall into the third evil, that of punishment. Even religious minds are frequently hard beset by the many evils of the present life, hunger, war, disease, loss of property, of reputation, of life. Rightly then, in fine, we pray,

7. *But deliver us from evil.*

That which we merely feel evil, is not truly evil in itself, unless it becomes so through our fault. From Thee, O LORD, come life and death, honour, poverty, and all things how, then, shall these be evil which proceed from the HIGHEST GOOD? Still, not seldom do they become evil, through our fault, *i.e.* through our impatience, timorousness, and want of faith. Strengthen Thou us by Thy Grace and comfort, and make all things work together for good to them that love Thee. Apply the caustic and the knife, as the physician doth on the sick, whose hope of life depends on these remedies, harsh though they be. Rebuke and chasten, as the father doth the son, for whom an inheritance is reserved. Try, test, purify me, as the goldsmith doth the gold which is tried in the fire. By fire refine and compact me, as the potter doth the vessel which is destined not for destruction but for honour, a vessel of glory for eternal life.

With these and such like meditations must the LORD's *Prayer be seasoned; else, what wonder if, so often uttered with the lips, it be so seldom relished in the heart?*

MEDITATION ON THE LORD'S PRAYER, gathered out of the epistles of St. Paul.

Our Father, which art in Heaven.

Blessed be GOD, even the Father of our LORD JESUS CHRIST, the Father of Mercies and the GOD of all comfort [a], Who hast predestinated us unto the adoption of children by JESUS CHRIST [b]; Who only hast immortality, dwelling in the light which no man can approach unto; with joyfulness we give thanks unto Thee, Who hast made us meet to be partakers of the inheritance of the saints in light [d]; for we have not received the spirit of bondage again to fear [e], but we have received the spirit of adoption, whereby we cry, Abba, Father. The Spirit itself beareth witness with our spirit, that we are the children of God; and if children, then heirs; heirs of GOD and joint heirs with CHRIST.

1. *Hallowed be Thy Name.*

Grant that we be followers of Thee as dear children [f]; and that we walk as children of light in all goodness, and righteousness, and truth, proving what is acceptable unto Thee; nor let us have fellowship with the unfruitful works of darkness [g], lest Thy Name be blasphemed among the Gentiles through us [h]. Let our conversation be as it becometh the Gospel of CHRIST [i], that we may be blameless and harmless, Thy sons, without rebuke, in the midst of a crooked and perverse nation, shining as lights in the world; holding forth the Word of Life to Thy glory in the Day of CHRIST [k], that we may walk worthy of the LORD unto all pleasing, being fruitful in every good work, and increasing in the knowledge of GOD [l];

[a] 2 Cor. i. [b] Eph. i.
[c] 1 Tim. vi. [d] Col. i.
[e] Rom. viii.
[f] Eph. v. [g] Ibid.
[h] Rom. ii. [i] Phil. i.
[k] Phil. ii. [l] Col. i.

grant that whether we eat or drink, or whatsoever we do, we may do all to the glory of GOD[r].

2. *Thy Kingdom come.*

Forasmuch as flesh and blood cannot inherit the Kingdom of GOD[s], for this cause we bow our knees unto Thee, the FATHER of our LORD JESUS CHRIST, that Thou wouldst grant us, according to the riches of Thy glory, to be strengthened with might by Thy Spirit in the inner man, that CHRIST may dwell in our hearts by faith[t], that sin reign not in our mortal body[u]. For Thou hast delivered us from the power of darkness, and hast translated us into the kingdom of Thy dear Son[x]. For we know that if our earthly house of this tabernacle be dissolved, we have a building of GOD, a house not built with hands, eternal in the heavens; but whilst we are at home in the body, we are absent from the LORD[y], so that we have a desire to depart and to be with CHRIST[z].

[r] 1 Cor. x.   [s] Ibid. xv.
[t] Ephes. iii.   [u] Rom. vi.
[x] Col. i.   [y] 2 Cor. v.
     [z] Phil. i.

For which cause we faint not, but though our outward man perish, yet the inward man is renewed day by day; for our light affliction, which is but for a moment, worketh for us a far more exceeding and eternal weight of glory, while we look not at the things which are seen, but at the things which are not seen; for the things which are seen are temporal, but the things which are not seen are eternal[a].

3. *Thy Will be done.*

For it is Thou, O LORD, that workest in us both to will and to do of Thy good pleasure[b]. Cause, therefore, that we be filled with the knowledge of Thy Will, in all wisdom and spiritual understanding, that we may walk worthy of the LORD unto all pleasing[c]; for this is Thy Will, even our sanctification[d].

Let us be unwilling to be conformed to this world, but let us be transformed by the renewing of our mind, that we may prove what is that good, and acceptable, and perfect Will of GOD[e]; for truly our

[a] 2 Cor. iv.   [b] Phil. ii.
[c] Col. i.   [d] 1 Thess. iv.
     [e] Rom. xii.

will towards good is, of itself, very weak; for we are not sufficient of ourselves to think any thing as of ourselves, but our sufficiency is of GOD [f]; grant us Thy grace that we may do it heartily, even as Thy ministering spirits, sent forth to minister for them who shall be heirs of salvation [g].

4. *Give us this day our daily bread.*

Godliness with contentment is great gain. For we brought nothing into this world, and it is certain we can carry nothing out. And having food and raiment let us be therewith content [h]. Let our conversation be without covetousness, and let us be content with such things as we have, for Thou hast said, I will never leave thee nor forsake thee; so that we may boldly say, The LORD is my helper [i]. Thou art at hand, O LORD, be we careful for nothing [a], but everywhere and in all things may we know both to be full and to be hungry, both to abound and to suffer need [b]; and, above all, may we exercise ourselves unto godliness, which is profitable unto all things, having promise of the life that now is and of that which is to come [c].

O let us not trust in uncertain riches, but in Thee, the living GOD, Who givest us richly all things to enjoy; grant to us to do good, to be rich in good works, ready to distribute, willing to communicate, laying up in store for ourselves a good foundation against the time to come, that we may lay hold of eternal life [d].

Thou art able, O GOD, to make all grace abound in us, that we, always having all sufficiency in all things, may abound in every good work. Thou that ministerest seed to the sower, wilt minister bread also for our food [e].

5. *And forgive us our trespasses as we forgive them that trespass against us.*

Since in our flesh there dwelleth no good thing, so that the good that I would I do not, but the evil which

[f] 2 Cor. iii.   [g] Heb. i.
[h] 1 Tim. vi.   [i] Heb xiii.
[a] Phil. iv.
[b] Ibid. iv.   [c] 1 Tim. iv.
[d] Ibid. iv.   [e] 2 Cor. ix.

I would not, that I do[a]; and by sin reigning in our mortal body we have obeyed it in the lusts thereof[b]: alas, how often have we yielded our members as instruments of unrighteousness unto sin[c]! and have despised the riches of Thy goodness, and forbearance, and long-suffering, not knowing that Thy goodness leadeth us to repentance, but after our hardness and impenitent heart have treasured up unto ourselves wrath against the day of wrath and revelation of Thy righteous judgment, Who wilt render to every man according to his deeds[d].

But, O most merciful FATHER, let Thy mercy come upon us, and showing forth the riches of Thy glory, make us vessels of Thy mercy, prepared unto Thy glory[e]; and where sin hath abounded let grace abound much more[f].

Behold, we forbear threatening to others, that we may have Thee our Master in Heaven propitious unto us[g]. Do Thou put on us, as Thine elect, bowels of mercies, kindness, humbleness of mind, meekness, long-suffering[h], that we may be kind one to another, tender-hearted, forgiving one another, even as Thou for Christ's sake hast forgiven us[i]; recompensing to no man evil for evil, but if it be possible as much as lieth in us living peaceably with all men, avenging not ourselves, but let us rather give place unto wrath, leaving vengeance unto Thee; neither let us suffer ourselves to be overcome of evil, but let us overcome evil with good[k]. Grant that we may follow after the things which make for peace, and things wherewith one may edify another[l].

6. *And lead us not into temptation.*

Mindful of our weakness, we implore Thee, most merciful FATHER, that no temptation take us but such as are common to man[m], lest, by any means, as the serpent beguiled Eve through his subtlety, so our minds should be corrupted from the simplicity which is in Christ[n].

[a] Rom. vii. [b] Ib. vi. [c] Ib.
[d] Ib. ii. [e] Ib. ix. [f] Ib. v.
[g] Eph. vi.
[h] Col. iii. [i] Eph. iv.
[k] Rom. xii. [l] Ib. xiv.
[m] 1 Cor. x. [n] 2 Cor. xi.

Thou art a faithful GOD, Who wilt not suffer us to be tempted above that we are able, but wilt with the temptation also make a way to escape that we may be able to bear it[c].

7. But deliver us from evil.

Lastly, stablish us and keep us from evil[d], bruise Satan under our feet shortly[e], that he get not an advantage of us, for we are not ignorant of his devices[f]: grant that we may put on the whole armour of God, that we may be able to stand against the wiles of the devil, and withstand in the evil day, and having done all to stand; having put on the breast-plate of faith and love, and for an helmet the hope of salvation[g]. Let us not trust in ourselves, but in Thee, O GOD[h]. And so are we confident of this very thing, that Thou, Who hast begun a good work in us, wilt perform it unto the Day of JESUS CHRIST[i]. We believe Thee to be faithful Who hast promised[k], for all *Thy* promises are Yea and Amen[l].

[c] 1 Cor. x.   [d] 2 Thess. iii.   [g] Ephes. vi. 1 Thess. v.
[e] Rom. xvi.   [f] 2 Cor. ii.   [h] 2 Cor. i.   [i] Phil. i.
   [k] Heb. xi.   [l] 2 Cor. i.

THE LORD'S PRAYER,

INTERMINGLED WITH VARIOUS PIOUS THOUGHTS SUITABLE FOR MEDITATION.

From Ludovicus de Ponte, Lessius, and others.

Our Father.

On many grounds hath He right and title to the name of *Father;*

1. On the ground of *Creation,* whereby He made us after His Own Image.
2. Of *Adoption* by grace, whereby He hath made us His heirs, and joint-heirs with His Only-Begotten. O rightly is He named *Father,* Who is ready so often to receive sinning men into the same grace, so as at last also to admit them to glory, which is the heritage of the sons of God. And verily, much did it cost the Son to purchase

this relationship of *Father* for us; it was by the Death of the Cross, and at the price of His Blood.

3. He is *Father* by His Providence, sustaining the body by so many of His creatures, supplied for food and healing, and so lovingly providing for the soul by so many assistances of grace and salvation: on this account only, rightly were He called Father: so He says, *Call no man your father upon earth, for One is your Father Who is in heaven;* and rightly, for *when my father and my mother forsake me* (what help indeed can they bring to the soul, or even to the body, without God?) *the Lord taketh me up.* He never forsaketh, unless forsaken.

4. By *Discipline* and Correction, for the Father rebuketh and chasteneth the son, whom He loveth.

5. By His *Indulgence* and His love. As a Father pitieth his children, even so the Lord hath pity upon them that fear Him.

If, then, He is *Father*, surely I am *son*. O exceeding dignity! How it behoveth me to perform the part of a true son, with love, observance, and obedience. If I, a servant, a worthless slave have been thus advanced, how unworthy it were to degenerate and offend so good a *Father!*

He would have us begin our prayer with addressing Him by this title, to excite in us confidence in approaching God, as being our Father, and assurance of obtaining our petitions; and since He rejoiceth in the name of Father, He delighteth in being so addressed. So then, with the affections of sons, let us approach Him, let us strive to please Him in all things, and beg for such things as may fitly be asked from such a Father.

Our.

Our, I say, not *My,*

1. Because, as He has One only Son by nature, He would have as many sons by adoption as possible, as well Angels as men, and that, in such wise, as that every one should joy in the blessing of filiation, as much as though he were the only one so blessed. For the blessings of God are not lessened by being communicated to many.

2. Since He is in such way Father of all generally, as yet to be Father of each separately, He will notwithstanding

be called *our*, to remind us of brotherly charity, without distinction of rank, dignity, or age, and that we must love each other as brethren, and pray for all without exception, and so the Prophet Malachi says, *Have we not all one Father? Hath not one God created us? Why do we deal treacherously every man against his brother?*

Yet nothing forbids me at times, as my affection may lead me, to call Him *My Father*, seeing that I am with as full right His adopted child as if there were no other.

Which art in Heaven.

He is indeed everywhere: by *Heaven* we mean,

1. To excite in ourselves Reverence towards that Majesty, Which sitteth in Heaven as on a throne.

2. To raise our minds to Heaven, where is the home and the heritage of the sons of GOD.

3. To reflect that we are here strangers and pilgrims, but that we should so live that our conversation should be in Heaven.

4. To remind myself, thitherwards to raise my eyes and my soul, whence only cometh my help.

Moreover, Heaven and the peculiar seat of God are those holy souls in which God dwelleth by grace, and which He specially enlighteneth by the light of His knowledge.

Thus far the introduction; the petitions follow.

1. Hallowed be Thy Name.

Be Thou esteemed, as Thou art indeed, Pure, Holy, Just, True, Righteous. God holdeth nothing so dear as to be esteemed and preached as Holy. Hence so often He saith, *Be ye holy, for I am holy*. Hence He was wroth with Moses and Aaron, because they had not sanctified Him at the waters of strife in the eyes of the children of Israel. Moreover, that is the only Song of the Blessed, *Holy, Holy, Holy*.

2, He saith not *Thy Power*, or *Thy Majesty*, but *Thy Name*, that He might embrace in one word all that is named of God among us, as being all holy, and therefore to be commemorated; and He is named Almighty, Wise, Creator, &c.

3. *Thy*, He saith, for that *Thine* alone is holy of Itself, and of *Thine* the righteous partake, as it were, a drop.

Not *ours* then, but *Thine;* to the King Eternal, Immortal, Invisible, the only God, be honour and glory for ever and ever; but unto us confusion of face. Why then do we so anxiously seek our own glory and a great name, whose desire should rather be to be unknown and to be despised?

4. *Hallowed be,* He saith simply, with no restriction, either *to certain persons,* for we should desire that all creatures do it, those in heaven, and those on earth, and those under the earth; or *to a certain time,* for throughout all time it is fitting that His Name be praised.

5. The Name of God is hallowed, when men believe that which He revealeth, hope for that which He promiseth, do that which He commandeth; worship God as He teacheth; and love Him with their whole heart, proving their love by their works, so that they who see our good works may glorify the Father, Who is in Heaven. It is a prayer worthy of a true and good son to desire nothing before or above the glory of his FATHER, and to prefer *His* honour to all things. Not unto us, O LORD, not unto us, but unto Thy Name give the praise, blessed be the Name of the LORD from henceforth, &c.

2. *Thy kingdom come.*

Yet He reigneth in heaven and in earth, in the sea, and everywhere. Whether they will or no, all things serve Him, and under His rule are all things. We pray, therefore,

1. For that kingdom, in regard to which He now reigneth by grace in the just, who are, in all things, subject unto Him.

2 For that, in regard to which He reigneth in the Blessed by glory. This last shall come to us, if we abide in the first.

Wherefore He saith, *Thy kingdom come,* as though following of its own accord; and, indeed, all long for this latter, though the former they desire not, as being conjoined with labour, for righteousness is acquired and preserved by mortification of the flesh, and by curbing of the desires which reign in our members.

3. Thy *kingdom* come; that complete and perfect kingdom when GOD shall be All

in all, at the resurrection of the just, which kingdom blessed souls are waiting for.

4. *Thy* kingdom come; not the kingdom of the world, which the children of this world seek after, which standeth in transient goods, infinite cares, and numberless perils; far less, the kingdom of sin, which I would were utterly overthrown. It is the part of sons, ever to pant after their native country, and to seek their paternal inheritance, in preference to all other things. *Woe is me, that I am constrained to dwell with Mesech, and have my habitation among the tents of Kedar. I desire to be dissolved, and to be with* CHRIST. *Like as the hart desireth the water-brooks, so longeth my soul after Thee, O* GOD, *&c.*

3. *Thy will be done in earth as it is in Heaven.*

1. Thy will, which alone is always good, right, and perfect in all things;—which by precepts, counsels, and inspirations He insinuateth into us, as well as by the commands of those who are over us in the Name of GOD. It is reason enough to make us perform these, that GOD so willeth, and biddeth in such sort, that, if I obey Him and keep His Commandments, I shall win life; if not, death.

2. *Thy* will, not *mine*, which is perverse; nor the will *of the flesh,* which is contrary to the Spirit; nor *of the world,* which is vain; nor *of the devil,* which is malicious; but *Thine,* which is the rule of righteousness: for what is Thy will, but our sanctification? For Thou requirest nought of us but for *our* good; not Thine Own, since our goods are nothing unto Thee.

3. *How* is it to be done? *As it is in heaven,* by the Angels, where there is no rebellion of a perverse will; so let it be done wholly, promptly, quickly, boldly, lovingly, vigorously upon earth, where resistance to Thy will stands in an unwillingness to be led gently with the cords of love, the cords of a man, and will only be forced, like a brute beast, by the might of Thy power, or dragged by the chains of Thy Justice. *Teach me, O* LORD, *to do Thy will, for Thou art my* GOD. *Behold, O* LORD, *I am Thy servant. O* LORD, *what wilt Thou have me to do? Speak,* LORD, *for Thy servant heareth.*

4. *Give us this day our daily bread.*

1. *The bread of grace and the word of* God. Man liveth not by bread alone; his soul too hath need of sustenance. The life of man is twofold; such also must the bread or food be, whereby he is nourished.

2. Above all, *the true Bread* Which came down from Heaven, the Supersubstantial Eucharistic Bread, Which confirms the heart of man, and strengthens his spirit.

3. *Bread for the body*, needful for the support of life; but His bidding us to look for it from the Divine blessing, shows that He would not have us anxious or too careful for this.

4. *Our*, not *my*, because it is common and to be shared among our brethren. We confess the same God, the Father of all, Who would have His gifts supply the needs, not of one or of a few, but of all.

5. *Daily* (if spiritual be meant, then) not *that* which is the portion of the few singularly beloved, of which I count myself unworthy, but that common, necessary portion, without which life cannot be supported; (if bodily, then) not so much as may minister to luxury and festivity, or be laid up for many years, but enough for use and daily needs.

6. *Give us:* we must pray for all as brethren, yea, even though they hate us; *Pray for them that persecute you, and speak evil of you;* and, *if thou see thine enemy hunger, feed him.*

7. *This day*, because He will have us pray daily and always be depending on His Providence, He calls us off from the superfluous care for the morrow, after the example of the Manna, which was supplied daily. *The eyes of all wait upon Thee, O* God; *give Thou them their meat in due season; open Thine hand and fill all things living with plenteousness.*

5. *Forgive us our debts, as we forgive our debtors.*

1. Many are the debts we owe to God; in many things we offend all, both in having done evil and left undone the good we ought to have done. Unless God of His mercy forgive, who can endure? If He will act with the rigors of justice, who can

answer one of a thousand? The only refuge is His mercy.

2. And this will fail us unless we pardon our neighbour his offences, small indeed when compared with the ten thousand talents we owe to God. Yet such is the goodness of God, He is ready to forgive the ten thousand, if we remit the thousand.

3. But take heed, He will forgive *as* thou forgivest, and this too thou addest in thy prayer. Dost thou forgive unwillingly, slowly, equivocally, with reservation? Fear and expect the same from God. He verily pronounceth sentence against himself who prayeth that his sins may be forgiven, and yet forgiveth not, and that heartily, them that trespass against him. *If Thou,* Lord, *wilt be extreme to mark what is done amiss, O* Lord, *who may abide it? &c.*[a]

6. *And lead us not into temptation.*

We pray, not that we be not tempted, for that is often for our good, and is wisely allowed by God, but that we fall not under temptation, or (also) that He suffer us not to be tempted, when He foreseeth that we shall fall. Temptation is often an occasion and the means of exercising virtue; but it rests with God so to rule the temptation and to help our infirmity, that we be not tempted above that we are able, but escape unharmed. *Try me, O* God, *and seek the ground of my heart; prove me and examine my thoughts; look well if there be any way of wickedness in me* [b].

7. *But deliver us from evil.*

From every kind of evil. As the Church prayeth, *Deliver us, we pray Thee, O* Lord, *from all evils, past, present, and future,* eternal and temporal, of soul and of body.

From *evil*, i. e. again, from the evil spirit, that he be not permitted to exercise his malice and envy against us.

Among *evils* are reckoned not those only of the soul, but such of the body also, of reputation, or of fortune, as may endanger or hurt the soul. *Though I walk through the valley of the shadow of*

---

[a] Ps. cxxx.   [b] Ps. cxxxix.

death, I will fear no evil; for Thou art with me. Lighten my eyes that I sleep not in death, lest my enemy say, I have prevailed against him.

Amen.

So be it, so be it. With fervent desire it shall be pronounced, for the LORD heareth the desire of the poor; and with great confidence, because we ask those things which He hath commanded to be asked, as saith St. John, *This is the confidence we have in* GOD, *that, if we ask anything according to His will, He heareth us, and we know that we have the petitions that we desire of Him.*

CHAPTER III.

VARIOUS LITANIES TO THE MOST HOLY TRINITY, AND TO THE PERSONS SEVERALLY.

[*Note, Pious Reader, that these and the following Litanies, gathered for the most part out of Holy Scripture, contain the names, titles, and attributes and praises, appropriated to the Divine Nature, or severally to the Divine Persons. More might have been collected, but the brevity of the work precluded it. This too may be added; if any one (more captious than pious) object that some of the epithets appear as nominatives, and not in the form of invocation, it is easy to supply the words,* Thou that art. *Let such an one, too, call to mind the practice of the Church, which recognizes the like form in more cases than one*[a].]

LITANIES TO THE MOST HOLY TRINITY.

LORD, have mercy upon us.
CHRIST, have mercy upon us.
LORD, have mercy upon us.

---

[a] Agnus Dei, qui, &c. Miserere nobis. *Also* Sanctus Deus, sanctus fortis, sanctus et immortalis, miserere nobis. The nominative form has been retained, as the precise words of Holy Scripture. [ED.

O God, the Father, of Heaven,
O God, the Son, Redeemer of the world,
O God, the Holy Ghost,
Holy Trinity, One God,
O God, from Whom, by Whom, and in Whom are all things[a],
Who Alone art God[b],
Who didst declare to Moses Thy Name, I am that I am[c],
The Lord, even the most Mighty God[d],
God, in Whom we live, and move, and have our being[e],
The Lord God, the strong and jealous, visiting the iniquity of the fathers upon the children[f],
To Whom Alone all honour and glory is due[g],
With Whose Majesty the earth is filled[h],
Who Only doest great wonders[i].
Who art higher than all that are in the earth[k],
Who Alone art good[l],
The God, Whose anger no one can resist[m],
Who art, and wast, and art to come[n],
The God of Abraham, the God of Isaac, and the God of Jacob[o],
The King of kings and Lord of lords[p],
Who loosest the bonds of kings, and girdest their loins with a girdle[q],
Who Only hast immortality, and dwellest in the light which no man can approach unto[r],
The Lord of Hosts, the God of Israel[s],
God, the God of the spirits of all flesh[t],
Who hast made the heaven and the earth, the sea and all that therein is[u],
Who helpest them to right that suffer wrong, Who feedest the hungry[x],

Have mercy upon us.

[a] Rom. xi. [b] Ps. lxxxvi. [c] Ex. iii. [d] Ps. l. [e] Acts xvii.
[f] Exod. xx. [g] 1 Tim. i. [h] Ps. lxxii. [i] Ps. cxxxvi.
[k] Ps. xcvii. [l] Luke xviii. [m] Job ix. [n] Apoc. i. [o] Ex. iii.
[p] 1 Tim. vi. [q] Job. xii. [r] 1 Tim. vi. [s] Is. xxxvii.
[t] Numb. xvi. [u] Ps. cxlvi. [x] Ib.

God, full of compassion and mercy, long-suffering, plenteous in goodness and truth ^y,
God, the righteous Judge, strong and patient ^z,
In Whose Hand is the soul of every living thing, and the breath of all mankind ^a,
Our God, a consuming Fire ^b,
A God of Truth, and without iniquity, just and right ^c,
God, Whose anger no one can resist ^d,
God, Who searchest the heart and triest the reins ^e,
Who openest Thine Hand, and fillest all things living with plenteousness ^f,
Great in counsel and mighty in work ^g,
Which doeth great things, and unsearchable, marvellous things without number ^h,
Who art a Father of the fatherless, and defendest the cause of the widow ⁱ,
Who loosest men out of prison, and givest sight to the blind ^k,
Our great Lord, Whose wisdom is infinite ^l,
The Lord, Who settest up the meek and bringest the ungodly down to the ground ^m,
Whose eyes are open upon all the ways of the sons of Adam ⁿ,
The One Lawgiver and Judge, Who art able to save and to destroy ^o,
Who healest those that are broken in heart, and givest medicine to heal their sickness ^p,
The Lord, Who killest and makest alive, Who bringest down to the grave and bringest up ^q,
That hast no pleasure in wickedness ^r,
That hast power to cast body and soul into hell ^s,
That formest the light, and createst darkness, That makest peace and createst evil ^t,

} Have mercy upon us.

^y Numb. xiv. & Ps. lxxxvi. ^z Ps. vii. ^a Job xii.
^b Heb. xii. ^c Deut. xxxii. ^d Job ix. ^e Jer. xvii.
^f Ps. cxlv. ^g Jer. xxxii. ^h Job v. & ix. ⁱ Ps. lxviii.
^k Ps. cxlvi. ^l Ps. cxlvii. ^m Ibid. ⁿ Jer. xxxii.
^o James iv. ^p Ps. cxlvii. ^q 1 Sam. ii. ^r Ps. v.
^s Luke xii. [Matt. x.] ^t Is. xlv.

That increasest the nations and destroyest them, That enlargest the nations and straitenest them again [u],
Whose eyes are ten thousand times brighter than the sun, beholding all the ways of men, and considering the most secret parts [x],
That discoverest deep things out of darkness, and bringest to light the shadow of death [y],
With Whom there is no respect of persons [z],
That takest the wise in their own craftiness, and carriest headlong the counsel of the froward [a],
That quickenest the dead, and callest those things which be not, as though they were [b],
The GOD of all flesh, for Whom nothing is too hard [c],
Who hast made the earth by Thy power, and hast established the world by Thy wisdom [d],
Who givest rain upon the earth, and sendest water upon the fields [e],
Who givest food to all flesh [f],
Who hast made all things for Thyself [g],
Who livest for ever and ever [h],
Who hast ordered all things in measure, and number, and weight [i],
Whom the Heaven and the Heaven of Heavens cannot contain [k],
Wonderful in Thy doing towards the children of men [l],
Before Whom the whole world is as a little grain of the balance [m],
Who workest all things after the counsel of Thine Own Will [n],
Who hast measured the waters in the hollow of Thy Hand, and meted out Heaven with the span [o],
Who rulest the raging of the sea, and stillest the waves thereof when they arise [p],

} Have mercy upon us.

[u] Job xii.   [x] Ecclus. xxiii.   [y] Job xii.   [z] Rom. ii.
[a] Job v.   [b] Rom. iv.   [c] Jer. xxxii.   [d] Ib. li.
[e] Job v.   [f] Ps. cxxxvi.   [g] Prov. xvi.   [h] Apoc. x.
[i] Wis. xi.   [k] 1 Kings viii.   [l] Ps. lxvi.   [m] Wis. xi.
[n] Eph. i.   [o] Isa. xl.   [p] Ps. lxxxix.

§ i.]   DEVOTIONS TO THE ALL-HOLY TRINITY.   35

Who comprehendest the dust of the earth in a measure, and weighest the mountains in scales ^q,
The LORD, the great GOD, and a great King above all gods ^r,
The King Eternal, Immortal, Invisible, the only Wise ^s,
Holy, Holy, Holy ^t,
GOD our Shield, and our exceeding great Reward ^u,
One GOD and FATHER of all, Who art above all and through all things and in us all ^x,
} Have mercy upon us.

Be propitious, spare us, O Holy Trinity,
Be propitious, hear us, O Holy Trinity,
From all evil, deliver us, O Holy Trinity,
From all pride and vanity of mind,
From greediness, gluttony, and indulgence of the appetite,
From anger, envy, and all ill-will,
From all luxuriousness and uncleanness,
From all sloth and undue gloominess,
By the Immensity of Thy Power,
By the Infiniteness of Thy Wisdom,
By the Abundance of Thy Goodness,
By the Eternity of Thy Glory and Thy Majesty,
By the Depth of Thy Knowledge and Thy Providence,
By the unspeakable Greatness of Thy Love and Pity,
By the Unfathomableness of Thy Justice and Thy Judgments,
In the Day of Judgment,
} Deliver us, O HOLY TRINITY.

We, sinners, beseech Thee to hear us,
That we may serve Thee in holiness and righteous all our days,
That we may worship Thee, the LORD our GOD, and serve Thee only,
That we may never take Thy Holy Name in vain,
That we may sanctify the holy and festal days of the Church by religious and pious works,
} We beseech &c.

^q Isa. xl.   ^r Ps. xcv.   ^s 1 Tim. i.
^t Isa. vi.   ^u Gen. xv.   ^x Eph. iv.

D 2

That we may pay all due honour, reverence, and obedience to our parents, bishops, superiors, and all who are to us in the place of parents,
That we may never, from anger, hatred, or envy, hurt the life, good name, or reputation of any man,
That we injure no man by hurt, theft, or any wrong whatsoever, whether by violence or guile,
That we may keep our heart from all carnal desires and unclean affections,
That we never bear false witness, or speak a lie against our neighbour,
That we covet not the goods of our neighbour,
That we may love Thee, our GOD, with all our heart, with all our soul, and with all our strength,
That we may love Thee above all things, and our neighbour, for Thy sake, as ourselves,
That we do not to another that we would not have done to us,
That Thou wouldest make all grace abound in us,
That we despise not the riches of Thy goodness, patience, and long-suffering,
That we may present our bodies a living sacrifice, holy, acceptable unto GOD,
That Thou vouchsafe to bring us to the kingdom Thou hast prepared for us from the foundation of the world,

} We beseech Thee to hear us.

LAMB OF GOD, That takest away the sins of the world, reconcile the Father to us,
LAMB OF GOD, That takest away the sins of the world, be propitious to us sinners,
LAMB OF GOD, That takest away the sins of the world, give us the HOLY SPIRIT.
O Blessed TRINITY, hear us,
O Adorable TRINITY, hearken unto us,
LORD, have mercy,
CHRIST, have mercy,
LORD, have mercy.
Our FATHER, Which art in Heaven, &c.

V. Blessed art Thou, O LORD GOD of our fathers,
R. Worthy to be praised and glorious for ever.
V. Blessed art Thou, O LORD, in the firmament of Heaven,
R. Worthy to be praised, glorious, and highly exalted for ever.
V. Let all Thy Angels and Saints bless Thee,
R. Praise Thee and glorify Thee for ever.
V. Bless we the FATHER, and the SON, with the HOLY GHOST,
R. Praise we and magnify we Him for ever.
V. O LORD, hear my prayer,
R. And let my cry come unto Thee.

LET US PRAY.

Almighty and Everlasting God, Who hast given us, Thy servants, grace by the confession of a true faith to acknowledge the glory of the Eternal TRINITY, and in the power of the Divine Majesty to worship the Unity, we beseech Thee, that, by stedfastness in this faith, we may evermore be defended from all adversities.

O GOD, Who declarest Thy Almighty power most chiefly in showing mercy and pity, multiply upon us Thy mercy, that we, running the way of Thy commandments, may obtain Thy gracious promises and be made partakers of Thy heavenly treasure.

Almighty and everlasting GOD, Who art always more ready to hear than we to pray, and art wont to give more than either we desire or deserve; pour down upon us the abundance of Thy mercy, forgiving us those things whereof our conscience is afraid, and giving us those things which we are not worthy to ask, through CHRIST our LORD. Amen.

LITANIES

TO GOD THE FATHER,

Gathered out of Holy Scripture.

KYRIE, eleëson, LORD, have mercy,
CHRISTE, eleëson, CHRIST, have mercy,
KYRIE, eleëson, LORD, have mercy,
Holy FATHER, hear us,
Righteous FATHER, hearken unto us,
O GOD the FATHER, of Heaven, have mercy upon us,
O GOD the SON, REDEEMER of the world,
O GOD, the HOLY GHOST,
O HOLY TRINITY, One GOD.
Our FATHER, Which art in Heaven [a],
The Blessed GOD and FATHER of our LORD JESUS CHRIST [b],
FATHER of mercies and GOD of all comfort [c],
Who comfortest us in all our tribulation [d],
The FATHER, GOD blessed for ever [e],
The FATHER, Who seekest worshippers in spirit and in truth [f],
The FATHER, of Whom are all things [g],
The FATHER of glory [h], and LORD of Heaven and earth,
Who hast sent Thine only Begotten SON into the world, that we may live through Him [i],
The FATHER of CHRIST, Who workest hitherto [k],
The FATHER of our LORD JESUS CHRIST, of Whom the whole family in heaven and earth is named [l],
Who hast chosen us in the SON, before the foundation of the world [m],
Who hast predestinated us unto the adoption of children by JESUS CHRIST [n],

} Have mercy upon us.

[a] Matt. vi. [b] 1 Pet. i. [c] 2 Cor. i. [d] Ib.
[e] Rom. ix. [f] John iv. [g] 1 Cor. viii. [h] Eph. i.
[i] 1 John iv. [k] John v. [l] Eph. iii. [m] Ib. i. [n] Ib.

Who hidest Thy mysteries from the wise and prudent, and revealest them unto babes [o],
Who hast blessed us with all spiritual blessings in heavenly places [p],
Who forgivest us our trespasses [q],
Who chosest us, that we should be holy and without blame before Thee [r],
Who givest the HOLY SPIRIT to them that ask Thee, [s],
The FATHER of Lights, from Whom every good gift and every perfect gift cometh down [t],
The FATHER, Who raisest up the dead and quickenest them [u],
The FATHER, Who seest in secret [v],
The FATHER, Who hast life in Thyself [w],
The Husbandman [x], That workest hitherto,
Who makest Thy Sun to rise on the evil and on the good [y],
Who sendest rain on the just and on the unjust [z].
Who numberest all the hairs of our head [a],
Who sparedst not Thy Own SON, but deliveredst Him up for us all [b],
Who callest us into the fellowship of Thy SON [c],
Who hast made us accepted in Thy beloved SON [d],
Whose SON took upon Him the form of a servant, that He might redeem His servants [e],
Who hast translated us into the kingdom of the SON of Thy love [f],
Who hast made us meet to be partakers of the inheritance of the saints [g],
Who hast bidden us to the wedding of Thy SON [h],
Who hast loved us and given us everlasting consolation [i],
Who didst so love the world, that Thou gavest Thine Only-Begotten SON [k],

} Have mercy upon us.

[o] Matt. xi.
[s] Luke xi.
[w] John v.
[a] Ib. x.
[e] Phil. ii.
[i] 2 Thess. ii.
[p] Eph. i.
[t] James i.
[x] Ib. xv.
[b] Rom. viii.
[f] Col. i.
[k] John iii.
[q] Matt. vi.
[u] John v.
[y] Matt. v.
[c] 1 Cor. i.
[g] Ib.
[r] Eph. i. [Col. i.]
[v] Matt. vi.
[z] Ib.
[d] Eph. i.
[h] Matt. xxii.

^l Who by a voice which came down from heaven, from the excellent glory, gavest honour to Thy SON¹,
Who wert well pleased in Thy SON ᵐ,
Whose good pleasure it was to give us the kingdom ⁿ,
Whose Face the Angels do always see in Heaven °,
Who hast bestowed such love upon us, that we should be called and be the sons of GOD ᵖ,
Who wouldest have us conformed to the Image of Thy SON ᵠ,
Who hast prepared a kingdom for Thine elect from the foundation of the world ʳ,
Who, without respect of persons, judgest according to every man's work ˢ,
In Whose House are many mansions ᵗ,
The FATHER, with Whom nothing is impossible ᵘ,
The FATHER, Who lovest the SON, and hast given all things into His Hand ˣ,
Without Whom no man can come unto the SON, except Thou, O FATHER, draw him ʸ,

} Have mercy upon us.

Be propitious, spare us, O LORD.
Be propitious, hearken to us, O LORD.
Be propitious, deliver us, O LORD.
From all evil;
From the power of Satan,
From anger, hatred, and all ill-will,
From the over-hanging perils of sin,
From eternal death,
By Thy deep Knowledge, whereby Thou fathomest the unfathomable,
By Thy immeasurable power, whereby Thou madest all things out of nothing,
By Thy sweet Providence, whereby Thou rulest all [things,
By Thine everlasting Love, wherewith Thou hast loved the world,
By Thine Infinite Goodness, wherewith Thou fillest all [things,
In the Day of Judgment,

} Deliver us, O LORD.

¹ 2 Pet. i.   ᵐ Ib.   ⁿ Luke xii.   ° Matt. xviii.
ᵖ 1 John iii.   ᵠ Rom. viii.   ʳ Matt. xxv.   ˢ 1 Pet. i.
ᵗ John xiv.   ᵘ Luke i.   ˣ John iii.   ʸ Ib. vi.

§ i.]   DEVOTIONS TO THE ALL-HOLY TRINITY.   41

We, sinners, beseech Thee to hear us,
That Thy Name be, always and in all places, hallowed,
That it please Thee that Thy kingdom come to us,
That Thy Will be ever done in us, as in Heaven so in earth,
That Thou vouchsafe to give us our daily bread,
That Thou vouchsafe mercifully to forgive us our debts,
That Thou vouchsafe to defend us under the shadow of Thy wings, and deliver us from all temptations,
That Thou vouchsafe to deliver us from all evil,
That Thou vouchsafe to give Thy HOLY SPIRIT to them that ask Thee,
That what we ask faithfully we may obtain effectually,
That Thou grant us, according to the riches of Thy Glory, to be strengthened with might by Thy SPIRIT in the inner man,
O FATHER, in the Name of Thy SON,

} We, beseech Thee to hear us.

LAMB OF GOD, that takest away the sins of the world, &c. (as in p. 36.)

V. Regard us, O GOD, our Protector,
R. And look upon the Face of Thine Anointed.
V. Remember us in Thy good pleasure, O LORD,
R. Visit us with Thy Salvation.
V. O LORD, show Thy mercy upon us,
R. And grant us Thy Salvation.
V. Turn us, O LORD GOD of hosts,
R. Show the light of Thy Countenance and we shall be whole.
V. O LORD, hear my prayer,
R. And let my crying come unto Thee.

LET US PRAY.

Order our doings, Almighty Everlasting GOD, in Thy good pleasure, that, in the Name of Thy Beloved Son, we may obtain grace to abound in all good works.

O GOD, the high Tower of the lowly and the strength

of the upright, Who hast so vouchsafed to teach the world by Thine Only-Begotten Son, that every action done by Him should be for our instruction; stir up in us the fervour of Thy Spirit, that the things which He by word or deed taught to our souls' health, we may have strength faithfully to imitate.

O God, from Whom all good things do come, grant to us Thy humble servants, that by Thy holy inspiration we may think those things that be good, and by thy merciful guiding may perform the same, through Christ our Lord.

LITANIES,

CONTAINING THE PRINCIPAL NAMES, TITLES, PRAISES, AND OFFICES OT THE WORD INCARNATE, OUR LORD JESUS CHRIST,

From the Scriptures of both Testaments.

Kyrie, eleëson, Lord, have mercy.
Christe, eleëson, Christ, have mercy.
Kyrie, eleëson, Lord, have mercy.
O God, the Father of Heaven, have mercy upon us.
O God the Son, Redeemer of the world,
O God the Holy Ghost,
O Holy Trinity, One God,
O Word, made Flesh [a],
O Word, full of grace and truth [b],
O Word of the Lord [c],
God, by Whom all things are made [d],
The Blessed Lord God of Israel [e],
The Only-Begotten Son of God [f],
The Beloved Son of God [g],
Saviour, Christ the Lord [h],

} Have mercy upon us.

[a] John i.   [b] Ib.   [c] Ps. xxxiii.   [d] John i.
[e] Luke i.   [f] John iii.   [g] Luke iii   [h] Luke ii.

§ i.]   DEVOTIONS TO THE ALL-HOLY TRINITY.   43

Great and Son of the Highest [1],
Son of the living God [k],
Emmanuel, that is, God with us [1],
The Only-Begotten Son, Who art in the Bosom of the Father [m],
The Beloved Son of God, in Whom the Father is well pleased [n],
The Almighty Word of the Lord [o],
Wisdom, set up from the beginning [p],
Blessed, Who comest in the Name of the Lord [q],
The Arm of the Lord [r],
The Salvation of our God [s],
The Image of the Invisible God [t],
To Whom a Name is given which is above every name [u],
Upholding all things by the word of Thy Power [x],
The Beginning of the Creation of God [y],
The First-Born of every creature [z],
The First-Born among many brethren [a],
The Heir of all things [b],
The Rose of Sharon and the Lily of the Valleys [c],
The righteous Branch of the Lord [d],
The Expectation of the Gentiles [e],
Wonderful, Counsellor, the Mighty God [f],
Angel of the Lord [g],
Angel of the Covenant [h],
Our God, Who hast shown Thyself upon the earth and conversed with men [i],
Seed of Abraham [k],
Star risen out of Jacob [l],
Lion of the tribe of Judah [m],
Stem of Jesse [n],

} Have mercy upon us.

[1] Luke i.   [k] Matt. xvi.   [l] Ib. i.   [m] John i.
[n] Matt. iii. [o] Wisd. xviii.   [p] Prov. viii.   [q] Luke xix.
[r] Isai. liii. [s] Isai. lii.   [t] Colos. i.   [u] Phil. ii.
[x] Heb. i.   [y] Apoc. iii.   [z] Colos. i.   [a] Rom. viii.
[b] Heb. i.   [c] Cant. ii.   [d] Isai. iv. [Jer. xxiii.]
[e] Gen. xlix. [10] [f] Isai. ix. [g] Ps. xxxiv.   [h] Malach. iii.
[i] Baruch iii. [k] Gal. iii.   [l] Num. xxiv.   [m] Apoc. v.
[n] Isai. xi.

Son of David º,
Son of Man ᵖ,
Jesus of Nazareth ᑫ,
Man compassed by a woman ʳ,
The Holy Thing born of the Blessed Virgin ˢ,
First-Born Son of Mary ᵗ,
Fruit of Mary's Womb ᵘ,
Jesus, Son of Joseph of Nazareth ˣ,
Truth, That hath flourished out of the earth ʸ,
At Whose Name every knee boweth, of things in Heaven, and things in earth, and things under the earth ᶻ,
In Whom are hid all the treasures of wisdom and knowledge ᵃ,
By Whom all things were made, and without Whom was not any thing made ᵇ,
In Whom dwelleth all the Fulness of the GODHEAD bodily ᶜ,
A High Priest for ever after the order of Melchizedec ᵈ,
A High Priest of good things to come ᵉ,
A High Priest, holy, harmless, undefiled, separate from sinners, and made higher than the Heavens ᶠ,
A High Priest, Who art passed into the Heavens ᵍ,
Meek and lowly of heart ʰ,
A Spouse beloved, white and ruddy, the chiefest among ten thousand ⁱ,
Head of the body, the Church ᵏ,
Head of all principality and power ˡ,
The good Shepherd, Who layest down Thy life for Thy sheep ᵐ,
The Shepherd and Bishop of our Souls ⁿ,
The Holy of Holies º,

} Have mercy upon us.

º Matt. i. ᵖ Matt. viii. &c. ᑫ John xix. &c. ʳ Jerem. xxxi.
ˢ Luke i. ᵗ Matt. i. ᵘ Luke i. ˣ John. i.
ʸ Ps. lxxxv. ᶻ Phil. ii. ᵃ Colos. ii. ᵇ John i.
ᶜ Colos. ii. ᵈ Ps. cx. ᵉ Heb. ix. ᶠ Ib. vii.
ᵍ Ib. iv. ʰ Matt. xi. ⁱ Cantic. v. ᵏ Colos. i.
ˡ Ib. ii. ᵐ John x. ⁿ 1 Pet. ii. º Dan. ix.

The Chief Shepherd [p],
The faithful and true Witness [q],
A Great Prophet [r],
A Prophet, mighty in deed and word, before GOD and all the people [s],
Of a truth that Prophet That should come into the world [t],
MESSIAH, the Desire of all nations [u],
Who wast sent to preach the Gospel to the poor, to heal the broken-hearted, to preach deliverance to the captives [v],
Anointed by the LORD with the HOLY GHOST and with power [w],
Anointed by GOD with the oil of gladness above Thy fellows [x],
Fairer than the children of men [y],
The great King upon all the earth [z],
King of the Jews [a],
King of Israel [b],
Higher than the kings of the earth [c],
The LORD our Lawgiver [d],
A Living Stone, Chosen of GOD, and Precious [e],
A Stone refused by the builders, become the Head-Stone of the corner [f],
A Stone cut out of the mountain without hands [g],
A Stone laid in Zion; a chief Corner-Stone, Elect, Precious [h],
Set for the fall and rising again of many in Israel [i],
The Light of the World [k],
The true Light, Which lighteneth every man that cometh into the world [l],
The bright and morning Star [m],

} Have mercy upon us.

[p] 1 Pet. v.   [q] Apoc. iii.   [r] Luke vii.   [s] Ib. xxiv.
[t] John vi.   [u] John iv. Hag. ii.   [v] Isai. lxi. Lu. iv.   [w] Acts x.
[x] Ps. xlv.   [y] Ib.   [z] Ps. xlvii.   [a] Matt. ii. &c.
[b] John i.   [c] Ps. lxxxix.   [d] Isai. xxxiii.   [e] 1 Pet. ii.
[f] Ps. cxviii.   [g] Dan. ii.   [h] Eph. ii. & 1 Pet. ii.
[i] Luke ii.   [k] John viii.   [l] Ib. i.   [m] Apoc. xxii.

The Sun of Righteousness [n],
The Way, the Truth, and the Life [o],
The true Vine, whereof we are the branches [p],
The Key of David [q],
The Door of the Sheep [r],
The Ark of the Testament of GOD [s],
The hidden Manna [t],
The Living and True Bread Which came down from Heaven [u],
The Bread of Life and Understanding [v],
The Bread which giveth life unto the world [w],
Our super-substantial Bread [x],
The Bread of GOD that strengtheneth man's heart [y],
The fat Bread which yieldeth royal dainties [z],
Rabbi, a teacher come from GOD [a],
The Prince of the kings of the earth [b],
GOD, the Prince of Peace [c],
Our Peace, Who hast made both One [d],
Master and Lord [e],
Lord of lords and King of kings [f],
Man of sorrows and acquainted with grief [g],
Who hast borne our griefs and carried our sorrows [h],
By Whose stripes we are healed [i],
Who hast loved us and washed us from our sins in Thine Own Blood [k],
Upon Whom GOD hath laid the iniquity of us all [l],
Led as a sheep to the slaughter [m],
As a sheep before her shearers, dumb [n],
Lamb without spot [o],
Lamb slain from the foundation of the world [p],
Who wert wounded for our transgressions, Who wert bruised for our iniquities [q],

} Have mercy upon us.

n Malach. iv. o John xiv.   p Ib. xv.   q Apoc. iii.
r John x.   s Apoc. xi.   t Ib. ii.   u John vi.
v Ecclus. xv. w John vi.   x Matt. vi.   y Ps. civ.
z Gen. xlix.   a John iii.   b Apoc. i.   c Is. ix.
d Eph. ii.   e John. xiii. f Apoc. xvii. g Isai. liii.
h Ib. i Ib.   k Apoc. i.   l Isai. liii. m Acts viii.
n Isai. liii. o Exod. xii. p Apoc. xiii. q Isai. liii.

§ i.]   DEVOTIONS TO THE ALL-HOLY TRINITY.   47

Who hast saved Thy people from their sins [r],
Our Prince and Saviour [s],
The Salvation of God sent unto the Gentiles [t],
The Propitiation for our sins [u],
Who art made of God unto us Wisdom, and Righteousness, and Sanctification, and Redemption [v],
The Apostle and High Priest of our profession [x],
Who camest not to call the righteous but sinners [y],
Who camest to seek and to save that which was lost [z],
Who madest Thyself of no reputation, and tookest upon Thee the form of a servant [a],
Who didst lay down Thy life for us [b],
Who hast purchased a Church with Thine own Blood [c],
Who camest not to be ministered unto, but to minister [d],
Who becamest obedient to God the FATHER even unto the Death of the Cross [e],
The One Mediator between God and man, the Man CHRIST JESUS [f],
The Mediator of a New Covenant [g],
The Author and Finisher of the faith [h],
Who didst deliver us from the wrath to come [i],
My LORD and my GOD [k],
The LORD, strong and mighty in battle [l],
The LORD of Hosts [m],
The First-Begotten of the dead [n],
The Resurrection and the Life [o],
Who wast dead and art alive [p],
Who wast delivered for our sins, and wast raised again for our justification [q],
Who hast made us kings and priests to Thy God and Thy FATHER [r],

} Have mercy upon us.

[r] Matt. i.   [s] Acts v.   [t] Ib. xxviii.   [u] 1 John ii.
[v] 1 Cor. i.   [x] Heb. iii.   [y] Matt. ix.   [z] Luke xix.
[a] Phil. ii.   [b] 1 John iii.   [c] Acts xx.   [d] Matt. xx.
[e] Phil. ii.   [f] 1 Tim. ii.   [g] Heb. viii.   [h] Ib. xii.
[i] 1 Thess. i. [k] John xx.   [l] Ps. xxiv.   [m] Zech. ii.
[n] Apoc. i.   [o] John xi.   [p] Apoc. i.   [q] Rom. iv.
[r] Apoc. i.

Who wert offered of Thine Own ill [r],
Our Passover [s],
Who hast the keys of death and hell [t],
To Whom all power is given in Heaven and in earth [u],
Who didst ascend up far above all Heavens [x],
Who sittest at the Right Hand of the MAJESTY on high [y],
Our Advocate with the FATHER [z],
By Whom we have access unto the FATHER [a],
Who art, and wast, and art to come [b],
Who hast in all things the pre-eminence [c],
Who livest for ever and ever [d],
The Everlasting FATHER [e],
The Temple and Light of the Holy City [f],
CHRIST, our Peace, Who hast made both One [g],
Our Hope [h],
The King of Glory [i],
The Brightness of the Everlasting Light [k],
The Brightness of the Glory and the express Image of the Person of GOD [l],
The Unspotted Mirror of the Power of GOD [m],
The Tree of Life [n],
The Light of Life [o],
The Well of Life [p],
The Author of Life [q],
Alpha and Omega [r],
The Beginning and the End [s],
The First and the Last [t],
Who art ordained of GOD, the Judge of quick and dead [u],
Who art over all GOD blessed for ever [x],

} Have mercy upon us.

[r] Isa. liii.
[s] 1 Cor. v.
[t] Apoc. i.
[u] Matt. xxviii
[x] Ephes. iv.
[y] Heb. i.
[z] 1 John ii.
[a] Eph. ii.
[b] Apoc. i.
[c] Col. i.
[d] Apoc. i.
[e] Isai. ix.
[f] Apoc. xxi.
[g] Ephes. ii.
[h] 1 Tim. i.
[i] Ps. xxiv.
[k] Wis. vii.
[l] Heb. i.
[m] Wis. vii.
[n] Apoc. ii.
[o] John viii.
[p] Ps. xxxvi.
[q] Acts iii.
[r] Apoc. i.
[s] Ib.
[t] Apoc. xxii.
[u] Acts x. & 2 Tim. iv.
[x] Rom. ix.

Be propitious, spare us, O LORD,
From all evil, deliver us, O LORD,
By Thy Eternal Generation from Thy FATHER,
By Thy temporal Nativity from Thy Mother,
By Thy most Holy Life and conversation,
By Thy most bitter Passion and Death,
By Thy glorious Resurrection and Ascension,
By Thy coming to Judgment,
By Thy Co-eternal Glory with GOD the FATHER,
} Deliver us, O LORD.

We, sinners, beseech Thee to hear us.

That we may seek first the kingdom of GOD and His righteousness [y],

That we may learn of Thee, for Thou art meek and lowly of heart [z],

That we may love our enemies, and do good to them that hate us [a],

That we may deny ourselves, take up our cross, and follow Thee [b],

That we may be wise as serpents, and harmless as doves [c],

That our light may so shine before men, that they may see our good works and glorify our FATHER which is in Heaven [d],

That we may lose our lives in this world, so as to keep them unto life eternal [e],

That we fear not them that kill the body, but Him which is able to destroy both soul and body in hell [f],

That we lay not up for ourselves treasure upon earth, but in heaven [g],

That we may never judge our neighbours rashly [h],

That, when we ask the FATHER in Thy Name, we may, according to Thy promise, have grace to be heard [i],

That all things which we would have men do to us, we may do to them [k],

} We beseech Thee to hear us.

[y] Matt. vi.   [z] Ib. xi.   [a] Ib. v.   [b] Ib. xvi.
[c] Ib. x.   [d] Ib. v.   [e] John xii.   [f] Matt. x.
[g] Ib. vi.   [h] Ib. vii.   [i] John xvi.   [k] Matt. vii.

That we take heed to ourselves, lest at any time our hearts be overcharged with surfeiting, and drunkenness, and cares of this life [1],

That, leaving the broad way that leadeth to destruction, all may strive to enter in at the strait gate which leadeth unto life [m],

That we may gladly and willingly take upon us Thy easy yoke and Thy light burden [n],

That we may carefully put out to interest the talents we have received from Thee [o],

That, receiving Thy Word into an honest and good heart, we may bring forth much fruit with patience [p],

That, being uncertain of the hour of our death and Thy Coming, we may ever study to be watchful and prepared [q],

That we may seriously prepare ourselves to give an account of our stewardship [r],

That, enduring by Thy grace unto the end, we may be saved [s],

We beseech Thee to hear us.

LAMB OF GOD, that takest away the sins of the world,
Have mercy upon us.
LAMB OF GOD, that takest away the sins of the world,
Hearken to us, O LORD.
LAMB OF GOD, that takest away the sins of the world,
Grant us Thy peace.
  Our FATHER, &c.

LET US PRAY.

O GOD, Who by Thy Co-eternal Wisdom didst create man when as yet he was not, and didst mercifully new-create him when he was lost, grant, we beseech Thee, that by the inspiration of the same wisdom, we may love Thee with all our mind, and run after Thee with all our heart, through the same JESUS CHRIST our LORD, Who liveth and reigneth with Thee in the Unity of the Holy Ghost now and ever. Amen.

[l] Luke xxi.   [m] Matt. vii.   [n] Ib. xi.   [o] Ib. xxv.
[p] Luke viii.   [q] Matt. xxv. &c.   [r] Luke xvi.   [s] Matt. x.

LITANIES

TO THE HOLY GHOST,

Gathered out of Holy Scriptures.

KYRIE, eleëson, LORD, have mercy.
CHRISTE, eleëson, CHRIST, have mercy.
KYRIE, eleëson, LORD, have mercy.
O GOD the FATHER of Heaven, have mercy upon us.
O GOD the SON, Redeemer of the world,
O GOD the HOLY GHOST,
O HOLY TRINITY, One GOD,
O SPIRIT, proceeding from the FATHER and the SON [a],
SPIRIT, That testifiest of CHRIST [b],
SPIRIT of truth, That teachest us all things [c],
SPIRIT, That guidest us into all truth [d],
SPIRIT, That didst come upon Mary [e],
SPIRIT, by Whose marvellous power the Incarnation of the LORD was effected in the Virgin's Womb [f],
SPIRIT of the LORD, That fillest the world [g],
SPIRIT of GOD, That dwellest in us [h],
SPIRIT of wisdom and understanding [i],
SPIRIT of counsel and might [j],
SPIRIT of knowledge and piety [k],
SPIRIT of the fear of the LORD [l],
SPIRIT of grace and mercy [m],
SPIRIT of holiness [n],
SPIRIT of power, and of love, and of a sound mind [o],
SPIRIT of grace and supplications [p],
SPIRIT of faith, peace, and love [q],
SPIRIT of lowliness and chastity [r],
SPIRIT of charity, goodness, and meekness [s],
SPIRIT of long-suffering, temperance, and continence [t],

} Have mercy upon us.

[a] John xv.   [b] Ib.   [c] John xiv.   [d] Ib. xvi.
[e] Luke i.   [f] Ib.   [g] Wisd. i.   [h] 2 Tim. i.
[i] Isa. xi.   [j] Ib.   [k] Ib.   [l] Ib.
[m] Heb. x.   [n] Rom. i.   [o] 2 Tim. 1.   [p] Zech. xii.
[q] Rom. viii.   [r] Gal. v.   [s] Ib.   [t] Ib.

SPIRIT of compunction [a],
SPIRIT of manifold grace [x],
SPIRIT of the LORD, Who, at the beginning of creation moving upon the face of the waters, didst brood over them and make them fruitful [y],
SPIRIT, by Whose inspiration holy men of GOD did speak [z],
SPIRIT, Whose unction teacheth us of all things [a],
SPIRIT, Who searchest all things, even the deep things of GOD [b],
SPIRIT, Who intercedest for us with groanings which cannot be uttered [c],
SPIRIT, Who didst descend upon CHRIST in the form of a dove [d],
SPIRIT, by Whom we are born again [e],
SPIRIT, by Whom the love of GOD is shed abroad in our hearts [f],
SPIRIT of the LORD, That restedst upon CHRIST [g],
SPIRIT of adoption of the sons of GOD [h],
SPIRIT, That helpest our infirmities [i],
SPIRIT, lovely, good, sweeter than honey [k],
SPIRIT princely, Who dost establish us [l],
SPIRIT, Who on the day of Pentecost appearedst, sitting in fiery tongues on the disciples of the LORD [m],
SPIRIT, with Whom the Apostles being filled, boldly confessed CHRIST [n],
SPIRIT, Who convincest the world of sin, of righteousness, and judgment [o],
SPIRIT, Who purifiest our hearts by faith [p],
SPIRIT, Who quickenest us [q],
SPIRIT, Who diversely distributest Thy gifts and graces [r],

Have mercy upon us.

[u] Rom. xi. [8.]   [x] 1 Pet. iv.   [y] Gen. i.   [z] 2 Pet. i.
[a] 1 John ii.   [b] 1 Cor. ii.   [c] Rom. viii.   [d] Matt. iii.
[e] John iii.   [f] Rom. v.   [g] Isai. xi.   [h] Rom. viii.
[i] Ib.   [k] Ecclus. xxiv.   [l] Ps. li.   [m] Acts ii.
[n] Ib. iv.   [o] John xvi.   [p] Acts xv.   [q] John vi.
[r] 1 Cor. xii.

§ i.]   DEVOTIONS TO THE ALL-HOLY TRINITY.   53

Spirit, Who dividest to every man severally as Thou wilt ˢ,
Spirit, the Discerner of the thoughts and intents of the heart ᵗ,
Spirit, Paraclete, Who abidest with us for ever ᵘ,
Spirit of discipline, That fleest deceit, nor dwellest in the body which is subject unto sin ˣ,
} Have mercy upon us.

From all evil, deliver us, Holy Spirit,
Be propitious, spare us, Holy Spirit.
Be propitious, hearken unto us, Holy Spirit.
From all sin,
From the temptations and snares of the devil,
From all presumption and desperation,
From questioning acknowledged truth,
From envying brotherly charity,
From all obstinacy and impenitence,
From all uncleanness of mind and body,
From the spirit of wrath, strife, and dissension,
From the spirit of fornication,
From every evil spirit,
By Thine Eternal Procession from the Father and the Son,
By the miraculous conception of the Son of God by Thy co-operation,
By Thy descent on Christ at His Baptism,
By Thy Appearance at the Transfiguration of the Lord,
By Thy coming upon the disciples of Christ,
In the Day of Judgment,
} Deliver us, Holy Spirit.

We sinners beseech Thee to hear us.
That Thou mayest spare us,
That, as we live in the Spirit, we may also walk in the Spirit ʸ,
That by the Spirit we may mortify the deeds of the body ᶻ,
That we grieve not the Holy Spirit of God ᵃ,
That we do not despite unto the Spirit of grace ᵇ,
} We beseech &c.

ˢ Ib.   ᵗ Heb. iv.   ᵘ John xiv.   ˣ Wisd. i.
ʸ Gal. v.   ᶻ Rom. viii.   ᵃ Eph. iv.   ᵇ Heb. x.

That we be careful to keep the unity of the Spirit in the bond of peace [c],
That, walking in the Spirit, we fulfil not the lusts of the flesh [d],
That we believe not every spirit, but try the spirits whether they be of God [e],
That, remembering our body is the temple of the Holy Ghost, we take heed not to defile it [f],
That we may instruct the erring in the spirit of gentleness and meekness [g],
That we may sow in the Spirit, and of the Spirit reap life everlasting [h],
That Thou vouchsafe to stir up and nourish in us poverty of spirit [i],
That Thou vouchsafe to make us meek and gentle [k],
That Thou vouchsafe to give us the grace of pious mourning and holy tears [l],
That Thou vouchsafe to create in us the hunger and thirst after true righteousness [m],
That Thou vouchsafe to pour into us sincere affections of charity and mercy [n],
That Thou vouchsafe to make us a clean heart and renew a right spirit within us [o],
That we may be peace-makers, and worthy to be called the children of God [p],
That we may patiently and constantly endure persecution for righteousness' sake [q],
That Thou keep us from blasphemy against the Spirit, to which pardon is denied both in this world and in that which is to come [r],
That we grieve not the Holy Spirit of God whereby we are sealed [s],
That Thou grant us to persevere unto the end in faith, hope, and charity,

We beseech Thee to hear us.

[c] Eph. iv. [d] Gal. v. [e] 1 John iv. [f] 1 Cor. vi.
[g] Gal. vi. [h] Ib. [i] Matt. v. [k] Ib.
[l] Ib. [m] Ib. [n] Ib. [o] Ps. li.
[p] Matt. v. [q] Ib. [r] Matt. xii. [s] Eph. iv.

LAMB of GOD, That takest away the sins of the world,
  Pour on us the HOLY SPIRIT.
LAMB of GOD, That takest away the sins of the world,
  Send forth on us the promised SPIRIT of the FATHER.
LAMB of GOD, That takest away the sins of the world,
  Give unto us the SPIRIT of peace.
            Our Father.
V. Make me a clean heart, O GOD,
R. And renew a right spirit within me.
V. Cast me not away from Thy Presence,
R. And take not Thy HOLY SPIRIT from me.
V. O give me the comfort of Thy Help again,
R. And stablish me with Thy free SPIRIT.
V. May the grace of Thy HOLY SPIRIT
R. Enlighten our senses and our hearts.
V. O LORD, hear my prayer,
R. And let my crying come unto Thee.

           LET US PRAY.

O GOD, unto Whom all hearts be open, all desires known, and from Whom no secrets are hid, cleanse the thoughts of our hearts by the inspiration of Thy HOLY SPIRIT, that we may perfectly love Thee and worthily magnify Thy Holy Name.

Grant, O LORD, we beseech Thee, that by the power of Thy HOLY SPIRIT our hearts may be mercifully cleansed from all impurity, and we may be defended from all adversities.

Almighty Everlasting GOD, by Whose SPIRIT the whole body of the Church is governed and sanctified, receive our supplications and prayers, which we offer before Thee for all estates of men in Thy Holy Church, that every order of the same, by the gift of Thy grace, may faithfully serve Thee, through CHRIST our LORD. Amen.

CHAPTER IV.

ROSARY, OBLATIONS, AND DAILY EXERCISES TO THE MOST HOLY TRINITY.

ROSARY OF THE MOST HOLY TRINITY.

USED AND RECOMMENDED BY ILLUSTRIOUS DIVINES.

It is recited as follows :—
After saying the Apostles' Creed, I believe in GOD, &c. *say*

O GOD the FATHER, of Heaven, have mercy upon us.
O GOD the SON, REDEEMER of the world, have mercy upon us.
O GOD the HOLY GHOST, have mercy upon us.
HOLY TRINITY, One GOD, have mercy upon us.

Then the Rosary is said in three divisions of Ten. At the beginning of each Ten, or at the three larger beads of the Rosary, the LORD's *Prayer is said, and the Angelic Hymn from Revelation* vii. Blessing, and glory, and wisdom, and thanksgiving, and honour, and power, and might, be unto our GOD for ever and ever. *At each of the smaller beads read the words of the Seraphic Trishagion,* Isai. 6, *and of the Ecclesiastical Doxology.* Holy, Holy, Holy, is the LORD GOD of Sabaoth; the whole earth is full of His glory. Glory be to the FATHER, and to the SON, and to the HOLY GHOST, As it was in the beginning, is now, and ever shall be, world without end. Amen.

Cornelius à Lapide *(on Isaiah* vi.*) bear switness that many learned and wise men have used this exercise with great profit; for this short doxology is, as he says,*

1. A profession of faith in the Most HOLY TRINITY, *against Infidels and Heretics.*

2. An exercise of religion, hope, love, gratitude, and other graces.

3. An incitement to devotion and spiritual joy, whereby thou mayest manfully endure adversities and temptations, nobly overcome all difficulties, and, after the example of the Royal

Prophet, always give thanks unto the Lord.

4. *We emulate in our degree the life and office of Angels, while hereby we endeavour and begin to praise* GOD *assiduously, which things the angels do in heaven without intermission; and we too, hereafter, shall along with them in the same place; for this is the true life and function of Angels, to praise* GOD. *Hereby we begin to be blessed and to have our conversation in heaven, for we pass beyond things of earth, and are taken up with* GOD *and with praising Him. So far* Cornelius.

Add to this, that we habituate ourselves to the practice and exercise of a right intention, so as to refer all things to the greater glory of GOD.

And, on the other hand, we gradually put off that evil and dangerous affection, so natural to us, of looking in all things to our own glory; we profess that to GOD *Alone is rightly due all glory, as the chief fountain of good, and to us nothing but confusion.*

To excite and keep alive these and such like pious affections, divers religious and learned men have illustrated the hymn, Glory be to the Father, &c. *with various devout thoughts and meditations.* See Card. Toletanus, *Serm.* 14 and 15, *on Ps.* xxxi.; Julius Mazarinus, *in thirty Sermons;* Cornelius à Lapide, *on Rom.* xi.; Mauburn *in his Roset. Exercit.*, p. 1. *dist.* 1. *tit.* 6. *c.* 7. *The following short exercise, among the rest, seems to good purpose.*

Glory be to the FATHER, Who, by His Power, created me in His Image, when as yet I was not; *and to the* SON, Who, by His Wisdom and Blood, restored me when I was lost; *and to the* HOLY GHOST, Who, by His grace and goodness, justified me a child of wrath, first in Baptism, and hath since, after frequent falls, often justified me still.

For all and each of these mercies, such and so great glory, *as it was in the beginning* before all creation, in equal, yea, in higher degree, be *now*, in the course of this present life, and *evermore*, even to the end of all things, *world without end*, Amen; to all eternity, be given from all the Blessed in the Heavenly Home, where there will be no satiety, or rest, or cessation from the Praise of GOD. Such and so great praise and glory even *now* I desire, in saying this Doxology, to pay in act and truth to GOD. See how pregnant in holy meanings is this short formula.

And so Cornelius[a] thinks that no act can be done, no prayer offered more holy, none more worthy of GOD, or pleasing to Him, none more profitable to man. He tells us that B. Nicolas Serarius, of the Society of Jesus, was the Author of this Rosary, concerning whom the following passage occurs in the Life prefixed to his works.

"It is indescribable with what depth of holy feeling he was wont to use the formula of praise with which the Church concludes all the Psalms. It was the beginning and the end of all his actions in public and in private. The ardour with which he pronounced it shone forth in his countenance. Did he hear it sung by the chanters with more than ordinary beauty, he seemed to exult in holy joy and triumph. The fulness of heavenly meaning, with reference to the Divine Nature, which flowed thence into his soul, the contemplation of the Divine Glory, which, by pondering thereon, grew day by day brighter in his bosom, he exhibited not only in frequent discourses, made as occasion offered, but he has left in writing, also, records of the same," &c.

Furthermore, to recite this chaplet of praise with greater profit and affection, note (from Thomas Saille in his Thesaurus Precum),

The three principal things which we may do by using this Doxology: 1. Praise the MOST HOLY TRINITY. 2. Render to the Same thanksgiving. 3. Petition for somewhat from It. Reflect, then, before beginning the Rosary, which of these things you intend, whether all at once, or one of them in each Ten, or One only through all of them.

2. Set before yourself some cause, either general or particular, on account of which you would praise GOD; e. g. I desire to render thanks to, or to praise GOD for the most Holy Nativity of CHRIST, His Passion, &c.; for my own calling, for this private or public blessing (specifying it), &c. So, too, reflect what you would pray for; any virtue or grace, deliverance from any temptation, or assistance in any particular matter. Whatever you pray for (if it be rightly), you cannot but be seeking greater glory to GOD.

[a] Loco citato.

THE DAILY EXERCISE

TO THE MOST HOLY TRINITY

Of Blaise Palma, Clerk Regular of St. Paul.

O Most Merciful LORD, my GOD, FATHER, SON, and HOLY SPIRIT, Who didst create me for Thyself, and to Whom for very many most grave reasons I owe the tribute of myself; I do now, with all the strength I am able, direct and offer unto Thy Divine Majesty all the thoughts, words, and actions of my whole life, specially of this day, uniting them with the Merits and Works of CHRIST, my most Dear Redeemer.

O that besides this my narrow heart, I had (of Thy Divine power to which nothing is impossible), infinite faculties, whose only desire, office, and constant aim it might be, unwearyingly to regard, confess, meditate upon, love and praise Thee, my GOD and my LORD!

And now I do protest before Thee and the whole Heavenly Court, that this is all my mind, this my longing and my desire, in every thought, word, and deed; yea, in every sigh, motion, and breath; this my single wish and intention, to unite with them, and to add my share to that multiplied energy of holy acts and hearts which please Thy Divine Majesty, that they with me may never cease that exercise, whereto by the gift of creation and preservation they are bound, which is, ever to know, to worship, and to love Thee.

And this duty I do now offer, and wish so to do, with all the perfection and sincerity possible; without respect, O LORD, to any reward or punishment; but simply for Thy sake, my Chief Good; for it is most meet that I should do so, and chiefly,

1. That I may profess Thy Supreme Majesty, Glory, and Excellence, and so join my heart most closely unto Thee.

2. That I may render thanks to Thee for Thy

numberless mercies, (whether general or particular) bestowed upon me.

3. That in some degree I may make amends for my sins, and find Thee propitious unto me, now and at the hour of death.

4 That I may obtain of Thee the help of Thy grace, and all that Thou knowest needful for me towards the attainment of final perseverance and the eternal fruition of Thee.

Thee, then, O my most loving LORD, I humbly pray, by the bowels of Thy mercies, vouchsafe to accept all these oblations, to preserve me from all sin, and give me grace that I may never barter any part of my heart for any transitory creature, but may entirely, such as I am, be joined to Thee Alone, O GOD my Creator, my LORD and my Chief Good, for ever.

A MOST BEAUTIFUL OBLATION OF OURSELVES,

Wherein, considering the titles of GOD, *as the Author of Nature, we may offer ourselves to Him, with reference to our whole condition by nature, enumerating our several faculties or parts of our body in this wise.— From Francis Bourgoineus, Presbyter of the Congregation of the Oratory, in his Lignum Vitæ.*

O Most High, Eternal, Adorable TRINITY, One GOD! I offer to Thee my soul which Thou createdst out of nothing; I offer my body which Thou formedst out of clay; I present to Thee my reason, my memory, my heart and will; every energy and capability of those faculties, all the actions, affections, thoughts, desires, &c., which shall or can proceed from them throughout eternity, I offer and dedicate to Thee.

Accept, O LORD GOD, all my senses and their powers, their exercises and uses; my eyes and every glance, my hearing, smelling, taste, and touch; all their desires and operations; in fine, every artery, vein, member, and bone of my body, with all their faculties, movements, and actions, &c.

All these for ever I offer, dedicate, consecrate, and devote to Thee: Vouchsafe to accept this sacrifice of my service as a sweet smelling savour.

ANOTHER OBLATION TO GOD,

Wherein, considering the titles of GOD *in the work of Grace, we dedicate ourselves entirely to Him, with reference to the condition of our spiritual life.—From the same Bourgoineus.*

O Most High, Powerful and Merciful GOD, Adorable and Incomprehensible TRINITY! I offer, consecrate, and yield unto Thee my soul with all its powers and energies, every capability of my will to love Thee, and of my reason to know Thee, unto my own humiliation and Thy glory.

I present and offer unto Thee every obediential power of my soul, to co-operate with Thy Divine Grace, and to fulfil all Thy will. O LORD, Thou knowest all my desire, and my groaning is not hid from Thee; accept all the possible desires of my will to praise Thee, to please Thee, and to serve Thee.

Finally, I offer and give to Thee all my affections, thoughts, words, and actions, all that I have done, all that I may hereafter do, my life, my time, my eternity, my whole being in nature and in grace; in fine, myself as a most vile and unworthly slave of Thy Almighty Power and Thy Goodness, and as wholly dependent on Thy Mercy. By this gift of myself, never (by Thy Grace) to be recalled, with full intention of mind, I desire that all that I have shall be Thine for ever.

A MOST PROFITABLE DAILY EXERCISE,

Whereby to our great increase in Grace and Piety we may offer ourselves and all our actions, to GOD, *by uniting them with the Actions and Merits of our* LORD JESUS CHRIST.

Wonderful is the advance in Grace and Piety, which proceeds from the exercise and use of a right intention, whereby we refer all our actions to the Glory of GOD *Alone.*

But far more profitable will this exercise be, if we unite our actions with CHRIST'S, *and so offer them to the Eternal* FATHER. *St. Paul exhorteth to this;* "Whether ye eat, or drink, or whatever ye do, do all to the Glory of GOD."—1 *Cor.* x; *and again,* "Whatsoever ye do in word or deed, do all in the Name of the LORD JESUS."—*Col.* iii.

In this way our petty doings, else most worthless, in this way our distresses, griefs, and miseries, yea, our every step, breathing, and sigh, being united to CHRIST'S *Actions and Merits, will be clad in the highest preciousness and dignity, and cannot but be most pleasing to* GOD *the* FATHER.

It is as though lead were dipped into molten gold, and so invested with the beauty and preciousness of gold: as though a vessel of water were poured into a cask of the choicest wine, and were wholly changed into the nature of wine. It is thus we are warmly clad in the Fleece of the LAMB, *Which taketh away the sins of the world. How can we, poor, and wretched beings, who have no confidence in our own merits or righteousness, please the* FATHER, *save through the* SON, *in Whom He is well pleased? For He is our Head, by Whose influxion the members are nourished, of Whose fulness we have all received. And how shall the Gracious* FATHER *despise us, when He looks upon the Face of His Anointed?*

AN OBLATION
TO GOD THE FATHER.

O Most Pitiful FATHER of Mercies, and GOD of all Comfort! I, though Thine unworthy creature and unprofitable slave, do humbly present myself to Thee, my most Gracious LORD and CREATOR; I come to Thee, a suppliant, not trusting in my own merits, but in the merits of Thy Most Dearly Beloved SON, our LORD JESUS CHRIST, desiring to be made partaker of Thy Grace and Bounty, by the aid of which in my every thought, word, and work, I may be able so to order myself according to the rule of Thy Will and Good Pleasure, as to present unto Thee, my LORD, my bounden service, acceptable and pleasing unto Thee.

To Thee, therefore, O Most Gracious FATHER, I offer my whole self, and all I have, (of all Thou art the Giver and the Preserver) for a most ready service and obedience unto Thee; and this I do in union with the Oblation which Thy Most Beloved SON, our LORD JESUS CHRIST, made, when He offered and commended Himself unto Thee, first, in His Infancy in the Temple, afterwards praying in the Garden, and lastly, dying on the Altar of the Cross.

Be propitious, Most Merciful FATHER, to me, a most miserable sinner; despise me not, the work of Thine Own Hands; but look upon the Face of Thine Anointed, Whom Thou hast given unto us for an Advocate and Mediator.

May His Dignity compensate for my vileness, and by His Merits may I obtain what I cannot by my own.

Vouchsafe, therefore, of Thy Infinite Goodness and Pity, mercifully to accept this my service (though it be worthless), to the greater Glory of Thy Name, and the salvation of my soul.

OBLATION

of our Sleep and Watching.

O GOD, most sweet unto my soul! I offer to Thee my sleeping and watching, in union with every sleep and watching, and with the Resurrection of Thy SON my SAVIOUR, whereby on the third day, raised from Death as from sleep, He, of His own power, took His Life again. Grant, I pray Thee, that I may so use the necessary rest of my body, and so spend my watchings, that all may redound to Thy greater Glory and the salvation of my soul.

OBLATION

of the Thoughts, Words, and Works, &c.

O Most Loving GOD! I offer to Thee all my thoughts, words, and works, all my labours and business, on this day or at any other time to be performed by me, in union with all the labours, actions, and toils which Thy Only-Begotten, our SAVIOUR, once took on Him, to redeem us miserable sinners.

All these I offer, in acknowledgement of the debt under which I lie to Thee, as my Supreme LORD, and giving Thee thanks for Thine unnumbered Blessings bestowed on me from my birth to the present hour.

Look upon me, O LORD, in mercy, and in all things so direct me according to Thy Divine Will, that by Thy Gift I may desire, and with all my might perform, the things which please Thee, to Thy greater Glory, and the salvation of my soul.

OBLATION
of the Refreshment and Care of the Body.

O Most Good God! I offer to Thee the necessary refreshment and care of my body in union with that Supper and refection, which Thy most sweet Son my Saviour instituted with His most dear Disciples, on the Eve of His Passion.

Grant me the help of Thy Grace, that I may moderate the care and refreshment of my body, so to sustain and preserve it, as to render it more fit to serve and honour Thee, and without hurt or disadvantage to my soul.

OBLATION
of Prayer and Pious Exercises.

O Most Merciful God! I offer to Thee my prayers and supplications of this day, and all the good works and exercises of religion, which by Thy help and assistance I may undertake.

May it please Thee, O Eternal God, to accept them in union with all the Merits and Prayers of Thy Son Jesus Christ, which He poured forth for us on Mount Olivet or elsewhere.

Grant to me always, O Lord, by the Love of Thy Most Dearly Beloved Son, a salutary issue to all my prayers, according as shall seem to Thee best to tend to Thy greater Honour, and my own salvation.

OBLATION
of Troubles, &c.

O Most Compassionate God! I offer to Thee all my tribulations, distresses, pains, and afflictions, which I either have suffered, or, according to Thy will, have to suffer, in union with the most bitter Passion of Thy Only Begotten Son, my Saviour, and in union with all the pains, torments, and afflictions which He refused not to undergo, that He might redeem me, a lost sinner.

Grant me Thy grace and help, O Most Good God, that I may never refuse to receive afflictions sent by Thee, or to endure them for Thy sake, but by bearing them with an equal and willing mind, may praise and glorify Thy Name, and seek and reap from them salvation for my soul. Amen.

OBLATION TO GOD THE SON.

O Most Good Lord JESUS CHRIST, Most Sweet unto my soul, SAVIOUR of the world! I, an unworthy sinner, yet redeemed by Thy Precious Blood, flee unto Thee my GOD and SAVIOUR with humble soul and the inmost affection of my heart.

And for that Thou, to redeem me, didst offer Thy whole Self on the Altar of the Cross to GOD the FATHER, as the Price of my redemption; I too, O Most loving JESU, do offer my whole self, whatever I am, whatever I shall be, unto Thee, with all I have and all I may hereafter have.

Receive, O LORD, I pray Thee, into the hands of Thy unspeakable pity both my soul and body, my senses, words, and actions, and in all things vouchsafe so to direct and govern me, that I may ever flee every occasion of sin, that I may never fall into the snare of the evil spirit, but may constantly so cleave to Thee, my GOD and my Redeemer, that neither life nor death, nor any lot which may befall me, may separate me from Thee.

I pray Thee, O most loving JESU, by that love which brought Thee down for our salvation from the Bosom of the Supreme FATHER into the womb of the Virgin, fill up the imperfect measure of my actions; for small, of a truth, is their value and worth, unless their defect be supplied out of Thy fulness.

Unite, I implore Thee, my most unworthy service with all that Thou didst do and suffer in Thy most perfect and ineffable charity and obedience; vouchsafe to offer it to Thine Eternal FATHER with the riches of the merits and satisfactions of Thy love, so that out of Thy abundance my poverty may be enriched, and the grace which of myself I in no wise deserve, I may through Thy mediation obtain.

I implore Thee, O Most Sweet JESU, by Thy holy Incarnation, Passion, and Death, and by all that Thou hast done for our salvation, have mercy upon my parents, brothers, sisters, friends, and benefactors, whether living or departed; communicate unto them the merits of Thy Precious Blood and of Thy Passion, that by the help of Thy grace they may so live

F

here, as finally to receive the rewards of eternal life in Heaven.

OBLATION TO THE HOLY GHOST.

O HOLY GHOST, One and True GOD with the FATHER and the SON, without Thee man hath nothing; for, regenerated by water and the HOLY SPIRIT, we are members of CHRIST JESUS and sons of His Church; which Church, by grace and goodness everflowing from Thee, Thou dost rule, protect, make fruitful, and sanctify.

To Thee, therefore, I offer my heart and my whole self; all I have and all I do, I humbly devote and consecrate to Thee.

Purify, I pray Thee, by the infusion of Thy gifts and grace, my senses and my heart, that I may ever serve Thee with a chaste body, and please Thee with a pure heart.

And because we cannot think a good thought without Thee, far less carry it into act, may Thy grace, I beseech Thee, always prevent and follow me, and make me ever to be given to all good works; and, as my doings cannot of themselves please Thee, mercifully accept them in union with the most holy works and Merits of CHRIST JESUS, that as He, being conceived by Thy overshadowing the most pure Virgin, became unto us a SAVIOUR, so we may feel our weakness and needs assisted by His grace, charity, and infinite Merits.

With Thy bright flame our senses light; Into our hearts Thy true love pour; Renew our breast's all-wasted might, With vigour that can waste no more. Amen.

CHAPTER V.

A METHOD OF ASPIRING AFTER AN INTIMATE UNION WITH GOD, BY INTERIOR ACTS OF VIRTUE;

OR,

EXERCISES, SPECIALLY FIT FOR THE TRUE WORSHIP AND LOVE OF GOD, AND FOR OBTAINING CHRISTIAN PERFECTION.

FROM BLAISE PALMA, CLERK REGULAR OF ST. PAUL, OFTEN PUBLISHED WITH UNIVERSAL APPROVAL IN ITALIAN.

PREFACE.

A Christian man, if he would live according to his name and calling, should constantly strive after union with Him Who is the End of his being, even GOD, and as far as is possible join his soul to HIM. As the easiest way and means thereto, St. Dionysius the Areopagite would have the faithful soul raise itself to GOD by constant aspirations and acts of holy fervour, of affection and desire, panting after Him with inward affection, holding converse and communing with Him; and he would have it long to cleave unto Him with a pure heart, fired with holy love.

This, says the same father, is that admirable and occult unitive wisdom, whereby, without previous meditation or search, the affection of the loving soul is raised upwards to GOD: this affection towards Him groweth in intensity by short, frequent, and ardent exercises of prayer and acts of virtue, so that it may be said, that the ground-work of perfection, specially of interior perfection, stands in certain definite acts and motions of the mind towards GOD and our neighbour; and such we here put down in the way of prayers. However, let him that useth these, take heed not thereby to intend to make any promise or vow which may bind him to new obligations, but let him exercise these Acts in the way of a free oblation and devotion; and then, the more often and earnestly he does this, the *greater benefit will he certainly reap, along with no unfounded hope of soon extricating himself from all earthly attachments, and of perfect union with* HIM *Who is his highest and true Good; i. e.* with GOD.

To which end, before all things (forsomuch as the end alone giveth to any work its value and praise) we will set down a solemn form of protestation, whereby the soul may in the presence of God frame a right intention and perfect direction of its will, so as, renouncing all things else, to make the glory and service of GOD *Alone, its end.*

I.

PURE INTENTION;

OR, A PROTESTATION OF ACTING PURELY FOR GOD, WITHOUT REGARD TO ANY ADVANTAGE WHICH MAY FLOW FROM THIS LOVE AND SERVICE.

" Whatsoever ye do in word or deed, do all in the Name of our LORD JESUS CHRIST." Col. iii.

1. O most Holy and Undivided TRINITY, FATHER, SON, and HOLY GHOST! I, Thy wretched and unworthy creature, do with fixed and constant purpose throw myself this day entirely upon Thy most holy and righteous Will; and do declare and protest with all my heart, that, renouncing myself, I desire to be wholly Thine, so as not to have any thing nor to desire to have any thing but Thee Alone; Thee Alone would I seek, Thee Alone I love, with purity, simplicity, and sincerity, without looking for any profit to myself. And I do now stedfastly purpose henceforth to serve and love Thy Divine Majesty, not through fear of punishment the pit and pains of hell; nor for the sake of consolations, or bliss hereafter, or aught desirable here; but chiefly that I may seek Thee Alone, desire Thee Alone, love Thee Alone; and surely Thou dost suffice me, for who but Thou suppliest the deficiencies of all things?

Wherefore to Thee Alone I yield and dedicate myself for ever, with so steadfast and inviolable a purpose, with such sincere affection of heart, that with this intent I would wish to love and serve Thee with my whole soul, though I should live for an infinity of ages. This is my purpose, this my determination, this my most fervent desire.

2. If it please Thee to give me sweet consolations, blessed be Thou; for so Thou wilt show Thyself a God of loving-kindness, such as Thou hast ever been, ever art, and wilt be: and I, in return, do give Thee infinite thanks; even as also I do if Thou withhold them. Yea, if Thou willest to lay pains, troubles, and vexations upon me, I bless Thee still and give Thee infinite thanks.

3. For the confirmation of this my purpose, I do now call to witness the whole Court of Heaven and all the inhabiters thereof; may they all intercede for me to Thy Divine Majesty, that this my purpose of seeking Thee Alone purely in all things, and nought besides, may daily grow in strength and be fulfilled.

Therefore to Thee again I turn, O my most Blessed Lord, and implore Thee, that Thou wouldest vouchsafe to accept this my purpose, and strengthen me to fulfil it; for without Thee I can do nothing. And confessing myself such, I repair to Thee I commend and yield myself wholly to Thee, and hide myself in the bowels of Thy pity. Receive me, then, O my God: embrace me, Thou that art my Hope: in all things, change me and transform me into Thyself, O most Sweet Father.

4 With this purpose, I resolve to practise myself in the exercises and acts of virtue which follow; which if sometimes I be unable to exhibit by my mouth or outward performance, yet in heart I do now intend and purpose to fulfil them at all times, and chiefly at the hour of my death, with my utmost endeavour and affection, and in the most perfect way that can be done by me or any other creature, even as Thou knowest it may be done. And now, behold, I offer them all to Thee, even as though they were drawn out by myself, and at the same time with all my heart I pray Thee vouchsafe to accept them of Thy infinite Goodness and Mercy. Amen.

II.
ACT OF FAITH.

"Without faith it is impossible to please God." Heb. xi.

1. *Faith, as the foundation of the others, holds the first place among the Theological Virtues, and is a habit of the intellect, infused by* GOD, *whereby the believer, being illuminated, assents and cleaves to the things which are, through the Church, revealed and proposed to him by* GOD.

I do, then, O most faithful and true GOD, most sure and original Truth, with all my mind, embrace this groundwork of faith. Prostrate on the ground, I most humbly adore and venerate Thee, in heaven and in earth, and do most stedfastly confess Thee in the most perfect and excellent way I am capable of: henceforth and for ever, I believe with my heart and confess with my mouth all things which, through the Holy Church, Thou hast uttered, revealed, and proposed to be believed; specially those which are contained in the Apostles' Creed, affirming that they are most sure, and that nothing thereof may ever be questioned or doubted of.

2. Therefore, before Thy Divine Majesty and all the Heavenly Court, I confess and I most stedfastly protest, that in the confession of this truth I desire to live and die. Ah! how do I desire that the whole world might acknowledge and confess Thee with stedfast faith; deeply, most deeply, do I grieve that it does not, as it should, believe Thee, worship and adore Thee.

3. I implore Thee, therefore, by the Precious Blood, the Life and Death of my LORD JESUS CHRIST, remembering[1] His most holy Mo-

[1] Substituted from Bp. Andrewes' Devotions, fifth day, "Making mention of the all-holy, undefiled, and more than blessed Mary, Mother of GOD and Ever-Virgin, with all saints, let us commend ourselves and each other and all our life to CHRIST our GOD;" add (seventh day), "Blessed, and praised, and celebrated, and magnified, and exalted, and glorified, and hallowed be Thy Name, O LORD, its record, and its memory, and every memorial of it; for the all-honourable senate of the Patriarchs, the ever-venerable band of the Prophets, the all-glorious college of the Apostles, the Evangelists, the all-illustrious army of the Martyrs, the Confes-

§ i.] DEVOTIONS TO THE ALL-HOLY TRINITY. 71

ther, and the holy Apostles, Disciples, Martyrs, Confessors, Virgins, and all the Saints and Elect, that Thou wouldest increase that holy light of faith in me and in all men, and kindle it in the unbelieving, that thereby all may more fervently acknowlege, bless, and adore Thee, as Thy holy Prophet desired, with whom I do cry, *Let the people praise Thee, O* GOD, *yea, let all the people praise Thee; let all the earth worship Thee and sing unto Thee; praise the* LORD, *all ye nations, &c.*

sors, the assembly of Doctors, the Ascetics, the beauty of Virgins, &c.

4. Yea, gladly I offer to Thee, if need be, my life and my blood to maintain the truth and confession of this faith. Would that, O Most Holy TRINITY, FATHER, SON, and HOLY GHOST, it might please Thee to give me the grace of undergoing martyrdom in its behalf; with Thy grace, not only would I, most readily, offer myself to any pains and hardships, but I would deem it the highest blessing, to be permitted to endure the utmost cruelties for the love of Thy truth. Hear and answer me, O most sweet GOD.

III.

ACT OF HOPE AND CONFIDENCE IN GOD.

"Cast not away your confidence, which hath great recompence of reward." Heb. x.

1. *Hope is a virtue infused into our mind by* GOD, *whereby we confidently look for Bliss through the Merits of* CHRIST JESUS *our Redeemer, and at the same time from the works wrought in us by the grace of* GOD.

Bending, then, and wholly prostrate before Thee, O my Almighty GOD, I adore and worship Thee: to Thee nothing is impossible or hard, even as the Word of Truth declares, *with* GOD *nothing shall be impossible.* And for that by this Thine Omnipotence Thou hast promised me heavenly glory, and to that end hast also called me that (O infinite loving-kindness!) I should share Thy bliss and be like Thee; by Thy help and the good works which by Thy special grace I purpose to perform, I hope and long to obtain from Thee, Who Alone canst give it, Eternal Life.

2. O truly Almighty God! most freely I confess, that, without Thy mediation, I cannot possess this infinite, promised good; and that Thou desirest and wishest to give it me, for to that end Thou hast given Thy Son to die for me.

3. I rejoice and leap for joy, most lovely Jesu, Who art Infinite Goodness, that through Thee Alone I can be blessed, for there is no other Name given under Heaven whereby we can be saved. Bliss would be none to me, did I not receive it through Thee, for all my hope and trust is in Thee; I will that in Thee Alone it continue fixed and firm, O most Gracious and most Sweet Jesu, Thou that art the chief and supreme Good of my heart.

Hence is it that I rejoice with such joy unspeakable, such glad consolation, and feel such confidence, as though the good that I long for were already mine; for I know that Thine Only-Begotten Son, through Whom Thou dost wish to bless me, is my Redeemer, and in all the difficulties which threaten me, my faithful Advocate.

4. Wherefore, Almighty Father, with my whole heart I most stedfastly hope to obtain from Thee (for Thou art Most Bountiful) all things needful for my salvation.

In the first place, the pardon of my many and grievous sins; and then, also, strength to overcome all difficulties which may assail me in this life; finally, the grace of perseverance, that I may rejoice in Thy blissful Presence for ever.

Though heaven, earth, and all creatures were to conspire against me, and I stood in the gates of death, still, most kind Father, I would desire ever to hope and trust in Thee, and say with the Prophet, *In Thee, O Lord, have I trusted, let me never be confounded; my hope also is in the* Lord, *therefore shall I not fall.* Amen.

IV.

ACT OF LOVE TOWARDS GOD AND OUR NEIGHBOUR.

"Thou shalt love the LORD thy GOD with all thy heart." St. Luke x.

1. *The love of* GOD *is a thing of so great dignity and excellence, that all the Blessed, all things that are and that shall be created, can do nothing more noble than to love* GOD. *An act of love standeth in wishing well to the object loved, rejoicing in the good it possesses, and wishing for it that which it hath not.*

I, then, O GOD, most lovely, and most Sweet LORD! desiring to exercise this most excellent act, do supremely rejoice, delight, and call Thee Blessed in Thine infinite attributes and perfections; that Thou Alone ART THAT THOU ART, and the Supreme Infinite Good; that Thou art GOD Inscrutable and Unbounded, Whom no creature can comprehend or adequately know.

2. I do call Thee Blessed for the supreme power, glory, dominion, and empire Thou hast, from Thine Own Self, over us and over all things. Verily, O LORD, if (which is impossible) I could possess aught which Thou hadst not, most gladly would I yield and give it unto Thee; yea, could I be GOD, I would not, that Thou Alone mightest be GOD, and have no peer.

3. I do wish also, and from my inmost heart desire, that all creatures in heaven, in earth, in the sea, wherever aught is, or can be, and may be found, would ascribe their being to Thee, and thankfully honour and serve Thee; that all, drawn by Thine Infinite Goodness alone, and by the excellency of Thy Majesty, would praise, magnify, and love Thee, for Thou only art most worthy of all love.

But specially I rejoice that all that creatures strive to do through love of Thee falls far short of Thy Dignity and Thy Greatness.

4. And for that Thou art of Thyself the Supreme Object of all love, with my whole heart I desire to love Thee with that perfection wherewith all the Blessed have loved, do, and shall love Thee to all Eternity. And with the same affection of

heart I offer to Thee that fervour and flower of charity wherewith Thou dost love, Thou hast loved, and shalt love Thyself to all Eternity.

5. My joy runneth over, infinitely do I bless Thee, that Thou dost Thyself supply the lack of mine and all Thy creatures' service, by loving Thyself. And this very love of Thyself I offer to Thee as thanksgiving for all the Glory, Honour, and Bliss that Thou enjoyest, together with all that Glory, Honour, and Praise which, with one consent, all spirits beatified and all the righteous of this world render unto Thee; in fine, Thy Being, Thy Glory, all the Good Thou hast, in Thyself and for Thyself Alone, I desire.

6. And this know, O Thou Who art my Love, that with so stedfast and constant will I purpose to love Thee, that though Thou shouldest be pleased neither in this life, nor in that to come, to give me any good; nay, though in this life Thou afflict me with all griefs, and in the other doom me to everlasting punishments, yet I would love Thee, and from my heart of hearts serve Thee, nor for one moment (if Thy Grace but help me), cease from loving Thee, or remit the ardour of my love. This, Most Merciful, vouchsafe to confirm and accept, I most humbly beseech Thee.

7. And since, O Most Merciful Lord, Thou biddest me love my neighbour also, I bless Thee for so sweet a precept, and do, to my utmost, incline my will to love him.

I desire to love him, and pray Thee to give him all good, both that he may be happier and may please Thee more; specially N. and N. towards whom my rebellious will has some aversion.

I pray Thee, forgive them all their sins; grant them to lay hold on the remedies needful for obtaining everlasting life; if Thou knowest of any gift of Thine which it is expedient for me to forego, that Thou mayest give it unto them; behold, O Lord my God, I refuse it not. The love with which Thou lovest them, overfloweth me with joy; and the perfection in which Thou arrayest them, Lord! I bless Thee for it.

8. If by Thy permission it so chance that any grieve or offend me, now, O Lord, before it come to pass, I

pray Thee pardon him and give him eternal life; and this I pray, because Thou lovest him, and because I desire to be like Thee in all things, so that I may never wish anything but what Thou Thyself wishest, O LORD my GOD. Amen.

v.

ACT OF ADORATION TO THE MOST HOLY TRINITY.

"Thou shalt worship the LORD thy GOD." St. Luke iv.

1. *The worship due to* GOD *only* (latreia) *is at the same time an internal and an external act, whereby the rational creature worships* GOD *by humbling itself, with the intent of adoring Him and confessing Him to be* GOD.

O GOD, of Infinite Majesty and Greatness, FATHER, SON, and HOLY SPIRIT! Lo! with all the lowliness and humility I can, placed before Thy Divine Majesty, O my GOD, I confess myself Thy creature, the work of Thy Hands, wholly dependent upon Thee; Thee, the absolute LORD of All, most worthy so to be accounted, and honoured by all, with the most utter heart-felt abasement prostrate on the ground, from the lowest depth of my nothingness, I adore with Divine Worship; to Thine Infinite Majesty I submit myself, and pay Thee all the reverence and honour I can.

2. I am content, yea, most content, to be nothing, to be able to do nothing, but by Thee; yea, apart from Thee, I would not wish to be aught or be able to do anything.

3. Therefore I invite and call on the blessed spirits [a], and all the Court of Heaven, yea, all creatures that are, to adore, venerate, and confess with me Thy Infinite Majesty; and I do now with them adore and confess Thee; yea, in this my present act I desire to unite all the acts of adoration wherewith Thou hast been, or it is fitting that Thou shouldest be approach-

[a] "O ye Spirits and Souls of the Righteous, bless ye the LORD, praise Him and magnify Him for ever. O Ananias, Azarias, and Misael, bless ye the LORD, praise Him and magnify Him for ever!" Benedicite.

ed, all these, united and combined in one, I offer and dedicate to Thee.

4. Finally, O my GOD, to Thee, the Absolute LORD of All Things, all things I consecrate; in particular, I offer and devote to Thee all my thoughts and words, all my actions, internal or external; this only imploring, that in me most perfectly be Thy Will fulfilled, with which most lovingly Thou madest me, and hast called me to serve Thee. Amen.

VI.

ACT OF PRAISE AND GRATULATION.

"Praise the LORD, all ye nations." Psalm cxvii.

1. *The praise given to* GOD, *as the Holy Scriptures teach us, consists in every act of virtue, whereby (whether the heart conceive it or the mouth speak it, whether it be a work done or any outward sign) the excellence of the Divine Virtue is set forth; and Gratulation is an act of joy, felt at the good possessed by another.*

I, therefore, O LORD, desire now, by the help of Thy Grace, to elicit these acts and to stir up my heart, saying, with intensest feeling of my soul, O GOD most praised, O LORD my GOD, my heart exults with joy, and with all my strength I proclaim, I declare, I set forth and herald to all the world Thy greatness past finding out, Thy excellence, Thy magnificence; that Thou art Infinite and Incomprehensible; Unchangeable and Everlasting; All-powerful, All-wise, All-good, Most Holy, and of Infinite Perfection, the Creator of Heaven and Earth, the First Cause, the Final End of all things, ruling and guiding all things with consummate Providence. For all these things' sake I joy and bless Thee.

2. And therefore now, with holy applause, with my whole soul, I laud, exalt, magnify, and adore Thee; O that, without ceasing, at all times, in all places of the earth, I could pay to Thee this service in that degree in which all creatures combined in one, all that have been, are, or shall be, exalt, magnify, and

glorify, shall glorify, have glorified, and could glorify Thee, O Lord my God.

3. Yea, I desire in this my act to render unto Thee all those praises which could at any time, can now, or may hereafter be rendered unto Thee, by the holiest Beings which Thou hast ever made; by innumerable worlds, unnumbered creatures, visible and invisible, which Thine Almighty Hand hath created. So great praises, so great honours, do I long to present unto Thee, as Thou knowest can be presented; yea, so great as are due to Thee.

But since this is beyond my strength, all such honours and praises at least I would ascribe to Thee as, assisted by Thy help, I am able to offer, and with such forces of love as Thou dost love Thyself withal; to which, as a slender and poor addition, I join the affection wherewith I praise Thee.

4. I bless Thee, I join my joy with Thine, gladly I confess that Thou, my God, art so great, so highly to be praised, that the strength of no creature in earth or in heaven can suffice to praise and magnify Thee worthily; and meanwhile, O Lord, right glad I am, that Thou Thyself dost abundantly fill up the lack of all Thy creatures.

VII.

THANKSGIVING.

"In every thing give thanks." 1 Thess. v.

1. *Thanksgiving is the express acknowledgement of a favour received, directed to the benefactor, in sign of requital.*

I confess Thee, O my most bountiful God, to be surpassing in Almightiness, most plentiful in pity, the Source of all good things; and I confess with thanksgiving that benefits untold, gifts most precious, have flowed from Thee to me from the moment of my conception to the present hour; such as are my creation, redemption, calling, the gift of the Holy Ghost, my preservation, and other blessings innumerable proceeding from these or contained in them (and all this notwithstanding my utter unworthiness). For all these, and especially for — and —, with intense gratitude of heart, with all my might, I bless Thee infinitely, even as Thy Love is infinite and Thy Goodness, whence they flowed to me.

2. Confessing thus my infinite debt to Thee, O Unbounded Goodness, unable and ignorant how to thank Thee as I ought and as I desire, I call on all creatures, visible and invisible, to thank Thee for me; and the thanksgivings which, in whatever kind, in whatever manner, they have rendered, do and through eternity shall render to Thee, all these I now offer to Thee in my own behalf; and in unison with them, with like affection, acknowledgment, and thanksgiving, I give Thee thanks.

3. Nor do I do this as though these blessings were my own, but because they are Thine. I am ready and willing to give them up, whensoever it shall please Thee to recal them; and I pray Thee to recal them whensoever Thou shalt deem it conducive to thy greater glory.

4. I also thank Thy Divine Majesty for that THOU ART THAT THOU ART; and for all the good thou possessest. Moreover, in the way of thanksgiving and grateful acknowledgment for all the gifts and benefits Thou hast granted or mayest grant to me, and all other creatures which have been, are, or shall be; specially for those which most abundantly Thou hast hitherto accorded to holy angels and to men, to the most Blessed Virgin, to the All-Holy Humanity of Thy SON our LORD; in that fashion and manner wherein Thou most delightest, I offer to Thee, O GOD, Thyself, Who art the fulfilment and complement of all things.

5. Nor yet content with this, further, in sign of gratitude, from this moment I give, dedicate, and surrender myself to Thee: earnestly desiring and willing to serve Thee faithfully and love Thee ardently for ever; and this gift, most trifling though it be, most unworthy of Thy Majesty, yea, already due to Thee (such as it is) on numberless accounts, I most humbly implore Thee, vouchsafe to accept. Amen.

VIII.

ACT OF OBLATION.

"The sacrifice of sanctification thou shalt offer unto the LORD."
Ecclus. vii.

1. O LORD, most excellent, my GOD, FATHER, SON, and HOLY GHOST! in all respects I confess myself Thine, both because Thou hast created and that Thou hast redeemed me, besides other blessings innumerable, for which, though I should a thousand times an hour offer myself to Thee, still I should remain infinitely Thy debtor, infinitely bound to Thee. Such, therefore, as I am, freely and fervently, to the utmost of my power, I consecrate and offer myself to Thee, I give Thee myself entirely, a perfect holocaust of soul and body, and of all I have and all that ever may be mine.

And this I desire to do in the way most pleasing to Thee, and that is most fitting I should offer and consecrate myself to Thee. And so with most willing mind, and with no reservation, I yield myself to Thy most holy precepts, and all indications of Thy will for ever.

And since I am now wholly Thine, I pray Thee so keep me that I may never be given back to myself, or become my own: may all I wish, do, or say be no other than what Thy most holy and righteous Will would have me will, do and say; may my not willing, not doing, not saying, likewise be Thy not willing, Thy not doing, Thy not saying; and this, simply and alone, when, how, and as far as it seemeth good to Thee, O most worthy LORD, that it should be through me.

2. Moreover, to Thee I offer all the riches and spiritual goods of all things created or laid up in the treasure-house of Thine Almightiness, in such sense that, were they all mine, I would with most glad heart yield them to Thee, or at the least, spend and use them only in Thy Love and Honour.

3. I offer to Thee all the spiritual goods, thoughts, words, and good works, which all men that ever have been, are, or shall be in this world have done, do, or shall do;

yea, all those thoughts, words, and good works, which men innumerable, even as many as Thy Almighty Power could create, could ever entertain or produce; so that were I able, I would wish to do them all out of love to Thee with all the energy that Thou knowest possible, and in the manner Thy Majesty doth most delight in.

4. No less[a] I offer to Thee all the sufferings, pangs, martyrdoms, all the bitter griefs of soul and body, which all men have ever suffered, do, or shall suffer, to the satisfaction of Thy Justice, and to the increase of Thy Glory; all that Thou knowest can be endured by all, by each, not in this world only, but in ten thousand, yea, innumerable worlds, in such sense that I would, did it so please Thee, and if Thou wouldest help me, willingly for Thy love's sake, my own and my neighbour's salvation, endure them all.

5. But chiefly I offer to Thee the Precious Blood, and Infinite Merits of my LORD JESUS CHRIST, and in union with these, under the feet of Thy Saints, and Thine Elect[b], all my thoughts, words, works, studies, occupations, acts of this day and my whole life.

Finally, I desire to make this oblation, with the most fervent affection Thou knowest possible; even as often as I draw my breath, that I may, through all eternity, be wholly Thine, wholly devoted unto Thee. Amen.

[a] On these solemn prayers see Preface

[b] Substituted from Bishop Andrewes.

IX.

ACT OF RESIGNATION TOWARDS GOD.

"Casting all your care upon Him." 1 Pet. v.

1. My Most Merciful LORD, in all things denying every affection of my heart, I resign myself wholly to Thee, with the utmost longing that Thou knowest possible; and as far as my strength can reach, I most fully desire to transfuse my will into Thy Divine Good Pleasure, in which alone, and nought else, I wish to find my own pleasure and repose.

Wherefore I pray that Thou wouldest dispose of me and all which is mine, in whatsoever way it seemeth good to Thee, and will conduce to Thy greater Glory.

And thus wholly resigned in Thee, I offer myself ready to accept from Thy Most Mighty Hand, whatever may happen to me in this life, whether weal or woe.

2. If then Thou wilt have me live, life I gratefully accept: if Thou wilt have me die, LORD, I am Thine: if Thou give me health, I receive the blessing: if Thou wilt have me sick, I accept sickness: if to be wealthy, riches: if poor, my will is poverty: if honoured, honour pleaseth me: if without honour, I embrace ignominy: wilt Thou have me enjoy consolation, Thy Will is mine: if desolation, I refuse it not: wilt Thou that I be in favour with men, such too is my will: or hated by them; lo! I will pray for my enemies, and bless Thee in persecutions.

3. Therefore I would not have eyes, but to see Thee; nor ears, but to hear Thee: nor a tongue, but to speak of Thee: nor a heart, but to love Thee: nor memory, but for the recollection of Thy sweetness: nor reason, but for the acknowledgment of Thy Majesty: nor hands, but to minister to Thee; nor feet, but to pursue Thy service: nor a body, but as a victim to Thee: nor life, but as a sacrifice to Thee.

4. Finally, so utterly without all reservation do I desire to be Thine, that no longer owner of myself, and renouncing all right in myself, to Thy Most Holy Will (for my own will I have already surrendered to Thee, and do now, and for ever, without recal surrender it), I would yield, make over, and resign all my thoughts and words, all my works internal and external, all my faculties and my being, which by Thy Grace Thou hast vouchsafed to bestow upon me.

Nor would I like or dislike, save in the manner, the time, and the degree that Thou likest or dislikest, so that Thy Good Pleasure may be my highest and ultimate desire, my joy and consolation, at all times, and in every thing. Wherefore, O Most Merciful LORD, stand by me with Thy Most Holy Grace (without which I know I can do nothing), that so all things may issue in Thy Honour and Glory, and Thy Most Holy Will may be most perfectly fulfilled. Amen.

X.
DELIGHTING IN GOD.
"Delight thou in the Lord, and He shall give thee thy heart's desire." Ps. xxxvi.

True joy is delight proceeding from those things which are God's; for the true matter of all joy standeth in God and in His excellence.

1. O how great reasons, therefore, have I for joy and exultation; inasmuch as Thou art That Thou art, God, of Infinite Power, Wisdom, Goodness, Beauty, Mercy, Justice, Faithfulness, and other attributes innumerable, the Well-spring and Principle of all good; and though so great, so perfect, Thou hast so deigned to exalt human nature, and unite it to Thyself, that it has become true to say, God is Man, and Man is God; God by nature; Man by vouchsafement and grace. Yea, Thou hast, besides, promised me endless happiness and bliss, and confirmed Thy promise by numberless evidences and signs as well in the Old as in the New Testament. O Infinite Condescension! O Infinite Goodness of our Lord and God!

2. Ardently, then, I desire and will, O Lord, that henceforth, Thy Grace helping me, my soul may find its delight wholly in Thee, from Thee only and the things which are Thine, and which draw me towards Thee. Truly he said well of Thee, who said, *My* God, *and my All*. Thou Alone art Goodness, the Treasure, the Paradise of Thy rational creature, here and hereafter.

3. And I loathe, and turn in disgust from this world and all that is in it. The sight thereof, to hear thereof, or think thereof, is to me as loathsome as a most filthy sewer, a putrified body, or a common draught-house. Compared with Thee, O Lord, all things I count as dung, yea, I hate them as infected with a plague.

4. I desire to feel delight at the taste of Thy Sweetness alone, to feel joy and pleasure only in what is Thine, to reject, hate, and abhor all worldly things, all

that would wean my heart from Thee. Help me to this end, O LORD, with Thy Goodness, that, gladly and perfectly serving Thee in this life, I may with Thy Blessed Saints see and enjoy Thee for ever in the life to come. Amen.

XI.

ZEAL FOR THE HONOUR OF GOD AND THE SALVATION OF SOULS.

"The zeal of Thine house hath even eaten me, and the rebukes of them that rebuked Thee are fallen upon me." Ps. lxix.

1. O MOST JEALOUS GOD, Who givest not Thy Glory to another, and Alone hast created all souls, Who wouldest therefore, among Thine other names, be called *Jealous*, even a JEALOUS GOD, I grieve, yea, I am racked with grief in the behalf of all those, who in all they do, leaving their true end, which is Thou Alone, the Highest and Only Good, seek for and love the passing and fading things of this world more than Thee; who, ceasing not to sin, yield themselves to their most cruel enemy, the devil; I cannot think thereon, or speak thereof, without great pangs of grief.

2. [Wherefore*, O my GOD, could I, a most vile sinner, of no merit before Thee, for Thy Love and Honour, endure all the pains and torments which all Thy servants have suffered, and thereby effect that none should ever after offend Thee, with my whole heart I would beg and implore this grace of Thee.

Yea, for love of Thee, I entirely renounce[b], if so it please Thee, all my good deeds and holy actions, if such there be, if ever indeed I have done aught really pleasing to Thee, and I offer them to Thee, the Eternal FATHER, united with the Merits of Thy SON, for the conversion of the whole world, that so Thou mayest be Honoured in earth, as Thou art in Heaven.

* This is inclosed in brackets, that none may use so high and aweful a prayer without reflecting whether they are fit for it. See further, Preface. [Ed.]

[b] i. e. could it be for GOD's glory he would renounce all reward, all but love. [Ed.]

And if all the stripes, due to others for their sins, could be laid upon me, so that they might be spared, and the fruit of this my pain might be for their good, even these I would beg of Thee; and now, if it please Thee, I humbly pray Thee to accept this my desire, such as it is, and to give grace to all perfectly to serve Thee, and so to love Thee as never more to offend Thee; but that all may praise and bless Thee continually, even as Thy Saints and Angels do in Heaven.

3. So highly do I prize Thy Honour and Glory, that I would choose to abide eternally in hell [c], and suffer all torments, rather than Thou shouldest, for one moment, be deprived of Thy Honour; for to Thee all honour is due, to me all pains, afflictions, and ignominy; rather than Thou shouldest lose the honour which is Thine, let me, I pray Thee, suffer all ignominy, distress, and misery.

If this suffice not for Thine honour, let all evils of soul and body come upon me, all but sin: and these what, and as great soever as Thou knowest to be possible; only do Thou, Whom my soul loveth, not forget me, but give me grace and endurance to bear them, as I am ready willingly to receive them, for love of Thee, and to honour Thee.]

[c] This is an application of St. Paul's prayer, "I could wish myself accursed from Christ." See further, Preface. [Ed.]

XII.

ACT OF THE FEAR OF GOD.

"Blessed are all they that fear the LORD." Ps. cxxviii.

Right fear is a certain anxious care of the heart, withholding a man from unlawfully using his members, his external senses and his inward affections; lest his soul be weaned, wholly or in part, from GOD, or seek delight in any creature, and so its spiritual heat grow cold.

1. O LORD, fearful and terrible, at sight of whom all spirits in heaven, earth, and hell do tremble, I now, contemplating Thy Greatness and Infinite Majesty, utterly confounded at my monstrous unworthiness, sink down into the abyss of my own nothingness, greatly fearing lest I

should offend thee, and be separated from Thy Divine Grace; for so it has befallen many who walked not uprightly in Thy sight.

2. Wherefore, when I do but reflect that I may offend Thee by venial and mortal sin, I shudder and tremble in every limb, most of all because I know how utterly weak I am, and that without Thy special Grace, I can do nothing.

4. At the same time I confess the great use and necessity of this fear, and therefore earnestly beg it of Thee; increase it in me, engrave it in my soul; I pray with the Psalmist, *make my flesh tremble for fear of Thee, and make me afraid of Thy judgments.*

PIOUS READER,

Similar acts of other virtues thou mayest find below in their proper places in the 4th section.

CHAPTER VI.

A MOST RELIGIOUS CONTEMPLATION OF THE ATTRIBUTES OF GOD,

FOR THE ELICITING OF VIRTUOUS ACTS AND AFFECTIONS.

FROM BLAISE PALMA, CLERK REGULAR OF ST. PAUL.

PREFACE.

Though all the Divine excellencies and perfection be in very truth incapable of discrimination from each other or from the Divine Essence, This being I AM, *Most High, Most Absolute, Most Simple; yet our minds, too dull to comprehend them as they are, strive to sip, as it were, of the Divine fulness, by the use of various conceptions and distinctions which we call the Divine Attributes, and which we ascribe to* GOD *as so many distinct perfections, though they are indeed most inseparably interunited.*

Though the knowledge of these be the most high and sublime science in the world, yet to those who possess it practically it will also be the most perfect rule for acquiring all virtues and spiritual goods, for that the knowledge of GOD *and imitation of His virtues is our perfection, as, on the contrary, ignorance of* GOD *is the source of all sin and misery. For to know Thee is perfect righteousness; yea, to know Thy power is the root of immortality.* Wisd. xv.

In like manner, then, as we have just described certain virtuous acts, it has seemed good to select a few of the Divine Attributes, that the devout Christian, having this lantern for his path, may come to the knowledge of GOD *and perfection of life, with the hope of attaining at length unto complete and consummated righteousness, even the fruition of* GOD *Himself in life everlasting.*

I.

THE ESSENCE OF GOD.

" This is life eternal, that they may know Thee, the only true GOD, and JESUS CHRIST, whom Thou hast sent." St. John xvii.

1. O LORD, Thou art most simple Essence, and therefore Absolutely Infinite in every kind of perfection, nor can aught be added to, or taken from Thee. Thou art incomprehensible as to all times, all places, all wills, and intelligences. For Thou passest beyond all space, encompassest all time, transcendest all mind, dost absorb all affection of men and angels, so that Thou only canst worthily comprehend, measure, understand, and love Thyself.

2. Thou art Unmeasured, filling, pervading, exceeding all created things that are or can be: immoveable, unlimited, uncircumscribed. For in this Infinity, Thou infinitely transcendest all limits, all imaginable space. Wherefore also in Nature, in Operation, in Thought, in Affection, Thou art Immutable; for shadow of variableness or change befalleth not Thee, ever constant in one will, in One I AM.

3. Thou art Eternal, without beginning or end: in the single point of indivisible eternity Thou embracest all duration, all vicissitude of

time; with Thee is no time save that most perfect *Now*, which with Thee answereth to all time alike; Thou art to Thyself the adequate and most perfect measure of Eternity.

4. Since Thy excellence then, O LORD, as I most stedfastly believe, is so great, with my whole heart, with deepest humility and reverence, I now adore and venerate Thee, and with the blessed and righteous spirits confess that THOU ART THAT THOU ART; before Thee prostrate on the earth I reverently bow, to Thee I submit myself in lowliest humility; and as thou art worthy of all love, with perfect and sincere love I will for ever love Thee.

And for Thy glory's sake, I would have all creatures for ever love, confess, reverence, honour, and praise Thee; to which end I offer Thee my life, strength, and faculties, all I have, all I can have.

5. Moreover, I rejoice and am glad, as often as I reflect that Thou, the LORD, art so Great, so Infinite, Incomprehensible, Immeasurable, Eternal, and that all the perfections before rehearsed are found in Thee.

6. With inmost affection, I confess Thy Blessedness, O LORD, in Thy Majesty, Glory, and Felicity, which Thou dost now, and shalt for ever possess; wherefore I call all created things in one voice to bless Thee, saying, *O all ye works of the* LORD, *bless ye the* LORD, *praise Him and magnify Him for ever, &c.*

7. And with twofold joy and consolation I abound, while I hope and consider, that this very good which is Thine, shall some time become mine, for Thou hast promised it to me, obtained, prepared it for me, and bountifully bestowed it on me through CHRIST, Thy Only-Begotten SON, my REDEEMER; which also I shall enjoy with Thee for ever, if I do but continue stedfast in Thy love. *And then shall I be satisfied, when Thy Glory shall appear.*

II.

POWER.

"With God all things are possible." St. Matt. xix.

1. O my God Almighty, Thou art that Power Which can do all things that It willeth: Which knoweth not weakness, Which tireth not with working; produceth all things from nothing, and with like ease, if It will, reduceth them thereto again; nought can resist It; all things obey It.

O adorable, tremendous Almightiness, in religious silence to be worshipped! Thou, O King Immortal, canst do all things of Thyself; originating from Thee, dependent on Thee, is all the power, might, strength, and active energy of all things. Thou madest all out of nothing, and by the support of Thy Influence preservest, and by the Hand of Thy Almightiness holdest them (as it were) in mid air, lest they fall back into their own nothingness. Thou canst of Thyself give and do, O Lord, not only all that men and Holy Angels can conceive, but all that Thine Own Infinite Wisdom can think; for Thine Almightiness is equal to Thy Wisdom, and equally with it it stretcheth and diffuseth itself: yea, *this* is the sole rule and measure of the former; for what measure can Power unmeasured have, other than Immensity?

2. I take delight, O Lord, I joy in Thy so great Majesty and Power; and I pray Thee, that, out of the consideration thereof, Thou wouldest imprint on my mind the deepest reverence and submission towards Thy Divine Majesty. I desire, too, that Thou dispose of me and of all creatures according to Thy Good Pleasure; for none can say to Thee, *Why doest Thou thus?* All things are Thine, and the works of Thy Hands.

3. Grant me, Lord, to have this most sure truth constantly before my eyes, *that Thou art ever with me;* and that the Hand of Thy Almightiness is ready with the thunderbolt of endless damnation, if I obey Thee

§ i.]   DEVOTIONS TO THE ALL-HOLY TRINITY.   89

not; and so may I never offend Thee.

Grant to my heart trust and security in Thee, that I fear none beside Thee, and that no creature may be able to sever me from love of Thee; for, compared with Thee, what are all creatures but *nothing?* What hurt, without Thy permission, can they do me? And if Thou permit any to afflict me, it is for my salvation, and to contribute towards the attainment of eternal life. All my trust, therefore, I place in Thee, and desire that it shall ever rest in Thee, Almighty LORD and GOD. Amen.

III.

WISDOM.

"Wisdom proceedeth out from GOD." Ecclus. xv.

1. O most wise GOD, Thou art that Wisdom that comprehendeth all that can be thought of: ignorance hath no place in Thee: Thou knowest all things, and canst neither be deceived nor err; most thoroughly, most distinctly Thou knowest all things—the present, the past, the future, the possible, the imaginable, the things that are, the things that are not, —to Thee, O my GOD, they are present, and set in Thy holy Sight.

2. Thou art the Archetype, the original Impress of all things; pure and pervading, Thou penetratest all, and, in all intimately existing, fitly disposest them. Yet though Thou reachest from one end to the other, from the summit to the abyss, and most thoroughly pervadest all things, Thou art not confounded or mixed with any, not stained with the least pollution, but ever abiding in Thine Own Beauty, Brilliancy, and Incorruption.

3. Thou art the Author and Maker, the first Type and Form, the Measure and End of all things; the Framer not only of the things that are, which have received their being and their form impressed on them by Thee, whether visible or invisible, but of those things also that *are* not, yet *can* be through Thy Almightiness, in number infinitely exceeding the things that have been made.

4. O admirable Wisdom, That circleth all eternity, receiveth into Itself all immensity, and draweth to Itself all infinity! all things in It have, in some sense, eternal being, eternal life; without beginning is It, without end, in all things free from change.

5. I take delight, O LORD, I bless Thy Name, and joy in Thy most profound Wisdom wherewith Thou searchest the heart. Could I one jot lessen this Thy Wisdom, so as to hide from Thee my sins and my wickedness, I would not do it: yea, I had rather be destroyed and fall into annihilation myself than that Thy Wisdom should be one jot diminished. O most wise LORD, from that inexhaustible Fountain of Thy Light, shed some ray into my soul, that I may thoroughly know the beauty of virtue and the filthiness of sin; that I may fly sin and pursue virtue, and that I may more and more love whatever tends to Thy glory and eternal honour. Amen.

IV.

GOODNESS.

"Thou art good and gracious, O teach me thy statutes." Ps. cxix.

1. O LORD, the Creator of all good, Thou art Good, not in one way, not in one kind of Goodness only, but absolutely, without beginning, without end; without limit, without measure, save that whereby Thou without measurement possessest and embracest all good.

Thou art the very Fulness and Universality of good, unto Whom all creatures, from the sublimest intelligence down to mere primitive matter, must refer all the good they have received.

Thou, in Thy most simple Essence, possessest all excellence, all perfection, all blessedness, all good; neither hath Thy Goodness and Perfection bound or limit, for that it is original and primal, dependent upon none.

2. From Thee all things sweet derive their sweetness; all things fair, their beauty; all things bright, their splendour; all things that live,

their life; all things sentient, their sense; all that move, their vigour; all intelligences, their knowledge; all things perfect, their perfection; all things in any wise good, their goodness.

3. Thou art Great, without quantity; Good, without quality; Infinite, without number; Beautiful, without figure; Eternal, without time; Immeasurable, without space; Pervading, without extension; Perfect, without multiplicity; Most Exalted, without position.

4. Thou art the Centre of the universe, towards Whom all things of their nature tend, and in Whom all find their rest; by Whom all are sustained; in Thee are the attractions of all love, the consummation of all desire, the limit of all motion, the satisfaction of all appetency.

O how great the might of that Thy supreme Goodness, when every creature hasteth with such eagerness to the shining of but a spark thereof! Every creature seeketh its own especial good, and with its whole strength presseth towards it: yet this is but a slight trace and sign of Thy Goodness. It mightily draweth every creature, it causeth strong perturbations in the world; for whatever among things created is moved, stirred, worketh, is moved and acted upon by the perception of good. If, then, so slight a shadow of good draw so mightily, what shall the very Truth do, Thy Infinite Beauty and Goodness, when openly beheld, yea, Thyself, O GOD, Thou Good Most Sweet, Most High!

5. Draw my mind unto Thee, Beauty inconceivable! Bind it unto Thee, free from attachment to created things, with a link indissoluble, the bond of never-ending love. What shall I seek or desire but Thee, O Fulness of all good; the Fount, the End, the Sweetness, the Strength and Marrow of all good? Farewell all else! Thee let me ever meditate upon and love; towards Thee let me strive; cleave to Thee Alone; abide in Thee; praise Thee, bless Thee, and serve Thee Only, with all the might of my soul and all my life. Let all passing things be cheap or precious to me, so far as they agree with Thy goodness; may this be to me the only measure of their worth. Perfect me, according to the secret good pleasure of Thy

Will, in thought and love of Thee; change me into Thyself, that I may be made one spirit with Thee; that I may live no longer unto myself, but unto Thee. Amen.

V.

HOLINESS.

"There is none holy as the LORD." 1 Sam. ii.

1. O LORD my GOD, manifoldly art Thou Holy! first, Thy Essence is the Origin and Root of all holiness and purity; and, then, the true Standard of all holiness. Thou art the efficient Principle, the Form, Archetype, and End of all the beauty of holiness, which is found in Thy creatures. Thou art Holy of Thyself, of Thine Own Essence, by a fundamental, true, and self-dependent holiness. So perfect is Thy Holiness, that nought can be taken therefrom or added thereto; for it is Thy Essence and universal.

2. I delight and rejoice in this Thy Holiness, the essential Source of all beauty and purity; whence all intelligent creatures derive their holiness and purity. Thou hast proposed it for our imitation; for of it Thou spakest, not of Thy Power, Thy Wisdom, or Thine exalted Majesty, *Ye shall be holy, for I am Holy* [a]. Not, indeed, so great holiness dost Thou look for in us, as is in Thy surpasing Sanctity, but some resemblance thereto, such as, with Thy grace, our frailty can receive.

3. This Thy Holiness and Purity I venerate, honour, love, and admire. Truly all reverence, honour, and love is due to It. By Its presence It hath sanctified, yea, sanctifies the whole world; so that, turn me which way I will, I see Thee present, and in Thine Omnipresence I venerate, praise, honour, and bless Thee, as in the sacred temple of Thy Glory. Yet in a special way Thou hast sanctified my soul (which is far more capacious, more august, than a world of matter), like a temple, for Thy worship, and consecrated it for an habitation for Thyself; so that in myself, in the shrine of my

[a] Lev. xi.

soul I can see Thee dwelling; here in holy silence I can converse with Thee and enjoy Thee; here propitiate Thee with service; here adore Thee; here seek of Thee purity and holiness: and this, O my LORD, I desire now, with all my heart, with all my soul, to do and to obtain from Thee.

4. I will strive, also, O LORD, and do now purpose, to avoid to my utmost all impure and inordinate affections, all pollutions of the soul, whereby Thy holy temple might be violated and profaned; for as Thou, LORD, must needs love above all Thy Sanctity, so must Thou needs greatly hate sin and detest all uncleanness.

5. Finally, to Thee, the Author, End, Rule, and Archetype of all holiness, from Which, after Which, and according to Which all things in Heaven and earth are sanctified, be glory, blessing, thanksgiving from all creatures in Heaven and in earth. Amen.

VI.

LOVING-KINDNESS.

"*He* the LORD *is kind*." St. Luke vi.

1. Thou art Good, O my LORD, because of Thy natural perfection, of Thy holiness, and of Thy beneficence, yea, Thy kindness, which is nought else but Thy natural inclination to impart the good Thou hast to Thy inferior creatures, as each is able to receive it.

O how truly kind showest Thou Thyself, O LORD, when, though Thou needest nothing, but wert all-sufficient to Thyself, Thou createdst all things out of nothing, and broughtest them from the abyss of their own nothingness, giving them being, form, beauty, desire of good, avoidance of evil, strength, functions, impulse, motion, position, measure, order, perfection, and bounds, as was good and convenient for each; nor didst Thou this for any advantage or profit to Thyself, but that they might be happy, and might, as each was capable, partake Thy Goodness and taste the fruit of Thy Loving-kindness. Therefore do all things praise Thee, and with silent voices celebrate Thy kindness. *The heavens declare the glory of God, and the firmament sheweth His handy-work* [b]. &c.

2. But brightest far of all doth Thy kindness towards man appear. Thou createdst us after Thine Image and Likeness, and didst mark us with the impress of Thy Countenance. Reason, memory, and will Thou gavest us, to make us recipients of Thy Glory and Blessedness. Thou hast, moreover, supplied us with Divine assistances and graces, that we might merit and obtain blessings so transcendent. Angels Thou hast set as our guardians and rulers; the whole world Thou hast created and filled with blessings innumerable for our dwelling-place and solace. What greater than these blessings? what more wonderful than such kindness can be imagined or conceived? And all this hast Thou done to bring us to Thy heavenly mansions, and make us sharers of Thy bliss.

3. Wherefore, O Lord, all I am, all I can, I bless Thee, and render boundless thanks to Thee for so wondrous kindness; I call on all creatures to laud and bless Thee: *O all ye works of the* Lord, *bless ye the* Lord, *praise Him and magnify Him for ever,* &c.

4. I rejoice, O Lord, in Thy kindness, wherewith Thou givest Thyself, yea castest Thyself to things so miserably vile, and delightest in healing the infirm, raising the abject, and exalting the abased. Where is the more grievous need, poverty, misery, there Thou art wont the more bountifully to pour forth Thy succour, the more readily to give Thy help: what greater sign of true loving-kindness?

5. I grieve and repent me for not having imitated this Thy kindness; I have been cruel, harsh, unmerciful to my neighbour; the blessings I have of fortune or mind I have not used in his behalf; —how often just the contrary! Wherefore with all my soul most humbly I implore Thy pardon, and intend, by Thy help, to amend this vice of unkindness, to be kind, gentle, and loving towards all, and I would do this through the desire to imitate Thy Divine kindness.

[b] Ps. xix.

Because from this Thy kindness, Thy love at once and immediately proceedeth, and is shed on all creatures, so that Thou wouldest have all partake of Thy blissfulness, inflame my heart, O LORD, I beseech Thee, with the same fire, that I too may be kindly-affectionate and full of charity. Amen.

VII.

PROVIDENCE.

"Thou hast beset me behind and before." Ps. cxxxix.

1. Thy Providence, O LORD, governeth all things, from the highest part of heaven to the lowest parts of the earth, from the most exalted spirit to the vilest worm. It thought, conceived, divided, and fitly ordered all things from eternity. Without its behest nought is born, nought dies, works, is moved, or rests.

Hence is it that all things void of reason, work so reasonably, uniformly in such wondrous order tending to their appointed end; while man, gifted with free-will and abusing it, ever recedeth from the order of Thy Divine and particular Providence, proposing to himself other ends than It appointed him.

Yet can he not escape Thy general Providence; the due punishment, decreed to sin and sinners, awaits him; and so, even in the reprobate, the order of Thy Divine Providence marvellously shines forth.

2. Woe is me that I so often have sought to flee Thy Fatherly Providence, and to live after my own foolish mind; therefore shunning the Hand of Thy Divine Providence, which was leading me unto life, I have incurred perils, errors, and sins unnumbered: yea, I have incurred the most just punishments decreed by counsel of Thy Providence for wretched sinners to the glory of Thy Infinite Justice ; I cast myself in folly from Thy mercy and kindness, and lo ! Thy Justice arrests me. O wretched me ! I was treasuring up for myself the penalties of justice ; I desired to shun the gentle yoke of Thy Hea-

venly precepts, and I was bringing myself under the cruel service of devils; I rejected eternal rewards, and all the while was meriting eternal punishment.

O folly, to be deplored with tears of blood! I repent, ah! my whole soul repenteth; most humbly I pray Thee for pardon.

3. I pray Thee, LORD, by all the marvels of Thy Most Sweet Providence, take away this folly from me, give me Thy Grace ever to have Thy Providence before my eyes; that I may feel that whatever good or evil befalleth me, cometh therefrom, and may receive it at Thy Hand as an exceeding blessing. Be this my solace in adversity; may it give me confidence in terrors, security in dangers, boldness in difficulties, patience in distress, calmness in tumults, rest of soul in anticipation of the future. May it take from me all anxiety, while, free from care, I depend simply on the kindness of Thy Providence: may it guide all my actions, and direct them to the end, as is expedient for Thy Glory and my salvation. What means soever it willeth to use, weal or woe, honour or shame, evil report or good report, plenty or want, sickness or health, life or death: I refuse none; I shrink from none; whatever Thy Providence wills, *that* I deem most right, most fit; *that* I embrace as most desirable.

This only is my heart's most fervent desire and longing, and may it ever be, to do, to say, to think, O my LORD, as Thou judgest best for Thy Glory and my salvation, so that in all things, above all things, I may contemplate, admire, love, honour, praise, and bless Thee for ever. Amen.

VIII.

MERCY.

"The earth is full of the mercy of the LORD." Ps. xxxiii.

1. O Most Merciful LORD, Thou art that Immeasurable Mercy, that infinitely exceedeth our utmost misery and sin. Thou didst first bring me forth from the darkness of nothingness, and gavest me life, and a noble

§ i.] DEVOTIONS TO THE ALL-HOLY TRINITY. 97

nature fashioned after Thine Image; with it, too, Thou hast bestowed the highest endowments, understanding, judgment, reason, memory, will. Then, by adopting me for Thy son, Thou hast exalted me from the low estate of nature, to the sublime estate of grace. And further, to these two first, Thou hast added another, the estate of glory, which is the most noble of all; for far more perfect and excellent are Thy gifts of glory than of grace. It is Thy measureless goodness and mercy that has destined me to this high degree.

Wherefore, O my soul, if thou hast reached the second degree, be it thy business to rise to this third also, specially remembering the many aids and assistances afforded thee; such as the Most Holy Sacraments, bequeathed and earned for us by CHRIST JESUS, our LORD, Who, to fill up the vast treasure of His Blessings, hath left us also the Most Holy Sacrament of His Precious Body and Blood.

2. Ah! LORD, enlighten my soul that I may know the Immensity of Thy Mercy; and when I know it, daily value it, and ever have it before my eyes as my rule and guide, until, freed from the chains of this wretched life, my soul bound by such precious blessings, and by the bands of so great benevolence, may be transformed into the same likeness, loving Thee with all its might, consecrating itself to Thee, and surrendering itself to Thy Honour and Holy Service.

My God, may I serve Thee my whole life long; may no thought possess me, but to do what tends to Thy Glory, whereto, as to the end of all my desires, may all my doings, my strength, and endowments, whether of nature or of grace, be directed. May my energies, whether of body or mind, intend, regard, pursue nothing else but to do Thy Most Holy Will. And, O that I somewhat resembled that Infinite Love of Thine, wherewith Thou hast ever followed me, that so I might not be altogether ungrateful to so great a Benefactor.

3. *Bless the* LORD, *O my soul, and all that is within me, bless His Holy Name.*

Bless the LORD, *O my soul, and forget not all His benefits;*

H

Who forgiveth all thy sins, and healeth all thine infirmities;
Who saveth thy life from destruction, and crowneth thee with mercy and loving kindness;
Who satisfieth thy mouth with good things, making thee young and lusty as an eagle.

And in like manner, bless ye the LORD with me, all ye Angels and Arch-angels; all ye Principalities and Powers; all ye Virtues and Dominations; all ye Thrones, Cherubim and Seraphim, bless ye the LORD and praise Him, redouble your endless praises to our common LORD; for He hath not dealt with us according to our sins, but according to His Great and Fatherly Mercy. Praise Him, ye Heavens, Earth, Sea, and all that is therein, yea, let them praise Him and magnify Him for ever. Praise be to God from every creature; blessing and thanksgiving to the LORD from all creatures, in all places of His Dominion, for ever and ever. Amen.

IX.

JUSTICE.

"Thy right hand is full of righteousness." Ps. xlviii.

"Who knoweth the power of Thine anger? or Thy wrath, according as Thy fear requireth?" Ps. xc.

1. None, O LORD, can duly express the greatness and multitude of the punishments Thou hast prepared for sinners, decreed some time to be endured, through Thine Almightiness. As Thy Mercy is Infinite, so is Thy Justice, which in infinite ways, not only in the world to come, but in this, (which specially is Mercy's,) shall be displayed against the wicked, that all may learn to fear Thee, and those whom the kindness of a most sweet Father moveth not, may, at least, be appalled by the severity of a most just Judge, Who will leave no evil unavengéd, no good unrewarded; for that with Thee, most just Judge, is no respect of persons.

2. I rejoice and take delight, O LORD, in this Thy Justice; could I one jot deprive Thee of it, so that my

sins might go unpunished, I would not have it so; nay, if my sin, my hardness, and obstinacy be so great as to shut out repentance, if I would die hardened, impenitent, in despair (which terrible evil avert, O my GOD!): but if I were so reft of sense, from this moment I declare my will that Thy Justice take its course, and doom me to endless pain; that since I refused to glorify Thy Mercy by voluntary and healthful penitence, I may, at least in torments, glorify Thy Justice.

3. But, O my Most Sweet LORD! While I am here, I can, by Thy Grace, appeal from the tribunal of Thy Justice to the tribunal of Thy Mercy: therefore now, once for all, with great confidence, O my LORD, with all my heart, with all my soul, with all my strength I appeal to Thy Mercy; I implore Thee, through JESUS CHRIST, Thy SON, forgive me my sins, lest I stand arraigned at the tremendous tribunal of Thy Justice. Religiously I protest that hereafter, with Thy Divine Help, I desire to amend my life, and live as becomes a faithful servant; thus, by true repentance, may Thy Mercy the more tenderly and sweetly be glorified. Amen.

X.

THE LAST END.

"I am Alpha and Omega, the beginning and the ending, saith the LORD GOD." Rev. i.

1. As Thou, O my LORD, art the first and highest creative Cause of all things, so art Thou their last end, and specially of Thy rational creatures. Wherefore it behoves me to leave the creature, and put no trust in it, in that it hinders me manifoldly in the pursuit of that happy and highest end for which Thou hast created me, even Thyself, my true, my sole and highest Good.

2. This then should be my heart's care, to be united to Thee in vision, love, joy; in this union stands my highest good and Thy highest Glory. All the delights and attractions of this life, compared with this Chief Good, I count for filth and dung. From this moment I direct

all my thoughts, acts, and desires to this end, nor will I flag or desist, until I reach it.

3. But since I am unequal of myself, O Lord, to attain so great a good; to Thee, O Most Merciful God, I come. By Thy measureless Goodness, whereby Thou createdst the world, and wert made Man, and didst willingly for man submit to death; by Thine Infinite Blessings bestowed on me, and Thy Good Pleasure from eternity, whereby Thou hast freely predestinated me to so exalted a height of glory, shut not against me the fountain of Thy overflowing Beneficence. Most ungratefully indeed have I wasted the time given me for holy works, but let this rather inflame Thy Kindness, and let Thy Help and Protection be the greater in proportion to my weakness. Call to mind the end, for which from Eternity Thou didst destine me: let not in me Thy Most Holy Counsel and Desire be frustrated.

4. Lighten my mind by the light of Thy Holy Spirit; guided by Him, may I perfectly know the vanity of this world, and detect the perils which lie hid in it. And may I know, no less, the greatness, the excellency, the sweetness of the unmeasured blessings which Thou hast prepared for me in Thyself, for which my whole heart gives thanks to Thee, and joyfully renounces all vanity.

5. O my Lord, may my soul think of nought else, may nothing else be firmly engraven in my mind, save this *last end:* despising all fading and passing solaces, may I lift up myself forthwith to the love of eternal things, and the desire of this my last, my happy end.

May my longings never tire, may my sighs and pantings after that happy hour never cease: may I unwearied fight against myself, as I now purpose to do, till I reach the end of the race, when all the saints, by the vision of Thee, by Thy love and ineffable consolation, shall rest in Thee, their highest Good and last End; when their intention shall be consummated, their earnest and ardent longing fulfilled, in the possession of their last End, their chief Good, for which they strove more than manfully, and gloriously overcame. Amen.

CONCLUSION.

An Alliance of Love with God.

Finally, my most sweet Lord, as I confess Thee to be my only Good, my chief happiness and bliss, I am bound on no account to separate from Thee; rather must I do my utmost ever to remain most intimately joined to Thee. Wherefore I desire and will endeavour to let no moment pass which may not confirm the things I have purposed and set down. To this effect, I desire, in lowliest reverence and humility, to form an alliance with Thy Divine Majesty, and by a perpetual covenant to ratify my desire, that, as I shall never cease to breathe so long as I live, even so, I may never cease to believe in Thee, to love Thee, to praise Thee, to give Thee thanks, to offer myself to thee, to surrender myself to Thee, to hope, to joy in Thee, to shun the world as I would a plague, to have a zeal for Thy honour and the salvation of souls, to fear Thee, to humble myself, to do penance, to purpose holy deeds, to love my neighbour, to cultivate chastity, poverty, and obedience, and to pray to Thee for all that I have now prayed for. Moreover, to acknowledge Thee, to adore Thee, and to confess Thee, my God, the Infinite, Immeasurable, Unchangeable, Eternal, Almighty, Wise, Good, Holy, Kind, Provident, Merciful, Just, and our Last End. And with all lowliness of mind I protest before Thy Divine Majesty and the whole company of heaven, that with all my soul I most heartily desire, with all possible purity, earnestness, and energy of intention, to observe all that I have said and set down: and this even so often as I breathe, and as often as I direct my soul to any act like unto this, pleasing in Thy sight. Accept it now, O Lord, both for the present and for ever; and of Thy most merciful good pleasure, ratify and confirm the desire of my soul throughout eternity. Amen.

CHAPTER VII.

RHYTHMICAL HYMNS ON THE MOST HOLY TRINITY.

Profitentes Unitatem,
Veneremur Trinitatem
  Pari reverentia.

Tres personas asserentes,
Personali differentes
  A se differentia.

Hæc dicuntur relative,
Cum sint Unum substantive,
  Non tria principia.

Sive dicas tres, vel tria;
Simplex tamen est usia,
  Non triplex essentia.

Simplex esse, simplex posse;
Simplex velle, simplex nosse;
  Cuncta sunt simplicia.

Non unius quam duarum,
Sive trium personarum
  Minor efficacia.

Pater, Verbum, sacrum Flamen,
Deus unus; sed hi tamen
  Habent quædam propria.

Una virtus, unum Numen;
Unus splendor, unum lumen,
  Cuncta sunt hic paria.

Patri Natus est æqualis,
Nec hoc tollit personalis
  Amborum distinctio.

Patri compar, Filioque;
Spiritalis ab Utroque
  Procedit connexio.

1. CONFESS we all the Unity,
   Adoring still the TRINITY
     With equal reverence.
   Asserting ever Persons Three,
   Differing each personally
     With mutual difference.

2. Spoken be this relatively,
   For they are One Substantially;
     Not three first principles.
   But Principles, or Persons, Three
   Not triple is their Entity,
     Their Being simple is.

3. Simple Being, simple doing,
   Simple Willing, simple Knowing,
     Simple and single all;
   Whether of One, whether of Two,
   Or of the Persons Three, yet so
     The power is still equal.

4. The FATHER, WORD, and SPIRIT Blest,
   One God they are; yet each possest
     Of some proprieties.
   In Power One, in Deity,
   In Brightness, and in Majesty,
     In each all equal these.

5. FATHER and SON, They are equal,
   And yet distinctions personal
     In each of them are found.
   Equal with FATHER, and with SON
   Equal, yet Each proceeding from,
     The SPIRIT, Holy Bond.

Non humana ratione
Capi possunt hæ Personæ;
  Nec harum discretio.

Non hic ordo temporalis,
Non hic situs, aut localis
  Rerum circumscriptio.

Nil in Deo præter Deum,
Nulla causa præter Eum
  Qui causat causalia.

Digne loqui de Personis,
Vim transcendit rationis,
  Superat ingenia.

Quid sit Gigni, quid Processus,
Nescit homo, licet gressus
  Tentet per sublimia.

Quisquis credit, non festinet:
Et à via non declinet,
  Abiens per devia.

Servet fidem, formet mores,
Nec deflectat ad errores,
  Credat quod Ecclesia.

Ut in una jam moramur,
Sic in una moriamur
  Fidei constantia.

Trinæ sit laus Unitati,
Sit et simplæ Trinitati,
  Coæterna gloria. Amen.

DE SANCTO SPIRITU.

Qui procedis ab Utroque,
Genitore, Genitoque,
  Spiritus Paraclite:

Redde linguas eloquentes:
Sed accende primum mentes
  Charitatis fomite.

6. These not by man's capacity
   Of mind can comprehended be,
     Nor their distinctions spied.
   No order temporal is this,
   To places, or to boundaries
     Of circumstances tied.

7. In GOD there is but GOD Alone,
   Cause beside Him of aught is none,
     Cause of all causes He.
   These Persons Three, man's utmost height
   Of reason it transcendeth quite,
     To speak of worthily.

8. What Begetting, what Proceeding,
   He, this height of heights though treading,
     Striving, yet cannot know.
   Hasten not, believer: hasting
   Lest, the pathway everlasting
     Leaving, askance you go.

9. Keep the Faith, your life adorning,
   Error's ways deceitful scorning,
     Hold all Church-Verity.
   So, one whilst yet on earth we abide,
   We may be one when death betide
     In faith's true constancy.

   Praise to the Three in Unity,
   All praise to the One TRINITY,
     And glory co-eternally.

HYMN TO GOD THE HOLY GHOST.

1. From Both proceeding, as from One,
   The FATHER, and the Eternal SON,
     Thou SPIRIT Paraclete,
   Give tongues to speak, but first our hearts
   Inflame with love's all-quickening darts,
     Thine own true genial heat.

Tu procedens à Duobus,
Coæqualis es Ambobus,
  In nullo disparitas.

Par Majestas Personarum;
Par potestas Singularum;
  Et communis Deitas.

Amor Patris, Filiique,
Par amborum, et Utrique
  Gloria consimilis,

Cœlos imples, terras foves,
Mare domas, cuncta moves,
  Permanens Immobilis.

Tu commutas elementa,
Per Te suam Sacramenta
  Præstant efficaciam.

Tu malignam vim repellis;
Tu subvertis et refellis
  Hostium nequitiam.

Te docente, nil obscurum;
Te præsente, nil impurum;
  Cuncta sunt splendentia.

Gloriatur mens jucunda.
Per Te sana; per Te munda
  Gaudet conscientia.

Quando venis, corda lenis;
Quando subis, atræ nubis
  Effugit obscuritas.

Sacer Ignis, pectus uris,
Non comburis, sed à curis
  Eruis, dum visitas.

Mentes prius imperitas,
Et sopitas, et oblitas
  Erudis et excitas.

Cor ad fidem facit pronum,
Ori muto reddit sonum
  Manans à te claritas.

2. Thou that proceedest from the Two
   With each Co-equal art, that so
      There's no disparity.
   Each Person hath like Majesty,
   Of Power a like efficacy:
      One common Deity.

3. Love of the FATHER and the SON,
   Compeer of Both, with Each Alone
      Alike majestical;
   Filling heaven, quelling ocean,
   Earth enfolding, Fount of motion:
      Changeless, though changing all.

4. Cold elements, by Thee informed,
   With sacramental Life are warmed;
      From carnal made Divine.
   Dæmon malice Thou refellest,
   Dæmon violence repellest,
      Worsting our foes malign.

5. Under Thy teaching nought's obscure,
   Within Thy Presence nought impure,
      All shines with light serene.
   Leap regenerate hearts with joy,
   Consciences without alloy
      Exult, by Thee made clean.

6. At Thy coming, hearts Thou quellest,
   At Thy entrance, clouds dispellest,
      Putting dark shades to flight.
   Sacred Fire, our breasts inflaming,
   Burning never—aye reclaiming
      From care's corroding blight.

7. Darkling minds Thy wisdom teacheth,
   Stony hearts Thy influence reacheth,
      Souls sunk in slothful trance
   Now with burning faith are glowing,
   Gift of Brightness from Thee flowing
      Mute lips have utterance.

O quàm felix, quàm festiva
Dies, in qua primitiva
  Conditur Ecclesia!

Vivæ sunt primitiæ
Nascentis Ecclesiæ,
  Tria plebis millia.

Panes legis primitivi
Una fiunt adoptivi
  Fide duo populi.

Nempe duos unum fecit,
Cum duobus se præfecit
  Lapis caput anguli.

Tu perversos corde vitas,
Sed sinceros mente ditas
  Dono sapientiæ.

Veritatem notam facis;
Et ostendis viam pacis,
  Semitas justitiæ.

Dat liquorem Helisæus,
Largum fundit rorem Deus,
  Ubi vasa vacua.

Utres novi, non vetusti,
Sunt capaces novi musti;
  Tu fac corda congrua.

Non hoc musto vel liquore,
Non hoc sumus digni rore,
  Si discordes moribus.

In obscuris vel divisis
Sancta nequit Paraclisis
  Habitare cordibus.

Consolator Alme, veni;
Linguas rege, corda leni.
Nihil fellis vel veneni
  Tui fert præsentia.

8. O happy day! O festive day!
   Whereon the LORD began to lay
      His Church's living stones.
   Three thousand souls, redeemed to-day,
   Are living still, and still for aye
      The Church her firstlings owns.

9. Two people, whom the Law made two,
   By faith become one bread, are now
      Adopted into one;
   For He hath made both one, Who made
   Himself of both the Living Head,
      Of both the Corner Stone.

10. Thou shunnest the perverse of heart,
    Pure souls that choose the better part
       With wisdom's gift to bless.
    All truths divine Thou makest known;
    By Thee the ways of peace are shown,
       The paths of righteousness.

11. As erst at great Elijah's word,
    Streams plentiful from GOD are pour'd
       Where vacant hearts are found.
    New bottles only can contain
    New wine, e'en so grace to retain
       Old hearts Thou makest sound.

12. Unmeet that soul for this new wine,
    These streams from heaven, this dew divine,
       Where reigns not heavenly love;
    For, sure, to darkling hearts and torn
    Thy holy comfort Thou wilt scorn
       To impart, Celestial Dove.

13. Come, blessed COMFORTER, to soothe
    Our hearts, our lips to rule with truth:
    Nor gall, nor asp's envenomed tooth
       Thy Presence can assail.

Nil jucundum, nil amœnum,
Nil salubre, nil serenum,
Nihil dulce, nihil plenum,
   Sine Tua gratia.

Tu, cœleste condimentum,
Medicamen et unguentum,
Aquæ ditans elementum
   Virtute mysterii.

Nova facti creatura,
Te laudamus mente pura;
Iræ prius ex natura,
   Gratiæ nunc filii.

O qui Dator es et Donum,
Tu qui condis omne bonum,
   Mentis dona gaudium.

Tange corda, terge sordes,
Vinclo pacis fac concordes,
   Adsis ad præsidium.

Sicut post Ascensum Christi,
Rudes linguis imbuisti
   Variis Discipulos;

Sic nos vise; sic dignare,
Dissidentes congregare,
   Una fide populos.

Demum mortis ab hac valle,
Duc ad vitam recto calle
   Lætos de victoria;

Ubi Patris, ubi Tui,
Et Æterni Verbi frui
   Mereamur gloria.   Amen.

No joy is found, no gaiety,
Nought healthful, no serenity,
No pleasant sweetness, no plenty,
   Where'er Thy graces fail.

14. Thou, Salt from heaven in mercy sent,
Thou, Medicine, and Anointment,
Endu'st the watery element
   With powers of mystery.
We, now become a new creation,
Pour forth to Thee this pure oblation,
We, children once of indignation,
   Now, LORD, Thy family.

15. O Thou the Gift, and yet the Giver,
Who all good things conservest ever,
   Our minds with joy fulfil.
O touch our hearts, our stains remove,
Bind us in bonds of heavenly love,
   Aid and defend us still.

16. Like as when CHRIST on high had sped,
Thy Gift of divers tongues was shed
   On Thy disciples rude:
So visit us: so one in mind,
Though diverse now, vouchsafe to bind
   Nations to faith subdued.

17. At length from this dark vale of death
Lead us to life by a straight path,
   Joyful in victory.
Thine and the FATHER's glory there,
And th' Everlasting SON's to share,
   Grant us eternally.   Amen.

TO

The Illustrious Penitents,

IN WHOM GRACE SHONE SO BRIGHT;

THE LIVING MIRRORS OF REPENTANCE,

WHO STILL YEARN OVER SINNERS:

To David, King and Prophet,

MAN AFTER GOD'S OWN HEART,

YET STILL A MAN, AND, BY HIS FALL, A WARNING UNTO US,

WHOSE SINGLE CRY (O MARVEL OF GOD'S PITY),

SOBBED FROM HIS HEART'S DEPTH, MERITED FORGIVENESS;

To Peter, Son of Jonas,

CHIEF OF THE APOSTOLIC CHOIR, BEARER OF HEAVEN'S KEYS,

ROCK OF THE CHURCH, PASTOR OF THE SHEEP,

WHO YET BY SUFFERANCE, FELL, THAT HE MIGHT

LEARN COMPASSION,

WHO FORGAT HIMSELF, FORSOOK HIS LORD,

CAME TO HIMSELF ERE LONG, AND THEN WEPT BITTERLY,

SO CONSTANT WAS HIS LOVE WHOM HE DENIED,

SUCH MIGHTY EFFICACY IN ONE LOOK OF CHRIST:

[AND TO

And to thee, Mary,

ONCE INFAMOUS AND SINNING,

BUT NOW A FRIEND, YEA MORE, A BEAUTEOUS BRIDE,

WHOSE SINS, THOUGH MANY, WERE FORGIVEN,

FOR THAT THOU LOVEDST MUCH;

O WONDROUS SHOWER OF TEARS,

THAT WASHED THE SAVIOUR'S FEET,

AND CLEANSED THE FILTH OF CRIME:

NOR BE THOU SEVERED FROM THIS COMPANY,

Blest Thief,

WHOSE CROSS BECAME AN EASY STEPPING-STONE TO HEAVEN;

THRICE HAPPY THIEF,

WHO SEEST THY KING IN HIM

WHO WAS THY FELLOW IN THE CROSS OF SHAME,

AND THE SAME DAY DIDST WIN THY PRAYER

AND DIDST BECOME HIS FELLOW IN HIS KINGDOM AND HIS GLORY:

Patterns of Penitents; Solaces of Sinners;

WE HAVE FOLLOWED YOU IN SIN,

MAY WE FOLLOW YOU IN PENITENCE,

THEN SHALL WE FOLLOW YOU AND REIGN WITH CHRIST.

PARADISE FOR THE CHRISTIAN SOUL.

PART III.

ON PENITENCE, OR THE CONVERSION OF A SINNER, WITH SUITABLE EXERCISES.

For Tuesday.

CHAPTER I.

COLLOQUY BETWEEN CHRIST AND A MAN ON THE MANNER OF EXERCISING PENITENCE.

§ 1. *Lament over the state and wretchedness of a sinner.*

MAN. Wretched man that I am, who shall deliver me from the body of this death? Why do I yet live, why cumber I the ground? I, who am a dry and unfruitful stock, ever ungrateful and injurious to my GOD, who do nought but heap up sin on sin, and treasure up for myself wrath against the Day of Wrath and revelation of the righteous Judgment of GOD? I know, yea, by sad experience I know, that in my flesh dwelleth no good thing, and that my body, which is corruptible, presseth down my soul. Wherefore I do evil and sin daily; and, which is worse, seldom or never do I recollect how sad it is that I do sin; and yet strive not, with worthy tears and groans, to appease the Countenance of my GOD, my CREATOR, Whom I so constantly provoke to wrath.

Woe is me! I have so much to wail, and nothing which ought to give me joy! Darkness of soul, a treacherous conscience, falls into sin, loss of Grace, entanglements of sin and perils of sinning; what can these produce but tears and moaning? O that my head were waters and mine eyes a fountain of tears, that I might weep day and night for the losses of the past, the perils of the future, and the sicknesses of my soul, which are multiplied without number! Ah, LORD, my GOD! what will become of me? I fail daily; I cease not to offend Thee. When shall I be healed of my infirmity? When shall I rise again, who am cast down in the mire of the pit? Is there yet, thinkest Thou, hope of recovery? Shall the dead man again live?

Lo, out of the deep do I call unto thee, O LORD! O hearken unto my voice! Of myself I have no hope: O that I had stronger hope in Thee! The strength of despair multiplies upon me; daily as my sin increases, so does my infirmity: and if I say, Now will I begin; now it is high time to awake out of sleep; now is the accepted time, now is the day of Salvation; straightway sin standeth before the door, and, like a heavy yoke, a talent of lead, presseth down my neck: my enemy lifteth up himself against me, and the habit of evil drags me, overcome and fettered, in its bonds.

Look upon my affliction, O LORD; deliver me from them that compass me about, for their terror gaineth strength upon me. My counsel is perished from me; my strength hath failed me; my arm is broken, and my sword cannot save me. Thou Alone art left to be my refuge; yet Thee, alas! I have so often forsaken, that I may well fear lest I be forsaken of Thee; yea now, O LORD, I fear lest I be cast out of the sight of Thine Eyes: for Thine Eyes are upon them that do evil, to root out the remembrance of them from the earth. O LORD! all my desire is before Thee, and my groaning is not hid from thee.

§ 2. *Conviction and confusion of the sinner.*

CHRIST. I have heard thy lamentations, O man, and the cry of thine heart hath come even into Mine Ears; for I am nigh unto them that are of a troubled heart, and am ready to save them that are of an humble spirit.

Yet hearken a little while to My just complaints. I break not indeed the bruised reed, nor quench the smoking flax; nor is it My act to lose any one of those whom My Father hath given Me. Yet consider, thyself, how justly My Wrath might burn like fire against thee? I created thee after My Image and My Likeness; and when thou wast the bond-slave of Satan, I redeemed thee with My Own Blood, that thou mightest serve Me. But now thou hast made Me to serve with thy sins; thou hast wearied Me with thine iniquities. Put Me in remembrance; let us plead together: declare thou, if thou hast whereby thou mayest be justified.

Am not I thy Father Who have possessed thee, Who made thee and created thee? But thou hast forsaken thy Father Who begat thee, and hast forgotten God thy CREATOR. If I be a Father, where is My honour? and if I be a Master, where is My fear? Behold, I have nourished thee, and brought thee up, My son, and thou hast rebelled against Me. Whence is it, that when thou mightest have been brought up in scarlet in thy Father's House and clothed in purple twice-dyed[a], thou chosest rather to go into a far country, to attach thyself to strangers, to embrace dunghills, to consume away in nakedness, with cold and hunger? What have I done unto thee, and wherein have I wearied thee, that thou shouldest forsake Me? Why hast thou forsaken Me, the Fountain of living waters, and hewed thee out cisterns, broken cisterns, that can hold no water?

I had chosen and betrothed thy soul to Me with the tenderest Love, but thou chosest to go after other lovers. I showed thee the smooth and the straight way; for I am the Way, the Truth, and the Life. Wherefore hast thou wearied thyself in the way of wickedness, yea, in deserts where there lay no way; where there was only destruction and unhappiness; and the way of peace thou wouldest not know?

Lo, I had given thee a Law of life and discipline, that in keeping My Commandments thou mightest show that thou lovedst Me, and mightest have life; but

[a] Prov. xxxi.

thou hatedst My Discipline, and didst cast My Words behind thee! How often have I called thee, and thou refusedst! How often stretched out My Hand, and thou regardedst not, and hast set at nought all My Counsel! Is not My yoke easy, and My burden light? Yet wouldest thou rather go and buy for thyself five yoke of oxen, and follow after thine own heart's lusts, which drown men in destruction and perdition! O, ye sons of men, how long will ye blaspheme Mine Honour, and have such pleasure in vanity, and seek after leasing?

MAN. I know it is so of a truth; and how should man be just with God? If I would justify myself, truth will condemn me. If I say I am perfect, Thou wilt prove me perverse. If I would contend with Thee, I cannot answer Thee one of a thousand. I have sinned. What shall I do unto Thee, O Thou Preserver of men? Lo, I confess my wickedness, and am a burden to myself. Why dost Thou not take away my iniquity? For my wickednesses are like a sore burden, too heavy for me to bear. I confess I have merited wrath, not indulgence. Wherefore, if Thou cast me out from Thy Face, Thou doest justly; but if Thou receive me, miserable and worthless, among Thy hired servants, Thou doest mercifully. O, let Mercy rejoice over Judgment, for Mercy is over all Thy Works.

Woe is me, miserable! In my way from the heavenly Jerusalem, a stranger and an exile, I have fallen among thieves, been stripped of my garment of immortality, and, covered with many wounds, been left half dead; and now my wounds stink and are corrupt through my foolishness. If thou heed me not, and pass by on the other side, who will have compassion on me, and bind up my wounds? If Thou pour not in the wine of consolation, and the oil of pity, who will make up for me the medicine that I need? If Thou wilt not pay the penny, even the Price of my Salvation, who is there that can?

§ 3. *The necessity of penitence, and earnest invitation of the sinner thereto.*

CHRIST. Be not so troubled, O man; fear not. Thy perdition cometh of thyself alone; thy help is of Me. I am the good Samaritan, the true Physician, Who therefore came into the world to heal the broken-hearted. Myself bare thy sicknesses, yea, I have made ready a salve for thy wounds out of My Own Blood. I desire not the death of a sinner; but rather that he should be converted and live: to that end I came to seek and to save that which was lost. I came not to call the righteous, but sinners; for they that are whole need not a physician, but they that are sick. Bethink thee of the words with which I invited all the sinners of the earth to come to Me; "Come unto Me, all ye that travail and are heavy laden, and I will give you rest."

Come thou too, and return to the Heavenly Country by another way, which I have shown to sinners, that they should walk therein. This way is penitence. If thou wilt have life, cease from *evil* and do *good;* remember whence thou art fallen, and repent, and do the first works. Bring it again to mind, O transgressor; see how bitter it is to have forsaken the LORD GOD, thy CREATOR. Lay aside all malice; cast away the works of darkness; bring forth worthy fruits of penitence; deny ungodliness and worldly lust. Henceforth live soberly, righteously, and godly, in this world. This is the way that leadeth unto Life, and there is none else.

MAN. O, how sweet are these words of Thine, O LORD, to my throat! yea, sweeter than honey unto my mouth! In the multitude of the sorrows that I had in my heart, Thy Comforts have refreshed my soul. O true saying, and worthy of all men to be received, that Christ came into the world to save sinners, of whom I am chief. Now, therefore, think upon Thy servant as concerning Thy Word, wherein Thou hast caused me to put my trust: take back the prodigal, the fugitive from Thy Presence; embrace him, at length returning to his most Sweet Father, with the Arms of Love. Cast me not away from Thy Presence; forgive Thy servant all his sin, and blot not out my name from the book of the living.

§ 4. *The sinner invited to speedy penitence.*

CHRIST. Lo, it is I ; I am He Who blot out thine iniquities for my Own Sake, and thy sins will I remember no more. It is I Who justify the ungodly, forgiving him all his sins for My Name's Sake. For mercy I love more than wrath, and I desire to spare more than to punish. Why, then, dost thou fear? Why tremble to approach a Bosom of so great Lovingness? I am readier to pardon than thou to penitence.

But take heed that thou tarry not to turn to the LORD: delay not from day to day. Great are the perils of procrastination. When thou art sick, thou tarriest not; at once thou sendest for the physician, anxious to check the evil at the beginning, lest when it has gained strength by time, medicine be then in vain.

And it is wise: but why not do the same when thy soul is sick? Thou art in greater peril than if the plague or poison had attacked thy very vitals. Slumberest thou? tarriest thou? Awake; hasten; turn to the LORD thy SAVIOUR, lest He devour thy soul like a lion and tear it in pieces, while there is none to help. Remember now thy Creator in the days of thy youth; beware of forming any sinful habit. No cord so strongly binds a man as evil habit. It is a second nature; and how hard is nature to get rid of. Dost thou give the world and the flesh thy flower, and the dregs to Me, Who gave thee all, and all too of the best; yea, Who, for thy sake, even from My Youth up, was in misery, and like unto him that is at the point to die?

MAN. This is to many a hard saying, O LORD; they cannot bear it. So they say, Come on, let us enjoy the good things that are present, and let us speedily use the creatures like as in youth; let no flower of the spring pass by us; let us crown ourselves with rose-buds before they be withered. Nor are there wanting among them who promised themselves length of days, and meanwhile spent their days in delights, as though it were time enough at the end to call to mind their past years in the bitterness of their soul, and then to pray Thee not to remember the sins and offences of their youth; as though it were just, that where sin abounded, Grace should much more abound. Thus in their heart spake the unwise; and that they do so, their life and works bear witness.

§ 5. *Penitence must not be delayed from the hope of living longer.*

CHRIST. I know that the multitude of the unwise is without number; but fret not thyself because of the ungodly, and if sinners entice thee, consent thou not. Walk not with them, refrain thy foot from their path; for, when sudden calamity shall come upon them, and their destruction cometh as a whirlwind, when distress and anguish shall come upon them, then shall they call upon Me, but I will not answer; for that they would none of My Counsel, they despised all My Reproof. Hear, O man, thou that delayest to live better through hopes of living longer; thou fool, what if this night, what if this hour, I require thy soul of thee; whither, thinkest thou, will it go? How many thousands has that fond hope, that mad presumption, deluded! Now they lie in the hell, death gnaweth upon them; and above all this thought tormenteth them, that they neglected to do good when they had time: for an unsure hope they neglected the sure remedy of Salvation; they wished to repent, but not *now*. That delay was ruin; their life, while it yet seemed new, was cut off as a weaver's thread; ere they knew that they were dying, they were dead; and at the last gasp thou knowest their penitence of what kind it was; they repented, yea, and still repent, but all in vain, that they had neglected penitence in the acceptable time, and refused, by the easy task of a few hours, to redeem the pains of Eternity.

O be thou wise through others' woe: take warning in so perilous a case! I have promised pardon to the penitent, not time to him who deferreth till the morrow. To-day, then, if thou wilt hear My Voice, harden not thy heart: thou knowest not when I shall come to thee, perchance as a thief in the night, at an hour that thou art least aware. Watch, therefore, and be ready at any hour.

What is thy life but a vapour that appeareth for a little while? What thy body, liable to a thousand accidents, dangers, and diseases, which a draught of wind, a slight fever, an unlooked-for accident, throws prostrate at a moment? So frail a support hast thou the hardihood to rest upon and trust to?

Do not so many daily instances of death prove such hardihood mere folly? Such cases, without regard to age, sex, or rank, yet not without My certain Providence and Counsel, are multiplied before thine eyes, that thou mayest learn how vain the hopes of man, how cheating are his thoughts; that thou mayest remember that the lot of others may be thine; and that he is wise and happy, who by another's evil mends his own.

MAN. Righteous art Thou, O LORD, and true is Thy Judgment; but spare me if I speak unto my LORD, which am but dust and ashes. Dost Thou take pleasure in the death of a sinner? Are not Thy Mercies over all Thy Works? Wilt Thou not in wrath remember Mercy? Hast Thou not said, I have no pleasure in the death of the wicked? And, as for the wickedness of the wicked, he shall not fall thereby in the day that he turneth from his wickedness? Shall there not, then, be time for penitence, so long as there is time for life?

§ 6. *Penitence not to be delayed through regard to the Divine Mercy.*

CHRIST. Thou art beside thyself, O man, whosoever thou art, that flatterest thyself with the hope of My Mercy, forgetful of My Justice: wilt thou then be evil because I am good?

What? is My Mercy and My proneness to pardon set forth, that thou mayest more securely sin, that thou mayest freely provoke Me to anger, and yet, at last, when thou hast filled Me with reproaches, confidently promise thyself My Mercy? Great, I own, is My Mercy towards sinners, while it is the time of mercy; but whence is thy hardihood, who hast so often by inward calls, so often by heralds of My Word, been warned, and yet hast resisted My Spirit, and, like the deaf adder which stoppeth her ears, refused to hear My Voice; whence is thy hardihood to hope for My Mercy at the last, who after thy hardness and impenitent heart treasurest up for thyself wrath against the Day of Wrath?

Shouldest not thou rather fear lest, peradventure, for thy contempt of My free Mercy so often proffered, thou be given over to a reprobate mind, and henceforth follow greedily the desires of thine heart, and so, when thou art sunk into the deep, thou become a despiser, and, no longer worthy of mercy, be reserved for justice only? Thus is the sinner smitten with appropriate vengeance: living and in health he forgat Me; dying, he forgets himself.

Say not, the Pity of the Lord is great, He will be pacified for the multitude of my sins; for mercy and wrath come from Him, and His Indignation resteth upon sinners. Walk whilst thou hast the light, lest darkness come upon thee; whatsoever thy hand findeth to do, do it with all thy might. Thou knowest not what thou shalt, yea or canst, do hereafter, when thy strength faileth. Now in thy youth amend thy ways, even by ruling thyself after My Word. Behold, now is the accepted time; behold, now is the Day of Salvation: if thou let this pass, O how rash to promise thyself another time for penitence! Late penitence is seldom true penitence. Sins then are not so much forsaken by thee as forsake thee, because strength for sinning fails. Is it not then strange that thou committest thy Salvation to so unsure a hazard, when in all other things thou lookest about carefully for the surest way? Now I offer thee My Grace; rejected now, justice may require that hereafter it be denied thee.

O that thou knewest the danger and the guilt of receiving My Grace in vain, and of repelling Me when I call thee! Like as the hart desireth the water-brooks, so wouldest thou pant after Me; thou wouldest give all diligence to make thy calling and election sure. Do therefore *now*, what thou wilt wish that thou hadst done, when no longer able, and which thou wilt bitterly lament thou hast not done, when thou hadst the power: *then* no longer wilt thou find medicine for thy grief. Whatsoever a man soweth, that shall he also reap; this life is seed-time, death will be harvest-time; if thou shalt have sown to the flesh, of the flesh shalt thou reap corruption. O sow now in tears what then thou mayest reap in joy!

Consider this, ye that forget God; O consider this, lest He pluck you away and there be none to deliver you.

Lo, I have left the ninety and nine sheep in the wilderness, and thee, the stray one, I am come to seek: now like a Good Shepherd, I am ready to take thee on My Shoulders to bring thee back to My Fold rejoicing: defraud Me no longer of My desire and My Angels of their joy, for they rejoice over one sinner that repenteth.

MAN. Truly I have gone astray like a sheep that is lost; seek Thy servant, O LORD; for that which was lost Thou camest to seek and save. Against Thee only have I sinned and done evil in Thy Sight; surely I am one, so wretched, so degraded, in whom Thy Glory may be magnified, if, according to Thy Promises, Thou give me Thy Mercy, and in me justify Thyself against the evil surmises of men, who, in their judgment of Thee, think not of Thee in Goodness, but deem Thee stern and cruel in taking vengeance of our sins. But I know Thee pitiful and good, and will return to Thee as a prodigal son to the Father of Mercies. Cast me not away from Thy Presence.

§ 7. *The examination of conscience, the first movement towards contrition and confession.*

CHRIST. Return, My son; why wilt thou feed away from thy home upon the draff of swine, when thou mayest with Me eat the pleasant food of children? Return with all thine heart, and I will take thee to My Embrace. But this do; first bethink thee of all the years and days spent in sin, in the bitterness of thy soul; heedfully examine thyself, diligently search out the hiding-places of thy conscience. If thou do this slightly and formally, many things will escape thee; the heart of man is wicked and inscrutable. Who can know it? There is nothing harder than to *know thyself:* yet, nothing more useful. It is in vain to know all things, if thou know not thyself. To know thy disease is the first step towards health.

MAN. In many things we all offend; Thou, O LORD, hast searched me out and known me; Thou countest all my steps; all things are bare and open to Thine eyes; Thou knowest well what is in man; Thou understandest my thoughts long before; but who can tell how oft he offendeth? O cleanse Thou me from my secret faults. I am afraid of all my works, for Thou wilt not hold me innocent; my sins are more in number than the hairs of my head, and I cannot look up. But Thou, O Very Light, that lightenest every man that cometh into this world, lighten the darkness of my mind, that I may see where I have gone aside from Thy Commandments, and may be put right again in the right way. Answer me and tell me the number of my wickednesses and my sins.

§ 8. *Contrition the first part of penitence.*

CHRIST. Thy own conscience will give thee thy answer, and that easily, if it be not seared or hardened: ask it seriously, it will answer thee: even unasked, does it not often vex thee and accuse thee, and secretly scourge thee when accused? Such sins, however, as after diligent examination still escape thee, trust them to My Mercy; vex not thyself with scrupulosity: I would have the ministry of penitence not a torment, but a consolation. Yet self-love not seldom inclines the heart of man to an evil way, and in his sins to plead excuses. Put thou aside all partiality; be to thine own self culprit, accuser, and judge, and when thou findest thyself guilty, spare not thyself; more and more strictly chide thyself, mourn from thy heart of hearts that thou hast offended and despised ME, thy GOD, thy CREATOR, and thy SAVIOUR, Whom thou wast bound to love supremely as the Highest Good of all.

Bethink thee how thou grievest at the loss of a petty trifle, but dost not grieve when thou hast suffered loss in thy soul and lost Me, thy Highest Good. If thou confess me LORD, where is My fear? If thou call me Father, where is My love? How oft have I whispered to thy heart, how often has thine own conscience said to thee, "Thy way is crooked; this is not the way to Heaven, this is the broad road that leadeth to destruction; they that pleased GOD walked not herein. How long wilt thou have such pleasure in vanity, and seek after leasing?" But thou hast cast My Words behind thee; and behold I stand at the door and knock, and how hardly am I allowed to enter!

MAN. Enter not into judgment with Thy servant, for in Thy Sight shall no man living be justified. Remember, O LORD, that Thou hast made me of clay, and wilt bring me back again to dust; and, since Thou hatest nothing that Thou hast made, have mercy upon me, and that soon, for I am come to great misery.

§ 9. *How to raise in us contrition, or sorrow for our sins.*

CHRIST. Bethink thee, O man, what I have done for thee: for what hast thou which thou hast not received? See how bitter and evil a thing it is, that thou shouldest have forsaken the LORD Who created thee, and been so thankless and despiteful to thy Highest Benefactor.

I created thee in My Image, after My Likeness, and I put a seal upon thee, even the light of My Countenance, that thou mightest confess and praise Me thy Creator; and I set thee over the works of My Hands. But when thou wast in honour, thou understoodest not: thou wast like unto the beasts that perish; like unto horse and mule, which have no understanding.

Yet all this time I have, like a Father, taken care of thee; kept thee and brought thee up, even as an eagle stirreth up her nest, and fluttereth over her young. I have given thee strength and health, have stood by thee and saved thee in danger and adversity; have given thee needful food, and bestowed on thee countless benefits: but these very Gifts have too often made thee wax more wanton, and thou hast abused them to My reproach. Thou hast waxen fat, thou hast grown thick, thou hast forsaken GOD Who made thee.

Yea, I have more grievous things against thee. When thou wast lost, the bond-slave of Satan, and due to eternal death, for thy sake I came down from Heaven, and was made Man: for thee I took the Form of a Servant, being Lord of all: so many griefs and pains I bare, and I redeemed thee at a great price, not with corruptible things, as silver and gold or precious stones, but with My Own Blood; and all this that thou mightest glorify and bear Me in thy heart and in thy body. What more could I have done for My vineyard that I have not done for it?

But what reward hast thou given unto Me for all the Benefits that I have done unto thee? Has it not been evil for good, and hatred for My good Will? I looked that thou shouldest bring forth grapes, and behold wild grapes! Thou hast sold thy soul without price, the Price whereof is My Blood. What but shadows and smoke are all these things for which thou so often lightly hazardest thy soul, wastest and slightest My Blood? What else the foul pleasures of the flesh, the vain hollow emptiness of the world, the desire of filthy lucre? All these things My Apostle, and the rest of them who love Me, counted as dung, that they might win Me; while thou so highly esteemest them, that often thou wouldest rather offend Me than man, wouldest forfeit Eternal Joys and Treasures for fleeting ones, wouldest rather despise My Commands than the judgment of the world.

Yet, what shall it profit thee to gain the whole world and lose thy soul? Is this the return thou makest Me, O foolish creature and unwise?

MAN. Who shall stand to speak with Thee? Who shall answer Thee one of a thousand? I confess that Thou art a long-suffering and patient GOD, and of great pity, Who hast mercy upon all, and hidest away the sins of them that are penitent. O that my head were waters, and mine eyes fountains of tears; for that I have not kept Thy Law, and have received my soul in vain, for which Thou yieldedst Thy Beloved Soul to Death! What shall I say unto Thee? O Goodness Immeasurable! I have sinned, but spare me. Do not Thou condemn me, Whose Will it was to be condemned for me.

CHRIST. I have loved thee with an Everlasting Love; sweetly and with blessings of greatest price I have called thee, to love Me in return: but thou, like an adulteress, hast run after many lovers; and so that thou mightest be the world's friend, thou hast not feared to become Mine enemy. Thou hast forsaken Me, the Fountain of Living Waters, and hast digged for thyself broken cisterns that can hold no water, whereas thou mightest have drawn water with gladness out of the Wells of thy SAVIOUR. Thou hast chosen to follow an enemy, who, for the service paid to him, and the hire of fleeting pleasure, recompenses endless torments, rather than Me Who crown them that follow Me with glory and honour.

§ 10. *Grief for sin, and hope of pardon.*

MAN. I have sinned, O LORD, and done evil in Thy Sight; but, GOD forbid that I should say with the wicked, my iniquity is too great for me to win pardon. Nay, Thou art plenteous in forgiveness; and though my sins are multiplied exceedingly, yet of Thy Mercy there is no numbering. Truly, I should despair, if I knew not the Loving-kindness of the LORD. The tempter sleeps not; but against him, my JESU, I set the remembrance of Thine abundant Sweetness, which Thou showedst to David in his heavy sin, to the adulteress, to the traitor, to Mary the sinner, to Peter who denied Thee, to the Canaanitish woman who cried to Thee, to the seditious robber on the Cross, to Thy very crucifiers. Let them, therefore, who know Thy Name, put their trust in Thee; for Thou, O LORD, never failest them that seek Thee; yea, Thou invitest them that seek Thee not.

I have gone astray like a sheep that is lost. For love of Thee, I mourn from my heart of hearts. O that I had never offended Thee! O that I might never hereafter offend Thee! O that I might be as in the former days, in the days when I yet enjoyed the Fatherly Sweetness of Thy Countenance.

[§ iii.] ON PENITENCE. 17

But even now look Thou upon me, and be merciful unto me, for I am desolate and in misery. Undertake for Thy servant for good, for whither shall I flee any more from Thy Face? Ever since I forsook Thee, without Thee it has always gone ill with me. Cast me not away from Thy Presence; deliver me not over with the evil-doers. Thy sacrifice is a troubled spirit; a broken and contrite heart do not Thou despise. Thou that searchest the heart and reins, Thou knowest my heart's desire, and my groaning is not hid from Thee.

CHRIST. Can a mother forget her sucking child, that she should not have compassion on the son of her womb? Yea, though she forget, yet will not I forget thee. I gave My Life for thee, and washed thee in My Blood: if thy sins be as scarlet, they shall be as white as snow; though they be red like crimson, they shall be as wool.

MAN. O how good and sweet is Thy Spirit, O LORD, in all things! Bless the LORD, O my soul, and forget not all His Benefits; Who forgiveth all thy sins, and healeth all thine infirmities: Who saveth thy life from destruction, and crowneth thee with Mercy and Loving-kindness; Who satisfieth thy mouth with good things, making thee young and lusty as an eagle. I thank Thee, O LORD, from mine inmost heart, that Thou hast thus long given me life and mercy, and that Thou hast not, as Thou mightest, cut me off in my sins, but hast in goodness spared me to bring me to repentance.

§ 11. *The second part of penitence, confession.*

CHRIST. That thou mayest be more fully restored to My favour after thus confessing thy unrighteousness to Me, go and show thyself also to the Priest, to whom I have given the power of binding and of loosing. Whoso hideth his wickednesses shall not be set right, but he that confesses and forsakes them shall obtain mercy. My son, be not ashamed to tell the truth for thy soul's sake. There is a shame that bringeth sin, and there is a shame that bringeth glory. Open, then, thy conscience frankly and sincerely to him who is

B

in My Stead, and he shall open heaven to thee*, for to this end the keys of the kingdom of heaven have been delivered to him.

Why be ashamed to say before a man, a sinner like thyself, what thou hast not been ashamed to do before Me? Wheresoever thou art, thou art laid open to Mine Eyes, Which behold the good and bad in every place. Away with this shamefaced-ness, *then* only profitable when thou wouldest sin, *then* harmful when thou wouldest repent. What is it to hide thy sins but to cover up thy wounds, and reject the physician's hand until they fester by reason of thy folly? Dost thou hold thy salvation cheaper than my credit? Fearest thou exposure to one man, like thyself, when thou shalt be accused and condemned in the eyes of the whole world?

What wilt thou, wretched, do in that day when I shall bring to light the hidden things of darkness, and disclose the counsels of the heart? Then shall there be nothing secret which shall not be known. Then that which hath been said and done in darkness shall be laid bare in the light before the world. Blush not, then, to say what thou hast not blushed to do.

O how many, through ill-timed shame, have found Mine ordinances, which are the vessels of grace and salvation, a stone of stumbling, and a rock of offence! Master this preposterous shame; humble thyself before My Priest, whom I have appointed in My place, as My

---

* No words upon the power of Absolution can contain more than those in which we receive our commission as Priests, combined with the form of Absolution prescribed for us to use when the sick "humbly and heartily desire it:" "Receive the HOLY GHOST for the office and work of a Priest now committed to thee by the imposition of our hands: whose sins thou dost forgive, they are forgiven; and whose sins thou dost retain, they are retained; and be thou a faithful minister," &c. Service for the Ordination of Priests.

"Our LORD JESUS CHRIST, Who hath left Power to His Church to absolve all sinners who truly repent and believe in Him, of His Great Mercy forgive thee thine offences; and by His Authority committed unto me, I absolve thee from all thy sins, in the Name of the FATHER, and of the Son, and of the HOLY GHOST. Amen." The Visitation of the Sick.

ambassador and thy counsellor and physician. Declare thy wickednesses, that thou mayest be justified.

MAN. I said I will confess my sins unto the LORD, yea, and to the man whom I revere as Thy vicegerent: and do Thou, O LORD, forgive the iniquity of my sin. I am human, and I know that in my flesh dwelleth no good thing; and if I say that I have no sin, I am a liar, and deceive myself. I have nothing of my own, but to err, to fall, to be ignorant, to be deceived; why should I deny it or hide it, or wish to seem more innocent or holier to man than Thou Who seest the very secrets of my heart, knowest me to be? Rather let me openly lay bare my sins to him, that he, whom Thou hast made my physician, may the sooner heal me.

§ 12. *Avoidance of occasions of sin, and of relapse.*

CHRIST. My son, thou hast sinned: sin no more. Yea, pray for thy past sins, that they may be forgiven thee. Washed, as it were, in Jordan, that is, in the bath of My Blood, thou hast by confession been cleansed from the leprosy of thy sins: return not like the sow to wallowing in the mire, or as the dog to his vomit: thou art made whole, sin no more, lest a worse thing come upon thee. Relapse is easy; if thy penitence be not serious, it is certain.

Resolve, therefore, stedfastly to bear all things rather than again offend Me. To this end it will be most profitable to know to what sin thou art most inclined, and on what occasions of sinning thou art most wont to fall, so that thou mayest fortify thy weakest part, and the side which is most exposed to danger.

Search therefore diligently and not lightly, the root from which sprung up in thy soul all those thorns and briers and hurtful buds. If thou cut that out, or at least keep it down, thou hast done much.

By how few is this seriously done! and so they stick in the same mire, accusing their conscience, not healing it. They put off their sins and purpose better, but soon they return to their vomit. Now they weep for what they have done, soon they repeat what calls for new tears; and thus they dally with Me all their life, till at last unexpected death snatches them away, and sinks them in the deep, and the pit of hell shuts its mouth upon them.

See, O man, that thou be not like these who thus abuse My patience and long-suffering, who so often receive My grace in vain, and crucify to themselves the Son of GOD afresh, and put Him to an open shame. I tell thee it is difficult to renew *them* again to repentance. For the earth which drinketh in the rain which cometh oft upon it, and bringeth forth herbs meet for them by whom it is dressed, receiveth Blessing from GOD; but that which beareth thorns and briers is rejected, and is nigh unto cursing, whose end is to be burned. And if one man persists in acting offensively to another, is he not at last quite shut out from his friendship and his favour?

MAN. Woe is me, O LORD. But now I rejoiced in Thy words of consolation, and now again Thou utterest words full of terror and bitterness; and what shall I say? I am confounded and am ashamed to lift up my face to Thee, for my wickednesses are more in number than the hairs of my head. Yea, I am very vile, ever returning to my old ways, and like a dog, abominable in Thine eyes, returning over and over again to its vomit. Whither shall I go then from Thy Spirit, whither shall I flee from Thy Presence?

CHRIST. Whither, O man, but to *His* mercy, Whose power thou hast set at nought by sinning? No one of you fleeth from Me aright, but by flying to Me; *from* My severity *to* My goodness. For whither canst thou fly where thou wilt not find Me present? If by these words of Mine I have made thee sorrow to repentance it is well: for godly sorrow worketh repentance unto sure salvation. But this one thing I warn thee,—profit by the peril and the loss of others, who confess with their lips their sins, but their heart is not right with GOD: so they go on repeating their sins, and at last perish.

How easy were it for many to escape sin if they would be earnest in shunning the *risks* of sinning! The thoughts of man are inclined to evil from his youth, and thinkest thou to be unharmed amid the very occasions and incentives to sin? Can a man hide fire in his bosom and his garments not catch fire; can a man walk on live coals and his feet not be burned? David, Solomon, Peter, and many others, have been famous for wisdom and holiness, yet in the *occasion* of sin they fell, and are examples to thee of man's weakness. Take warning by them; if they fell so easily, thou mayest fall: canst thou dare then to be self-confident, and in the midst of peril promise thyself security? Blessed is the man that feareth always.

§ 13. *Good resolution.*

Man. I have sworn, and am stedfastly purposed to keep Thy righteous judgments; but what can I do without Thee? In vain I purpose, unless Thy grace be with me, and Thou stretch out Thy Right Hand to the work of thy Hands. I *would* serve Thee, but I cannot without Thee: Thou hast given the will, give me the power too. Stablish this thing, O Lord, which Thou hast wrought in me; cast me not away from Thy presence, and take not Thy Holy Spirit from me. Pierce my flesh with Thy fear; wound my heart with Thy love, and may Thy love and fear be feet to me, that I may walk always in the way of Thy Commandments.

§ 14. *The third part of penitence, satisfaction* [or making amends].

Christ. Walk thou before Me, and I will be with thee in all thy ways, and order thy steps. But knowest thou not that *so* much torment is due to the sinner as he has magnified himself and revelled in delights? Is it not just, that as has been the sin, such shall be the stripes [b]? If thou art wise, anticipate the sentence of the Judge, and take vengeance on thyself, lest thou be cast into prison, whence thou shalt not come forth till thou hast paid the very last farthing. It is

[b] "If thou beginnest to judge thyself, to be displeased with thyself, God will come to have mercy upon thee. If thou willest to punish thyself, He will spare." S. Aug. Serm. 270, c. 12. See Tert. de Pœnit. c. 9. "In what measure thou sparest not thyself, in the same, be assured, God will spare thee," and Note o.

easier now to make amends to Divine Justice, while it is the time of mercy and the day of salvation; it is easier to pay the penalty here, than to reserve it to the time when I shall judge righteous judgment.

Turn thee, then, unto Me with all thy heart, with fasting, and with weeping, and with mourning. By pursuing pleasures and carnal delights thou hast oft offended Me; it is but just that thou shouldest chastise thy body, and bring it into subjection, that as thy flesh by pampering has led thee to sin, by bruising it may bring thee back to pardon.

Redeem [c] too thy sins with almsgiving: nothing so much bends me to have mercy, as when I see you, moved with brotherly love, show pity to the needy and distressed. But if thou shut up thy bowels of compassion against them, take heed lest when *thou* cry thou be not heard. Wilt thou make amends for thy sins? Lo, how good a thing is prayer with fasting and alms!

But the best amends of all most pleasing to Me, most profitable for you, is to direct the whole force of thy penance against thy sins and their root. Specially, therefore, and earnestly give thyself to the exercise of those virtues which are most opposed to the vicious inclinations of thy mind, and which are most galling to the flesh in its weakest part. If the head be wounded, you would not apply a plaister to the feet; so, each vice, like each disease, has its proper remedy. Hatred of sin alone can secure true penitence; when that becomes bitter to thy soul which was before pleasant to thy flesh, then thou repentest truly, and reconcilest Me to thyself.

Does my counsel seem harsh to thee? Far more harsh are the things from which I would preserve thee by My counsels. But, tell Me, have you not endured up to this time far harsher things for the world and the flesh? Their pleasure and Satan's suggestions thou hast done promptly and willingly; when I instructed, counselled, entreated thee, by My love and my Blood, to carry about my mortification in thy body, thou hast refused. Say, is it otherwise?

Lo, I will convict thee and set before thy face. Did any hope of gain, or honour, or advancement, gleam upon

---

[c] Dan. iv. 27. See Pref. to Avrillon's Guide for Lent, p. xxviii.

thee, wouldest thou not move every stone, wouldest thou not go any distance by land or sea? Wert thou attacked by sickness, rather than run the risk of thy life wouldest thou not spend all thy substance on physicians, and bear caustics and the knife? Wert thou to receive injury, loss, or reproach from any one, what wouldest thou not undergo to defend thine honour, profit, or good name? Yet how little hast thou done to please Me! And yet, if thou hadst laboured a little, thou hadst found great rest; hadst thou done for heaven a tenth of what thou hast done for the world, thou shouldest have lived safe and happy; for My Yoke is easy, and My Burden light.

This thou couldest scarce credit, and no wonder; thou hadst not tasted how gracious the Lord is, nor relished those things that are above, for thou feddest on those which are on the earth. But what fruit hast thou from those things whereof thou art now ashamed; for the end of those things is death? Being made free from sin, thou art become the servant of righteousness; as therefore thou hast yielded thy members as servants of uncleanness and of iniquity unto iniquity, so now yield them as servants of righteousness unto holiness; then shalt thou know how sweet and good I am to those that are of an upright heart.

MAN. Of a truth, O Lord, when I turn me to all in which I have hitherto vainly toiled, I find in all nothing but vanity and vexation of spirit, and that there is nothing abiding under the sun. But Thou, O Lord, abidest for ever. It is good for me then, O Lord, to hold me fast by Thee, and to put my trust in Thee Alone: and what shall separate me from the love of Thee? O let not life, or death, or any other creature. Yet how shall I come to Thee and be joined to Thee, unless Thou draw me with the cords of Thy love? Draw me, that, like as the hart to the waterbrooks, I may run to Thee. Help me for the glory of Thy Name, for Thou art God my Saviour.

This colloquy has exceeded the bounds I at first intended. It matters not; for well does that subject merit greater exactness, which is of daily, necessary use; for we sin daily. And perchance this closer examination may save us from sinning so often, or at least so foully.

CHAPTER II.

LITANIES OF PENITENTS, GATHERED OUT OF HOLY SCRIPTURE.

By the use whereof the sinner is invited to the hope of pardon and the practice of penitence.

LORD, have mercy.
CHRIST, have mercy.
LORD, have mercy.
O CHRIST, hear us.
O CHRIST, graciously hear us.
O GOD, the Father of Heaven, have mercy upon us,
O GOD, the SON, REDEEMER of the world, have mercy upon us.
O GOD, the HOLY GHOST, have mercy upon us.
O Holy Trinity, One GOD, have mercy upon us.

PART I.

O GOD, Who wouldest not the death of a sinner, but rather that he should be converted and live [a],
Who sparedst not the Angels that sinned, but didst thrust them down to be tormented in hell [b],
Who calledst Adam after his fall to the acknowledgement of his fault and to repentance [c],
Who castedst forth from Thy Presence impious Cain, despairing of pardon [d],
Who in mercy deliveredst, by the ark, Noah from the flood and the overthrow of the ungodly [e],
Who broughtest out Lot from the midst of sinners [f],
Who at last fearfully punishedst Pharaoh, feigning repentance and hardened in heart [g],

} Have mercy upon us.

[a] Ezek. xxxiii.   [b] 2 St. Pet. ii.   [c] Gen. iii.   [d] Ibid. iv.
[e] Ibid. vii.   [f] Ibid. xix.   [g] Exod. xiv.

Who deliveredst Thy people Israel, when they called to Thee in trouble, from the hard bondage of Pharaoh[h],
Who gavest the law to Moses in the Mount, after fasting forty days[i],
Who forgavest the sins of Thy disobedient people at the prayer of Moses[k],
Who savedst Jonah, when he called to Thee, from the belly of the whale[l],
Who sparedst the Ninevites, when they repented in sackcloth and with fasting[m],

PART II.

Who, through Nathan, broughtest David to confess his fault[n],
Who didst put away David's sin when he confessed and repented in sackcloth[o],
Who gavest David the choice of three plagues, when he sinned in numbering the people[p],
Who sparedst Ahab when he humbled himself and repented[q],
Who heardest Judith when she prayed in sackcloth and ashes for the people[r],
Who deliveredest Hezekiah, with the people, from the army of the Assyrians, when he called on Thee in sackcloth, ashes, and fasting[s],
Who heardest penitent Manasseh, and restoredst him to his kingdom[t],
Who madest Esther, in her fasting, find grace in the eyes of king Ahasuerus[u],
Who deliveredst Mordecai from the gallows, when he called on Thee in sackcloth and ashes[x],
Who succouredst the Maccabees, when they fasted and called on Thee in sackcloth and in ashes[y],

} Have mercy upon us.

[h] Exod. xiv. [i] Ibid. xxxiv. [k] Ibid. xxxii. [l] Jonah ii.
[m] Ibid. iii. [n] 2 Sam. xii. [o] Ibid. [p] Ibid. xxiv.
[q] 1 Kings xxi. [r] Judith ix. [s] 2 Kings xix. [t] 2 Chron. xxxiii.
[u] Esther xiv. [x] Ibid. xvi. [y] 1 Macc. iii.

Who hast commanded the Priests to weep, pray, and sacrifice for the people [a],

PART III.

Who camest into this world to save sinners [b],
Who, when coming to redeem the world, sentest John before Thee to preach repentance [c],
Who gavest the same, marvellous in his rough food and apparel, as a mirror of penitence [d],
Who fastedst forty days and forty nights [e],
Who, rich in mercy, for the great love wherewith Thou lovedst us, when we were dead in sins, didst quicken us together in CHRIST [f],
Who gavest Thy preventing grace to Matthew, sitting at the receipt of custom [g],
Who barest witness that the publican who smote his breast with grief and humility, received the grace of justification [h],
Who deliveredst the paralytic, after remitting his sins, from his disease [i],
Who, in the parable of the prodigal returning to his father, hast given sinners the hope of pardon and indulgence [k],
Who openedst to the Samaritan woman the well of living water [l],
Who broughtest salvation to Zaccheus' house, when he repented and restored fourfold [m],
Who mercifully heardest the Canaanitish woman when she persevered in prayer [n],
Who mercifully absolvedst the woman taken in adultery [o],
Who receivedst publicans and sinners, and didst eat with them [p],

} Have mercy upon us.

[a] Joel ii. and elsewhere. [b] 1 Tim. i. [c] St. Matt. iii.
[d] Ib. [e] Ib. iv. [f] Eph. ii. [g] St. Matt. ix.
[h] St. Luke xviii. [i] Ib. v. [k] Ib. xv. [l] St. John iv.
[m] St. Luke xix. [n] St. Matt. xv. [o] St. John viii. [p] St. Luke v. xv.

[§ iii.] ON PENITENCE. 27

Who forgavest the many sins of Mary Magdalene who loved much [q],
Who in mercy lookedst upon Peter who denied Thee, thus moving him to confess his fault, and shed tears of penitence [r],
Who on the Cross promisedst Paradise to the penitent thief [s],
Who didst no sin, and barest our sins in Thine own Body on the tree [t],
Who was bruised for our iniquities [u],

PART IV.

Who lovest all things that are, and hatest nothing that Thou hast made [x],
Who triest Thine elect like gold in a furnace [y],
Who givest time and place for repentance for sins [z],
Who scourgest every son whom Thou receivest and lovest [a],
Who rebukest and chastenest them whom Thou lovest [b],
Who wouldest not that any should perish, but that all should turn to repentance [c],
Who camest to seek and to save that which was lost [d],
Who hast mercy upon all, and winkest at the sins of men, because they should amend [e],
Who wast made a propitiation for our sins [f],
Who hast pity on sinners who turn to Thee in weeping, fasting, and mourning [g],
Who wouldest mercy and not sacrifice [h],
Who camest not to call the righteous but sinners to repentance [i],
Who of Thy goodness leadest us to repentance [k],

} Have mercy upon us.

[q] St. Luke vii. [r] Ib. xxii. [s] Ib. xxiii. [t] 1 St. Pet. ii. [u] Is. liii.
[x] Wisd. xi. [y] Ib. iii. [z] Ib. xii. [a] Heb. xii. [b] Rev. iii.
[c] 2 St. Pet. iii. [d] St. Luke xix. [e] Wisd. xi. [f] 1 St. John ii. [g] Joel ii.
[h] St. Matt. ix. [i] Ib. [k] Rom. ii.

Who didst wonderfully call Saul, when persecuting and laying waste the churches[1],
Who didst enlighten him, fasting for three days and praying [m],
Who after repentance rememberest all our sins no more [n],
O GOD, the gracious and merciful, slow to anger and of great kindness, Who repentest Thee of the evil [o],

} *Have mercy upon us.*

PART V.

Be gracious; spare us, O LORD.
From all evil, Good LORD, deliver us.
From all sin, Good LORD, deliver us.
From a sudden and wicked death, Good LORD, deliver us.
By Thy Baptism and Thy Holy Fasting, Good LORD, deliver us.
By Thy Toils and Thy Griefs, Good LORD deliver us.
By Thy Blood Thou sheddedst for the remission of our sins, Good LORD, deliver us.
In the Day of tribulation and anguish, and of Thy awful Judgment, Good LORD, deliver us.

PART VI.

We sinners do beseech Thee to hear us,
That it may please Thee to bring us to true repentance,
That, condemning ourselves, we may escape Thy condemnation [p],
That we may bring forth in time worthy fruits of penitence [q],
That, as we have yielded our members as servants of uncleanness and iniquity, so we may now yield them as servants of righteousness unto holiness [r],

} *We beseech Thee, &c.*

---

[1] Acts ix.   [m] Ib.   [n] Ezek. xviii.   [o] Joel ii.
[p] 1 Cor. xi.   [q] St. Matt. iii.   [r] Rom. vi.

That we give not place to the Devil and that the sun go not down upon our wrath [s],
That, denying ungodliness and worldly lusts, we may live soberly, righteously, and godly [t],
That we may chastise our bodies, and bring them into subjection [u],
That sin may not reign in our mortal body [x],
That we yield not our members as instruments of unrighteousness [y],
That we love not the world, neither the things that are in the world [z],

PART VII.

That we may not be conformed to the world, but transformed by the renewing of our mind [a],
That we be not over-wise above what is fitting, but that we be wise unto sobriety [b],
That we be not drunk with wine, wherein is excess [c],
That, as true members of Christ, we crucify our flesh with its passions and lusts [d],
That no corrupt communication proceed out of our mouth, but such as is good to the edifying of the faith [e],
That all bitterness, and wrath, and anger, be put away from us [f],
That we become not desirous of vain glory [g],
That we put off the old man and his deeds, and put on the new man in righteousness and true holiness [h],
That we live not according to the flesh, but in the Spirit mortify the deeds of the body [i],
That we never despise the riches of Thy goodness, patience, and long-suffering [k],

} We beseech Thee to hear us.

[s] Eph. iv. [t] Tit. ii. [u] 1 Cor. ix. [x] Rom. vi.
[y] Ib. [z] 1 St. John ii. [a] Rom. xii. [b] Ib.
[c] Eph. v. [d] Gal. iii. [e] Eph. iv. [f] Ib.
[g] Gal. x. [h] Eph. iv. [i] Rom. viii. [k] Ib. ii.

That coming boldly to the throne of grace, we may obtain mercy and find grace to help in the time of need [1],

That, putting on the armour of God, we may be able to resist the wiles of the Devil [m],

That we may work out our own salvation with fear and trembling [n],

That we may count all things but loss for CHRIST [o],

That being dead to sin, we may live to righteousness [p],

That through the many tribulations of this world, Thou vouchsafe us entrance into the Kingdom of God [q],

That it may please Thee to burn and purge us here, and to spare us in Eternity,

That it may please Thee graciously to hear us,

We beseech Thee to hear us.

O SON of GOD, We beseech thee to hear us.
LAMB of GOD, That takest away the sins of the world, Spare us, O LORD.
LAMB of GOD, that takest away the sins of the world, Graciously hear us, O LORD.
LAMB of GOD, That takest away the sins of the world, Have mercy upon us.
O CHRIST, hear us.
O CHRIST, graciously hear us.
LORD, have mercy.
CHRIST, have mercy.
LORD, have mercy.
    Our FATHER.
V. And lead us not into temptation,
R. But deliver us from evil.
V. O Lord, deal not with us after our sins:
R. Neither reward us after our iniquities.
V. O Lord, remember not our old sins.
R. Have mercy upon us soon, for we are brought very low.

[1] Heb. iv.   [m] Eph. vi.   [n] Phil. ii.
[o] Ib. iii.   [p] 1 St. Pet. ii.   [q] Acts xiv.

V. Help us, O God our Saviour;
R. And for the glory of Thy Name, deliver us, O Lord; and be merciful unto our sins, for Thy Name's sake.
V. O Lord, cleanse Thou me from my secret faults:
R. Keep Thy servant also from presumptuous sins.
V. Remember not, O Lord, our iniquities, neither the iniquities of our forefathers;
R. Neither take Thou vengeance of our sins.
V. Deliver not the souls of them that confess Thee, O Lord, to the blood-thirsty;
R. And forget not the souls of Thy little ones for ever.
V. O Lord turn not Thy Face from my sins;
R. And put out all my misdeeds.
V. O give me the comfort of Thy help again.
R. And stablish me with Thy free Spirit.
V. O Lord, hear my prayer;
R. And let my cry come unto Thee.

LET US PRAY.

O God, Who rejectest not the greatest sinner, but in loving pity art reconciled to him by penitence, mercifully regard our lowly supplications, and give us strength to fulfil Thy Commandments.

O God, Who justifiest the wicked, and wouldest not the death of a sinner, we humbly beseech Thy Majesty bountifully to protect with heavenly succour, and to preserve, by Thy continual help, us Thy servants, who trust only in Thy mercy; so that we may constantly serve Thee, and that no temptations may separate us from Thee.

O God, Who desirest not the death of sinners, but their repentance, most mercifully regard the weakness of our mortal nature, and strengthen our endeavours by Thy goodness, that of Thy infinite mercy we may obtain pardon for our sins, stedfastness in Thy service, and finally, with joy, the rewards promised to those who persevere unto the end, through our Lord Jesus Christ, &c.

CHAPTER III.

VARIOUS PRAYERS FOR PENITENTS.

Prayers against the seven deadly sins, which may be said after each of the Penitential Psalms.

1. *Against Pride.*

O LORD JESUS CHRIST, meek and lowly of heart, Who hast, by word and deed, bidden us to take Thyself for an Example of humility; for when Thou wast in the Form of GOD, and equal to the Eternal Father, Thou didst humble Thyself, and take the Form of a servant, being made Obedient unto death even the Death of the Cross;

Take away from us all proud swelling of soul, that so, looking down on no man, and glorying only in Thee, we may think lowlily of ourselves, and praise Thee Alone with humble heart; and if we seem to have aught that is good, may we confess that it is not our own, but cometh down from Thee, the Eternal Fountain of all good; and so give Glory, not to ourselves, but to Thy Name, for ever. Amen.

2. *Against Avarice.*

O most bountiful GOD, our goods are nothing unto Thee: Thou sheddest abundantly Thy blessings upon us, and biddest us to impart willingly to our poor neighbours the temporal goods which Thou bestowest, and therefore commendest frequent works of charity and almsgiving;

Incline our hearts unto Thy testimonies, and not to covetousness; and make us willingly to bestow our temporal goods for Thy Name's sake, and glad to communicate.

Pluck Thou out of our hearts covetousness, which is the root of all evil. Far from coveting that which is another's, help us to give that which is our own, not grudgingly, nor of necessity, but with a full hand and merciful heart; that so, being cheerful givers, we may be loved of Thee, and may obtain the Kingdom prepared from the foundation of the world. Amen.

3. *Against Gluttony.*

O Lord JESU, the Mirror of Abstinence, Who, to commend to us salutary abstinence by word and deed, didst take our mortal Flesh, and fastedst forty days and as many nights; Who hast taught that not by bread alone, but by every word that proceedeth out of the Mouth of God, doth man live; make us to taste the honied richness of Thy words, which are sweeter than honey and the honeycomb, that, rejecting all delicate meats and provocatives to gluttony, we may live soberly and piously in this world; that, content with simple and moderate fare, we may receive Thy Gifts with thanksgiving, and serve, not our bellies as god, but Thee, the Living God Who dost so mercifully feed us. Amen.

4. *Against Luxury.*

O Lord JESU CHRIST, the Guardian of chaste souls, and Lover of modesty; Who to show how Thou dost delight in cleanness, vouchsafedst to take human flesh of the Womb of the most pure Virgin-Mother; mercifully look on our weakness. Make us a clean heart, O LORD, and renew a right spirit within us. Make us to curb the lust of the flesh by the rein of continence; to conquer all incentives to evil desire, and to pierce the flesh with the fear of Thee: so may this bosom enemy be overcome, and we serve Thee with a chaste body and please Thee with a clean heart. Amen.

5. *Against Envy.*

O most loving JESU, pattern of Charity, Who makest all the commandments of the Law to stand in love to GOD and man; grant us to love Thee, our GOD and REDEEMER, with all our heart, with all our soul, and with all our mind; for Thou hast first so dearly loved us, that Thou hast given Thy Life for us.

And make us to love our neighbours from our inmost heart; may we hate him alone by whose envy sin came into the world. So, rejoicing in our neighbour's joy and mourning with his sorrow, may we take pleasure in no man's evil fortune: but, putting far from us all incitements to envy, may we come to Thee, Who art Very Love. Amen.

6. *Against Anger.*

O most meek JESU, Who like a Gentle Lamb taken to sacrifice, and like a Sheep led to the slaughter, openedst not Thy Mouth, but dragged, mocked, spit upon, smitten, yea, fastened to the Cross, not only returnedst not evil for evil, but prayedst to GOD the FATHER for sinners; plant in our hearts the virtue of meekness and patience, that so, keeping under the fierceness of wrath, we may, with a gentle heart, overcome evil with good, and love our enemies; and, kindled with mutual beneficence as with burning coals, we may be inflamed to love each other, and with one mind and one mouth and with brotherly love, honour Thee our FATHER, upon earth, and finally att*** to Thee in heaven. Amen.

7. *Against Sloth.*

O LORD JESU, Who for our sake didst think no toil too heavy, but enduredst weariness, frequent hunger, thirst, and all manner of discomforts, yea, spentest often the whole night in prayer; put away from us all sloth and inactivity, both of body and mind; make us ready and wakeful to serve Thee in watchings, fastings, and prayers. May we lay ourselves out to Thy Glory and the salvation of our neighbours. O let not our soul slumber in languor, but when Thou hast enlarged our heart by love to Thee and man, may we run with diligence the way of Thy Commandments, lest peradventure our lukewarmness be nauseous unto Thee, and Thou begin to spue us out of Thy Mouth.

Kindle in us the Fire of Thy Love; help Thou our weakness, that, strengthened in Thee and by Thee, we may take heed by good works to make our calling sure. Whatsoever our hand findeth to do, may we straightway do it, with the desire to please Thee only, and then be Thou our Exceeding Great Reward. Amen.

*Three short and fervent Prayers for Pardon and Amendment.
(From the Prayers of German. P. Canisius.)*

PRAYER I.

O most sweet LORD JESU CHRIST, I, unworthy sinner, call to Thy Memory all the Holy Thoughts which from Eternity hitherto Thou hast ever had, and, above all, of that one, whereby Thou, Eternal Word, thoughtest to become man.

O most merciful LORD, I pray from my heart of hearts that Thou in turn wilt pardon me all the vain, foul, and evil thoughts, which up to this time I have, against, or beside Thy Will, entertained, or in any way caused others to entertain.

Our FATHER.

PRAYER II.

O most piteous LORD JESU Christ, I, miserable sinner, call to Thy Memory all the good and health-giving Words which Thou ever utteredst on earth.

I pray Thee humbly, O good JESU, forgive me all the words which up to this time I have uttered against Thy Will, or caused others to utter.

Our FATHER.

PRAYER III.

O most sweet JESU CHRIST, I, unworthy sinner, yet redeemed by thy Precious Blood, call to Thy Memory all the Good Works which, for our Salvation, Thou wroughtest in the earth.

I beseech Thee, most piteous LORD, pardon me whatsoever by my ill-doing, I have, knowingly or unknowingly, committed against Thy Law and the Glory of Thy Name, or have caused others to commit.

And now, O most kind LORD, direct and order all my thoughts, words, and works, according to Thy good pleasure, to the praise of Thy Name, and conform them to the perfect rule of Thy most holy Life and Conversation. Thine I am, O LORD, and will be, in life and death; into Thy Hands, I commend myself, and all I am.

Our FATHER.

THE PRAYER OF A PENITENT.

(From the same.)

O JESU CHRIST, SAVIOUR of the world, Who mercifully invitest all sinners, and whosoever cometh to Thee castest not out, but lovingly receivest, cherishest, and restorest; I call to Thy Memory that Boundless Love whereby Thou didst offer Thyself on the Cross for us, and with the most plenteous Shedding of Thy Precious Blood didst pay to the utmost the full price of our Salvation, and didst expiate the sins of the world.

By that most sacred and effectual penance wrought in Thy most Holy Life, Thy Sinless Death, I humbly pray Thee, forgive me all my sins, as Thou willingly forgavest the thief while hanging on the Cross, and promisedst him Paradise.

Lo, I cast all my sins into Thy most Deep and Sorrowful Wounds. What in me is wanting of contrition and penitence, O do Thou vouchsafe mercifully to supply out of the riches of Thy satisfactions and Thy merits, of all Thy Griefs, Pains, and Toils, which Thou willingly tookest upon Thee in Thy most Holy Body, and chosest to sustain for us even to the most bitter Death.

And as Thou, the Fountain of all clemency, didst of Thy mere Love, and with the longing sigh of Thy Inmost Heart, pray for Thy enemies, yea, sheddedst Thy Blood for Thy very torturers; O make me, unworthy though I am, partaker of Thy most Holy Life and Passion. Let not the fruit thereof be lost for me, but, freed from all my sins and the pains they merit, may I turn wholly unto Thee, to worship and to love Thee.

O SAVIOUR, of Sovereign Clemency, let me never more crucify Thee by my sins; but, by the virtue and merit of Thy Cross, give me true sorrow for my past sins, strength to overcome present temptations, and henceforth to hold on the way of penitence and the Cross, and to persevere in good works even to the end; for unto Thee I desire to live, and in Thee to die.

I commend to Thee my body and soul, and all I am; my friends and benefactors. O JESU, Son of David, have mercy upon us. Make us all with full purpose decline from sin, and fulfil Thy Commandments, to Thy greater Glory and our own salvation. Amen.

A MOST CHOICE PRAYER OF ST. BERNARD FOR PARDON OF SINS.

In union with Thy Grief, whereby Thou tookest on Thee the cause of my grief, and undertookest a Remedy for my sins, O LORD JESU CHRIST; and together with the whole body of mourners and true penitents and such as seek after Thee in truth, I confess to Thee all my sins, the ill deeds committed, the good deeds omitted, or done carelessly, or without pure intention, even as Thou knowest them in number, measure and weight; and the days of my life lost, by offending Thee or diminishing Thy Praise, by falling from my chief Good, and leading my neighbours also to fall along with me.

Now therefore, O LORD, accept the residue of the years of my wretched life, and for those which I have lost in my living, because I lost sight of Thee: my broken and contrite heart, O GOD, do not Thou despise. My days have departed, and perished without fruit: I cannot recall them: but may it please Thee that I may recollect them in the bitterness of my soul.

O LORD, the deep of my most profound misery calleth the deep of Thy Unfathomed Mercy. Shut not up Thy Lovingkindness in displeasure, and let not the fountain of Thy exhaustless Mercy be dried up for me by reason of my sins, O Thou Who hast mercy upon all, Who hatest nothing that Thou hast made, and hidest away the sins of men, for their penitence.

It is Thine, O LORD, to forgive sins; pity me now in the time of pity and of grace; and while the time of amendment lasts, grant me to attain the glory of Thy Blessing, that in the Day of consummation the word of cursing smite me not.

Make me to quit, O LORD, my habitual sins, and to do works well-pleasing unto Thee; and henceforth, by Thy Help, to practise the zeal wherewith I have hitherto practised sin, in doing Thy Will, that where sin hath abounded, Thy Grace may again abound.

I pray Thee by Thyself, pardon me all my sins, negligences, and ignorances. O destroy me not with my iniquities, and lay not up my wickednesses in anger for ever.

Bethink Thee, LORD JESU, that it is not Thine to lose aught of that Thy FATHER hath given Thee; but Thy Property is always to have Mercy and to spare; to destroy none, but to save; for Thy FATHER sent Thee into the world not to condemn the world, but that by Thee we may have life; that Thou mayest be not against us, but on our side: for what we owed, Thou hast paid; what we sinned, Thou hast atoned; what we neglected, Thou hast supplied.

Now, then, O LORD, and in my extremity, let Thy full, yea, Thy overflowing Satisfaction, Thy bitter Death the Price of Thy Blood shed forth, the renewal of Thy Satisfaction, the venerable Mystery of Thy Body and Blood[a], which is daily offered to Thee in the Church for the salvation of the faithful[b], (wherein Thou art at once Priest and Sacrifice[c], at once He that offereth, He to

---

[a] "Vouchsafe me, in the Holy Catholic Church, to have my own calling, and holiness, and portion, and a fellowship of her *sacred rites* and prayers, fastings and groans, vigils, tears, and sufferings, for assurance of remission of sins, for hope of resurrection, and translation to eternal life." Bp. Andrewes' Devotions, First Day, Tract 88, p. 24.

[b] "Remember, O LORD, Thy servants and Thy handmaidens, and all present, whose faith and devotion are known unto Thee, who offer this sacrifice of praise for themselves and all others, for the redemption of their souls, for the hope of their salvation and safety," &c. S. Greg. Sacram. See other Liturgies, and Johnson's Unbloody Sacrifice, c. 2. s. 2, p. 290. "We offer up CHRIST, sacrificed for our sins, propitiating our merciful GOD both for them and for ourselves." S. Cyr. Cat. Myst. v. 110, p. 276. Oxf. Tr. "What of the very Body and Blood of CHRIST, the only Sacrifice for our Salvation? Although the LORD Himself says, 'Except ye eat the Flesh of the Son of Man,' &c., doth not the same Apostle teach that It hurteth those who use It amiss?" S. Aug. c. Cresc. i. 21. See others in Johnson, l. c.

[c] "We have seen the Chief Priest coming to us; we have seen

Whom the offering is made, and the Offering Itself) let these avail me to merit Grace here, which I merit not, and to obtain rest and glory hereafter, which Thy most Bitter Death hath won.

Thine Eyes, O LORD, have seen my substance, and that so imperfect; but in Thy Love,

and heard Him offering His Blood for us; we, Priests, follow as we can, in offering sacrifice for the people; poor in merit, yet of high esteem through our Sacrifice; for although CHRIST now is not seen to be offered, yet He is offered on the earth when the Body of CHRIST is offered; yea, it is manifested that He Himself offereth in us, Whose Word sanctifies the Sacrifice which is offered." S. Ambr. in Ps. 38, § 25. "And would that to us also, when burning incense on the altar, and bringing the Sacrifice, an angel would stand by, yea, rather Himself would stand by. For thou mayest not doubt that the angel standeth by, when CHRIST standeth by,—when CHRIST is offered." Id. in S. Luc. i. 11. "Aforetime, the lamb or the bullock was offered, now CHRIST is offered; but He is offered as Man, as capable of suffering; and He offereth Himself as a Priest, to remit our sins; here in the express image (Heb. x. 1, as opposed to the 'shadow,') there in truth, where He interceded as an Advocate with the Father for us." Id. de Off. i. 48, fin.

for Thou art merciful and easy to be intreated for sin, impute it not to me for endless punishment, O Thou Who hast fore-ordained all things best, most perfectly, most wisely to that which is supreme and perfect good: and let me not be blotted out of the Book of Life, but give to me the portion that falleth unto me for my support, even of Thy Precious Passion, in return for which Thou wouldst have man for Thy fellow-heir in the land of the living.

Let, then, the thought of man's weakness, O LORD, incline and move Thee to compassion; Thou knowest whereof he is made, and that Thou hast not set man on the earth in vain; O preserve me, the work of Thy Love; let not Thy Labour have been in vain for me; let not the shedding of Thine Immaculate Blood be fruitless for me.

O Thou Who makest purification for sins, grant that, cleansed from the filth of my sins and enlightened in soul, I may know Thee by the eye of faith: and knowing Thee, may I ever direct my heart to Thee, press and pant after Thee, till at last I may attain, by a happy death, to come to Thee, CHRIST JESU, Who livest and reignest with God the FATHER, in the unity of the HOLY GHOST, for ever and ever. Amen.

CHAPTER IV.

THE LORD'S PRAYER

WITH SPECIAL REFERENCE TO THE USE OF PENITENTS.

A MODE OF RECITING THE LORD'S PRAYER

With reference to the Parable of the Prodigal Son, with a view to elicit compunction.

From P. Christ. Mayer *in Indust*.

Our Father.

O MOST Loving Father, Who hast more anxious care, and yearnest more for Thine unworthy sons than any father, yea, than any mother for the son of her womb; to what misery am I come, of my own fault, and wantonly departing from so good a FATHER; squandering His Grace and the goods He so bountifully gave me. In bygone days I was cherished in a most sweet Father's Bosom, nourished in His House, and I shared in His Table: I was a son, and lacked nothing. Now I dwell in a far-off country, amid strangers and foreigners, a wanderer and an exile, naked and an hungred.

1. *Hallowed be Thy Name.*

On how many accounts was I bound, and in how many ways could I once have hallowed and glorified Thee, the Father of Infinite Majesty, Power, Wisdom, and Goodness, and requited Thy love, prevented as I was with so great blessings, supplied with full abundance. Woe is me that I did it not! Lo, from this moment I desire, ardently as my heart of hearts can yearn, to do this now for ever.

2. *Thy kingdom come.*

With what folly have I preferred the hard slavery of the world, the flesh and the devil to Thy sweet Yoke: and now, wearied in the path of sin and perdition, fervently I pant again after my FATHER'S Kingdom, the Kingdom of Thy Grace and Glory, where is peace and joy in the HOLY GHOST!

3. *Thy will be done.*

Of how many evils has my perverse will been the cause to me; I have used it amiss against Thy Most Holy Will, and contracted the guilt of sin, while I ought to have used it towards obtaining Grace and Glory! Henceforth not my will, but Thy Most Holy Will be done with me always and in all things; and be it done by me as it is by the Blest in Heaven.

4. *Our Bread.*

Most bountiful Father, Who from the plenteousness of Thy House fillest Thine elect, from whom I have with greatest folly separated myself; how many hired servants in my Father's House have bread to the full, and I perish with hunger! Woe is me; once I was brought up in purple, and ate the children's bread, now I scarce fill my belly with the husks of swine. O that I might, if not as a son, yet as a hired servant, feed on the bread of Thy Grace!

5. *And forgive us.*

Lo, prostrate in Thy Presence I cry to Thee, Father, I have sinned against Heaven, and in Thy Sight, and am no more worthy to be called Thy son; make me as one of Thy hired servants. I grieve that I have ever offended Thee; forgive me, as I too forgive all for Thy Sake.

6. And lead us not.

Now, O LORD, Thou hast received me to favour with the Kiss of Peace, Thou lockest me in the Arms of Love; but I pray Thee (for Thou knowest my infirmity) suffer me not to be severed from Thee, henceforth for ever, nor to go astray after the desires of my heart.

7. But deliver us.

Save and deliver me from all the ills of this life and that to come, so far as they may impair Thy Glory, or endanger my Salvation; so may I serve Thee perfectly without hindrance here, and enjoy Thee blissfully in Heaven, where no ill shall be, but Thou shalt be all in all, and the supreme Good of them that love Thee, for ever. Amen.

THE LORD'S PRAYER,
AGAINST THE SEVEN DEADLY SINS.

The LORD's *Prayer is most full of holy meanings, and is like a full armoury, or, if you will, an universal antidote against the diseases and plagues of the soul, all which shoot forth from the bad root of the seven deadly sins. Against these then is the* LORD's *Prayer profitably used.*

This sevenfold evil principle is described in the Book of the Revelation as a beast with seven heads; this hateful enemy of man ceases not to assail us with one or other of its heads, and to shed on us its infectious poison; when one is cut off, another rises; and when this is weakened, another gathers strength; and so they succeed each other.

Yea, and sometimes they all assail us in a body, as any man who has care for his salvation knows by experience at times.

Wherefore our SAVIOUR, *Who has bequeathed to us this struggle to exercise our virtue, and multiply our attainments, has also given to our hand His Prayer of seven petitions, that with these we may transpierce each of that monster's seven heads; saying thus,*

Our Father which art in heaven.

Lift up thine eyes to GOD thy Father, Who dwelleth in Heaven, and beholdeth the proud from afar off; Who is near all them that call upon Him, and to those who are of a contrite heart. Think Who and how great thy Helper is, in the Heavens: how powerful, how good; for He is GOD, and thy Father. Fear not, therefore, in this conflict; trust in GOD and His Fatherly Love to you, as did the Prophet: the LORD is the strength of my life, whom then shall I fear? And now direct thy first arrow,

1. *Hallowed be Thy Name,*

against the first of the monster's heads, which is Pride.

For since Pride, which is the beginning of all sin, puffs us up to self-conceit, or the pursuit of our own honour, praise, and advancement, we shall do wisely in dispersing this infection by referring all praise and glory to Him Who is Alone, in Himself, truly holy and great, and to Whom therefore Alone, praise and glory is due. Let us then say, O our heavenly Father, *hallowed be Thy Name,* not our name, but *Thine;* and be *Thy Holy Name* confessed, glorified, and praised in all things, and by all.

This is truly meet and right; whereas nothing is more unmeet than for man, who is a sinner, dust and ashes, filth and a worm, to exalt himself by claiming what is due to God; as saith the Apostle, *To God Alone be honour and glory;* and the Prophet thus renounces, with abhorrence, human glory, *Not unto us, O Lord, not unto us, but unto Thy Name give the praise.*

Let us, too, be like-minded, and say, *Hallowed be Thy Name.* If we seek not our own glory, there will be One to seek it for us: if we honour GOD Alone in all things continually; them that honour Him, He will honour, them that despise Him He will lightly esteem. As for those that usurp the Glory due to GOD, confusion shall cover them.

2. When the head of Pride has been thus cleft in twain, oft-times the devil betakes him to avarice: when *honour* has failed, his next tempta-

tion is *gain*. He inspires men's souls with the desire of this world's goods, and he makes it his business that they shall spend all their time and all their life in pursuing and securing these, rest their hope in them, and count much wealth to be their happiness.

If we, on the other hand, measure how vain these are, how fleeting, how insufficient to satisfy man's heart; and yet that GOD has promised them to us, so far as need shall require, without any anxious care of our own, if we seek first the Kingdom of GOD and His Righteousness; then, better far, if looking down upon things of earth, we lift up our eyes to that Heavenly Kingdom, that inheritance in Heaven, uncorrupt, undefiled, and that fadeth not away, which none can attain but they who give not their heart to riches, who hold cheap the kingdom of this world and its gay things, and who, while they sigh continually after the treasures of the Kingdom of Heaven, pray from the heart,

Thy Kingdom come,

That Eternal Kingdom where we shall be filled with the plenteousness of Thy House, and be satisfied when Thy Glory shall appear: for we believe verily to see the goodness of the LORD in the land of the living. O what, how great that goodness! Eye hath not seen, nor ear heard, neither hath entered into the heart of man to conceive what GOD hath prepared for them that love Him.

Yea, and meanwhile, may *Thy Kingdom* of Grace and Righteousness *come* to us; for that will make us, though poor in riches, rich in attainments and good works. Though we live poor, many good things will be ours if we fear God; for, in truth, riches are not worldly goods, but Christian virtues and Gifts of Grace.

3. But take we heed, lest, in seeking the Kingdom of GOD, languor and a spirit of slumber creep over us; for, *not every one that saith, Lord, Lord, shall enter into the Kingdom of Heaven, but he that doeth the Will of My Father Which is in Heaven.* The next struggle, therefore, after avarice, will be against *sloth :* and use this arrow,

Thy will be done in earth as it is in Heaven.

That is,—O may we, who dwell on earth, do Thy Will like the inhabitants of Heaven. In Heaven, God is praised with joyous exultation. In Heaven, the angels are prompt to do His Will with glad alacrity. O that it were done, with like devotion, alacrity and eagerness, by us on earth. However, even heartily to desire this, is of price with Him, Who sees into every will, and loves the good one.

4. But, seeing that our frail bodies need the nourishment of food and drink, and that there is a pleasure which goes with the supply of this necessity, the Devil takes advantage of it, and tries to entangle us in the sin of gluttony, by tempting us to—excess in the quantity or quality of our food. Therefore must we pray GOD earnestly, Who made us thus frail and liable to the necessity of daily refreshment, and say,

Give us this day our daily bread.

O merciful GOD, vouchsafe to us of Thy Goodness our necessary food, and so direct us that we turn not that supply of our necessities into a business of pleasure; that what Thy Bountiful Hand bestows we use not for luxurious living, but for the support of nature; and that we bring the flesh's appetite under the law of God and right reason. Vouchsafe also to give us the Bread of heavenly wisdom that we may taste how gracious the Lord is, and refuse the enticements of gluttony: in comparison with His Sweetness, may we loathe the delicacies of the flesh as we would the husks of swine.

5. But, while gluttony is being kept down, the malice of the Devil oft-times contriveth occasions of anger and impatience, that overcome by the sin of wrath, we may be reft of the fruit of abstinence, and in the midst of our very fasts become hateful to God: like those of whom Isaiah said, that they *fasted for strife and debate.*

Against this pestilential head of the Beast is a shaft aimed vigorously by the man who prays from his heart,

Forgive us our trespasses, as we forgive them that trespass against us.

We have daily need to pray GOD for forgiveness of our sins, for in many things we all offend; and if GOD be extreme to mark what is done amiss, who shall abide it? His Forgiveness we shall not gain, unless we refrain our anger against those who do us wrong, and heartily forgive them: then may we say, with open forehead and with confidence, Forgive us, LORD, for we too forgive.

And surely these few added words may strike carefulness and alarm into us; for what if thou forgive not? What if with reservation and not fully? What, if outwardly only and with craft, while all the time thou foster wrath in thy mind, and meditate revenge? Then, indeed, thou callest upon GOD against thee, not in thy behalf; to be thy Judge, and not thy Father; and thou shalt hear the words, Out of thine own mouth do I judge thee, thou wicked servant; thou desiredst me to forgive thee, as thou forgavest, &c.

O let us then take heed and do, what the Lord adviseth, *When ye stand to pray, forgive if ye have ought against any;* else, if man lay up wrath against his fellow, how shall he seek forgiveness from GOD?

6. If now we have learned to be gentle and meek under any injury, there is fear lest this meekness become softness, and the Devil thus ensnare us, and gradually beguile us into *luxury:*

And when we look and see how far and wide this plague of *luxury* is spread among men, so that it is as true now as of old that all flesh has corrupted its way, we may well dread this fatal head of the Beast. The Wise Man, saith, *It hath cast down many mighty men, yea, strong men have been slain thereby.* Let us, then, meekly pray GOD to help us, (for it is of His Gift only that we are continent,) and say.

Lead us not into temptation.

O let us not, LORD, be tempted, for we are weak; and if we be left to our own strength, we shall without fail be overcome; so sadly are we inclined to evil.

7. Even though, thus far, the wicked enemy be baffled, he gives not over yet: with his darling sin, most his own—even envy *(for by envy of the Devil sin entered into the world)* he plots the soul's destruction; turning the happiness of our neighbour into our cross and torment. It is this that gives us an evil eye to our neighbour; we grieve at his good success and take delight in his misfortunes.

From this worst and devilish sin, we pray for deliverance by the last petition,

Deliver us from evil,

the evil, namely, of envy, which makes us utterly evil; the poison, whereof the Evil one is full, and wherewith he poisons and inflames man. What is worse than for a man to convert the good of others into his own evil, when he might, by rejoicing with him, make it in a way his own good, and so become himself better, happier, nearer to and worthier of the Sovereign Good, which is Supreme?

METHOD OF SAYING THE LORD'S PRAYER TO GOD THE FATHER, THAT BY THE VIRTUES AND MERITS OF HIS SON OUR SINS AND SHORTCOMINGS MAY BE EXPIATED.

Our Father.

O most Holy Father, by that immeasurable love whereby Thou gavest us to be called, and to be, the sons of God, from my inmost heart I pray Thee, forgive me that I have hitherto neglected to pay Thee, my most Loving Father, the honour and the love I owe Thee; that I have often grievously offended Thee by my sins, and that I have often basely cast Thee, by my sins, out of my heart, which ought to be Thine, and wherein Thou oughtest, as in heaven, to have Thy Resting-place.

O most Gracious Father, look upon the Face of Thine Anointed Son, and have mercy upon me. I unite my supplication with that infinite Love of Thine, whereby Thou didst beget Thy Coequal Son from everlasting, and then at the fore-ordained time wouldest have Him made man for us. I pray Thee, in virtue of that most abundant Satisfaction, made to Thee for me by the Same, Thy well-beloved Son, our Sinless Brother, JESUS CHRIST, that in Thy Goodness Thou wouldest accept, in compensation for all my sins and shortcomings, that most burning love of His Divine Heart, and that most worthy praise and honour, which in His profound humiliation He paid to Thee.

1. *Hallowed be Thy Name.*

O most sweet Father, I pray with all the affection my heart can feel, forgive me that I have not sanctified, with becoming honour, reverence and religious worship, Thy most Holy Name; yea, rather have oft-times done despite to it, and have continually disgraced with my unholy life the name of Christian, which by Thy Grace I bear.

O most High Father, vouchsafe, I beseech Thee, to accept, in expiation of all my guilt, that most absolute sinlessness of Thy most Dear Son's Life, in which, for thirty-three years and more, while He dwelt on earth, He never ceased to glorify Thy Blessed Name, to praise and sanctify it by so many signs and miracles, words and works.

2. *Thy kingdom come.*

O Father of Mercies, I pray Thee, pardon me in Thy great Clemency, that I have never, with becoming zeal and fervour, sought Thee, the King of Heaven and Earth, and thine Everlasting Kingdom, wherein alone is true peace, rest, and joy.

I pray Thy most Sweet Mercy, vouchsafe to receive the All-holy Labours of Thy Son, in Whom Thou art well-pleased (whereby He made me and all men co-heirs with Himself in Thy Kingdom); receive them in expiation of all those my negligences and short-comings, which, while I sought and minded so lukewarmly the things that are above, and with such eagerness the things of earth, I so miserably have committed.

3. *Thy will be done.*

O most merciful Father, forgive me of Thine Infinite Goodness, that I have not always preferred Thy Divine and most supreme Will to mine; that I have so often re-usurped my own will, though I had once vowed it to Thee, and that I have not promptly, reverently, and cheerfully embraced Thy most Gracious Will in Thy disposal of me.

I pray Thee, O Everlasting FATHER, accept, in satisfaction for all my disobedience, whereby I have gone contrary to Thy Commandments, the most ready resignation of the Heart of Thy most Loving SON, and that His most Perfect Obedience, whereby He became obedient unto Thee, even to the Death of the Cross.

4. *Give us this day our daily bread.*

O most bounteous FATHER, Who openest Thy Hand, and fillest all things living with plenteousness, and hast of Thy Rich Providence fed me too from my youth up until now, both in body and soul, notwithstanding my unworthiness; I pray Thee, from my heart of hearts, pardon me my ingratitude, that I have so often, whether by setting my heart too much upon them, or by inordinate indulgence in them, or by neglecting to bless Thee for them, abused Thine Own Gifts, whether, of mind or body, so as to do despite to Thee, and bring condemnation on myself.

I beseech Thee, O my FATHER, by the Love of Thy Well-beloved SON, vouchsafe to accept His Fasts and Hunger, Thirst, and wonderful Abstinence, and all His Giving of Thanks before receiving food, which He was wont to offer to Thee: accept them in satisfaction for all the carelessness and ingratitude with which I have ever received and enjoyed Thy Gifts.

5. *And forgive us our trespasses, as we forgive them that trespass against us.*

O FATHER of immeasurable goodness, if Thou shouldest mark our sins and wickednesses, who shall stand? So grievously, in many things, do we all offend! I pray Thee, therefore, of Thine Everlasting Love, mercifully forgive me my sins, wheresoever, whensoever, howsoever committed: forgive me, if at any time I have not satisfied Thy Commandment in wholly forgiving others, or if I have not loved my enemies from my heart.

O most Righteous God, I pray Thy Majesty, accept, in satisfaction for me, the infinite Price of the Blood of Thy most Well-beloved Son, and that most touching Prayer, in which, while hanging on the Cross, He desired Thee to forgive His enemies.

6. *And lead us not into temptation, but deliver us from evil.*

O most Loving Father, of Thy Inestimable Love pardon me that hitherto, so far from striving with all earnest diligence to resist my lust and corrupt desires, I have rather consented to the evil suggestions of the world, the flesh, and the Devil; and therefore am I worthily exposed to many evils. If, therefore, O Lord, Thou, in the counsel of Thy Divine Providence, wilt have me feel, yet let me not fall under temptation.

Vouchsafe to accept, O Almighty God, the Glorious Victory of Christ, Thy Son, over the world, Satan, and the flesh, and His most Holy Life, with all His Toils and Griefs, to make up all my heedlessness and weakness; so mayest Thou deliver me from all evil, and lead me to all good, even to Thyself, with Whom Alone is, Who Alone art, Good; my God and my All. Amen.

CHAPTER V.

INSTRUCTIONS AND EXERCISES FOR CONFESSION.

A short Instruction towards its profitable use.

In religious discipline and a devout life, no exercise is so frequent as Confession; and yet in many persons it yieldeth little or no fruit, being performed merely out of habit, and in a cursory manner,—not with the desire of true piety and improvement in holiness.

I. *Reflect, then, that the frequent devout use of this sacred ordinance is a most easy means of making rapid advances, in a short time, in the way of perfection. For,* 1. *By it sins, and the desire of sins, are put off.* 2. *The desire of virtue and of spiritual advancement is called into energy.* 3. *Grace and the love of* GOD *is multiplied.* 4. *Cleanness of conscience is obtained, calm and security; the dread of death is lessened,* &c.

II. *Rouse within yourself, or renew a fervent desire and a firm resolution of approaching this sacred ordinance with suitable dispositions, circumspection, and devotion; considering,*

1. *The inestimable end of this ordinance, even the forgiveness of sins, the cure of the soul's maladies, the renewal of fervour, the increase of acceptableness, grace, glory,* &c.

2. *The easiness and efficacy, whereby we apply to ourselves the Merits of* CHRIST, *and become partakers of the rich Treasures of Divine Grace, by the frequent, serious, and loving use of this ordinance.*

3. *Such inducements as the following: the Will of* GOD, *Whose Sole Desire is our sanctification; His Innumerable Blessings; the weight of sin; the shortness of life, and the uncertain duration of the state of grace; the fear of the strict Judgement, the terror of Eternity, the bitterness of pains hereafter,* &c.

III. *Ask for* GOD'S *Grace to enable you to confess, detest, lay bare and amend your sins, and this by His Infinite Mercy, which so movingly invites thee, and waits for thy repentance.*

IV. *Call to mind your sins in a certain order, such as may help you to remember them. See how you have sinned by thought, word, or deed, against* GOD, *your neighbour, or yourself. Sum them up, in brief, omitting all mere generalities, all that is not to the purpose or unnecessary, and all such things as many dwell on, more to excuse than to accuse themselves. Do this fully, by enumerating all the sins which weigh on your conscience, according to their distinguishing character and their number, either precisely or as near as may be with the essential circumstances that belong to them, and constitute their differences. Do it distinctly; expressing each sin in its own simple obvious words: distinguishing what is certain from what is doubtful, grave from venial, deliberate from unpremeditated, purposed from inadvertent, fully consented to from half-consent,* &c.

V. *Above all, strive for true contrition of heart:*

1. *That you may grieve for these and the sins of all your life, simply and solely for the love of* GOD, &c.

2. *That you may form a*

firm and a determined resolution to amend all these sins, especially your besetting sins, and those which your will most readily consents to; to shun all opportunities and occasions of committing them; and to serve and please GOD henceforth more perfectly. Do all this with the trust of a child in the Fatherly Compassion of GOD. And it may be very useful to you to use often and habitually the following act of contrition; more especially before prayer, or when in danger of falling, or after you have fallen, in temptation, before going to sleep, with one sincere sigh, O JESU, I do love Thee, and I grieve from my heart that I have offended Thee. O JESU! amo te et doleo ex corde, quia offendi Te.

SOME ORDINARY MEANS OF AMENDING AND REMEDYING OUR FAULTS AND SHORTCOMINGS.

I. *Form a serious and fervent resolution, and renew it frequently, to be on your guard against all sins, and especially your besetting sins.*

II. *In the morning, protest before* GOD *your abhorrence of such temptations as are most apt to overcome you, or most difficult to overcome; detest them, and solemnly determine that your will neither has nor shall have any part in them.*

III. *Before setting about any work of more than ordinary consequences, prepare for it thoughtfully and seriously; renew your resolution to amend what is commonly amiss in you, and pray for Grace, with at least short ejaculations.*

IV. *Look to the end and object of all you take in hand, and be scrupulously careful not to wander from it, and that none of your ordinary faults overtake you; what thou doest do in earnest.*

V. *Ever dart frequent and affectionate sighs to* GOD, *and so bring home to yourself a sense of His constant Presence.*

VI. *Contemplate* CHRIST *as the living Mirror and Pattern of all Perfection, and strive to imitate Him; and do it the most earnestly by remembering that you bear the name of Christian.*

VII. *In temptation take refuge with child-like love and trustfulness, in* JESUS,—*in His most Gracious Heart and His Sacred Wounds; so will all temptation pass quick away. Renew the resolution to which you call* GOD *to witness in the morning against these temp-*

[§ iii.] ON PENITENCE. 53

tations. Ratify thy devotion generously. Repair betimes to thy spiritual father: ask his counsel, and obey it.

VIII. *Renew thy zeal to root out N. or N., thy fast-rooted sins, by a particular examen, by the exercise of mortification, &c.*

A PRAYER PREPARATORY TO CONFESSION.

Maker of Heaven and earth, King of kings and Lord of lords, Who hast made me out of nothing in Thine Image and Likeness, and hast redeemed me with Thine Own Blood: sinner that I am, I am not worthy to name Thee, to call on Thee, to think on Thee in my heart.

I humbly pray Thee, I meekly entreat Thee, look on me, Thy wicked servant, in mercy. Have mercy on me, Thou Who hadst mercy on the woman of Canaan and Mary Magdalene; Thou that sparedst the publican and the thief upon the Cross.

I confess my sins to Thee, most Merciful Father; if I wished to hide them, I could not, from Thee, LORD. Spare me, O CHRIST, Whom I have so late and so much offended by thought, word, and deed; yea, and in whatsoever way I could possibly sin against Thee, by my fault, by my fault, by my most grievous fault, poor miserable sinner.

Wherefore, LORD, I pray Thy pity, Who didst come down from Heaven to save me. Thou raisedst David from his fall. Spare me, O LORD: O CHRIST, spare me, Who sparedst Peter when he had denied Thee. Thou art my Creator and Redeemer, my Lord and my Saviour, my King and my God.

Thou art my Hope and my Trust; my Guidance and my Succour; my Comfort and my Strength; my Defence and my Deliverance; my Life, my Health, and my Resurrection; my Light and my Longing; my Help and my Protection.

I pray and entreat Thee, help me and I shall be safe; direct me and defend me; strengthen me and comfort me; confirm me and gladden me; enlighten me, and come unto me. Raise me from the dead; I am Thy creature, and the work of Thy Hands.

LORD, despise me not; I am Thy servant, vile though I be, worthless, and a sinner.

Such as I am, good or bad, I am Thine. Whither shall I go for refuge but to Thee? If Thou cast me off, to whom shall I go? If I find wrath with Thee, with whom shall I find ruth?

Own me as Thine own who fly to Thee for refuge though worthless, vile, unclean. Though I be worthless and unclean, Thou canst cleanse me; though blind, Thou canst enlighten me; though sick, Thou canst heal me; yea, though dead and buried, Thou canst raise me up. Thy Mercy is more than my iniquity; Thy pity than my impiety; Thou canst remit more than I commit; Thou canst spare more than I can err.

Despise me not, then, O Lord; neither regard the multitude of my iniquities; but, according to the multitude of Thy Mercies, have mercy upon me, and be gracious to me, the chief of sinners.

Say unto my soul, I am Thy Salvation, O Thou Who hast said, I desire not the death of a sinner, but rather that he should be converted and live. Turn Thee unto me, O Lord, and be not angry against me.

I implore Thee, Most Pitiful Father, I pray Thee meekly of Thy Great Mercy, bring me to a holy end, and to true penitence, perfect confession, and worthy satisfaction, for all my sins. Amen.

A PRAYER BEFORE CONFESSION.

O Lord God, Who lightenest every man that cometh into the world, let the light of Thy Grace shine into my heart, that I may fully know my short-comings and my sins, and may confess them with that true sorrow and contrition of heart, which befits me before Thee [and the Priest, Thy minister]; and may make full amends for them, and amend them to Thy Honour and Glory, and to the salvation of my soul. Amen.

PRAYER AFTER CONFESSION.

I bless Thee, most Loving Jesu, that Thou hast patiently waited for me to be penitent, and graciously given [promised] me pardon and remission of my sins. Accept I pray Thee, my humble Confession that I have made; and all that has been wanting to the full and entire enumeration of my sins, or to befitting sorrow for them, do Thou vouchsafe to supply out of the Fountain of Thy Mercy and the Treasure of Thy Passion, and to have me fully absolved in heaven; and grant me the help of Thy Grace, that henceforth I may avoid sin, and serve Thee more faithfully; and to this end may I enjoy the prayers of all Thy Saints that have ever pleased Thee from the beginning of the world: for lo! I have sworn, and by Thy help am stedfastly purposed to keep Thy Righteous Judgments, Who livest and reignest God, for ever and ever. Amen.

ANOTHER PRAYER BEFORE CONFESSION.

Accept my Confession, O most loving, most Gracious LORD JESU CHRIST, on Whom Alone my soul trusts for salvation. Give my heart contrition, and tears to my eyes, that I may weep day and night, all my negligences, with meekness and purity of heart.

Let my prayer come before Thee, O LORD. If Thou be angry with me, to whom shall I seek? Who shall have pity on my iniquities? Remember me, O LORD, Thou that calledst the woman of Canaan and the publican to repentance, and receivedst Peter when he wept. Hear my prayers, O LORD my GOD.

O Good JESU, SAVIOUR of the world, Who gavest Thyself to death and the Cross to save sinners, look on me, a miserable sinner, who call upon Thy Name; remembering how evil I am, forget not how good Thou art. If I have done that for which Thou mayest condemn me, Thou hast not undone that whereby Thou art wont to save.

Spare me then, Thou that art my SAVIOUR, and pity my sinful soul; loose its chains, heal its sores. LORD JESU, I desire Thee, I seek Thee, I yearn for Thee; show the light of Thy Countenance, and I shall be whole.

Regard me not alone, O LORD, but in communion with Thy holy Saints, and send forth Thy light and truth into my soul, to show me in full truth all the shortcomings which I must confess, [and to teach and help me to lay them bare without reserve, and] with a contrite heart; O Thou Who livest and reignest with GOD the FATHER.

PRAYER AFTER CONFESSION.

May the Confession I have made, O LORD, be well-pleasing and acceptable in Thy Sight; and whatsoever is wanting, whether now or at other times, in the sufficiency of my contrition, or, the simplicity and unreservedness of my Confession, may Thy Love and Pity supply: and according to that Love vouchsafe to have me fully and entirely absolved in heaven; Who livest and reignest.

A PREVAILING ACT OF CONTRITION, IN THE FORM OF A PRAYER, TO OBTAIN REMISSION OF SIN.

The following parts go towards the performance of such an act:
1. *An Act of faith.* 2. *Sorrow for sin.* 3. *Love of* GOD *above all things.* 4. *Resolution for the future.* 5. *Self-oblation through* CHRIST. 6. *Hope of pardon through* CHRIST. 7. *Petition for the Grace and Help of* GOD.

O LORD JESU CHRIST, Very GOD and Very MAN, my Creator and Redeemer;

2. I grieve, with my whole heart, that I have offended Thee, my LORD and my GOD;

3. Whom I love above all things;

4. And I fully purpose to sin no more, to shun all occasions of sin [to confess, and to fulfil the penance which may be enjoined me]:

5. And in satisfaction for my sins, I offer to Thee Thy most Sacred Life, Thy Passion, and Thy Death, and the whole Price of Thy Blood, which was shed for us; all my works and all my life.

6. And I trust that of Thine Infinite Goodness and Mercy, Thou wilt, by the Merits of Thy Precious Blood, forgive me all my sins;

7. And that Thou wilt pour on me the Richness of Thy Grace, whereby I may live holily, and serve Thee perfectly to the end; Who, with the FATHER and the HOLY GHOST, livest and reignest, GOD Blessed for ever. Amen.

AN ADMONITION TOUCHING THE ACT OF CONTRITION.

Contrition is a thing of such price and so prevailing, as to be able, even in an instant, to extinguish an infinite number of most grievous sins, to reconcile man to GOD, *and recover the blessed Eternity which sin has* forfeited, supposing a man to die without the means of Confession; for a broken and contrite heart GOD will not despise. Now contrition rests mainly on loving GOD above all things, and consists of three Acts:

1. The first is grief, that GOD, Who is most worthy to be loved and worshipped by all above all things, should have been offended.

To have Him for a Friend, which blessing is forfeited by any deadly sin, is an infinite good, far above all other good things; whence also the evil, which by any deadly sin is incurred, is an infinite evil, far beyond all other evils; the loss, therefore, of so vast a good, and the endurance of so vast an evil, ought to afflict us more than the loss of all the goods of this life in our health, fame, life, our all. To perish ten thousand times were child's play, compared with that to which a single sin subjects us, the everlasting burnings of hell.

2. The second is resolution to sin no more, and to make restitution of any unjust gain.

And with this stedfast resolve, a man makes an oblation of himself to keep all GOD's laws: I am stedfastly purposed, O LORD, to keep Thy Commandments: all that Thou biddest, O my GOD, I will do with all my might.

3. The third is hope of pardon, and prayer for Grace towards earnest amendment of life.

To accuse oneself, and not to mend oneself, is to tempt GOD: nor is it of any avail to pray for pardon of sin, and yet go on sinning. However, the Blood and Death of our LORD JESUS inspires good men with confidence to pray and hope for this exceeding Gift, that, though we have sinned so often and so grievously, He will give us earnest amendment of life and therewith forgiveness.

ACCUSATION OF SELF AND PURPOSE OF AMENDMENT, AFTER FALLING INTO THAT WHICH WE KNOW TO BE OUR BESETTING SIN.

O MY most loving GOD, ungrateful and undone, after long wandering astray in forbidden acts, lo, I come back to Thee: I seek Thy Love, who have myself made Thee mine enemy. Again have I sinned: often before I had fallen, I have fallen again. Ah, LORD, into that very sin, which Thou most abhorrest (and I knew it), my very worst sin; into that very sin I have again fallen.

O I knew what need I had of watchfulness, and yet I took no heed: and I have offended Thy Majesty, O GOD; I have lost Thy Grace, I have forfeited Heaven, I have ruined myself: and why? for nothing, for mere vanity; for what else is the pleasure, (or profit, &c.) which I pursued?

I knew, O LORD, that Thou meritest my love above all things; I own, O my GOD, that Thy Law and Thy Honour, O my GOD, ought to be dearer to me than all creatures; and yet I so madly love myself, that, over and over again, I have set my paltry credit, or gain, or lust, before Thee, Thy Honour, and Thy Law.

Ah, how am I yet carnal! and though I should deny it, my works condemn me. The world is not crucified unto me; it lives and breathes in full strength in me; I am full of evil inclinations, foul desires, lusts and infinite wretchedness, yet I am none the humbler; yea, I love to be admired and thought much of.

My life is a mere ebb and flow, the merest inconstancy and changeableness; my senses go rambling, with full licence, whithersoever they will. O what varied and foul imaginations continually flit about and infest my soul! What a hard immoveable stone I am, O my GOD, when penitence is spoken of, and yet how ready to talk at random! how deaf to admonitions for my soul's health, and how greedy after gossip and trifles; and how strange to me and distasteful sound words which speak of GOD and Heaven, but how open my ears are to earthly gains and bodily comforts!

When I am to pray, I wholly loathe it; but feasting never comes amiss. I am a tortoise in GOD's Worship, swifter than an eagle after sports and jests. I creep after what is good, and have wings for evil; ready enough for suspicions and envy, but how hard to find excuses for my neighbours! indulgent and soft to myself, strict and stern with others. If I am but touched, I am on fire, and my tongue, at least, if not my hand, is ready to strike; no one does me hurt but I begin to think how I may revenge myself.

And for the fires of lust, O GOD, Thou knowest how they embrace me: I may hide them and dissemble them here, but to Thee, Eye of the world, they are all open; there is no secret of the heart which can be hid from Thee. How oft do I resolve, and what great re-solutions! And then how strangely, yea, how wickedly are they all forgotten!

Well may I then lament that I live so lamentably, yea, lament that I lament so little, and that I feel not my misery as I ought.

Lo, I have been a sluggard in religion, swift and active after sin. LORD, I would be so no more. I will cease to be myself, the self I have been. *I have said, Now I begin;* no man happily wins his way to Heaven, who begins not every day.

Trusting, therefore, in Thy Help, O LORD, I am most stedfastly purposed to shun my old sins and every occasion of sinning, with all my might. O may this change be through the Right Hand of the Most High.

My GOD and my LORD, create in me a clean and pure heart: renew, O LORD, a right spirit within me; so may I at last seriously amend my life, love Thee from the ground of my heart, and so persevere unto the end of life.

FORM FOR RAISING PIOUS FEELINGS OF LOVING GRATITUDE, CONTRITION, &c., BEFORE OR AFTER CONFESSION.

Ex P. Christ. Mayer in Indust.

JESUS, GOD of my heart, infinitely pitiful and long-suffering, infinitely Sweet and Amiable, how hast Thou with the Father and the Holy Ghost, multiplied upon me, among Thy other Elect, the inestimable Riches of Thy Mercy and Long-suffering, Thy Goodness and Charity, even until now; by looking so oft on me as Thou didst on Peter, notwithstanding my ingratitude; by calling me back so oft into the way of life, when wandering far from Thee, as Thou didst the Magdalene, notwithstanding my unworthiness; by washing me white so often in Thine Own Blood, in my uncleanness; by receiving me so oft with the kiss of peace, though Thy prodigal son; and by so oft inviting me to Thy loving intimacy, though Thy unfaithful spouse.

Truly Thou art a GOD of Pity and Mercy, Long-suffering, and of great Mercy.

Truly Thou art good to all men, and Thy mercies are over all Thy works. O let Thy works sing praise unto Thee, specially Thy Works of Mercy and Pity; and let Thy saints, who have known Thy loving-kindnesses, bless Thee and sing of Thy Mercies for ever.

I acknowledge, venerate, and embrace the Bowels of Thy great Mercy, which Thou hast shown towards me and all Thy Elect, them that have already apprehended, and them that still are on their way. In union with their love, and with all the possible love of all possible created beings, I give Thee thanks, and will for ever, for that unspeakable superabundance of Eternal Love, whereby with them Thou hast mercifully kept me from the sins into which I might have fallen; Thou hast so patiently borne with me in my repeated daily falls; hast, when fallen, so pitifully called me to repentance; hast, when penitent, so graciously taken me back to Thy Favour, yea, hast hitherto vouchsafed me so bountifully an effectual desire of amendment, Grace in full to live thenceforth more holily, and a stedfast hope of perseverance and attaining to Thy Glory.

For these and other unnumbered blessings of Thy Goodness, O that I had praised Thee and blessed Thee all my life long! O that I had ever loved and glorified Thee with infinite honour and love! O that I had never, O that I might never offend Thee henceforth for ever!

But, alas! how have I *not* acknowledged, loved, and glorified Thee, for all Thy Goodness! What have I given unto Thee for all Thy Gifts unto me, but sins, ingratitude, negligences innumerable? I grieve for these from the ground of my heart, and for all and each of the sins of my past life; not, O LORD, for fear of punishment or loss of Glory, but simply because of Thee, O my GOD, most infinitely amiable, because they sorely displease Thee, Whom I love, and will love for ever, above all things.

Fervently I desire, firmly I resolve, by the help of Thy grace, to amend all my sins, specially —— by means of ——, and with renewed fervour to spend myself wholly in Thy Service, &c.

And by that same Love and Infinite Charity, whereby, with the FATHER and the HOLY GHOST, O good JESUS, Thou hast so oft turned the Eyes of Thy Loving Mercy towards me, ungrateful sinner, and all penitents, hast patiently borne with me, hast washed me white in Thy Blood, and still continuest to look upon me, bear with me, and wash me white; remember, O LORD, and have pity on all Thy Holy Church, its heads and members, &c.

And may "the citizens of the Heavenly Jerusalem, the innumerable company of angels, the general assembly of the first-born written in heaven, and the spirits of just men made perfect," "bless, praise, and magnify the LORD" for ever, with me and for me, for this and all His Blessings vouchsafed to them and me, or that shall be vouchsafed for ever; and may I obtain, through their prayers, the grace perfectly to glorify Him as I journey now on my way, and hereafter as inhabitant with them of the Heavenly Country, sing in unison to Him for ever, with Cherubim and Seraphim; Holy, Holy, Holy, LORD GOD of Sabaoth! Blessing and Glory, &c.

ANOTHER MOST BEAUTIFUL FORM OF STIRRING OUR AFFECTIONS, AFTER CONFESSION.

From the same. Ibid.

I. O JESU, Infinite Object of all love, whence is it that Thy great Goodness should so pity, Thy great Majesty should so stoop, Thy great Charity should so love me, a vile earthworm, so foul a sinner, so ungrateful a servant, so faithless a spouse, a son so prodigal, as to vouchsafe so oft to look on me with the eyes of Thy Mercy when wandering far from Thee, to bring me back from straying, to enlighten me when blind, to raise me when fallen, and to invite me to the Kiss of Peace? Holy, Holy, Holy, LORD GOD of Sabaoth!

O be Thou confessed, loved, and infinitely glorified, in number infinite, by all, in all, over all, for Thine own sake, to all Eternity and more!

How dost thou multiply upon me, up to the present moment, Thy Mercy, Charity and Goodness! I embrace it with confession, reverence, and love, and with all conceivable affection of all conceivable created beings, I give Thee thanks now, and will for ever.

How scantily, how imperfectly, have I returned Thy Love, and glorified Thee, Who art most worthy of infinite love, honour, and service! Nay, rather how often have I thus offended Thee! I confess, I abhor, my exceeding ingratitude towards Thee, and I grieve from my heart for Thy Sake. Pardon me; fill up by Thyself what is wanting in me. From this moment, Thee and Thy most Holy Good Pleasure, with arms of love and all conceivable devotedness of affection, (yea, though Thou shouldest annihilate me, or, which of Thy Infinite Goodness Thou wilt not do, reprobate me,) most closely I embrace, and will so do for ever.

Grant that I may perfectly know, and will, and do, what Thou willest and knowest, and all others with me, by Thy Tears, Thy Sweat, Thy Blood.

JESUS, God of my heart, grant me grace to amend all my sins, especially——; to advance in this virtue——, to reform these actions——, and to persevere in my holy calling.

May I live in Thee, die in Thee, and abide eternally in Thee. May I be wholly Thine, and Thou mine, O JESU, for ever, through Thy Own Merits. Amen.

Here perform the [enjoined] act of penitence.

II. The like Grace, Indulgence, and Mercy, show, O good JESU, to all for whom Thou didst vouchsafe to die, and for whom I am especially bound and wont to pray, by Thy Tears, Sweat, and Blood; by giving to the dead everlasting rest, that, cleansed from sin, enjoying Thy Perpetual Light, they may most perfectly love and praise, and sing Glory to Thee; by preserving, advancing, and helping the righteous in their state of Grace, that so, by serving Thee in holiness and righteousness all the days of their life, they may go from strength to strength, till Thou be seen of them in bliss in the heavenly Sion: by looking pitifully, with the eyes of Thy Mercy, upon all sinners, converting them mercifully, to own, fear, and love Thee; so that they too, washed white in Thy Blood, may sing Thy Mercies now upon earth, and hereafter for ever with all Thy saints, in heaven.

EXHORTATION TO PENITENCE,

BY DOMINIC, THE CARTHUSIAN.

Homo Dei creatura.

MORTAL, who art GOD's creation,
Why so little meditation
On the vast eternal station,
    Wherein death will leave thee?
Couldst thou know how great that Glory,
It so strong would come before thee,
Things so vain and transitory
    Ne'er could thus deceive thee.

Couldst thou know how great the sorrow,
Which, in hell that knows no morrow,
Can from hope no comfort borrow,
    Thou thy chains hadst broken:
And ere yet thou art belated,
All aghast and consternated,
Those thy sins hadst mourn'd and hated,
    Thought, and done, and spoken.

Such of saints the joy and pleasure,
Such the torments without measure,
Such of each the endless treasure,
    That no thought can know;
Till the soul, by life forsaken,
Shall in endless bliss awaken,
Or is suddenly o'ertaken
    With eternal woe.

When the grave from sight shall sever,
Vain to know is the endeavour,
If in bliss or pain for ever,
    And but little mention;

There is then a show of sorrow,
But his goods they share to-morrow,
And his kindred thence will borrow
    Envy and contention.

Death the good and bad inherit,
But the lot the undying spirit
Doth for good or evil merit,
    Distant is for ever :
They may hold the pomp funereal,
They may feast upon thy burial ;
Thou hast lost the eternal trial :
    They can aid thee never.

No avail is then in grieving,
No delay for thy retrieving,
And no place for thy relieving ;
    All shall be bereft thee.
Wouldst thou rise,—a hand hath bound thee,
And a dread abyss surrounds thee,
Till the Judge's Eye hath found thee :
    Nothing then is left thee.

If no Saviour thou hast gained,
If no Advocate attained,
When the time to thee remained
    For thy preparation ;
Who in changes shall defend thee ?
Who in Judgment shall attend thee ?
Who as surety shall befriend thee,
    In thy consternation ?

Angels e'en of Peace attending,
Then shall weep in sorrow bending,
Yet, the Righteous JUDGE defending,
    Own the Judgment true ;
And what soundeth more astounding,
All God's creatures then surrounding,
Thine own conscious soul confounding,
    Ratify thy due.

Then its guilty deeds reviewing,
Conscience-self, in sadness ruing,
Witness to its own undoing,
    Shall the sentence own.
In the soul, of GOD forsaken,
Fiends shall have such terrors shaken,
That the soul shall then awaken
    Unto griefs unknown.

Held of saints in reprobation,
In itself all desperation,
Shall it then in desolation
    Turn unto that gloom,
Where no change for ever neareth,
Where no door of hope appeareth,
But, as Abraham witness beareth,
    None from thence can come.

Never yet the tongue hath spoken,
Sense of man hath found no token,
Ne'er on thought of man hath broken,
    Those unnumber'd pains,
Which are in that word, Damnation,
Where of sins each variation
Hath its own allotted station,
    Portion'd to its stains.

Angry flames with sulphur glooming,
Foulest darkness scarce illuming,
And a woe the soul consuming,
    Fill their cup of sadness;
Where the death that never dieth,
Where the thirst that nought supplieth,
And the soul mid scorpions lieth,
    Causing burning madness.

Many there the dismal places,
And of anguish the dark faces,
As in all earth's varied spaces
    Here are visible.

Here of woes our darkest trances
Are of those but feeble glances,
Which eternity enhances,
    And no tongue can tell.

Such of saints the boundless treasures,
Such of angels are the pleasures,
GOD Himself their fulness measures,
    Which no eye hath seen.
Seeing GOD in glad fruition,
Fulness without inanition,
Happy, loving, sweet condition,
    Peaceful, bright, serene.

Of Thy MAKER there in Heaven
Unto thee may sight be given,
Happy Vision, whence is driven
    All that doth offend;
Sight which ne'er of parting heareth,
Joy which never disappeareth,
Nothing more of evil feareth,
    And shall have no end:

Where bright Angels' forms are shining,
Saints on JESUS' Breast reclining,
Where no death, and no declining,
    And no fear of dying;
Into Bliss's Fount ascending,
Chief of goods, all goods transcending,
In itself, and without ending,
    Every good supplying.

Such as ear hath ne'er received,
Such as heart hath ne'er conceived,
Such as man hath ne'er believed,
    But to whom 'tis given—
What the spirit there enjoyeth,
Free from all that her annoyeth,
In the Vision which ne'er cloyeth,
    Sight of GOD in Heaven.

But thus warn'd by things revealed,—
Half disclosed and half concealed,—
Soon for good or evil sealed,
   When our race is run:
Let us now awake from sleeping,
And the holier pathway keeping,
In this world for ever weeping,
   Sins that we have done.

Nor live like the brute creation,
Lest when death hath fix'd our station,
We be found in desolation
   Which no thought can bear.
Pray o'er sins which thee have stained,
And o'er woes which CHRIST sustained,
While the time hath yet remained,
   And for Heaven prepare.

Lo, how soon the world decayeth,
How short-liv'd its beauty stayeth,
And its glory that betrayeth,
   Coming soon to nought,
And it then to hell descendeth!
Let the bliss which heart transcendeth,
And the life which never endeth,
   Ever fill thy thought.

So from death be sorrows driven,
If our joys be now in Heaven,
And to God all Glory given,
   Of all good the Store!
To Him, Who is our Salvation,
Be all Love and Adoration,
Glory, Praise, and Domination,
   Now and evermore.

ON PENITENCE,

FROM ANCIENT WRITERS.

BETHINK ye of the real character of repentance; for there are many who are ever saying that they are sinners, yet go on sinning, and find pleasure in it. This is profession, not correction; self-accusation, without cure; declaration of sin, not eradication. Sure penitence there is none, without hatred of sin and love of GOD. When thou so repentest, that thy former delights now taste bitter to thee; and what once gave pleasure to thy body, now afflicts thy very soul; then dost thou groan aright, and say to GOD, Against Thee only have I sinned, and done evil in Thy Sight. (Auct. Serm. 177, ap. S. Aug. App. olim Serm. 7, de tempore.)

ST. GREGORY.

True repentance stands in mourning for past sins, and in forsaking that for which we mourn. He that deplores his sins, and then goes and does the like, is either ignorant of true penitence or a hypocrite. (Hom. 34, in Evang.)

ST. AMBROSE.

Why delay till to-morrow? Thou mayest gain to-day. Beware, lest thou miss to-day, and lose to-morrow too. It is perilous to lose one hour: the whole of life is made up of single hours. (Epist. 82.)

ST. CÆSARIUS.

Behold GOD's Judgment upon sinners: he that in life forgat GOD, in death forgets himself. (Hom. 13. See too S. Aug. Libr. 50. Homil. 41. Serm. 393.)

ST. AUGUSTINE.

GOD, Who hath promised indulgence to thy repentance, hath not promised a to-morrow to thy delay. (In Ps. 144.)

END OF SECTION III.

TO THE

Most High God,

Sovereign Ruler of this mighty Ocean,

WHOM THE WINDS AND THE SEA OBEY,

UNDER WHOSE COMMAND THE CHRISTIAN PEOPLE

ARE SAILING TOWARDS THE HARBOUR OF ETERNITY,

IN THE SPACIOUS SHIP OF THE CHURCH,

OVER THIS WORLD'S WIDE EXPANSE, THROUGH MANIFOLD STORMS;

AND PURSUE THEIR COURSE HAPPILY,

THEIR SPECIAL AIDS BEING

THE POLE-STAR OF FAITH, THE ANCHOR OF HOPE,

THE LABOURING OAR OF CHARITY.

THE HELM OF PRUDENCE DIRECTS THEIR COURSE,

THE MAST OF JUSTICE KEEPS THE VESSEL UPRIGHT,

THE CABLES OF FORTITUDE BIND IT FIRM,

THE PLUMMET OF TEMPERANCE FORESTALLS DANGER:

REASON, SITTING AT HER WATCH,

TAKES NOTE OF ENEMIES, OF STARS, OF CHANGES OF WEATHER;

HUMILITY TURNS ASIDE FROM ROCKS AND WHIRLPOOLS,

POVERTY AVOIDS PIRATES,

CHASTITY SHUNS SYRENS,

OBEDIENCE REPEATS THE CHEER OF ENCOURAGEMENT;

[PENITENCE

PENITENCE, MOREOVER, AT INTERVALS, CLEARS OUT THE HOLD:
AND PRAYER, FASTING, ALMS, AND ALL OTHER VIRTUES,
SPREAD WIDE THE SAILS.
BUT WHAT HELP OR MIGHT IS THERE IN THEM ALL,
EXCEPT THE FAVOURING GALE BREATHE ON THEM,
EVEN THE GENTLE ZEPHYR OF THY GRACE,

O Thou Supreme Ruler and Inspirer,

WITHOUT WHOM WE CAN DO NOTHING,
OF WHOM IS ALL OUR SUFFICIENCY?
AND LO! A GREAT TEMPEST HATH ARISEN IN THE SEA,
AND IS GRIEVOUSLY TOSSING OUR VESSEL.
LORD, SAVE US, WE PERISH!
THE WAVES OF THE SEA ARE MIGHTY, AND RAGE HORRIBLY,
BUT YET THE LORD, WHO DWELLETH ON HIGH,
IS MIGHTIER.

O Thou great Ruler of the World,

WHEN WILT THOU REBUKE THE WINDS AND THE SEA,
THAT THERE MAY BE A GREAT CALM?
WHEN WILT THOU GIVE US DAYS OF PEACE,
AND TO SING OUR JOYFUL ALLELUIA, SAYING,
"WE HAVE PASSED THROUGH FIRE AND WATER,
AND THOU HAST BROUGHT US OUT INTO A PLACE OF REST?"

PARADISE FOR THE CHRISTIAN SOUL.

PART IV.

CONTAINING VARIOUS EXERCISES HELPFUL TO THE PURSUIT OF VIRTUE AND CHRISTIAN PERFECTION.

A PRAYER,

TO BE USED BEFORE READING ANY BOOK OF PIETY.

BLESSED is the man whom Thou instructest, O LORD, and teachest him out of Thy law. Yea, LORD, blessed indeed is he. Under Thy guidance he cannot err, for Thou art the Way: under Thy teaching he cannot be deceived, for Thou art the Truth: neither, under Thy protection, can he perish, for Thou art the Life. Therefore teach Thou me goodness, and discipline, and knowledge. I hear on all sides many lessons of virtue and piety; much do I read which Thy servants have with pious diligence written about the means of obtaining Thy grace, and about Thy warnings and commands; but how shall I understand them, unless Thou enlighten my understanding? And how shall I obey, unless Thou also inflame my affections? To will, indeed, is present with me, but how to perform I find not. Surely, without Thee I can do nothing; but I can do all things by Thee, of Whom is all our sufficiency.

Whilst, therefore, I am reading what is piously written in books, do Thou, I beseech Thee, write the same with Thine own Finger upon the tablet of my heart. Fair words soothe the ear; but without Thee they affect not the mind. In vain, truly, doth man, one like myself, speak to me,—how piously, how learnedly, how eloquently soever he may speak,—unless Thou, O LORD, speak inwardly to my heart. Speak, therefore, LORD, for Thy servant heareth. Or, if he hear not, do Thou cause him to hear, Thou Who makest both the deaf to hear, and the dumb to speak.

But, above all, make Thou my heart to burn within me, whiles thou art speaking to me. Teach me to do Thy will, that I fall not into that greater condemnation, to have known what Thou wilt, and done it not. For the servant that knoweth his lord's will and doeth it not shall be beaten with many stripes. But I am Thy servant; give me understanding, therefore, that I may learn Thy commandments; give me grace also, that I may keep them with my whole heart. My soul longeth from henceforth to obey and to please Thee only, and to cleave for ever unto Thee, O GOD, Who art the Strength of my heart, and my Portion for ever!

CHAPTER I.

THE DOCTRINE OF HOLY LIVING HANDLED IN A CONFERENCE BETWEEN CHRIST AND MAN.

§ 1. *Aspiration after the way of salvation.*

MAN. O Eternal Wisdom, my LORD and my GOD, how excellent is Thy Name in all the world! Thou hast created all things out of nothing by the might of Thy Right Hand; and of Thy boundless goodness Thou didst form me, when as yet I was not, after Thine Own Image: and when I was lost, Thou didst redeem me with Thy Blood; and didst give up

Thy Precious Soul unto death, in order that I might obtain life!

Thou hast also lifted up upon me the light of Thy Countenance, that I might acknowledge Thee as my Chief Good. Wherefore also my soul longeth after Thee, O GOD, even as the hart desireth the water-brooks. O when and how shall I appear before the Face of God! In this desert, trackless, and thirsty land, in this region of horror and waste solitude, I find no certain and secure path.

Do Thou, therefore, the True Light, Who lightenest every man that cometh into the world, shine upon me who sit in darkness and the shadow of death, to guide my feet into the way of peace and salvation. Lighten my darkness. Tell me what I shall do that I may obtain eternal life. Thou Who teachest the way of GOD in truth, show Thou me the way that I should walk in, that I may come unto Thee Who art my Salvation and my Life!

CHRIST. Thou dost well to ask for the way that leadeth unto life. For there is a way that seemeth right unto a man, but the end thereof are the ways of death. Strait, indeed, and narrow is the way that leadeth unto life, and few there be that find it; but broad is the way that leadeth to destruction; and, ah! how many are those who walk therein! These care not at all, where two ways part, yea nor, in the midst of so many turns and by-paths, to ask for the straight way, or to inquire for a guide who knoweth the way.

Hence the wicked walk ever round and round, and, missing the path of peace and truth, they perish miserably. I will show thee, therefore, O man, what is good, and what I, the LORD, require of thee, surely to do justly, and to love mercy, and to walk carefully with thy GOD.

MAN. I know, O LORD, that the way of man is not in himself; neither does it belong to man to walk and to direct his steps. He knows not at all his own end; a stranger and a pilgrim upon earth he knows neither his entrance upon it, nor his departure out of it. Without Thee we are as stray sheep not having a shepherd. O Thou Good Shepherd! seek after Thy servant. Guide me in Thy truth, and teach me, for Thou art my GOD and SAVIOUR. Look well if there be any way of wickedness in me, and lead me in the way everlasting.

§ 2. CHRIST *is the Way of Life, through the keeping of His commandments.*

CHRIST. Thou desirest to know the way. Behold, I am the Way, the Truth, and the Life; the Way, in My Example; the Truth, in My Promises; the Life, as your Reward. He that followeth Me shall not walk in darkness, but shall have the Light of Life. I have given you an example, that ye should follow My steps; that, as I have done, so ye should do also. Look fixedly, therefore, upon My Life, and do according to the Pattern which was showed thee on the Mount. Yea, learn of Me, for I am meek and lowly of heart. For I came not to do Mine own will, but the will of Him that sent Me. And I was obedient to GOD the FATHER even unto death, the Death of the Cross.

Go thou, therefore, O man, and do likewise. Be thou humble and obedient; and if thou wouldest enter into life, keep the Commandments. Now, the first and great commandment is this, Thou shalt love the LORD thy GOD with all thy heart, &c.; and the second is like unto it, Thou shalt love thy neighbour as thyself. He that hath My commandments and keepeth them, he it is that loveth Me. For to show obedience is the proof of love.

MAN. Ah! my CREATOR! stretch forth Thy Right Hand to the work of Thy Hands, that I may not err from Thy commandments. O that my ways were made so direct that I might keep Thy statutes! For in the law of the LORD is my delight. But, O wretched man that I am! I delight indeed in the law after the inward man, but I see another law in my members warring against the law of my mind, so that I cannot do the good I would, and the evil that I would not, that I do. So prone to evil are the thoughts of man even from his youth! and the corruptible body weigheth down the soul. How shall I love Thee as Thou willest and oughtest to be loved? For the measure of our love to Thee is to love Thee without measure, because Thou Thyself exceedest all measure.

CHRIST. My commandments are not grievous; much less are they impossible. For My yoke is easy, and My burden light. If thou dost not believe Me, let so many thousands of My faithful servants who have cleaved to Me with their whole heart convince thee. Yea, even boys and tender virgins, weak both in sex and age, will put thee to shame. Behold! how are they numbered among the children of GOD, and their lot is amongst the saints! Through love of Me they crucified the flesh with its affections; they spurned the world and its allurements; they boldly contemned threats and torments of all kinds; they overcame Satan manfully; and thus taking My yoke upon them with joy, they followed Me, their REDEEMER, with their whole heart. And canst not thou do as did such youths and virgins?

MAN. These are they which fly as clouds. But I am weak and creep limpingly on the ground. Their power was greatly strengthened; and I cannot attain unto it.

CHRIST. Consider, therefore, O man, (I speak after the manner of men because of the infirmity of thy flesh,) consider those who are wise to do evil and rejoice in their evil deeds, even the heifers of Ephraim who are taught and love to tread out the corn,—the children, I mean, of this world. See with what earnestness they toil and sweat, to what a degree they harass themselves, that they may scrape together a little of the perishable goods of earth. Why and whence is it, that in their generation they have more strength than the children of light? Why is it, that when they thus yield their members servants to iniquity unto iniquity, thou art not able to yield thine as servants to righteousness unto holiness? Make the trial, at least; and if thou labour ever so little, thou shalt find great rest. Thou shalt see how much easier it is to gain heaven than earth, to please and to serve Me than the world. Thou shalt see, moreover, the misery of those who tread such uneasy paths; for labour and sorrow and unhappiness are in the path of those who know not the way of peace; whereas My ways are smooth and pleasant. Why then do ye love vanity and seek after leasing? Why do ye weary yourselves in the ways of iniquity? How long, O ye children of men, will ye, with a heavy heart, be deceitful upon the weights? What will it profit you to gain the whole world and to lose your own souls?

MAN. To whom shall I go from Thee, O LORD? Thou hast the words of eternal life. Thy testimonies are very sure. Blessed is the man whom Thou instructest, O LORD, and teachest him out of Thy law. Show me Thy ways, and teach me Thy paths. Make me to go in the path of Thy commandments, for therein is my desire; but remove far from me the way of wickedness.

CHRIST. Attend unto My words, for they are spirit and they are life. I am He that teacheth thee profitable things. Blessed is the man who heareth Me and keepeth My words. But vain are all men, in whom there is not the knowledge of GOD. Behold, with few and easy lessons will I instruct thee in the way in which thou shalt walk. I will lead thee by the paths of righteousness, on which, when thou shalt have entered, thy steps shall not be straitened, and when thou runnest thou shalt not stumble. But do thou diligently hearken unto My sayings, and lay them up in thy heart. For if thou wilt keep My commandments, they shall preserve thee.

MAN. Speak, LORD, for Thy servant heareth. Yet give me understanding, that I may learn Thy commandments, and keep them with my whole heart. Teach me to do Thy will, for Thou art my GOD; lest Thy servant, knowing Thy will, yet doing it not, be worthy to be beaten with many stripes.

§ 3. *The consideration of the end of our creation.*

CHRIST. Before all things, reflect often and seriously on the purpose for which thou wast created. For thou art aware that, without a knowledge of the end, means can never be rightly ordained. Consider, therefore, for what intent thou art made man, made, moreover, after My Image and Likeness; why, in preference to all other animals, thou hast been endued with that noble gift of reason; why thou art placed in this world as in a most stately theatre; why, in fine, thou hast been redeemed by the countless labours of My whole Life and by My Precious Blood—why, moreover, supplied with sacraments and aids of heavenly grace. For, thinkest thou, I have created the children of men for nought? And for what purpose have I conferred on them so many gifts of soul and body? Is it that they may give themselves up to the heaping up of wealth? that they may seek after honour and the glory of a name? that they may build spacious and splendid houses as if they were to live here for ever? that they may lay house to house, and join field to field? that they may be engrossed by farms and yokes of oxen? that they may be clothed in purple and fine linen, and fare sumptuously every day? that they may give themselves up to pleasure and idleness, to sports and pastimes? that they may eat and drink, and pass their days in indulgences, supposing that this is their portion? Ah! wicked imagination, and far below the largeness of My bounty! For a far higher end than this have I made and redeemed mankind.

MAN. Praise the LORD, O my soul. I will praise Thee, O LORD, with my whole life. For what is man that Thou art mindful of him? or why hast Thou inclined Thy heart towards him, Thou Who hast need of nothing? Wast Thou in want of our good things, that Thou madest us? But what have we that we have not received? Thine own is the earth and the fulness thereof. Thou didst make us that Thou mightest show forth in us the riches of Thy goodness and of Thy glory. For since Thy nature is the Highest Goodness itself, it could desire nothing more than to communicate and diffuse itself. Who is able, O LORD, to declare the wonders of Thy power, Thy wisdom, and Thy goodness? What shall I render unto the LORD for all the benefits that He hath done unto me? Bless the LORD, O my soul, and forget not all His benefits. May my tongue cleave to the roof of my mouth, if I am not mindful of my CREATOR!

CHRIST. O that thou wert wise and didst understand, and couldest estimate at its right value thine end and the blessing of thy creation! Hear, therefore, and understand. Surely I have given thee understanding, and I have set Mine eyes upon thee, that thou mightest not be like unto horse and mule which have no understanding to know their Creator; but I have given thee understanding, that thou mightest acknowledge Me to be thy GOD and thy LORD: I have given thee a will that thou mightest love Me, and desire only heavenly things; memory, that thou mightest be mindful of Me and of My kindnesses; a tongue, that thou mightest praise Me: I have given thee, in fine, all the senses and all the faculties, both of body and of mind, that thou mightest use all these to the glory of My Name; and when thou shalt have faithfully discharged this duty, then, after all, will I be Myself thy Reward. I am thy Chief Good, in the enjoyment of which all thy desires shall be completely satisfied. For nothing that is less than the greatest can fill a soul which is capable of entertaining the Highest Good.

Behold, O man, this is the end for which thou art formed. On this account art thou placed in this world as a pilgrim and a stranger, not having here any abiding city, that thou mayest seek one to come. On this account art thou set in this course, that, when thou hast run and striven vigorously, thou mayest at length receive the reward and crown of righteousness.

But O how blind and wretched are they who know not nor understand these things; and so care for nothing less than for that on account of which they were formed; and, as if they possessed souls in vain, take thought only for things present, and are engrossed by those things after which the Gentiles seek who know not God; nay, things which are sought after by the very brutes who have no understanding to perceive the end of other things. Hence, like the beasts, they wallow in their own mire. Thus are they corrupt and become abominable in their doings, as if there were no GOD nor any knowledge in the Most

HIGH; or as if the end of man and beast were as one and the same, and their condition equal. And thus, seldom, or rather never, do they think on heaven and its glories!

MAN. True, O LORD, Thou hast lifted up the light of Thy Countenance upon us. For together with the light of reason, or the gift of understanding, are our souls impressed with the traces of Thy goodness, Thy love, and grace. And hence Thou hast also put joy into my heart, springing from the consideration of so excellent a gift, and of the good things which Thou hast purchased for them that love Thee and make good use of Thy gift. For Thou art the Portion of my inheritance and of my cup; Thou shalt maintain my lot. Whom have I in heaven but Thee, and there is none upon earth that I desire in comparison of Thee, Who art the strength of my heart, my God, and my Portion for ever!

§ 4. *Upright and pure intention.*

CHRIST. Seeing that thou knowest, then, the end of thy creation, even My Glory, take care that in all thy actions thou have a regard thereto, and aim at it as thy mark: see, in fact, that thou do all thy works to the glory of My Name. The exercise of a pure and upright intention is, as it were, the sum of all piety and perfection. If thine eye be single and look right onward, thy whole body shall be full of light. Whether, therefore, thou eatest, or drinkest, or whatsoever thou doest, remember that thou do all to the glory of My Name.

The labour is light, but the fruit thereof abundant; the sowing is scanty, but it yields a most plenteous harvest. The art is easy of attainment; but it is one which, out of lead or other common metal, produces gold; in other words, it draws forth and increases the love of GOD out of any work, however humble or profitless it may otherwise be.

For, by the grace of a right intention, thy labours, be they in themselves most lowly or indifferent, or merely natural, are endued with the character of worth and virtue; they gain the Divine favour; they miss nought of temporal good; but while they will be performed with more ease and pleasantness to thyself, they will, at the same time, be more pleasing to Me.

O how many lose the fruit of their labours by the fault of a corrupt intention. And yet they commonly flatter themselves, as a people that had wrought righteousness, and delight themselves in the multitude of their works; which still they perform with small desire for My Glory, or affection for true piety: they do them rather to be seen of men, or for the rewards of this life rather than for those of the life to come. Nevertheless it shall come to pass, that when I receive the congregation, I shall judge according unto right. Surely, in that Great Day, when I shall search Jerusalem with candles, then will I bring to light the hidden things of darkness, and I will make manifest the counsels of the heart.

O how many things which now give content will then cause bitterness! How many which now look pleasant will then appear abominable! For, when I come to Judgment, and to render to every man according to his works, and especially according to the *intention* of his doings, what will multitudes of you bring forward that is worthy of praise or reward? Verily, I say unto you, they have already had their reward; they have had that which they sought after, the glory of the world, the splendour of a name, the gains of the flesh, wealth, gifts, dignities: and what remaineth that I should reward them with? They who are led—be it even to acts of piety and devotion—by a view to their own advantage or credit, rather than by zeal for My glory and the desire to please Me, these serve not Me, but themselves, and the world, and the flesh. And how, then, can they presume to look for a reward from Me?

Behold the vanity of men who wear themselves out with foolish and unprofitable toil. They sow much, and bring in little; they eat, but have not enough; they drink, but they are not filled with drink; and they who earn wages, put them into a bag that is pierced through with holes. But be thou, O man, more prudent; and take heed lest, in doing many things, thou shouldest, in fact, do nothing, and thus lose all the fruit of thy labour. Why dost thou spend thy gold for that which is not bread, and thy silver for that which satisfieth not? How long dost thou halt between two opinions? If I am the LORD thy GOD, then follow Me with all thy heart. If thou preferrest or lovest anything before Me, why dost thou call thyself by My Name? Why dost thou take on thee My badges? If servitude delights thee, to serve Me is to reign. If thou seekest after glory, the highest glory is to follow after the LORD. Them that follow Me I will honour; but they that despise Me shall be lightly esteemed. If thou pursuest after gain, ask it of Me Alone, and whence canst thou look for greater? For neither hath eye seen, nor ear heard, neither hath entered into the heart of man, what I have prepared for them that love Me. O that thou wouldest oftener have respect unto this recompense! No labour, surely, would then seem grievous to thee. For the hope of reward is the sweetener of labour; and, behold, I will be thy exceeding great Reward.

MAN. Thou art worthy, O LORD, to receive praise, and glory, and honour, from all Thy creatures; why not, then, from me also, who am made after Thine Image, and purchased by Thee at so costly a Price, that I might glorify Thee my GOD in my body and in my spirit? Who planteth a tree or a vineyard and eateth not of the fruit thereof? But, Thou, O LORD, hast formed me and planted me in this earth. Thou hast brought this vine, even my soul, out of Egypt, and hast set me in this condition of life, N., this calling, N., this post of duty, N. Be it far from me, that when Thou shalt look for grapes, I should bring forth nothing but wild grapes.

O that my soul were as a watered garden that is fertile in good fruits; that is to say, in solid virtues. Let there not be in it any unproductive flowers which only please the eye, specious virtues merely, and works which are good only in appearance, and which dry up quickly as the hay. May every spurious plant be rooted out, which the FATHER of Truth hath not planted, but the author of vanity and pride. Oh that I were as a tree which is planted by the water-courses, and which yieldeth to Thee its fruit in its season; lest when Thou comest, and findest not upon it the fruit of true piety, Thou curse the barren stock, and order it to be cut down and cast into the fire.

Wherefore my soul sigheth after Thee, mine eyes look up to Thee, O Thou that dwellest in the heavens. Let me not keep mine eyes bent on earth, neither let me labour for vile dross, rather than for Thy glory and the love of Thee and the rewards of the heavenly life. Let me not take delight in the chase after empty honours, to whom eternal life is offered. Thy Apostle counted all things but dung, that he might win Thee. And truly, what remaineth to us of all these things, after they shall have passed away, but that which causes shame? O how shall we, one day, wish that we had laboured more earnestly for Thee, seeing that we should not have laboured in vain. Behold, O LORD, I give up my heart to Thee in an everlasting covenant, and to Thee I dedicate all my works. Let Thy Name be sanctified in me, and blessed throughout all ages.

CHRIST. Take heed lest thou seek the good which belongs not to thee. Seek after thine own good, O man. For each kind of being has its own peculiar good; but do thou seek after that which is proper to thyself. There is none good but the High God; what, therefore, canst thou need who hast the chief Good so nigh thee? There are, indeed, inferior good things which constitute the distinct happiness of other creatures. What, for instance, forms the happiness of the beasts of the field, but to eat their fill, to escape from want, to sleep, to exist, to be in health, to reproduce their kind? Is it such a good as this thou seekest after, thou that art joint-heir with the SON of GOD! Is it thy joy to be the fellow of the herds? Elevate thou thy hope to the Good of all goods. (See S. Aug. on Psalm cii.)

MAN. It is good for me to hold fast by the Chief Good, even by Thee, my GOD, and in Thee to place my hope. I will offer unto Thee a free-will offering, and I will confess unto Thy Name, O LORD, for it is good. For whom have I in heaven but Thee, and what is there on earth that I desire in comparison of Thee?

CHRIST. Yet do I not utterly withhold from thee the inferior goods—the other creatures of my hand; for I have not made them for nought. But mark! thou must make no other use of them, neither are they to be loved and sought after, further than as they may be helps to thee or means to the attainment of thy proper end. Happy is the man who, out of all that is created, draws forth the love of the CREATOR; who out of creatures, which otherwise become entanglements to the feet of the unwise, makes for himself a ladder, as it were, to heaven!

MAN. I look upon all these things, made by Thee, O LORD, for my service; and behold, they are beautiful and very good. How much fairer, then, how much more excellent and lovely art Thou, the Maker of them all! If the mere drops and sprinklings of good afford so much delight, how much more to be beloved is the Spring, yea, the vast Ocean itself of all goodness! O that my soul might love Thee supremely, nay, love nothing else but for Thine own sake!

§ 5. *The practice of self-denial; or, watchfulness over the heart and senses.*

CHRIST. That wish of thine is good; but in vain dost thou aspire after the love of Me, unless thou hate thyself. The love of the flesh and the love of the CREATOR cannot agree together; he, therefore, that loveth his own life shall lose it; but he that hateth his life in this world shall keep it unto life eternal. If, then, ye live after the flesh, ye shall die; but if, through the SPIRIT, ye mortify the deeds of the flesh, ye shall live. Without this healthful hatred of thyself thou canst not be My disciple. Mortify, therefore, thy desires, thy senses, and thy members which are upon the earth, and see that thou do not everything that thou inclinest unto.

In the first place, keep thy heart with all diligence, for out of it are the issues of life. I have committed unto thee a most precious treasure; but thou carriest it about enclosed in an earthen vessel, which is in more imminent peril than glass itself,—even the casket of thy heart, which is the object of the plots of a multitude of enemies; and which thou thyself, moreover, dost betray, whenever thou keepest ill guard over thy senses or misusest them.

O how few are there who take serious heed unto their ways, that they offend not in their tongue! And yet the injuries and sins of but one tongue, no tongue can sufficiently recount. But if any one thinketh that he is religious, and yet bridleth not his tongue, this man's religion is vain. Dost thou not know, by thine own experience, that many a time some feeling of love for Me, some relish for devotion acquired after lengthened labour, has been easily dissipated and driven away by a few vain and idle words? See how mighty an influence upon the furtherance of piety has the control of but a single tongue. Yet few consider this; notwithstanding experience may have taught them, that in the multitude of words there wanteth not sin; and notwithstanding that I, Eternal Truth, have said, That every idle word that men shall speak, they shall give account thereof in the day of judgment.

A strict watch over the other senses is, moreover, of great avail to this end; namely, that man may advance in love of Me, and may persevere unto the end. O how many souls have the eyes made a prey of! Let Eve, Dinah, David, and many others, be as warnings unto thee; happy and wise he who by the fall of others is made cautious against his own. Turn away thine eyes, then, lest they behold vanity. Yea, rather, with Job make a covenant with thine eyes, lest through them thou give entrance to some blind desire, some hurtful passion. It will be easier for thee not to admit it, than when once admitted to cast it out.

Hedge about thine ears with thorns, that thy heart may not lie open to devouring beasts — to slanderers, revilers, and filthy-talkers. When thou sittest down to a feast, put a knife to thy throat; that is, restrain thine appetite, taste not greedily of every dish, and see that in taking food thou serve not pleasure rather than the necessity of nature. Rather do thou deny thyself some portion of thy repast, and offer it unto Me in My members.

Consider what delights I relinquished for thy sake; of what bitter things I willingly partook; and do thou, in like manner, deny thyself much, which, though pleasant to the flesh, is hurtful to the spirit. And that thou mayest the easier refrain from things forbidden, restrain thy desires even in things lawful; knowing that I have prepared far higher joys for those, who through love of Me have despised these vanities.

MAN. Shame covereth my face, O LORD, when I look on Thee engaged in various labours, even from Thy youth, and beset on all sides with hardships and severities; while we, Christians in name, fall so far below Thy example. For what, throughout Thy life, didst Thou teach us,— Thou Who, for the joy that was set before Thee, enduredst the Cross, despising the shame,—but to set light by pleasures, to deny ourselves, to take up our Cross, and to follow Thee? Thou, in truth, didst know how to refuse the evil, and to choose the good. But Thou didst choose what was rugged and irksome to the flesh. That, therefore, is the best for us; that the most profitable; that chiefly to be chosen.

Yet how few are there who, in this, follow Thee! All seek their own; that, forsooth, which is pleasing to the flesh; and we feel no shame at being delicate members of a thorn-crowned Head. We are, and would be thought to be, thy disciples and servants. But, alás! how much more readily do we listen to the world, and the prince thereof! With what greediness do we gratify the desires of the flesh! O LORD, all my desire is before Thee, and my groaning is not hid from Thee.

CHRIST. Henceforth, then, do thou follow My steps; and continually endure in thy body the mortifying power of My Cross. Chastise thy body and bring it into subjection. Behold Mine elect, men of strong virtue, how did they hate their lives in this world, that they might keep them unto life eternal; yea, this was truly to love them. O that thou also wert convinced that the world passeth away, and the lust thereof; that thy life also fleeth as a shadow, and as a vapour that appeareth for a little while! What, in truth, wilt thou at the last wish that thou hadst done? What will then remain to thee of all thy joys, but anguish, and tribulation, and affliction of spirit? O how will men bemoan their self-deception, when wailing takes the place of their last enjoyments, though they now vaunt themselves for that which is most vile, and count it pleasure to lie amongst the thorns! For in the end of man shall his deeds be discovered; and in the sadness of his last hour shall he forget his choicest luxuries. O, if thou couldest but taste the bitterness which ends their joys and pleasures, surely thou wouldest cry out, There is death in the pot!—death in the delights of the flesh! Thou wouldest have no taste for that which, when tasted, bringeth forth death; neither wouldest thou drink of that cup, the wine whereof, though now it moveth itself aright, at the last biteth like a serpent, and as an adder poureth out poison. For all the ungodly of the earth shall suck out the dregs of My cup; fire and brimstone, storm and tempest, this shall be their portion to drink.

When thou art sick, thy physician prescribeth to thee, perchance, an abstinence from certain kinds of food, very grateful, it may be, to thy taste: and from the love of life and of health thou followest his advice: how much more oughtest thou to hearken unto Me, Who am the Author to thee both of life and of eternal health and salvation! How long, then, as a little child wilt thou love childishness, and, as a fool, desire that which will do thee hurt?

MAN. Blessed be Thou, O LORD, for ever, for that Thou thus admonishest me, that I, too, put not forth my hands to the cup of Babylon. Wherefore, from henceforth my soul renounceth [vain] delights. But I will be mindful of Thee, O JESU, and so shall delights never fail me; for there are delights at Thy Right Hand; and Thy delights are to be with the sons of men.

Let others, then, take the

timbrel and the harp, let them feast on fat things, and clothe themselves in soft raiment; let them stretch themselves upon their couches, and leave tokens of their joyfulness in every place; but as for me, I will delight myself in the LORD; this shall be my chief, my sole delight, to refuse for Thee all other delight, that I may taste how sweet the Lord my GOD is. But this Thou wilt not cause us to perceive, unless we be weaned from the milk, and drawn away from the breasts, of earthly pleasure; neither wilt Thou give manna from heaven, unless the flesh-pots of Egypt have come to an end; so impossible is it to delight at once in both, highest and lowest.

Nevertheless I feel—(for why should I dissemble before Thee Who knowest my inmost thoughts?)—I feel how strong is the force of pleasure, by which I see that even cedars of Lebanon have been overthrown, and stars, as it were, have fallen from heaven. How then can I, compassed with infirmity, presume upon myself?

§ 6. *Self-distrust; and the practice of constant prayer.*

CHRIST. This is the beginning of wisdom and of salvation, to feel how weak ye are, and that ye are not sufficient of yourselves to think anything as of yourselves, much less to do aught; but that all your sufficiency is of Me.

Without Me ye can do nothing. As the branch cannot bear fruit of itself, except it abide in the vine, no more can ye, except ye abide in Me. If the hammer be not moved by the hand of the workman, or the pen by the fingers of the writer, what can either of them effect?

MAN. Truly, O LORD, except Thou build the house, their labour is but lost that build it. In vain do we sit down to erect a tower, who have not in ourselves the means wherewith to finish it. But Thou workest all our works in us which pertain unto salvation. Without Thee I can do nothing; but I can do all things through Thee Who instrengthenest me.

CHRIST. With good reason, then, do I withdraw Myself from the sons of pride, who trust in their own strength, and boast themselves in the multitude of their riches; that being left to themselves they may see that they are nothing, and can do nothing, without Me, and that I Alone am He Who giveth the will, and the power, and the performance.

MAN. In Thee, O LORD, we live, and move, and have our being. Thou, O good JESU, art my Strength, and my Praise; Thou Alone art become my Salvation. Wherefore I will not trust in my bow; it is not my sword that shall save me. Our hand hath not the pre-eminence; but the Right Hand of the LORD bringeth mighty things to pass, &c.

CHRIST. Be careful, then, for nothing: but with all prayer and supplication let your requests be made known unto GOD. Lean not upon a staff of reed, but upon thy Beloved; cast all thy care upon Him, and thou shalt see the change of the Right Hand of the Most High, Who Alone doeth great wonders. Thou hast seen from time to time, that some have made but slow progress, and that others have altogether fallen away. Know thou, that this came to pass through their self-confidence, and their neglect of prayer. Hence it is that I have so often warned you, yea and My Apostle also, that ye ought always to pray, and not to faint. And though this may to many seem hard, yet how easy it really is, they well know, who, in the midst of their business, studies, conversations, are wont, without effort, to lift up their minds to GOD. Even but to raise the eyes towards heaven with deep longing of the heart is earnest prayer, and affects My Heart with the utmost tenderness. For prayers of this kind must gush forth from the affections of the mind. Such, for instance, as grief for sin, hatred of the vanity of the world, weariness of this life, longing for the life to come, admiration of the wonderful works of GOD, trust in GOD, zeal for the Divine honour, but, chief of all, that ardent love of Me, by which the soul pants to be united with its Beloved.

The flame of such affections is for the most part enkindled by meditation, and kept alive by frequent ejaculations; the matter of which is supplied sometimes by the desire after those graces most essential to salvation, at other times by those things which are the objects of the senses. Hence sang the man after Mine Own Heart, *Thou, Lord, hast made me glad through Thy works, and I will rejoice in the operations of Thy Hands.*

To make this use of the creatures is not in the power of all men; but of such only as have their senses exercised to discern both good and evil. For the unwise man doth not well consider these things, and a fool doth not understand them. But do thou, in this way, tread in the steps of that same Prophet of Mine, and imitate him in his breathings after Me, in frequent and short, but ardent aspirations. Take the following as examples, a few out of a multitude.

O Lord! how wonderful are Thy works! In wisdom hast Thou made them all; the earth is full of Thy riches.

O that my ways were made so direct, that I might keep Thy statutes!

Woe is me that I am constrained to dwell with Mesech [that my sojourning is prolonged].

Create in me a clean heart, O God! &c.

Like as the hart desireth the water-brooks, so longeth my soul after Thee, O God! My soul is athirst for God, &c.

Lighten mine eyes that I sleep not in death; lest mine enemy say, I have prevailed against him.

I will love Thee, O Lord, my Strength; the Lord is my strong Rock and my Defence, and my Deliverer.

The Lord is my Shepherd; I shall not want: He maketh me to lie down in green pastures.

Blessed be the Name of the Lord from this time forth for evermore.

One thing have I desired of the Lord, which I will require, even that I may dwell in the house of the Lord all the days of my life, &c.

§ 7. *Practice of the Presence of* God.

Christ. This habit of frequent ejaculation will produce another effect not less helpful to thy progress in piety: namely, the heartfelt recollection of My constant Presence with thee; and thus thou wilt perform all thy actions as one who is every where in My sight.

Walk, therefore, before Me, and be thou perfect. Wouldest thou do that which is evil? Seek thee out a place where I cannot see thee, and there, in security, do what thou wilt. Knowest thou not, that I fill heaven and earth, and that all things are naked and open unto My Eyes? For Mine Eyes, which exceed the brightness of the sun, are in every place, beholding the evil and the good. How is it that so many, like the unbridled horse or mule, rush headlong into every kind of wickedness? and wherefore do the sons of men practise evil without fear? Surely, because they believe not that I am present with them, and they set not GOD before their eyes. But think thou upon the LORD in all thy ways; think, I say, on Me, and I will direct thy steps. Observe, how much the sight of some grave and good man availeth to keep another humble and in the path of duty. How carefully and diligently dost thou do all things in his sight! yea, how cautiously dost thou forecast that thou do nothing bad or unseemly in his sight! And wilt thou dare to do that in My Sight, which thou wouldest not dare if a man were to look on thee? Hast thou greater awe of the eyes of man than of God, the LORD, thy Judge, Who hath power to cast both body and soul into eternal fire?

MAN. Whither shall I go from Thy Spirit, and whither shall I flee from Thy Face, Who art present in my inmost self, and searchest my heart and my reins? But ah! why do I not live as it behoveth one who believes this? Alas, for the dulness of our heart! We act, and live, and speak, just as if Thou walkedst in the circuit of Heaven, and regardedst not our ways. I am afraid of my fellow-worm, a man like myself, and I fear not my GOD, the King of the Universe, the Judge of all the kings of the earth! Have mercy on me, JESU, Thou Son of David! And what is my desire but to see Thee,— to see, I say, that Thou art about me, yea, within me;

for Thou art not far from any one of us. God forbid, then, that I should not henceforth set Thee always before me, for Thou art on my right hand, that I may not be moved. O what great necessity is laid upon me to live well and holily, who am, at all times and in every place, in the sight of that Judge Who discerneth all things.

§ 8. *The regulation of the life or actions; and the care of our time.*

CHRIST. Take care, then, that all thy works be done decently and in order. The man who knows that some great one is an observer, nay, a censor of his actions, will take serious heed to do nothing confusedly and in disorder, lest he should be offensive in his eyes. How wilt thou act, then, seeing I behold all thy doings? In the first place lay out thy actions in a settled order, and, as far as thou canst, mark out for thyself each hour of the day. See what is to be done in each, and give thyself wholly to this one thing at its allotted time.

Dost thou marvel at this advice, as if it were too minute, and scrupulous? Know thou, that all things which are from God are well ordered. Knowest thou not how great a lover of order am I, Who have created all things in a certain order, weight, and measure? Verily Satan, Mine enemy, hateth order, and is the author of confusion; seeing that he is always looking towards that place where there is no order, but where eternal horror dwells. Hence, when thou art engaged in any pious exercise, it is none other than his craft which suggests to thee that other things are to be done and cared for, in order that he may withdraw thee from that. But do thou, as thou wouldest escape his snare, cleave closely to that one thing thou art about; cast off the thought of other things, or set it aside for awhile. Do every thing in its own time. Adapt thyself to thy several affairs. To those more serious and pressing matters, those which concern My glory and thine own salvation, devote, as they most justly demand, the better portion of thy time. Follow not the perverse and foolish conduct of many who bestow the greatest care on things of least account, and the least on those of greatest moment; who keep for My service the refuse of their time, when they shall have spent the better portion of it on the business of the world, and the cares of the flesh. O how unjustly do they estimate the real value of things! Hence confusion seizeth upon them; hence they reel to and fro, and stagger like a drunken man, and their wisdom is utterly taken from them.

But be not thou like unto them; rather do thou lay out thy affairs in a pious and wise order, seeking first the Kingdom of GOD and His righteousness; so shalt thou enjoy great peace of mind. For order is the parent of peace; it enables us to know, both what we ought to do, and when to do it; it restrains the flightiness of thought; it furthers and brings to perfection whatever we undertake; it prevents idleness; whilst the very course of time reminds thee of its proper employment, and each hour exacts its peculiar work.

MAN. True are Thy warnings, O LORD! and grateful are they to my mind. But how can I carry them into effect? Thou knowest, O LORD, how much of our time is, even against our will, snatched, as it were, from us by engagements, by business, by the visits of friends and converse with them, and other necessary duties of life. Moreover, Thou seest, O JESU! Thou seest how heavily this corruptible body weigheth down the soul, and the earthly tabernacle oppresses the mind that would meditate on heavenly things.

CHRIST. This it is which is so highly displeasing to Me, —that there are so few who are sensible of the preciousness of that time which I have granted to man to perfect repentance, to grow in grace, and attain to heavenly glory. Behold, the accepted time flieth away, never to be recalled, and no man layeth it to heart; the day of salvation passeth away, and no one takes blame to himself, that occasions of well-doing have perished, never to return.

But do thou avoid, as much as lieth in thee, the thieves of time—friends, vain talk, and trifling occupations,— and because the days are evil, redeem the time, and devote it to thy better friends, to Me and to thine own soul. Is My demand grievous and irksome? Consider how much time is given to the body, to food, to sleep, to recreation, to conversation, to festive meetings and the like; and wilt thou not give the very smallest portion of it to GOD, to thy soul, to eternity? O how lavish men are of their time, when they would serve vanity! how sparing, when they are to be employed in piety, to which all time is justly due!

This too I exhort thee, My son. Be not employed in many matters; lest, being distracted amid manifold things, thou be not equal to each. He who falls somewhat short of active pursuits shall find wisdom. For the bed of thine heart is but narrow, and the scanty coverlet cannot enfold both. The worldly-wise know well, that no one overwhelmed with occupation can attain to a sound judgment. How shalt thou, then, entangled by a multitude of affairs, attain unto true piety? Look upon men of business. O couldest thou search their inmost hearts, thou wouldest see how miserably they are torn to pieces, as it were, by briars and thorns; and how in the midst of so many cares and toils their spirit is by degrees exhausted, their affections dried up, and all relish for holy things gradually and insensibly destroyed. This is the way to hardness of heart; thence they pass on to aversion; and at length into contempt and perdition. What marvel? Strangers have devoured their strength, and they knew it not.

If thou wouldest gain wisdom from the mishap of another, (which is indeed the part of a wise man,) give good heed and consider that I am GOD, Alone, above all things, worthy of thy service. What wilt thou be advantaged, if neglecting Me, thou art troubled about many things, and with the loss of thy soul shouldest gain the whole world? Be it, thou art called to a life of labour, and thou canst not entirely disengage thyself from business. I too will not, that thou shouldest be wanting to the duties of thy calling. Only take good heed that thy occupations be useful, honest, and necessary. Thus thou wilt discover that thou art wanting to time, rather than that time is wanting to thee. At least let thy soul turn oftener to its rest, and consider to whom thou art most indebted. Surely it is to the LORD, Who, above all others, has conferred benefits upon thee.

Once at least every day, therefore, go up with Moses into the Mount, that thou mayest hold converse with Me. Withdraw awhile from the crowd, and enter into thy closet, and take refuge, as it were, from the tempest in the haven of quietude; and when thou hast shut thy door, speak unto Me in secret, and I will there, as in a solitary place, speak to thy heart about the things which belong to thy peace. Behold Judith also, that devout heroine; she had an oratory in the upper part of the house, into which she was wont daily to enter, together with her handmaidens, for prayer. Thinkest thou this was a hindrance to her counsels and her affairs? No man was so prudent or so successful as she; none of the leaders of the people brought such help and safety to all that region.

Needest thou some profitable exercise in this daily retreat; it will readily occur to thee, when thou shalt have begun to hold more converse with Me, and less with the world. Behold now, pray, read. When thou prayest, thou speakest unto Me; when thou readest books of piety, I am speaking unto thee; and what can be more honourable, what more profitable, what more pleasant to man?

MAN. O how small a thing is it, O LORD, that Thou demandest of us! All the time of our life, indeed, is due to Thee Alone. For there is not a moment of our time in which we are not in the enjoyment of Thy benefits; there ought to be none also free from our praise and grateful memory of Thee. O that I might do what Thou hast taught us, that my whole day might pass away amid Thy ordering. O that I might so far heed others as never to forget Thee; and prefer above my chief joy the love of Thy glory and of the heavenly Jerusalem.

§ 9. *A Guide of life; or a spiritual instructor.*

CHRIST. Take heed, that thou be not wise in thine own eyes; for so shalt thou easily come to ruin. Woe to him that is alone; for when he falleth, he hath not another to help him up. Discourse with the wise about the affairs of thy soul. There is none so wise, but that he sometimes needeth the counsel of one that hath more wisdom than himself. A wise man will hear and will increase wisdom; but he that hateth reproof is brutish.

O how many doth self-love deceive! how many are blind in their own cause, who yet have too keen eyes in the things of others! Behold David. Who more holy, or dearer to Me, than he? But he fell and sinned grievously, and yet (although he could inflict a severe sentence enough on him who took the poor man's lamb) he did not acknowledge his sin till he was openly rebuked by My servant Nathan. Even My servant Moses, although I spake with him face to face, listened with good will and profitably to the counsel of Jethro his father-in-law, a heathen man. So did Paul attend humbly to Ananias; the eunuch of Queen Candace to Philip; the centurion Cornelius to Peter.

Do thou also take unto thyself a faithful guide of life; one who is not ignorant of the devices of Satan; whom thou mayest consult in doubtful matters; to whom thou mayest lay open the secrets of thy heart, and whose guidance thou mayest safely follow. And though he prophesy unto thee true and hard rather than soft and smooth things, yet hate him not. Better are the wounds of a friend than the deceitful smiles of the flatterer. Take heed that thou follow not them who love iniquity, and hate their own souls; and so, having itching ears, seek out for themselves smooth teachers, and turn away their ears from the truth. Take heed, I say, and trust not those who speak to thee only smooth things; who say peace and there is no peace. Doth not the physician destroy the sick man whom he spareth? Thus they who pronounce thee happy are they who deceive thee.

Consider well, therefore, to whom thou entrustest thy soul. If thou wert about to travel on a strange road and in the darkness of night, wouldest thou choose a guide ignorant of the way? If thou wert afflicted with some dangerous disorder, wouldest thou have an ignorant and unskilful physician? or a compliant one who by indulging might destroy thee? No one commits the care of his horse or his cattle except to one experienced and trustworthy; and thinkest thou it is of little moment to whom thou entrustest thy soul? Lastly, to him wilt thou safely commit thy soul, who knows how to take care of his own. If the blind lead the blind, shall they not both fall into the ditch? And to whom will he be good who is evil to himself?

MAN. It is of man to err and to be deceived. I confess it, O LORD. O that Thou wouldst provide for me a guide that hath a zeal for GOD according to knowledge, fitted to instruct me in the spirit of gentleness and meekness; who seeks not his own things, but the things which are JESUS CHRIST's; who, in fine, out of love to Thee and to his neighbours, would not spare me, that Thou, O LORD, mayest spare both. Let the righteous smite me in pity, and reprove me; but let not the oil of the flatterer anoint my head. And in him I shall hear not so much man, as Thee speaking in him. For truth, whencesoever it cometh, is from Thee, Who art the Primal Truth.

§ 10. *Daily Self-examination.*

CHRIST. There is yet one thing which must be the object of daily serious attention, or the labour in other respects will be lost. And this is the daily examination of conscience; which is of such vast importance that, without it, it is vain to hope for the continuance of a pious and spiritual life, or for any solid growth in grace. For since the knowledge of sin is the first step towards salvation, how can a man entertain any serious thoughts about amendment of life, compunction of spirit, or progress in piety, who cares not ever to discover his own faults? How shall he be anxious to obtain pardon and remission of his sins from Me, who knows not in what he has offended? How can he seek to be healed, who knows not his disease? Nay, he flattereth himself that he is every whit whole, and is pleased with himself as if he were a good man and had done no evil: he saith, I am rich and have need of nothing; and knoweth not that he is wretched and miserable and poor and blind and naked.

O man! wouldest thou but look within thee, thou wouldest be displeased with thyself, and thou wouldest please Me; but because thou knowest not thyself, thou art pleased with thyself and displeasest Me. How many know many things, but know not themselves! Whereas all is vain which profiteth not for eternity. How many are busied about others and the things of others, and neglect themselves! But let what will come of others, do thou, My servant, if thou wouldest be wise, before all things incline thy heart to My ways, and have compassion on thy soul; than which nothing in this life can be dearer to thee or more precious; of which if thou shouldest suffer the loss, and yet gain the whole world, what would it profit thee?

MAN. Alas, O LORD, in many things we offend all. But who can understand his errors? Yea truly, if we say that we have no sin, we deceive ourselves and the truth is not in us. O how great is the dulness of our hearts, that we examine not our ways whether our hearts condemn us! But having the conscience seared, we dissemble our offences, as a people that had done righteousness, and care little to make progress in the ways of the LORD.

CHRIST. If ye will judge yourselves, surely ye shall not be judged. But if ye shrink from self-scrutiny, shall ye not undergo a severer judgment? Wherefore if, perchance, in the course of the day, ye say anything in your hearts, if ye purpose, or in spirit do, anything that is evil, (for out of the heart proceeds all wickedness,) I exhort you, for these things be ye pricked in heart, bemoan and repent of them, when, withdrawn from the crowd and noise of the world, ye go into your closets, and are about to compose your bodies to rest.

O how little do they consult for themselves, who drag out the whole day in toil and business and care and turmoil, and then, wearied and drowsy, hurry to their beds, and find it burdensome to employ the very smallest portion of time in prayer and self-inspection. What shall I say of those who rise up early in the morning that they may follow strong drink; that continue until night till wine inflame them; that close the day with feastings and banquetings, with sports and jests and idle tales, and then, like the sottish Holofernes, oppressed with sleep and wine, or even as the very beasts, lie stretched upon their beds? O fools! what if this very night death should seize upon you? Whither would your miserable souls be hurried? Will not the tree, as it falleth, so remain? What if they wake no more out of that sleep? Will they find aught of their wealth in their hands? What if these wretches, still reeking with their excess, should be placed before their Judge? O how fearful will it be for such to fall into the hands of the living GOD! O consider this, ye that forget GOD, lest He tear you in pieces and there be none to deliver you.

MAN. Lighten mine eyes, O Lord, that I sleep not in death: lest mine enemy say, I have prevailed against him. It is, I confess, more the life of beasts than of men thus to close and thus to begin the day in forgetfulness of GOD, without Whom we cannot, for one moment, live or move or have our being. Grant unto me that I may never climb up into my bed, nor suffer mine eyes to sleep nor mine eyelids to slumber, before that, in bitterness of my soul, I shall have retraced in thought the day that has passed: and so, with an humble and contrite heart, which Thou wilt not despise, being reconciled unto Thee, I may lay me down in peace and take my rest.

CHRIST. Do this, O man, and live. Examine thyself daily, especially at eventide, with seriousness and strictness; summon, as to the Judgment-seat, the words, the deeds, the thoughts of the whole day. Review thy offences, both what thou hast done, and what thou hast left undone. Enquire strictly what pains thou hast taken to reduce to practice the saving monitions which I have hitherto given thee; and whereinsoever thou shalt discover that thou hast offended, take blame to thyself, and heartily grieve for it: appoint to thyself some punishment; make good resolves for the ensuing day; seek grace from Me to this end; but above all give thanks for the favours thou hast on that day received. Finally, commend thy body and soul to Me. Thus shalt thou sleep in security.

But, on the other hand, great is the boldness, nay dangerous the rashness, to lie down to sleep with a conscience laden with sins, and without reconciliation with

Me, Who am offended at them. Add to all this, that unless thou practise this examination daily—and that not lightly and superficially, but diligently and deeply, thou wilt stick fast in the same filth of sin; during months, nay during many years, the same vices will live in thee, and even acquire strength; they will so far prevail, that at length thou wilt have no power to expel them; seeing that thou hast neglected to root out, with the harrow of discipline and daily examination, those thorns and briars, which the earth that is nigh unto cursing, the corrupt nature, from time to time bringeth forth to thee.

MAN. I will give thanks unto Thee, O LORD, at all times; Thy praise shall be ever in my mouth. Blessed art Thou, O LORD, Who hast taught me from my youth up; O forsake me not in mine old age when I am grey-headed. O that my ways were made so direct that I might keep all the precepts I have now heard from Thee; lest being a servant that knew his Lord's will but did it not, I deserve to be beaten with many stripes.

CHAPTER II.

VARIOUS EXERCISES UPON THE LORD'S PRAYER.

I.—STEPS TOWARDS PERFECTION, ACCORDING TO THE ORDER OF THE LORD'S PRAYER.

§ 1. THE LOVE OF GOD; HIS OMNIPRESENCE; AND THE REVERENCE DUE TO HIM.

Our Father which art in Heaven.

Thou dwellest in the heavens as on the throne of Thy Glory; but Thou knowest the depths afar off, and Thou lookest searchingly upon all our ways; for Thine Eyes are brighter than the sun. From the throne of Thy Majesty Thou beholdest in every place both the wicked and the good; but upon Thy beloved children Thou lookest with special favour and loving-kindness. Grant unto me, I beseech Thee, what Thou commandest, that I may love Thee, and walk before Thee; that I may also fear Thee, not as the criminal his judge, but as a child his father; and may I study to be perfect, even as Thou, my Heavenly Father, art perfect!

§ 2. PURE INTENTION, OR ZEAL FOR THE GLORY OF GOD.

Hallowed be Thy Name.

This, O Good JESU! do I earnestly and above all things desire, that at Thy Name every knee should bow; that all things should be done, by me and by all, with an upright and pure intention to the glory of Thy Name; that Thou, O Most Holy Redeemer of the World! mayest be known and adored by all men. O that our light might glorify Thee our Father Who art in heaven!

§ 3. LOVING DESIRE AFTER HEAVENLY THINGS.

Thy Kingdom come.

We are strangers and pilgrims upon earth; yet to this end were we born, and, which is more, made after Thine own Image, yea, redeemed by Thy Blood, that we might be partakers of Thy kingdom (for we have here no continuing city, but we seek one to come); that seeking after the things which are above, not the things which are upon the earth, we may have our conversation in heaven. O that we sought first the kingdom of GOD and His righteousness! for about all other things, Thou, O LORD, makest us feel secure. What, indeed, should there be in the world, (which altogether lieth in the wicked one,) that could so delight me, as to make me unmindful of Thy Kingdom, where our desires shall be satisfied with all good? What could there be, which could separate me from Thee? Away with all the kingdoms of the world, and all the glory of them. One day in Thy Kingdom is better unto me than a thousand; verily, all other kingdoms are vain, transitory, and perishing; of Thy Kingdom alone shall there be no end.

§ 4. RESIGNATION; AND CONFORMITY TO THE DIVINE WILL.

Thy Will be done in earth, as it is in Heaven.

Be it, in every thing, done

by me, in me, and as to me, in respect of my body and my soul, and all that is mine. All the angels, all the elements, the sea and the winds, and all created things obey Thy Voice: how much more then should I, a worm of earth, but yet Thy servant, do Thy Will! O that Thy Will were my chief, my sole delight; as it is indeed my true bliss, to will what God willeth. For whom have I in heaven but Thee, and what is there on earth that I desire in comparison of thee, O GOD, Who art the Strength of my heart, and my Portion for ever?

§ 5. MODERATION IN THE USE OF THE CREATURES.

Give us this day our daily bread.

We ask not what may minister to our self-indulgence, but what may be sufficient for our necessities. The eyes of all wait on Thee, O LORD, and Thou givest them their meat in due season. Thou openest Thine Hand, and fillest every living thing with plenteousness. Lo! I also cast all my care upon Thee, since Thou carest for us. Give me but food that is needful for me; and grant that having food and raiment I may be therewith content; in every thing giving thanks unto Thee Who art the Giver of all things. O let me not abuse the abundance of Thy gifts to luxuriousness, excess, and idleness. O how many, when their corn and wine and oil have increased, have grown fat and waxen gross, and have forsaken GOD Which made them. Godliness with contentment shall be to me great gain.

§ 6. THE LOVE OF OUR NEIGHBOUR THROUGH OUR ENEMY.

And forgive us our trespasses, as we forgive them who trespass against us.

O how sweet is Thy Spirit, O LORD! Dost Thou thus teach us to pray? as though the measure of Thy grace and favour dependeth upon our conduct, and upon the affections of our heart towards our neighbour! O strange and wondrous form of prayer! And at the same time the pledge of Thy love! Behold, such as we are towards our neighbours, such wilt Thou be towards us. Shall I then be hard and unyielding in forgiving my neighbour, that I may find Thee the same? Nay, rather will I be slow to anger; neither shall the sun go down upon my wrath. Keep me, O LORD, from being implacable, revengeful, and mindful of a wrong, lest Thou also remember my old sins, and tear me in pieces in Thy wrath. Shall I not freely remit unto my neighbour one penny, that Thou also mayest remit unnumbered talents unto me? tion turn to my improvement, none to my ruin.

§ 7. FORTITUDE UNDER TEMPTATION.

And lead us not into temptation.

What is the life of man on earth but a temptation? Yet, suffer me not to be tempted above that I am able. I can do nothing without Thee; but by Thee all things, if Thy grace strengthen me. Grant that I may prevent the temptations of the flesh by mortification and avoiding occasions of sin. May I, being strong in faith, resist that roaring lion, that goeth about seeking whom he may devour! May I despise the judgment of the world! May I never for an instant prefer things temporal to things eternal! Let every tempta-

§ 8. ACKNOWLEDGMENT OF THE DIVINE PROVIDENCE.

But deliver us from evil.

For while we are thus striving to attain the heights of virtue, we are assailed on all sides by a multitude of evils; yet over them all Thy Divine Providence has sovereign sway. To this Thy prophet beareth witness, when he saith, *Shall there be evil in the city and the* LORD *hath not done it?* the evil, that is, of punishment, such as war, famine, sickness, poverty, and the like. That we may not pervert these into the evil of sin, we do most earnestly beseech Thee. For this would be the greatest of all evils; whereas they will not be evil to us, if they do not separate us from Thee, the Chief Good. To Thy power, Thy wisdom, and Thy goodness it belongeth, O LORD, so to direct those evils, that they may all work together for good to them that love Thee. For so great is Thy power, that Thou wouldest not permit any evil to exist, if Thou wert not able to bring out of it a greater good.

II.—THE LORD'S PRAYER ADAPTED TO THE THREE THEOLOGICAL AND THE FOUR CARDINAL VIRTUES, OR A METHOD IN WHICH THOSE SEVEN VIRTUES MAY BE SOUGHT AFTER AND EXERCISED IN THE SEVEN PETITIONS OF THE LORD'S PRAYER.

Our Father which art in Heaven.

O ETERNAL FATHER, Who hast prepared for Thy children an inheritance in the heavens, and blessings out of sight—(yet Thou ownest no degenerate sons, and requirest in Thy children lives worthy of such a Father, even of Thyself)—grant that we may study to be perfect, even as Thou, our Father, art perfect. We are not sufficient of ourselves, but all our sufficiency is of Thee. Therefore in the Name, yea, in the words of Thy Well-beloved Son, we ask for those graces and gifts without which we cannot please Thee, nor attain to Thy Kingdom.

§ 1. FAITH.
Hallowed be Thy Name.

When GOD is worshipped with a true and living faith, then is His Name best hallowed. I believe, O LORD, that Thou art Almighty, infinitely Wise, and supremely Good; true and faithful to Thy promises, yea, Truth Itself. LORD, increase my faith; help Thou mine unbelief, that I may sanctify Thee in faithfulness and truth.

Marvellous are Thy works and Thy judgments, O LORD; yet are they true and righteous altogether. Thy Name is excellent in all the earth; and there is no word impossible with Thee. Thy testimonies are very sure; and therefore holiness becometh Thine House, the Church. For what can be more unseemly than to believe these things, and yet so to live as to deny by our deeds what we profess with the mouth, even the knowledge of Thee? Be this far from me. Rather may a lively faith rule in me, that by a life consistent with my belief I may sanctify Thy glorious Name for ever! For what good will the name of a Christian do me, apart from a Christian's life?

§ 2. HOPE.
Thy Kingdom come.

That kingdom which Thou

hast prepared for us from the foundation of the world. Of Thine infinite love, Thou hast made us heirs of Thy kingdom, even joint-heirs with Christ. I hope, therefore, to see the goodness of the LORD in the land of the living. For, O Thou boundless Goodness! dost Thou call me in so many ways, and couldest Thou reject me at last? Dost Thou invite and draw me, and wilt Thou suffer me utterly to fall by the way? In Thee, O LORD, have I trusted; I shall never be confounded. This hope is laid up in my bosom. This strengthens my heart, so that I shall not faint at any tribulations. For I believe that my REDEEMER liveth, and that He will fill me with joy with His countenance, when He shall bring me into His kingdom. O Hope! which maketh not ashamed! O what comfort in our difficulties is the expectation of so high a reward!

§ 3. LOVE.
Thy will be done.

Inflame my heart with the love of Thee, O most loving FATHER; and then to do Thy will and to obey Thy commandments will not be grievous to me. For to him that loveth, nothing is difficult, nothing is impossible; because love is as strong as death. O may love, fill and rule over my heart. For thence there will spring up and be cherished between Thee and me a likeness of character and an union of will, so that I may choose and refuse what Thou dost. My will could not henceforward rebel against Thine; but in thy law would be all my desire. What clearer mark can there be of true love and regard? He that hath Thy commandments and keepeth them, is it not he that loveth Thee? Of a truth, the manifestation of obedience is the proof of love.

§ 4. TEMPERANCE.
Give us this day our daily bread.

As the body is sustained by food, so is the mind by temperance; yea, sobriety and moderation are beneficial to both body and soul. Grant unto me, therefore, that with the curb of right reason I may guide myself in the use of the pleasures which pertain to this life, lest through sufeiting and gluttony my heart become sluggish, and the corruptible body, immersed in sensuality, press heavily on the spirit that would rise in meditation towards heavenly things. Rightly, then, do I beg that this good may be given unto me day by day; because the bait of pleasure lies concealed under almost all the creatures of which we make daily use, and lies in wait for us on every side.

§ 5. JUSTICE.

And forgive us our debt.

It is the office of justice to give unto every one his due. And what is it that we owe to our neighbour, but that we love another? that we bear each other's burdens, and to fulfil Thy law? in short, that we do unto others as we would they should do unto us? It is but just, moreover, that we who seek of Thee the remission of ten thousand talents, our far heavier debt, should not refuse to remit to our fellow-servant one hundred pence, his trifling debt to us. Give me, therefore, O Lord, a desire and a love for justice such as this; that I may not, through my neglect of it, fall into the hands of Thy justice. For if man harbour wrath against his fellow-man, how can he look for pity from Thee? Is it not just that with what measure he meteth, it should be measured to him again?

§ 6. FORTITUDE.

And lead us not into temptation.

The life of man lies open to divers temptations: yea, it is itself one entire temptation. Strengthen my heart, therefore, with the virtue of fortitude, that I may be neither drawn aside by prosperity, nor overwhelmed by adversity; and so I be separated from Thee. Thou knowest what should be my fortitude, that I may be able to resist. Surely thou, O Lord, art my strength, and my salvation. Have mercy on me, therefore, for I am weak. And they, moreover, that are mighty, have sought after my soul. O that Thou Who art mightier than they, Thou that art strong and mighty in battle, wouldest suddenly come upon them; then, indeed, shall not my heart be afraid; for Thou art with me. If GOD be for us, who can be against us? For Thou wilt not suffer us to be tempted above that we are able, but wilt, with the temptation, also make a way to escape.

§ 7. PRUDENCE.

But deliver us from evil. Amen.

He, Whom prudence guides, will readily escape from every ill—prudence, which is the sound judgment of active minds. Give me, therefore, O LORD, this virtue; that whatsoever I do, I may do it prudently, and in all things look to the end. For where prudence prevails, evils even work together for good; but where it is wanting, virtues themselves are changed into vice; even goods become evils. Grant, therefore, that I may not (as when the blind runneth headlong) stumble against or rush upon evil; but let Thine Eyelids go before my steps. Give me the simplicity of the dove; but, even before that, give me the

wisdom of the serpent; that as he by interposing his body wardeth off the blow from his head; so I may give my body and my limbs to the torture, rather than suffer injury to my soul; which of all evils is the greatest.

III.—METHOD OF SAYING THE LORD'S PRAYER, SO AS, BY INTERPOSING MEDITATION, TO EXCITE DEVOUT AFFECTIONS.

(From F. Christ. Mayer.)

Our Father.

O LORD of Heaven and Earth, Who, with Thine Only-begotten Son and the Holy Ghost, art of Infinite Majesty, Power, Wisdom, and Goodness, and art, therefore, worthy of infinite honour and love; Fountain of all good, from Whom, with assured trust, we may expect all the blessings of nature, of grace, and of glory.

1. *Hallowed be thy Name.*

Mayest Thou be sanctified, loved, glorified, by me and all Thy creatures, for all Thy perfections, Thy Power,

Wisdom, Goodness, Mercy, and Justice; for all Thy judgments and decrees, in respect to myself, all men and all things; for all Thy works of nature, grace glory; for all that Thou hast permitted; for all thy benefits in every possible way, for Thine own sake, infinitely above all things, now, ever, to all eternity, and beyond. O that Thou hadst been ever thus glorified by me and by all, and that Thou mayest henceforth, even for ever, be thus glorified and sanctified.

2. *Thy Kingdom come.*

O that Thou mayest absolutely reign in me and in all, now by Thy grace, hereafter by glory. O that my soul may seek above all things the kingdom of GOD, that it may savour and long for the things which are above, not the things which are on the earth. O that, weary of its present exile, where sin reigneth, where ambition, pride and the like hold sway, it may unceasingly pant after that blessed life, and the possession of the eternal kingdom. O that it had been ever thus; that from this moment it may henceforth be perfectly thus; that at length we may reign with Thee, and with all Thy saints to all eternity!

3. *Thy will be done,*

May Thy most holy will be done by me and by all pilgrims here below, in the perfect performance of Thy precepts, Thy counsels, and all Thy good pleasure; purely for Thine own sake, as exactly, readily, and constantly, all the days and moments of our life on earth, as it is done by the blessed, those who have attained, with an insatiable desire of pleasing Thee according to Thy good pleasure. O that we had all ever done this in mind, in heart, and in deed; and may it henceforth be done as Thou willest, with all possible perfection!

4. *Our daily Bread.*

All the gifts, as well bodily as spiritual, which are needful for the attainment of grace, perseverance, and glory, do Thou, of Thine infinite goodness, mercifully vouchsafe to bestow upon us;

this day, and all the days of our life, as it seemeth good to Thee. and for Thy great glory.

5. *And forgive us.*

Out of the boundless treasury of Thy Mercy pardon us all the sins we have committed in thought, word, deed, or by omission; all our ingratitude to Thee for Thy so many benefits; all the injuries we have done to Thee, or to our neighbours, as we also with our whole heart most fully forgive all, all their offences; (that being reconciled to our brethren, we too may, in our turn, the more readily find grace in Thine Eyes;) and that, both out of pure love to Thee Who art infinitely worthy of love, and with constant and unwearied effort even to the latest breath of life.

6. *And lead us not.*

Suffer us not at any time to yield to any temptations of the world, the flesh, or the devil; but grant us in Thy strength gloriously to triumph over all now, henceforth, at the hour of death; to the display of Thy greater glory of Thine infinite Power, Wisdom, and Goodness.

7. *But deliver us.*

Mercifully preserve and deliver us from all evils both of body and soul, present and to come; so far as they may let or retard us in the attainment of perfection, perseverance, and salvation, and in the promotion of Thy glory; that so we may, without hindrance, more perfectly love and glorify Thee in time, more blessedly hereafter in eternity: and that not so much for gain as for the increase of Thy glory.

Amen.

May what I ask be done, as Thou wilt, when Thou wilt, how Thou wilt, through Thy tender Mercy and the Merits of Thy Son. And I would that all these devout desires may be renewed by me and by all, if so it might be, out of pure and disinterested love of Thee, most intensely, as is pleasing in Thy sight, in every moment of the season of grace!

CHAPTER III.

A LITANY OF CHRISTIAN VIRTUES GATHERED OUT OF HOLY SCRIPTURE.

Lord, have mercy.
Christ, have mercy.
Lord, have mercy.
O Christ, hear us.
O Christ, graciously hear us.
O God, the Father, of heaven, have mercy upon us.
O God, the Son, Redeemer of the world,
O God, the Holy Ghost,
O Holy Trinity, One God,

Who didst create our first parents in original righteousness and innocence^a,
Who hadst respect unto Abel when he brought his offering in an excellent spirit of devotion^b,
Who didst save Noah in the ark from the deluge, being found righteous in the midst of a perverse generation^c,
Who madest Lot and Abraham illustrious by their praiseworthy hospitality^d,
Who didst adorn Abraham with wonderful obedience and faith^e,
Who didst promise unto Isaac and to his seed the blessing of all nations^f,
Who didst strengthen Jacob with wonderful confidence and patience in adversity^g,
Who didst endow Joseph with singular love of modesty and chastity^h,
Who didst declare Moses, the leader of Thy people, and the meekest of all men, to be most faithful in all Thine houseⁱ,

} Have mercy upon us.

^a Gen. i. ^b Gen. iv. ^c Gen. vii. ^d Gen. xviii. xix.
^e Gen. xxii. ^f Gen. xxvi. ^g Gen. xxix, &c. ^h Gen. xxxix.
ⁱ Num. xii.

Who didst inspire the same with signal love towards his neighbour, and with zeal for the welfare of his brethren [k],

Who didst put into the sons of Levi great zeal for the avenging of Thine honour [l],

Who didst appoint Samuel the Prophet, who loved justice and was free from all corruption of bribes, to be a Judge to Thy people [m],

Who didst raise on high King David, the man after Thine own Heart, for the praise of justice, mercifulness, and piety [n],

Who didst adorn Solomon with wondrous wisdom, peace, and glory, above all the kings of the earth [o],

Who didst endue Tobit with remarkable patience, and with compassion towards his neighbour [p],

Who didst ennoble Judith, a widow of singular chasteness and piety, with confidence in prayer, and with glorious greatness of soul [q],

Who didst by the faithfulness of Esther and Mordecai deliver Thy people from being wholly cut off [r],

Who didst give Job, a man of wonderful and rare endurance, to be unto us all a mirror and pattern of patience [s],

Who didst arm Elijah the Prophet with singular zeal and boldness of spirit, against the idolatrous and false prophets [t],

Who didst imbue King Josiah with holy ardour for Thy law and worship [u],

Who didst adorn the prophet Daniel with singular abstinence, sobriety, and wisdom [v],

Who didst cause the Three Children, on account of their confession of Thee, to enter boldly into the burning fiery furnace, and to come out thence unhurt [w],

} Have mercy upon us.

[k] Exod. xxxii. [l] Ibid. [m] 1 Sam. vii. xii. [n] 2 Sam xiii.
[o] 1 Kings iv. [p] Tobit ii. [q] Judith viii. [r] Esther viii.
[s] Job i. &c. [t] 1 Kings xviii. [u] 2 Chron. xxxiv.
[v] Dan. i. [w] Dan. iii.

Who didst arm Mattathias and Judas Maccabeus against their enemies, with singular zeal and with love of the laws and religion of their country[x],

Who didst keep the seven Maccabees, together with their mother, unsubdued in the midst of tortures[y],

Who didst choose Mary, that most highly-favoured Virgin, to be a most pure Spouse and Mother[z],

Who didst adorn the same with the gift of singular chastity, humility, obedience, and all virtues above all other Thine Elect[a],

Who didst wonderfully refresh with Thy Coming the aged Simeon, that just and devout man, waiting with longing desire for the redemption of Israel[b],

Who didst refresh with the sight of Thee, Anna, the daughter of Phanuel, who served Thee continually with fastings and prayers in the temple[c],

Who didst stir up the three Magi with great zeal to seek out and to worship the new-born King of heaven and earth[d],

Who, by the leading of a star, didst enlighten the same Magi with conspicuous faith, to recognise in the little Infant, the God-Man[e],

Who didst send John the Baptist, of marvellous abstinence and austerity of life, as Thy Forerunner and preacher of repentance[f],

Who madest him bold to reprove, with zeal and love of the truth, the crime of the impious king[g],

Who didst choose for Thy disciples and apostles, unlearned, poor, and simple men; and yet by them didst bring the whole world under Thy Gospel[h],

Who didst vouchsafe unto John, illustrious for the gift of purity, the privilege of singular love[i],

Who didst commend the faith of the Canaanitish woman, and her perseverance, when she besought Thee in prayer[k],

} Have mercy upon us.

[x] 1 Mac. ii. iii.   [y] 2 Mac. vii.   [z] Luke i.   [a] Ibid.
[b] Luke ii.   [c] Ibid.   [d] Matt. ii.   [e] Matt. ii.
[f] Matt. iii.   [g] Mark vi.   [h] Matt. iv.   [i] John xiii.
[k] Matt. xv.

Who didst manifest Thine approval of the Centurion's and the Ruler's faith, by miraculous cures[l],

Who didst extol with singular commendation the humility of the Publican[m],

Who by a miracle didst mark Thine approbation of the multitude who, during three days, maintained their desire to hear Thee[n],

Who, on the day of Pentecost, didst, by the fire of the Holy Ghost, confirm the hearts of Thine Apostles in the love of Thee[o],

} *Have mercy upon us.*

Be merciful unto us; spare us, O Lord.
Be merciful unto us. O Lord, deliver us.

That denying ungodliness, and worldly lusts, we may live soberly, righteously, and godly, in this present world[p],

That we may do good while we have time[q],

That we may walk worthy of the vocation wherewith we are called[r],

That, forbearing one another in love, we may endeavour to keep the unity of the Spirit in the bond of peace[s],

That we may be doers of the word, and not hearers only[t],

That having food and raiment, we may be therewith content[u],

That we may owe no man any thing, but to love one another[v],

That we may provide things honest, not only in the sight of God, but in the sight of all men[w],

That we may present our bodies a living sacrifice, holy, acceptable unto God, which is our reasonable service[x],

That we may recompense to no man evil for evil[y],

That by good works we may give all diligence to make our calling and election sure[z],

} *We beseech Thee to hear us.*

[l] Matt. viii. John iv.   [m] Luke xviii.   [n] Mark viii.
[o] Acts ii.   [p] Titus ii.   [q] Galat. vi.   [r] Ephes. iv.
[s] Ibid.   [t] James i.   [u] I Tim vi.   [v] Rom. xiii.
[w] Rom. xii.   [x] Ibid.   [y] Ibid.   [z] 2 Pet. i.

§ iv.]   ON THE PRACTICE OF VIRTUE.   43

That we be not weary in well-doing^a,
That we may rejoice in the LORD alway^b,
That before all things we may seek not our own, but the things which are JESUS CHRIST'S^c,
That we, who in word confess GOD, may not in works deny Him^d,
That whatsoever we do in word or deed, we may do all things to the glory of GOD^e,
That we may restore the erring in the spirit of meekness and gentleness^f,
That all we do may be done with charity^g,
That we may bear one another's burdens, and so fulfil the law of CHRIST^h,
That we receive not the grace of GOD in vainⁱ,
That, considering the conversation of the Saints, we may follow their faith and patience^k,
That, in our warfare for GOD, we may not entangle ourselves with the affairs of this life^l,
That in all things we may take the shield of faith, wherewith we may be able to quench all the fiery darts of the most wicked one^m,
That we may so run in the race of this life, that at length we may obtain the prizeⁿ,

⎫
⎬ We beseech Thee to hear us.
⎭

O LAMB OF GOD, That takest away the sins of the world Increase our faith.
O LAMB OF GOD, That takest away the sins of the world, Inspire us with hope.
O LAMB OF GOD, That takest away the sins of the world, Enkindle in us charity.
O CHRIST, hear us.
O CHRIST, hear us.
LORD, have mercy.
CHRIST, have mercy.
LORD, have mercy.
Our FATHER, &c.

^a Galat. vi. ^b Phil. iv. ^c Phil. ii. ^d Titus i.
^e Col. iii. 1 Cor. x. ^f Galat. vi. ^g 1 Cor. xvi.
^h Galat vi. ⁱ 2 Cor. vi. ^k Heb. xiii. ^l 2 Tim. ii.
^m Ephes. vi. ⁿ 1 Cor. ix.

LET US PRAY.

O GOD, Who makest all things to work together for good to them that love Thee, pour into our hearts such stedfast love to Thee, that our longings, which by Thy inspiration we conceive, may not be turned aside by any temptation.

O GOD, Who resistest the proud and givest grace unto the humble, grant unto us the virtue of true humility, which Thine Only Begotten set forth in Himself to His faithful servants; that we may never be lifted up so as to provoke Thine indignation against us, but rather, being subdued, may receive the gifts of Thy grace.

Burn, O LORD, our heart and reins with the fire of the HOLY GHOST; that we may serve Thee with a chaste body, and please Thee with a clean heart.

O GOD, Who by the endurance of Thine Only Begotten hast bruised the pride of the old enemy, grant to us, we beseech Thee, worthily to call to mind what He lovingly endured for us; that so, by His Example, we may patiently bear our adversities.

O GOD, Who justifiest the ungodly, and willest not the death of a sinner, we humbly beseech Thy Majesty, with Thy heavenly aid, graciously to protect us, Thy servants, who lean only on Thy mercy, and to keep us with Thy continual defence; that no temptation may ever separate us from Thee, but, that running unwearied the race of virtue, we may at length receive the Prize, through our LORD.

CHAPTER IV.

VERY PIOUS EXERCISES; OR, THE PRACTICE AND ACTS OF SUNDRY VIRTUES.

(From Ludovicus Palma, Clerk Regular.)

*** Other very devout and useful exercises of his thou hast in the first section.

I. *An act of compunction and hatred against sin.*

"Eschew evil for good; seek peace and ensue it."—Psalm xxxiv. 14.

I. *Contrition consists in the hearty detestation of all the sins we have committed, chiefly as having offended* GOD; *with a firm purpose of confessing them, and of sinning no more; together with the hope of pardon.*

O´ my GOD, and my Mercy! with true contrition I bend the knees of my heart, and with the deepest grief of mind humbly accuse myself, and before Thy Divine Majesty acknowledge my fault, confessing all my sins, and all the abominations which I have committed in the whole course of my life, by pride, by avarice, by sensuality, by envy, by gluttony, by anger, by sloth, and by all the wickednesses which flow from them; for, to my shame, I have been too much inclined and poured out among them. I most earnestly repent and grieve that I have sinned, not out of love to the reward promised to the righteous, of which I am not worthy; neither, again, out of fear of the punishments to be inflicted upon the wicked, of which I am every way most worthy; but on this account alone, that I have offended Thee, O my GOD! Who, of Thyself, art supremely good, and above all to be adored; yea, Who art Love Itself, Goodness Itself, Majesty Itself.

2. And for the great love which I owe to Thee, and which I bear towards Thee, O LORD, I hate, detest, and abominate sin, self-love, the inordinate love of the crea-

tures, and all else which might hinder me from being joined and united to Thee by the holy love of Thee.

Whereinsoever either in thought, word, or deed, whether through frailty, or ignorance, or wilfulness, I have sinned against Thee, my GOD, against my neighbour or myself, in whatsoever way, with the whole affections of my heart I confess it to be my fault, my most grievous fault. It repenteth me that I have sinned; and I mourn that at this hour I do not feel so great hatred of sin, nor have such deep grief, nor so ardent a desire to bewail the past, nor so firm a purpose to eschew all future sins, as I wish and ought to have, that it might answer to these my so great abominations.

3. Therefore, I beseech Thee, my GOD, accept that infinite hatred wherewith Thou Thyself hatest sin, to make up that which I ought to have, and in the place of that grief wherein I am lacking, I offer to Thee, O most Merciful FATHER, the sorrows of JESUS CHRIST, Thy SON, my REDEEMER, as well as the Sacrifice of His spotless Life, and that holy fervour and zeal which drew Him to that most ignominious and most bitter Death, in order that He might destroy sin.

4. Ah, JESU! my most compassionate Saviour! I fall down before the feet of Thy mercies, beseeching Thee, by that love which drew Thee down from heaven to the Virgin's Womb, that Thou wouldest apply to me the Merits of Thy most bitter Passion, and of that most precious Blood which Thou didst shed for sinners, of whom I am chief; and thus supply all that is lacking in me, and forgive me all my faults, sins, negligences, and ingratitude.

Grant, I beseech Thee, that all these things may henceforward be far from me; and although, through the frailty of my nature, I can never be wholly free from sin, yet, O Infinite Goodness! grant me at least this grace, that I may never sin mortally. This is indeed what Thou Thyself willest, desirest, askest for us, and commandest; give what Thou commandest, and command what Thou wilt.

Cause, O LORD, that from henceforth, in the stead of

those vices, holy virtues of every kind may be engraven in my soul, and all this to Thy glory and praise, now and ever, and through endless ages. Amen.

II. *An act of good resolve.*
" I have sworn and am stedfastly purposed, to keep Thy righteous judgments."—Psalm cxix. 106.

1. O most mighty GOD, I know, by the light of Thy grace, how greatly I am bound to do good works, and to follow after virtue; to decline from evil and to flee sin; therefore now, wholly distrusting self, and wholly trusting to and leaning on Thy holy grace, I purpose, and with the whole power of my free will, with most entire and deliberate consent, I resolve never more to commit sin, and infinitely to prefer, hourly to wear out my life, than grievously to offend Thee, my GOD; or to attempt to do, say, or think any thing that is contrary to Thy good pleasure; but to flee as a serpent all occasions of sin, and whatever is displeasing to Thee; forasmuch as whatsoever Thou willest, I will also, and hate whatsoever Thou hatest.

And if at any time it happen—O may it never be!—that I should do or leave undone any thing contrary to Thy will, I now protest beforehand, that whatever it be, it shall not be with my own mind and will, but from some malicious suggestion and sudden impulse, contrary to this my firm resolve. Do Thou, O LORD, grant that I may abide stedfast in this purpose, and that, allowing nothing of this sort to creep over me, I may by the aid of Thy grace be fully master of all the desires and motions of my heart.

Wherefore, I now freely renounce all consent to whatever is opposed to Thy will; and I entirely lay down all free will, whensoever I may be enticed to evil, and be in danger of offending Thee, or amid whatever tends to ill.

2. I further resolve for the future to keep most perfectly all Thy divine precepts, and the promises and vows which I made to Thee in Baptism, or at any other time; I will endeavour also, as far as I may, by the help of Thy grace, to imitate Thy most

holy Life, and to attain the habit of all those virtues which are most pleasing to Thee: in all things to perform Thy most righteous Will, and in all things to hold down my own, which is bent to evil; subjecting it, out of love to Thee, to all my superiors, equals, and inferiors; and, finally to walk in the way of perfection, by the help of all those means which Thou my Master, hast, in Thy holy Gospel, pointed out both by word and example.

3. Help me, therefore, O LORD; for without Thy special aid I am unable to follow out or to fulfil these my good resolves; give unto me a lively faith, strong and stedfast mind, that as Thou, of Thine own Nature, canst not sin, so I may, by Thy grace, be incapable of it.

4. Finally, I beseech Thee, that Thou wouldest deign by Thy judgment to accept and to approve of this declaration of my will; that all things may be and be done to Thy honour and glory, to the salvation of my soul, and of my neighbour, and agreeably to Thy most holy Will; to which I give up and devote myself, with my whole being, which Thou hast bestowed upon me. Amen.

III. *An act of humility and self-abasement.*

" He that humbleth himself shall be exalted."—Luke xvi. 11.

1. *Humility is that virtue which restrains us from the immoderate exaltation of self to the disparagement of another.*

And how shall I, a most vile worm of earth, when I see Thee, my GOD, humbled to the endurance of the most ignominious Death, through love of me, how, I say, shall I dare to lift up myself, and not rather hide myself beneath the earth? And yet I must acknowledge myself to be so proud and ungrateful, that I believe the creature is not to be found, which, if it had received such great grace, and so many blessings as I, would not have served Thee with far greater fervour of spirit than I. Yea, and because I do not acknowledge this truth from the heart, and as it really is, I confess myself to be most proud, and in truth more vile than all others; and so, by reason of my vanity and foolish pride, am deservedly execrable and hateful to Thee, my GOD.

2. Woe is me! my pride hath so blinded me that I cannot discover myself, nor see, O LORD, that the more gifts I receive from Thee, so much the more base is my ingratitude, and the more heinous my sins; and so much the more strict will be the account I must give up to Thee. Truly, therefore, am I a viler sinner than all others; and I believe that no one hath ever departed so far from Thee as I have by my offences. Yea, I believe that even the greatest sinners, if they had had the helps that I have received, would have returned to Thee with greater readiness, and would, perhaps for ever, and with greater sincerity of heart and affection, have loved and honoured Thee. Surely they would bewail their sins more deeply, and serve Thee more faithfully than I.

3. I am amazed, O LORD, how Thou canst endure the sight of me, Thy creature, who am so ungrateful to Thee. And therefore I count myself altogether unworthy to serve Thee, and that Thou shouldest hear my prayers; unworthy of all grace and heavenly inspirations; yea, most unworthy, because I look so little to Thy light, and therefore have long since wholly deserved to be cast away by Thee, and left in darkness and error; unworthy, moreover, because I am so disobedient and rebellious against Thee, though I dwell in the midst of Thy faithful ones, and in the house of Thy servants; from whom, would they treat me according to my deserts, I ought to hear nothing but contumely and reproach. Nay, it would be right to banish me far away from the society of all men, lest perchance I should infect any of them with the ulcerous corruption of my abominable vices.

4. I would, indeed, that my extreme worthlessness and wretchedness were known to all, that all might hold me in just abhorrence, and in their zeal for Thy glory treat me as I deserve.

5. I marvel, O LORD, at Thine inestimable kindness towards me, in that Thou hast hitherto borne with me, and hast not—as my most extreme ingratitude towards Thee merited—cast me down

into the lowest pit of hell. Yea, I acknowledge that, for my ingratitude, I alone among all Thy creatures am unworthy of Thy Divine care, providence, and love, wherewith Thou tendest them; and when I look in upon myself, I shudder as at a thing beyond expression base, odious, and abominable; and I beseech Thee, O Eternal Light, that I may know myself more and more, lest I should at any time perversely exalt myself above others.

O LORD, out of the lowest depths of misery do I cry, and call upon the abyss of Thy pity and love—grant me this grace. Amen.

IV. *An act of petition to God.*

"Whatsoever ye shall ask the FATHER in My Name, He will give it you."—John xvi. 23.

1. O my most gracious LORD and GOD, although I am Thine by creation, preservation, redemption, justification, special calling, and natural condition, I desire further to be, yea I am Thine, by the most special choice of my own free will; so that, for any grace, I cannot knock at any other gate than Thine, Thou Who art the Fount and Source of all good.

2. Neither ought I to desire, ask, or wish for aught from Thee, save that alone which is most pleasing to Thee, and most regards Thy glory; and if it chance at any time that my will should be moved with the desire of aught else, I now beforehand abominate and detest it, and will that it be not; and I pray Thy Divine Majesty, that Thou wouldest never hear me in such desires. Yea, to this end I ask first and chiefly, and with the utmost earnestness whereof I am capable, I beseech Thee, that Thy most perfect Will may be always done in me; and that my own will may have no weight whatever, so that nothing may henceforth be found in me which is not Thine Own.

Yet since my will cannot be altogether inactive, I wish that which way soever it may be borne, it may not be borne by itself only, but ever joined with Thine, O LORD, which Alone is holy and right. Thus by Thy grace do I desire, thus do I resolve with myself, thus do

I protest in the presence of Thy Heavenly Court.

3. Wherefore, O LORD, whensoever I ask any thing of Thee, I design to ask nothing except through Thy Son JESUS CHRIST, and in the union of my own poor will with His most holy desires. Therefore, gracious FATHER, though not my own desires, yet at least the gracious desires of Thy Son merit acceptance. Thus dost Thou show justice towards Him, mercy to me: and to Thine own Self Thou dost conciliate honour and glory. The Will of Thy most sweet SON, my GOD, willeth, desireth, demandeth that I be meek and lowly in heart, patient, kind, full of charity; it desireth that I live unto Thee, die unto myself. Grant, Gracious FATHER, unto Thy SON, that this His good and holy desire be fulfilled; for thus will Thine own Will be satisfied; and His honour, and the praise and glory of the whole Most Holy Trinity be enhanced.

4. O LORD, forasmuch as I am not able of myself to perform any thing that is good, grant unto me this grace, that I may allow Thee to do whatsoever Thou wilt; and that my doing may be to lie still in Thy Hand, that Thou mayest do with me that thing only which is most pleasing to Thee.

And that there may not be any thing in me offensive to Thee, do Thou adorn me with holy virtues, giving unto me the increase of faith, hope, and charity; humbleness of mind, purity of heart, and all those virtues, gifts, and graces which Thou knowest to be needful for me; and whatsoever of Thy grace Thou wouldest have to be in me, whether in body or soul; that so I may be able the better to please Thee, the more worthily and faithfully to serve Thee, and the more perfectly to love Thee.

I pray, moreover, that Thou wouldest give me grace to arrive at that degree of perfection, which from eternity Thou willest me to attain; and grant unto me, also, the aids, means, and dispositions needful for the attainment of the same.

5. Further, with all the earnestness of my soul, I entreat of Thee true contrition for my sins, and the full forgiveness of them; and that

Thou wouldest grant me for the time to come to choose to die ten thousand deaths in the body, rather than even once to die in my soul.

6. So good art Thou, most loving LORD; so dost Thou Thyself, of Thy mercy, excite me to pray, that I, dust and ashes, may presume to ask not only what Thou hast, but that also which Thou Thyself art. I, then, Thy lowest suppliant, beseech with all the humility of mind of which I am capable, that I may enjoy Thee Only and Alone; that in Thee Alone I may find ease and rest, and not in any gifts of Thine, however excellent, noble, precious, or divine.

7. I pray for the clearest enlightening of mind, chiefly for the knowledge of three things. First, that I may most perfectly, learn Thy good pleasure, and may entirely perform Thy most holy Will. Then, that I may know my own vileness, ingratitude, and unworthiness of all good. Finally, that I may have a perfect knowledge of all moral virtues, and may follow after them; so that the simple, pure, and sincere love of Thee, my God, may more and more prevail in me.

8. Lastly, I beseech Thee, that it may please Thee to accept my prayers, not as they come from me, but as inspired by Thee; and to unite them with the prayers of thy SON JESUS CHRIST, of His most holy Mother, of the holy Angels, Apostles, Martyrs, doctors, virgins, confessors, and of the whole Church as well triumphant as militant, for the attainment of all those graces and gifts, whether of soul or body, both for myself and my neighbour. Neither do Thou regard my person, O LORD, but the merits of JESUS CHRIST Thy SON, from Whom every just work and every holy desire doth proceed. All which, may it tend to the everlasting glory and honour of the All-Loveable, All-Adorable, All-Glorious Trinity. Amen.

V. *An act of renunciation of pleasures for the preservation of chastity.*

".... they neither marry nor are given in marriage, but are as the angels of GOD in heaven." —Matt. xxii. 30.

1. O GOD, most pure, and most worthy Possessor of the hearts of men, with the ut-

most willingness I give up unto Thee the entire possession and direct control of all that is mine, renouncing every earthly affection and sensual delight; so that if it were possible for me to enjoy all the pleasures and all the delights of sense and of the flesh which are commonly enjoyed and tasted by all men, and which they long after; and if I could indulge in them even without sin, nevertheless I would give them up with the utmost freedom of will, and most readily eschew them; as I do now renounce and eschew them, in order that I may the better please Thee, live to Thee more purely, and more conform myself to Thee.

2. Moreover, I repudiate not only all carnal pleasures whatever, but also all delights which spring from the senses; such as those of the eyes, that they may not look on those objects which appear beautiful, delightful, or curious to the sight, or on any created thing which may affect them.

Thus also I renounce every other delight which my senses may take in any of the creatures, and this I desire with my whole heart, in order to take the greater delight in Thee, and to become more pleasing to Thee. For when I shall have broken through the meshes of all enticements, and have cleansed my heart from every earthly taste and delight, then will it the more readily conform itself to Thee, and be at one with Thy Heart, O my most Sweet JESU! and thus shall I be able to enjoy Thy Blessed Countenance, even as thou hast said, *Blessed are the pure in heart, for they shall see God.* Extinguish, therefore, in me, O LORD, and utterly root out every lust of the flesh and of the senses.

3. Yea, that I may the better serve and please Thee, and may love Thee more purely, I not only renounce all the above delights, pleasures, and enjoyments, but I also resolve not anxiously to long after even those of the spirit, save in so far as they may excite in me a loathing of what is sensual, and may lead me onward so as to find my whole delight, pleasure, and comfort in Thee Alone, and in the good pleasure of Thy most holy Will. Amen.

VI. *An act of renunciation of temporal goods out of an affection for poverty.*

"Whosoever he be of you that forsaketh not all that he hath he cannot be My disciple." —Luke xiv. 33.

1. KING of kings and LORD of lords, my GOD, my consolation aboundeth exceedingly, and my heart singeth for joy, when I consider that Thou art the Absolute LORD of all things, and, among them all, even of me the last and least of all. Wherefore I would not belong to aught but Thee, neither would I possess or have aught as my good and treasure but Thee; so that if the possession and lordship of the whole world were offered to me, with all its wealth, splendour, and power, I would on the instant reject it, even as at this present moment I do voluntarily and freely reject it; nor it alone, but all other things also which the heart of man can wish for in this life; and that from love to Thee Alone.

2. And though I have renounced all things, lest some one in particular should hold down my soul, I profess, O LORD, that if it should be Thy Will that I should now be stripped of the garment I am clothed withal, and be deprived of all comforts, I would bear it with a calm spirit, that I might be the more conformed to Thee, Who didst hang naked on the Cross for me, and that in my bareness I might be the more pleasing to Thee, O LORD JESU!

If I should be driven away and shut out from the home in which I dwell, and it should be more pleasing unto Thee, O LORD, that I should dwell with wild beasts in the woods, or have my habitation in any other mean place, I would be content.

3. If I should ever be deprived of the better kinds of food and fruits of the earth, and should have nothing to support my life beyond a hard crust of coarse bread and water, I will be content therewith, yea, give thanks for it, forasmuch as, on account of my manifold sins, I am not worthy even of that. O LORD, imprint this truth on my mind; help me, and suffer me not to take the very faintest pleasure in those vain goods of the world, or in any created thing, however choice or

precious. But may all my good, my treasure, and my wealth, be in Thee, and may my heart rest in Thee Alone. Amen.

VII. *An act of the renunciation of our own will, from a principle of obedience.*

"If any man will come after Me. let him deny himself, and take up his cross daily, and follow Me."—Luke ix. 28.

1. Ruler and Prime Mover of the Universe, Whom all things obey, GOD of Infinite Majesty, my heart burneth with desire whenever I think with myself (and very frequently do I so think) how I may be able to please Thee, and to conform myself in all things to Thy good pleasure. And therefore willingly and freely do I now offer and make over my whole self to Thee; and especially my own will, the free possession of which I give up and resign to Thee; seeing that I have nothing, save this, in my own power. This, therefore, in and by all things, with the most full exercise of holy obedience do I submit to Thy most holy Will, utterly renouncing with firm resolve, and with all my power, my own free choice and will.

2. And in reliance on Thy grace, I purpose ever to obey Thee in every thing, as well in what is difficult as what is easy; embracing anew and most freely accepting all Thy holy precepts, and, as far as the nature of my calling and office may admit of it, Thy counsels also; desiring that they may be a constant guide, and lantern unto my feet, and a light unto my paths. May Thy words be sweet unto my throat, and the fulfilment of them above honey and the honey-comb. May Thy Will be as a crown upon my head; and to do whatsoever Thou, O my GOD, vouchsafest to command or to persuade, be as a collar of gold about my neck. I would that my will should never hereafter in the slightest degree rebel against Thee, but ever be most exactly conformed to Thine, so that even a single opposing thought or motion may be to me a grief and a torment.

3. Out of love to Thee, also, do I submit my will to all my superiors, in all those matters which are agreeable to Thy divine law, or not expressly contrary to it. However difficult and irk-

some may be their commands, I propose, nevertheless, with Thy help, promptly to obey them.

4. Ah, LORD, take, O take from me at least utterly my own will; let there no longer be any mark or trace of it in me, but let all mine be Thine. Burn it out and reduce it to ashes with the fire and glow of Thy love; that, all evil being wholly taken away and consumed, I may at length come out altogether pure and pleasing unto Thee. Amen.

VIII. *An aspiration of the mind towards God.*

"I opened my mouth and drew in my breath."—Psalm cxix. 131.

1. O my GOD! for that unmeasured love wherewith Thou ever encompassest me, would that I could love Thee in return, even as Thou dost merit and oughtest to be loved.

2. O my LORD! Thou GOD of Love, Infinite Goodness, I would, that as in Thee and by Thee I live, and move, and have my being, so my whole life, action, and being, may turn to Thy honour and glory.

3. O FATHER of mercies! make me, I pray Thee, such as Thy Son hath merited, and Thy Holy Spirit desireth me to be.

4. I desire to love Thee, O LORD, because Thou art supremely good; to be careful about myself for no other reason than because I am Thine, and because the preservation of myself belongeth to Thy honour. And therefore I protest that all the care which I may hereafter take of myself shall not be as of what is mine, but Thine; that is, I will love myself not for my own sake but for Thine.

5. May this be pleasing to Thee, my GOD; and do Thou accept it, O LORD, for the love of Thy most Beloved Son, JESUS CHRIST my REDEEMER, in Whom Thou art well pleased.

IX. *Acts to be drawn forth out of any good we hear or see of a neighbour.*

"I am a companion of all them that fear Thee, and keep Thy commandments,—Psalm cxix. 63.

1. O LORD, my GOD, when I hear and see that my neighbour, and in particular that [N.], is obedient to Thee, and performs or designs any good thing, I re-

§ iv.]   ON THE PRACTICE OF VIRTUE.   57

joice and joy therein exceedingly. His good I count as my own, and I offer and present it to Thee as mine, together with all the good deeds which all Thy saints have heretofore performed, and which they still perform in this life to Thy eternal glory, just as if I myself had done and were now doing them.

2. I give thanks unto Thee, O LORD, for the good thoughts and for the aid which thou hast vouchsafed to this person as well as to all other my neighbours, and which Thou dost still vouchsafe, so that they may do, speak, and think what is good; and I thank Thee for this, just as if the same favour had been manifested to my own soul.

3. I, moreover, enter and throw myself into the very heart of this person, and of all Thy servants and handmaidens, that together with them I may, from the heart, do all that they do or desire to do, in Thy worship and service. For Thou knowest, O LORD, that I will altogether perform the same, if Thou willest I should do so, and wouldest grant me grace, strength, opportunity, and power to do it. May I never suffer myself to be deterred by any difficulty or any fear from performing it.

4. Increase in him, O LORD, I earnestly beseech Thee, all good, grace, and worth, with every virtue which he, by Thy inspiration, desireth, or which Thou knowest him to need; that whatever service he performeth pleasing unto Thee, may be yet more pleasing, and may be offered with greater perfection.

5. Finally, O LORD, I beseech Thee to grant that whosoever shall see such good in him, may be kindled by his example to meditate the like, and set hmself to accomplish it, according to the purpose of Thy will, and to Thy greater service and glory. Amen.

X. *Acts to be drawn forth out of any evil we hear or see in our neighbour.*

" With what judgment ye judge, ye shall be judged: and with what measure ye mete, it shall be measured to you again."- Matt. vii. 2.

1. O LORD, of Infinite Perfection, whensoever I hear or see any evil of my neighbour, especially spi-

ritual, I greatly sorrow for human frailty, common though it be to all; and chiefly do I sorrow over the failings of [N.]. Nevertheless I do not believe that that evil is so great as it appears to me, or as it is said to be; nay, perchance, it may be no evil at all; and may not appear to Thy most clear Sight such as it does to our erring eyes. Yet, O LORD, Searcher of our hearts, if there be any fault, I deeply grieve for the fall of my brother; and yet more for the offence done to Thee.

2. In behalf of his failure, and in satisfaction of the offence to Thee, I offer unto Thee the Precious Blood of JESUS CHRIST, Thy SON, Who was so greatly humbled and bruised for our iniquities. I set before Thee His love, His clemency, and long-suffering amidst our continued failings.

3. But, alas! I myself have done the very same, or given Thee no less offence in some like way. Woe is me! Yea, I should have offended Thee still more grievously, had not Thy grace preserved me. Wherefore with my whole heart do I give thanks to Thee for the help afforded me without any desire of mine.

4. I know well, O LORD, that out of any evil Thou art able to draw forth greater good, otherwise Thou wouldest not have permitted evil. Let this fault, therefore, turn out to Thy greater glory, and to the greater humility and self-knowledge of him who hath sinned.

5. Lastly, close up, I beseech Thee, the eyes of all, lest they should thence derive boldness to commit the like. Restrain their tongues by the remorse of conscience, that they take not occasion therefrom to speak evil, and that out of one lesser failing through human infirmity, many others spring not forth through human wickedness and want of charity.

XI. *Acts of charity to be drawn out of every thing, good or evil.*

"All things work together for good to them that love God."— Rom. viii. 28.

1. O most kind Lord, I delight greatly, not only in all that love which all just and holy men in this world bear to Thee, but much more in that wherewith Thou art

embraced, as well by those who, freed from the body and tarrying in the outskirts of the heavenly kingdom, are most earnestly longing for Thy Face, as by those, both men and angels, who, admitted into the inmost abodes of bliss, enjoy the full Vision of Thee.

2. O could I love Thee with all that ardour with which all they do love Thee, how cheerfully and gladly would I offer it! But since I cannot, I rejoice that they, at least, do so who better can. And I desire that they may ever do so more and more, and continue throughout eternity in that same love, according to Thy Good Pleasure.

3. And, again, O LORD, I am greatly displeased and grieve, that very many other of Thy servants love Thee so carelessly, and that many, for thy love, requite Thee with injuries. I beseech Thee, O LORD, of Thine infinite Goodness, forgive them, and grant them thy grace, whereby they may amend themselves, and may even now begin to love Thee above all things, and in all things to perform Thy most holy Will.

4. But what shall I say of those who, formed by Thee after Thine own image and likeness, and endowed with countless blessings, yet, infidels and ungodly, do not even acknowledge Thee, Whom above all things they ought to love. O what deep grief, what floods of tears, ought this to call forth in me, O LORD, Who art to be loved most highly! Would that I could have all their hearts and wills in my power, that I might inflame them with the love of Thee! Behold, O LORD, I offer them all to Thee, cleansed, in my design at least, from all their sins, such as I would they were, and Thou canst make them, pure and holy, to Thy honour and glory.

O how vast would be my happiness, could I supply their defect, by exercising towards Thee those acts of love which it behoveth them to exercise; could I supply the failures not of them alone, but of the bad angels also, and of lost souls, who, in the stead of love and praise, burn with accursed hatred and rage against Thee, far worse than with the flames of hell. But since I fail, even for my own part, sufficiently to love and praise Thee, I supply in desire at least, both my own default and that of others, as far as, and in the way which, best I can.

5. Meanwhile it yieldeth me great comfort to know that Thy Divine Majesty, by an infinite exercise of Its own will, both satisfieth for all, and also fulfilleth all the duties of love; since with an Infinite Love Thou dost love Thyself. Wherefore I greatly rejoice; and, with all humility, do I set before Thee this love, and offer it both for myself, and in stead of all those also who omit to do it, O GOD, my Love, my Chief, and only Good!

A prayer of S. Thomas Aqinas, very profitable for the attainment of many and great virtues.

Grant to me, I beseech Thee, O Almighty and Merciful GOD, ardently to desire, prudently to search out, truthfully to acknowledge, and perfectly to fulfil, whatsoever is pleasing to Thee.

Order my condition to the praise and glory of Thy Name; and what Thou requirest me to do, grant that I may know, be able, and will: and grant me grace to do it as I ought, and as may further my salvation.

Let my way to Thee be, I beseech Thee, safe, right onward and perfect; not faltering either in prosperity or adversity, not lifted up by prosperity or depressed by adversity. In prosperity may I give Thee thanks; in adversity preserve patience. Let me not rejoice or grieve at any thing, save as it leadeth to Thee, or from Thee. May I seek to please no one, and fear to displease no one, save Thee.

Grant that I may do all things in charity; and whatsoever appertaineth not to Thy service, to count as dead. Grant that I may not perform my actions out of custom, but refer them to Thee with devotion.

May all passing things be valueless in my sight for the sake of Thee; and all that is Thine precious to me, and Thou, my God, more than all. May all labour be sweet unto me, which is for Thee: and all rest wearisome, which is not in Thee.

Grant unto me, O most sweet LORD, frequently and fervently to lift up my heart unto Thee, and where insoever I fail, to make amends by sorrow, with full purpose of correcting it.

O my GOD, make me humble without feignedness, cheerful without relaxedness, grave without dejection, sober-minded without heaviness, active without lightness, truthful without double-mindedness, fearful without despair, hopeful in Thee without presumption, chaste without any taint, reprove my neighbour without displeasure, and build him up both by word and example without elation, be obedient without gainsaying, patient without murmuring.

Give me, O most sweet JESUS, an ever-watchful heart, which no restless imagination may ever lead away from Thee; stedfast, which no unworthy affection may draw down from Thee; dauntless, which no tribulation may tire out; free, which no vehement pleasure may make its own; upright, which no sinister intention may turn aside.

Vouchsafe to me, O my most sweet GOD, an understanding to know Thee, diligence to seek Thee, wisdom to find Thee, a conversation well-pleasing unto Thee, perseverance sweetly and trustfully awaiting Thee, trustfulness which shall blessedly embrace Thee; grant me to be nailed to Thy Pains through penitence; to use Thy blessings on the way through grace; and at length, in our heavenly home, to enter into Thy joys in glory; Who with the FATHER and the HOLY GHOST livest and reignest, &c.

CHAPTER V.

OTHER EXERCISES ON THE PRINCIPAL VIRTUES.
From "The Way of Eternal Life."

1. *An exercise of lively faith.*

O Truth! O Goodness! Who both here and every where art most present with me, I believe on Thee; and I profess before Thy whole Court, that these things [N.], and whatsoever else hath been written, done, and said by Thee, are most sure, and that they are profitable for my instruction; and that I have no excuse if I believe them not, and show it not by Thy grace in works.

Thou art All-Mighty, All-Wise, All-Good, and shall I not believe Thee? And shall I not embrace these [N.] testimonies of Thy will? They are, indeed, entirely to be believed, and altogether lovely, whether I listen to reason and the wise, or look into the nature of things. O that I had ever hearkened unto Thee, and had never offended Thee, Who art all Good! O that I had honoured Thee by my life, and had shown forth my faith by my patience!

But henceforth, even for ever, I will believe in Thee, and love Thee, in deed and in truth. Do with me for ever, what seemeth good to Thee; and I, by Thy grace, will, from my inmost love for Thee, do what I know to be Thy Will; and whatsoever Thou hast revealed for my salvation, that will I embrace, and all Thou willest, O Thou my Life, and All my Good. Amen.

2. *An exercise of hope.*

Thou knowest, O my GOD, Thou knowest, that of ourselves we are not sufficient to do any thing, as neither this [N.], as of ourselves. Therefore do I, dust and ashes, flee unto Thee, that by Thee, and though patience and comfort of the Scriptures, I may have hope, and, hoping in Thee, may not be confounded. For dost Thou, Who art Goodness, thus [N.] call me, and couldest Thou cast me out? Dost Thou thus invite me to follow Thee, and draw me unto Thee, and wilt Thou suffer me to faint in the way?

Hoping in Thee, O LORD, I know I shall never be confounded, although I find a law in my members warring against the law of my mind, and am unworthy of Thy grace. But since Thou hast given Thy Body and Blood for my price, and art ready to give Thyself to me, this day, for a pledge of salvation; and since Thou hast prevented me with so many blessings [N.], and hast so often commanded us to ask and promised to give, Thou, O Goodness, O Truth, wilt surely give me that which I shall ask, that I may hope in Thee with my whole heart. Although Thou shouldest slay me, O my Hope and my Life, yet will I hope in Thee; yea, though the hosts of this world and of all vanity should rise up against me, yet shall it be my portion to keep Thy law, and to follow Thee. For whither shall we go from Thee, O Good JESU? Art not Thou my Life? Hast not Thou the words of eternal life?

3. *An exercise of charity.*

O Charity, O my God, give me understanding, and I shall learn Thy commandments, whether Thou speakest by epistle or by Thy creatures unto my heart. For whatsoever I learn to my salvation, Thou, ever most present with me, teachest me with most inward love, ·O my Health and Medicine of my soul! And how great the love wherewith Thou teachest me, who am nothing before Thee! Dost Thou need my goods, that Thou shouldest with such free love present me with so many good things, and with Thy charity?

For Thou, O Eternal FATHER, so lovedst the world as to give Thine Only-begotten SON. So didst Thou love me, O most merciful JESU, Son of GOD, as to give Thy Life unto death for me. And can Thy commands and Thy counsels be grievous unto me? I will love Thee, then, O GOD my strength! O how good is it for me to hold me fast by Thee!

What, then, shall be able to separate me from Thy charity? Can tribulation, or distress, or famine, or nakedness, or peril, or persecution, or the sword? For Thy love is strong as death; and many waters, so I trust, shall not be able to quench Thy Charity; that fire, that is, which Thou camest to send on the earth, and which Thou willest earnestly to be enkindled. Amen.

4. *An exercise for the love of our neighbour.*

O Charity, O my GOD, I believe on Thee, and I hope in Thee, and with my whole heart I love Thee, and my neighbour for Thy sake,

For by this shall all men know that we are Thy disciples, if we have love one towards another.

This, Thou saidst, is a commandment like unto the greatest. For he that loveth his neighbour hath truly fulfilled the law; and he that loveth not, abideth in death. If then we ought, above all things, constantly to have mutual charity among ourselves, I will, from henceforth even for ever, to cherish this virtue above all things, and to be Thy disciple; to judge no one; to sadden no one by word or deed; but to solace, to help, to be forward to honour all men, to love all men in Thee, and to do to all men, even to the lowest, what I would do to Thee, O most loving JESU!

For Thou hast said, "A new commandment I give unto you, that ye love one another as I have loved you." Since, therefore, Thou didst deign to lay down Thy life for us, yea, for me, so ought I also, and so do I desire, not only to give up wealth or convenience, but to lay down my life also for my brethren.

But give me, O JESU! to love, not in word and in tongue, but in deed and in truth; that whatsoever I would that men should do unto me, that I may do unto them; or rather, unto Thee; for with what measure I mete, Thou wilt measure to me again, and wilt give Thyself to me, Who art my Hope, my Refuge, and my Salvation.

5. *An exercise of spiritual joy.*

What joy have I in this wilderness, O my GOD, save Thee Who art all Good? But alas! afar off art Thou, although near and within me, and I see Thee as through a glass, darkly. What or what manner of joy then can I have while I sit in this darkness, and see not Thy light, O Sun of Righteousness? Yet, nevertheless, I will greatly rejoice in the LORD, yea, I will be joyful in GOD my JESUS, since after darkness I hope for light.

O that my heart and my flesh may rejoice in Thee, the Living GOD. For even in this vale of tears I meet on all sides with causes for joy. For every creature serveth me, and the heavens declare Thy glory, and speak to me of Thy Love.

I see the walls of the heavenly Jerusalem placed before my eyes, that I may not forget Thee nor my home. May my tongue cleave to the roof of my mouth, if I do not remember Thee. Thou, LORD, hast made me glad through Thy works, and I will rejoice in the operations of Thy Hands.

And whereas I read it written, "Delight thou in the LORD, and He shall give thee thy heart's desire,"—wilt Thou not give me mine, even to joy in Thee, my LORD, and exult in Thy glory, and that to Thee every knee doth bow? O that I may so joy, as stedfastly to put back from me the joys of this life and enjoy Thee; and endure unweariedly all weariness, and whatsoever shall seem good to Thee. For 1 am Thine; and as the hart desireth the water-brooks, so longeth my soul after Thee, O GOD!

6. *An exercise for trust under perils.*

Behold, O GOD our Defender, and be Thou my stay and my refuge; for I believe in Thee, O LORD, and I hope in Thee, and with my whole heart I love Thee. O my GOD, be not Thou far from me; my GOD, look upon me and help me; lo! the purchase of Thy Blood, I am standing in a slippery place, and surrounded on all sides with snares and pits for my soul; oh! draw me forth with the cords of Thy love!

O, who will give me wings like a dove, that I may flee away and fail not; that, by Thy grace, I may follow Thee, my Shepherd, and cleave unto Thee with my whole heart!

This poor man is left unto Thee, O JESU! O Father of mercies, without Whom I can do nothing, I beseech Thee be Thou a guardian and helper to me an orphan; for Thou art my GOD, my only Hope, my Protector, the Horn also of my salvation, and my Refuge. Amen.

7. *An exercise of gratitude towards* GOD.

I will give thanks unto Thee, O LORD, with my whole heart; I will tell of all Thy wondrous works. For Thy knowledge is too wonderful for me, because of Thy mercy towards me. For whence is this to me, that Thou shouldest remember me, and brevent me with so many [N.] plessings of goodness, and of Thy most loving charity?

May my tongue cleave to the roof of my mouth, if I do not remember Thee as my Chief Joy. For Thou art most Mighty, I a vapour, yea, nothing; Thou art most Wise, yea, Light itself, I darkness and ignorance; Thou art Goodness Itself, my righteousness is as filthy rags; and yet Thou bestowest these things [N.] upon me, and Thou openest Thine Hand unto me, and fillest me with all blessing.

Wherefore my heart is inditing a good matter, and I devote my works and my whole self to Thee, that Thou mayest do Thy will with me in good things or in evil, in time and for eternity. I give myself up to Thee, Who gavest Thyself for me. I give myself in return to Thee, that Thou mayest live in me, and I die unto Thee, and love Thee with my whole heart. Amen.

8. *Another exercise of gratitude for* God's *unnumbered blessings.*

What shall I render unto Thee, O my God, for all the benefits Thou hast done unto me, heart, body, and soul? For I believe in Thee, I hope in Thee, and truly with my whole heart I love Thee.

Behold, I will pay my vows to Thee, my Lord, in the presence of all Thy people, and I have hope that Thou, Who hast given me the beginnings of these desires wilt enable me also to perform them.

Thy many blessings assure me of this; Thy Body and Thy Blood, and, above all, Thy Love, are pledges to me that Thou wilt not leave me nor forsake me. Let the people praise Thee, `O God, yea, let all the people praise Thee.

O let my mouth be filled with Thy praise, that I may sing of Thy glory and honour all the day long. I will bless Thee, O Lord, at all times, and that not with my lips only, but by my life. O that my light may so shine before men, that they may see my good works, and glorify Thee Who art in heaven. Amen.

9. *An exercise for the grace of resignation.*

O Christ Jesu! my Refuge, my LORD, I believe and hope in Thee, and with my whole heart I love Thee. And as in Thee we live, and move, and are, to Thee will I live, and move, and be, from this moment even for ever.

For whom have I in heaven but Thee? and there is nothing on earth that I desire in comparison of Thee. If there be any thing, I renounce it with my whole heart, that I may love Thee with my whole soul. Yea, truly, what can we miserable beings, wish for out of Thee, who in Thee Alone have all things?

Behold, Thou hast set before mé in this thing [N.] water and fire, death and life, sorrows and joys, hopes and fears; what shall I desire, what dread? Towards what shall I stretch forth my hand? I know not my going out or my coming in. O JESU! I know not; Thou knowest: do with me what pleaseth Thee; Thine am I with my whole heart.

My times are in Thy hands. In death or in life I will lift up mine eyes unto Thee. I will stretch forth my hands towards Thy holy place. I will bless Thee, O LORD, for ever and ever.

O Thou, my Only Hope, CHRIST JESU, my GOD, Thy Will be done as in heaven so in earth. Be that done, be that done, not what I will, but what thou wilt. Behold, I am as it were a beast before Thee; yet am I always with Thee; therefore, henceforth, even for ever, do I cast all my care upon Thee, both on public and on private matters; for I know that Thou, O GOD, Most Highest, hast a care for both; yea, even for me also. Although Thou knowest me and my nothingness, keep me, I beseech Thee, for Thine own sake, as the apple of Thine Eye; hide me under the shadow of Thy wings.

And since there is no evil in the city which Thou, O most loving LORD, hast not done, whereof should I complain? Let Thy will, Thy will be done! And since there is no good thing but from Thee, to whom shall I look but unto Thee? I will wait in silence for Thy salvation, O my GOD, and I will love Thee with my whole heart. Amen.

10. *An exercise for the grace of humility.*

Thou commandest me, Good Master, to learn of Thee, that I may be meek and lowly in heart. But whence, I pray Thee, should I, who am a vapour, yea, a nothing, who know not whether I be worthy of hatred or of love, deceive myself? If I am nothing, if I have nothing which I have not received, and all is Thine, to whom can I prefer myself? Every good gift and every perfect gift is from above, and cometh down from the Father of lights. And thanks be to GOD, thanks be to GOD, thanks be to GOD, I see what I am, where I am, of what sort I am. Where, alas, may I be this day? What shall I, or what might I, do this day? Of myself, all evil; and, if any good, through Thee. For we are not sufficient of ourselves to do any thing as of ourselves, but our sufficiency is of Thee, and all our works Thou hast wrought in us.

Shall the axe, then, boast itself against him that heweth therewith? and that, before Thee, O GOD Most Highest, Who exaltest the lowly and despisest the proud, even the angels, in the imagination of their hearts, and pullest down every haughty one. I desire, therefore, by Thy grace, to lie down with Thee in the lowest place, to complain of no one (for Thou doest all things justly), to envy no one; for of Thee, and in Thee, and by Thee, are all things, O GOD of my heart and my All.

11. *An exercise for the contempt of earthly things.*

O Eternal Wisdom! O Truth! O Good Master! Who hast uttered things hidden from the foundation of the world, grant unto me, to be of the same mind with Thee, to speak as Thou. I would call them blessed whom Thou callest blessed, and who are ever with Thee, as The Saints and Elect, the poor, namely, and the meek, the patient, and the peacemakers.

Grant that I may think of the world and the lust thereof, as Thou, my GOD, dost think of it. Doth not every thing that is, pass away like a ship, a flower, a bird, a stream, like smoke and vapour? For what and where are they now, who since the world have been, or from of old, were in this place, city, and country? Where, then, will they, too, shortly be, who now are? Passed away are those of old, and their trace is no where to be found; pass away will these also.

Vanity of vanities, all is vanity. I know, I know; and Thou art the only Truth, the only Goodness; which I love above all things, for which I resign all things. For what profiteth it me, or any man, to gain the whole world and lose one's own soul? What profiteth it?

For truly the eye is not satisfied with seeing, nor the ear filled with hearing, nor the soul with all these things of earth; for all things without us are commonly in us by knowledge only; nay, the mind reposes in the thoughts of things as much as in the things themselves; and my heart cannot find rest in any thing, unless it repose on Thee.

Why, then, do I run in vain? Why do I beat the air? Why do I seek the judgment of any man, or respect his sentence? With me it is a very small thing that I should be judged by any one, or of man's judgment.

What need, then, have I to seek after other things with which I cannot be filled? and which, if I shall have first sought Thee, Thou wilt freely add unto me. They err, then, who trust in vanity and speak lies; they conceive mischief and bring forth iniquity; they hatch cockatrice's eggs and weave the spider's web. Since Thou hast said, Whosoever he be that forsaketh not all that he hath, he cannot be My disciple, I renounce all things, and cleave unto Thee, my GOD, my sole Good. Amen.

12. *An exercise for poverty.*

O King of kings and LORD of lords! Who art here present with me, and sustainest me every where, hast Thou not truly said, Blessed are the poor in spirit? O certain truth! And I am unwilling to be blessed, and to have Thy kingdom, and be like unto Thee, my King and my GOD, and hereafter to sit with Thee, and with Thee judge. Truly Thou hast chosen the poor in this world, and Thou art wont to hearken unto the desire of the poor.

Choose me, then, and hearken unto me; for lo, for Thy sake, do I sincerely and with my whole heart renounce, in inclination at least, all things small or great, that I may, hereafter, be able to say, Lo! we have forsaken all things and have followed Thee; what shall we have therefore? What? Treasure exceeding great in heaven. And what is that? Thou Thyself, most loving JESU! for Thou art my Treasure, in Whom is all my heart and all my desire.

Naked came I out of my mother's womb, and naked shall I return thither; and, bared of all, do I long to follow Thee, O JESUS, bared of all; to be perfect and sell all, that in Thee, both here and for ever, I may find an hundredfold, yea, All. Amen.

13. *An exercise for obedience.*

Thou didst humble Thyself, O LORD, my GOD and my King, and didst become obedient unto Death, even the Death of the Cross, that I might learn of Thee, to be meek and lowly in heart. And shall I not follow Thee Who thus invitest me? Shall I not listen to Thee Who sayest, Whosoever heareth you, heareth Me; and whosoever despiseth you, despiseth Me?

I will follow Thee by grace. Surely to obey is better than sacrifice, and to hearken than the fat of rams; for rebellion is as the sin of witchcraft, and stubbornness is as iniquity and idolatry. Therefore, by Thy grace I will, for Thy sake, be subject to every creature, especially to my superiors, whether good or froward. And I will freely sacrifice myself to Thee, Who wast offered up for my sins and bruised for my iniquities, that in no one thing may my own will be found.

Nor will I ask, as neither did Abraham, wherefore Thou enjoinest me anything; for Thou art eternal Wisdom, and I, a child, who know not my coming in or going out. Thou art Goodness Infinite, and vouchsafest to care for me, as if I were the only living being; and I know that he that is obedient shall discourse of victories.

What is it, then, O LORD

JESU, my REDEEMER, that Thou wouldest have me to do? My heart is ready, my heart is ready. Give what Thou commandest, and command what Thou wilt to Thy servant, the son of Thy handmaid. For I am come to do Thy will, my GOD; I have willed, and do will, that Thy law shall be in the midst of my heart. Amen.

14. *An exercise for chastity.*

O JESU CHRIST, Son of the Virgin, most Beloved of my soul, Whose Eyes behold me in every place, blessed indeed are the pure in heart, truly blessed are they, for they shall see Thee. This is all my wish and all my desire.

I have heard Thy preacher say, "He that loveth pureness of heart, for the grace of his lips, the king shall be his friend." I therefore love it, that Thou, most loving LORD, mayest be my Friend, Who hast given me grace to receive that word, which all receive not; viz., that I should not marry, but, as an angel of GOD, should care only for the things that are the LORD's; that my soul being wholly fair, and without spot or wrinkle, may hereafter be worthy to hear that word, Come, come, from Lebanon, My sister, My spouse; come, thou shalt be crowned.

But forasmuch as I know that I can no otherwise be continent, than as Thou, O GOD, dost give me to be so, I beseech Thee, by the bowels of Thy Mercy, to keep my soul, for I am holy; that I may shun those occasions, and that conversation [N.], and may, with the utmost diligence, guard my senses, that I may escape that flame which devoureth even unto death; but let the fire of Thy love consume me, that fire which Thou wouldest earnestly have kindled. Amen.

15. *An exercise for patience.*

I hear Thee, O most Patient JESU, and I see Thee as most Present with me, a man of sorrows and acquainted with grief; I hear Thee saying, both by precept and by example, that in patience I should possess my soul; he that would come after Me, let him take up his cross and follow Me.

I desire, therefore, to take up the cross and to follow

Thee. For I learn that Thou wilt not suffer me to be tempted above that I am able. Thou knowest my strength, the burden of the beast, such as I am with Thee. And I know that good and evil, poverty and fair station, are of Thee, my GOD; neither is there evil in the city which the LORD hath not done. And if we have received good at Thy Hand, wherefore should we not endure evil?

I will bear Thine anger, O LORD, for I have sinned against Thee. I will count it all joy, as Thy Apostle exhorteth me, when I fall into divers temptations; and I will think upon Thee, O most loving JESU, Who, for me, didst endure such contradiction against Thyself, that my patience, being much more precious than gold, may be found to the praise and glory of Thy Name, Who hast suffered so many and such great things for me, that Thou mightest enter into Thy glory. And I hope that this [N.] our light affliction, which is but for a moment, may work out for us a far more exceeding and eternal weight of glory. Amen.

16. *An exercise for abstinence.*

O Eternal Wisdom! must not both our ears still tingle with that first command of Thine which Thou gavest to the first man in his innocence, In the day that thou eatest, thou shalt surely die? And would we still hearken unto our Eve, and give place to this our worst enemy, and obey our belly as a god? would we eat, yet never be satisfied with the swine-husks? The righteous eateth and satisfieth his soul; but the belly of the wicked is insatiable.

Is not every one that striveth for the mastery temperate in all things? Now they do it to obtain a corruptible crown, but we an incorruptible.

For the love of Thee, therefore, Who for me didst hunger forty days, and wast athirst, and wert, on the Cross, given gall mingled with vinegar to drink, I will not, for vile meat, for a momentary pleasure, destroy Thy work, O my GOD: but if it be Thy will, I will gladly follow Thee, O LORD, with the Nazarites; I will drink neither wine nor strong drink, wherein is excess; but I desire with Daniel and Elias, with John and with all Thy Saints, to live soberly, righteously, and godly, and to look for that blessed hope and Thy glorious Appearing, O GOD, my Fulness, my All, my only True Good. Amen.

17. *An exercise for the renewal of fervour of spirit.*

O LORD JESU! my King and my GOD, Thou, for me, didst endure hardships from Thy very Childhood. All Thine Elect bear the burden and heat of the day. Sun, stars, elements, and all Thy creatures serve me, that I may serve Thee. What do not the children of this world do for the most worthless goods? How do they sweat and torment themselves for the vapour of honour, for the shadow of pleasure! And shall I, Thy servant, bought at so rich a price, hired at so high a reward, shall I stand all the day idle? No; I will rather with joy take Thy easy yoke, Thy light burden; I will carry it and glorify Thee in my body; and, by Thy grace, whatsoever my hand is able to do, that will I do earnestly for Thee, Who thus workest all in all for me; and so hast Thou wrought out salvation for me in the midst of the earth. For he that soweth sparingly shall reap also sparingly; but if we be not weary in well doing, O how abundantly shall we reap in due season, and bring in our sheaves with joy! Then shall we be satisfied with the plenteousness of Thy house, and eat bread in Thy Kingdom for ever, if in this brief moment of life we eat bread in the sweat of our brow, and seize on Thy kingdom by violence.

Why, then, should my slack hand procure poverty for me, whereas the hand of the diligent maketh him rich? I hear one saying, He that gathereth in summer is a wise son, but he that sleepeth in harvest is a son that causeth shame. Behold, now is the acceptable time, and the season of harvest this present life; now are the days of salvation, in which we may bind together many sheaves of virtues and of Thy grace; the winter cometh, in which no man can work. Death tarrieth not; and time flies away never to be recalled. Grant unto me, that, ever mindful of these things, I may give diligence by good works to make my calling and election sure;

lest I grow lukewarm, and Thou spue me out of Thy mouth.

18. *An exercise for the mortification of curiosity.*

O LORD JESU CHRIST! in Whom are hidden all the treasures of Wisdom and Knowledge, O that I knew Thee, that I knew myself! O that I knew Thy Will! For that knowledge alone sufficeth me, by which I may be for ever wise unto salvation, and know Thee, see Thee, and in Thee possess all things; and this the more, and the more perfectly, the less a vain curiosity shall have here distracted me amid diverse things. One thing is needful; and this is life eternal; to know Thee Alone.

Are these things true? Do I believe them with a living faith? do I live, think, speak, and act before Thee as if I believed them? And do I hope in Thee, O my only Hope? and do I love Thee, O Infinite Goodness, here most intimately present with me?

LORD, I believe; help Thou mine unbelief. In Thee Alone do I hope, and I know I shall not be confounded. Vanity of vanities; yea, all things are vanity; and as, from love to Thee, I grieve above all things that I have offended Thee, so with my whole heart do I love Thee above all things. And what is there that can yet separate me from Thee? O JESUS! O my Life! O most endearing Charity! O GOD of my heart, and my All! Why then, O my soul, should I seek to pry into things too deep and too mighty for me? Why should I turn mine eyes unto vanity, and not rather unto Thee, O JESU, in Whom Alone is our salvation? But, alas! the uncultured soil of our heart, through our neglect, brings forth only thorns and briers; our soul, finding no rest in itself, is forced to wander forth abroad; slothful to look into itself, carelessness of self makes it curious as to all besides. And yet all wisdom, knowledge, experience is vain, which profiteth not for eternity. What is it all, then, but vexation of the spirit, which cannot be satisfied, nor rest in any creature but in Thee Alone, in Whom are all things? O happy soul! to whom Thou Alone art all things, who in Thee seeth all

, things, and from Thee receiveth, and to Thee directeth all things, O God of my heart, and my All!

19. *An exercise for peace and tranquillity of mind: to be frequently used by the devout soul.*

For the peace of GOD *passeth all understanding.*

I know, O LORD JESU! Who art most Present with me, that Thy Abode is in peace. Thou Alone, our Peace, art my Centre and Rest, and all my Good. What, then, do I any more wish or hope for, beside Thee? What can I fear or grieve for, out of Thee? Thou art my Love; Thou art my Fear.

O my LORD, abide with me, I beseech Thee, and in Thee let my soul find rest, and let it delight itself in Thee; for what is there that can be compared with that peace which is in Thee, seeing that it passeth all understanding; and better than a continual feast is that repose and quiet of the spirit in whom Thou dwellest.

Be it far from me, LORD, that this thing [N.] should trouble me; that I should seek this or grieve for that out of Thee. Nothing can bring me any good if I lack Thy peace. And what can I lack if I have thee, Who art all Good? Why for these briers and filth [N.] should I lose Thee, Thou Chief Good of man,—Thee, the Peace of my soul? Let the children of this world keep to themselves what they list. But I will joy in Thee, yea, I will rejoice in GOD my JESUS! and Thou, I hope and pray most humbly, wilt disperse this cloud of vanity, and show me the light of thy Will, and wilt cause Thy peace and serenity to fill and gladden my heart. Had I all things, should not I without Thee be nothing, and amidst all have nothing? And ought I not to renounce all, if I would be Thy disciple? To what end, then, should I have them, if with them I cannot have Thee? if they take away or diminish my only true good, even the peace of my soul? And yet for this very end, that the heart may rest in them, are these things sought and searched after: but whoever found that rest? Verily, the heart is ever restless, until it rest in Thee Alone. It, which can contain the Highest Good, can never be filled or satisfied with aught that is less than Thee.

This I know; this I believe; this all past ages, all creatures proclaim.

Why, then, do I not reject that lesser good? Why do I shut out that evil, which, while it is far off, and, as it were, without the walls, by its very look and bearing as an enemy, disturbs my soul? Be this far from me, O LORD; turn this away from Thy servant, whose peace and all whose good is to rest in Thy Will. Thou knowest all which, public or private, is for the glory of Thy Name, and for my salvation. But I, seeing that I have it not, what should I hope or fear, whereat should I grieve or be glad, but as is Thy Will?

And truly whatever happeneth, nothing I know will be, not a hair fall from my head, nor a leaf from a tree, nor a grain of sand be moved, without Thy Providence. Wherefore I ought neither to wonder nor to complain at any event; for Thy Will is lone, and shall be done: yea, and mine too, because I have so often yielded it up to Thee, as I now, too, yield it, Whose I wholly am, as all besides. Wherefore I most humbly pray that Thou, O Eternal Wisdom! wilt never do any thing, or permit it to be done, according to my foolish will. May all things be to me rather according to Thy word and good pleasure. Let Thy will alone be that most favouring gale, by whose breath, amid the countless waves of this present life, I may be borne safely into the haven of salvation and of a blessed eternity. Amen.

20. *An exercise respecting the right use of worldly goods: most profitable for the rich in this world; in order that the " Woe unto you that are rich" may be changed into the blessedness of the poor.*

Read, O ye rich, and understand.

O most gracious GOD, Whose is the earth and the fulness thereof, Who needest not our goods, but dost so largely communicate to us Thy good things, I acknowledge that from Thy bounteous Hand I too have received all these good things.

But are they, in truth, good things? O Good Jesu! Thou Eternal Truth, tell me, I beseech Thee. For This word of thine pierces and torments me, *Woe*, Thou sayest, *Woe unto you that are rich, for ye have received your consolation;* and Thou testifiest that that rich man had in his life-time received his good things, but was at length buried in hell.

Can we, then, boast ourselves in these good things, and call them happy who possess them, when Thou, Eternal Truth, hast denounced a *woe* against them? Moreover Thou addest, *Verily, I say unto you, that a rich man shall hardly enter into the kingdom of heaven:* and again, *It is easier for a camel to go through the eye of a needle, than for a rich man to enter into the kingdom of heaven.*

Are these things true? Yea, most true, for they are the words of Eternal Truth. How then can we call these things good, and strive to procure them with so much care and toil? Is it that they will make the possessors of them good, and so the more pleasing to Thee, the Chief Good? But I learn that Thou hast chosen, not the rich but the poor in this world. Again, *He that maketh haste to be rich shall not be innocent.* And again, *They that will be rich fall into temptation and a snare, and into many foolish and hurtful lusts, which drown men in destruction and perdition.*

But, perchance, they may help us to serve Thee with greater ease. Yet I hear Thee say, *Ye cannot serve God and Mammon.* And again, *He that loveth gold shall not be justified. For there is nothing worse than the love of money.* And, *Blessed is the man that hath not gone after gold, nor placed his hope in the treasures of money.* Thou hast declared, moreover, *Blessed are the poor in spirit, for theirs is the kingdom of heaven.*

O Voice of the Lord, that breaketh the cedars and discovereth the thick bushes! do I believe this, O my God? Do I in truth believe Thee, O Eternal Truth? Ah! wretched man that I am, whom a few fleeting goods, lent for a short moment, bring into such peril, that through them I may be separated from Thee, the Chief Good, and plunged into perdition and the extremity of woe!

What shall I do unto Thee, O Thou Preserver of men? Wherefore hast Thou put me in so slippery a place and condition? What shall I do, that, through temporal goods, I lose not those which are eternal? Thou hast commanded, that if riches increase, I should not set my heart upon them; that I should not be high-minded; that I should honour Thee with my substance, yea rather, with Thine own; for I brought nothing into this world, neither can I carry any thing out. I am Thy steward; but, alas! when Thou comest to take account with Thy servants, how shall I be found faithful?

I am in a strait on every side. But behold! I know what I will do. Rather than perish eternally, I will give up every thing for Thee; and Thou wilt give me back things far better. Strait is the gate, and narrow is the way. Rather than be shut out from Thee, I will most freely lay aside all things, or rather, I will lay them up with Thee. For I know that Thou art able to keep that which I have committed unto Thee, Who reservest Thyself for me, O my GOD and my All!

Thou, O Eternal Truth, hast said, not only to those who lead a monastic life, but to every Christian, *Whosoever he be that*, in heart at least, *forsaketh not all that he hath, he cannot be My disciple.*

I, therefore, give up all things, and most humbly beseech Thee by the bowels of Thy mercy, that I may be able to be Thy disciple, O LORD, our Salvation and our Life! Thou hast no pleasure in the perdition and death of any one: take from me, therefore, the lust of the eyes; and accept this my desire, by which in heart I renounce all things, prepared to do so in deed also, rather than offend Thee; and to be poor with Lazarus rather than rich with him who fared sumptuously every day.

With good will, then, do I offer to Thee my heart and all that is mine; that is, Thine. Dispose of them as it preaseth Thee; for if they be Thine, as in truth they are, I am unjust if I claim to myself what is Thine by right.

Be it then, that violence

of man, or waste of war, or malice of Satan, or injuries of seasons, or any other calamity deprive me of them, 1 will look unto Thee Alone; with Job I will say in patience and humility, *the* LORD *gave, and the* LORD *hath taken away; blessed be the Name of the* LORD.

If a poor man, or rather Thou Thyself by a poor man, ask assistance of me, I will freely give it, for Thou askest back Thine own; and yet such is Thy love, Thou promisest an hundredfold. Can I distrust Thee, and can I ever send any from me sorrowful and unrelieved? Never! and this I purpose before Thee and Thy heavenly Court.

Further, whatsoever, either by reason, or by the counsel of the wise, or by Thy inspiration, I may learn to be for Thy greater glory (not mine), that I am ready to do. What must once be forsaken at death, that, through love of Thee, I do now in heart forsake. What must be lost, I willingly now lose; that they may be laid up for Thee, and so for me with Thee. I now renounce all things, that I may be Thy disciple.

If the world cannot understand this, since its portion is to lay up treasure here, join house to house, aggrandize families, live in splendour, walk in state, seek a great name; may I at least, by Thy grace, long to be amongst Thy disciples and faithful stewards, as one soon to give up an account of my stewardship, and to answer Thee, when Thou askest why I have not put out Thy talents to usury; for I cannot deceive Thee. I know what I should require from my own servant; I know what Thou dost demand from me. O let me not be as the servant which knew his LORD's will, and did it not!

Myself, then, and all that is mine, with my whole heart, do I give back to Thee. Lo! in heart I am already poor. Lo! I have left all things, and follow Thee. What shall I have, therefore? Thee, my GOD, and all Good!

Thou art my exceeding great Reward. Thou art my lot and my inheritance. And why should not this suffice me? Even now Thou givest me Thyself, that is, Thy Body and Blood; and Thou dost promise me, moreover, an hundredfold, and life eternal. I believe Thee, for Thou art Truth; but every man is a liar. I believe Thee, for Thou art supreme Goodness, and canst not be surpassed in benefits. For what is in Truth Thine own, do we give Thee back. O GOD of my heart! receive them, as with a sincere heart I offer them; and when it shall please Thee, me also, poor in this world's goods, but enriched with Thy gifts, do Thou receive into Thine everlasting habitations. Amen.

CHAPTER VI.

CONTAINING EXERCISES FOR THE MORNING AND EVENING.

MORNING PRAYER.

In order to pass the day aright and piously, it is of the utmost importance to begin it well. As soon, therefore, as thou wakest in the morning, unite the thought of GOD *with the opening of the day, and beware that no other have the first-fruits of your thoughts and actions, save* GOD. *No day will pass ill and unhappily which thou hast begun with Him. For from the Fount of all good what can flow but good?*

The five parts of Morning Prayer:
1. *Be grateful.* 2. *Offer up thine heart.* 3. *Design Thy daily task.* 4. *Shun sin.* 5. *Seek aid Divine.*

1. *Thanksgiving.*

O Eternal GOD, I praise Thee and I thank Thee from my inmost heart, that Thou didst create me after Thine own image; and hast redeemed me with the Precious Blood of Thy Dear Son; and, in addition to other unnumbered blessings, hast so mercifully preserved me to this moment, protecting me from evils and dangers during the past night, and bringing me safely to the beginning of this day. What shall I render unto Thee, O LORD, for these and all the other benefits Thou hast bestowed upon me?

2. *Self-dedication.*

Behold, O LORD, I cheerfully give up all to Thee, from Whom is all that I have. My body and soul, the powers of both, and all the thoughts, words, and works of this day, I truly and purely dedicate to the glory of Thy Name; that in all these things Thy Blessed Name may be for ever praised and glorified: and this I do in union with all the works which, in the most perfect love, our Saviour wrought on earth for our salvation; that so out of the abundant Merits of Thine Only-Begotten Son, in Whom Thou art ever well-pleased, my weakness may be strengthened and my defects supplied.

3. *Disposal of one's actions.*

But what wilt Thou have me to do, that I may please Thee? I know, O LORD, that we must render to Thee a strict account of our whole life, when Thou shalt come to reckon with Thy servants. And, therefore, I justly dread all my own acts, knowing that Thou wilt not spare the guilty; and not knowing the hour when Thou wilt come and summon me to give up an account of my stewardship. What, if it be to-day! Therefore I will give myself more diligently to the duties and works [as N. or N.] befitting my state of life [N.] and calling [N.] in which, by Thy grace, Thou hast placed me; I will endeavour to do all things decently and in order.

And whereas Thou dost command us to seek first the kingdom of GOD, I will give myself but sparingly to outward cares and duties, lest time should fail for the chief of all affairs, the work of my eternal salvation. I know it is vain to toil for, yea, or gain all things, and lose Thee, the Only Highest Good. O may my soul rather seek Thee before all things and in all things, my GOD and my All!

4. *Avoidance of sin.*

O that my ways, O LORD, were made so direct, that I might this day keep Thy statutes! Truly I would not walk in the ways of sinners, rugged ways, full of sorrow only and misery. For although at first they appear to be good, yet the end thereof leadeth unto death. I have sworn, and am stedfastly purposed to keep Thy righteous judgments. I have said I will take heed to my ways, that I offend not in my tongue. I will turn away mine eyes, lest they behold vanity. May I keep my heart with all diligence. I know that such and such occasions [N. and N.] have often proved injurious to me; and how shall I again this day expose myself to such peril? For the love of Thee, O LORD, Whom Alone my soul longeth to serve and to cleave unto Thee, I will not do it.

5. Petition for Divine grace.

But, O LORD, what will it profit me to will those things, unless Thou give me the power also to perform them? In vain does man propose, unless Thy grace dispose him. Thou knowest my frailty, that I am poor and miserable, and can do nothing, yea, can think no good thought, without Thee; but all my sufficiency is of Thee Alone. Arise Thou, therefore, and help me, and by Thy effectual grace give me strength, that the good I will, I may be able to bring to good effect; that by the guidance of Thy grace I may so live this day, that, with all who are departed this life in Thy faith and fear, I may live with Thee, and rejoice in Thee, and praise Thee, throughout eternity. Amen.

AN EXERCISE

OF GREAT VALUE AND EFFICACY, OR AN ACT OF SELF-DEVOTION AND COVENANT WITH GOD.

(From Philip Rovenius, Archbishop of Philippi and Vicar of Holland, in his Instit. of Christian Piety, *and P. Mart. a Matre Dei Excalc. Carmel. in the Gymnas. of Christ. Phil. Whom see more at length on the efficacy and excellence of this exercise.)*

The devout Christian, who is desirous to praise GOD without ceasing, may make some such covenant with GOD as

[§ iv.] ON THE PRACTICE OF VIRTUE. 83

follows; namely, that on certain signals, such as the sound of a bell, the sight of the sky, or when he beats his breast, &c. (for such signals may be fixed upon and multiplied at pleasure), he should will, and take pleasure in, whatever deed, good and pleasing to GOD, *hath ever been done in time past, or is done to-day, or shall be done hereafter, or which could be done. Further, that he willeth so often to offer himself to* GOD; *mourn for his sins; renew the vows he may have made; worship, praise* GOD, *&c.*

The force and efficacy of this act may be gathered from its reverse. Suppose that any one should resolve, that whenever he heard a bell, or looked on the sky, &c., he would so often will, approve, and take pleasure in whatever evil had ever been, or ever should be done, and would wish he were a partaker in it, what a mass of sin would he bind around him! If, then, such an act has such efficacy for evil, why should it not, when applied to good, have immense force and value? But, to give a form of such a compact,—

O most benign FATHER of mercies, my GOD, my LORD, and my Creator, of Whom, and through Whom, and in Whom are all things, for in Thee we live and move and have our being, and, therefore, by right of supreme dominion all things serve Thee, I also, by the same right, am Thine, even as I now yield myself up to Thee as Thy servant for ever by an everlasting covenant; that every moment of my life, and all things within me and around me, may bless Thy Name! But since the necessities of this present life will not allow us to give our minds unceasingly to Thy praise, I desire to enter into this compact with Thee, O my Lord.

Whensoever I shall gaze upon the sky, or smite my breast, or cast my eyes upon any sacred picture; whensoever I shall hear the hour strike, or church-bell ring, or take a book into my hands; whensoever I shall be conscious of temptation from the flesh, the world, or the devil, in any thing affecting faith, hope, charity, chastity, patience, humility, &c. I profess now for then, that I will, so often, to perform and to exercise in the best manner and form I can the following acts, although, perchance, at the very time it may not be in my mind.

On all such occasions, then, I rejoice and from my heart give thanks unto Thee for Thine infinite Perfections, that THOU ART THAT THOU ART, GOD Almighty, All Wise, All Good, All Merciful, All Just, &c.; the chief Good of every rational creature; that Thou art in want of nothing, seeing Thou art altogether Blessed in Thyself, and sufficient for Thyself; but all our sufficiency is of Thee.

I rejoice also, O LORD, and with Thee joy from my inmost soul, on account of the good works, which, for love of Thee, have ever been done in time past, are done on this day, or shall hereafter be done; and for all other things which may be done by those whom Thou hast created or art able to create; and this I do with all the perfection of which I am capable.

I rejoice on account of those things which our LORD JESUS CHRIST, the Virgin Mary, the holy Angels, the Patriarchs, Prophets, Apostles, Martyrs, Confessors, Virgins, and all the Saints and faithful have done to Thy glory; and for the love also which they shall bear towards Thee eternally, and for the praises which they shall unceasingly offer unto Thee.

I present unto Thee all the Sacrifices of the Holy Eucharist which have hitherto been offered in Thy Church, or are hereafter to be offered even to the end of the world; and I do this with the desire of adoring and praising Thee as GOD, of Supreme Majesty, Power, Wisdom, Goodness, &c., and of thanking Thee, and of appeasing Thee, and of obtaining from Thee the blessings of grace and glory.

For love of Thee I grieve from my heart for all and each of my sins. I hope for pardon from Thine infinite Mercy. And I resolve, with the help of Thy grace, never more to offend Thee.

I grieve, moreover, for the many sins which, from the beginning of the world up to this time, have been committed by any man, and that Thou wert so grievously offended by them. [I wish from my heart that any ever so slight amends could be made for them, even with my blood[1].] O may, in the place of every sin, a thousand acts of obedience be, in each moment of eternity, paid to Thee by the holy Angels, and all the blessed!

Out of love to Thee, I forgive from my heart all who have offended or in any way injured me; and I desire for them that for each offence Thou wouldest bestow on them some special grace or benefit. And I desire that they may never fall into Thy displeasure.

Into Thy hands I commend myself, and all that is mine, especially the end of my life; that Thou mayest, both in time and in eternity, do with me, as being Thine more than mine, what shall please Thee, and shall seem to Thee to be most for Thy glory.

Lastly, I present unto Thee the best I can, and as best I can; but chiefly the Life, Passion, and Blood of our LORD JESUS CHRIST, by way of thanksgiving for all the blessings of body and of soul which I have hitherto received from Thee, and shall hereafter receive; more especially for the love wherewith Thou hast loved me from eternity; and that I may obtain the grace of perseverance to cleave inseparably unto Thee.

This present act, in respect to each of its parts, and whatever else is involved therein, I wish to ratify, whensoever any of the signals shall occur, now fixed upon, or to be fixed upon hereafter; yea, as often as creatures have been or can be formed by Thee; as often as I shall draw my breath; finally, as often as it is possible or even imaginable for them to be repeated and multiplied. And this I do simply from love to Thee, and all the good and holy ends which any one can have.

O LORD, what I have said, I wish to be said, done, accepted, and confirmed, with the greatest affection, efficacy, and fruit that may be.

It will suffice to say this exercise in its complete form, once in the day, especially in the morning, or before or after the Holy Communion. But it may be frequently repeated at the occurrence of the appointed signals. And this will not be difficult

---

[1] See notes on Part I.

to do, since it may be done, virtually, by a simple and single reflection or direction of the mind. Also by saying O JESU! *or,* O my GOD, and my All!

A VERY USEFUL PRAYER,

WITH WHICH A PERSON MAY, IN THE MORNING, COMMEND HIS ACTIONS AND ALL THAT HE HAS TO GOD, IN UNION WITH THE MERITS OF CHRIST.

(From the Prayers of P. Canisius, of the Society of JESUS.*)*

I praise Thee with my whole heart, and I give thanks to Thee, O LORD my GOD, for that, when I was nothing, Thou didst create me after Thine own image; so that I might be capable of enjoying the Chief and Eternal Good, even Thine own Self. And when I was lost, being a child of wrath, and exposed to eternal malediction, Thou didst yet, out of the might of Thy boundless love, redeem me by Thy most Holy Life and Passion, by Thy Death and Precious Blood.

Wherefore, as from Thy Hand Alone I receive every good, so of what kind soever it be, I willingly offer it in return, for ever, together with my whole self also, to the praise and glory of Thy Supreme Majesty.

Moreover, though I was unworthy of all grace and kindness, nay rather, full of uncleanness, and worthy of punishment, Thou didst so mercifully bestow on me the Holy Ghost, together with His gracious gifts. And besides all this, Thou hast prepared for me everlasting joys and blessings in heaven.

I beseech Thee, also, by Thine Infinite Goodness, O most merciful SAVIOUR, JESU CHRIST! that Thou wouldst keep me, this day, from all sin; that I lose not Thy grace, but that I may employ my heart and every purpose thereof, my understanding and my will, all the powers of my soul and body, to Thy sole worship and honour, that so my thoughts words and works may in all things be pleasing to Thee.

But because, being so very imperfect, I am not able to do any thing, no, not even to think any thing as of myself, which may be pleasing in the Eyes of Thy Divine Majesty, or profitable to myself, or possess any worth, but all our sufficiency is of Thee; I therefore most humbly beseech and beg of Thee, that Thou wouldest vouchsafe to supply my want and deficiency out of the infinite riches of Thy Charity, and the exhaustless treasury of Thy Merits.

Thus, then, I may offer and commit unto Thee, O LORD JESU CHRIST, my most unworthy, and in themselves most vile, works, that Thou mayest unite them to those most meritorious and most holy works of Thy whole Life, which Thou didst perform with that most ardent and perfect love, wherewith Thou wroughtest all things, in the earth, for our salvation, according to the good pleasure and for the glory of Thy Eternal FATHER.

Finally, I pray Thee, that whatsoever it is right for me this day either to do or suffer, Thou wouldest not only mercifully accept, but also by Thy most Holy Incarnation, Life, Passion, and Death, make it profitable to my salvation; that so the welfare of my soul may be more and more holpen, and all my life more perfectly conformed to the pattern of Thy most Holy Life and Passion; and that by this means I may be better fitted to promote the well-being of my neighbour, and to preserve peace and charity with him. But above all things, that I may with my whole heart perform the will, and further the service and love, of Thy Divine Majesty. Amen.

A BENEDICTION TO BE USED MORNING AND EVENING.

From the same.

The Peace of our Lord JESUS CHRIST, and the Virtue of His most Sacred Passion, the sign of the Holy Cross, and the triumphant title JESUS OF NAZARETH, KING OF THE JEWS; His Immaculate Birth of the Blessed Virgin Mary, the guardianship of holy Angels, especially of my peculiar guardian, and the prayers of all GOD's elect, be between me and all my enemies, visible and invisible, both now and at the hour of my death. Amen. In the Name of the FATHER, and of the SON, and of the HOLY GHOST. Amen.

EVENING PRAYER.

In the evening, when thou art about to betake thyself to rest, take heed that thou forget not GOD, *by Whose favour thou hast passed through this day, and all thy life hitherto ; and which, perchance, may not be prolonged until the morning, if thou make not thy peace with* GOD *this night. Thy very bed, in some measure, impresses upon thee the thought of death ; for in it thou layest the unclothed body as in a grave ; and what is sleep itself, but the brother and image of death ? Too exceeding reckless is he, who having offended* GOD, *and not made peace with Him, dareth to entrust himself to the night, and to sleep. Rather, prepare thyself for thy nightly repose, as if some one whispered in thine ear,* This night shall thy soul be required of thee. *Remember, therefore, to pray with the Prophet,* Lighten mine eyes that I sleep not in death; lest mine enemy say, I have prevailed against him.

Five points to be observed at Evening Prayer :

1. *Give thanks to God.* 2. *Beg light.* 3. *Search well thy soul.* 4. *Ask pardon for thy faults.* 5. *Check Sin's control.*

1. *Thanksgiving.*

O Infinite Goodness ! I thank Thee from my inmost heart for all Thy blessings, which, this day and through my whole life, Thou hast so bountifully bestowed upon me, so utterly unworthy. Praise and glory be to Thee, from me and from Thine Elect in heaven and in earth, and from all Thy creatures for ever and ever.

2. *Prayer for light.*

O Eternal Wisdom! in many things, alas ! we all offend; but who can understand his errors ? Do Thou, O true Light, enlighten my darkness, that I may see and know what is lacking to me. Thou knowest all the secrets of the heart, and markest all my steps. Grant, therefore, that in bitterness of my soul I may fully recall before Thee all wherein I have this day offended against Thee, in thought, word, or deed.

the practice of this grace [N.] *thou most needest, or in the rooting out of the fault* [N.] *which most besets thee, &c.*

3. *Sifting of conscience.*

O GOD! Who searchest the hearts and reins, I, wretched man, have this day sinned against heaven and before Thee; how, then, can I hide any thing from Thee, Who didst foresee all my ways, and hast known my thoughts long before? What can I do unto Thee, O Thou Preserver of men? Alas, my LORD, I have sinned; and my faults are not hidden from Thee; and if I judge myself; my heart condemns me chiefly for these things.

Here examine thy conscience; and to that end retrace the course of the whole day; consider well where thou hast been; with whom thou hast had any intercourse; what thou hast thought, said, and done. And remember especially to examine thyself with respect to thy station, office, or calling; thou wilt thus more readily perceive thy sins, both of commission and of omission. Consider seriously, moreover, what progress thou hast made in

4. *Prayer for pardon.*

O FATHER of mercies! Who hast no pleasure in the death of sinners, look upon me in the multitude of Thy mercies. I cast all the offences of this day and of my whole life into the abyss of Thine eternal love wherewith Thou hast loved us. I grieve from my inmost heart that I have been so ungrateful for Thy many blessings to me, and that I have so often offended Thee, my GOD, and my Chief Good. I beseech Thee, by the Death, and by the Love of Thy Son, JESUS CHRIST, spare me, a wretched sinner, and of Thine exceeding Mercy, forgive me all that I have this day, or ever committed, either against Thee, my neighbour, or myself.

5. *Resolution of amendment.*

O Almighty GOD, without Whose power man is nothing, I firmly resolve, before Thee and all the company of heaven, to follow more closely the rule of Thy will; to amend my ways; to attend more diligently to the duties of my calling; to avoid all sins, and the occasions of them, &c.

This, indeed, is my will; but without Thee it will not avail. Do Thou, then, Who givest me the will, give me also the power to perform. Grant what Thou commandest, and command what Thou wilt; that so I may live soberly, righteously, and godly in this present world, and in the world to come may, with all Thy Saints, praise Thee eternally.

O LORD, let my desire come up before Thee as incense. Of Thine infinite Mercy, despise not Thou this my evening sacrifice.

Unto Thee, O GOD, I commit myself, that I may be defended from the snares of my enemies, who are ever wakeful whilst we sleep, and are ever ready to do us hurt. Be Thou, O GOD, our defence; so shall no evil approach to hurt us.

O LORD GOD, give unto us the increase of faith, hope, and charity. Root out from among us all sin and wickedness, all discord and infidelity, all errors and vain conceits.

Rebuke the erring, convert the unbelieving. Bring back into the unity of Thy Church, all those that are in schism, and show unto them the light of Thy grace. Defend from all adversity, both of body and soul, the pastors and governors of Thy Church, and all other rulers, emperors, kings, princes, bishops, and all who are in authority.

Convert sinners to true repentance. Preserve the righteous in the good way. Confirm all their thoughts, words, and works. Have mercy upon all men, O LORD, and strengthen in Thy service those who are dedicated to Thee. Sustain all those who labour; raise up those who are oppressed with grief; heal the sick; supply the wants of all who are in need; grant unto travellers a return to their home; bring to a haven of safety those in perils of sea; give joy to those who are labouring with child; and deliverance to captives.

Forgive all who have sinned with me, or whom I have led to sin. Recompense one hundredfold those whom I have injured, offended, or deceived. Direct in the way of life all united to me by kindred or friendship, my parents, brothers, and sisters —all whose labour or help I make use of; all who pray for me, or desire my prayers for them; and all who think kindly of me. Hear them in what trouble soever they call upon Thee. Vouchsafe both to our enemies and to ourselves unbroken charity. May we all have patience, kindness, and pity, and may envy, wrath, and bitterness be far from us.

Further, O most merciful FATHER, have mercy upon all who have fallen asleep in CHRIST, especially on my parents, and on those with whom I have had familiar converse, or whose possessions I have inherited; on all, moreover, who have departed in Thy faith. Grant, unto them, O LORD, eternal rest, and let perpetual light shine upon them.

Eternal FATHER, I beseech Thee, by the Life and Death of Thy well-beloved SON, and by the bowels of Thy mercy, grant unto me that I may persevere in holiness, and die in Thy favour.

O Good Jesu, I beseech Thee, by the love of the Eternal FATHER, and the last Words on the Cross wherewith Thou didst commend Thy Spirit to Thy FATHER, receive Thou my spirit at the close of my life.

O GOD the HOLY GHOST, have mercy upon me; and by Thy holy inspiration strengthen me at all times, and chiefly in the hour of my death.

O most holy TRINITY, One GOD, have mercy upon me, now and in the hour of death. Amen.

An aspiration to be uttered at each of the hours.

O GOD of infinite mercy! I grieve, for love of Thee, that I have ever offended Thee. I love Thee with my whole heart. I adore and praise Thee through the glowing charity and infinite merits of Thy most well-beloved SON, together with the love of the HOLY GHOST. And I beseech Thee to give me continual increase in Thy love, preventing and directing all my doings to Thy Glory.

END OF PART IV.

TO THE

BELOVED AND MOST TO BE LOVED

OF THE HUMAN RACE,

𝕵𝖊𝖘𝖚𝖘 𝕮𝖍𝖗𝖎𝖘𝖙,

WHOSE DELIGHTS ARE TO BE WITH THE SONS OF MEN:

TREE OF LIFE,

PLANTED IN THE MIDST OF PARADISE,

WHOSE FRUIT GIVETH IMMORTALITY TO THEM THAT EAT THEREOF:

PASCHAL LAMB,

SPOTLESS THANK-OFFERING,

TO BE EATEN FOR A PERPETUAL MEMORIAL

OF OUR DEPARTURE FROM EGYPT:

TRUE MANNA FROM HEAVEN,

WHICH HATH IN ITSELF EVERY SWEET SAVOUR:

BREAD OF ANGELS,

YET FOOD OF WAYFARERS,

WHICH, AS THEY JOURNEY THROUGH THIS WILDERNESS,

𝕲𝕺𝕯,

LAVISH, AS IT WERE, OF HIMSELF, HATH GIVEN TO MORTALS TO EAT:

TRUE VINE,

WHICH, BY ITS CELESTIAL SAP,

MAKETH EVERY BRANCH THAT ABIDETH IN IT TO GROW

AND TO BE FRUITFUL;

YEA, AND YIELDETH WINE ALSO, MAKING THE VIRGINS CHEERFUL,

AND GLADDENING THE HEART OF MAN:

MYSTIC PELICAN,

WHICH NOURISHETH ITS YOUNG

WITH THE BLOOD OF ITS OWN BOSOM:

GOOD SAMARITAN,

WHO POURETH INTO OUR WOUNDS

THE WINE OF LOVE AND THE OIL OF PITY:

PRIEST FOR EVER

AFTER THE ORDER OF MELCHIZEDEK,

WHO BROUGHT FORTH BREAD AND WINE, EVEN HIS VERY SELF·

THE GREAT HIGH PRIEST

HOLY, HARMLESS, UNDEFILED, AND SEPARATE FROM SINNERS,

WHO NEEDETH NOT FOR HIS OWN SINS,

AS FOR THE SINS OF OTHERS, TO OFFER UP SACRIFICE:

THE GOOD SHEPHERD

WHO FOLDETH HIS SHEEP IN A PLACE OF RICH PASTURE,

YEA, FEEDETH THEM WITH HIS OWN BODY AND BLOOD.

What greater could He give Who gave Himself to us,

AT BIRTH, TO BE OUR FELLOW;

AT SUPPER, OUR FOOD;

AT DEATH, OUR RANSOM;

IN HIS KINGDOM, OUR REWARD!

PARADISE FOR THE CHRISTIAN SOUL.

PART V.

OF DEVOUT COMMUNION, WITH PRAYERS AND VARIOUS EXERCISES FOR THE USE BOTH OF CLERGY AND LAITY.

CHAPTER I.

A CONFERENCE, OR MEDITATION, ON A RIGHT AND PROFITABLE ATTENDANCE AT HOLY COMMUNION, APPROPRIATE TO EVERY CONDITION.

1. *An Earnest Exhortation, or Invitation to Holy Communion.*

CHRIST. Come unto Me, all ye that labour and are heavy laden, and I will refresh you. For I am the Good Shepherd Who have laid down My life for My sheep, and I feed them with that sweetest food of life, even with My own Body and Blood. For I have made a great Feast, that I might shew forth the riches and the power of My Kingdom. Come ye, therefore, and eat of My Bread and drink of the Wine which I have mingled for you; for My delights are to be with the sons of men. I desire, by every right and wont of true and faithful friendship, to make you partakers of My grace and glory; that is, of all My Goods. And therefore came I from heaven into this world, and was made Man, endured countless labours, torments, yea Death itself, and with

B

great desire have I desired to eat this Passover with My disciples.

But that I might leave with you a perpetual memorial of this My exceeding great love, and pledge of future glory, I have given Myself. Behold, I have given My Whole Self to you; born to be one with you; eating with you, to be your Nourishment; dying, to be your Ransom; and at length reigning, to be your Reward. And what could I give greater or more excellent? or what more could I have done that I have not done?

MAN. Of a truth, O LORD, Thou art gentle and meek, and full of compassion. O how excellent is Thy Name in all the earth! But what is man that Thou art mindful of him, or the son of man that Thou visitest him, and takest such account of him? Is he not dust and ashes? Is not every man living altogether vanity? And dost Thou deign to open Thine eyes on such an one? to come unto him and make Thy abode with him? What shall I render unto the Lord for all the benefits that He hath done unto me? Thou, O LORD, art rich towards all men, and rulest over all things; yea, all things are Thine: but, as for me, I am poor and needy; and Thou wantest not any of my goods. Were I to give Thee all my substance, yea, and mine own self also, how could that ever be a worthy return for all Thy benefits?

CHRIST. Offer unto GOD the sacrifice of thanksgiving, and pay thy vows unto the Most Highest. Most acceptable to the Eternal FATHER, and well-pleasing unto Me, is the Oblation and Reception of my Body and Blood. Do this, therefore frequently, but withal, reverently, in remembrance of Me. For to this end I have ordained that these Holy Mysteries should continue in My Church, that thou mightest cherish a perpetual memory of My love and of My Redemption of thee. I know that thou canst not make Me any other return: but canst thou not render a grateful mind, and the recollection of so vast a benefit? Assuredly thou canst: and in no way more aptly than in the devout and frequent use of this Mystery; and if thou slight it, take heed lest thou too be reckoned among those ungrateful and unworthy, and be shut out from the Supper.

MAN. O how plentiful is Thy goodness, O LORD, which Thou hast manifested towards them that fear Thee! Thou Who, to prove Thy goodness towards Thy children, dost fill the hungry with good things, even with that most sweet Bread Which came down from heaven. O how pleasant to my taste are those words of Thine, with which Thou dost so lovingly invite me unto Thee! But, ah! who am I, O Thou Great King above all kings, that I should eat Bread from Thy Table all the days of my life?

2. *The dignity and excellence of the most venerable Sacrament.*

CHRIST. That is it, which I wish thee to ponder diligently; lest, haply, if thou lightly esteem the benefit which I have prepared for My faithful servants, thou shouldest at length become lukewarm, and thy soul should loath this Food as if it were too light, and I also begin to spue thee out of My Mouth. O how happy art thou, O Christian, Mine own, didst thou but know thy blessings; who art placed in so rich a pasture, and to whom it is given to enjoy so mighty a benefit and so august a Feast! But, more than all art thou blessed, O Priest, whom, by a singular privilege of honour, I have chosen to myself from among the people, that thou shouldest stand before Me, as My friend and private counsellor, at My Table, and shouldest thence take Food, yea, and dispense It, moreover, to the rest of My faithful ones. To thee, assuredly it is given, what is withheld from Angels, (and for what merit of thine?) in the exercise of a most wonderful, tremendous, and truly Divine, office, to call down, as it were, the LORD of glory from His Throne, so as to be present upon the Altar, to take Him in thy hands, and to give Him unto others. At this the heavens are astonished, and the Angels, full of wonder, venerate the Mystery, when they see Him beneath them, Whom, above them, they continually adore. And doth man, yea a Priest, dare to approach this same Mystery with a cold, impure, and distracted mind? And does he who is so often fed with Angels' Food still hanker after the husks of swine?

MAN. Great indeed, is the honour put on man; greater still on the Priest. Deeply, therefore, beyond doubt, is each of them bound to live conformably to so high a dignity. But, alas! O LORD, I behold the transgression and am troubled; and in how many things do I myself fail! Thine Eyes behold my imperfections. I find, also, a law in my members warring against the law of my mind, and bringing me into captivity to the law of sin; so that the good I would, I do not; but the evil that I would not, that I do.

3. *The utility and necessity of the most sweet Sacrament of the Eucharist.*

CHRIST. Behold, for this very purpose do I offer thee My grace and help, yea, in this Sacrament, I bestow on thee Myself, the Fountain of grace and the Author of all good. I know that without Me thou canst do nothing; but lo, I am the Living Bread Which have come down from heaven; that Bread, I say, Which strengtheneth man's heart, and Which if thou receive frequently and with reverence, thou wilt soon perceive the change of the Right Hand of the Most High: for then shall thy soul be filled as with marrow and fatness; thou shalt be strong and mighty to do good works, and in the strength of that Food thou shalt walk through the wilderness of this world, even unto the Mount of God, Of what enemy can he be afraid who has Me for his ever present and inmost help? He will say boldly with the Apostle, *If GOD be for us, who can be against us?* And, *I can do all things through* CHRIST *Which strengtheneth me.* Or, with the man after My own heart, *Though I walk through the valley of the shadow of death, I will fear no evil; for Thou art with me.*

MAN. Everlasting praise and glory be unto Thee, O LORD, for Thou hast prepared a table before me against them that trouble me. O that I might henceforth derive from it strength and courage to fight against mine enemies! How is it that I have hitherto failed in this, and that my strength has been brought low in weakness? Why have I so easily yielded to temptation and adversity? Is it not that I have set light by Thy Table, and have forgotten to eat my Bread; and that hence my strength hath failed me through want? Or, have I not too often presumed to eat it unworthily and irreverently?

CHRIST. Thou hast said, O man. For as the life of the body must be sustained by food, which continually repairs the waste which the natural heat occasions, so, of a truth, must the vigour of the spirit be restored by frequent Food, lest it waste away by the heat of concupiscence. Thou askest, What is that Food? Behold, *My Flesh is meat indeed, and My Blood is drink indeed.* This is the daily Bread, the Bread Which came down from heaven, with which, if the faithful, and especially My priests, frequently and worthily refresh themselves, they shall retire from My Table like lions breathing fire, terrible to their enemies, yea, to Satan himself[a]. There is no surer remedy against the fiery darts of the wicked one, and against temptations, especially of the flesh, with which thou hast, else, a daily struggle, and but seldom victory. For the desires of the flesh are extinguished most easily by the water which is drawn from the wells of Salvation; from Mine, that is, which I have opened to all in this Sacrament; and the Wine which gladdeneth the virgins, and which is here drunken. For I Alone satisfy the empty soul, and fill the hungry with good things, and with delights that shall never decay. I give unto her Bread which hath in it every manner of delight. And what good shall not he have, to whom I, the Source and Author of every good, vouchsafe to come? Come ye, therefore and eat of My Bread, and drink of the Wine which I have mingled, yea, drink ye abundantly, My well-beloved.

4. *The frequency with which we ought to approach the All-Holy Mysteries.*

MAN. Yet I see, O LORD, that to many Thine is a hard saying, and all cannot re-

---

[a] So saith S. Chrysos. Hom. 46, in S. Johann.

ceive it. For, not to mention those who walk in darkness, and, not believing the word of truth, say, *How can this Man give us His Flesh to eat?* we see every where many others readily yielding to the arguments which recommend them to unfrequent Communion.

CHRIST. I know how prone to ill are the minds of men; by what light and trifling causes they suffer themselves to be drawn aside and hindered from My worship and service; who also too eagerly catch at every occasion of serving the world, the flesh, and vain pleasures! O how easily do they give credence to the devil when he entices them to pleasure, invites them to eat the forbidden fruit, and, lying, promises that they shall be as gods! Whereas, when I offer My Flesh as Food, and so lovingly exhort and invite them to eat thereof, and promise that, so eating, they shall be partakers of the Divine Nature, and live for ever, they refuse to believe and obey Me! Me, Who am the Way and the Truth and the Life!

Behold, moreover, and recognize in this matter the craft of Pharaoh, who, envious of My Honour, will not let My people go, that they may sacrifice to Me in the wilderness, but keeps them busied in the midst of Egypt with works of clay, and bricks and straw, (for what else are the things of earth, the silver and gold, the wealth, and honours, and cares of this world?) that they may have no leisure to serve Me. And yet how active and unwearied are men in labours by which they eat only the bread of affliction; while yet with much less toil they might eat the Bread Which hath in itself every delight, and every sweet savour!

Not so did My faithful ones of old: not so. But walking in simplicity of heart, and full of love and zeal, they continued stedfast in the breaking of Bread and in prayers. Thus, of a truth, by the daily use of this Food did My Church, in the first ages, grow and increase; so that, through their longing after It, they readily despised all things, and would not suffer themselves to be seduced by any blandishments, or threats, or torments.

Call to mind, O Christian, but chiefly thou who art of

My Clergy, those beginnings of the new-born Church, when the heart of believers was one, and their spirit one: admire their zeal and love. Behold, the greater was their contempt of the things of earth, the greater was the care for My worship and honour. But where is now that fervour? where now that inebriation of the Spirit, that peace and joy in the HOLY GHOST? Alas! how is the gold become dim, how is the most fine gold changed!

O ye sons of men, how long so heavy of heart? how long will ye love vanity and seek after leasing? Wherefore do ye leave the Tree of Life? wherefore do ye forsake the fountain of Living Water, and seek out for yourselves broken cisterns, which can hold no water? Surely, if ye knew the gift of GOD, and Who it is That inviteth you, and offereth Himself to be your Food, ye would run with great quickness; there were no need to compel you to come to this Great Supper, this Marriage-feast. But these things are hidden from the wise and prudent of this world, who savour not the things that be of GOD. Yet the poor in spirit know them, the few who find in this one heavenly Morsel greater delicacies than in all the joys of the world.

MAN. I blush, O LORD, and am confounded within myself, whensoever I hear or think upon these things; when I look upon the ways of the first believers and upon our own. Alas, how great the disparity! Yet despise us not, O GOD of our Salvation; make us such as Thou wouldest have us to be. Arouse the torpid, enlighten the blind, lift up the lame, compel the sluggish to come in, that Thy table may be filled. Teach me to do Thy Will, for I am Thy servant, that I may make an offering of a free will unto Thee, and praise the Name of the LORD; that like as the hart desireth the water-brooks, so may my soul long after Thee, that my soul may have a desire and longing for Thy courts, O LORD. Wherefore shall I not, of mine own accord, come, yea run, that I may draw water out of the wells of Salvation? Why shall I not go willingly to the Altar of GOD even unto the GOD Who gladdeneth my youth?

5. *The hindrances to frequent Communion.*

CHRIST. With the sword of zeal and of love do thou, therefore, break through all the obstacles wherewith thou seest others every where to be kept back. But, first of all, put a limit to the business and cares of this world, with which, as with thorns, the mind of man is torn; and take heed that thou be not engaged in a multitude of affairs. Why wilt thou so miserably, and in such manifold ways, rend asunder thy heart, by the union of which thou wouldest be far happier? Why art thou troubled about many things, and neglectest that one thing which above all others is needful, and at the same time most pleasing to Me, the care of thy soul? Is not the soul more than the body? And what will it profit thee to gain all things, and to lose thy soul? There is nothing more displeasing or offensive to Me, than to hear such words as these:—I have purchased a farm—I have bought a yoke of oxen—I have married a wife, and therefore I cannot come. Have I not long ago plainly and severely condemned these and all the like excuses? Look to thyself, whether it be right that I should be put on one side for such vanities as these.

MAN. I confess, O LORD, that it is too unworthy, for the sake of such empty and perishing things, to forsake Thee and Thy Table, which in Thy great love Thou hast furnished with so many and such rich delights; not for Thyself, not for Angels, but for us men. Yet Thou Thyself knowest how hard it is for man, amidst so many affairs, both private and public, amid the cares and necessary duties of this life, to keep his mind collected and properly disposed duly to partake of such great Mysteries.

CHRIST. Hasten then thou the more to Me, by Whose counsel and Providence all things are carried on. For the more difficult thy affairs and the greater thy need of prudence, so much the more do thou have recourse to the Tabernacle, and seek counsel of the LORD. Thou hast there the Fountain of wisdom, the Angel of deep counsel. If therefore, thou lackest wisdom, ask it of Me, and it shall be given thee. O if thou knewest how many they are that weave spiders' webs, and labour for nought! How many do manifoldly ill, because they ask not at the Mouth of the Lord! It is in vain that ye rise before the dawn to go forth to your labours and to your business, unless I, the Sun of Righteousness, forecome your efforts with My light.

MAN. Of a truth, O LORD, the designs of men are laid in fear, and all our forethought is uncertain. Thou, therefore shalt henceforth be my Light and my Guide, and Thy Righteousness shall be my Counsellor; therefore will I the oftener go with Moses to the tabernacle, that I may take counsel of the LORD.

6. *Whether one ought to abstain from Holy Communion in compliance with the prejudices and opinions of men.*

CHRIST. Yet very many are there also, who, through fear of men and their judgments, but seldom take their place at My Table. But thou who knowest that the Great Judge Alone is to be feared, since He has power to cast into hell—thou who desirest to please Me, why dost thou depend more upon the word of the people than on Mine? Is not every man a liar? Am not I Truth Itself? Give diligence, therefore, before all things, to please and obey Me, and be not conformed to this wicked world. But if thou wilt yet please men, thou canst not be My servant:

And yet, if thou shouldest suffer persecution and reproach for living piously and serving Me, it behoveth thee to rejoice rather than to grieve that thou art thought worthy to suffer shame for My Name; for this is indeed the part of a true Christian. Meanwhile comfort thee through the consciousness of a good will. The day cometh, when I, the Supreme Judge, will make manifest all the counsels of the heart, and will condemn the judges of wicked thoughts. Then shall they indeed be overwhelmed with horrible fear, but thou shalt stand with great boldness, if now thou shalt have stood fast with patience; for to him that overcometh will I give the hidden Manna and a new name.

MAN. Lord, let it be with me a very small thing that I should be judged of man's judgment. For that Great Day will reveal all things. May I desire to please, and fear to displease Thee Alone! But will it be pleasing to Thee, if, conscious of my own unworthiness and of Thy Majesty and of the reverence due to such high Mysteries, I nevertheless presume to come so often unto Thee? Ought I not to fear lest familiarity should produce contempt? So think many; and for myself, I shall perchance perform more holily and reverently, and with greater delight and profit, what I shall perform more rarely.

7. *Whether, on the plea of humility and reverence, one ought to abstain from frequent Communion.*

CHRIST. I entreat you, O My faithful ones—yet in this not faithful enough—that ye no longer call evil good, and disguise your sloth and lukewarmness with the garb of virtue, deceiving your ownselves; for it will be difficult to deceive Mine Eyes, which are brighter than the sun. Does infrequency, or delay, or postponement, dispose you to become more worthy of My Table? Behold I know what is in man, I Who know the secrets of the heart. But your own consciences, which I see through in their inmost recesses, shall bear me witness how prepared ye come to Me after lengthened delay. I will accuse you and arraign you before My Face, because impious is this piety, and irreligious the reverence which disguiseth sloth with the title of godliness, and under a seeming reverence skilleth to feign zeal for religion. But iniquity lieth against itself. Doth the sick man come nearer to health, the longer he puts off the physician? Does a man grow warmer, the farther he withdraweth from the fire? But I am the Physician Who have borne thine infirmities; I am He Who came to send fire on the earth, and what will I but that it burn and inflame your hearts?

But I will speak with more plainness to thee, O man, that thou mayest confess how grievously, with many others, thou errest in this matter. That the Sacrament of My

Body and Blood conferreth grace, unless he that partaketh of It interpose some obstacle, this thou dost certainly confess. The more frequently, then, thou receivest It, wilt thou not obtain the more grace? But as grace increaseth, there is increase also of faith, hope, charity, devotion, reverence, purity, and all the other virtues which enlighten the understanding, excite the affections, purify the heart, and the like. And is not this the adorning, this the wedding garment which I chiefly require from thee, that thou mayest come worthily to My Table?

Thou seest, then, how one communion disposeth towards another; so that he will come best disposed towards to-morrow's communion, who shall bring with him the effect and fruit of to-day's. Nor hast thou reason hence to fear contempt. Among men, indeed, contempt may easily spring out of familiar converse, because, by frequent intercourse, the defects, imperfections, and faults of any one become more known; but the more frequently and familiarly thou art conversant with Me, the more and higher perfections wilt thou discover in Me, and so wilt thou observe towards Me the greater honour and reverence.

But this is too plain to need proof although the father of lies would advise the contrary, and persuades many who, making light of My glory, and little anxious about their own salvation, walk after the desires of their heart. Hence, knowing that a stricter watch over themselves—and continual caution should accompany frequent Communion, they, who hate discipline, had rather give up frequent Communion than their evil habits, that, unbridled, as it were, they may go the more freely after their own lusts. For they esteem it a kind of freedom to go without Communion and Sacrifice, whereas to serve Me is to reign. But if, perchance, on some solemn festival, or when the duties of their station require it, they communicate, or celebrate the Holy Office, they cherish devotion for a little while, until they have performed their duty; then presently they return to their former mind and habits, as the dog to his vomit, or the sow to her wallowing in the mire. Hear, O heavens, and give ear, O earth, for I call on you to be witnesses of My complaint, since men, to whom I have given understanding, heed Me not, *I have nourished and brought up children, and they have rebelled against Me : the ox knoweth his owner, and the ass his master's crib: but Israel doth not know, My people doth not consider.* How ill, I say, do men requite Me! men, whom I have created and redeemed, that they might serve Me! to nourish whose bodies I have given so many good things of the earth, but for their souls My Own Body and Blood! Of a truth, like the brutes which have no understanding, or rather, more stupid than they, they own not their Benefactor. For the brutes, they indeed, rude though they be, yet know their own masters, obey them and answer to their call, at whose stalls they are fed with a mouthful of hay; but these, although it is given them to sit at My Table and to partake daily of a Heavenly Feast, yet, alas! ungratefully regard not their Benefactor.

8. *The complaint of* CHRIST *against lukewarm and negligent Priests.*

But to you most of all, O Priests, who despise My Name, does this My complaint apply. Have I not chosen you for My ministers, and stewards of the Mysteries of GOD; giving unto you a power, such as I have not given to the kings and princes of the earth; no, not even to the Angels themselves? But which one among you revolves this seriously in his heart? Who kindles a fire upon Mine Altar for nought? Who, of his own free will, offereth Sacrifice unto Me? Is it not, as with the people so with the Priest? Do not all seek their own? Every one hasteneth unto his own house, but My House is desolate.

Often to do the Priest's office, to stand daily at My sacred Altar, and to offer Sacrifice to GOD, is now everywhere vile, and the business of common Priests, as of those who must live of My Altar. But those whom I have nourished and brought up more tenderly, these have despised Me. For having waxen fat and grown thick, and being covered with fatness, they have forsaken GOD Which made them: and they who eat of My Bread, and live in splendour on My patrimony, even they lift up the heel against Me. Do the nobles of a royal court esteem it an honour to be occupied about farms and cattle or other meaner offices, while the country folk sit down daily at the king's table?

Will not much be required of them to whom much is given? The cares of the world, the training up of their offspring, the traffic and the business of this life, will more readily excuse the laity; but ye who are separated unto Me for the work to which I have chosen you, that ye may be My soldiers, and therefore should not be entangled in the affairs of this world, what excuse will ye make? All other matters are alien from you; this one thing especially is your own: to serve GOD. For I have chosen you out of all the people, that ye may stand before Me, and minister unto Me and worship Me, and burn incense before Me; that ye may henceforth be, as it were, ambassadors and intercessors with GOD for the offences of the people.

To you, therefore, it especially belongs often to perform the functions of the Priesthood, and to praise His Name, as those who above all others owe to GOD honour and worship, aid to your neighbours, refreshment to the departed [b], help to sinners, and to yourselves especial care. But all these ye defraud at once, whensoever

[b] "Not in vain do we make mention of the departed in the course of the Divine Mysteries, and approach GOD in their behalf, beseeching the LAMB, Who is before us, Who taketh away the sin of the world; not in vain, but that some refreshment may thereby ensue to them."—S. Chys. Hom. 41. 8. in 2 Cor. xv. 46, p. 592, Oxf. Tr. On Phil. i. 24, (Hom. 3,) he says it is Apostolic. "Not in vain did the Apostles order that remembrance should be made of the dead in the dreadful mysteries. They know that great gain resulteth to them, and great assistance; for when the whole people stand with uplifted hands, a priestly assembly, and that awful Sacrifice lies displayed, how shall we not prevail with GOD by our entreaties for them? And this we do for those who have departed in the Faith." See also Tert. de Cor. c. 3; S. Cypr. Ep. i. S. Aug. Conf. ix. 32. 35. fin.

without lawful hindrance ye neglect these holy Mysteries. And seemeth it unto you a trifling wrong, that so great and august a power, freely conferred upon you by Myself, should through your negligence be unexercised and unproductive, and that ye receive the grace of God in vain?

O how much good may Priests do, how much evil avert, when they rightly discharge their office! But how shall ye be able to stand in My Judgment, when I shall take account of My servants, and demand with increase the talents which I have given unto you?

Behold, the land is utterly desolate, because there is none that layeth it to heart. The enemy hath spread out his hand upon all her pleasant things. The spoilers have come up on all sides, and have trodden My portion under foot; and My cattle have been made a prey, and My sheep become meat. But ye, O Priests, have not gone up into the gaps, neither made up the hedge for the house of Israel, that ye may stand in the battle in the day of the Lord. But ye eat the lambs out of the flock, and calves out of the midst of the herd, drinking wine in bowls of gold, and anointing yourselves with the chief ointments, and there is none who is grieved for the affliction of Joseph.

Is it, then, that ye look for defence against such evils solely to the numbers and the weapons of warriors? But in vain do ye put your trust in princes, in the children of men, in whom there is no help. Ye deceive yourselves, if ye think that the battle depends upon the strength of armies. Piety is by far the most powerful sinew of war, since it availeth for all things. But how rarely is this to be found in men who follow camps, where excess, lust, rapacity, blasphemies, and every vice holds sway! And what marvel, then, if by such men the cause of peace, of country and of religion be perilled? It belongs to God to give aid, and to put to flight; but it is yours, O Priest, to stand between the living and the dead, until the plague be stayed. It is yours with Moses to lift up pure hands unto God; so should Joshua more readily prevail, and destroy the Amalekites. It is yours, I say, to stand between the porch and the Altar, and to say, Spare Thy people, O LORD, spare them. It is yours to present My Blood unto My Father, that, being appeased by this Sacrifice, He may lay aside the scourges of His wrath, nor permit the innocent blood to be shed, nor suffer those to come into reproach who have been redeemed at so dear a Price.

These are the weapons of your warfare, with which ye ought to recover and to defend the peace and safety of the Christian Commonwealth. Who among you is wise and will observe these things, that he may please GOD in his generation, and that reconciliation may be made in the day of wrath?

Search the Scriptures, turn over all histories, and ye will find that I have never sent forth the rod of My anger and vengeance, unless provoked thereto by sin; neither have I drawn it back again, until the Priests, with pious zeal, have risen up and appeased My indignation. Wherefore, also, the neglect or misuse of My worship and sacrifices has almost ever been a sign of great impending desolation and destruction.

And this, because they who know not the LORD, and understand not the dignity and office of the priesthood, are deprived of a blessing for which they are unthankful. And in this My righteous judgment, it cometh to pass that the kingdom is taken away from those that are unworthy of it, and given to a nation bringing forth the fruits thereof; and they that despise Me, are lightly esteemed.

MAN. Alas! O LORD, how is the gold become dim, how is the most fine gold changed! Heathen, ungodly, aliens, robbers, have come into Thine inheritance; they have defiled Thy temples and Thy sanctuaries: evils have surrounded us whereof there is no number. But we, what shall we say to these things? There is no evil in the city which the LORD hath not done. For Thou visitest our offences with the rod, and our sin with scourges.

CHRIST. When I shall take a set time, I will judge according unto right. I will require My flock at the hand of My shepherds, and I will seek them out.

MAN. Righteous art Thou, O LORD, and true is Thy

judgment; but spare our offences. Look upon us, and behold our reproach, and be not angry with us for ever. Let Thy Priests be clothed with righteousness, and be holy because Thou art holy; that they may do honour to their ministry, and offer the Sacrifice of righteousness: for the offering of the wicked is an abomination.

9. *Reverence; or Preparation through the feeling of Fear with which the Holy Mysteries are to be approached.*

CHRIST. Whereas I urge a frequent attendance at My Holy Table, I would not have thee unmindful of the reverence with which thou oughtest to come there. In Zaccheus love and readiness were greatly pleasing to Me; but not less, fear and reverence in the Centurion. The former received Me with joy into his house; but the latter, conscious of his infirmities, durst not receive Me under his roof. But best is it to unite both affections, and to come to My Table, with the two feet, as it were, of *fear* and of *love*.

Faith, moreover, will excite fear in thee; for if thou believe with a firm faith that I, the LORD GOD, Who fill heaven and earth with My Majesty, Whom the Angels adore with trembling, am really and truly present in this Sacrament, how shalt thou not approach with trembling? Without doubt, whatever sin is committed in this, thou wilt say it is through want of faith. No one impure, or defiled with sin would come, if he believed that I, the Source of all purity, and the Avenger of all impurity, am present here.

Behold, how plainly he, who knew My secret counsels and was the faithful interpreter of My Will, Paul, My elect servant, gave this very warning; *Let a man examine himself,* he saith, *and so let him eat of that Bread and drink of that Cup; for he that eateth and drinketh unworthily, eateth and drinketh damnation to himself, not discerning the Lord's Body.* What plainer?

MAN. The lightning of these words terrifieth me. Who can read, or hear, or think of them without dread? Who can presume to come to the tremendous Sacrament of Thy Body and Blood? Even the heavens are not clean in Thy sight: how much less man, that is but a worm and corruption! I will, therefore, say rather, with another of Thine Apostles, *Depart from me, for I am a sinful man, O Lord*; lest if, perchance, I approach Thee rashly, I be guilty of Thy Body and Blood.

CHRIST. My Apostle does indeed make use of words most sharp and full of fear, yet withal most true. Yet he does it by way of caution to you, lest the Bread of Life should become to any one, through his own fault, a poison unto death. And yet how few are there, who ponder, as they deserve, the words of the Apostle, most weighty though they be. How few, the rash and careless approach of many to these tremendous Mysteries sheweth! See with what levity and unpreparedness multitudes come hither? as if they knew no difference between this most Precious Food and other common repasts; and as if they thought nothing of less account than to receive Me; or rather, as if they believed that no one was less present than Myself.

But alas! what just cause of complaint, even in this respect, have I against you, O ye Priests who bear My Name! you, I say, who so dishonour Me as to handle and receive the Sacrament of my Body and Blood with such irreverence! You, who dare to place the Ark of the LORD by the side of the idol Dagon; who fear not to approach My sacred Body with hearts and bodies defiled by so many sins! What agreement is there between light and darkness? What concord between CHRIST and Belial? Let the idol of covetousness, of luxury, of lust, of vanity, or whatsoever it be, fall down flat; else will the Ark bring destruction upon you rather than salvation. What have ye to do with the Ark of the LORD, O foolish Philistines, O impious Christians? I have no pleasure in you; neither will I accept an offering at your hand. To what purpose is the multitude of your sacrifices unto Me? I am full: bring no more vain oblations; incense is an abomination unto Me. Your hands are full of wickedness. Even of old it was said unto the Priests: *The Priests shall be holy unto their* GOD, *and shall not profane His Name: for the incense of the* LORD, *and the bread of their* GOD *do they offer; therefore shall they be holy*. And again: *Let the Priests which come near to the* LORD *sanctify themselves, lest He break forth upon them, &c.* See, also, herein, what strict holiness and purity were prescribed. The man that had a blemish, or any other defect of body, is forbidden to offer bread or sacrifice to the LORD. They are commanded to be holy who had to do only with the figure and the shadow: what, then, ought ye to be, who handle the Substance and the Reality, yea, the Holy of Holies Itself! What proportion is there between the finite and and Infinite? Or, what comparison between loaves, oxen, and sheep, and the SON OF GOD Himself? Is it not just, that in proportion to the difference of dignity, should be also the difference of sanctity?

But now how often is the Very, True, Sacrament of My Body and Blood polluted by impure hearts, and lips, and hands! and yet ye live securely, as a nation that had done righteousness! Is it that, because sentence is not speedily executed against the wicked, therefore the sons of men do evil fearlessly? Did the sons of Aaron sin so grievously, when they entered unworthily into the Sanctuary, and offered strange fire? Or the Bethshemites, when, with prying eyes, they looked into the Ark; of whom more than fifty thousand were destroyed for their irreverent curiosity? Did Uzzah offend so heinously when he put forth his hand to stay the Ark, with an officiousness which seemed to him pious? Or, did Belshazzar sin more grievously, who touched the hallowed vessels with unworthy hands? And yet these and many others did either the fire consume, or the earth swallow up alive, or some other heavy vengeance suddenly cut off! With such great severity were impiety and irreverence towards My sacrifices and things dedicated unto Me punished of old!

O happy are ye, if ye wash your hands in the blood of offenders, and let the ills of others be a caution to yourselves, that henceforward ye may offer unto Me the Sacrifice of righteousness out of a pure heart and a good conscience. For the sacrifice of the wicked is an abomination unto Me; and they who unworthily offer Me [c], now that I reign in heaven, sin more grievously than they who crucified Me when I was on earth. For these, if they had known Me, would never have crucified the LORD of Glory. But those, albeit they confess that I am GOD, and truly present in this Sacrament, yet fear not to deal with Me thus unworthily.

MAN. Righteous art Thou, O LORD, when I plead with Thee, and all Thy ways are in truth; and there is none on earth that can reprove Thee, and say, What doest Thou? Thy Will alone is the most righteous rule of Thy doings. Nevertheless, I will speak unto the LORD,

[c] "When we sacrifice, Christ is present, Christ is immolated." S. Ambr. in S. Luc. 1. "In many places is offered, not many Christs, but every where One Christ, being whole here and there, One Body, not many bodies." S. Chrys. Hom. 17, in Ep. ab Hebr. "We offer up Christ, sacrificed for our sins, propitiating our merciful God, both for them [those who have fallen asleep] and for ourselves." S. Cyril. Jer. Lect. Myst.

though I be dust and ashes. Thou callest upon us, O LORD, to come frequently to Thy Sacrament; yet, on the other hand, whom dost Thou not frighten away by such examples of severity? Ought I not justly to fear, lest with Uzzah and the Bethshemites, I perish at the sight and touch of the Ark of Thy Most Holy Body? Lest, not having on a wedding garment, I be cast out from Thy Supper? For there is not a man upon earth that liveth and sinneth not. In many things we offend all; and who shall dare to approach Thee? I desire, indeed, to do so; but if Thou shouldest mark iniquities, O LORD, who shall stand? All my desire is before Thee, O LORD; and my groaning is not hidden from Thee.

CHRIST. Let My words make thee not faint-hearted, but humble: a troubled spirit is to Me a grateful sacrifice; and if thou wilt present that beforehand, thou mayest safely offer the Sacrifice of My Body and Blood. An humble and a contrite heart I will not despise. It was a pleasure to Me to eat and to converse even with sinners; for the whole have no need of a physician, but they that are sick.

That Thou mayest, therefore, come worthily to My Table, in the first place, cleanse thy conscience, by sincere confession and true contrition, from every deadly sin, and from every desire towards it. And that thou mayest come yet more worthily, and more acceptably to Myself, and mayest receive more grace, be diligent to put off sins of infirmity and every evil inclination of the mind, and whatsoever thou knowest to be displeasing in My Sight. In short, the more pure thou comest to Me, the greater grace shalt thou receive.

Mark well what I did at My Last Supper, when I instituted this Sacrament. Before I would admit My disciples to the Sacred Supper, I washed their feet; that by this ceremony, full of mystery, I might declare the necessity of purity of mind in those who would come worthily to my Sacraments. For he that is washed, or clean from heavier sins, needeth not save to wash his feet, that is, to have his dispositions of mind purified. For as he that walketh on the ground, although he walk warily, can yet scarcely avoid defiling his feet with mire and dust; so is it difficult for you to live on earth, and not to be sometimes defiled with earthly things. Wherefore as the affections of the mind are often defiled by converse with what is earthly, so are they often to be cleansed; and then, most of all, when ye would approach Me, the Very Fount of Purity.

Meanwhile, those daily shortcomings, which I frequently permit for the better trial of virtue, and for the preservation of humility (so that ye have no love in them, but do make efforts to overcome them), need not frighten you away. For I know how to have compassion on your infirmities; and it is more grateful to Me that ye should be drawn to Me by love, than withdrawn by fear. For My law is a law of love, rather than of fear.

MAN. Blessed be Thou, O LORD, Who, in Thy gentleness, dost instruct me so kindly and lovingly. With so much greater readiness, therefore, and confidence will I henceforth come unto Thee; if only, as far as in me lies, and by the help of Thy grace, I be guiltless of any deadly sin, or of design to commit it. But for effacing venial sins[d], which are not altogether a hindrance, there are many and ready means, through Thy gift, O LORD. This one thing I know, that with the LORD there is Mercy, and with Him is plenteous Redemption.

10. *Preparation, or a nearer approach to Holy Communion, by means of Love.*

CHRIST. Having set down the foot of fear, which is, as it were, a distant preparation, approach now nearer with the other, and, as it were, the right foot of love. In the first place, be very careful to come with upright and pure intention, that thou mayest take this Heavenly Food, not out of custom, nor for any inferior end, but out of love to Me, and concern for thine own salvation, and with hungering desire after It. The food which is eaten with hunger and appetite is both more pleasant to the taste, and more nourishing to the body; that food is both unpleasant and injurious which is taken into a loathing stomach. So, also, do I fill the empty and the hungry souls with good things: but the disdainful rich I send empty away.

MAN. Alas, wretched that we are! Why doth not the love of Thee urge us onward? Why do not hunger and nakedness goad us on? Why do not our wounds and perils arouse us?

CHRIST. Taste ye and see how gracious I am, how Powerful, Good, Bountiful, and full of pity. See also how wretched, and miserable, and poor, and naked thou art: but the eyes of all wait on Me, and I give them their meat in due season. Yet few care to think on these things: and, therefore, their soul loatheth this bread as most unsatisfying; and thus they, to whom it is given to enjoy the delights of My Table, still sigh after the flesh-pots of Egypt; and they who might eat the bread

---

[d] S. Augustine often says that these, as distinguished from deadly sins, are effaced by the daily use of the Lord's Prayer; *i. e.* when bearing them in mind and forgiving others, a person uses our Lord's own words for us, "Forgive us our trespasses." [Ed.]

of children, long rather for the husks of swine.

But when Thou sittest down to meat with Me, consider seriously the things that are put before thee; what, and how precious is the Food which is offered to thee. When the children of Israel of old time saw the Manna from heaven, they said amazed, *Man hu, What is this?* How much more oughtest thou to be amazed, O Christian, who art fed, not with Manna shaped by Angels' hands, but with My Body, conceived by the operation of the HOLY GHOST! Oughtest thou not the more to think upon and to admire the excellency of this Food, and that, not coldly and carelessly, but so that, whilst thou art musing, the fire may kindle? Thou knowest how, of old, the Paschal Lamb (a figure of this Sacrament) ought to be partaken of. Nothing of it was to be eaten raw or sodden with water, but only roasted with fire. So, also, ought this Food to be prepared with the fire of love, that it may taste the sweeter, and profit more.

What helpeth most hereto is meditation on My Life and Passion, in which My love burned so ardently, that many waters could not quench it. As a memorial of that great love, I instituted this Sacrament. If thou be slow to love, be ashamed not to requite love. In this, and similar exercises of devout affection, the unction of the Spirit will more fully instruct and direct thee.

To devote a small portion of time to an exercise so pious and useful, before thou comest to so high a Mystery, will not seem burdensome or grievous to thee, if thou considerest with what a multitude of rites and ceremonies and with what preparation the sacrifices of the old law were to be performed. Read Numbers, Leviticus, &c., and be amazed, and reason thus with thyself: If this were done in the shadow and the figure, what in the Very Substance and Truth?

But, indeed, what can be more unworthy or offensive to Me, than to see, that nothing commonly is performed with less care and solicitude than My worship and Sacrifice, than which there is, yet, nothing on earth more sublime, nothing more excellent? Every one hasteth to his own house, but My House is deserted. Men hasten to business and conversation; and of that Guest, the King of kings, Who cometh from Heaven to thee, not that He may be refreshed by thee, but that He Himself may refresh thee, there is little thought. Wouldest thou thyself, when invited by a friend, be willing to be so received by him, so inhospitably treated, so unceremoniously sent away?

Those royal maidens (Esther ii.) had to be trained for a whole year, that when at length they were to appear before King Ahasuerus, they might find favour in his eyes: and shall it be burdensome to a Priest, or to any one of My faithful, to bestow one little hour, or even the fourth part of an hour, that so he may stand before the King of kings duly adorned and prepared, and thus find grace in His Eyes?

MAN. Alas! the blindness and the hardness of the heart of man! not to heed so unspeakable a gift, not more to reverence it! that all other things should be done with such exceeding care and accuracy, and that we should prepare ourselves for the Holy Table of the LORD so casually and carelessly! Behold, O LORD, I acknowledge my iniquity against myself; but yet Thine Eyes see my imperfection. Thus speak I unto Thee, O LORD, and I hear Thee in return thus speaking unto me (and is not Thy Word very fire?); yet my heart languisheth and is cold, and my soul is unto Thee as a barren and thirsty land. I bear a Fire in my bosom; and why doth not my heart burn within me? The Fount of living water is before mine eyes; and why doth not my heart pant after Thee, even as the hart panteth after the water-brook?

CHRIST. O faithful souls, which I have loved with an everlasting love and redeemed at so great a Price, whom I have hitherto fed with such Precious Food, and am willing still henceforth to feed! O ye, My friends and My guests, take heed unto yourselves, and be not careless in a matter so weighty, so difficult and full of danger; where the issue (mark Me well!) is so diverse; life or perdition, according to the character or deserts of each. Behold, thou hast a Fountain, yea, an Ocean of graces, from which every one draweth the more abundantly, the larger is the vessel that he bringeth. Open thy mouth wide, O man, and I will fill it. Enlarge the bosom of thy soul with longings after charity, devotedness, and perfection. I, Who Alone satisfy the longings of the heart, will replenish thee with the gifts of My Grace, that so thou mayest abide in Me, and I in thee. And, having Me, what canst thou want besides? For all things are Mine, and with Me.

MAN. Abide with Me, O Lord, and set Thyself as a seal upon my heart. Draw me, that I may run after Thee in the odour of Thine ointment. Kindle in me the fire which Thou camest to send upon the earth. O that I might love Thee, O Lord, my Strength, my Refuge, and my Deliverer! O that I could embrace Thee with that most burning love of Angels and of Thine Elect! so that nothing might separate me from Thee. For Thou, O God, art my Lot and my Portion for ever; it is good for me to hold me fast by Thee; for whom have I in heaven but Thee, and what is there upon earth that I desire in comparison of Thee?

CHAPTER II.

AN EUCHARISTIC LITANY, FOR THE USE BOTH OF PRIESTS AND COMMUNICANTS, GATHERED OUT OF HOLY SCRIPTURE.

NOTE.—*The passages included between brackets [ ] are for Priests alone, and may be passed over by others.*

Lord, have mercy.
Christ, have mercy.
Lord, have mercy.
O God, the Father of Heaven, Who so lovedst the world as to give Thine Only-Begotten Son to take upon

Him our flesh and to suffer death upon the Cross, Have mercy upon me,

That I may receive Him with entire affection and with the inmost feelings of love; and that I may give up my whole self, all that I am, to Thee, and live not to myself, but to Thee.

O Eternal Father, Who out of love to us sparedst not Thine Own Son, but gavest Him up for us all, Have mercy upon me,

That I may with a grateful heart meditate on this work of such exceeding love, and commemorate it in this sacred Mystery.

O Most Holy FATHER, Who didst send Thy SON into the world, not to condemn the world, but that the world through Him might be saved, Have mercy upon me,

That His Body and Blood may not be unto me for judgment and condemnation, but for life and salvation.

O FATHER, of Infinite Wisdom, Who with wonderful Counsel hast wrought our salvation in the midst of the earth, and hast willed that Thy Son, Whom from Eternity Thou hast begotten Equal with Thyself, should, in time be born of a Virgin, and should be in this Sacrament in a new and wonderful manner, and be present with us even to the end of the world, Have mercy upon me,

That I may never be ungrateful for the blessings of such Thine unspeakable grace and love.

O FATHER, supremely Excellent, with Whom we have an Advocate, JESUS CHRIST, Who is the propitiation for our sins, Have mercy upon me,

That through Him I may obtain from Thee pardon and forgiveness of all my sins; for, Behold, He is the Lamb of GOD *That taketh away the sins of the world.*

O FATHER, Most Mighty, Who with a loud voice didst bear witness that He is Thy Beloved Son in Whom Thou art well-pleased, Have mercy upon me,

And, because by my own doings I am not able to please Thee, look upon the Face of Thy CHRIST, *that through Him I may find grace in Thy sight.*

O FATHER, Most Bountiful, Who, according to the pro-

mise of Thy Most Well-beloved Son, wilt give unto us whatsoever we shall ask in His Name, Have mercy upon me,
> *That I may obtain this one thing, for which I earnestly pray; that I may never receive the Mysteries of the Body and Blood of Thy* SON *unworthily, nor to my condemnation.*

O FATHER of the fatherless, on Whom the eyes of all do wait, and Thou givest them meat in due season, Have mercy upon me,
> *And give me this my Daily Bread, even that Living Bread Which came down from heaven; that It may strengthen and nourish my heart unto life eternal.*

II.

O GOD the Son, REDEEMER of the world, Who, of Thine Infinite Love, didst undertake the work of our redemption; and, taking flesh in the most chaste womb of the Virgin Mary, wast made in the likeness of Man, and wast found in fashion as a Man, Have mercy upon me,
> *That I may cherish in my inmost heart the memory both of this Thy boundless love and of Thy most Holy Incarnation, whensoever, by means of this Sacrament, Thou shalt be born, as it were, in my soul.*

JESU, Most Sweet SAVIOUR, Who hast prepared a table before us against all them that trouble us, Have mercy upon me,
> *That mine enemies may never prevail against me; and that I may fear no evil, because Thou art with me, and in this Sacrameut most inwardly present to me.*

JESU, most Worthy of all love, Who hast said, Come unto Me, all ye that labour and are heavy laden, and I will refresh you, Have mercy upon me,
> *That 1 may be delivered from the weight of my sins, which are like a sore burden upon me, too heavy for me to bear; and with this heavenly Food do Thou refresh my heavy and fainting spirit.*

JESU, Most Pitiful, Who hadst compassion on the

multitude who had long waited on Thee, and when they had nothing to eat, didst, by a wonderful exercise of Thy power, feed them all to the full, Have mercy upon me,

That I may not faint by the way, being deprived of that Heavenly Nourishment.

JESU, Most Bountiful, Who hast given unto us the True Bread, that yieldeth royal dainties; and Who feedest us with the marrow of wheat, Have mercy upon me,

That my soul may be satisfied even as it were with marrow and fatness; and that my heart may never be withered, so that I forget to eat my Bread.

JESU, Most Benign, Who exhortest us to receive Thee, saying, My Flesh is meat indeed, and My Blood is drink indeed; and, Unless ye shall eat the Flesh of the SON of Man, and drink His Blood, ye shall have no life in you, Have mercy upon me,

That I may worthily eat this Bread and drink this Cup, so that I shall hunger no more, nor thirst any more, nor die eternally.

JESU, Most Sweet, Whom Zacchæus received with joy into his house; and Whom the Centurion, out of reverence, did not dare to invite under his roof, Have mercy upon me,

That I may ever combine the feelings of them both, love and fear, whensoever I receive Thee into my house.

JESU, Most Lowly, Who didst vouchsafe to consort and to eat, even with publicans and sinners, saying, The whole need not a physician, but they that are sick, Have mercy upon me,

And vouchsafe to be the Guest of me also, a sinner, and heal my soul which is sick even unto death.

JESU, Great and Marvellous King, Who, that Thou mightest display the power and riches of Thy kingdom, hast prepared for us a great Feast, and hast deigned so lovingly to invite to it all the subjects of Thy kingdom, Have mercy upon me,

That I may come to this Divine Feast with joy and alacrity, yet never without being clothed in a wedding garment.

Jesu, Most Loving, Who, before Thy Passion, desiredst with desire to eat this Passover with Thy disciples, Have mercy upon me,
> That as the hart panteth after the water-brooks, so my soul may in this Sacrament pant after Thee, the Living God.

Jesu, Most Pure, Who when Thou wert about to institute this Sacrament, didst first, with Thy Knees upon the earth, wash the feet of Thy disciples, in token of the purity and cleanness which Thou wouldest enjoin upon us when about to receive these holy Mysteries, Have mercy upon me,
> And wash me throughly from my wickedness, and cleanse me from my sin: wash, not my feet only, but also my hands and my head; so that my affections and deeds and intentions may be pure, whensoever I desire to be a partaker of Thy Table.

Jesu, Most Gracious, Who hast planted the Tree of life in the midst of the Garden, that is, of Thy Church, as a remedy for all the diseases of the soul, and even its very death, Have mercy upon me,
> That I may there gather the fruit of life and immortality, and that by it my youth may be renewed as the eagle's.

Jesu, Most Bountiful, Who hast given Thyself to us, Born, to be one with us; Living with us, to be our Food; Dying to be our Ransom; and Reigning, wilt at length give Thyself to us as our Reward, Have mercy upon me,
> That for these so great benefits my soul may bless Thee at all times; and that all that is within me may bless Thy Holy Name.

Jesu, Most Truthful, Who giving Thyself to be Meat and Drink, didst say, This is My Body Which is given for you, and, This is My Blood which is shed for you, Have mercy upon me,
> That I stagger not in faith at the words of Thy mouth; for Thou art the Truth Itself, in Whose mouth there is no guile nor deceit; Thou art also a Mighty God, with Whom nothing is impossible.

JESU, Most Tender, Who, when Thou wast about to depart out of this world unto the Father, didst leave us a lasting monument of Thy great love; and in this Sacrament didst appoint a Memorial of Thy wondrous works, commanding us to do this in remembrance of Thee, Have mercy upon me,
> *That I may be always most mindful of Thee, and may constantly adore Thine ineffable Power, Wisdom, and Goodness shining forth here; and may never forget all Thy benefits.*

JESU, Most Meek, Who, at Thy Last Supper, wouldest not shut out even Judas from the company of the disciples and from Thy Table, Have mercy upon me,
> *That I, who am, alas! Thy most unworthy and unfaithful servant, may yet never, with Judas, be guilty of Thy Body and Blood.*

JESU, Most Thankful, Who, when this Mystery was accomplished in the sight of Thy disciples, didst give thanks to the Eternal Father, and having sung an hymn, wentest out into the garden, Thy wonted place of prayer, Have mercy upon me,
> *That I may never retire from this surpassing Feast with a thankless heart; but that seriously reflecting on so great a benefit, my soul may more and more burn with love towards Thee.*

JESU, PRIEST FOR EVER, Who didst offer Thyself as a Victim upon the Altar of the Cross; GOOD SHEPHERD, Who didst lay down Thy life for Thy sheep, and dost feed them with Thy Very Body and Blood, Have mercy upon me,
> *And whereas I have gone astray as a sheep that is lost, seek out Thy servant, and bear me on Thy shoulders back to Thy fold, and feed me in that green pasture wherein Thou hast placed me.*

JESU, Most Compassionate, Who, under the form of a stranger, didst join Thyself to the disciples who were going to Emmaus, and at length madest Thyself known to them in the breaking of Bread, Have mercy upon me,

That as I believe Thee to be truly present with me under these visible forms, although I see Thee not with mine eyes, so I may at length be counted worthy to behold Thee with unveiled face; and as meanwhile Thou vouchsafest to uphold me on my way with Thy sweet converse, and to feed me with the Food of Thy Body, my heart may burn within me with love and longing for Thee.

III.

O GOD, the HOLY GHOST, Who, by the wonderful exercise of Thy Divine Power, didst effect the mystery of the Incarnation of our LORD JESUS CHRIST in the Virgin's womb, making her in an ineffable manner fruitful, and sanctifying her, that she might be a fit receptacle for the SON OF GOD, Have mercy upon me,
That I also may, in this Sacrament, receive the same my Lord and my God, with pure affections and a clean heart; and may be able henceforward, by works of holiness to manifest Him openly.

IV.

HOLY TRINITY, ONE GOD, Who, openest Thine Hand, and fillest all things living with plenteousness, Have mercy upon me,
That the Bread Which strengtheneth man's heart may be given to me to eat, and that in the strength of that Food I may walk through this wilderness even to Thy Holy Mount.

HOLY TRINITY, ONE GOD, Who didst command the children of Israel in memory of their deliverance from the hard bondage of Pharaoh, to eat the Paschal Lamb, that type of our Saviour, Have mercy upon me,
That as often as I partake of these Divine Mysteries I may, with grateful heart, reflect upon the works of our Redemption.

HOLY TRINITY, ONE GOD, Who while the children of Israel were passing through the wilderness, didst feed them with manna from heaven, even with Angels' Food, which

possesseth in itself all manner of delight; but when after awhile they loathed it, didst punish them with severity, Have mercy upon me,
> *That with the cleansed palate of my heart I may taste and see how gracious the Lord is; and that my soul may never loathe that Food as light and unsatisfying.*

HOLY TRINITY, ONE GOD, Who didst of old, not once only, chastise with heavy punishment irreverence and wrong in regard to sacrifices and the ark, figures only and shadows of this our Sacrament, Have mercy upon me,
> *That warned by these examples, I may give all diligence to treat these Holy Mysteries the more warily, more holily and devoutly.*

[HOLY TRINITY, ONE GOD, Who of Thine Infinite Clemency, hast chosen me into Thy Ministry, and, raising the poor out of the mire, hast willed that I should exercise the priesthood, and offer gifts and Sacrifices unto Thee for a sweet-smelling savour, Have mercy upon me,
> *That my life and conduct may be answerable to this so high and holy calling; and that I may always with pure hands and clean heart offer unto Thee the Sacrifice of praise, and pay my vows unto Thee, the Most Highest.*

HOLY TRINITY, ONE GOD, Who wouldest have Thy Ministers to be Holy, saying, Be ye holy, for I am holy, Have mercy upon me,
> *That my heart being weaned from all worldly cares and carnal desires, I may serve before Thee in holiness and righteousness all the days of my life.*]

V.

A LITANY PRAYING ALMIGHTY GOD FOR GRACES CORRESPONDING TO THOSE WHICH HE HAS BESTOWED ON THE SAINTS AND CHURCH IN HEAVEN, WITH WHOM WE HAVE COMMUNION.

O GOD, Who didst choose Mary, Blessed among women, for that most profound Mystery of the Incarnation of the LORD; and didst prepare her by the HOLY GHOST to conceive in her most pure womb the LORD of heaven and earth, to bear Him for nine months, and to give birth to the SAVIOUR of the world, Have mercy upon me,

That I, Thine unworthy servant may, in this Sacrament [or Sacrifice], with a pure spirit receive, bear within me [and dispense to others] that Same Lord, even Thy Son.

O GOD, Who didst order that Angels and Archangels should humbly adore their LORD, made Man for us, and should with amazement worship their King lying in a manger; should bring the tidings of great joy that a SAVIOUR was born; and now that He reigneth in heaven, always minister unto Him; yea, when the Priest celebrateth, should in adoring hosts* encompass His very Altar, Have mercy upon me,

That I may always treat this Bread of Angels with due reverence; and that my heart may be so strengthened by the frequent participation of CHRIST, *that mine enemies may never prevail against me.*

O GOD, Who didst elect Joseph to be the betrothed husband of Mary, Mother of GOD, and to be the foster-father of CHRIST JESUS; and didst give him grace to bestow on her diligent care and kindness, and to pay to his supposed Son all worship and honour, Have mercy upon me,

That I may also be as a servant in this Holy Family; and that to CHRIST, *especially in this venerable Sacrament, I may ever pay due worship and reverence.*

VI.

O GOD, Who didst inspire Holy Simeon with patient expectation and ardent longing to see the Messiah and didst at length vouchsafe unto him to see Him with his eyes and to take Him up in his arms, saying for joy, LORD, now lettest Thou, &c., Have mercy upon me,

---

* See S. Chrys. de Sac. vi. 4, S. Greg. the Great, and others.

That I also may ardently desire to see JESUS *in glory; and with no less longing may ever pant after Him, truly present in this Sacrament, and most sweetly enfold Him in the arms of my soul.*

O GOD, Who by the leading of a star didst bring the Magi from a distant country, and guide them to the new-born King of kings; and didst give them grace also humbly to offer Him their gifts, falling down to the ground, with singular faith and deepest devotion, Have mercy upon me,

That I also may come with like faith and devotion to adore the Same King, truly present in this Sacrament, and to honour Him with my offerings, mean though they be; or rather, that I may be presented with His gifts, and received with the same clemency as they.

O GOD, Who didst inspire all the Holy Patriarchs and Prophets, prefiguring by divers types and shadows the mysteries of this Sacrifice and Sacrament, with earnest longing and many prayers and sighs to breathe after the Messiah; Have mercy upon me,

That I may with piety approach, and into a pure heart receive, not the shadow but the Substance, not the figure but the Reality: not the ark but the Holy of Holies; not sheep or oxen, but the VERY SON *of* GOD *Himself.*

O GOD, Who didst consecrate the tender bodies of the Holy Innocents, as Infant Martyrs to the New-born CHRIST, and didst in them hallow the very years of infancy and innocence, Have mercy upon me,

That I may go with innocency to the Altar of GOD, *and with this [Sacrifice and] Sacrament may present myself a living sacrifice, holy, acceptable to my* GOD.

O GOD, Whose servant St. John Baptist, when visited by CHRIST and His Virgin Mother, did for joy leap in his mother's womb, yet afterwards did not think himself worthy to unloose His shoe-latchet: and yet Thou didst vouchsafe to him, that by the Voice of CHRIST Himself he should be called the greatest among those born of women, and more than a prophet; and that, baptizing Him, he should touch His Sacred Head, Have mercy upon me,

That I also may go with joy unto the Altar of God, Who gladdeneth my youth; and yet that I may not appear before His tremendous Majesty without fear and deep humility.

VII.

O GOD, Eternal Father, by Whose revelation, not taught by flesh and blood, St. Peter did confess that JESUS was the CHRIST, the SON of the Living GOD; from Whom also he received the command to feed His sheep, and the keys of the kingdom of heaven, Have mercy upon me,
> *That with lively and unshaken faith I may confess JESUS CHRIST in this Sacrament the true GOD and my LORD; and that owning Him truly and really present here, I may offer Him due reverence.*

O GOD, Who didst cause St. Paul of a wolf to become a lamb, of a persecutor to become a preacher of the Gospel; of a vessel unto dishonour to become a chosen vessel unto Thee; and having taken him up into the third heaven, didst in a wonderful manner instruct him in heavenly mysteries, so that in words of weightiest import he declared the institution and right use of this Sacrament, Have mercy upon me,
> *That whensoever I would approach these awful mysteries, I may, according to his monition, seriously examine myself, and take anxious heed that I receive them not to my condemnation and death, nor be ever guilty of the Body and Blood of the LORD.*

O GOD, Whose servant St. John, the beloved of the LORD, did in the Last Supper, out of singular love to his Master and confidence in His love towards him, lie on the bosom of his LORD, and did thence imbibe those heavenly streams which he afterwards poured forth in his Gospel; and, as an eagle, took a higher flight that he might gaze on the Mysteries of the Divine and Incarnate Word, and then disclose them unto us, Have mercy upon me,
> *That I may be drawn by love to CHRIST my SAVIOUR, present in this Sacrament, rather than be kept back from Him by fear; and that with holy affiance I may lean*

upon my Beloved, and with joy draw Living Water out of the wells of salvation.

O GOD, Who by Thy SON JESUS CHRIST didst in that Last Supper confer the Priesthood on all Thy holy Apostles, and gavest them power to consecrate these holy Mysteries, when, by the previous washing of their feet as a symbol of purity, He had admonished them of the necessity of inward cleanness, and so admitted them to eat of the True Lamb, even the Body and Blood of their LORD,

Grant that I may hold in due honour and reverence the grace and office of the Priesthood, [conferred upon me by the laying on of hands of Bishops their successors,] and that I may never come to the participation of these Divine Mysteries without having first purified my conscience.

O GOD, Who didst inspire the Holy Evangelists to record by clear testimony the institution of this Sacrament, Have mercy upon me,

That I may ever venerate, and partake of this great Mystery with full faith, lively hope, and fervent charity.

O GOD, Who didst give such grace to the holy Disciples of the LORD, that, together with the first believers, they continued daily in the breaking of bread, so that the faithful were of one heart and one soul, and none of them said that aught of the things which he possessed was his own, Have mercy upon us,

That we also who are partakers of One Bread and One Cup may come to the Sacrament of peace and love in the unity of peace and in the bond of charity; and that, all speaking and minding the same things, we may thus with one mind and one mouth glorify GOD, *even our* LORD JESUS CHRIST, *Who is our Peace, making both one.*

VIII.

O GOD, Who didst strengthen the holy Martyrs to make an offering of their body and blood unto CHRIST, the King of Martyrs, Who offered up His own Body and Blood for us on the Altar of the Cross,

*Grant that I, by spiritual martyrdom, may mortify my
members which are upon the earth; and whensoever I
would [celebrate] partake of the Sacred Mysteries, may
first present myself a living sacrifice to* GOD, *acceptable,
holy, and well-pleasing unto* GOD, *a sacrifice of righteousness for an odour of sweetness.*

O GOD, Who didst give grace to all holy Bishops and
Confessors, Priests of the LORD, as Ministers of CHRIST and
faithful dispensers of Thy Mysteries, holily to perform the
office of the Priesthood, frequently to offer for the people
a Sacrifice acceptable unto Thee, and unweariedly to feed
the same with the Bread of the Word and the Sacrament,
Have mercy upon me,

*That I also may with all diligence perform the office of
a faithful [Priest] Christian, that I may never be found
to have despised the healing gifts of salvation, or to have
received the grace of* GOD *in vain.*

IX.

O GOD, Who didst give such grace to holy Anchorites
and Ascetics of old, that going forth from the Egypt of this
world, that is, dead to the world, removed from the breasts
and weaned from the milk which the world giveth to drink,
they longed no more for its flesh-pots, but, manfully trampling on the desires of the flesh, their souls were fed in the
wilderness of this world with the Food of Angels, the
Manna from Heaven, the Living Bread, until they came
to the Land of Promise, flowing with milk and honey, Have
mercy upon me,

*That I too may loathe the miserable meats of Egypt, despising the pleasures of the world, out of longing for
This Heavenly Food, and that I, having the children's
Bread given me to eat, may have no pleasure in the husks
of swine.*

O GOD, Who didst give grace to all holy Virgins and
Widows, with more than manly soul, to hold a stedfast
purpose of continence and chastity, and so to offer their
bodies a living sacrifice to their Bridegroom the living GOD,

and now to be admitted to the Marriage-Supper of the LAMB, Have mercy upon me,

That I, through that Wine[b] *Which maketh virgins to grow, may imbibe a love of chastity, and with the love of a pure heart be ever held in an indissoluble bond of union with the Bridegroom, and from my inmost soul and with my whole affections embrace Him, truly Present in this Sacrament, and be admitted to His Holy Kiss*[c].

X.

O GOD, Who didst give grace to Thy servant, Mary Magdalene, together with her sister, to receive CHRIST into her house, and there, abstaining from serving, to sit at the Feet of the LORD and hear His words; and before, at the Pharisee's feast, to wash the Feet of the LORD with large streams of tears, and to wipe them with the hair of her head, thus showing openly both her love for the LORD and her grief for her sins: and, at length, as He hung upon the Cross, to cleave unto Him, and with burning, eager love, to seek Him in the tomb, Have mercy upon me,

That I also may withdraw my heart from the cares of the world, and may seek above all things to give myself to GOD *in all holy retirement; and that, whensoever I would draw near to my* LORD *in this Sacrament, I may first offer to my* GOD *the tears of a contrite heart, and with joy cleave unto Him Crucified, desiring not to glory in any thing save the Cross of my* LORD JESUS CHRIST.

O GOD, Who hast brought all Thy Blessed and Elect Saints to that haven, whither we, unhappy, are but tending, where now, in their home, with open face, in beatific

---

[b] Zech. ix. 17.

[c] Cant. i. 2, " Let Him kiss me with the kisses of His Mouth," is interpreted of the H. Comm., as the highest union with our LORD here below, by S. Ambrose, Ep. 42, § 15, " We kiss CHRIST with the kiss of Communion " (add de Isaac, c. 8, and the de Sacram. v. 2; see further note q, on S. Cyprian Ep. vi. p. 15. Oxf. Tr.) Hence a profane Communion is likened to the kiss of Judas.

vision, they behold, and, with enlarged mouth, do feed upon That Bread, Which we see only through a glass darkly, and receive veiled under another Form. O how, amidst so many storms and perils, do we need Food for the way, that we may win our way! CHRIST is our Food for the way: He is the Way, and the Truth, and the Life, the sole Solace of our pilgrimage, Have mercy upon us,

That we may at least be supported by Him by the way, until with them we too are satisfied with the plenteousness of Thine house, and drink of Thy pleasures as out of a river.

PRAYER.

O GOD, Who, under this marvellous Sacrament, hast left us a memorial of thy Passion, grant, we beseech Thee, that we may so venerate the sacred Mysteries of Thy Body and Blood, that we may ever feel within us the fruit of Thy Redemption; Who livest and reignest with the FATHER in the Unity of the HOLY GHOST, One GOD, world without end. Amen.

CHAPTER III.

THE LORD'S PRAYER APPLIED, IN VARIOUS EXERCISES AND PIOUS MEDITATIONS, TO THE PRACTICE OF DEVOUT COMMUNION.

When about to approach to the Holy Feast in which CHRIST *Himself is received, we shall do well first to make use of the words also of* CHRIST, *and the very Prayer which we have received from His sacred Lips, by way, as it were, of Grace before Meat.* *The Priest, indeed, says this Prayer at the beginning of the Office for Holy Communion; but he may very profitably meditate upon it before he says that Office; and every Communicant also may hence readily draw forth devout affections. With the deep affec-*

tions, then, of our minds, let us say,

Our Father.

Most Mighty, most Wise, most Merciful, Who, that Thou mightest show Thy sweetness towards Thy children, dost fill the hungry with that most sweet Bread Which cometh down from heaven, and with Fatherly love dost wonderfully nourish, cherish, and preserve whatsoever Thou hast made! behold, even I, though one of the vilest of Thy children, lift up mine eyes with confidence unto Thee *Who art in Heaven*, beseeching Thee, that with the Eyes of Thy Fatherly Goodness Thou wouldest look down upon me, miserable and in want; living far away from the Face of my FATHER, among the sons of Eve, in the vale of tears; an exile and pilgrim on the earth, yet sighing unto Thee my most sweet FATHER. And what now should I rather ask of Thee, than that

1. *Hallowed be Thy Name.*

For this is the main wish and desire of my heart, that all that I do, say, think, may tend to the glory of Thy Great Name. And now, especially, when I am coming to the Sacred Mysteries of the Body and Blood of Thy SON, this only do I purpose, this only do I desire, that Thy Supreme Majesty, Power, Goodness, and Wisdom may be praised; to Whom all honour and glory, eternal praise and thanksgiving, are due from every creature, for that Thou hast so loved us as to give us Thine Only-Begotten SON both as our Food, and as the Price of our salvation. For which, since we can never worthily praise Thee, O may Thy SON Himself glorify Thee! for Thou, also, hast exalted Him above all things, and hast given Him a Name which is above every name.

2. *Thy kingdom come.*

That kingdom, of the happiness and delights whereof we have in this Sacrament the foretaste. For Thou hast given us the Body and Blood of Thy SON as an earnest of future glory; and thus, by the grace of adoption, Thou hast made us Thine heirs, joint-heirs with CHRIST.

Meanwhile, while we are yet pilgrims in exile far from the LORD, make us so to use this sacred Pledge, that Thy Kingdom of grace may daily more and more advance in us till at length Thy Kingdom of Glory come unto us.

3. *Thy Will be done.*

And what is Thy Will, but our sanctification? especially when we draw near to this Holy of Holies. It is Thy Will, moreover, that we eat the Flesh of the Son of Man, and drink His Blood; otherwise, we shall have no life in us. But who that is conscious of his weakness could presume to do this, hadst not Thou, together with Thy SON, so lovingly and condescendingly both willed it and commanded it? For to will and to do is to Both the same. Because, therefore, Thou so willest, let what Thou wilt be done, and as Thou wilt; for Thou willest that we be holy, because He, to Whom we draw near, is Holy, yea, the Holy of Holies, Thy SON. But who can make holy, save Thou? Give what Thou commandest. Grant that we may treat holy things, holily only, purely, and devoutly.

Whence, *as in heaven*, the saints, with enlarged mouth, pure heart, and burning love, feed on this living Bread with face unveiled, *so on earth* may we also with great desire and pure affection feed on Him, veiled under the Forms[a] of Bread and Wine, until together with the Elect we too shall enjoy Him as He is, and be satisfied with the plenteousness of Thine House.

4. *Give us this day our Daily Bread.*

For the eyes of all wait upon Thee, O LORD, and Thou givest them their meat in due season. Thou openest Thine Hand and fillest all things living with plenteousness. And canst Thou, then, fail me? Thou knowest, O LORD, that the soul, no less than the body, needeth to be restored by food, that it may live. For as the natural heat wasteth away the one, so doth the burning of desire consume the other. But blessed sons, who in the House of so great a FATHER,

[a] "Hereafter shall follow Sermons—of the due receiving of His Blessed Body and Blood, under the Form of Bread and Wine." Homilies, Part 1. end.

(the Church), have bread so abundantly. Here the bread of grace and of the Word of GOD is broken copiously. Here the bread of Sacraments, and especially that Living Bread Which came down from heaven, Which was born in Bethlehem (the house of Bread), the Bread of Angels, the heavenly Manna, is set before all. O precious and noble Food! O the great love and mercy of the Eternal FATHER! For to me, who neither sow nor reap nor gather into barns, is given from heaven the Wheat of the Elect, the Bread of Life. Thou, O LORD, hast sown It in the midst of the earth; Thou hast reaped It with the sickle of death; Thou hast stored It up in the granary of Thy Church, and givest It wholly to nourish Thy children.

Grant unto me, then, O Most Gracious FATHER, that I may often be worthily refreshed with this Bread: yea, that I may partake of it daily—if not sacramentally, at least spiritually—that It may daily do me good. For as I offend and fail daily, it is but reason that I daily also receive relief, to recruit my strength. O that in this wilderness I may be so sustained by this Heavenly Bread, this Provision for the way, that in the strength of that Food I may journey on even unto the mount of GOD.

5. *And forgive us our debts.*

Alas! how numerous and how heavy are they! for in many things we all offend. Poor and wretched indeed are we; we have been unable to pay, nor are we able.

But behold, O LORD, with Thee there is Mercy, and with Thy SON, Whom in Thy pity Thou hast given to us, there is plenteous redemption. He the Just One, Undefiled, and wholly Innocent, what we owed, He hath paid; wherein we sinned, He hath atoned; He hath abundantly satisfied Thy Justice, giving us the exhaustless treasury of His Merits, and the Infinite Price of His Blood.

But all this treasure we possess, laid up as a deposit in the precious shrine of the most Holy Sacrament.

This Treasure, then, do I now offer unto Thee, O Eternal FATHER, that Thou mayest take thence what Thou demandest of me for my debts. I have nothing wherewith to pay; but the Merits of Thy SON are superabundant, so that thence my debts may be discharged.

For His sake, therefore, forgive us, *as we also forgive our debtors*. We forgive them, indeed, lest we should not be of the bond of charity, and so come unworthily to the Sacrament of unity and peace, and in vain seek healing from GOD, while, man against man, we retain anger. For what communion can we have with the Body and Blood of the LORD, if we be not joined in the communion of peace and love with the members of His Mystical Body, even our neighbours?

It behoveth us, therefore, when we would approach the Altar, first to be reconciled to our brethren if they have aught against us, and then to come and offer our gift. This, Thy SON both taught us to do, and this He did Himself. For whilst He hung upon the Cross, and was paying the debt of all, He forgave His enemies, and besought Thee on behalf of His murderers, saying, "Father, forgive them," &c. Forgive me, therefore, my debts, on behalf of which Thy SON offers His Merits: for if, setting these aside, Thou shouldest mark iniquity, O LORD, who shall stand? &c.

6. *And lead us not into temptation.*

O LORD, Who hast prepared a Table before us against all those that trouble us, and settest thereon Bread Which strengtheneth the heart of man against all the temptations of the world, the flesh, and the devil, give unto me, through this Heavenly and Life-giving Food, strength and courage, that I may never yield when tempted, but cleave stedfastly unto Thee.

May I not seek to be the friend of this world, nor to be conformed to this world; but, by virtue of this Heavenly Food, may I be transformed into Thee; and may I seek to please, and fear to displease Thee Alone! May this earth be vile in mine eyes, since here I gaze upon Heaven, and embrace the LORD of the whole world!

Let not carnal pleasures any way move me, to whom it is given to feed on the Flesh of the Spotless Lamb, and on the Heavenly Manna, in Which I find delights far greater, yea, every sweet savour.

And what power can Satan have over me, since GOD is with me? For if GOD be for us, who can be against us? &c.

7. *But deliver us from evil.*

For in this life we are exposed to manifold accidents and misfortunes; and these are to be accounted evils, in so far as, through our frailty, they cast us down and withdraw us from Thee. For to be led away from Thee, the Chief Good, is, indeed, the chiefest of all evils. But who shall deliver us from this evil but Thou, the Fountain of all good, and He Whom Thou hast given us to be our Advocate with Thee, and the Author of all bliss and salvation, JESUS CHRIST, Who, by His own Blood, hath delivered us from sin and death?

By This Mediator, do Thou make all things to work together for our good, seeing there is salvation for us in none other. As therefore He is truly present in this Sacrament, so may He be with us every where! May He feed, rule, preserve, protect, lead us, according to His most merciful lovingkindness, as the sheep of His pasture! Whatsoever betide us, it will not be evil, so it separate us not from the Chief Good. For it is good for me to hold me fast by GOD, and to put my trust in the LORD GOD. For whom have I in heaven but Thee? and there is nought on earth that I desire in comparison of Thee, &c.

¶ *This meditation on the Lord's Prayer may be used as well after as before Communion.*

THE LORD'S PRAYER

ACCOMMODATED TO THE FOUR ENDS OF SACRIFICE; OR THE FOUR KINDS OF OBLATIONS.

(*For the use of both Priests and People.*)

Sacrifices under the Old Law were of divers kinds; the whole Burnt-offering;

the Peace-offering, which again was two-fold, one as a Thank-offering for blessings received, the other as supplicatory for future blessings; and lastly, the Sin-offering. See Levit. i.—viii.

Four kinds of Sacrifices therefore are ranged under the following names:

1. Adoratory, *or the Sacrifice of praise; which is offered to* GOD *simply to His praise and to the honour of His Supreme Majesty, and to express our love of His Supreme Goodness. Hence the victim was to be burnt entire, to denote,* 1. *The Supreme Dominion of* GOD *over all things.* 2. *That all things are to be referred to Him as their ultimate end.* 3. *That we ourselves belong wholly to* GOD, *&c.*

2. Eucharistic, *or the Sacrifice of thanksgiving; by which thanks are offered for the Divine blessings of peace.*

3. Impetratory; *by which we beg of* GOD *grace and blessings both bodily and spiritual, both for ourselves and others.*

4. Propitiatory; *whereby we implore pardon for sin, and win the favour of* GOD *to us.*

The whole virtue and efficacy of these various sacrifices are remarkably comprised in the one single Sacrifice of the New Law.

It will therefore be a pious and profitable way both of celebrating and partaking of the Holy Communion to refer that sacred service to these four ends; towards which the LORD's Prayer, according to the following method, will be a suitable help.

Our Father Who art in Heaven.

O LORD, Holy FATHER, Who hast comprised the multitude of legal sacrifices in the offering of the One Sacrifice of the New Law; and Who didst, on Mount Calvary, Thyself, show unto us, in Thy Beloved SON,— that Chief Priest, yea the Great High Priest of both covenants,—a pattern of a perfect oblation, according to which we are to do; grant we beseech Thee, that by Thy grace we may be conformed unto the image of Thy SON, Who vouchsafed to be made like unto us, in the form of a servant.

And as He, on the Cross, offered Himself up, both Body and Soul, unto Thee His Eternal FATHER, with shedding of Blood, after the order of Aaron; and in an unbloody manner also at His Last Supper, after the order of Melchizedech[b]; so may we also, after His example, daily present our bodies a living sacrifice, holy, acceptable unto Thee, a reasonable service; and our souls also with all their powers and faculties, as a holocaust of praise, a sacrifice of thanksgiving for gifts received, of supplication for blessings to come, and that Thou mayest look graciously upon us, and forgive us our sins.

I.—THE SACRIFICE OF PRAISE.

Hallowed be Thy Name.

O LORD JESU CHRIST, Who, out of the love of the Eternal FATHER, and seeking, in and through all things, not Thine own but His Glory, didst give up Thyself for us as an Offering and Sacrifice to GOD for a sweet-smelling savour; I praise, and with my whole heart adore Thy Supreme Power, Goodwill, Wisdom, Justice, Mercy, &c., which so wondrously shine forth in this Sacrifice and work of Redemption.

I rejoice that by this Offering the vain idols of the Gentiles and their profane sacrifices were abolished, and that pure and true worship and honour were restored to Thee, the Living and True GOD. Wherefore I now offer unto Thee the sacrifice of praise, and pay my vows unto the Most High. I believe in Thee, and I hope in Thee, and I love Thee above all things: and I give up myself wholly unto Thee, and make an offering of my whole mind, and will, and memory, as a perpetual holocaust; and that, until

Thy Kingdom come.

That kingdom which Thou hast prepared for us from the beginning of the world, O Thou Great King, and Prince of the kings of the earth, Who didst reign from the Cross, and cast out the prince of this world; Who hast loved us, and washed us from our sins in Thy Blood, that Thou mightest make us kings and priests unto GOD.

O JESU, my King and my GOD! behold I, Thy servant and the son of Thy handmaid, make choice of Thee this day, in this Holy Communion and Sacrifice, to be

---

[b] See S. Greg. Nyss., &c., in "The Holy Eucharist a Comfort to the Penitent," p. 22.

my King for ever; and I offer myself to Thee as Thy servant for ever. To Thee only will I henceforward offer the sacrifice of praise; and I will call upon Thy Name. Blessed be Thy Name, O LORD, from this time forth for evermore.

II.—THE SACRIFICE OF THANKSGIVING.

Thy Will be done.

Even Thine, O LORD JESU CHRIST, Who didst come into this world, that Thou mightest do the Will of Thy FATHER and finish the work which He gave Thee to do, our Redemption. Wherefore, also, that Thou mightest fulfil it, Thou becamest obedient to GOD the FATHER even unto Death, the Death of the Cross. And from the merit of this obedience, all grace, life, and salvation, yea, all good, hath in such copious streams flowed down upon us.

But what return shall I make unto the LORD for all the benefits that He hath done unto me? Nothing, I know, can be more pleasing to Thee, than that Thy Will should in all things be done by us.

Behold, therefore, in union with Thy most sacred Sacrifice, in which Thou didst of Thine own Will submit Thyself to the Will of the Eternal FATHER (for Thou wast offered up because Thou willedst), and which Sacrifice I now commemorate in this Communion, I do now freely and entirely submit my will to Thine; and I desire exceedingly that this Will may be most fully done by all men, every where, and always; and *that*, by way of thanksgiving for all Thy blessings of creation, redemption, preservation, providential guidance, &c.

Bless the LORD, O my soul; and all that is within me bless His Holy Name, &c.

III.—THE SACRIFICE OF PRAYER.

Give us this day our daily bread.

O most Loving FATHER, by Whose Infinite Bounty Thy SON JESUS CHRIST was given to us to be our Guide, Physician, Shepherd, Nourisher, &c.; for Thou didst so love the world as to give Thine Only-Begotten Son.

He, then, that spared not His own SON, but delivered Him up for us all, how shall He not with Him also freely give us all things? More especially, since that SON Himself gives ground for such great confidence in Him, saying, *Verily, verily, I say unto you, whatsoever ye shall ask the* FATHER *in My Name, He will give it you.*

When, therefore, we ask for Bread, will He give us a stone? or for an egg, a scorpion?

Behold, O Eternal FATHER, I present before Thee His Name, and with It the Infinite Merits of that Perfect Sacrifice which He made on the Cross; and I beseech Thee to *give us our daily bread,* bread for our bodies, but chiefly, the Bread of the soul; asking under the one, for all things needful to the present life, that we may the better serve Thee; and under the other, for the food of the soul, even the gifts of grace, and whatsoever belongeth to the strengthening of the heart; so that we may not faint in the way whereby we are going towards our Country, where we shall be satisfied with the plenteousness of Thy House, &c.

IV.—THE SACRIFICE OF PROPITIATION, OR DEPRECATION.

And forgive us our trespasses.

O FATHER of Mercies, with Whom we have an Advocate, our LORD JESUS CHRIST, Who was made the Propitiation for our sins, and Who reconciled us to Thyself by His Blood, when He offered Himself a Sacrifice for sin upon the Altar of the Cross. O costly Ransom! O what plenteous Redemption! what superabounding satisfaction for my sins, yea, for the sins of the whole world!

This do I now present and offer unto Thee, O Holy FATHER! now that in this Communion I renew the remembrance of It.

I offer unto Thee, moreover, in sacrifice, my body, and all my members, that by the willing mortification of them, I may present the sacrifice of a troubled spirit. An humbled and a contrite heart, do not, I beseech Thee, O LORD, despise. But look on the Face of Thy CHRIST, Who bare our sins in His own Body on the Tree: by Whose stripes we are healed.

But what will it profit us

to be delivered from our past offences, if we be not fenced against them for the time to come? We beseech Thee, therefore,

Lead us not into temptation.

For the imagination of man's heart is evil from his youth. O LORD, Thou knowest our misery, and the weakness of Thy creatures, and how we can do nothing without Thee. I beseech Thee for Thy Mercy's sake, and for the merit of that Propitiatory Sacrifice Which was finished on the Cross, that Thou wouldest put away from us all stumbling-blocks, temptations, perils, occasions of sin, by which Thou foreseest that we may be led again to sin.

Be it far from Thee to give us up, in Thine anger, to the desires of our heart, and to suffer us to be tossed about by temptations, as by the waves of the sea, without rudder or oar. Rather, O GOD of Truth and Faithfulness, be Thou with me in trial, and suffer me not to be tempted above that which I may be able to bear.

Wherefore I present unto Thee the Sacrifice of Thy Body and Blood, that Thou mayest give me strength against the temptations of the world, the flesh, and the devil. If Thou, LORD, art with us and for us, nothing can hurt us.

But deliver us from evil.

O LORD! Who willest not that any should perish, but that all men should be saved, put away from us, we beseech Thee, penal evils also, by which we possibly might be led to do the evil of sin, even to offend Thee, and make shipwreck of our salvation. Mercifully turn from us the scourges of Thy wrath, wars, famine, pestilence, &c.

We acknowledge that we worthily deserve to suffer these things; for we have sinned against Thee, our Brother, yea, our FATHER, and are no more worthy to be called Thy sons.

Yet for Thine own sake, O LORD, and for Thy Name's sake (for it is good), remove Thy strokes away from us, and in Thy Mercy turn away from us all evil things; or grant, at least, that all, even evil things, may work togather for good to them that love Thee.

To this end, I offer to

Thee, O JESU! the Sacrifice or Communion of Thy Body and Blood, yea, rather, Thyself, as an antidote and remedy for every ill. Though I walk in the midst of the shadow of death I will fear no evil, for Thou art with me.

¶ *Another Paraphrase upon the* LORD'S *Prayer, adapted to the Seven Words upon the Cross, will be found in Chap.* vii.

CHAPTER IV.

A SHORT METHOD FOR THE DEVOUT AND PROFITABLE PARTICIPATION AND CELEBRATION OF HOLY COMMUNION.

In order to reap the benefit which is to be derived from the Sacrament and Sacrifice of the Eucharist, it is of the greatest moment, in what manner we approach It.

Be assured, then, that it is a very imperfect method, and one void of spiritual consolation, to be content with the bare repetition of certain pre-composed forms of prayer, in common use, before and after Communion. Greater diligence in preparation, surely, is required for this Sacrament, so awful, so abounding in exceeding gifts of grace, which yet, in effect, correspond with the mind and disposition of the receiver.

For this Sacrament is the Food of the soul, of no less use and necessity to it, than is its own peculiar food to the body. Now that food, we know, does most good, and yields the greatest nourishment, which is eaten with hunger; and to produce this sensation, some exercise, previously to eating, should be made use of; for this absorbs and dissipates the vicious humours which might accumulate in the system: and the natural heat thereby excited whets the stomach, so that it becomes both more desirous of food, and more fit for its digestion; whence the food supplies wholesome nourishment to the whole body.

E

What, according to the same mode of reasoning, is to be done, that the Food of the soul (the Sacrament of the Body and Blood of CHRIST) may do us good, because partaken of with appetite, you have here in few words:

The mind must be employed in devout meditations and holy exercises. For these will gradually expel the depraved affections of the mind, and the warmth of charity and the flame of Divine love will be enkindled in it, so that it may the more earnestly desire that Heavenly Food, and be the more fitted to receive It with profit and advantage.

If you neglect such previous exercise, you will receive this Food without hunger or desire, and thus you will have small relish for It; and what remains but that your soul should at length loathe that Food as light and unsatisfying? Because, forsooth, thou tastest not how sweet the LORD is in that Heavenly Feast, which, though It contain within Itself every sweet savour, yet will It not satisfy with goodness any but the soul that is empty, and that hungereth after It.

We will, therefore, give some exercises suited to increase the hunger for this Food and benefit from It. Thou must use them in the way of pious aspirations, not casually and superficially, but with earnest affection, and utter them in the heart rather than with the lips.

For the affection of the mind is the one thing which must season and recommend every work of piety, else it will become distasteful and wholly insipid.

Every one is at liberty to lengthen these exercises. We have but furnished a method and a form. Yet I fear there are some who will turn away from this and any similar exercise, as being too long to be made use of as often as they intend to communicate.

Yet, would that they but well weighed and considered the Majesty of this Sacrifice and Sacrament, that they might more earnestly desire to draw benefit and spiritual refreshment from It! Nothing is difficult to him that loveth. He never wearies of labour and toil, whose heart burns with the desire of heavenly grace.

If, however, we have not always time for it, still it will be useful frequently to prepare *in this way for Holy Communion.*

Yet I see not with what face any of us can complain of prolixity in this matter, who in other matters, and those vain and trifling, are but too lavish and prodigal of time.

How few are there who do not, every day, most readily give up one entire hour (not to say more than one), to the care and refreshment of the body! And shall it be thought a hardship to devote as much, nay, even one quarter of an hour, to the Heavenly Feast? Yet in the one the mortal body alone, in the other the immortal soul takes food.

What! shall all our bodily and common affairs be transacted with so much care and diligence, with such accuracy and attention: and shall the business of the soul and of salvation, and this the chief of all, be treated with such carelessness and haste?

AN EXERCISE

BEFORE COMMUNION.

The several points to be observed in this exercise, may be reduced to three principal. 1. Self-Examination. 2. Kindling of devotion. 3. Prayer for Grace.

FIRST POINT.
SELF-EXAMINATION.

The necessity of this is shown by,

1. The sacrifices of the Old Testament; which although signs only, or shadows and figures of this Sacrament, yet were not to be offered except by the pure and holy. It is indeed wonderful with what manifold rites and ceremonies, those who offered them were to be cleansed for that purpose. See Exod. xxxviii. Levit. xxii., &c.

2. Those most solemn words of the Apostle, in which he asserts that those who receive unworthily are guilty of the Body and Blood of the LORD. *O what great need, to listen earnestly to his warning, or rather threat:* "Let a man examine himself, and so let him eat of that Bread and drink of that Cup!"

3. *Reason itself; because holy things must be handled holily only. But what is more holy than this Sacrament, in which the Holy of Holies is Himself Present?*

I. *In the first place, then, examine thy conscience; and if thou shalt find it guilty of grievous sin, thou shouldst clear it by a special confession; lest thou come unworthily, and so eat judgment to thyself. Lesser infirmities and disorderly affections of the mind thou must endeavour to put away, that so thou mayest derive the fuller benefit from this Sacrament. Then, cherish the deepest grief for thy sins, with firm resolution of amendment.*

O my Most Loving GOD, my CREATOR and my SAVIOUR! I grieve from my inmost heart that I ever offended Thee, my LORD and my GOD! Whom I ought to love above all things; because Thou art good to all, and hast bestowed very many blessings upon me; while I, alas, wretched and ungrateful sinner that I am, have returned Thee evil only for Thy good.

But be Thou merciful unto my sins, O LORD. For now I firmly purpose and resolve no more to offend Thee, and to shun all occasions of sin. And therefore do I now desire to receive this Sacrament, that I may be strengthened in the love of Thee, and may be defended against all occasions of sin; that Thou mayest abide in me, and I in Thee.

II. *See whether thou comest to these Sacred Mysteries with an upright and pure intention, or only out of custom, or for some by-end. To sift the intention is of very great use, because the intention gives the character to every act, and on it depends its worth. The exercise may be of this sort.*

I desire, O GOD, to offer to Thee this Sacrifice to the praise and glory of Thy Name, and to the benefit also of my own soul, and of Thy whole Holy Church [c].

An offering of a free heart will I, therefore, give unto Thee, and I will praise Thy

[c] "We entirely desire Thy Fatherly Goodness mercifully to accept this our Sacrifice of praise and thanksgiving, most humbly beseeching Thee, that by, &c., we and all Thy whole Church may obtain remission of our sins and all other benefits of His Passion." Eng. Lit.

Name, O Lord, for it is good.

For what else can I seek for, besides Thee, O my GOD, and my All? If I have Thee, what have I not? If I worship Thee for Thine own sake, Thou wilt be my exceeding great Reward. What have I in heaven but Thee, and what is there on earth that I can wish for apart from Thee? For Thou Thyself art the Portion of mine inheritance, and of my cup; Thou art He Who shalt maintain my lot.

The intention may be made yet more special, by having regard unto the ends to which, according to the meaning of the institution, the Sacrifice and, by consequence, the Sacrament ought to have respect. For it is

I. ADORATORY,

Or a Sacrifice of praise; to be offered to GOD *in acknowledgment of His Supreme dominion, and as it were the highest worship due to His Supreme Majesty.*

O LORD! Worthy art Thou, for Thy Supreme Excellency, Wisdom, and Power, to receive praise and glory and honour from every creature. Therefore will I praise Thee, O LORD, with my whole heart, and glorify Thy Name for ever. I will offer unto Thee the Sacrifice of praise, and pay my vows unto Thee, O Thou Most Highest, &c. Be Thou blessed, and praised, and glorified, and exalted above all for ever.

II. EUCHARISTIC,

Or a peace-offering; to be presented unto the LORD *as a thanksgiving for His numberless benefits.*

What shall I render unto the Lord for all the benefits that He hath done unto me? Who hath so often forgiven me all my iniquities, and crowneth me moreover with mercy and loving-kindness; Who continually satisfieth my desires with good things, and with such kindness provideth both for my body and my soul. I am less than the least of all Thy Mercies, O Lord; for great is Thy mercy toward me, &c.

O LORD, because Thou hast made me, I owe Thee myself; and seeing that by Thy SON, Who for me became

Man, Thou hast re-made me, I owe Thee more than myself.

But what am I? dust and ashes. And all besides? A breath and vanity. And Thou too, O LORD, needest nought that is mine. Behold therefore Thy Beloved SON! Him do I offer unto Thee, O FATHER, seeing that I can present nothing better nor more grateful than Him in Whom Thou art well-pleased.

III. PROPITIATORY,

Or, Deprecatory; to be offered to GOD *as a means of obtaining the pardon of our sins.*

O LORD! invited so lovingly to Thy rich Feast, what shall I do, miserable, poor, naked, and without the wedding garment; conscious, too, of so many sins by which I have merited Thy wrath rather than Thy grace? Behold the Mediator between GOD and Man, CHRIST JESUS, Thy SON! Him do I offer unto Thee; Him, Who did no sin, yet became the Propitiation for our sins, and washed us in His own Blood, &c.

O LORD, look upon the Face of Thy CHRIST; and see what labours in His Life, what agonies in His Passion, what pains in His Death, He endured for us. All these do I offer unto Thee as the satisfaction for my sins; and that by means of this Sacrifice, that, by virtue of It, Thou mayest impart to me the virtue and efficacy of those Sufferings, and mercifully forgive my offences, and take not vengeance of my sins.

IV. IMPETRATORY;

To be offered unto GOD *in supplication for the obtaining of blessings bodily and spiritual, and for turning away all evil, and that for ourselves, our friends and enemies, the righteous and sinners, the living, the dead, &c.*

O LORD! Rich in blessings, and Bountiful in gifts; of Whom, and through Whom, and by Whom are all things! I am poor and needy. But what may we not obtain from Thee, Who hast given unto us the Very Fountain of all grace, even Thine Only-begotten SON; and together with Him hast bestowed on us all good? In Him Thou hast laid up the countless treasures of grace, wisdom, and goodness, that He might be rich towards all.

Him therefore do I offer unto Thee, that through Him Who intercedeth for us, and Who is worthy to be heard in that He feared, to Thy Church Thou mayest give enlargement and peace; to the righteous, perseverance; to sinners, pardon; to the departed, refreshment[d]; to us all, Thy grace, and, in the end, life everlasting, &c.

v. *This Mystery being instituted by* CHRIST *in remembrance of His Passion, it is very profitable to thee, and very pleasing to* GOD, *to offer It, specially directing thy mind to the memory and veneration of the Passion of the* LORD.

SECOND POINT.

KINDLING OF DEVOTION.

When about to approach to these awful Mysteries, content not thyself with thy ordinary habit of devotion, but take all pains to excite within thee some special acts of devotion. To this end it will much avail,

[d] See above, on p 18. note.

amid the exercises of the highest virtues, to meditate on the following points, (for in meditation the fire of devotion is kindled), namely, Who cometh in this Sacrament; to whom He cometh; wherefore; in what manner; how often He cometh, and the like.

I. FAITH

Is to be exercised by considering that CHRIST *Himself, Very* GOD *and Very Man, Who was born, Who suffered, and died for us, is verily and indeed here present, &c.*

O CHRIST JESU! Very GOD and Man, of One Substance, Majesty, and Power with the FATHER, I believe and confess with firm faith that Thou art verily and indeed Present in this Sacrament. For Thou, the Truth Itself, didst say,

THIS IS MY BODY.

I believe whate'er the SON of GOD hath told;
What the Truth hath spoken, that the truth I hold.
Lord, increase my faith, &c.

This exercise of faith is in the highest degree beneficial, because on the true belief of this point rests all the devotion of this Sacrament. For if we believe with lively faith that

CHRIST, *Very* GOD *and Man, is present in this Sacrament, how can we treat such sacred and awful Mysteries with such slight reverence and devotion?*

II. HOPE

Is to be exercised by the consideration that GOD *is most Compassionate, Merciful, Gentle, Wise, &c.*

O Lord of Hosts! blessed is the man that hopeth in Thee. Why art thou, then, so vexed, O my soul; and why art thou so disquieted within me? Hope thou in GOD, the Fountain of all goodness, and the Author of all grace, Whom thou hast Present in this Sacrament. Draw near to Him with full trust, for He is Good and Gracious, and of great mercy unto all them that call upon Him. He Alone can give all things, for He is LORD over all; yea He willeth to give all things, for He is supremely Good.

O God, my Hope! therefore doth my heart rejoice, because, when I receive Thyself in this Sacrament, I have good hope that Thou wilt withhold nothing, Who hast given Thyself to us. In Thee, O Lord, do I trust; O let me not be disappointed of my hope.

III. CHARITY.

It is exercised by the consideration that GOD *is supremely Good, Excellent and Bountiful, and so Loving towards us, &c.*

O Most Sweet SAVIOUR, CHRIST JESU! how great was the force of Thy love which drew Thee from the Bosom of the FATHER into this vale of tears, to take upon Thee our flesh, and endure unnumbered miseries, wrongs, yea the Cross and Death; and all this solely for the sake of us, miserable men, and for our salvation!

O what exceeding love! Thou mightest have condemned, and Thou didst prefer to save us. We were guilty, and Thou, the Innocent, dost suffer punishment, that Thou mightest free the guilty.

Out of love, therefore, didst Thou come down to us into the flesh: and when at length about to depart out of this world, Thou didst leave this Sacrament to us as a pledge of love, that in a wholly new and wonderful manner Thou mightest ever abide with us, Whose delights are to be with the sons of men.

O LORD! how worthy art Thou to be loved, Who hast done so much for love of us! I will love Thee, therefore, O LORD my Strength. The LORD is my strong Rock and my Refuge and my SAVIOUR.

O GOD, Who art Love! He that abideth in love, abideth in Thee. I desire to receive Thee in this Sacrament, that I may be the more firmly bound to Thee in the bonds of love. Who shall separate me from the love of CHRIST my SAVIOUR? O that neither life nor death, nor change of state, nor any other creature, may ever have power for this!

IV. HUMILITY AND REVERENCE.

By meditating that GOD *is of Supreme Majesty, and yet cometh from the Throne of His Glory to thee the meanest worm of the earth, &c.*

O LORD our GOD! how excellent is Thy Name in all the earth! Thou art the King of heaven and earth, Whom Angels praise, Dominions adore, Powers dread. But what is man that Thou art mindful of him, giving unto him a Memorial of Thy marvellous works? or the son of man that Thou visitest him, coming to him in this Sacrament? O LORD, I am not worthy that Thou shouldest come under my roof, but speak the word only, &c.

V. HUNGER AND DESIRE,

By considering, first, the manifold fruits and graces of this Sacrament, and then thine own miseries and wants.

O Holy Bread! Bread Which strengtheneth man's heart, Which whosoever eateth shall live for ever; but he that eateth not hath not life. How amiable are Thy tabernacles, O LORD of Hosts! My soul hath a desire and longing to enter into Thy courts, O LORD, where Thou dost dispense that Bread, and givest Food to them that fear Thee.

Bow down thine ear, O LORD, and hear me, for I am poor and in misery; refresh my hungry soul, that so, in the strength of that Food, I may walk through the wilderness of this world even unto the mount of GOD, until with enlarged mouth I shall feed on Thee in Thy Kingdom, and be satisfied with the plenteousness of Thy House.

VI. *Finally, Meditation on our* LORD'S *Passion is of the greatest efficacy in exciting the devotion of the heart.*

THIRD POINT.

SUPPLICATION FOR GRACE.

Forasmuch as all our diligence and all our preparation must be too little to suffice for such high Mysteries, we shall do well, after all, suppliantly to beg of GOD *grace, help, and assistance.*

I. *Beseech* GOD, *therefore, through the Merits of His* SON, *to give thee grace to receive this Sacrament worthily.*

O Thou Great FATHER of mercies! look upon the Face of Thy CHRIST, Who, with the most perfect love, was obedient to Thee unto Death, even the Death of the Cross, and by virtue of His Merits, give me grace that I may show acceptable obedience to Thee. Grant, I beseech Thee, that through His Merits and Intercession, I may obtain those things which I am not worthy to ask.

II. *Having laid before* CHRIST *thy sins, thy imperfections, and all thy necessities, ask for pardon, through the Merits of His Passion and His Blood, and for grace to communicate devoutly.*

O JESU, SAVIOUR of the world! Who camest to save sinners, and saidst, Come unto Me, all ye that labour and are heavy laden, and I will refresh you; lo, I, a sinner, dare to come unto Thee; for with Thee there is plenteous Redemption.

I come unto Thee, from Whom I have erred and strayed as a sheep that is lost; but, O Thou Good Shepherd, Who didst lay down Thy Life for Thy sheep, Who camest to seek and to save that which was lost, seek Thy servant, O LORD, for I do not forget Thy commandments.

I come unto Thee, pierced with many wounds, grievously oppressed with so many evil passions: but LORD, if Thou wilt, Thou canst make me whole. Thou knowest that it is the sick who need a physician.

But Thou art that Samaritan, the true Physician of souls, Who hast borne our griefs; Thou art He Who gavest, as the medicine for my soul, the Sacrament of Thy Precious Body and Blood.

Have mercy, therefore, upon me, O LORD, and heal my soul; for I have sinned against Thee. A troubled spirit is a sacrifice to Thee, O LORD! a broken and a contrite heart Thou wilt not despise. This do I first offer unto Thee, that I may the more safely offer the Sacrifice of Thy Precious Body and Blood.

Break Thou, therefore, the bonds of my sins. For thus shall I worthily offer unto Thee the Sacrifice of praise, and call upon the Name of the LORD.

III. *Betake thyself humbly to the* HOLY SPIRIT, *that by His gifts He may make in thee a fit habitation for* CHRIST JESUS, *as He did in the Virgin, Mother of* GOD.

[*What is included in brackets, is designed for Priests only.*]

O Most Merciful GOD! without Thy hallowing flame nought in man is free from blame; for of Thee is all our sufficiency. Without Thee we can do nought that is good, or becoming our state and calling. Keep my soul, for I am holy; my GOD, save Thy servant who putteth his trust in Thee. I am holy through the gift of faith and of grace, wherewith Thou didst sanctify me in Baptism.

[I am holy also by the office of priesthood which Thou hast called me to perform. For it is holy; and, worthily to answer to it, I ought to be holy; that is, separate from earthly things, pure, chaste, and adorned with many gifts of grace and virtues. They were to be holy, who had to do with the figure only and the shadow of this Sacrament. How much more I, who have to do with the very Substance and the Truth!]

But who can bring a holy and clean thing out of that which is unclean? Thou, of a truth, O GOD the Sanctifier! Who art the Holy of Holies, of Whom is all our sanctification!

IV. *Lastly, if, after such previous exercises, thou shouldest not yet, in the actual reception of this Sacrament, experience those affections, fervour and love, for which you long, and which the dignity of the Sacrament requireth, be not dejected in spirit; but humbly beseech* GOD, *that He would accept the desire at least of your heart, and the affection of a right will.*

O God the Searcher of my heart, I desire to receive (O that I could really!) this wonderful and heavenly Sacrament, with all the piety and devotion, all the affection, desire, and fervour of the Angels, and of Thine elect, as it is meet for me to do. O LORD, all my desire is before Thee. My heart is ready, O GOD, my heart is ready; I offer unto Thee my whole heart and my all. LORD, hear the desire of the poor; let Thine Ear hearken unto the preparation of his heart. Let thy Divine and boundless Goodness supply what my human weakness lacketh.

¶ *Observe, that this exercise, as well as those which follow, is so constructed, as, by the omission or alteration of a few parts, to be made use of both by the priests who celebrate, and by the people who communicate.*

They may be used also in the way of spiritual communion, by those who have not access to actual communion.

We add various exercises, longer, or shorter; divers meats, as it were, at the same table: in order that variety may prevent loathing, which is wont to arise from the frequent repetition of one and the same. Different persons, of different tastes, require a variety of exercises.

ASPIRATIONS AT THE TIME OF COMMUNION.

The visit of so Great a Guest is to be received with the greatest reverence and most deep devotion. Thou wilt therefore use frequent acts of lively Faith, Hope, and Charity; thou wilt acknowledge and set forth the Majesty, Goodness, and Mercy of God; thou wilt confess thine own misery and frailty. Hence thou wilt hold converse with CHRIST, *now Present, with the desires and affections of thine inmost soul. For this purpose thou mayest make use of short but burning aspirations, whereof there are many in the Psalms and Gospels; but rather conceiving them in the heart than uttering them with the lips. But when thou hast retired from the Altar, thou wilt do well to dwell upon them at greater length in stillness.*

We here subjoin a few; which will be found profitable

both during Holy Communion and at other times.

I will love Thee, O Lord my Strength; the LORD is my strong Rock, and my Refuge, and my SAVIOUR.

What is man, that Thou art mindful of him; or the son of man, that Thou visitest him?

Truly GOD is loving unto Israel; even unto such as are of a clean heart.

O give thanks unto the LORD, for He is gracious; and His mercy endureth for ever.

O praise the LORD, all ye nations; praise Him, all ye His people.

For His merciful kindness is ever more and more towards us; and the truth of the LORD endureth for ever.

Like as the hart desireth the water-brooks, so longeth my soul after Thee, O GOD!

It is good for me to hold me fast by GOD, and to put my trust in the Lord GOD.

Whom have I in heaven but Thee? and there is none upon earth that I desire in comparison of Thee.

My soul doth magnify the LORD, and my spirit rejoiceth in GOD my SAVIOUR, &c.

Blessed is the womb that bare Thee, &c.

Whence is this to me, that my Lord cometh unto me?

Blessed is He that cometh in the Name of the LORD. O Lord, I am not worthy, &c.

The diligence of each, or rather the unction of the Spirit, will readily suggest similar passages. To the same purpose serve also the following breathings of love.

Who art Thou, O LORD, and what am I?

Dost Thou come unto me, O King Most High, even to the very lowest of Thy servants?

Thou, Who didst come from the Bosom of the FATHER into the most pure womb of the Virgin, wilt Thou come also into this unclean vessel, this den of filth?

I know, O LORD, love urgeth and overcometh Thee. Even so, come, O LORD, tarry not. But let there come with Thee, I beseech Thee, that much-to-be-desired Goodness, Compassion, Charity, and Pity, by which my wretchedness may be forgiven and holpen.

Behold, O LORD, I now

have Thee, Who hast all things. I possess Thee, Who canst and possessest all things. Therefore, O my GOD, and my All! do Thou wean my heart from all other things out of Thee, in which there is nought but vanity and vexation of spirit. On Thee Alone may my heart be fixed; in Thee be my rest, where my Treasure is, the highest Truth, and true Bliss, and blessed Eternity.

Let my mind, O LORD, perceive the sweetness of Thy Presence. Let it taste how sweet Thou art, O LORD! that allured by love of Thee, it may seek for nought, wherein to joy, out of Thee, since Thou art the Joy of my heart, GOD and my Portion for ever.

Thou art the Physician of my soul, Who with Thine own Stripes hast healed our wounds. But I am that sick man, to heal whom Thou camest down from heaven: heal my soul, therefore, for I have sinned against Thee.

Thou art the Good Shepherd, Who didst lay down Thy life for Thy sheep. Behold, I am that sheep which was lost; and yet dost Thou vouchsafe to feed me with Thy Body and Blood; lay me now upon Thy Shoulders. What wilt Thou refuse me, Who hast given Thyself? Tend Thou me, and I shall lack nothing in that green pasture wherein Thou hast folded me; until I shall be led out into the pastures of eternal life.

O Thou True Light, that lightenest every man that cometh into this world, lighten mine eyes that I sleep not in death, &c.

O Thou Fire that ever burnest and never failest, behold, I am lukewarm, yea cold. Kindle Thou my reins and my heart, that they may glow with love to Thee. For Thou camest to send fire on the earth, and what willest Thou but that it be kindled?

O King of heaven and earth, rich in mercy! Behold I am poor and needy; Thou knowest what I most want. Thou Alone canst enrich and help me. Help me, O GOD, and out of the treasures of Thy goodness supply Thou my poor soul.

O my Lord and my God! Behold, I am Thy servant; give me understanding and kindle my affections, that I may know and do Thy Will.

Thou art the Lamb of

GOD, the Lamb without spot, Who takest away the sins of the world; take from me whatever hurteth me and displeaseth Thee; and give me what Thou knowest will please Thee and be good for me.

Thou art my Love and all my Joy. Thou art my GOD and my All. Thou art the Portion of mine inheritance and of my cup. Thou shalt maintain my lot.

O my GOD and my All! Grant, I beseech Thee, That the fiery and sweetly-flowing force of Thy love may absorb my soul, that I may die unto the world out of love for Thy love, Who from love to me didst deign to die on the Cross, O my GOD and my All!

CHAPTER V.

AN EXERCISE AFTER COMMUNION, FOR BOTH PRIESTS AND PEOPLE.

It is a matter of very great importance, to know how to employ the time after Communion, during which CHRIST *especially remaineth with us, and how to gain the full benefit of the Presence of so great a Guest. No time, indeed, can be more fit for doing whatsoever pertaineth to salvation, than when we have with us, and dwelling in us, the very Author of Salvation.*

Beautifully and piously, according to his wont, saith Thomas à Kempis, in his fourth book on the Imitation of CHRIST: "Thou oughtest not only to prepare thyself to devotion before Communion, but carefully also to preserve thyself therein, after thou hast received the Sacrament. Nor is the careful guard of thyself afterwards less required, than devout preparation before. For a good guard afterwards is again the best preparation for the obtaining of greater grace. For if a person gives himself up at once too much to outward things, he is rendered thereby greatly indisposed [to devotion]."

Judge from thine own self, what thou oughtest now to do. Were any to invite thee to his house, and as soon, almost, as he had received thee, to leave thee, as weary of thy society, and give himself to some foolish and empty trifling, not thinking thee worthy of familiar converse, or of any office of kindness and courtesy, wouldest thou not call this rude and unseemly; and even eschew such a friend, as one little mindful of his duties?

Consider, then, what must be said of those who when they have received GOD *into their house, (and what and how great a Guest is He!) forthwith turn their backs upon Him, and go their way, nor, even for a little while, care to hold converse with Him. What is this but to slight, yea rather grievously to offend thy Guest? More especially, when He is One Who cometh to thee, not to be refreshed by thee but Himself to refresh thee.*

Why, then, thus hastest thou? What seekest thou beside thy GOD? *More will He teach thee than all books; more delight thee than all friends; more good bestow than all the arts, wealth, sciences, &c. of the world.*

Conduct, then, thou thy Guest into thine inner chamber, that is, thy heart. "Beware of much talk" *(saith the aforecited Thomas),* " remain in secret, and enjoy thy GOD; for thou hast Him Whom all the world cannot take from thee."

That thou mayest practise this, we will supply thee with an easy exercise; comprised chiefly in three points.

FIRST POINT.

AN ACT OF THANKSGIVING.

1. *In order to excite in thyself due thankfulness, exercise acts of lively faith; mingling these with affections of humility, reverence, admiration, and the like.*

O most Merciful SAVIOUR, CHRIST JESU, how good and gracious art Thou, and of great mercy unto all that call upon Thee! For when as yet we were not, by Divine Power didst Thou create us; when we were Thine enemies, Thou camest down from heaven and with wondrous wisdom didst redeem us; and because, without Thee we are unable, either in body or soul, to live, or move, or have our being, Thou dost of Thine Infinite Goodness, still preserve us by so many Sacraments and helps of grace; yea, in this Sacrament, Thou dost in a most wonderful manner give unto us Thy Body and Blood, that is, Thyself; O love! O compassion! O unheard-of, awful Mystery!

Dost Thou, my GOD, vouchsafe to come unto me? The King and LORD of Highest Majesty to His lowest servant? GOD to man? The CREATOR to the creature?

Whence is this to me, that Thou, O LORD, comest unto me? from whom Thou mightest well depart, because I am a sinful man. What is man, that Thou art mindful of him, or the son of man that Thou visitest him? Knowest Thou not what I am? dust and ashes, an unclean vessel, food of worms! And to such an one dost Thou come from heaven? O LORD our GOD, how excellent is Thy Name in all the earth!

II. *Here exercise acts of thanksgiving and praise to GOD for such great blessings.*

What reward shall I give unto the LORD, for all the benefits that He hath done unto me? O that my lips were opened, and my mouth filled with praise, that I might sing of Thy glory and honour all the day long, and tell of all Thy wondrous works!

Let my soul, touched by so many and such great benefits, magnify the LORD, and my spirit rejoice in GOD my SAVIOUR; for He hath regarded the low estate of His servant; He that is Mighty hath done to me great things; He hath filled the hungry with good things.

Bless the LORD, then, O my soul, and let all that is within me bless His Holy Name. Bless the LORD, O my soul, and forget not all His benefits, Who forgiveth all thy sins; and, by virtue of this Sacrament, healeth all thine infirmities, &c.

III. *Forasmuch as of thyself alone, thou art wholly unequal worthily to set forth such great blessings, invite all saints, yea, all creatures to praise GOD. As the Three Children, unharmed in the fiery furnace, called upon all creatures in heaven, earth, and sea, to praise GOD, saying with one voice, O all ye works*

F

of the LORD, *bless ye the* LORD, *&c. how much the rather ought we so to do, when we have received Him within us, by Whom we are delivered from death and from the flame of eternal fire!*

Great art Thou, O LORD, and highly to be praised; but who can express Thy mighty acts, or show forth all Thy praise? Though all my members were changed into tongues, and every breath of my life into Thy praises and thanksgivings, still should I fall far short of all Thy mercies. Therefore, owning my insufficiency, this is my one earnest desire, that all Thy creatures should, with me and for me, praise and bless Thy Name for ever.

But, above all, O most merciful GOD, accept the praises and thanksgivings which Thy SON our SAVIOUR, when He took upon Him our nature, did, from the moment of His Incarnation, through the whole course of His life, continually offer up. And those thanks especially, which, when He instituted this Sacrament, as if even then acknowledging that we were unequal to return thanks for so great a blessing, lifting up His Eyes towards heaven, He gave thanks to Thee, O GOD, His ALMIGHTY FATHER, in the name of us all.

Let all Angelic Spirits also bless and praise Thee, who continually stand with holy fear about Thy Throne, and chant with unceasing voice, saying, Holy, Holy, Holy!

I desire, also, with all my heart, to unite my unworthy thanksgivings with those of all Thy Saints and friends now reigning with Thee in Heaven; in the Communion with whom we believe; those which the Blessed Virgin, Mother of Thy Only-Begotten SON, offered up to Thee when she conceived, carried, and bore in her most chaste Womb, Him Whom I now hold within my breast; those which she and all Thy Saints, receiving Him in this Holy Sacrament, have devoutly offered up here upon earth; and those which they now sing to Thee, feeding with open face on the Bread of Life, and drinking of the river of Thy pleasure. Make me a companion, O GOD, of them that fear Thee, and keep Thy Commandments.

O that I could in like way gather together into my one self the affections and fervency of all the pious faithful, and all the longings, desires, and attainments of all who please Thee on earth! and thus with entire intensity of soul, love and honour Thee, for that great love and honour which Thou hast vouchsafed to me in this Sacrament.

For I avow, that how numerous soever have been the devout, who have been already, are, or shall be, in the world, who with due preparation, devotion, and profit have ever received, or shall receive this most Divine Sacrament, if all their efforts, desires, grateful and pious affections, could meet together in me alone, I would, indeed, freely and willingly turn all to the praise and glory of Thy Name, and the thanksgiving due unto Thee. And yet (I confess it unfeignedly, O LORD) I should still be an unprofitable servant, unable worthily to praise Thee since Thou art above all praise. But spare me, O LORD, for I am poor and needy; and, at least, the desire of the poor, and the offering of a good will, Thou wilt not despise. O let all the works of the LORD bless the LORD, praise Him, and magnify Him for ever!

SECOND POINT.

OBLATION.

1. *Offer unto* GOD *the* FATHER *His* SON, *together with the whole treasury of His Merits.*

O FATHER of mercies, and GOD of all comfort, how hast Thou loved us! So, in truth, as to give Thine Only-Begotten SON, once as our Ransom, daily as our Food. What shall I, vile creature, render unto Thee for so great love? That, than Which Thou couldest give nothing of greater dignity; I receive nothing greater. Him do I offer unto Thee, O my FATHER, even Thy most Well-Beloved Son, Whom for my salvation Thou hast so lovingly offered up; and so graciously given to be received [offered [e]] in this Sacrament [and Sacrifice] which we celebrate in perpetual Memory of that benefit.

[e] See above, p. 19, note.

Whom should I rather offer unto Thee, O Eternal FATHER! than Thy Beloved SON, in Whom Thou art well-pleased? What other intercessor shall I, guilty, set forth before Thee, than Him Who is the Propitiation for my sins? our Advocate, our Great High Priest; sprinkled not with blood of others, but with His own; a Holy Sacrifice; the Lamb without spot; Who did no sin, yet bare the sins of the world, and with His own Stripes healed our infirmities?

Behold my Hope, my whole Trust, CHRIST JESUS, Thy SON, my SAVIOUR. Despise not, I beseech Thee, this Offering, albeit the vileness of the offerer doth merit it; but look graciously upon It, I beseech Thee, because infinitely greater is the worth of the Offered. Look upon the Face of Thy CHRIST, Who, for our salvation, having been obedient to Thee, even unto Death, offered Himself on the Cross as a Sacrifice for us.

Is not He that Guiltless One, Thy Son, Whom, to redeem Thy servant, Thou didst deliver up? Remember, O loving FATHER, that this is He, Whom, although Co-equal with Thyself, Thou didst, of Thine Own Essence, beget from all eternity, still Thou wouldest that He should take upon Him our flesh, that, partaker of our humanity, He might make me partaker of His Divinity.

Behold in the SON, what may move Thee to compassionate Thy servant; and whilst the Wounds of Thy Beloved SON lie open before Thee, let my sins, I beseech Thee, be covered. And whereas my flesh hath provoked Thee to anger, let the Flesh of Thy SON turn Thee to pity.

Receive, then, O HOLY FATHER! ALMIGHTY, EVERLASTING GOD! this Holy and Spotless Sacrifice of Thy SON, which I, Thine unworthy servant, offer unto Thee, together with all His Virtues, Merits, Wounds, Torments, Stripes, Sighs, and sacred drops of Bloody Sweat.

In the unity of that love wherewith He offered Himself unto Thee upon the Altar of the Cross; to the praise and glory of Thy Name; in thanksgiving for all Thy benefits conferred on me and on the whole human race; in expiation also of my sins; for the supply of all my shortcomings; for the solace and refreshment [f] of all the faithful, living and departed, &c., through the Same, Whom here I offer unto Thee, our LORD JESUS CHRIST, Thy Son, &c.

11. *Offer thyself to* CHRIST, *Who so lovingly vouchsafed to offer Himself for thee.*

O most loving SAVIOUR, how great is Thy Mercy towards me! whom, though a vile and worthless sinner, Thou hast purchased at so great a Price, even Thy most Precious Blood.

For, to deliver me, the slave of Satan, Thou, the Very Son of GOD, didst, upon the Altar of the Cross, offer Thyself to GOD the FATHER, as the Price of our redemption: and that Thou mayest spare and strengthen me, dost now give Thyself as my Food.

What shall I render unto the LORD, I who am poor and needy, for all the benefits that He hath done unto me? Wouldest Thou that I should give Thee my heart? Nought can be more just. Shall not my spirit be subject unto GOD, from Whom cometh all my salvation?

By every right indeed doth He claim my soul to Himself, Who for mine laid down His Own. My heart is ready, O GOD, my heart is ready. Behold my soul and my body. Receive me all, Who didst make me all, and when I was wholly lost, didst give Thy Whole Self for me.

But what an exchange, to give back myself for Thee! the servant for the LORD! man for GOD! the ungodly for the Holy and the Just! a defiled sinner for the Spotless Lamb!

But Thou, O LORD, Who hast thought me worthy for whom to give no other than Thyself; now too, I humbly beseech Thee, turn not Thy Face away from me, neither do Thou despise me, O GOD my SAVIOUR.

Receive Thy servant for good, Who for me didst take the form of a servant. Receive the man, Who for me wast made Man. Receive the sinner, Who didst come to save sinners. Seek for the lost sheep, Who didst come to seek and to save that which was lost; Who art

[f] See above, p. 13, note.

the Good Shepherd and the Spotless Lamb That takest away the sins of the world.

Receive also my bounden service, which I, unworthy, have offered before the eyes of Thy Majesty, in union with that Sacrifice, in which Thou didst offer Thyself an Oblation for me unto GOD the FATHER, upon the Altar of the Cross.

Unite my vile service with all that Thou hast done and suffered out of most perfect Love and Obedience, and vouchsafe to offer it to the Eternal Father united with the riches of Thy Satisfactions and Merits, that out of Thine Abundance my penury may be enriched, and the grace, of which in myself I am utterly unworthy, I may through Thy Mediation obtain.

Into Thy Hands I commend my spirit; for Thou hast redeemed me, O LORD, Thou GOD of Truth! It is good for me henceforth to hold me fast by Thee, and to place my hope in Thee, O LORD. For Whom have I in heaven but Thee? and there is none on earth whom I desire in comparison of Thee. For Thou art the Portion of mine inheritance and of my cup; Thou shall maintain my lot.

THIRD POINT.

PETITION.

1. *Hesitate not here eagerly and earnestly to ask largely both for thyself, and for thy neighbours. Thou hast here a boundless Treasury of heavenly wealth. Ask what thou wilt. The eagerness of the asker calls forth the bounty of the Giver. Open thy mouth wide, and* GOD *will fill it. In the first place, humbly ask pardon for the sins, the negligences also, and the failures of which thou hast been guilty in the use of this Sacrament.*

O most Merciful Saviour! in the multitude of Thy mercies and of Thy goodness have I come to [Thine Altar], to the Table of Thy Supper, from which, conscious of my wretchedness and my iniquity, I ought, of right, to abstain, lest haply by a rash approach I become guilty of Thy Body and Blood.

But, O most Sweet LORD, remember not Thou mine offences and mine ignorances, but remember rather Thine own mercies, O LORD, that Thou enter not into judgment with Thy servant, since in Thy Sight shall no man living be justified.

If Thou, O Lord, shouldest mark iniquities, O LORD, who shall stand? Who will dare to approach Thy Table? Who can endure the rigour of Thy Justice? Or who can stand before Thy Divine Majesty, in Whose Sight the very heavens are not clean?

Behold, O Lord, against myself do I confess mine unrighteousness; do Thou, I beseech Thee, forgive the wickedness of my sin. Against Thee only have I sinned, and done evil in Thy Sight. But do Thou, Who camest to save sinners, save me, and cast me not away from Thy Presence, for whose salvation Thou didst freely deliver up Thyself as a Ransom; for whose sustenance Thou hast given Thyself to be the Food. O how strong will be the confidence of the sinner, who knoweth such mighty compassion of the SAVIOUR!

What, then, O CHRIST my SAVIOUR, could hinder me from coming to Thee, Who didst come down from the highest heaven for my salvation? I am feeble, indeed, and sore smitten; but shall I therefore flee from Thy Face?

Nay rather, therefore alone do I come to Thee, because I am weak; for the whole have no need of a physician, but they that are sick. And Thou Alone art the Physician of my soul, Who by Thine own Stripes hast healed our infirmities. Heal Thou my soul, therefore, O LORD! for I have sinned against Thee.

Mine iniquities, as a sore burden, are too heavy for me to bear; and who shall lighten, who shall carry for me my burden? Thou, O LORD! The Lamb of God That takest away the sins of the world; Who didst bear the Cross upon Thy Shoulders, that Thou mightest bear our iniquity; Who hast said, Come unto Me, all ye that labour and are heavy laden, and I will refresh you. And why should I not come to Thee, Who Alone canst lighten the burden of my sins?

I am defiled by vices and evil affections, and therefore do I flee unto Thee; for who else can bring a clean thing out of an unclean, save Thou?

O LORD, Who hast washed us from our sins in Thine Own Blood, wash me, I beseech Thee, from mine iniquity, and cleanse me from my sin.

I am that prodigal and rebellious son, who, having fled from Thee, have wasted all my substance, and am now suffering the extremity of want. Whither shall I go, if I return not to Thee, my most loving FATHER? For Thou art the FATHER of mercies and the GOD of all consolation, Who dost ever receive into Thy favour the children which return unto Thee, and dost cherish and embrace them with Fatherly love.

I indeed am not worthy to be called Thy son; yet Thou art willing to be accounted and to be my FATHER. Be Thou, therefore, merciful and gracious unto me, receive Thy banished child, clothe his nakedness, appease his hunger. Even as a father pitieth his children, so do Thou, O Compassionate and Merciful LORD, have pity on me. For hast Thou any pleasure in the death and perdition of a sinner, Who, that I might live, didst deign for me to die?

Behold with what trust I come to Thee, O CHRIST my SAVIOUR! sinful man though I be. But of Thine Infinite Mercy, do Thou spare me, although I came not to this awful Mystery with that care, preparation, and devotion that I ought.

Remember, O LORD, whereof I am made; the spirit, indeed, is willing, but the flesh is weak, and the earthly tabernacle weigheth down the mind that museth upon many things. O LORD, all my desire is before Thee, and my groaning is not hidden from Thee.

11. *Seeing that thou now hast with thee thy* GOD *and* SAVIOUR, *thy Guide, Physician, Teacher, thy Father and every Good, at once Almighty and All-Good, and One Who is both able and willing to give thee all things profitable to salvation, therefore with great trustfulness do thou pour out thy heart before Him, lay open to Him thy distress, and seek the aid of His grace for thy necessities.*

O most Gracious GOD! I desire with all my heart to serve Thee, henceforward, in righteousness and holiness, all the days of my life. O that my ways were made so direct that I might keep Thy statutes!

This is my most earnest desire, to wean my heart from all created things, and be wholly united unto Thee, that by virtue of this Sacrament I may abide in Thee, and Thou in me. I desire to cleave unto Thee; for Thou art GOD my SAVIOUR, my Light, Guide, Physician, Master, yea, my FATHER and my All.

O that I could present my body a living sacrifice, holy, pleasing unto Thee! May I live; yea not I, but may CHRIST live in me, Whom I now possess within me. I have sworn, O GOD! and am steadfastly purposed to keep Thy righteous judgments.

But, O LORD! to will indeed is present with me, but to perform I find not; because I find another law in my members warring against the law of my mind, so that the good I would, I do not. Unto Thee, therefore, O LORD! do I lift up mine eyes; for Thine Eyes see my imperfection.

Look, I pray Thee, on my infirmity with the eyes of Thy mercy; for without Thee I can do nothing good, but of Thee is all our sufficiency. Make Thou me, therefore, to go in the path of Thy commandments; for therein is my desire.

Deliver me from mine enemies, O LORD, Who hast prepared before me a Table (of which by Thy grace I have now been made partaker) against them that trouble me. Show some token upon me for good, that they who hate me may see it and be ashamed, because Thou, LORD, hast holpen me and comforted me.

Give me understanding, and I shall keep Thy law; yea, I shall keep it with my whole heart. Try me, O GOD, and seek the ground of my heart; prove me, and examine my thoughts. Look well if there be any way of wickedness in me, and lead me in the way everlasting. Make Thy way plain before my face; that I may turn aside from the path, the ends whereof are the ways of death.

O Thou Searcher of my heart! Thou seest how frail I am, and how prone to this (N.) or that (N.) fault. I indeed purpose to avoid a fall, and yet I do fall, unless Thou uphold me with Thine Hand.

By Thy grace, therefore, O LORD, help Thou my weakness.

III. *Reflect upon the virtues befitting the Christian, and especially in thine own station or calling: and ask for especial grace, by virtue of this Sacrament, to perform them.*

O CHRIST JESUS, Meek and Lowly in heart! Who, although Thou wast in the Form of GOD, yet didst make Thyself of no reputation, taking upon Thee the form of a servant; and even now condescendest to be handled by any unworthy Priest, and givest Thyself under the form[g] of bread and wine; and so allowest Thyself to be treated shamefully and contemptuously by many who discern not the LORD's Body; grant unto me, that my heart be not haughty, nor mine eyes lofty; that I exercise not myself in great matters which are too high for me; that I be not highminded, but that I may fear.

O my LORD! Who, though Thou wast rich, didst take the form of a poor servant, incline my heart, O GOD, unto Thy testimonies, and not to covetousness; that I may delight in the way of Thy commandments, as in all manner of riches; that having food and raiment, I may be therewith content, &c.

O Spotless Lamb! Who wast willing to be born of a pure Virgin, give unto me purity of mind and body, by means of That Which Thou dost here give unto us, even the new Wine which maketh the maidens grow[h]. Create in me a clean heart, O GOD, &c.

O CHRIST JESU! Who wast led as an innocent lamb to the slaughter, and enduredst so many injuries and reproaches, grant unto me the spirit of patience and of gentleness. May I learn of Thee to be meek and lowly of heart, &c.

O CHRIST my SAVIOUR! Who, when Thou wast thirsty, didst taste of the vinegar and the gall, and hast in this Sacrament prepared for us all spiritual delights, take from me the desires of gluttony. Grant that I may serve Thee, my GOD, and not my own belly or my pleasure: take from me the desires of gluttony, that my heart may never be weighed down by

---

[g] See above, p. 40, note.   [h] Zech. ix. 17, margin.

surfeiting and drunkenness, &c.

O LORD, Who in the garden didst, with Bloody Sweat, pray long and most fervently, make me to praise Thee with my whole heart, that my spirit slumber not, through weariness in Thy worship and service. Restore unto me the joy of Thy salvation, &c.

O LORD! Who, of true charity, didst pray for Thine enemies, make me to love my neighbour as myself, and to do good to them that hate me, &c.

O most Sweet SAVIOUR and Searcher of the heart! Thou knowest what is in man, and ponderest all my ways. Thou knowest best, of what virtues and gifts I stand most in need in this state (N.) and office (N.) in which by Thy grace I am placed.

Grant unto me, therefore, Thy grace, Thou, Who in this Sacrament hast given us so rich a Treasury of grace, even Thyself, the Author of grace, and hast now so mercifully admitted me to partake thereof. What good indeed will not accrue to him, to whom the Fountain of all good deigns to come? When Thou didst of old enter the house of Zacchæus, Thou saidst, *This day is Salvation come to this house.* Thou hast now entered, O CHRIST! into the house of my soul. Say unto it, I beseech Thee, *I am thy Salvation.* For what Thou sayest is done; and Thou Alone art GOD my SAVIOUR.

Help me, O GOD of my salvation; and for the glory of Thy Name deliver me and save me; for what is JESUS but a SAVIOUR? Of a truth there is none other Name under heaven given among men, whereby we must be saved.

O LORD, forasmuch as Thou hast graciously come unto me, I will not let Thee go, unless Thou bless me; Thou Who dost open Thine Hand and fill all things living with plenteousness!

O that I may receive a blessing from the LORD, and righteousness from the GOD of my Salvation! that so I may go from strength to strength, until I shall see, face to face, the GOD of gods in Sion, Whom I now see veiled in the Sacrament, and as through a glass darkly.

IV. *Pray, moreover, that the benefit of this Sacrifice or Sacrament may be applied to* thy neighbours, those chiefly who have been specially commended to thee.

O Lord! Whose bowels of mercy are open to all; Who willest not that any should perish, but wouldest have all men to be saved, and therefore didst for all suffer Death and institute this Sacrament; O my God, save Thy servants who hope in Thee; O think upon Thy congregation which Thou hast purchased and redeemed of old.

Save Thy people, O Lord, and bless Thine heritage. Govern them and lift them up for ever.

Help Thy servants, I beseech Thee, whom Thou hast redeemed with Thy Precious Blood. Send them help, O Lord, from Thy Sanctuary, and strengthen them out of Zion.

Have mercy upon my parents, brethren, friends, benefactors, especially N. N. Impart to them the Merit of Thy Precious Blood, shed for our salvation, that they may have grace to serve and please Thee in the present life, and so, at the last, may come to the glory of the life everlasting, and enjoy Thee for ever; that by the help of Thy grace they may so order their present life, as finally to receive in heaven the rewards of life eternal. (*Here also add the departed.*)

AN ADMONITION

ADDRESSED TO ALL CHRISTIANS, ESPECIALLY PRIESTS, ON THE DEVOUT USE OF THIS SACRAMENT.

The devout Christian in his retirement, as time shall permit, may dwell, more or less on the above points, both before and after Communion, that he lose not the taste and benefit of Food so Precious.

For whence is it, that they who so often attend upon Divine Sacraments, remain yet so cold, sluggish, and weak? They eat, and are not satisfied; they drink, and are not filled; they sow much, and gather in little. Is not He Who in this Sacrament is verily and indeed taken and received, a consuming Fire, ever burning, never decaying? Is He not the Light of the world? Is not His Flesh meat indeed and His Blood drink indeed?

Why then is not our soul replenished with Food, so Precious and so Rich, even as it were with marrow and fatness? Why are we, who are fed so often with the Bread of Angels, yet delighted with husks of swine? Why do we not shine, who so often receive the Light, yea, the Sun Himself? Why are not our lives and actions as sunbeams? Why do we not enlighten the world? Why, so often and so closely approaching the Fire, do we not burn? Why not kindle others also?

It is, that we engage in so high a work carelessly, as a thing to be gone through and done; we are led to it rather by custom than by affection. We neglect meditation, during which this fire is wont to be kindled.

Think often on these things, O Christian, but thou chiefly, O Priest, that ye receive not so often this so great grace of GOD in vain!

AN EXERCISE

OF GREAT BEAUTY AND EFFICACY, TO BE USED AFTER COMMUNION.

(From F. Antonio Molina Carth. in Instruct. Sacerd., who says that a more useful form than this cannot be conceived.)

O FATHER of mercies and GOD of all comfort! Who, out of the abundance of Thine Infinite Love, hast given unto us Thine Only-begotten SON, that whosoever believeth in Him should not perish, but have everlasting life; and that out of the exhaustless treasury of His Merits our wants may be supplied; lo, I, miserable sinner, but by Thy mercy called into the fellowship of Thy SON, have now also been made partaker of His Body and Blood. And I now enfold Him in my bosom and possess Him as mine own, most closely united with me.

And as such,- in the union

of that love wherewith He once gave Himself for us on the Altar of the Cross, and now giveth and communicateth Himself to us in the Sacrament of the Altar, do I now offer Him unto Thee, together with all His Merits and Virtues, to Thy eternal praise and glory; that in Him Thou mayest be perfectly well-pleased; and that we, who by our own deeds are not able to please Thee, may by the Merits, and Intercession of Thy most Wellbeloved SON, be perfectly pleasing to Thee.

I offer unto Thee, O most Holy FATHER, all His Charity, Piety, Obedience, Humility, Poverty, Gentleness, Patience, with all the other virtues, which He had surpassingly, that by them all my defects may be supplied.

And, since I cannot thank Thee as I ought, for all the benefits conferred upon me, I offer unto Thee all the Praises which He Himself offered, whilst He was visibly on earth amongst men, and those which He now offereth unto Thee in glory.

But forasmuch as I cannot satisfy Thee for my debts, that is, my sins; I offer unto Thee all His Labours, Fastings, Watchings, Weariness, Prayers; whatsoever in fine He did or suffered, from the first moment of His Conception, until He gave up the Ghost on the Cross; all the Anguish, Griefs, and Torments of His Passion, all His Blood poured out for me, all the Wounds for me received, and the Death which He endured in my stead.

Behold, this is the Treasure, most Merciful FATHER, in which I repose all my hope; these are the Riches, which I offer in satisfaction of all my debts.

Holy FATHER, look upon the Face of Thy CHRIST, and since He is Thy Beloved SON in Whom Thou art ever well-pleased, Who now is most inwardly united with me, look upon me also, I humbly beseech Thee, with the Eyes of Thy mercy. Under His Protection and Defence, under the shadow of His Merits, do I appear before Thee, that, looking chiefly upon Him, Thou mayest regard me also with mercy and favour, Whom He has purchased and made His servant for ever.

Suffer not, I beseech Thee, that soul to perish, which so

often receiveth into itself Thy Son, Who, sent by Thee, came into the world to seek and to save that which was lost. Grant this unto me, through Thine Infinite Mercy. Amen.

CHAPTER VI.

CONTAINING OTHER EXERCISES FOR COMMUNICANTS.

A SHORTER HELP

TO DEVOUT COMMUNION, SUITABLE TO BOTH PRIESTS AND PEOPLE, AND WHICH MAY BE USED BOTH BEFORE AND AFTER COMMUNION.

1. *Direct your intention aright.*

O Most High and Most Mighty God! to the Praise and Glory of Thy Supreme Majesty; in remembrance of the most Holy Life, Passion, and Death of Jesus Christ my Saviour; and in thanksgiving for all the gifts and blessings which Thou hast bestowed on me an unworthy sinner, and upon Thy whole Church; for the pardon of my numberless sins; and for my salvation; and of my neighbours (N.), for the bliss of the departed (N.) do I, unworthy sinner, desire to [call to mind, or to] receive the Mysteries of the Most Holy Body and Blood of Thy Son. Of a truth, O Lord, in Thee Alone is all that can satisfy the desires of my heart. For whom have I in heaven but Thee? and there is none on earth that I desire in comparison of Thee. Wilt not Thou Thyself be our exceeding great Reward?

2. *Exercise an Act of Contrition.*

But together with the Sacrifice and Sacrament of

the Body and Blood of Thy Son, my SAVIOUR, I humbly offer unto Thee, my LORD, the sacrifice of a troubled spirit. For I grieve from my inmost heart, that by my sins I should ever have offended Thee my GOD, the Chief Good, and to me so Bountiful, Who so often refreshest me in this Sacrament; and by these sins especially (N. and N.) which Thou, O Searcher of hearts, knowest, and which I too, a miserable sinner, with sorrow confess in the bitterness of my soul. O that I had never offended Thee! But a broken and a contrite heart, Thou, O GOD, wilt not despise; Thou, Who of Thy love to us, hast given Thine Only-begotten SON, that He might wash us from our sins in His Own Blood.

3. *Exercise Faith.*

I firmly believe, indeed, O good JESU, and with lively faith confess, that Thou Thyself, Equal with GOD the FATHER in glory and power, Very GOD and Very Man, art really and truly Present in this Sacrament; Thou, Who, sent from heaven, didst come on earth to seek and to save that which was lost. And therefore wast Thou truly born of the Virgin, didst suffer, wast crucified, and diedst and in remembrance of Thy Love didst leave us Thy Body and Blood in this Sacrament.

4. *Exercise Hope.*

And why should I not hope in Thee, O Thou Supreme Hope and only Salvation of my soul? or whither shall I flee, save unto Thee, O JESU, my only Refuge, Who with Thy All-holy Lips hast said, Come unto Me, all ye that labour and are heavy laden, and I will refresh you?

O how sweet are these Thy words unto my throat; yea, sweeter than honey unto my mouth! And therefore do I come with boldness to Thy Altar, where, filled with hope, I receive Thyself. For if I have Thee, what shall I not have? For Thou art He Who hast and canst do all things, and Thou art good over all.

The LORD is my Shepherd; therefore shall I lack nothing; He shall feed me in a green pasture; where the Good Shepherd Himself, Who laid down His life for His sheep, doth feed us with none other Food than with His own Body and Blood.

What wilt Thou not give to man, to whom Thou hast given Thyself! Surely, Good JESU, Thou wilt not suffer me to lack anything for my salvation, who so often receive and have with me Thee, the Author of Salvation. No, of a surety, because of Thy Name, which is JESUS.

5. *Exercise Charity.*

For truly Thou art GOD my SAVIOUR; and Thou art Good above all good. And therefore do I love Thee, O CHRIST JESU, Who, of Thine exceeding Love for me, didst come in the Flesh, and lovedst me even unto Death, and as a sign of this love, hast given Thyself in this Sacrament. I love Thee, indeed, above myself and all things; certainly I most earnestly desire thus to love Thee, and for ever to cleave to Thee Alone. O that, by virtue of this Sacrament, so mighty an union of love may grow together between Thee and me, that nothing may be able to separate me from the love of CHRIST my SAVIOUR!

6. *Renew your Resolves.*

But whatsoever things oppose this my desire and Thy Command, or whatsoever even hinders the taste and sweetness of this Heavenly Manna, as this (N.) or that (N.) I seriously and sincerely resolve to shun, and that out of love to Thee Alone. O that Thine abounding and effectual grace may, in the virtue and union of this Sacrament, assist the purpose of my will, of itself (Thou knowest, O LORD!) so unsteady and frail. Thine Eyes see my imperfections; but of Thee is all my sufficiency.

7. *Exercise Humility.*

But how shall I dare to approach Thee? Art not Thou, O GOD, the LORD, my Creator and my Redeemer, the King of heaven and earth &c.? And what am I? A vile worm of earth, dust and ashes; and (what is fouler yet) so often a disobedient and ungrateful sinner against Thee, &c. Of a truth, O LORD, I am not worthy that Thou shouldest come under my roof. Yet remember, O LORD, that Thou, being LORD of all, didst take upon Thee the form of a servant and come to us, and didst converse as a Friend with publicans and sinners. And at length Thou didst humble Thyself even unto Death. Let that lowliness, I pray Thee, move Thee not to despise me, vile and low as I am; but do Thou mercifully come unto me, or graciously receive me, coming unto Thee.

8. *Ask for Grace.*

I beseech Thee, therefore, O Eternal FATHER! by the strength of that most mighty love, which drew down Thine Only-Begotten SON from Thy Bosom into the Virgin's womb, that for us men He might become Man.

I beseech Thee by the vehemence of that desire wherewith He desired to eat the Passover with His disciples at the Last Supper, and to perfect the work of our redemption: by the strength also of that love whereby, when He instituted the Sacrifice and Sacrament of His Body and Blood, as a Memorial of His boundless love and as a pledge of future glory, He gave Himself to them and to us all to be our Food.

I beseech Thee also by virtue of that most burning love, whereby He offered Himself up to Thee, His Eternal FATHER, upon the Altar of the Cross as a Sacrifice and Ransom for the redemption of us sinners; so direct me, by Thy saving grace, and make me ever so worthily to receive the sacred Mysteries of His Body and Blood, that I may thence obtain abundant benefit and strength against all the snares of the world, the flesh, and the devil, and may shun all vices, especially this. (N.)

May I more diligently practise, moreover, the virtues most needed in my condition, as charity, humility, purity (N. and N.); and study to serve Thee daily more faithfully.

9. *Offer thyself and all to* GOD.

For what other return can I give to Thee, O LORD, for all the benefits which Thou hast done unto me? Do I not owe my life, my body, my soul, my all, to Thee, Who hast freely given me all, yea Thy very SON Himself, Who for me laid down His Life and Soul?

Truly, O LORD, I owe my whole self to Thee, Who, to redeem me, the guilty, didst give wholly Thy Guiltless SON. O that I could present my body a living sacrifice, holy, well-pleasing unto GOD! O that my soul may live unto Thee, and all that is mine may serve Thee! Behold, my heart is ready, O GOD, my heart is ready. I beseech Thee, O LORD, Who lookest upon the heart rather than the hand, despise not Thou Thy poor servant, who hath nought to offer Thee more pleasing than Him in Whom Thou art well-pleased; and then bringeth Thee two mites, my soul and my body, which I singly and wholly make over to Thy service and all Thy good pleasure.

10. *Join thy Oblation or Communion with the Oblation and Merits of* CHRIST.

But do Thou, my most Sweet Redeemer, Mediator and Advocate with GOD the FATHER, despise me not: but graciously offer and commend to the Eternal FATHER the oblation of an unworthy sinner, together with Thine All-Holy Works, which Thou wroughtest, done in sovereign charity.

Unite this my duty and service with that most Precious Sacrifice, by which, in most eminent charity and obedience, Thou didst offer up Thyself to GOD the FATHER upon the Altar of the Cross.

Behold, O LORD, I am poor and needy; but Thou art rich in Merits and in Mercies; and for whom hast Thou heaped up the riches of Thy Goodness rather than for miserable sinners? Relieve then my poverty out of the boundless treasury of Thy Merits; and out of the abundance of Thine infinite Love perfect all my doings. And now especially do Thou mercifully fill up what is lacking in my too slight and

11. *Represent unto* GOD *the* FATHER *the Merits of the* SON.

O Eternal FATHER! look upon the Face of Thy CHRIST. Behold, This is Thy Beloved SON, in Whom Thou art well-pleased; and yet Thou didst so love the world, as to give Thine Only-Begotten SON for the salvation of the world. Yea, to redeem the servant, Thou didst deliver up the SON! Him, too, Thou didst will to be our Mediator and Advocate with Thee, that what by our own we could not, by His Merits we might obtain from Thee. His Sacrifice offered upon the Cross for us, His Works and Merits, as they are most perfect, so they cannot but be most pleasing unto Thee.

O that this abundance may supply my lack, so that, for the honour and love of Thy SON, Thou mayest now favourably accept the service of so vile a servant.

A SHORT PRACTICE

OF DEVOUT COMMUNION; FOR THE USE OF BOTH PRIESTS AND PEOPLE, AS WELL BEFORE AS AFTER COMMUNICATING.

Make here the Acts of the principal virtues.

O Most sweet SAVIOUR, CHRIST JESU! I adore Thee with my whole heart; and, with the inmost affections of my soul, I give thanks unto Thee, that with such great love Thou didst redeem us, miserably lost, with the Price of Thy Blood; and that, in memory of this Thy Love, and as a pledge of future glory, Thou didst, with such wondrous Power, Wisdom, and Goodness, give to us Thine own Body and Blood for our Meat and Drink. And lastly, that, out of Thine unspeakable Mercy, Thou hast vouchsafed to call to these Divine Mysteries me, the most worthless sinner, amongst the number of Thy [Priests] servants.

But, alas! wretched man that I am! who have hitherto lived so unworthily of my calling, and have so often and so heinously offended Thee, my GOD, by my sins (especially these, N.)! But now, I grieve for them from my inmost heart, out of love for Thee above all things: and I purpose henceforth to serve, please, cleave to Thee alone.

And therefore now, coming to the Table of Thy Feast, do I, with the whole affections of my heart and a pure and single mind, offer, to the praise and glory of Thine Eternal Majesty, and in commemoration of Thy most Holy Incarnation, Life, Passion, and Death, that most costly Sacrifice of Thy Body and Blood, Which Thou Thyself didst once for all offer for us upon the Altar of the Cross.

In thanksgiving also for all the gifts and blessings hitherto bestowed, or hereafter to be bestowed on all the company of the Elect, and on me, though most unworthy; in propitiation for my sins; for the salvation also of the faithful living (N.), and bliss of the departed. (N.)[k]

And I would that I could celebrate [could have celebrated] this so mighty work of Thy love with all the affection, fervour, and longing of Thy friends, whether now reigning triumphant in heaven, or still militant on earth.

With my heart indeed I believe, O my JESU; and with my mouth I confess, that the Eternal FATHER, GOD, supremely Blessed in Himself, Mighty, Perfect, and needing nothing, did, according to His infinite Mercy, so love the world as to give Thee, His Only-Be-gotten SON, to be our SAVIOUR.

I believe also that Thou Thyself, Equal in all things to the FATHER, didst, from the might of Thy boundless Charity, come down from the Bosom of the FATHER into the Virgin's Womb, and for us men was made Man.

I believe that out of love for us, Thou didst, at the Last Supper, institute this Sacrament, and didst give to us to eat Thy Very Body and Blood, that is, Thine

[k] See above, p. 13, note.

Own Self[1]. And lastly, being obedient to Thy FATHER even unto Death, Thou didst offer up Thyself as a Sacrifice for us upon the Altar of the Cross.

And therefore do I hope in Thee, and with great confidence do I come to Thee, O LORD! Who for our sake wast willing to do such marvellous things, and to endure things so dreadful. For what wilt Thou refuse, Who so lovedst us as to give Thyself?

I love Thee also, O Good JESU! with all the strength of my heart; and I will always love Thee henceforth even for ever, if Thou givest it.

But what shall I render unto Thee, O LORD, for so great a Gift, and for all the benefits which Thou hast done unto me? Behold, I renounce myself, and fully resign myself, all that I am, body and soul, and all that is mine, to every good pleasure of Thy most gracious Will.

Yet what have I, that I have not received? What is man, compared with his Maker? What can a vile creature, a worm of earth, a miserable sinner, an unprofitable servant, give unto GOD, his Creator and his LORD?

I acknowledge that I am poor and needy; and therefore do I humble myself under Thy Mighty Hand. But do Thou, O LORD JESU! as my Advocate and Mediator, rich in merits and in mercies, undertake my cause.

And out of the treasury of Thy boundless love do Thou help my need; and represent to Thy Eternal FATHER the Price of Thy Blood and of all Thy Merits; and thence supply all lacking in me; and especially, alas! the too slight and imperfect preparation with which I come to these most sacred Mysteries; that thus, through Thee, the offering of my most unworthy service may be pleasing unto Him.

Grant also, O Good JESU! by all Thy mercies, that I may ever honour this awful Mystery and Wondrous Gift of Thy love with due faith, reverence, and gratitude; and receive It now and ever with a pure and glowing heart; may I give diligence also to adorn the station (N.) to which, by Thy special grace, Thou hast been pleased to call me, with charity, purity,

---

[1] He that eateth Me. S. John vi. 57.

humility, gentleness, patience, sobriety, &c., and with all such behaviour as is pleasing to Thee, and becometh a [Priest] faithful servant of Thine. And all this, that my service may be more pleasing to Thee, to Thy greater glory, the good of Thy Church, and my own and my neighbour's salvation.

Wherefore, lastly, I humbly beseech Thee, that by the virtue of Thy Body and Blood Thou wouldest effectually wean my heart from all hurtful affections (such as N.) which hinder the taste and profit of this Sacrament; and unite and incorporate me most closely with Thyself, that I may taste how sweet Thou art, O LORD; and be made one spirit with Thee; that Thou mayest abide in me, and I in Thee; and so nothing may ever be able to separate me from Thee. For it is good for me to hold me fast by Thee, &c. For whom have I in heaven but Thee, and there is none upon earth that I desire in comparison of Thee, O GOD, my Portion for ever!

A SHORT AND USEFUL METHOD

OF STIRRING UP THE AFFECTIONS BEFORE AND AFTER COMMUNION.

(From F. Christ. Mayer.)

O JESU, Worthy of all love, GOD of my heart, whence such great condescension, such great love from such High Majesty to me, most unworthy sinner, that Thou shouldest vouchsafe to look on me so tenderly with the Eyes of Thy Mercy, so lovingly to visit me, so mercifully to refresh me, so fatherly to cherish me, so sweetly, powerfully, wonderfully, to lead me on thus far towards the glory, as I hope, fore-ordained for me?

Blessed for ever be Thine Infinite Goodness, Love, and Mercy, by which, together with the FATHER and the HOLY GHOST, Thou hast from eternity so loved me, ungrateful; decreeing thus to create, redeem, endow, call, preserve, glorify me, with all Thine Elect, and by which (goodness, &c.) Thou hast, in time, thus actually created, preserved, endowed me, body and soul; hast at so great Price of Thy Tears, Sweat, and Most Precious Blood, of old redeemed me; hast so bountifully applied to me, and now ceasest not so to apply, that same Price; thus justifying, thus calling, thus preserving, thus uniting me with Thyself, thus inviting me to the reward of glory.

I acknowledge and embrace Thine eternal Love towards me and all Thine Elect, and with all possible affection of them and all creatures possible, from my inmost soul I give Thee thanks.

I acknowledge and detest my so great ingratitude towards Thee, and most inwardly bewail it; and with like affection I adore, praise, glorify Thee, my LORD and my GOD; I lower myself below all, into the centre of my own nothingness, and bow down to Thy Majesty; seeing that by Thy grace alone I am what I am.

In Thee, O Ineffable Truth, do I believe; in Thee, my only Hope, do I hope, wholly mistrusting myself. Thee do I love, and will love for ever above all things, O infinitely loveable Fountain of all good. I rejoice at all Thy Perfection, Bliss, Glory, and good Pleasure; and resign myself to Thee, even for death or nothingness. To be wholly Thine, and so to abide for ever, is my desire; as Thou vouchsafest to be wholly mine. My whole life I offer freely to Thy service; and countless lives, if I had them, I would willingly offer.

All the pious desires of glorifying Thee, which I ever had, I renew; all evil desires I revoke and hate, and protest that they are and shall be contrary to my will. O that I had always thus loved Thee, and never offended Thee, nor might hereafter for ever offend Thee!

I grieve for all my sins, because they are displeasing to Thee, Whom I love above all things. I desire and resolve seriously to amend all my ways, especially this particular fault (N.) and with fresh fervour to give myself wholly to Thy service, striving to do perfectly all which is to be done; chiefly, to exercise this virtue (N.), or to reform this ordinary action (N.).

To make amends for the past, I give up myself wholly to Thy good Pleasure; I pray and hope for pardon, together with grace to the last, through Thee, O Good Jesu, into the abyss of Whose Merits I plunge myself.

Do Thou, in Thine everlasting Charity, vouchsafe to supply all my imperfections by Thy most Holy Merits; and conform me in all things to Thy Will, and bestow on me effectual grace for the amendment of these defects, the exercise of these virtues, or for the reform of my ordinary actions, and perseverance in Thy calling and grace, even unto the end; so that Thee, O Jesu, in Whom I have believed, in Whom I have hoped, Whom I have loved, in the way, I may, with all Thine Elect, in our home, see, love, praise, glorify, eternally.

2. By that same love of Thine, wherewith, with the Father and the Holy Ghost, Thou hast so loved the world, O Good Jesu! be mindful of and have pity upon Thy whole holy Church; its heads, prelates, princes, pastors; all conditions therein, ecclesiastical, secular, religious; all who can most promote or hinder Thy glory, and the salvation of souls; remember my parents, brethren, benefactors, and friends who have commended themselves to me; all who have saddened me, or whom I have saddened, offended, neglected to aid; all whom Thou hast decreed to direct into the way of salvation, by means of me, unworthy; all, living and departed, for whom Thou didst vouchsafe to die.

On all these be pleased to have mercy. Give rest to the departed, grace to the living, that they may most perfectly please Thee, even as Thou knowest and willest; and this, through Thine Own Merits, which I offer unto Thee, that Thou mayest represent them (together with my most extremely imperfect longings, attempts, and services) to Thy Eternal Father, to Whom Thou wast once obedient, even unto Death, and now sittest at His Right Hand, a Glorious

High Priest, to make intercession for us.

O FATHER, look upon the Face of Thy Beloved SON, and through Him have mercy upon us, and give us Grace, that, with the Same Thy Beloved SON and HOLY SPIRIT, we may, with all Thine elect, know, love, praise, and glorify Thee, now and for ever.

Have mercy upon us, O LORD, have mercy upon us, and help us, as Thou knowest to be needful for us, both in body and soul. Thou knowest all things, Thou canst do all things, Who livest and reignest world without end.

A PRIVATE PRAYER

FOR PRIESTS BEFORE CELEBRATING HOLY COMMUNION.

O Most High and Adorable Trinity; One, True, and Eternal Deity; my GOD, Creator, Saviour, and Governor; Most Mighty, Wise, Good, Just, and Merciful; I, Thy creature, although unworthy, desire to praise Thee, and serve Thee; forasmuch as I acknowledge that I was created, and by Thy singular grace have been called, to praise Thee. But Who art Thou? GOD and LORD of all; King of heaven and earth; Great and greatly to be praised. But I am a vile worm of earth, dust and ashes; and, what is more unworthy, so often disobedient towards Thee, and an ungrateful sinner! And how can I dare to come and offer sacrifice unto Thee, and to praise Thy Name, O LORD?

Yet, a troubled spirit is a sacrifice pleasing unto Thee; a contrite and a humbled heart, O GOD, Thou wilt not despise. I grieve, therefore, with my whole heart, that I ever offended Thee, O. my GOD, and my Chief Good. Turn away Thy Face from my sins; and look upon the Face of CHRIST, Thine Only-Begotten SON; for He is the Beloved, in Whom Thou art well-pleased; on Whom, as Man, Thou hast so largely heaped the rich gifts of grace, that out of

His Fulness all we might receive.

I therefore, although an unworthy sinner, yet by Thy grace Thy priest and servant, offer unto Thee, O Great GOD, the Sacrifice of the Body and Blood of my LORD JESUS CHRIST; and this I most earnestly desire to do with all the affection, zeal, and longing, with which the saints who now rejoice with Thee in heaven have at any time offered It, or the pious still living on earth now offer It.

I offer It also in union with that boundless Love wherewith Thou so lovedst the world as to give Thine Only-Begotten SON to us; in union with that Love, whereby He Himself came from Thy Bosom into the Virgin's womb, and was made Man; in union with that wondrous Sacrifice, which the Same Thine Only-Begotten instituted at the Last Supper in the presence of His Disciples, and at length consummated, dying upon the Cross.

And at the same time I offer unto Thee the Price of His Blood, all His Labours, Sorrows, and the whole treasure of His Love.

And I offer It, first indeed to the supreme glory of Thy Divine and Eternal Majesty, the worship and adoration due to Thee, as Supreme GOD, LORD, and Author of all. To the honour, moreover, and in commemoration of the All-Holy Humanity, Incarnation, Nativity, Passion, Death, Resurrection, and Ascension of our LORD JESUS CHRIST.

Again, I offer to Thee this Sacrifice as a thanksgiving for such admirable gifts and graces conferred on the All-Holy Humanity of Thy SON JESUS CHRIST; and for that so exceeding great love wherewith Thou gavest Him to us, to be our Father and Master, our Advocate and Mediator; for the numberless gifts of grace and virtues, with which Thou didst adorn the most Blessed Virgin, the Mother of Thy SON; the Holy Angels, and all Thine Elect [and amongst others, Saint (N.), or the Saints, whose festival or memory the Church this day celebrates]; for all Thy benefits, also, and aids of grace, bestowed both generally and in particular upon the whole congregation of the faithful; and for those especially, wherewith Thou dost forecome and follow the fore-ordained, and dost effectually guide them to their end.

I give Thee special thanks also, through this most acceptable Oblation of Thy Son, for all the blessings which Thou hast so bountifully bestowed upon me from the beginning of my life, to this very hour; but chiefly, that for no merit of my own, but solely by the good pleasure of Thy goodness, Thou hast vouchsafed to take me, unworthy sinner, among Thy Ministers to execute this office of the Priesthood,—venerable even to the Angels themselves,—to celebrate and to dispense the All-Holy Mysteries of the Body and Blood of Thy Son, to the praise and glory of Thy Name, and the salvation of Thy faithful people.

Moreover, seeing that Thy Son is the Propitiation for our sins and for the sins of the whole world, I offer this Sacrifice unto Thee, O God Most High, for the pardon of the injuries, reproaches, blasphemies, and all sins, committed every where throughout the world, against the glory of Thy Name; alas! how many and grievous! but yet Thy Mercy is greater, and with Thy Son is plenteous Redemption; yea, more plenteous than all the offences of the world is His Satisfaction. Behold, the Blood of Thy Son crieth unto Thee from the earth, yet not for vengeance, but for pardon. Spare, O Lord, spare Thy people, whom Thy Son hath redeemed with His Blood.

Finally, because in this Sacrifice we handle the Very Fountain of all grace, the Author of all our salvation, I offer unto Thee this Sacrifice of Thy Son, that, asking through His Blood and in His Name, we may obtain that which of our own desert we could not.

For His Sake, therefore, look upon the Church, His Spouse, and present it to Thyself beautiful, without spot or wrinkle. Increase in her, faith, hope, charity. Break Thou the pride of her persecutors and enemies. Root out heresies and schisms. Pour the light of Thy truth upon people aliens from the Faith, and bring them into Thy fold. Let not so many souls perish, which have been formed after Thine Image, and redeemed by the Blood of Thy Son.

Provide for Thy Church faithful Bishops and Pastors, as workmen diligent and unreproveable, who may watch anxiously for the flock committed to them; and after the example of Thy Son, the Chief Shepherd, may not hesitate to lay down even their own lives for their sheep.

Give unto all whom Thou vouchsafest to call into Thy Clergy or the condition of the religious life, holiness of manners and life; kindle in them such zeal for Thine honour and the salvation of their neighbours, that they may be found faithful as Thy Ministers, and Stewards of the Mysteries of God.

I beseech Thee, also, O King of kings! in behalf of Christian Kings, Princes, and Magistrates; that Thou wouldest give them peace and concord, zeal and love for justice, faithful care of their subjects, constancy in defence of the Faith and of the Church.

Look in mercy upon all congregations committed to them; and graciously defend all the members of the Church and state; that each in his several calling may worthily and laudably serve Thee. Give perseverance unto the righteous; to the advancing, earnestness; but chiefly give to sinners repentance. For Thou hast no pleasure in the death of him that dieth; but that the dead might live, Thou wouldest that Thine Own Son should die. Do Thou, then, draw sinners unto Thee with the cords of Thy love; for, indeed, they cannot come to Thee, unless Thy love draw them.

Hear Thou, O gracious God, especially the prayers and desires of those, whose care most lieth upon me; as my parents, relations, friends, benefactors, and especially those whose souls are committed unto me, and of whom Thou wilt one day require an account from me. Direct them all, I beseech Thee, in the way of eternal salvation, that by Thy help they may desire whatsoever is pleasing unto Thee, and perform it with all their strength.

Look upon all who are tempted, sick, or placed in difficulties and dangers; be Thou the kind Comforter of the afflicted, the Father of the fatherless, the gracious

Judge of the widow, and the Defender of all faithful Christians. For the eyes of all are towards Thee, until Thou have mercy upon them. Spare our enemies also, O LORD; grant that they may love Thee above all things, and their neighbours for Thee.

Look, also, upon all souls of the faithful departed (especially N. and N., for whom Thou knowest me to be bound to pray). Let this, the great Price of our redemption [m], be unto them a full and abundant refreshment [n], even the Blood of Thy SON, one drop whereof is sufficient to do away the sins of the whole world.

Behold, O LORD, forasmuch as Thou hast willed that I should undertake the office of Priesthood, for all these do I act as ambassador with Thee. O let the lifting up of my hands, even this unbloody Sacrifice, be set forth in Thy sight as the incense!

But, O LORD, seeing that I myself am compassed with infirmity, how shall I praise Thee, since praise is not seemly in the mouth of a sinner? Or how shall I come as an intercessor for the sins of others, who am in hazard for my own? Behold, therefore, our only Advocate and Mediator, Who can both worthily praise Thee, and make intercession for us, even Thy SON. For He is for us both Priest and Victim, the Offerer and the Oblation. He is the guiltless Lamb, in Whom there is no spot, neither was guilt found in His Mouth. He, when He crieth unto Thee, deserveth to be heard, in that He feared. He setteth before Thee an Infinite Treasure and Price, for the longings, necessities, straits, and perils of all, for whom He Himself became obedient unto Thee, even to Death, and as a Good Shepherd laid down His Own Life.

For His Sake, therefore,

---

[m] "When the Sacrifice of our Ransom was offered for her [S. Augustine's mother], when now the corpse was by the grave's side."—S. Aug. Conf. ix. 32. "She desired only to have her name commemorated at Thy Altar; whence she knew that holy Sacrifice to be dispensed, by which the handwriting that was against us is blotted out—unto the Sacrament of which our Ransom, Thy handmaid bound her soul by the bond of faith."—§ 36 and 37.

[n] See above, p. 13, note.

grant unto me also, that I may diligently adorn this state to which Thou hast vouchsafed to call me, with all the virtues due and needful to it, as charity, zeal, chastity, gentleness, humility, and the like. Make Thou me such a minister to Thee as Thou wouldest have me to be; help me, O Lord, and command what Thou wilt. For who can bring a clean thing out of an unclean? Canst not Thou, Who out of nothing makest all things?

And therefore, O Lord, I beseech Thee, from mine inmost heart, that, by virtue of the Body and Blood of our LORD JESUS CHRIST, Thou wouldest join and incorporate me most inwardly with Him, that I may be made one spirit with Him, that He may dwell in me, and I in Him; and that there may not be any thing which either now, or for ever, may be able to separate me from that love which is in CHRIST JESUS our LORD. Amen.

Here may be selected from the 4th Book of Thomas à Kempis, On the Imitation of Christ, Prayers and Exercises most spiritual and helpful towards devout Communion.

An Oblation before the Sacrifice of the Eucharist, by S. Bonaventura.

Behold, O heavenly FATHER, making remembrance of that Death of Thine Only-Begotten Son our LORD JESUS CHRIST, I offer unto Thee this Sacrifice which He Himself once offered for my salvation, and that of the whole world. Behold, I lay before the Altar of Thy Majesty that living Oblation which Thou in great compassion didst send to be immolated on the Altar of the Cross for us. Remember, therefore, His most Holy Sweat, as it were drops of Blood falling down upon the ground.

Look upon that Virgin-Flesh, cruelly scourged with rods, wounded with smitings and blows, swollen with stripes, defiled with spittle, bloody with gore, torn with thorns, fastened through with nails, pierced with the lance.

Let that love, then, which drew Thy Son down and overpowered Him, that He might weigh down in the balance of the Cross the sins of the whole world, constrain Thee also, O FATHER, to be merciful to us miserable. Look, I beseech Thee, not on our sins, but upon the Face of Thy CHRIST. For we cast down our prayers before Thee, trusting, not in our own righteousness, but in Thy manifold and great mercies.

CHAPTER VII.

OF DEVOUT ATTENDANCE ON HOLY COMMUNION.

ADMONITION

CONCERNING THE EXCELLENCE AND NECESSITY OF THE EUCHARISTIC SACRIFICE, AND THE REVERENCE DUE TO IT.

He that fails to partake of the Holy Eucharist, whenever opportunity offers, or performs the duty with carelessness and indifference, is either ignorant of the dignity and benefit of that great Sacrifice, or, certainly does not duly value it.

For in the Eucharist the entire Price of our salvation, and the whole treasure of Christ's Merits, is offered to each individual Christian; and the chief mysteries of the Faith and of our Redemption are, as it were, enacted afresh.

He, then, is careless about his salvation, ungrateful to GOD, and too lukewarm in duties of piety, who does not frequently commemorate the blessing of his redemption with devout meditation, and with feelings of gratitude towards GOD: and so neglects the treasures purchased at so rich a Price, even the Blood of CHRIST; the greatest safeguard of the Christian life.

Surely the SAVIOUR *requireth of us a frequent and grateful remembrance of His Passion, and of His love towards us, whereof He left to His Church so noble and excellent a Memorial, when He said, "As often as ye shall do these things, ye shall do them in remembrance of Me."*

It will not, then, be out of place to note here some things which may both make manifest the dignity and benefit of this great Sacrifice, and also draw the faithful to a greater reverence and devotion.

For who of the faithful (says S. Gregory, *Dial.* lib. iv. c. 58) can doubt, that, in the very moment of offering, the heavens are laid open at the words of the Priest; that in that Mystery of JESUS CHRIST the choirs of Angels are present; the highest are associated with the lowest, earthly things are joined with heavenly, and things visible and invisible are made one?

To the same purpose speaks S. Chrysostom (Of the Priesthood, lib. vi.). At the time, *saith he,* that the Sacrifice is performed, Angels are standing by the Priest, and the whole host of celestial powers crieth aloud; and the space about the Altar is filled with choirs of Angels in honour of Him Who is present: a thing we may most readily believe, from the nature of the Sacrifice then offered.

He means, could it be thought that those Blessed Ones, those ministering Spirits, that Court as it were of so great a King, could leave their LORD without the reverent attendance of His retinue[a]?

Listen, again, to a wonderful yet most true sentiment, expressed by a deeply pious and learned author[b]. If the

---

[a] Add S. Ambrose, in S. Luc. c. 1. "And where we, too, kindle the Altars and offer the Sacrifice, may the Angel stand by; nay, rather, may he show himself. For thou mayest not doubt that the Angel is present when CHRIST is present, when CHRIST is offered." S. Chrys. de Sacerdot. l. c. states, that he had heard one relate, that an aged and very admirable man, and used to see visions, told him that this sight had once been vouchsafed to him, and at that time [the Eucharistic Sacrifice] he had, on a sudden, seen a multitude of Angels, as far as he might, clothed with bright apparel, and encircling the Altar, and stooping down, as you might the soldiers standing in the presence of the Emperor. "And I," adds S. Chrysostom, "believe it."

[b] F. Ant. Molina, De Inst. Sacram. Tract. 3, c. 9.

love, *saith he*, wherewith all the Saints altogether, from the very beginning of the world have been enkindled, and shall be henceforth even to the end; if the good deeds of all, and the praises offered to GOD were heaped together; if the torments of martyrs who with heroic courage have poured out their blood and their lives for CHRIST; if the virtues of confessors, patriarchs, prophets, monks, hermits, and all others who, by another kind of martyrdom, more protracted, and, in a certain sense, more hard to endure, have afflicted themselves, and subdued their rebellious appetites by fastings, watchings, and prayer; if, lastly, all the services performed unto GOD, although most pleasing unto Him, past, present, and to come, were joined therewith, they would not compose such perfect praise and honour as is comprised in that one Eucharistic Sacrifice, celebrated by the lowest and the poorest of Priests.

And lest he should seem to be speaking unreasonably, he adds, And for this reason; because in every Eucharistic Sacrifice CHRIST is the chief Priest, Who, as such, in fact offers the Sacrifice. But it is the office of the Priest to worship GOD. Wherefore in the Eucharist it is CHRIST Who chiefly worships and honours the FATHER, that He may supply our deficiency.

And it is certain that all created beings together cannot give so much honour to GOD, as can the SON of GOD. And so the Sacrifice of the Eucharist, on the part both of Him Who offereth, and of Him Who is offered [c], excels in the highest degree all devotion and worship which can be offered by creatures, either individually or conjointly.

Wherefore (*as the same author well adds*) let Priests consider what vast treasures they hold in their hands. It

[c] S. Ambr. in Ps. 38. "We have seen the Chief Priest coming unto us; we have seen and heard Him offering for us His Blood; let us Priests follow Him as we can, offering Sacrifice for the people, although weak in desert, yet in honour through the Sacrifice, for although now CHRIST seemeth not to be offered, yet He is offered on earth, when the Body of CHRIST is offered, yea, He Himself is clearly shown to offer in us, Whose Word sanctifieth the Sacrifice Which is offered."

is a shame and a disgrace that there should be any who readily, and for a thing of nought, deprive both themselves and others of a treasure of such vast magnitude. *Thus far the aforesaid author, a man of great religion and gravity.*

Consider now, *saith yet another*[d], how sad and lamentable it is to see a Priest in the performance of the Divine Mysteries, surrounded on every side by the companies of Angels, who are filled with astonishment and awe at the things which he is doing and saying, and in their admiration cry aloud one to another, Holy, Holy, Holy, and all the while the Priest standing in the midst, is altogether cold, and, as if devoid of sense, heeds not what he is doing, understands not what he is saying, and so hurries to the end, so confuses the signs, and so slurs over his words, as if he were driven on and chased by robbers at his back. We proclaim aloud that in the Sacrament of the Altar, CHRIST Himself is present; and yet some so handle the Mysteries as if they thought there were nothing less true.

But others, also, who wish to attend with profit at the Eucharist, should be mindful of the reverence due to such high mysteries. It is very much to be deplored, that there should be any among Christians, who though with the body present in Church, are at the same time wandering in mind and with their eyes, tell stories, bandy about nonsense, make jokes, stand as if spectators of some comedy, and take no account of those things which the Priest, in the performance of the sacred rites, is doing and setting forth. What can be more disgraceful to a Christian man, than to look on thus irreverently and indevoutly upon this Memorial of the Sufferings of CHRIST *his Redeemer?*

What can be more unseemly than when, by the Sacrifice, we renew the memory of the Sorrows of CHRIST *and His most Bitter Passion, and call to mind the blessing of our Redemption, that a Christian man should stand by with so slight a feeling of the due gratitude and piety, nay (which is worse), that he should not only be regardless of the blessing, but fling back on so loving*

---

[d] See Bellarmine, Serm. 9, for the 4th S. in Advent: and On the Art of Holy Dying, i. 14.

a Benefactor injuries and shame, with laughter, idle discourse, and jests. What else is this, than, where sins should be blotted out, to heap new sins upon the old, and, to his great condemnation, to convert medicines into poison?

How ill does this waywardness of men consist with the sanctity of the place! Holiness becometh the House of GOD, forasmuch as the Holy of Holies dwelleth there. You may say, that such persons believe not that He, the Great King of heaven and earth, the LORD, the Judge of quick and dead, is present in this Sacrifice; for that, whereas Angels praise Him, Dominions adore, Powers tremble before Him, they amuse themselves with tales and jests. S. Chrysostom and other Fathers commonly speak of these Mysteries no otherwise than as "dreadful," as "tremendous," at which Christians ought not to be present but with fear.

To this end, therefore, we will here supply some exercises, and frequent methods for devout and profitable attendance at the Holy Eucharist, that each may thence select what may be most agreeable to him, or that by variety the mind may be refreshed, and the weariness avoided, which may possibly be produced by the frequent repetition of one method.

Moreover, if any one should wish to make use of the first of the following methods, namely, the adaptation of the LORD's Passion, it is not necessary that he should make use of each meditation in exact correspondence with the several parts of the Divine Office (though that may be done with great ease, according to the form here given), but that he may dwell on this or that, according to the state of his mind. The same might be used as a preparation for spiritual Communion.

A METHOD OF PRACTICE

FOR DEVOUT COMMUNION; IN THE WAY OF EXERCISE ON THE PASSION OF OUR LORD.

The Sacrifice and Sacrament of the Holy Eucharist may be regarded as a true and lively representation of that Bloody Sacrifice which CHRIST *accomplished and offered to the Eternal* FATHER *upon the Altar of the Cross, by the immolation of His Body and Blood.*

A very good method, therefore, of attending on Holy Communion, and rich in spiritual benefit, will be, with devout affection, to go over in our minds the work of our Redemption, by applying the mystical celebration of this Sacrifice to the particulars of our LORD's *Passion.*

FIRST EXERCISE

FOR DEVOUT COMMUNION.

1. INTERVAL OF SILENCE BEFORE THE COMMENCEMENT OF THE DIVINE OFFICE.

Before the Priest goes within the Altar-rails, and while he is offering his secret prayer, consider, O my soul, with what intense desire the Fathers of old waited for the Coming of Messiah in the flesh.

O Eternal FATHER! Who hast so loved the world as to give Thine Only-Begotten Son for our redemption, what shall I render unto Thee for so rich a gift, for such great love? Behold Thine own Only-Begotten Son, than Whom nought can be more dear to Thee, nought more precious to us.

O with how many sighs, with what burning longings was He looked for by all nations! until at length, sent forth from Thee, He took the form of a servant, and, clad in the mortal garment of our flesh, He veiled the Majesty of the Godhead, and from the Virgin's womb came forth into the world; and becoming obedient to Thee even unto death, He redeemed us from death eternal.

Behold, O Lord, I desire, in this Sacrifice of the Eucharist, to commemorate this labour of such vast, such boundless love, to Thy Glory, and in remembrance of Thy Son. Do Thou, I beseech Thee, O Lord, take possession of my heart, and direct it by Thy grace, that I may do this piously, devoutly, and becomingly, so that this my service may be pleasing to Thee, and beneficial to my soul.

Here and on the following articles, all or some, according to the opportunity and judgment of each person, may be subjoined the following

ASPIRATIONS UNTO CHRIST.

Comprising an Exercise of the most exalted virtues.

O Lord, what great things hast Thou done, what hast Thou endured, from the force of Thy boundless love towards me! But what return have I made? or what shall I make unto Thee?

I mourn from my inmost heart that I ever offended Thee, Who hast so greatly loved me.

I believe in Thee with lively faith, O Thou Eternal Truth! that Thou Thyself art God and Man, my Lord and my Saviour!

I hope in Thee, O Lord, O Thou the only Hope and true Salvation of my soul!

I love Thee also above all things with my whole heart, O Thou my Chief Good! O may the all-glowing power of Thy love take me wholly into itself, so that nothing may ever separate me from the love of Christ Jesus my Saviour! For whom have I in heaven but Thee, and what is there on earth that I desire in comparison of Thee!

2. AT THE CONFESSION

which we make, both Priest and people, in the recitation of the Commandments, look how Christ, *calling with Him His disciples, and upon Him the sins of the whole world, to the Mount of Olives, and there falling down upon His Face, prayeth; and in anguish at His impending Passion and Death, but more on account of His horror at our sins, His Sweat becomes as it were drops of Blood falling down upon the ground.*

And can I ever again offend Thee by my sins, O most Sweet LORD! Who hast done such great things, and suffered so much for us? &c.

We may reflect too upon the wretchedness of man! How easily do we fall! But we rise not again, unless the mercy of GOD *help us. For this therefore we should frequently, nay constantly entreat. And this we are taught by the recurring petition,* "LORD *have mercy upon us, and incline our hearts to keep this law." For the conversion and recovery of a sinner are difficult, and the greatest work of the Divine Mercy.*

Alas! most merciful JESU, how inconstant and unstable have I been in my good resolutions! How often have I, forgetful of my promise, with Peter, denied Thee, O Lord! But how seldom have I bewailed my transgressions with tears of real grief! O that with Peter I could do this also!

3. IN THE PRIEST RETURNING TO THE ALTAR

to continue the Sacrifice, see how CHRIST, *as a meek Lamb comes forth and offers to the impious betrayer the Kiss of His blessed Mouth; and by that sign surrenders Himself to His enemies as they enter into the garden.*

And shall I, for some empty creature, betray or forsake Thee, O most meek LORD, Who didst hold me so dear, that, for my deliverance from the hands of mine enemies, Thou wouldest Thyself be delivered into the hands of wicked men?

4. AT THE COLLECT AND EPISTLE,

Think of the collected accusations of the people against CHRIST, *the council in the house of Caiaphas, and the various insults, spittings, buffetings, and mockeries which He then endured.*

O most Meek LORD, what great things hast Thou done and suffered for us! &c. as p. 105. col. 2.

5. AT THE GOSPEL, CREED, AND SERMON,

The reading of which is passed, as it were, from one end of the Altar to the other, and from the Altar to the Pulpit, look, in imagination, upon CHRIST *transferred from Caiaphas to Pilate; how He was examined by the ungodly respecting His doctrine and His disciples; how He was accused on account of His preaching the Gospel, and so was assailed with a multitude of injuries and reproaches.*

O LORD, of infinite Wisdom; Thou camest down from heaven to be our Master, that Thou mightest teach the way of God in truth, and lead us from earth to heaven. But that Thou mightest discharge Thine office the more perfectly, Thou didst begin to do before Thou didst teach, and yet didst Thou suffer reproach. In Thy words was simple truth; in Thy deeds integrity; in all Thy conversation sincerity; (for who could convince Thee of sin?) nevertheless Thou, the LORD, Master and Judge of all men, sufferedst Thyself to be judged and rejected by the wicked and ungodly!

O that I may receive the seed of the Word, Thy Gospel, into a good and fertile heart, and bring forth much fruit with patience!

6. AT THE OFFERTORY AND OBLATION,

Think, O my soul, how CHRIST *was sent from Pilate to Herod, and from the latter back again to the former; and was everywhere mocked, despised, and reviled.*

O Thou Fairest above the sons of men, O Thou Desire and Expectation of the Gentiles! art Thou only the Reproach of men and the Outcast of the people, Thou upon Whom the Angels desire to look; in Whom the Eternal FATHER is well-pleased! Thou wast offered for us, because Thou willedst; and, alas! art Thou thus despised? Behold, LORD, I offer myself wholly unto Thee; despise me not, I beseech Thee, Thou Who didst vouchsafe to offer Thyself wholly for me.

7. AT THE EXHORTATION, CONFESSION, AND ABSOLUTION,

Think of CHRIST *pronounced faultless by Pilate, when he washed his hands; how He was brought forth before the people, and yet by that infuriate rabble was declared guilty of death, and esteemed worse than the robber Barabbas.*

O how often have I also, with depraved affections, preferred the creature to GOD my Creator! O most blameless LORD! what great things hast Thou done and suffered for us, &c. *as above.*

8. AT THE PREFACE.

Think deeply on the intense grief of CHRIST, *and the anguish of His Mind, when He perceived that great hatred and extreme fury of the Jews, wherewith, though Pilate sought in every way to let Him go, those impious men demanded His Crucifixion and Death, &c.*

Art not Thou He, O LORD, to Whom, when Thou enteredst into the city a few days before, all the people gave praise, shouting Hosanna! Blessed is He that cometh in the Name of the LORD! Art not Thou He to Whom the Angels sing, Holy, Holy, Holy! Ah! sad and unlooked for change! Surely I may learn from Thee, O LORD, how to rely on human favour, how to trust in the children of men in whom there is no help; truly, it is good for me to hold me fast by Thee Alone, and to place my hope in Thee, O LORD, O most patient LORD! what great things hast Thou done and suffered for us, &c.

9. AT THE PRAYER "WE DO NOT PRESUME."

Consider how CHRIST *was most cruelly scourged by the impious attendants, how He was crowned with thorns, given up by Pilate to be crucified, and then, laden with the heavy Tree of the Cross, went up in great pain to Mount Calvary.*

Alas! O LORD, whither hath my great wickedness, and Thine own boundless love brought Thee? I have deserved the scourge of Thy wrath, and Thou, the Guiltless, art scourged for me! Eternal torment awaited me, and Thou hast drawn it aside and borne the Cross upon Thine own Shoulders! Truly, O Lord, hast Thou borne our griefs and carried our sorrows! O most Gracious Lord, what great things hast Thou done and suffered, &c.

10. AT THE CONSECRATION OF THE ELEMENTS;

Think of Christ *lifted up on the Cross stripped and exposed to the gaze of all the people.*

Note.—*This and the two following prayers may be said while the Priest and others are communicating before we go up to the Altar.*

O Christ Jesu! I adore Thee Who wast lifted up from the earth, that Thou mightest draw all unto Thee. I see Thee on the Cross with outstretched Arms, as though Thou wouldest embrace us, and I hear Thee crying out, Come unto Me, all ye that labour and are heavy-laden, and I will receive and refresh you.

O Lord! if I come to Thee too slowly, draw me, O Jesu, with the cords of that love which Thou didst show, dying upon the Cross. To know and to seek Jesus, and Him Crucified, be this my chief, my sole delight. God forbid that I should glory save in the Cross of our Lord Jesus Christ!

O Eternal Father! behold, here is Thy Beloved Son in Whom Thou art well-pleased. Look upon the Face of Thy Christ, and turn away Thy Face from my sins, on account of which Thine Only-Begotten humbled Himself, being made obedient unto Thee, even to the Death of the Cross. Behold, here is our Advocate with Thee, and the Propitiation for our sins. For He bare our sins in His own Body on the tree, and with His Stripes we are healed.

With the Publican then, in deepest sorrow, I smite my breast, guilty of those so grievous sins, which alone drew down such heavy punishment upon Thine Only-Begotten. For His sake, therefore, be merciful to me a sinner.

Behold the Voice of Thy Son's Blood crieth unto Thee

from the earth, not for vengeance, but for pardon. Let His Passion and Death, I beseech Thee, be the remedy and the remission of all my sins. Let the Torments and the Wounds of His Body be the healing of my soul.

Reflect, moreover, on the separation of the Soul of CHRIST *from His Body, that is, on the Death which He, as an innocent Lamb led to the slaughter, endured that He might take away the sins of the world. Think, also, upon His descent into hell.*

O LORD, dost Thou, the Author of life, die, that I, guilty of death, may live? Who will grant unto me, that I may die unto the world and the flesh, and live to Thee Alone? And that, being delivered from the depths of hell, I may rejoice with Thee in glory? O LORD, what hast Thou done and suffered, &c.

11. DURING COMMUNION AND DISTRIBUTION.

Whilst the Priest is partaking of the Sacred Mysteries (and dispensing them to others), think on the laying of the Body of CHRIST *in the sepulchre; and do thou also prepare to lay Him up in thine own breast; and to this end exercise lively Acts of faith, hope, and charity.*

I adore Thee, O LORD JESUS, with lively and true faith, as by virtue of Thy wondrous Power, Wisdom, and Goodness truly present in this Sacrament; Thy Body and Thy Soul, Thy Flesh and Thy Blood; and I hope in Thee, O Thou Fount of all goodness and mercy! for I am not worthy that Thou shouldest come under my roof; but speak the word only, Thou who canst do all things by Thy sovereign Will alone, and my weak and miserable soul shall be healed.

I love Thee, O LORD, Who art so loving to me, with my whole heart, more than myself and all things; and therefore do I now desire to receive Thee, that I may feed on Thee, and be changed into Thee, and be made one spirit with Thee, so that nought may separate me from Thee, but that I may cleave unto Thee for ever.

Grant, O LORD, by these Mysteries, the Precious Gifts of Thy love, that I may embalm Thy Sacred Body with the spices and sweet odour of virtue, and that, wrapped in the fine linen of a pure conscience, I may lay It in a new and clean heart. O that Thou mightest for ever abide and rest in me, and I in Thee!

12. AT THE LORD'S PRAYER,

Which consisteth of seven Petitions, reflect, O my soul, on the seven last and most sacred words which CHRIST uttered on the Cross.

1. *Our* FATHER *Which art in heaven, hallowed be Thy Name.*

O grant unto me, O LORD, that I may worship, love, fear Thee, the FATHER of us all, and for Thy sake may embrace my neighbour with true and sincere love; even as Thou hast instructed us by Thine own example, when hanging upon the Cross and dying for Thine enemies, Thou didst pray for them, saying, *Father, forgive them.* O rare and wondrous love! O that we, who profess the Name of CHRIST, may imitate it! No one, indeed, more honoureth Thy Name, O CHRIST! or more clearly proveth himself to be Thy disciple, that is, a Christian, than he who after Thy Example, and out of love of Thee, hath learnt to love even his enemies.

2. *Thy kingdom come;*

That kingdom, of which Thou didst promise the thief on the cross that he should be a partaker, saying, *To-day shalt thou be with Me in Paradise.* O that I may be found worthy to hear that most sweet declaration at the hour of my death!

Give unto me, O LORD, the faith, the hope, and the penitence of that thief; and my heart will not be afraid of any evil tidings.

3. *Thy Will be done in earth as it is in heaven.*

It is Thy Will, indeed, O JESU, that even those most dear to Thee should be partakers of Thy Cross; yea, Thou willest that this should be the sign and mark of Thy love. Lo, we see this in Thy most sweet Mother, and in the Disciple whom Thou lovedst. They were witnesses and spectators of Thy Crucifixion; but, alas, with what crucifixion of their own hearts!

Of a truth, that this sword of grief should pierce through those so-loved souls, even that of Thy most dear Mother—this was of Thy will; yet this also, that comfort should not be wanting to the afflicted.

Wherefore Thou saidst, *Woman, behold thy son;* and to the Disciple, *Behold thy Mother.* O unequal exchange, that for the SON of GOD His Mother should receive the son of Zebedee, &c., but since it was Thy Will, Thy Mother acquiesced.

O LORD! behold I am Thine. Willest Thou that I should be partaker of Thy Sufferings? O GOD, my heart is ready. Willest Thou that I should be partaker of the consolation also? My heart is ready. Let all Thy Will be done in me. For as Thou wouldest have it done in heaven, that is, in Thine Elect and in those who love Thee most, why should I shrink from it? I desire to please Thee in all things; and to obey Thee in all things; but give Thou me grace. I refuse not to suffer with Thee; but increase Thou my patience.

4. *Give us this day our daily Bread.*

For if Thou, O LORD, remake me not, surely I shall soon be unmade. O LORD, Who feedest me from my youth even to my old age and my hoar hairs, forsake me not when my strength faileth me. Remember that for my sake Thou didst cry unto the FATHER, as if abandoned in Thy distress, *My* GOD, *why hast Thou forsaken Me?* The eyes of all wait upon Thee, and Thou givest them meat and strength in due season, I also cry unto Thee in my famine and distress. If Thou look away from me, who will look upon me? If Thou forsake me, who will take me up? If Thou reject me, who will refresh me?

5. *And forgive us our trespasses;*

Because Thou hast so plenteously poured out Thy Blood, that there might be plenteous Redemption for us; and that at so great a Price Thou mightest pay to the uttermost our debts, which none could pay, save Thou. O the love, O the longing for our salvation! Wherefore, faint with love, and, now, all bloodless and parched, upon the Cross, Thou criest, *I thirst;* yet for what, but for the Cup of Suffering and Death, that by drinking it to the very dregs, Thou mightest wash out all our debts, all our transgressions?

6. *And lead us not into temptation,*

But rather, as the Good Shepherd, lead and direct us as the sheep of Thy pasture, and, as our Mediator, commit us to the care of Thine Eternal FATHER, to Whom, when dying, Thou didst commend Thyself, saying, FATHER, *into Thy Hands I commend My Spirit.* Suffer us not to perish, O LORD, Who didst come to seek and to save that which was lost.

7. *But deliver us from evil,*

For to what end were the countless toils, and labours, and pangs of Thy whole Life? To what purpose was the whole work of Redemption, which Thou saidst was *finished* by Thee on the Cross, but that we might be delivered from all evil; that we might rejoice in Thee, the One, True, Sovereign Good? O may it be given to me to have the fruition of it! Amen. So be it, O CHRIST JESU! so be it, my Life and my Salvation, my GOD and my Portion for ever!

O most Merciful JESU, how unsteadfast and soon moved have I been in good purposes! how often have I too, unmindful of my promise, with Peter, denied Thee, Lord! But how seldom have I with tears of real sorrow wept my sins! O that with Peter, this too may be given me! and that henceforth, persevering in good, I may gladden the Angels, and together with them, may sing unto Thee, GLORY TO GOD IN THE HIGHEST.

13. AT THE POST-COMMUNION,

Think on CHRIST *rising from the dead and appearing unto many.*

O that I also may now truly rise from the death of

sin, and henceforth walk with Thee in newness of life! For Thou didst die for our sins, and wast raised again for our justification. O LORD, what great things hast Thou done and suffered for us, &c., *as before.*

14. AT THE GLORIA IN EXCELSIS,

Including the threefold petition, " Have mercy upon us." Think on Peter, who after such fair professions of constancy and faithfulness, denied his LORD *three times; neither did he repent until after the merciful* LORD *had looked upon him. But afterwards he received the Angel's message, and made that threefold profession of love; that we might know how the Angels rejoice over one sinner that repenteth, whereof the Angelical Hymn here seasonably reminds us.*

15. AT THE BLESSING,

Think that CHRIST, *having now fully accomplished the work of man's Redemption, ascendeth into heaven as a glorious Conqueror; and the Apostles, having received* CHRIST'S *blessing, are gone into the world to preach the Gospel to every creature.*

O most Glorious JESU! shall I, with grovelling spirit, cleave to earth, knowing Thee to be my FATHER in the heavens? Do Thou lead me with Thyself on high, that I may seek after, and savour of, the things which are above, not those on the earth. Grant that my conversation may be in heaven.

O CHRIST JESU! Who sittest upon the heavens as upon the throne of Thy Majesty, and yet vouchsafest to be present on the Altar, and to be offered by the hands of the Priest, I praise Thee, I adore Thee, I love Thee with my whole heart, and I will not let Thee go except Thou bless me.

Be Thou our Mediator, where Thou sittest at the Right Hand of GOD; and unceasingly make intercession for us with the FATHER; show unto Him Thy Blood, Thy Wounds, and all Thy Merits. How can there be refusal there, where so many signs of love exist? O LORD, what great things hast Thou done and suffered for us! &c.

CHAPTER VIII.

MISCELLANEOUS PRAYERS FOR SEVERAL PORTIONS OF THE OFFICE OF HOLY COMMUNION.

One of the chief duties of Christian piety is frequently and devoutly to partake of the Holy Communion. Before all things, therefore, raise thyself to attention and reverence by meditation on that Divine Majesty, which is indeed present everywhere, but here more especially.

Then unite and conform thy intention to that of the priest; that is, offer up this Sacrifice together with him, and do as far as it is lawful for thee, what he does.

For the priest is, as it were, the mouth, the interpreter, the ambassador of Christian people: of those especially who are present at the celebration of the Holy Eucharist, and are one in intention with the celebrant.

Thus in the ancient Liturgy it is said,

Remember, O LORD, &c., all who stand around, whose faith and devotion are known unto Thee, for whom we offer unto Thee, or who offer unto Thee, this Sacrifice of praise, for themselves and all theirs, for the redemption of their souls, for hope of salvation and well-being, and to Thee do they pay their vows, the Living, True, and Eternal GOD.

And in our own, in the Prayer for the Church militant:

We humbly beseech Thee most mercifully to accept our alms and oblations, and to receive these our prayers which we offer unto Thy Divine Majesty;—and to all Thy people give Thy heavenly grace, and especially to this congregation here present, &c.

And afterwards,

We, Thy humble servants, entirely desire Thy Fatherly Goodness, mercifully to accept this our Sacrifice of praise and thanksgiving, most humbly beseeching Thee, &c. And here we offer and present unto Thee, O LORD, ourselves, &c., humbly beseeching Thee, that all we, who are partakers of this Holy Communion, may be fulfilled with Thy grace and heavenly benediction.

A FORM

FOR RIGHTLY DIRECTING THE INTENTION BEFORE HOLY COMMUNION.

(*From P. Christ. Mayer.*)

Accept, O Holy Trinity, One GOD, this most holy Sacrifice of the Body and Blood of our LORD JESUS CHRIST, which, with all the sacrifices which have at any time been offered, or are yet to be offered, in union with that All-holy Sacrifice offered by the Same our LORD at the Last Supper, and on the Altar of the Cross,—I, Thine unworthy servant, offer unto Thy Divine Majesty by the hands of the Priest, with every affection of piety whereof I am capable, out of pure love for Thine Infinite Goodness, and in conformity with the most sacred intention of the Same our LORD, and our holy Mother the Church.

1. To the highest and everlasting glory, love and good-pleasure of Thy Divine Majesty.

2. In acknowledgment of Thy Supreme Excellence and dominion, and of our subjection and dependence on Thee.

3. For the perpetual Memory of the Passion and Death of the Same our LORD.

4. In everlasting thanksgiving for all the benefits hitherto conferred, or throughout eternity to be conferred, through the most Sacred Humanity of our LORD, on all the blessed Elect, and on me, who am most wholly unworthy.

5. For the forgiveness of

my own sins, and of the sins of all the faithful, living or departed.

6. In particular, for the attainment of these (N. N.) or this (N.) especial grace. Then for these persons (N. N.) particularly commended to me, and all for whom I am wont and bound to pray, beseeching of Thee, for the departed, rest, and for the living, grace to know, love, glorify Thee, perfectly now in this present way, and hereafter blessedly in their home. Accept and perform this my desire, and vouchsafe Thy abounding grace and blessing devoutly to accomplish it. Amen.

A VERY BRIEF FORM

FOR THE EXCITEMENT OF CONTRITION AND DEVOTION, AND FOR THE RENEWAL OF THE INTENTION BEFORE HOLY COMMUNION.

(From the same.)

O JESU! infinitely worthy of all love! Who, by the Will of the FATHER and the Co-operation of the HOLY GHOST, didst not once alone vouchsafe to give Thyself to be one of us, our Food, Sacrifice, Ransom, and Reward, but art pleased daily to offer Thyself to me anew! how great is Thy Bounty, Charity, Pity, towards me, who am so ungrateful! How great towards Thee is my ingratitude, dulness, and wickedness, who repay Thee with so many and such great evils and sins, for Thy many and great benefits! I grieve for these ... and for all the offences of my whole life, simply because I have offended Thee, Thou Who art infinitely Good. I desire to amend all, and make amends for all, as Thou willest. Supply, forgive, receive me to the kiss of peace, I entreat Thee, by Thy Tears and Bloody Sweat, and by this Holy Sacrifice.

O that I could attend on

this most Divine Memorial of Thy Passion, this monument of Thy Power, Wisdom, and Goodness, this summary of all Thy marvellous works, with that attention, devotion, reverence, which are demanded by the Presence of Thy Divine Majesty, the company of so many attendant Angels, the magnificence of so many Mysteries here enacted!

I desire to do this, my GOD, with all the affections of my heart, to Thy Supreme Glory, Love, and Goodpleasure; by way of thanksgiving for all Thy benefits; for the forgiveness of my sins, and of the sins of all the faithful, to obtain for (N. and N.) and all, living and departed, pardon, grace, glory.

And that I may do this worthily, give me, I beseech Thee, abundant grace and blessing, for Thy Merit's sake.

PRAYER BEFORE COMMUNION.

O Most Gracious FATHER of Mercies, and GOD of all consolation, Who so lovedst the world, that Thou sparedst not Thine Only-Begotten Son, but, to restore us, gavest Him up to the Suffering of the most bitter Death of the Cross; and hast moreover willed that this Oblation of Him, most pleasing to Thee, should be daily renewed in Thy Church, that its benefit may be applied to ourselves; grant to us, we beseech Thee, that we may attend on this wondrous and salutary Mystery of Thy Divine Power, Wisdom, and Goodness, with such earnestness, reverence, and devotion, that, by the Offering of this Unbloody Sacrifice, we may partake most effectually of that Sacrifice of Blood; through the Same our LORD.

OF THE COLLECTS.

A Collect may be defined to be a prayer in which the Priest presents to GOD *the necessities and dangers, or the wishes and desires of the whole people, or the Church, collected together into one short form. And when he says,* Let us pray, *he invites all present to say this prayer, as it were with one heart and spirit.*

AN INTERCESSORY PRAYER

EXPANDING AND APPLYING THE GENERAL PETITIONS OF THE COLLECTS.

Almighty, Everlasting GOD, vouchsafe, we humbly beseech Thee, to look down from the height of Thy Sanctuary, upon this congregation, and graciously hear and accept the prayers of Thy Church, offered to Thee on behalf of us all by the ministry of Thy Priest.

According to Thine Infinite Mercy, grant unto us pardon of our sins, soundness of mind, health of body, all needful supports of life; give peace in our time, moderate weather, fruitfulness of the earth.

Preserve the unity of the Catholic faith; root out heresies; confound the devices of our enemies; extend the true faith; give unto us fervent charity and piety; heartfelt devotedness of mind; endurance and longsuffering under afflictions; and joyful hope. Finally, bestow upon us all things which are needful for the welfare both of our souls and bodies, but above all, whatever may promote the increase of Thy glory. Through our LORD JESUS CHRIST.

AT THE EPISTLE.

Listen with close attention, as if thou heardest the Prophet or the Apostle himself instructing, warning, or reproving thee.

A PRAYER.

O Eternal GOD! Who never ceasest, by the public ministry of Thy Church, by the doctrine and warnings of Apostles, Prophets, and other holy men, to stir up us, Thine unworthy servants, to the worship and love of Thy Name, and to defend us against the snares of the world, the flesh, and the devil; grant, we beseech

Thee, that we may all ever embrace, from our hearts, those wholesome truths and warnings, and may earnestly endeavour to fashion our whole life and manners, according to them.

And lest, at length, it should turn to our deeper condemnation, by so many instructors and preachers to have known the way of truth, Thy Holy Will, and not to have done it, give us grace and strength, that what we so often know we ought to do, we may be able to bring to good effect. Amen.

AT THE GOSPEL.

In accordance with ancient and pious custom, we are wont to hear the Gospel standing. First, as a mark of reverence shewn to CHRIST *as present with, and instructing us.*

Then, that we may profess ourselves to be disciples of CHRIST, *ready both to hear His doctrine with our ears, and shew it forth in our lives.*

Again, that we may shew openly that, as soldiers under CHRIST *our Captain, we seek for the weapons of our warfare, wherewith to fight against our enemies, out of the Faith and Doctrine of* CHRIST, *and that we are ready to do or suffer anything in defence of His Truth.*

Again, that we may be on the watch, lest the fowls of the air, that is, spirits of the air, the enemies of our salvation, should devour the good seed of evangelic truth, or lest, haply, the cares of the world, like thorns, should choke it, so that it bring forth no fruit.

Moreover, when, as is sometimes the case, the Epistle having been read at one end of the Altar, the Gospel is read at the other by the Priest who is the celebrant, this may serve to signify that the Gospel was first preached to the Jews as the peculiar people, but on their rejection of it, the Apostles turned to the Gentiles.

A PRAYER ON THE GOSPEL.

O LORD JESU CHRIST, Who didst come as a Teacher from God; and when on earth, and visibly conversing with man, didst teach us the way of God in truth, Thou ceasest not at this day also still to teach us by the writings of the Evangelists, and by the preachers of Thy Word.

Give us understanding to receive Thy life-giving doctrine. Inflame our affections also with longing desire after Heavenly Wisdom, and teach us to do Thy Will; that so the faith which is produced by the hearing of the Gospel, and which we profess with our lips, may be confessed also by our lives and conduct: lest it be to our deeper guilt and punishment, that, knowing the Will of the LORD, we did it not. For, both to know and to do is the work of Thy grace alone; seeing that of ourselves we are unprofitable servants, and all our sufficiency is of Thee.

AFTER THE GOSPEL IS READ.

Glory be to Thee, O CHRIST, Who by Thine own Self, and by Thy Apostles, hast vouchsafed to preach the Gospel to the world, and to shed upon the unbelieving the light of the true faith.

After the Gospel, follows the Creed, or Profession of Faith; and with reason, because faith cometh by hearing the Word of GOD, and great multitudes of people have embraced the Faith of CHRIST *through the preaching of the Gospel. Repeat it aloud with the Priest, but with lively faith and devout affection; for thus thou wilt excite in thyself ardent zeal for the Faith of* CHRIST, *and so, constancy and perseverance. For nothing is of greater force to excite in us the love of* GOD, *than a lively and strong belief of those things which are contained in the Creed.*

At the time of the celebration of the Communion, the Priest addresses to the communicants an Exhortation; which, with the Confession, the Absolution, and the comfortable words of our SAVIOUR CHRIST *and of His Apostles, which follow, constitute an earnest preparation of the minds of the people, that they may, with due attention, reverence, and piety, follow the solemn act of Consecration, and subsequent participation of the Body and Blood of* CHRIST.

Wherefore, when he saith, Lift up your hearts, *we ought to remember that, casting aside all earthly cares and thoughts, we should raise our minds to high and heavenly things; especially because as we reply,* We lift them up unto the LORD, *we shall be guilty of falsehood, if, entangled by things of the world, we profess with the mouth what is not in our hearts.*

While the Priest is preparing to place the Elements upon the Altar, say one of the following prayers.

O LORD JESU CHRIST, SON of the Living GOD, and of the blessed Virgin, in remembrance, and to the praise of Thy boundless Love, with which Thou gavest Thyself wholly to us upon the Altar of the Cross, lo, I this day offer unto Thee this present Sacrifice of the Holy Eucharist, as well as all those which are celebrated throughout the world by the Priests' hands, that they may, by Thee, be set before Thine Eternal FATHER, in union with, and in virtue of, that Oblation in which Thou Thyself, dying on the Cross, didst offer Thy most Sacred Body and Blood for the salvation of the world.

Grant that the Oblation of that Same Body and Blood, here, in a Mystery, made in an unbloody manner, under the form[a] of Bread and Wine, may effectually obtain its proper fruit; and that so the living may obtain grace, the faithful departed rest and peace, and those for whom the Sacrifice is offered, mercy and life eternal.

May this same Sacrifice also, by which the benefits of Thy Death and Passion are conveyed to us, be accepted as a thanksgiving for Thy countless benefits conferred upon us, and be a means of obtaining for us pardon and remission of our countless sins, whether of omission or commission, and of their deserved punishment, Who livest and reignest, &c.

OTHER SHORTER PRAYERS.

Accept, O Holy Trinity, this Oblation, which, in conjunction with the Priest, we offer unto Thee in Remembrance of the Passion, Resurrection, and Ascension of JESUS CHRIST our LORD, that it may tend to our salvation. Through the Same our LORD CHRIST. Amen.

The LORD send thee help from the sanctuary, and strengthen thee out of Sion; remember all thy offerings, and accept thy burnt-sacrifice.

---

[a] See above, p. 40, note.

Another.

The LORD accept this Sacrifice at thy hands, to the praise and glory of His Name, and to the benefit of us and of His whole holy Church.

Another.

Let Thy Priests, O LORD, be clothed with righteousness; he especially who now stands at Thy Altar and prays for us, that Thou wouldest spare Thy people, and not give Thine heritage to destruction. O that he may be holy, as Thou, Whom he serveth, art Holy; that by the purity of his life, he may approve himself worthy to minister at Thy Altar, and with due reverence may honour Thine All-Holy-Mysteries, and the Majesty of Thy Name.

Behold, this Sacrifice which he now offereth, and whatsoever he hath hitherto offered, or shall hereafter offer, do I now offer unto Thee, in union with that reverence with which Thou Thyself, O Great High-Priest, didst offer Thyself as a Holocaust for us, and hast willed that Thy Ministers should offer Thee in the Church.

PRAYER, *after the* HOLY, HOLY, HOLY.

Blessed be Thou, O LORD JESU CHRIST, SON of the Living GOD, Who, in Thy pity for us, didst come down from heaven, and on the Altar of the Cross didst freely offer Thy Body and Blood which Thou hadst taken of the Virgin, as a true Sacrifice for our sins.

Praise and glory be to Thee, because, of the Same Thy Body and Blood, Thou hast ordained not only that we should partake, as the Bread of Life in the Sacrament, but that a Sacrifice should be offered upon the Altar by Priests, and be celebrated even unto the end of the world.

A PRAYER

DURING THE PAUSE BEFORE THE PRAYER OF CONSECRATION.

(From P. Christ. Mayer.)

O Most Gracious FATHER, accept this Holy Sacrifice at the hands of the Priest, in union with that All-Holy Sacrifice which Thy Beloved SON, throughout His whole Life, at the Last Supper, and upon the Cross, offered unto Thee, for me, for (N. N.) and for all for whom He vouchsafed to die.

Look upon the Face of CHRIST, Thy most dearly Beloved Son, in Whom Thou art well-pleased, and by the everlasting Love, wherewith Thou hast so loved us, by the infinite Merits of the Same Thine Only-Begotten; by His Incarnation, Advent, Nativity, Circumcision, Tears, Labours, Passion, and Death; by the Infinite Love with which He did, spake, and suffered so much for me:

Remember and have pity upon Thy Church, and upon the rulers thereof; all Prelates and Princes, all the Clergy thereof, whether in colleges, set apart for Thine honour and service, or in parochial ministrations, as those who can most advance or hinder Thy Glory, and the salvation of souls:

Remember also my parents; brethren; my friends and benefactors; all who have especially commended themselves to me (N. N.); those who have done me wrong; whom I have wronged, offended, neglected to assist, and those whom Thou willest, through me, to direct into the way of salvation;

On all these do Thou have mercy, O FATHER of mercies, as Thou knowest and willest, giving them grace most perfectly to please Thee, to acknowledge, fear, love, glorify Thee, with the Same Thy Beloved SON and HOLY SPIRIT, now and for ever, world without end.

Another.

Hail! Life-giving Victim, offered for me and all mankind upon the Cross of suffering; O CHRIST, Eternal King, Man crucified for men, look upon Thy All-holy Flesh, for me fastened to the Cross with nails, and pierced with the spear.

And let that love, I beseech Thee, which drew Thee down, and overpowered Thee, to expiate the sins of the whole world, in the balance of the All-Glorious Cross; let that compassion have force with Thee, to have pity upon me, full of miseries, Who never ceasest to pour forth streams of mercy; and preserve my soul and body unto everlasting life.

A PRAYER.
(*From P. Christ. Mayer.*)

O JESU! SON of GOD, and of the Virgin Mary, my LORD and my GOD, Infinitely worthy of all love, Who for love of me didst vouchsafe to be crucified, and to die upon the Cross, I adore, I love, I glorify Thee, together with the FATHER and the HOLY GHOST, with all the affection of which all creatures are capable; and from my heart I desire, that Thou mayest be adored, loved, and glorified, to an infinite degree by all, in all, and above all, in every possible manner, freely, for Thine own Sake, now, always, and through eternity.

I believe in Thee; I hope in Thee; I love Thee, and whatsoever Thou lovest, for Thee; I grieve, simply for love of Thee, that I ever offended Thee. Pardon, forgive, atone, by Thine own Self.

Behold, from this moment my heart is ready at every hint of Thy Will. I am Thine, and so will I be for ever; possess me, and conform me wholly to Thy Will.

O FATHER, look upon the Face of Thy Most Well-Beloved SON, Whom I offer unto Thee as a sacrifice of praise, of thanksgiving and atonement; and, by His Tears and Bloody Sweat, by His Groans and Sighs, by His Labours and Obedience, by His Griefs and Tortures, by His Infinite Merits, have mercy on me, on (N. N.) and all for whom He died, and give us grace always perfectly to love Thee, to embrace and obey Thine All-Holy Will, in time and in eternity.

By the Same Thy Beloved SON have mercy, O most merciful FATHER, on the souls of the faithful departed (N. N.), commended especially to me, and on all for whom Thou wouldest have me chiefly to pray; graciously bestowing on them pardon and everlasting rest, that they may for ever bless and praise, and glorify Thee, to Whom all praise, honour, and glory are due.

RHYTHM OF ST. THOMAS AQUINAS.

Prostrate I adore Thee, Deity unseen,
Who Thy glory hidest 'neath these shadows mean.
Lo, to Thee surrender'd my whole heart is bow'd,
Tranc'd as it beholds Thee, shrin'd within the cloud.
Sight, and touch, and taste, are all in Thee deceived,
'Tis the hearing only safely is believed.
I believe whate'er the SON of GOD hath told,
What the Truth hath spoken, that for truth I hold.
'Twas the Godhead only on the Cross was veil'd,
Here the Manhood also is from sight conceal'd.
Both alike believing, Thee One CHRIST I own,
Suing, like the robber, at Thy mercy's Throne.
Thy dread Wounds, like Thomas, tho' I cannot see,
His be my confession, LORD and GOD, of Thee.
LORD, my faith unfeigned evermore increase,
Give me hope unfading, love that cannot cease.
Oh, Memorial wondrous of the LORD's own Death,
Living Bread, That givest all His creatures breath,
Grant, my spirit ever by Thy Life may live,
To my taste Thy sweetness never-failing give,
Pelican most tender, Thine own children's Food,
Cleanse my heart's uncleanness with Thy Precious Blood.
Lo, one Drop, Dear JESU, all the world could save,
From sin's foul pollution all creation lave.
JESU, Whom, now veiled, I by faith descry,
What my soul doth thirst for, do not, LORD, deny.
That Thy Face unveiled I at last may see,
With the blissful Vision blest, my GOD, of Thee.

ANOTHER, ON RECEIVING THE BREAD.

Hail, true Body, born of Mary,
  Victim true, of true maid born,
Thrill'd with true pains, hanging weary
  On the Cross for man forlorn.

Whose pierc'd Side for our Salvation
  Did with true Blood overflow!
Foretaste of Thy consolation
  In death's trial may we know.

Oh, Merciful! oh, Pitying One!
Oh, JESU! Mary's Gracious Son!

Prayer after receiving the Bread.

Grant that as I have been admitted to see Thee now, under the form [b] of Bread, so when Thou shalt come to Judgment, I may be found worthy, in sure trust and joy, to behold Thee in Thy Glorious Majesty, and may enjoy Thee for ever, in the kingdom of Eternal Brightness, where, with the FATHER and the HOLY GHOST, Thou livest and reignest GOD, for ever and ever.

On receiving the Cup.

All hail, most Precious Blood, flowing from the Side of my LORD JESUS CHRIST, and washing out the stains of every sin, old and new;
  See p. 40, note.

cleanse, sanctify, and preserve my soul unto everlasting life. Amen.

The following verses from the Hymn, Te Deum Laudamus, *may also be here repeated with great profit.*

Thou art the King of Glory: O CHRIST.

Thou art the everlasting SON: of the FATHER.

When Thou tookest upon Thee to deliver man: Thou didst not abhor the Virgin's womb.

When Thou hadst overcome the sharpness of death: Thou didst open the Kingdom of Heaven to all believers.

Thou sittest at the Right Hand of God: in the Glory of the FATHER.

We believe that Thou shalt come: to be our Judge.

We therefore pray Thee, help Thy servants: whom Thou hast redeemed with Thy Precious Blood.

A PRAYER

FOR PARDON AND GRACE BY VIRTUE OF THE HOLY EUCHARIST.

Almighty FATHER, Who hast so loved the world as to give Thine Only-Begotten SON, that whosoever believeth in Him should not perish, but have everlasting life; I beseech Thee, by the Same Thy beloved SON, Whose most Blessed Passion, and Glorious Resurrection, and Ascension into Heaven I call to mind, bring Thou my soul out of prison, that I may give thanks unto Thy Name.

Deliver me from the bonds of my sins; and although for my own deserts I have cause to fear a sentence to death, yet through the Intercession of the Same Thy Beloved SON, Who ever sitteth at Thy Right Hand, mercifully restore Thou me to life.

I know not, whom else I may engage as an Intercessor with Thee, save Him Who is the Propitiation for our sins, Who sitteth at Thy Right Hand, making intercession for us, my Advocate with Thee, GOD the FATHER; the Great High Priest, sprinkled not with blood of others but with His own; a holy, well-pleasing, perfect, Sacrifice, offered and accepted, for a sweet-smelling savour; the Lamb without blemish, Who did no sin, yet bare our sins, and with His Stripes healed our infirmities. This is He Whom Thou hast smitten for the sins of Thy people, although He is the Beloved, and in Him Thou art ever well pleased.

Look, O most Tender FATHER, upon the Humanity of Thy Beloved SON, and have mercy on the weakness of Thy poor creature. Behold the punishment of the REDEEMER, and forgive the offence of the redeemed.

O King of Saints, I beseech Thee, by this Holy of Holies, by this my REDEEMER, make me to run the way of Thy commandments, that I may in spirit be united to Him who abhorred not to be clothed in my flesh, JESUS CHRIST, Blessed for ever. Amen.

In Commemoration of the Departed.

We pray Thee also, O Lord, Holy Father, for the souls of the faithful departed, especially—, that this great Sacrament of Thy Love may be to them salvation, joy, and refreshment. O Lord my God, grant them this day a great and abundant Feast of Thee the Living Bread, Who camest down from heaven, and givest life unto the world; even of Thy holy and blessed Flesh, the Lamb without spot, Who takest away the sins of the world; even of that Flesh, Which was taken of the blessed Virgin Mary, and conceived by the Holy Ghost; and of that Fountain of Mercy, which, by the soldier's lance, flowed from Thy most sacred Side; that they may be thereby enlarged and satisfied, refreshed and comforted; and rejoice in Thy praise and Thy Glory. Amen.

Have mercy upon me also, O Lord, Thine unworthy servant, according to the multitude of Thy mercies; and having granted unto me, in this world, the pardon of my wickednesses, suffer me not to be punished with the ungodly in the world to come.

But grant unto me some small portion with Thy saints in heaven, who being fitly framed together into Thy members, and being made one Body in Thee, in grateful return for Thy Precious Blood, Which was shed for them, wherewith Thou didst wash them, shrank not from shedding their glorious blood for Thee and the brethren; who loved Thee in their life, and in death followed Thee, and so obtained triumphal crowns; with these, though falling short of their worth, yet, by Thy mercy alone, do Thou make me a partaker, and hear their prayers for me. Amen.

AT THE LORD'S PRAYER.

O Father of Mercies, we who, though unworthy, are called Thy servants, dare to call Thee our Father, and ourselves Thy children; seeing that Thy free Goodness hath by Thy Son adopted us to the honour of that title. And the Same Thy Son hath given us boldness thus to address Thee, in that He gave unto us a Form of Prayer.

Acknowledge, then, the Prayer of Thy Well-beloved SON, which He taught us, and mercifully grant by the Same Thy SON, whatsoever, taught by Him, we ask of Thee through Him, when we say, *Our Father, &c,*

[See further, the Paraphrase on the Lord's Prayer, Part I. c. ii. p. 15.]

Deliver us, we beseech Thee, O LORD, from all evils, past, present, and to come; and graciously give peace in our time, that, being holpen by the aid of Thy mercy, we may ever be both free from sin, and safe from all unrest: through the Same LORD.

In the primitive Church, the faithful in Christ had a custom in their sacred assemblies to "greet one another with a holy kiss," with great affection of benevolence and charity; accompanying it with the salutation, Peace be with thee. *And this they did chiefly before the reception of the Eucharist, that laying aside all hatred and malice, they might with greater safety draw near to the Sacrament of peace and charity.*

This practice, excellent in itself, was, in course of time, abused; and was in consequence laid aside. Since, however, we should be in love and charity with all, especially if we would partake of the holy Mysteries of Christ worthily and to our spiritual benefit, it may be of use to the exercise of this affection, that we say the following

PRAYER.

O LORD JESU, Who, after that Thou wast risen from the dead, didst utter that most sweet voice of peace to Thy chosen Disciples, saying, Peace be unto you; which also, just as Thou wert going to Thy Passion, Thou hadst intreated for them, saying, My peace I give unto you; My peace I leave with you; take away our sins from us, I beseech Thee, O Spotless Lamb of God, put far away from us our iniquities, which have separated between Thee and us, that, obtaining remission of our sins, we may have peace with Thee; peace, which, with-calm delight, results in the testimony of a good conscience; so that in Thy heavenly kingdom we may obtain that never-ending peace which passeth all understanding.

AT THE BLESSING.

When the Priest at the close of the Holy Office, pronounces the blessing on the people, bow down thy head with reverence; and, as looking for the blessing of GOD *from heaven, say, with firm faith,*

May the Almighty and Merciful GOD, the FATHER, and the SON, and the HOLY GHOST, bless and keep us.

After which say, privately,

Behold, O Eternal FATHER, the salutary Sacrifice of the Eucharist is done. May It be acceptable to Thee, inasmuch as in It Thy SON, in Whom Thou art ever well-pleased, is set forth before Thee. May He now, I beseech Thee, perform the office of a Mediator and Advocate, where He sitteth at Thy Right Hand, and maketh intercession for us. Remember all His patience, love, and pity; and vouchsafe to listen to one who prayeth in the Name of Thy Beloved SON; for He Himself hath said, If ye shall ask anything in My Name, He will give it to you. This one thing I ask, O LORD, let this Sacrifice be well-pleasing to Thee, to the glory of Thy Name; and may it be profitable to the salvation of all Thy faithful servants. Amen.

A DEVOUT PRAYER
TO BE SAID AFTER HOLY COMMUNION.

O most merciful LORD, Who hast not disdained to admit us miserable sinners, even at this solemn hour, into Thy Presence to glorify and praise Thee; forgive me all the failings which have come upon me in this very time of prayer, in that other thoughts have taken hold of my mind, or have carried it away in vain desires. Oh let not my enemy boast against me, that I have not taken heed of sin, even in the very time of praise, confession, and Communion. Amen.

Another.

Ah! wretched man that I am, who give praise to my GOD so carelessly. Behold, my LORD in His most bitter Passion for me throughout the whole night had no rest, and cannot I watch with Him one hour?

Help me, O LORD my GOD, that I may sing praises unto Thee with understanding; and always perform an acceptable service; Who livest, &c.

Or say what followeth with earnest attention.

Bless ye the LORD, all ye works of His; Bless the LORD, O my soul, and all that is within me bless His Holy Name. O that I might love Thee, and give thanks unto Thee, and my whole spirit might praise Thee, O LORD, with the fervour of all Angels and Saints.

Accept, I beseech Thee, O Eternal FATHER, as a thank-offering, the Life and Death of Thine Only-begotten SON; and, thereby grant unto me that I may live to Thee, and serve Thee with all the members of my body, and all the powers of my soul.

O LORD, this my desire is before Thee, but Thine Eyes have seen my imperfections [N.], yet, behold, O LORD, I pay my vows [N.] unto Thee, in the presence of all Thy people; and mindful of Thy benefits and of Thy boundless love, I dedicate and devote to Thee all my doings. I believe in Thee, and hope in Thee, and with my whole heart do I love Thee, O my GOD, my Truth, my Mercy, my Refuge, and my All!

COLLECT.

O GOD, Who, in this marvellous Sacrament, hast left us a Memorial of Thy Passion, grant, we beseech Thee, that we may so reverence the sacred Mysteries of Thy Body and Blood, that we may continually perceive within us the fruit of Thy Redemption.

ON SPIRITUAL COMMUNION [c].

Spiritual Communion is the calling into exercise of the most excellent Acts, of faith, namely, of hope, and of charity; by which, when deprived of the actual participation of the Sacrament, the effects of the Sacrament, that is, Union with Christ, may be obtained. (S. Thom. Aq. 3. p. q. 8. a. 1. ad 3.)

First, then, we must awaken in us a true and lively faith as to this Sacrament; which may be sustained by thoughts of the Divine Power, Wisdom, Goodness, and Truth.

Add to this, the exercise of hope. For what can the Good and Merciful GOD, *Who hath given Himself, refuse? What cannot He do for us, although not present in the Body, He Who, while absent, healed the Centurion's servant and many others?*

Lastly, stir up love, and with ardent desire of the heart, pant and long for CHRIST *as for a Living Fountain, of Which whoso drinketh, shall never thirst. Long, therefore, to be united and incorporated into* CHRIST *by the virtue of His Body and Blood; so that being made, as it were, one spirit with Him, thou mayest never be separated from Him.*

This Spiritual Communion is of great power and benefit: so that it often brings no less fruit and grace, than to many persons doth Sacramental Communion itself; whence it may be inferred of how great account it ought to be to thee, especially since it may be renewed oftentimes in the same day, and never without new accession of grace and charity.

---

[c] In the Office "for the Communion of the Sick," Spiritual Communion is thus spoken of.

"If a man, either by reason of extremity of sickness, or for want of warning in due time to the Curate, or for lack of company to receive with him, or by any other just impediment, do not receive the Sacrament of CHRIST'S Body and Blood, the Curate shall instruct him, that if he do truly repent him of his sins, and stedfastly believe that JESUS CHRIST hath suffered death upon the Cross for him, and shed His Blood for his redemption, earnestly remembering the benefits he hath thereby, and giving Him hearty thanks therefore, he doth eat and drink the Body and Blood of our SAVIOUR profitably to his soul's

A PRAYER

FOR SPIRITUAL COMMUNION.

Behold, I stand poor and needy, at the Table of the Great King and my most loving FATHER, at Thy Table, O CHRIST JESU; and [d] since I may not now receive Thee Sacramentally, I say with the Centurion, whose servant, as many others also, Thou didst heal when absent, "LORD, I am not worthy that Thou shouldest come under my roof; but speak the word only, and Thy servant shall be healed." Enter, I pray Thee, into my soul, and cleanse it from its evils and imperfections [N.], and adorn it with virtues and excellencies [N.]; feed it with Thy Body and Blood; that as a dog it may eat from its Master's Table, and be fulfilled with the richness and fulness of the heavenly benediction.

ANOTHER PRAYER

FOR SPIRITUAL COMMUNION.

O LORD JESU! I acknowledge that Thou art the True Bread Which didst come down from heaven to feed

health, although he do not receive the Sacrament with his mouth."

The same principle applies to any case in which a Communicant is deprived, by change of place or any incidental circumstance, of the frequency of Communion which had been vouchsafed to him, or which his soul would desire; and so its use might become daily.—[ED.]

[d] The original has a fuller form, which might be used, if, from any cause, a Communicant were, on good grounds, deterred from actually receiving the Holy Communion, yet was unwilling to go away altogether. It stands thus: [and I believe Thee, O Eternal Truth, that Thou freely vouchsafest to come from the highest heavens, on the consecration by Thy Priest, to visit me; nevertheless, conscious of my weakness and of my sins, I do not dare to receive Thee sacramentally, but I say] &c.

us with Thine own Self, [and [e] with wonderful sweetness, stupendous power, and marvellous condescension, hast hidden Thyself under these visible forms [f]; I know that Thou desirest earnestly to feed my soul.]

I believe that in Thee [as Thou art here] are hidden infinite treasures of spiritual gifts, and the largest riches of grace, all which my poor and needy soul panteth ardently to partake.

I believe the word which Thou hast spoken, He that eateth Me shall live by Me. Behold, O Living Bread, I, wretched that I am, well nigh perishing with hunger and cold, exposed to many infirmities, I approach to Thee, that, eating Thee, I may more fully and more truly live by Thee, may be gathered into Thee, and cherished by Thee. I trust that Thou wilt not loath my unworthiness, weakness, and want.

I do most truly confess that I am not worthy that Thou shouldest come under my roof; [and [g] therefore I do not venture to bring Thee now into the home of my heart, by actual feeding on Thine All-Holy Body;] but I know and believe, with the Centurion, that Thou, even when absent, that is, without Sacramental Communion, canst, with one word, heal, enrich, and sanctify me. For if the gazing on the brazen serpent had such efficacy, that it had power to heal those bitten by fiery serpents, shall not the faith whereby I contemplate Thee have more power to heal the bites of the infernal serpent? It was the type, Thou the Truth; it the shadow, Thou the Substance. If the touch of the hem of Thy Garment could expel incurable diseases, what may it not avail to touch Thy All-Holy Body and Thy Divine Blood, if not by my body, yet by my mind, through longing and earnest trust?

If the shadow of Thy disciple Peter could drive away all diseases of the body, what sickness of the soul shall be able to stand its ground, and not rather give place, instantly, before the Brightness of Thy Divine Majesty?

Come, therefore, to me, O LORD, and heal my sin-sick

---

[e] This might be used under the same circumstances as above note [d].   [f] See at p. 40, note.

[g] May be used as before.

soul, appease its hunger, strengthen its weakness. Thou Who, by the Will of the FATHER and the Co-working of the HOLY GHOST, hast by Thy Death given life unto the world, quicken me, feed me, sanctify me, by this Thy All-Holy Body and Blood; deliver me from all sin, make me ever to cleave to Thy commandments, and never let me be separated from Thee. Amen.

Lauda Sion Salvatorem.

Praise thy SAVIOUR, Sion, praise Him!
High in choral anthems raise Him,
   Guide unfailing, Shepherd strong!
Dare thy best, His Name exalting:
For all praise is weak and halting,
   Task too high for thy frail tongue.

Lo, thy praises not disdaining,
Living Bread and life-sustaining
   Is to-day before thee set.
Even the Same we touch and take It,
As when o'er His Board He brake It,
   Where the Brethren Twelve were met.

Full and clear ring out our chanting,
Joy nor order'd grace be wanting,—
   'Tis th' adoring spirit's mirth,
Well the solemn day beseeming,
With the grave glad memory beaming
   Of our Banquet's awful birth.

Here th' old paschal Lamb hath ending,
And the New, CHRIST'S Law attending,
   Crowns the Board of our new King.
Old, in all, gives place to New,
And the shadowy to the True,
   And the night to Day's clear spring.

In that Feast the Lord's Anointed,
What He wrought, the Same appointed:
  "This memorial keep of Me."
Taught His lessons well and truly,
Bread and Wine we offer duly,
  Victim of our peace to be.

Bread His Flesh, in truth and spirit,
(Christians this high lore inherit,)
  And the Wine becomes His Blood.
Heart perceives not, eye descries not,
But courageous Faith denies not,
  Faith o'er-mastering nature's mood.

In each Kind, to sense forbidden,
Glorious, aweful things are hidden;
  Signs, not things, are all we see.
Blood out-pour'd, and Flesh is broken,
Yet in either wond'rous Token
  CHRIST entire hath sworn to be.

None may separate, none may break Him:
Without maim in all who take Him,
  CHRIST, the LORD, abideth whole.
Whether one or thousands taste Him,
One nor thousand mouths may waste Him:
  He to all deals equal dole.

Good and bad one Bread are sharing,
But unequal, past comparing,
  Is their portion, Wrath and Love:—
Life to Saints, to sinful livers
Death.—O mark, of like receivers,
  How unlike the ends may prove!

When they break the holy Token,—
Waver not: the word is spoken:—
What is veil'd, by all unbroken,
  Doth in every part abide:

Of the Substance is no rending;
In the Sign our act hath ending,
When we break :—nor change, nor spending,
   E'er befalls the Signified.

See for food to pilgrims given
Angels' Bread, true Bread from Heaven :—
Feed the children, morn and even;
   To the dogs no portion cast!
Here is Truth, old Types fulfilling ;—
Isaac bound, so meek and willing,
Lambs reserved for Paschal killing,
   Manna strewn where Israel past.

Shepherd Good, true Bread and Living,
JESU, be to us forgiving :
Thou protecting, Thou relieving,
In the Land of all the living,
   Cause Thou us all good to see.
Thou all-ruling, all-espying,
Feed'st us, here, till hour of dying:
There, upon Thy Bosom lying,
We with Thine Elect are sighing
   Fellow-heirs and friends to be.
                 Amen. Alleluia.

Pange lingua.

Of the Body bright and gracious,
   Tongue, rehearse the mystery,
And the Blood, all pure and precious,
   Which He shed, our world to buy,
King of all its realms so spacious,
   Fruit of high-born Purity.

Given to us, His Birth and nursing
   Taken of that holiest Maid,
Here and there His Word dispersing,

In the world awhile He staid;
Then, a wond'rous Law rehearsing,
  End of weary sojourn made.

At His final Supper sitting
  With His own, that awful even,
All th' old Law for aye completing,
  Paschal meat made Meat from Heaven,
To the Twelve, for solemn eating,
  By His own Hands see Him given.

Word made Flesh! the bread of nature
  Thou by Word to Flesh dost turn,
Wine, to Blood of our CREATOR;—
  If no sense the work discern,
Yet the true heart proves no traitor;
  Faith unaided all shall learn.

Then in love and heart's prostration
  Own we this great Sacrament.
Gospel Rite, come take thy station,
  Ancient lore, be gone and spent!
Faith, thine earnest adoration,
  Passing eye and touch, present!

Praise, and glad notes heaven-ward speeding,
  To the FATHER and the SON,
Blessing, Glory, Power exceeding,
  And Salvation dearly won:
To the Spirit of Both proceeding,
  Equal, endless benison.

END OF PART V.

PLYMOUTH:
PRINTED AT THE PRINTING PRESS OF THE DEVONPORT SOCIETY
OF THE HOLY TRINITY.

TO THE BELOVED

WHITE AND RUDDY,   CANT. v. 10.

SPOUSE OF BLOOD,

Jesus Christ,

WHO BEING IN THE FORM OF GOD,

BY NATURE, NOT BY ROBBERY, EQUAL TO GOD,

EMPTIED HIMSELF

BY TAKING ON HIM FOR SERVANTS A SERVANT'S FORM:

To Him Who is Fairer than the sons of men,

AND YET MAN FOUND NO COMELINESS OR BEAUTY IN HIM,

FOR THAT HE WAS MADE A WORM,

AND NO MAN:

To the Desire of the Everlasting Hills,

And Expectation of the Gentiles,

WHO YET WAS SCORNED AND COUNTED FOR THE LAST OF MEN:

To the Blessed One,

WHO CAME IN THE NAME OF THE LORD,

AND YET WAS MADE A REPROACH OF MEN AND AN OUTCAST

OF THE PEOPLE;

WHO DID NO WICKEDNESS, NEITHER WAS GUILE FOUND

IN HIS MOUTH;

AND YET WAS NUMBERED WITH THE WICKED,

AND BARE THE SINS OF MANY: [TO THE

To the Lion of the Tribe of Judah,
WHO YET WAS LED AS A SHEEP TO THE SLAUGHTER,

AND, AS A LAMB BEFORE HER SHEARER, WAS DUMB:

To the Man of Sorrows,
WHO TROD THE WINE-PRESS ALONE,

AND OF THE PEOPLE HAD NO MAN WITH HIM,

WHO TRULY BARE OUR SICKNESSES AND WAS BRUISED FOR OUR SINS:

To the Good Shepherd,
WHO LAID DOWN HIS LIFE FOR HIS SHEEP:

To the High Priest of good things to come,
WHO BY HIS OWN BLOOD ENTERED IN ONCE INTO THE HOLY PLACE,

HAVING OBTAINED ETERNAL REDEMPTION:

To the Great King of Heaven and Earth,
WHOM WINDS AND SEA OBEY,

WHO YET HUMBLED HIMSELF, BEING MADE OBEDIENT

TO GOD THE FATHER,

EVEN TO THE DEATH OF THE CROSS.

WORTHY ART THOU, O LORD, TO RECEIVE MIGHT,

DEITY, AND WISDOM;

FOR THAT THOU WAST SLAIN AND HAST REDEEMED US TO GOD

IN THY BLOOD.

BLESSING AND HONOUR AND GLORY AND POWER BE UNTO THEE

FOR EVER AND EVER. AMEN.

PARADISE FOR THE CHRISTIAN SOUL.

PART VI.

ON THE LIFE AND PASSION OF OUR LORD JESUS CHRIST.

For Friday.

CHAPTER I.

A DIALOGUE ON THE WAY HOW WE ARE PIOUSLY TO MEDITATE ON AND IMITATE THE LIFE AND PASSION OF OUR SAVIOUR.

§ 1. *An exhortation to ponder on the work of Redemption.*

APOSTLE. *Let this mind be in you which was also in Christ Jesus, Who, being in the Form of* GOD, *thought it not robbery to be equal with* GOD, *but made Himself of no reputation, and took upon Him the form of a servant.*

Hear, O man! not good and faithful servant, inasmuch as being in the nature and condition of a servant, yet unwilling to serve, thou didst strive to grasp at freedom and equality with thy LORD.

Hear and behold, how that Christ, being in the Form of GOD, not by robbery, but by nature equal with GOD, (for that He is equally Almighty, Eternal, Incomprehensible, &c.,) did empty Himself, and not only took upon Him the form of a servant, and was made in the likeness of men, but fulfilled the ministry, also, of a servant, humbling Himself, and becoming obedient to His FATHER, even unto Death.

But lest it seem to thee a small thing that, being the SON and Co-equal, He did yet, as a servant, serve the FATHER, far more than a servant, His own servant He served. Thou wast made, O man, to serve thy CREATOR. And what could be more just than that thou shouldest serve Him by Whom thou wast created, without Whom thou canst not live, nor move, nor exist? What more blessed, what more sublime, than to serve Him, Whom to serve is to reign? Yet didst thou say, I will not serve. And lo! thy CREATOR, thy LORD, &c. cometh, ready to serve His servant, His obstinate, rebellious servant: He came not to be ministered unto, but to minister: He came, that thou mightest sit at meat, and He might serve; that thou mightest rest, and He toil and labour; that thou mightest be healed, and He bear thy sicknesses; yea, that thou mightest live, and He die for thee.

O Good and Faithful Servant, more faithful than Jacob, Who served not seven years, but three and thirty years and more for thee! How truly did He serve, with all fidelity, patience, and long-suffering! not lukewarmly or unwillingly; for He rejoiced as a giant to run His race of obedience; not feignedly, for after all His many and heavy labours He laid down His life besides; not murmuringly, for scourged, though innocent, He opened not His mouth; He became as a man that heard not, and in Whose mouth were no reproofs. And what more as a servant was He bound to do for thee? What could He have done for thee which He hath not done? O hateful pride of man who scorned to serve, which could not be humbled but by the example of the servitude (and such a servitude!) of his own very LORD!

CHRIST. O man, if thou hast ears to hear, hear what My chosen Apostle saith to My faithful; for he knows My secrets and speaketh from My Mouth. He it is who carried My name before kings and princes of the earth; he it is who determined to know nothing else but JESUS, even Me, crucified; and so though among the perfect he speak the hidden wisdom in a mystery, to *thee* he speaketh Me, CHRIST Crucified, to the unbelieving an offence, and to them who perish foolishness, but to thee and to those who are saved, the Power of GOD and the Wisdom of GOD. So now he hath well put before thine eyes the example of My humility, wherein I, thy GOD and LORD, did in labour serve thee from My youth up, till I died upon the Cross; if so be that even thus thou mayest learn subjection and humility, and to bless Me for My humility and goodness. O what hard service didst thou make Me serve by thy sins! how thou didst make me toil by thine iniquities! and what toil? unto weariness, hunger, and thirst? Nay, but unto sweat, sweat rolling to the earth in drops of blood; Nay, but unto Death, even the Death of the Cross!

MAN. O LORD! what is man that Thou hast respect unto him? or the son of man that Thou regardest him? O how great hath been Thy toil, O LORD, in serving me! Truly it were meet and right that at least henceforth Thou shouldest rest, and that Thy servant, were it only that it is his turn, should serve Thee. At how great a price hast Thou, O LORD, purchased my service, wholly unserviceable unto Thee! Thou Who, didst Thou need the ministry of any, couldest suddenly have more than twelve legions of angels at Thy every beck! Oh! with how sweet and merciful a contrivance of loving-kindness hast Thou recovered the subjection of Thine obstinate servant to Thyself, overcoming his evil with good, confounding his pride by Thy humiliation, with blessings overcoming his ingratitude! So hath wisdom conquered wickedness. So hast Thou heaped coals of fire upon the head of Thine enemy, whereby he might be kindled to love and obey Thee.

Thou hast overcome, O LORD, Thou hast overcome the rebel. I yield myself to Thy bondage; I submit my neck to Thy yoke. Only vouchsafe that I may serve Thee; suffer me to labour for Thee. Receive me as a servant for ever; behold I am Thy servant, though unprofitable, indeed, unless now too Thy grace, even both preventing and following, be with me and work with me. It preventeth, first exhibiting to us patterns of humanity and patience; may it follow us, helping us to imitate the patterns it exhibits. O how blessed shall we be, if herein we hearken to the counsel of Thine Apostle, bidding us that that mind be in us, which we know, O JESU, before to have been in Thee! O that I might seriously keep all these words, and ponder them in my heart, that so in my meditation the fire of Thy love may burn, and I may thenceforth run after Thee in the savour of Thy good ointments! I have gone astray like a sheep that is lost; who will guide me into the right way that leadeth unto life, that I may find it and keep it?

§ 2. *Christ proposed for our imitation.*

GOD THE FATHER. I, in the beginning, created man upright, even after My own image and likeness: but he, when he was in honour, knew it not; and so he who was created that he might be a partaker of the Divine Nature, now is compared unto the beasts that perish, and is become like unto them.

This is the first Adam, who by transgressing My commandment was cast out of Paradise and was made liable to death and perdition. And him, O miserable! have all imitated, who are by natural generation descended from him, and they have become partners of his guilt and punishment. Yet I would not that wretched man should perish, nor do I take pleasure in the death of a sinner; nay, I so loved the world that I gave My only-begotten Son, that all who believe in Him may not perish but have everlasting life.

This is the second Man, Heavenly from heaven, Who passed a life not earthly, but heavenly, upon earth. Him, therefore, have I given to be a Guide and Teacher to the Gentiles, that whosoever should follow Him should not walk in darkness, but should have the light of life. Him I sent as a Chief Pattern and Living Example from Heaven, and proposed It for imitation (perfectly adorned with all gifts, graces, and virtues,) to all whom I foreknew and predestinated to be conformed to the image of My Son, that they too may be co-heirs with Him of My kingdom. The first man, indeed, is of the earth, earthy; the Second Man is the LORD from heaven. As therefore ye have borne the image of the earthy (by transgressing My commandments as did your first Parent Adam), so bear ye the image of the heavenly (by following the example of Christ), serving Me in holiness and righteousness all the days of your life.

Look unto the Author and Finisher of the Faith, JESUS, Who for the joy that was set before Him endured the Cross, despising the shame.

Lo, He is fair before the sons of men, in Whom dwelleth all the fulness of the Godhead, not as a shadow, but bodily. This is My beloved Son in Whom I am well pleased; hear Him and follow Him. Wilt thou please Me, strive to imitate Him; by so much wilt thou be dearer to Me as thou art more like Him. Nay, like as Isaac then only blessed Jacob when he was clad in the garments of his first-born, neither wilt thou receive blessing from Me, unless thou be clad in the fleece of the Immaculate Lamb, *i. e.* the garments or virtues of My Only-begotten.

Cast away, therefore, the works of darkness and put on the armour of light, yea, put on JESUS CHRIST. Look upon and act in accordance with the pattern which I have shown thee; walk before Me in the way wherein My Beloved went before, when He appeared on earth and dwelt among men, and gave you an example, that according as He did, ye should do also.

MAN. Blessed be GOD, even the Father of our LORD JESUS CHRIST, the Father of mercies and the GOD of all comfort, Who art rich in mercy; for Thy exceeding love, wherewith Thou lovedst us, when we were dead in sins, Thou hast quickened us together with CHRIST (by Whose grace we are saved), and hast raised us up together and made us sit together in heavenly places in CHRIST, that Thou mightest show in the ages to come the abundant riches of Thy grace. O how sweet are Thy words unto my lips, by which Thou callest us to fellowship with Thy Son! But is it I who shall follow God? A servant, the LORD; sinner of earth, the King of Heaven; the least, the Incomprehensible; the lowest, the Supreme; and one so weak, the Almighty?

§ 3. GOD *became man that He might be imitable.*

CHRIST. I came down from heaven, and whereas I was

invisible I became visible: and for that thou wert unable to endure the brightness of My Majesty, I emptied Myself and took the form of a servant, and was made in the likeness of men, and was found in fashion as a man; that *thus* at least Thou mightest follow and imitate Me, Whom to follow is great glory, and to attain, your highest happiness.

For when by the sin of the first man all his posterity had fallen from their state of happiness, they could not be restored without some guide to go before them. Who then was this? A man? But as their natural condition was one, so were they held under the same condition of sin. Could an angel? Not even could an angel's satisfaction be plenary and equivalent to the Divine justice. GOD Alone was equal to the task: but GOD is invisible. In order, then, that He might be exhibited to man, to be seen by all, and to be securely imitated by man, I, Who am GOD, became man, like unto you and subject to death, that every action of Mine might be your instruction, and My Divinity shine forth before you in manhood.

Why, then, dost thou halt where the two ways meet? Seekest thou the straight and royal road of salvation? I am the Way; by Me, if any man enter in, he shall be saved. Art thou in doubt how to esteem the honours, wealth, delights, pleasures of this life, the judgments of men and the like? Consider how I esteemed them; embrace My judgment with confidence; thou canst not be deceived; for I am the Truth. Fearest thou affliction, or suffering, or death, for My name's sake? Lo, I am the Life, thy Salvation, thy every good; and though thou die, yet shalt thou live. For I am come that thou mayest have life, and that thou mayest have it more abundantly; in brief, I am to thee the Way by My example, the Truth in My promise, the Life in My reward.

MAN. We adore Thee, O CHRIST, King of Israel and of the Gentiles also; Prince of the kings of the earth; to Thee, O CHRIST, we offer the sacrifice of praise for the multitude of Thy goodness, which thou hast shewn to us, a wicked seed, corrupt and lost children. When we were yet thine enemies, Thou didst remember Thy mercy. Thou sawest the affliction of Thy people, and, inwardly touched with the sweetness of love, Thou didst meditate over us thoughts of peace and redemption; and as though it had been a small thing for Thy love to appoint a Cherub, or a Seraph, or one of the Angels, to fulfil the work of our Salvation, Thou didst Thyself vouchsafe to come to us by the command of the FATHER, Whose exceeding love we have experienced in Thee.

O transporting and admirable condescension! GOD of immeasurable glory, Thou didst not despise to become a despised worm. GOD of all, Thou wouldst appear servant of all. Was it not enough that Thou shouldest be FATHER to us and LORD? Thou hast vouchsafed to become our Brother.

O what great thanks am I bound to render unto Thee, *(Thos. à Kempis,* b. iii. ch. 18,) that Thou hast vouchsafed to show unto me, and to all faithful people, the good and the right way to Thine eternal kingdom! For Thy Life is our Way; and if Thou hadst not gone before and sought us, who would have cared to follow? Alas! how many would remain behind and afar off, if they considered not Thy most noble example! Behold we are even yet lukewarm, though we have heard of Thy so many miracles and instructions; what would become of us, if we had not so great light whereby to follow Thee?

§ 4. *What the name of Christian should remind us of.*

CHRIST. Wouldest thou please Me, O man: if so, *follow Me;* this, most of all, will please Me. Nothing is more right, nothing pleaseth a father more, than that his son should follow him. Be thou then a follower of Me as a most dear child. To what end thinkest thou that thou art called by My Name, but that thou shouldst follow My steps? Woe unto those who bear so glorious a Name to no purpose, and unworthily; who are called Christians, and are not; who with their mouth say that they know Me, but by their deeds deny Me. Very many there be who care little to follow Me, and live, indeed, a Christian life. Better had it been for such not to have known the way of truth, the Faith in Me, than, after they have known it, to hold it in unrighteousness. Alas! how sad is it for Me to see every where so much profaned My tokens and My Name.

If every one who saith that he abideth in Me, ought himself so to walk even as I : far more should they who say that they abide for Me, and exercise a commission in My Name, *i. e.* the Dispensers of the Mysteries of God, and My Ministers: if *they* do not follow Me, they have no excuse. Now, however, those who ought to follow Me most closely, are often the most bitter to persecute Me; and those who eat of My bread do magnify themselves against Me. What is this that My beloved do, in My house, much wickedness? How is it that among these, no less than among the children of this world, envy and strife, pride and ambition, avarice and gluttony, luxury and pride, prevail?

Are not these the works of the flesh and of darkness? I am the True Light; and whoso followeth Me, walketh not in darkness. What agreement hath Christ with Belial; light with darkness? Thinkest thou, then, that those deserve to be called by My Name, numbered with My inheritance, or are rightly called the children of ight, who love darkness rather than light? Those only who are like one another, become and continue friends; shall I then call those My friends who are so unlike Me? Shall I account those to be My disciples who abhor My discipline, and cast My words behind them? Shall they be My ministers who say, *Lord, Lord,* but do not the things which I say?

Man. Teach me to do Thy will, for Thou art a Teacher come from God, and verily teachest the way of God in truth, as One having authority. Thou hast begun to do and to teach: grant that we may follow Thee, and conform our life to the reflection of Thine. For whom Thy Father hath chosen, these He hath called to be conformed to the image of His Son. O that, most loving Jesu, Thou wouldest grant me, that as I have borne the image of the earthly, so, hereafter, I may bear the image of the Heavenly, and seek to be conformed, not to this wicked world, but to Thee, and that I may follow Thee whithersoever Thou goest. For he that saith he abideth in Thee, ought himself also so to walk even as Thou: but how shall I be able? *Thou* rejoicedst as a giant to run the course, and who shall be able with equal steps to walk with Thee?

§ 5. *To follow Christ is glorious, pleasant, profitable.*

CHRIST. Try to follow, at least, at a distance, and to run towards the destined prize of thy high calling. Lo, with what industry do the children of this world seek for wealth and honour: with what endurance do they study to be conformed to the world, and to please men; how anxious by complaisance to catch at the favour of princes and the mighty! With what alacrity and boldness do soldiers expose their lives before the eyes of their leader, and rush fearlessly into any danger! Yet, what is the reward of all these after so great labours and toil? What but a morsel of earth, wind and smoke, vanity and vexation of spirit? For they all do pass away like a shadow, and nothing under the sun abideth in the same stay. Surely, with less toil thou canst serve and please Me; with less labour gain heaven and immortality: and wilt thou neglect it?

Wherefore, O ye sons of men, have ye so much pleasure in vanity, and seek after leasing? Know this, that the LORD hath set apart His Holy One, even *Me* did He distinguish with so many, so wondrous gifts and virtues, that My life might be unto you a mirror to gaze on and imitate. Then follow Me.

Why walk ye the hard ways of the world and of the flesh? Lo, destruction and unhappiness are in the ways of sinners; but My ways are fair ways, My yoke also is easy, and My burden light. I make the crooked straight, and the rough places plain. I bring home the wanderers, I refresh the toiling, and I crown them that persevere.

Whoso, therefore, serveth Me, let him follow Me. To follow the LORD is great glory. For where I am, there shall also My servant be; and he shall inherit a kingdom which hath been prepared for him from the beginning of the world. If thou knewest its glory, nothing would seem to thee hard to do or suffer; the days of toil would seem short to thee, through the greatness of thy desire and love. For My kingdom suffereth violence, and the violent take it by force; and thus must thou assail heaven, by losing thy *own* life, by conquering thyself and the sinful motions of thy mind, breaking away the desires of the flesh. This is not difficult to one who loveth; yea, it will become pleasant, specially if he, at the same time, look forward to the recompense; for the hope of the reward is the solace of the toil.

But be it so, that it is toilsome, wilt thou therefore refuse it? Dost thou, too, desire to sit with Me in My kingdom, but art unwilling to drink the cup which I drank? Shalt thou be called a soldier of CHRIST, and wilt thou dread the sharpness which thy Leader embraceth? Thou art deceived, O man, thou art deceived, if thou thinkest to pass to delights out of delights, to rejoice here with the world, and hereafter to rejoice with Me in heaven. Not one of the Saints was crowned without a contest.

Look upon Me; behoved it not that I should suffer, and so enter into Mine Own glory? and art thou to enter into a glory which is not thine own without toil and endurance? Act then with fortitude, endure with patience; the labour is short and for a moment, the reward is lasting and eternal.

MAN. I am ready, O LORD, and am no more troubled. I will run the way of Thy commandments, when Thou hast set my heart at liberty.

§ 6. *The following of Christ standeth in the denial of self and perpetual mortification.*

CHRIST. In the first place, then, if thou wilt come after Me, deny thyself and take up thy cross and follow Me. I, for thy sake, came down from My throne; I laid aside My Majesty and became partaker of thy low estate, that thou, putting off the old, mightest put on the new man, which is created after GOD, and mightest mortify thy members which are upon the earth. I underwent death on the Cross for thee; do thou, at least, crucify thy flesh with its vices and lusts, and die to evil desires: unless thou shalt thus have died with Me, thou shalt not be able to live with Me.

MAN. I confess, O LORD, that he is worthy of death, who refuseth to live unto Thee. Who shall grant to me, O most kind JESU, that I may die unto myself through love of Thee, and live unto Thee? But love overcometh all things, and what shall not Thy love do? Thou, the highest of all, didst become lowest of all: who brought this to pass? Love *(they are the words of St. Bernard)*, ignorant of dignity, mighty in affection, effectual in persuasion. What more powerful in force? Love triumpheth over GOD, and shall it fail to rule me? Shall not the love of my GOD be able to expel the love of self?

But then I must hate myself in order to love Thee. I am bid lose my life that I may find it and Thee, my every Good. Lo, my heart is ready. I desire to be Thine with my whole heart: but all who are Thine, crucify the flesh with its vices and lusts. Circumcise, O LORD, the flesh and foreskin of my heart, that I may be reckoned in the number of Thy sons. Thou, O LORD, must be circumcised, before Thou take on Thee the Name of Saviour; I cannot reap the price of Thy Blood and Salvation unless I bear Thy mortification, as a seal, in my body. O that it were my chiefest pleasure to delight in the LORD, and to know no pleasure besides Thee! At least, let my soul refuse to be comforted, mindful of Thee Alone; for at Thy Right Hand there is pleasure, for evermore. No pleasure, O LORD, shall draw me, if but Thy love draw me.

Draw me then, O LORD, after Thee, Thou Who by love drawest all things unto Thyself, that I may run in the sweet savour of Thy ointments. For, therefore, hath the kindness of GOD our Saviour appeared unto all men, teaching us, that denying ungodliness and worldly lusts we should life soberly, righteously, and godly in the present world.

CHRIST. It is even so, my son; to thyself thou owest soberness, righteousness to thy neighbour, and to GOD, godliness. The constant endeavour after a pure mind is, as it were, a continual martyrdom. In vain thou seekest rest and peace in this life, for this life is a warfare upon earth. The time shall be when thou shalt rest from thy labours; the things which thou hast sown in tears, thou shalt then reap in joy; thou shalt then eat the labour of thy hands. O well is thee, and happy shalt thou be! thou shalt rejoice like men in harvest, and as men rejoice when they divide the spoil.

The present, however, is the time of labour, and why fearest thou? I, from My youth up, was in labours for thee. I ran through the streets and the broad ways, never giving myself rest, never indulging myself in ease; in hunger and thirst, in heat and cold, I wrought out thy salvation in the midst of the earth. I, though in possession of spiritual bliss, even in the flesh, restrained My glory, which else had spread itself from My Soul over My Body; and I did so, that from the absence of all consolation, My Passion might be more abundant and more bitter.

Hence was it that when I was praying in the garden, shuddering at death, out of the heaviness of My heart, I poured forth a bloody sweat, and on the Cross cried out, as though forsaken by GOD the FATHER. And wilt thou every where be seeking delights and conveniences of the flesh? Wilt thou be nourishing thy flesh in delicacy and softness? O consider rather My life, and when thou findest Mine so unlike thine own, be confounded in thyself. Well does a servant of Mine advise, while exhorting you to imitate Me, "rightly," he says, "mayest thou be ashamed, when thou beholdest the life of CHRIST, and reflectest that thou hast not yet striven more to resemble Him, though thou hast long been in the way of GOD. O how ill assorted are the comforts of the flesh and the contemplation of My Passion. Yet they who fulfil the desires of the flesh in the lusts thereof, often wonder that their souls are unmoved in meditating upon My Passion. Verily, were they partakers of the sufferings, they should be, likewise, of the consolation.

So, when David ascended with bare feet the mount of Olives, his whole household followed him in like guise. Uriah would not go down into his house, or rest upon a soft couch, because his leader Joab, the Ark, and his fellow-soldiers, abode in tents in the open fields. And wilt not thou feel shame at finding leisure for the delights of the flesh, while thou art a soldier under the banner of the Cross? eating, and drinking, and passing thy days in good things; a delicate member, while thy Leader and thy Head is crowned with thorns?

MAN. Shame hath covered my face, for that I am still so far from Thy paths. O that henceforth the same mind might be in me, which, O kind JESU, I see was in Thee! that I might study so to be affected by the goods of this life, and every creature, as I know Thou wert affected; for Thou art the very Truth and Eternal Wisdom, and he that loveth that thou lovest, most surely loveth not amiss; because as Thou canst not be deceived, so neither canst Thou deceive. He that followeth Thee, O eternal Way, cannot wander; he that adhereth to Thee, O immortal Way, shall become one Spirit with Thee, and shall not die everlastingly. O that I may live, yet not I, but Thou, O CHRIST, in me.

§ 7. *The humility and Submissiveness of Christ to be imitated.*

CHRIST. If thou wilt that I live in thee, take My life again and again, as the rule and pattern whereby to order thy life and character; and above all, diligently consider My Passion, in which all virtues shine more eminently, like roses amid thorns.

See Who I am and what I have done. When I was in the Form of GOD, equal, not by robbery but by Nature, to GOD, in glory and majesty, I emptied Myself and took on Me the form of a servant, I came too, not to be ministered unto, but to minister. Will man, then, still magnify himself upon earth? Will he still walk in great matters which are too high for him? See Me prostrate at the feet of My disciples, washing them and wiping them. And what meant I by this but to set you an example, that as I have done, so should you also do?

Wherefore, then, art thou proud, O earth and ashes? How is it, ye sons of men, that ye presume to lift up your horn on high? Why do ye love the highest places at feasts, and the chief seats?

Why strive ye so earnestly which of you shall be accounted greatest? Nay, rather learn of Me, not how to frame a world, or raise the dead, to give sight to the blind, or to do other wonderful works, but, *that I am meek and lowly of heart.*

The treachery of My betrayer was not hid from Me, yet did I at supper, stoop down before him on My knees and vouchsafed to take into My Hands, to wash and wipe those feet which were swift to shed My Blood: nay, I turned not away from him when he approached to kiss My Mouth, but joined My Lips (in which no guile was found) all sweetly unto his, which were full of wickedness, and said, Friend, wherefore art thou come? And does it seem hard or grievous to thee to show thine enemy the first signs and tokens of humility, or to be the first to speak a word of gentleness?

MAN. O most lowly JESU, truly from Thy cradle to Thy Death, Thou hast taught us lowliness; and of a surety the disciple is not above his master, nor the servant above his lord. How then should I feel loath, an unprofitable creature, to become, after Thy example, lowly and of no account? How shall I dare to walk in great matters which are too high for me? Verily, it were past endurance, that when the Most High LORD of all humbles Himself so low, a mean poor earth-worm should be inflated and puffed up.

O that I had ever rather be a door-keeper in the house of my GOD than dwell in the tents of ungodliness, and be humbled with Thee, O LORD, that with Thee I might likewise find grace to be exalted in the Day of visitation; for I know that Thou resistest the proud, but givest grace only to the humble.

§ 8. *Poverty and contempt of earthly things commended to us by the example of Christ.*

CHRIST. Yet since it is hard, and the happiness of few not to be high-minded but humble in the midst of riches and the good things of this life, I have shown thee a path of more security.

I despised them all to teach thee not to set thine heart on riches or the fading goods of earth, but to lay up treasure in heaven, where neither rust nor moth corrupteth.

Did not I, though rich and LORD of all, in need of nothing, become poor for your sakes? Of a truth, at my very Birth, I embraced poverty, and ever after carried it with Me in My Life and in My Death. The earth and its fulness, is it not Mine? Yet, when I was born, I scarce had where to lay My head, and was laid in the manger of an unclean stable, because there was no room for Me in the inn. It is the poor I have pronounced blessed; My Mother and My Apostles were poor, poor in this world, but rich in faith. I lived poor, naked and needy I died upon the Cross; and was at last buried in another's tomb. Consider how My extreme poverty condemns your insatiable covetousness. O foolish men! Be sure, that whoso renounceth not all that he hath, (at the least in intention, so as to be ready to do so in act, should My honour, his own or his neighbour's salvation, require it,) cannot be My disciple.

Consider what discouraged that young man who desired to follow Me; he felt it hard and grievous to give up his riches, and so, he went away sorrowful. And why do so few follow Me even now? Is it not that they go away after gold, and from the least even unto the greatest are given to covetousness? While, therefore, they serve mammon, they neglect Me; for no man can serve two masters.

O shame to a Christian man! To take to himself My Name, and to be so unlike Me! To follow after covetousness, which is idolatry, as though he had received his soul for nothing; to boast himself in the multitude of his riches, and, like the Gentiles which know not GOD and my providential care, to be troubled about many things, to be careful only about the present, how he may lay up treasure for himself on the earth. O ye sons of men, how long will ye blaspheme Mine honour, and have such pleasure in vanity, and seek after a lie? Do ye trust to see the goodness of the LORD in the land of the living? Is it thus that ye aspire to those eternal blessings which I have prepared for them that love and follow Me? Is this the way that I have pointed to you? Do thou at least, O man, call to mind My poverty, My wormwood and my gall.

MAN. O King of kings, Whose is the round world and all that therein is, and yet Thou vouchsafest to become for our sakes stripped of all; truly blessed is the man, who considereth Thee, the Poor and Needy. Rightly hast Thou called the poor in spirit blessed, for theirs is the kingdom of heaven. O that I may have grace to become with Thee poor and destitute, that in Thy poverty I may be made rich. Grant to me first to seek the kingdom of GOD and His righteousness; not to be overcareful for the necessaries (God forbid that the luxuries should be cared for by me) of the body and this life; for, to the man who would follow Thy steps, they are burdensome and heavy weights. O that I knew how to be full and to be hungry, both to abound and to suffer need, and could learn, in whatsoever state I am, therewith to be content, for great gain indeed is godliness with contentment.

§ 9. *How the admirable Patience of Christ is to be imitated by us.*

CHRIST. Truly blessed is the man whose GOD is the LORD. For the earth is the LORD's, and all that therein is. What then can he lack who hath for his Friend Him that hath all things? The more enriched shall every man be in things eternal, as he sits looser to things of earth. If, then, thou wilt leave all things, at least in intention, and follow Me, thou shalt receive an hundred-fold, and inherit eternal life.

But if thou wilt follow Me, thou must needs yet further prepare thy soul for temptation. For all who will live godly in Me must suffer persecution. How, indeed, shall a man be crowned except he strive lawfully? Look, then, on Me, the Pattern of all long-suffering; there is nothing but can be borne patiently, if My Passion be called to memory.

Think, then, what and how much I suffered, and all that thou shalt suffer will become easy to bear. Not to speak of the sharp pains and anguish of My bodily suffering, call only to mind the insults, the scoffs, the rebukes of the revilers, which fell on Me; and with what fault of Mine? I healed the sick, fed the hungry, gave sight to the blind; I went about doing good to and healing all; I did among them works that none other man did. Who ever could convict Me of sin? And yet they sharpened their tongues, as a sword, against Me; they called Me a glutton and a wine-bibber, a blasphemer, the carpenter's son. I cast out devils, they said, through the chief of the devils, and had a devil Myself; I was a Seducer and seditious, a Samaritan, and a friend of publicans, yea, numbered with malefactors, accounted guilty of death, and a robber was preferred before Me; I was a scorn of men and the outcast of the people. These things I suffered, leaving you an example that ye may follow My steps. Why are ye vexed, then, O men? What need have ye to sigh, if perchance ye have to bear injurious words? Think, again, what contradiction of sinners I endured against Myself; then will ye not be weary and faint in your minds.

Would ye have all men friends and well-wishers, when I found them enemies and detractors? If ye be tried with no affliction, how shall your patience be crowned? Surely, if I, Who was innocent and all unspotted, escaped not envy and evil-speaking, ye cannot expect to be without them here. Me it behoved first to suffer, and so to enter into My glory.

Thou errest, thou dost err, O man, if thou look for any other life. Shall the disciple be above his Master? or the servant above his LORD? Forasmuch, then, as I suffered in the flesh, arm thyself also with the same mind; and rejoice rather than be sad, if thou be counted worthy to suffer reproach for My Name's sake. This, above all, must every disciple in My school learn and know, that to do valiantly and to bear evil is a Christian's part, and a token of My friendship. Were suffering really evil, I had not chosen it; nor had I given My Mother and My dearest friends the Cup of

My Passion to drink. I knew well how to reject the evil and choose the good; yet, when joy was put before Me, I chose the Cross, despising the shame. Suffering, then, is not evil. Never to suffer any thing is worst of all; best of all is to suffer with Me, beneath My Cross.

For whom the LORD loveth He chasteneth, and scourgeth every son whom He receiveth. If thou be without chastisement, whereof all are partakers, see whether thou be not a bastard, and no true son. All chastening, indeed, at the present seemeth not to be joyous but grievous, but afterwards it beareth the peaceable fruit of righteousness to them that are exercised thereby.

MAN. LORD, I do, indeed, desire to be, and to be numbered among Thy sons; and therefore, I refuse not to be corrected by my Father: and this shall be my consolation, if when Thou afflict me with grief, Thou spare me not; only rebuke me not in Thine anger. I desire to suffer with Thee, O CHRIST JESU; may I now be partaker of Thy sufferings, that I may hereafter be of Thy consolations; for this I know, that if we suffer together, we shall also reign together.

§ 10. *The consummate Love of Christ must be especially admired and imitated.*

CHRIST. But in all and above all, consider My love, wherewith I desired and accomplished the work of your salvation. So great was it, that many waters of pains and afflictions could not drown it. For your sakes My FATHER spared not His Own and Only SON; I spared not Myself; surely I loved you unto the end, and, as a good Shepherd, I laid down My life for My sheep; and greater love than this can no man have, that a man lay down his life for his friends.

MAN. Nay, but, O LORD, Thou hast had greater, for Thou hast laid down Thine for Thine enemies. For while we were yet enemies, Thou didst by Thy Death reconcile us both to Thyself and to the Father. What love shall appear to be, ever to have been, or be capable of being, like unto this love?

For scarcely for a just man will one die; but Thou didst suffer for the impious, dying for our sins. Thou camest freely to justify sinners, to make slaves brothers, prisoners co-heirs, exiles kings. Whom will not Thy love inflame, O Jesu, Which inflameth and enlighteneth all things? It goeth forth from the uttermost part of heaven, and there is nothing hid from the heat thereof. Thou rejectest not publicans and sinners, but receivest them and eatest with them; yea, to Thy very enemies, who heap on Thee injuries, scoffs, and death itself, Thou art earnest to do good. O wonderful! what marvels hast Thou wrought upon the earth!

§ 11. *In the cross of Christ is a summary of virtue.*

CHRIST. Wouldst thou learn all this in one short summary? Lo, then, the school of all virtue and perfection is Mount Calvary; the chair of the Teacher is the Cross. Hither have I ascended, and with outstretched arms have invited all men unto Me, saying, Come unto Me, all ye that labour and are heavy laden, and I will refresh you: thus lifted up from the earth, have I drawn all things unto Me by the mighty power of My doctrine, even by My example and My love.

Consider what progress My Apostle had made in this discipline, when he professes that he knoweth nothing save JESUS CHRIST and Him crucified: hence he bare My Marks in his body, and with confidence exhorted others, Be ye followers of me, even as I am of CHRIST.

Ascend thou to the mountain of myrrh and the hill of frankincense! But alas! how few care to ascend thither with Me! Many more do I find to share My Table than My Cross. How many thousand men had I once satisfied with bread! how many sick had I healed! how many blind and lame had I made whole! Where were they all when I was going, bearing My Cross, to the Mount? Who was there then to plead My cause? I trod the winepress alone, and of the people there was none with Me. I, all alone, bare your sicknesses; all My acquaintance fled from Me; I was clean forgotten, as a dead man out of mind. Learn by My example not to make flesh thine arm; put not your trust in princes, nor in any child of man, for there is no help in them.

I was reckoned too with malefactors and robbers; yet I humbled Myself and became obedient even unto the Death of the Cross; and wilt thou refuse to humble thyself or to acquiesce in a small matter, when I, in a matter so difficult, exercised obedience so perfect?

I hung naked on the Cross, and the little blood that still flowed in My Body, I shed it all forth for thy salvation; and wilt thou set thy heart on riches? or wilt thou feel it irksome to give Me, in My poor brethren, though but a draught of cold water, or to bestow on Me a trifling alms?

Look upon My virgin flesh, rent so cruelly with sores and wounds, and thou wilt blush at pampering thine in luxury and pleasures.

I, beaten with Scourges, crowned with Thorns, pierced through with Nails, fixed to the Cross, filled with reproaches, condemned to a most shameful death, in all My oppressions minded not My pains, neither opened I My mouth to utter one word of complaint, or defence, or threatening, or malediction against My torturers. As a sheep was I led to the slaughter, and as a lamb before her shearers is dumb, so I opened not My Mouth; how then art thou often on slight occasions, yea, without occasion, so grievously agitated with anger and impatience?

Consider that draught they offered Me in My thirst, and then consider whether thou canst pamper thy flesh with delicacies, fare sumptuously, drink the choicest wine, and be the slave of thy appetite and thy pleasure?

Against envy and hatred set My unfathomable charity, when I prayed even for My enemies; and for the very authors of My Death, refused not to die.

MAN. O how abundant art Thou in pardon! O how plentiful is Thy goodness, O LORD! how much higher are Thy thoughts than our thoughts! how constant is Thy mercy even to the wicked! They cry, *Crucify;* Thou criest, *Forgive;* O marvel, O word of blessing, the like whereof never hath been heard!

CHRIST. Then, My love and earnest zeal for thy salvation flagged not in My tedious agony, nor was I hindered by languor from consummating all things. Remember thou too to fight the good fight, to finish thy course, and persevere unto the end, if thou wilt be safe, and win the crown laid up for thee.

Look upon, O man, and do according to the pattern showed thee on the Mount. Behold here the mystical Serpent lifted on high, so shalt thou be straightway cured of the bites of the old serpent, and be made whole of all thine infirmities.

MAN. I see and confess that the highest and most profitable knowledge is, to know JESUS and Him crucified. GOD forbid then that I should glory, save in the Cross of my LORD JESUS CHRIST; for the word of the Cross, while to them that perish an offence and foolishness, is to them that are saved, the power of GOD and the wisdom of GOD. O that through Thee, O JESU, the world were crucified unto me, and I unto the world! and that I were willing to forego all knowledge, save of Thee in Whom are hid all the treasures of the knowledge and wisdom of GOD! Blessed is the man whom Thou teachest, O LORD, and leadest him in Thy way. Teach me not only to know, but to do Thy will, O GOD.

CHRIST. Yea, for then shalt thou be My disciple indeed, when, not in words only, but, yea much more in deeds thou shalt do all that I command thee. But O how few thus truly love and follow Me! And what marvel: for to most men it is irksome to know and meditate on what I have done and taught; and are they likely to follow Me? I am clean forgotten as a dead man out of mind: and if they forget Me, can they love Me? Love cannot stretch forth towards One unknown.

Be thou then well assured in thyself, that nothing can so much inflame thy love for Me, that nothing is so profitable for the salvation of men, as the habitual meditation of My life and Passion. Hard must be that heart, hard as iron, which the power of so great love softens not. Who will dare to sin, if he takes to heart the agonies I suffered, to deliver man from the yoke of sin and death? All this thou forfeitest, and treadest under foot My Blood, as soon as thou consentest knowingly to sin. What, dost thou hold thy soul cheap, for which I laboured in the world three and thirty years? Wilt thou sell for nought that which I purchased at so great a price, even with My own Blood, and which I held dearer than My Life?

See, O man, where thou art; thou art placed between the highest blessings, and the sorest punishments; those, by many toils and pains, I have prepared for them that love Me: these await the degenerate and them that despise Me. If thou wilt be blessed, follow Me. What fearest thou? My ways are ways of pleasantness; when thou enterest therein, thy steps shall not be straitened; I have made the crooked straight, and the rough ways plain. My yoke is easy, and My burden light. I, Who am thy Leader, will also be thy Helper, and at the end, thy exceeding great Reward.

§ 12. *Conclusion and Thanksgiving for the Life and Passion of* CHRIST. (From St. Bernard.)

Let every tongue give thanks unto Thee, O FATHER, for the superabundance of Thy love, in that Thou sparedst not Thine own SON, but deliveredst Him up to death for us all, that we might have Him as a faithful Advocate before Thee in heaven.

For, behold, crowned with glory and honour, He standeth before Thy Face for us, at the Right Hand of Thy Majesty; for He is our flesh and our Brother. Look, O LORD, upon the Face of Thine Anointed, Who became obedient unto Thee, even unto Death; nor let the scars of His Wounds be hidden from Thy Eyes for ever, that Thou mayest remember the satisfaction Thou hast received from Him.

And to Thee, O LORD JESU, O most Mighty, Whose Name is Jealous, what thanks can I, Thy creature, render to Thee, who am mere dust, a poor vessel of clay? What couldest Thou have done for my salvation, that Thou hast not done for it? The waters of Thy Passion drowned Thee; they covered Thee wholly from the sole of Thy foot, and passed over Thy head, that Thou mightest draw me wholly out from them; yea, they entered even into Thy soul: for Thou abandonedst Thy soul to death, that my soul, abandoned to destruction, Thou mightest restore to me.

Thou hast bound me by a twofold obligation; I am debtor to Thee for the gift of Thine own soul and for mine; for mine which Thou hast twice given me; once in creation and once in redemption: what have I beside it, which I can more justly give Thee back?

But for Thine own precious Soul, so sorely smitten, what worthy return man can give, I find not; for though for it I could give Thee heaven and earth, and all their glory, most surely neither thus could I reach near the pressure of the debt. If I give Thee back, as I both ought, and as I can, myself, this, too, O LORD, cometh of Thy gift.

I must needs love Thee, O my LORD, with my whole heart, with all my whole soul, with all my whole strength; and follow Thy footsteps who hast vouchsafed to die for me. And how shall this be wrought in me but by Thee? O may my soul cleave after Thee; for all its strength hangeth upon Thee. And now, O LORD, my REDEEMER, I adore Thee as Very GOD: I trust in Thee, I hope in Thee; with all the longings I can, I pant after Thee: help my imperfection. I incline my whole being at the glorious signs of Thy Passion, wherewith Thou wroughtest my salvation. The royal standard of Thy victorious Cross, in Thy Name, O CHRIST, I adore. Thy thorny diadem, the nails ruddy with Thy Blood, the spear plunged into Thy sacred Side, Thy Wounds, Thy Blood, Thy sepulchre, Thy glorious and triumphant resurrection and glorification, O CHRIST, meekly I adore and glorify.

For the odour of life breathes upon me in all these; by the life-giving odour of these raise my spirit, LORD, from the death of sin; by the virtue of these shield me from the cunnings of Satan, and so strengthen me that I may find the yoke of Thy commandments sweet, and that the burden of the Cross, which Thou biddest me carry after Thee, may feel light unto my soul.

For what is my strength, that, as Thou commandest, I should sustain, with unbroken mind, so manifold tribulations, that hedge me round about? Are my feet like hart's feet, that I should be able to come up to Thee,

Who runnest swiftly along the thorns and roughnesses of Thy Passion?

But hear my voice, O LORD, and incline upon Thy servant Thy sweet Cross, which is a tree of life to them that lay hold upon it: so will I run (as I hope) vigorously, and bear after Thee, unwearied, that other Cross which mine enemies may lay upon me. Put Thou upon my shoulders that most Divine Cross, whose breadth is charity, whose length is eternity, whose height is almightiness, whose depth is wisdom unsearchable: fasten to it my hands and my feet, and conform Thy servant wholly to Thy Passion, O LORD.

CHAPTER II.

THE LORD'S PRAYER,

OUSLY APPLIED TO CHRIST AND HIS PASSION.

I.—METHOD OF SAYING THE LORD'S PRAYER, WITH THE COMMEMORATION OF THE PRINCIPAL TITLES OF CHRIST.

Our Father, which art in Heaven.

O most sweet FATHER, JESU CHRIST, Who hast regenerated us, children of wrath and perdition by our first birth, which we had from Adam, to be sons of GOD and heirs of everlasting life, in Thy Blood, so that Thy prophet called Thee well, the *Father of the age to come;* Thee, the FATHER and Author of a new creation, even of our regeneration; the FATHER of a love strange and hitherto unheard of, we confess, we worship, we adore. How good a FATHER Thou art, how inclined to help Thy children, behold, Thou provest by giving us a model for prayer, yea, suggesting the very words wherein, easily and surely, we may obtain whatsoever we ask of Thee, or of the FATHER in Thy Name.

O FATHER of our LORD

JESU, look upon the Face of CHRIST Thy Son, as often as, formed by the instruction He hath given, we meekly pray to Thee.

And hear Thou, too, O our FATHER JESU, whensoever in humble words we address Thee, saying,

Hallowed be Thy Name.

O JESU, great High Priest, Who in Thy days didst please GOD, and wast found righteous, and wast made an Atonement in the time of wrath, Who, not by other blood but by Thine Own, didst enter once into the Holy place: for such an High Priest became us; holy, innocent, undefiled, separate from sinners, Who needed not, as other High Priests, to offer sacrifices, first for his own sins and then for the people's.

Behold, Thou art holy, and Thy Name is holy. So wast Thou designated by angels at Thy birth; yea, before Thy birth; and the Everlasting FATHER hath given Thee a Name which is above every name, that at Thy Name every knee should bow. Worthy is Thy name to be praised from the rising up of the sun to the going down of the same. How then shall we poor worms of earth contribute to the hallowing of Thy Name? Most holy in itself, still must it be by us *hallowed,* that is, set forth and honoured, yet most of all by obedience and a holy life. Be ye holy, saith the LORD, for I am holy. But who shall make us holy and clean, who were conceived of unclean seed, save Thou, O Priest for ever, Who hallowest all things, Who lovedst us and didst deliver Thyself up for us, an oblation and sacrifice to GOD, that Thou mightest hallow to Thyself a Church, having neither spot nor wrinkle? Sanctify us in Thy Truth, that we too may sanctify Thee, and that our light may so shine before men, that they, seeing our good works, may glorify Thee and Thy FATHER, Which is in Heaven.

Thy kingdom come.

O JESU, great King above all the kings of the earth! O King of glory, Who at Thy first coming, camest to us meek and lowly, not striking terror into us by majesty and power, but refreshing us in our misery with lowliness and mercy. Born of a royal lineage, Thou art King in the house of Jacob; and of Thy kingdom there shall be no end. Thy kingdom indeed is not of this world; yet, when standing before the governor, Thou didst not deny that Thou wast a King. Yea, on Thy Cross, Thou displayedst the title of royalty. And, moreover, the Eternal FATHER hath crowned Thee with glory and honour, and unto Thee is given all power in heaven and in earth.

O King, best, greatest of Kings, may Thy kingdom of grace now come to us, and hereafter of glory. Far be it from us that, as sons of Belial, we should despise Thee or refuse to have Thee King over us; rather we will, O King of peace and wisdom, that Thou reign over us; for in righteousness and mercy is Thy throne established. Good luck, then, have Thou with Thine honour, according to Thy worship and renown, and rule Thou in us, as of good right Thy subjects. Be Thou, LORD, also in the midst among Thine enemies, and rule them with a rod of iron, that we, delivered out of their hand, may serve Thee in holiness and righteousness all the days of our life. So may the glory of Thy kingdom be magnified, and wax daily more and more.

Thy will be done.

O JESU, LORD and Master, Who camest to teach and do Thy FATHER's will, O LORD, I am Thy servant, and the son of Thine handmaid: what then wilt Thou have me to do? My heart is ready, ready to do what Thou biddest, to shun what Thou forbiddest. I know that not every man that saith, "LORD, LORD," but he that keepeth Thy commandments, he pleaseth Thee. O JESU, Teacher! have mercy upon me, and teach me to do Thy will; lest, if I be a servant knowing his LORD's will and not doing it, I be worthy to be beaten with many stripes. Give what Thou biddest, and bid what Thou wilt.

Give us this day our daily bread.

O JESU, good Shepherd, Who camest from heaven to

visit Thy sheep as a shepherd visiteth his flock; and Who feedest Thy sheep in most rich pastures. But Who feedeth a flock and eateth not of the milk and flesh of the flock? Yet *Thou* feedest Thy sheep with Thine own Flesh and Blood, yea, and layest down Thy life for Thy sheep.

Behold, O good Shepherd, I have wandered like a sheep that is lost; I have strayed where there is no way, finding no pasture. Seek again Thy sheep, lay me on Thy shoulders, and restore me to the pasture-ground, where Thou didst once place me: then shall I lack nothing, in body or in soul. For the one Thou wilt bring food out of the earth. O strengthen the other with the bread of heaven, lest I faint by the way.

Forgive us our trespasses, as we forgive them that trespass against us.

O JESU, most gracious REDEEMER, Who lovedst us and gavest Thyself for us, to redeem us from all iniquity, and purify unto Thyself an acceptable people; we had sold ourselves for nought, and had to be redeemed without money; yet have we been bought with a price, and how great a price! not with corruptible things as silver and gold, but with Thy Precious Blood have we been redeemed. Forgive us, therefore, our debts, for which Thou hast paid so abundant a price. If Thou shalt be extreme to mark iniquities, who shall abide it, while there is none to deliver, none to help? For who can forgive sins but Thou only? No brother shall redeem his brother, no man his fellow; for with Thee Alone, O Redeemer, Most High, is mercy, and with Thee is plenteous redemption.

And lead us not into temptation.

O JESU, most gracious SAVIOUR and Physician, Who camest into the world to save sinners, Who Thyself barest our griefs and carriedst our sorrows, Thyself tempted in all things like as we are, yet without sin, that Thou mightest be touched with the feeling of our temptations. Thou hast said, that the whole need not a physician, but they that are sick; lo, we are a crowd of sick, looking for help and health from Thee: Thou seest how infirm and weak we are, that of ourselves we cannot resist the evil or pursue the good, so inclined to evil are the thoughts and imaginations of men's hearts. The spirit is willing, but the flesh is weak; alas, how easily does it fall under temptation! But Thou, O SAVIOUR, save us! Thou, O heavenly Physician, give strength, bring help! Thy grace is a potent medicine; we can do all in Thee, if Thou but strengthen us.

Behold, O good Samaritan! man hath fallen among thieves; he lieth by the wayside, exhausted with many a wound, half dead, abandoned by all. Behold in my house lieth a paralytic, even my spent soul, powerless to do the deeds of holiness: come and heal it.

Yea, if it seem good to Thee, use the caustic and the knife; for so does the physician, not out of hatred, but for love of the sick man. Pour wine and oil into the wounds; be it that one stings, yet the other soothes. The physician spares not the sick man lest he die: he strikes, to cure; he giveth bitters, to purify.

Temptation is a bitter cup; but Thou, O wise Physician, knowest how to mix it as each man needs, as each case requires; so that with the temptation Thou mayest also make a way to escape. And so I am ready to drink Thy Cup, (yea with Thee too, for Thou wast the first to drink it,) not questioning but that if Thou present it mixed, it must be salutary.

Lo! I am in Thy Hand; if Thou willest, Thou canst make me whole; heal me, LORD, and I shall be healed; save me, and I shall be safe.

But deliver us from evil.

O JESU, most merciful Judge, to Whom the FATHER hath committed all judgment, not to condemn the world, but that the world through Thee might be saved; when Thou shalt manifestly come in the clouds of heaven with power and great majesty, to set apart Thy people and reward every man according to his works; then, O JESU, be a gracious Judge to me, and enter not into judgment with Thy servant, for in Thy sight shall no man living be justified; rebuke me not then, I pray, in Thine indignation, but let mercy triumph over judgment, and reward us not after our iniquities.

O JESU, deliver me from evil in the evil day, for that is the worst of evils; evil slayeth the ungodly, and his end is worst of all, for it is separation from Thee, the chief Good. O that I may not in that awful day tremble at the fearful tidings, "*Depart from me, ye cursed.*" It is good for me to cleave to Thee; O that I be not separated from Thee for ever. Amen, Amen.

II.—METHOD OF RECITING THE LORD'S PRAYER, WITH REFERENCE TO THE SEVEN EFFUSIONS OF THE BLOOD OF CHRIST.

While GOD, *in general, gladly inclines His Ear to our prayers, He testifies in His Prophet that there are prayers and vows which are an abomination to Him, for, saith He,* your hands are full of blood. *Now, however, nothing contributes so much to the prevailing power of prayer, as for a man to stretch forth his soul and his hand, warm with the Blood of* CHRIST. *Ye are come, saith the Apostle, to* JESUS, *the Mediator of the New Testament, and to the Blood of sprinkling, which speaketh better things than that of Abel: yea, better indeed; for the blood of Abel crieth aloud, vengeance, but the blood of* CHRIST, *pardon and mercy. Wilt thou then pray to good effect? Receive the cup of Salvation, and so call upon the name of the* LORD.

Our Father, which art in Heaven.

O FATHER of our LORD JESUS CHRIST, Who, for our sakes, didst not spare the only SON of Thy Bosom, even as He spared not Himself, but delivered Himself up for us of His own will, and loved us unto the end. Love, it is said, subdueth all things; what? doth it GOD Himself, than Whom nothing is greater or stronger? O mighty love! Many waters could not quench love, to prevent *Thy* willing, and Thy SON pouring forth by so many sluices all the Blood of His most Holy Body. Lo, I come to draw water gladly out of the wells of salvation. I lift my hands heavenwards to Thee, dipped and dyed in His rosy Blood. Lo, this is Thy Beloved Son, in Whom Thou art well-pleased. Look upon the Face of Thy Christ; see whether this be Thy Son's coat or no, sprinkled with so precious Blood. Consider why He is red in His apparel; and then, on us miserable sons of Eve, but now Thy sons by adoption, through the Blood of Thy Only-Begotten, turn the eyes of Thy mercy. Shall we meet with repulse when there speaketh for us not the blood of Abel, of bulls or calves, but the Blood of the Immaculate Lamb, Thy Only-Begotten Son Jesus Christ?

O Jesu, Beloved, white and ruddy, Husband of blood, Who hast redeemed us to God by Thy Blood, mercifully admit me, who would enter into the holy place by Thy Blood. Lo! I will receive the Cup of Salvation (of Thy Blood) and will call upon the Name of the Lord. And, therefore, above all I pray,

1. *Hallowed be Thy Name.*

For there is, O Jesu, no other more holy name under heaven, given among men, whereby we must be saved; none more worthy to be honoured than Thine, O most Holy Jesu! *that* Name above every name which was given Thee when first after Thy Nativity, in Thy Circumcision, Thou didst begin to pour forth for us Thy tender infant Blood. O may That Blood grow warm in our hearts, and stir in us zeal and fervour to spread abroad for ever the glory of Thy Name. Blessed be Thy Name, O Jesu, from this time forth for evermore.

2. *Thy kingdom come.*

For Thou art a King, O Jesu, a great King above all gods and all kings of the earth. But, alas! how art Thou esteemed by the wicked? How do they honour Thee as king, with what diadem crown, with what obeisances adore Thee? As a mock and sham king they jeer Thee, twisting for Thee a crown of sharp hard thorns, and driving it deep into Thy Head.

By the shedding of this most Holy Blood, may Thy kingdom come to us, wherein Thou crownest us now with mercy and loving-kindnesses; and hereafter may Thy kingdom come, wherein we are crowned with glory and honour. May Thy Blood obtain this for us, shed for us in Thy Coronation.

3. *Thy will be done.*

O Jesu! Who most willingly for our sake resignedst Thy will to the good pleasure of Thy Father, being made obedient unto Death, when in the Agony at Mount Olivet Thy Heart was, through anguish, very heavy, so that Thy sweat, like drops of blood, fell from Thy whole Body.

How can I help resigning my will for Thy sake; behold, I submit it unto Thine; Thy will, not mine, be done; be it so: though tribulation come down upon me, and my spirit be vexed within me even unto horror and to sweat, yet will I desire, *Thy will be done.* O be this given to me, by Thy Bloody Sweat.

4. *Give us this day our daily bread.*

O Jesu! sinners have ploughed upon Thy Back, and furrowed Thy Body with scourges and rods, as the earth is furrowed with the share, the rake, and mattock. But what a rich harvest, what plenty of fruit, does the ground of Thy Body bear for us, after so cruel culture! While here we are fed on the bread of tears, and eat our bread in the sweat of our brow, we are also nourished with the Bread of life and understanding; our soul is filled even as it were with marrow and fatness; in the strength of this meat we walk through the desert of this world; and at last eat and drink at Thy table, satisfied with the richness of the house of God. Grant this, O Jesu, by Thy Blood, which Thou sheddest for us in Thy Scourging.

5. *And forgive us our trespasses.*

O most patient Jesu! Whose Blood was so often shed for us, for the remission of sins, for once and again were Thy garments torn off Thee violently and cruelly, whereby Thy bleeding wounds were often opened afresh, widened, and enlarged, to Thy most excruciating anguish; and all this Thou barest because man had lost, by sinning, the garment of innocence; and when it had been restored him, had again and again, by repetition of his sins, befouled it.

I pray Thee by Thy sacred Wounds, renewed by the cruel despoiling of Thy garments, and by the Blood, that streamed so plentifully from them, *forgive us our trespasses.* For, as witnesseth Thy beloved Disciple, the Blood of JESUS CHRIST cleanseth us from all sin. O may we put off the garment of our old man with his deeds, and put on the new man, which, after GOD, is created in righteousness and true holiness. May Thy Blood, O JESU, cleanse our consciences from dead works to serve the living GOD.

6. *And lead us not into temptation.*

O JESU, Who with transpierced hands and feet wast so inhumanly fixed to the Cross, and from so many fountains, as it were, and sluices, didst pour forth in abundance Thy Blood; behold my lot is in Thy hands; when I am falling Thou upholdest me; when fallen, Thou raisest me; and when standing, Thou protectest me; into Thy hands I commend myself: hide me under the shadow of Thy wings, from the face of them that trouble me and persecute me. O may I stand fast in the faith against every temptation; fastened with Thee, O CHRIST, to Thy Cross, that neither life nor death nor any other creature may separate me from the love of Thee.

7. *But deliver us from evil.*

O JESU! the refuge of the afflicted; lo! wretched man walketh in the midst of evil and of snares; what shall he do to escape? Where seek a home where he may lie hid in safety? Where, but in the bosom of Thy most sweet Heart, to which an access has been opened to us by the Spear that pierced Thy Side. There will I enter fearless; there will I dwell secure; even as a dove in a cleft of the rock, in a secret place of the mountain side; there is my strength hidden; it will be good for me to be there, and to fix there a tent where no evil can come near, nor any plague. For from it came thereout Blood and water, to be a washing away of sins, a strength for the weak, a remedy for misery, and against all that can threaten salvation, a house of sure defence. O good JESU! deliver me from all evil, since Thou dost so lovingly open to me the bosom of Thy love, Thy most sweet Heart, even Thyself, the Fountain of all good. Amen, Amen.

III.—METHOD OF SAYING THE LORD'S PRAYER, WITH REFERENCE TO THE SEVEN WORDS OF CHRIST ON THE CROSS.

Our Father, which art in Heaven,
1. *Hallowed be Thy Name.*

O LORD JESU, Holy of Holies, of one glory and majesty with the FATHER in Heaven; whiles Thou wert on earth and conversedst with men, in all Thy life, yea, and in Thy Death, Thy only care was everywhere and at all times to seek and set forth Thy FATHER's glory. Thou seemedst indeed deserted of Thy FATHER, when in those strait agonies of death, Thou criedst, *My* GOD, *my* GOD, *why hast Thou forsaken Me.'* (when the inflowing of Thy Godhead and glory stayed a little while, that Thy solitary Manhood might feel all death's sharpness;) but that very forsaking did but enhance Thine own and Thy FATHER's glory. Thou becamest obedient to Death; wherefore GOD hath highly exalted Thee, and given Thee a Name above every Name.

O JESU, forsaken thus for me, cast me not from Thee, specially in the hour of death: when my strength faileth me, leave me not, for the glory of Thy Name: lest mine enemy say, GOD hath forsaken him; I will persecute him and take him, for there is none to deliver him. O GOD, be not Thou far from me; despise me not, O GOD of my salvation. Even in desolation, and under stripes, may I confess Thee, my gracious FATHER, and say with the man of tried patience, It is as the LORD will; blessed be the Name of the LORD.

2. *Thy kingdom come.*

That kingdom, O JESU, whereof the penitent thief,

when crucified with Thee, confessed Thee Lord, saying: Remember me when Thou comest into Thy kingdom; whereon Thou straightway promisedst that he should be with Thee: *To-day shalt thou be with Me in Paradise.* Grant me, JESU, to seek those things that are above, where Thou sittest at the Right Hand of GOD; to mind the things above, not those that are on earth. But, above all, give me a truly broken and contrite heart, such as Thou wilt not despise; and at the last may I say with great confidence, like the thief, *Thy kingdom come;* remember me, O LORD, Who once for me didst hang betwixt thieves upon the Cross, and now reignest with the Blessed in Heaven. O may I, too, then be found worthy to hear, To-day shalt Thou be with Me in My kingdom.

3. *Thy will be done.*

O most obedient JESU, Who for us becamest obedient to GOD Thy Father unto death, even the death of the Cross; to that Thou didst testify concerning the work of man's redemption (O how arduous a work!) committed by Him to Thee, that it was *finished.*

O JESU! grant me earnestly to fulfil the work of *my* calling and my office, and a good hope, after fighting the good fight and finishing my course, of receiving a crown of righteousness from Thee. If I do that Thou commandest, Thou wilt do what Thou hast promised.

4. *Give us this day our daily bread.*

O JESU! Who art very jealous for our salvation; that was it for which, while hanging on the Cross, Thou *thirstedst;* what else didst Thou pant after but our salvation? Surely with desire desiredst Thou to eat this food and drink this cup. What, was so sore a thirst needful to expiate our gluttony?

O that I so thirsted for my own salvation as Thou didst for that of others! Yet what good could my salvation do Thee? It was Thy free love of me that so parched Thee; and would that I too thirsted in turn, as well for my own salvation as my brethren's. Both *ought* to be as sweet and pleasant food to us. Thou hast made every man his brother's keeper, and the people's sins Thou hast given to the priests for food; far be it that their soul should loathe it because it is vile and hard. O that zeal for the LORD's house did eat them up, and that they who are set in charge over the Church took no food, received no profit, save for zeal of the LORD's house!

5. *And forgive us our trespasses.*

O most merciful JESU! Who wast wounded and diedst for our sins, Who so wouldest not the death of a sinner, that Thou prayedst for mercy for Thy very murderers, FATHER, *forgive them!* (O unheard-of love! O unutterable mercy!)

By this mercy, I beseech Thee, pardon me and forgive me my trespasses. Lo, I also am ready, moved by Thy teaching and example, heartily to forgive my enemies; lest I seek mercy of Thee in vain, harbouring wrath against my neighbour.

6. *And lead us not into temptation.*

O most sweet JESU! Who wast Thyself tempted in all points, and was sinless; Who temptest no man, neither canst be tempted with evil, Who art the refuge and strength of all that are tempted, their very present help in trouble: how didst Thou prove this upon the very Cross, when in Thy yearning love for Thy dearest Mother and Thy dear disciple, Thou *commendedst each to the other,* for mutual service and help; comfort in adversities, and support in trials.

Let me too, O LORD, in like manner be Thy care, that I fear not what the devil or man doeth unto me: may I ever have Thee before my face, as though I stood beneath the Cross; for Thou art on my right hand, that I should not be moved.

7. *But deliver us from evil.*

O most mighty JESU, for love is strong as death; this led Thee to die; yea, gave Thee victory over death and all evil. On the point of deliverance from the woes and miseries of this mortal life, tranquilly and calmly *Thou commendedst Thy Spirit into the hands of the Everlasting Father*, as willingly yielding up to Him the life and breath Thou hadst received: knowing that He was able to raise Thee up again to life, now no more subject to woe or death.

Grant me, O JESU, so to pass through the pains, the toils, the woes and miseries of this life; that at the end of it, like a confiding child, I may with ready will yield my soul to Thee my Creator: and do Thou from the woe, the terrible woe, of eternal damnation, deliver me; for Thou hast redeemed me, O LORD GOD of truth. Amen, Amen.

CHAPTER III.

LITANIES ON THE LIFE AND PASSION OF OUR LORD JESUS CHRIST.

LORD, have mercy.
CHRIST, have mercy.
LORD, have mercy.
O GOD, the Father of Heaven,
O GOD, the Son, Redeemer of the world,
O GOD, the Holy Ghost,
HOLY TRINITY, One GOD,
JESU, the desire of all nations [1],
JESU, sent into the world by the Father [2],
JESU, conceived of the Holy Ghost [3],
JESU, the Word made Flesh [4],
JESU, in the form of a servant [5],
JESU, Who in thy Mother's womb didst visit and gladden John [6],
JESU, born of the Virgin Mary [7],
JESU, wrapped in swaddling-clothes [8],

} Have mercy upon us,

[1] Hag. ii.   [2] Gal. iv.   [3] Luke i.   [4] John i.
[5] Phil. ii. [6] Luke i.   [7] Ib. ii.   [8] Ib.

Jesu, laid in the manger [9],
Jesu, suckled with virgin milk [10],
Jesu, shown to shepherds in the manger [11],
Jesu, willingly circumcised according to the Law [12],
Jesu, adored by the wise men [13],
Jesu, presented in the temple [14],
Jesu, taken in the arms of just Simeon [15],
Jesu, carried into Egypt [16],
Jesu, sought by Herod for death [17],
Jesu, brought up at Nazareth [18],
Jesu, found among the Doctors in the temple [19],
Jesu, subject to Thy parents [20],
Jesu, baptized by John [21],
Jesu, tempted in the desert [22],
Jesu, sojourner among men [23],
Jesu, chooser of the poor and ignorant for Thy disciples [24],
Jesu, gracious helper of all in sickness [25],
Jesu, transfigured before the fathers on the Mount [26],
Jesu, weeping for compassion over Jerusalem [27],
Jesu, meek king entering Jerusalem [28],
Jesu, zealous for God's house against the buyers and sellers [29],
Jesu, sold for thirty silverlings [30],
Jesu, bent to wash Thy disciples' feet [31],
Jesu, Who didst keep the Passover with Thy disciples [32],
Jesu, Who gavest us Thy Body for food, Thy Blood for drink [33],
Jesu, prostrated in prayer [34],
Jesu, in Agony bathed in Bloody Sweat [35],
Jesu, strengthened by an Angel [36],
Jesu, betrayed by Judas with a kiss [37],

} Have mercy upon us.

[9] Luke ii. [10] Ib. [11] Ib. [12] Ib. [13] Matt. ii.
[14] Luke ii. [15] Ib. [16] Matt. ii. [17] Ib. [18] Ib.
[19] Luke ii [20] Ib. [21] Matt. iii. [22] Ib. iv. [23] Ib.
[24] Ib. [25] Ib. [26] Ib. xvii. [27] Luke xix. [28] Matt. xxi.
[29] Luke xix. [30] Matt. xxvi. [31] John xiii. [32] Matt. xxvi. [33] Ib.
[34] Ib. [35] Ib. [36] Ib. [37] Ib.

Jesu, bound roughly by the servants [38],
Jesu, forsaken by Thy disciples [39],
Jesu, taken before Annas and Caiaphas [40],
Jesu, buffeted by the servant [41],
Jesu, accused by false witnesses [42],
Jesu, judged worthy of death [43],
Jesu, spat upon the Face [44],
Jesu, blindfolded [45],
Jesu, struck with blows [46],
Jesu, hated without a cause [47],
Jesu, Who gavest Thy Body to the smiters, Thy cheeks to them that plucked off the hair [48],
Jesu, thrice denied by Peter [49],
Jesu, delivered bound to Pilate [50],
Jesu, mocked and set at nought by Herod [51],
Jesu, clad in a white robe [52],
Jesu, rejected for Barabbas [53],
Jesu, cruelly cut with scourging [54],
Jesu, bruised for our iniquities [55],
Jesu, counted for a leper [56],
Jesu, clad in a purple robe [57],
Jesu, crowned with thorns [58],
Jesu, mocked with a reed for a sceptre [59],
Jesu, demanded for crucifixion by the Jews [60],
Jesu, condemned to a most unworthy death [61],
Jesu, delivered to the will of the Jews [62],
Jesu, overladen with the heavy Cross [63],
Jesu, led as a sheep to the slaughter [64],
Jesu, presented with drugged wine and gall [65],
Jesu, fixed naked to the Cross [66],
Jesu, Who lovedst us and washedst us in Thy Blood from sin [67],

} Have mercy upon us.

[38] Matt. xxvi. [39] Ib. [40] Ib. [41] Ib. [42] Ib.
[43] Ib. [44] Ib. [45] Ib. [46] Ib. [47] John xv.
[48] Isa. l. [49] Matt. xxvi. [50] Ib. xxvii. [51] Ib. [52] Ib.
[53] Ib. [54] Ib. [55] Isa. liii. [56] Ib. [57] Mark xv.
[58] Matt. xxvii. [59] Ib. [60] Ib. [61] Luke xxiii. [62] Ib.
[63] John xix. [64] Isa. liii. [65] Mark xv. [66] Matt. xxvii. [67] Apoc. i.

[§ vi.] ON THE LIFE AND PASSION OF OUR LORD. 39

JESU, Who for the joy set before Thee enduredst the Cross, despising the shame [68],
JESU, Who gavest Thyself for us an offering of a sacrifice to GOD for a sweet-smelling savour [69],
JESU, reckoned among transgressors [70],
JESU, crucified between two thieves [71],
JESU, distinguished by Pilate with a royal superscription on the Cross [72],
JESU, intercessor with the FATHER for Thine enemies [73],
JESU, made a scorn of men [74],
JESU, blasphemed by the passers-by [75],
JESU, derided by the Jews [76],
JESU, mocked by the soldiers on the Cross [77],
JESU, reviled by the robber [78],
JESU, promiser of Paradise to the penitent thief [79],
JESU, Who commendedst John to Thy Mother for a Son [80],
JESU, Who saidst, Why hast Thou forsaken Me [81]?
JESU, presented with vinegar in Thy thirst [82],
JESU, Who declaredst that all things written of Thee were accomplished in the Cross, [83]
JESU, Who in dying commendedst Thy Spirit to Thy [FATHER [84],
JESU, ever heard by the FATHER for Thy piety [85],
JESU, made obedient even to the Death of the Cross [86],
JESU, pierced by the lance [87],
JESU, from Whose side came water and Blood [88],
JESU, Who bare our sins in Thy Body on the tree [89],
JESU, by Whose stripes we are healed [90],
JESU, made for us a Propitiation [91],
JESU, taken down from the Cross [92],
JESU, wrapped in clean linen [93],
JESU, laid in the new sepulchre [94],
JESU, Who descendedst after death to Hell [95],
JESU, Who diedst for our sins, and rose again for our justification [96],

Have mercy upon us.

[68] Heb. xii. [69] Eph. iv. [70] Mark xv. [71] Matt. xxvii.
[72] John xix. [73] Luke xxiii. [74] Ps. xxii. [75] Matt. xxvii.
[76] Ib. [77] Luke xxiii. [78] Ib. [79] Ib.
[80] John xix. [81] Matt. xxvii. [82] John xix. [83] Ib.
[84] Luke xxiii. [85] Heb. v. [86] Phil. ii. [87] John xix.
[88] Ib. [89] 1 Pet. ii. [90] Ib. [91] 1 John ii.
[92] Mark xv. [93] Matt. xxvii. [94] Ib. [95] 1 Pet. iii. [96] Rom. iv.

JESU, exalted into Heaven [97],
JESU, placed with the FATHER at His Right Hand [98],
JESU, crowned with glory and honour [99],
JESU, King of Kings and Lord of Lords [100],
JESU, Who hast prepared for us a place in Thy FATHER's house [101],
JESU, our Advocate with the FATHER [102],
JESU, Who pouredst the HOLY GHOST the Comforter, on the disciples [103],
JESU, Who shalt judge the quick and dead [104],
JESU, Who shalt drive the reprobate into endless fire [105],
JESU, Who shalt bestow on the elect the kingdom prepared for them [106],

} Have mercy upon us.

 Be gracious, spare us, JESU.

From all evil,
From sudden, unprepared evil death,
From the snares of the devil,
From anger, hatred, and every evil motion,
From everlasting death,
By the mystery of Thy holy Incarnation,
By Thy Advent,
By Thy Nativity,
By Thy Circumcision,
By Thy receiving of Thy all-holy Name,
By Thy Baptism and holy Fasting,
By Thy labours and watchings,
By Thine Agony and bloody Sweat,
By Thy buffetings and stripes,
By Thy crown of thorns,
By Thy Cross and Passion,
By Thy thirst, tears, and nakedness,
By Thy five most sacred Wounds,
By Thy Death and Burial,
By Thy Holy Resurrection,
By Thy admirable Ascension,
By the sending of the Holy GHOST, the Comforter,
In the Day of judgment,

} Deliver us, JESU.

---

[97] Acts i. [98] Ps. cix. [99] Ib. viii. [100] Apoc. xix. [101] John xiv.
[102] 1 John ii. [103] Acts. ii. [104] 2 Tim. iv. [105] Matt. xxv. [106] Ib.

We sinners, JESU, beseech Thee, hear us.

That being dead unto sin, we may live unto righteousness [1],
That we delight not in glorying, save in the Cross of our LORD JESUS CHRIST [2],
That for love of Thee the world may be crucified unto us, and we unto the world [3],
That we continually carry about in the body the mortification of the Cross [4],
That we study to crucify the flesh with its affections and lusts [5],
That as Thou hast suffered for us in the flesh, we may be armed likewise with the same mind [6],
That we may be able to take up our cross daily and follow Thee [7],
That what is gain to us, we may count as loss for Thee [8],
That we strive above all things to know JESUS Crucified [9],
That Thy Blood may cleanse us from dead works to serve the living GOD [10],
That being bought at a great price, we may glorify GOD in our body [11],
That being dead unto sin, and buried with Thee, we may walk henceforth with Thee in newness of life [12],
That once cleansed from dead works, we beware lest we crucify Thee, the SON of GOD, again, and put Thee to an open shame [13],
That ever looking to the Ensample left us by Thee, we may follow Thy steps [14],
That as we are partakers of the sufferings, we may be also of the consolation [15],

} We beseech thee, JESU, hear us.

LAMB of GOD, that takest away the sins of the world, Spare us, JESU.

[1] 1 Pet. ii. [2] Gal. vi. [3] Ib. [4] 2 Cor. iv.
[5] Gal. v. [6] 1 Pet. iv. [7] Matt. xvi. [8] Phil. iii.
[9] 1 Cor. ii. [10] Heb. ix. [11] 1 Cor. vi. [12] Rom. vi.
[13] Heb. vi. [14] 1 Pet. ii. [15] 2 Cor. ii.

LAMB of GOD, that takest away the sins of the world,
Hear us, JESU.
LAMB of GOD, that takest away the sins of the world,
Have mercy on us, JESU.
Our FATHER.

COLLECTS

ON THE LORD'S PASSION, ANSWERING TO THE SEVEN
CANONICAL HOURS.

AT MATINS.

O LORD JESU, by the love wherewith Thou lovedst Thine own even unto the end; by the Bloody Sweat which fell down from Thee in the garden; by the spite and griefs which Thou enduredst when Thy disciple sold Thee, and the wicked Jews bound and rent Thee; unbind the chains of my sins, and bind this my soul with the most strait bonds of Thy love, which cannot be unloosed; Who livest, &c.

AT PRIME.

O LORD JESU, Who at the Hour of *Prime* wast brought before Pontius Pilate, the Heavenly before an earthly judge, and wast falsely charged by the wicked priests of evil deeds; help us miserable sinners in the Judgment Day, that we be not doomed with wicked men to endless punishment, but be made worthy of the fellowship of Thy saints in heavenly places; Who livest, &c.

AT TIERCE.

O LORD JESU, Who at the *third hour* of the day wast beaten with scourges, and crowned with thorns, grant that we Thy servants, having our bodies subdued by voluntary chastisement, may be deemed worthy members of Thee, our thorn-crowned Head; Who livest, &c.

AT SEXT.

O LORD JESU, Who at the *sixth hour* of the day didst hang with pierced hands and feet from the wood of the Cross, and didst fasten thereto with the same nails the hand-writing of our condemnation; grant to my soul that, thus set free from the service of sin, I may ever bear in my heart of hearts, as the symbols of my deliverance, those Thy most holy wounds; Who livest, &c.

AT NONES.

O LORD JESU, Who at the *ninth hour* of the day, when all was finished, didst bow Thy Head and yield Thy Spirit to Thy Father, and breathedst into mankind, who lay in death, the breath of life; grant that I, who do owe myself wholly to Thee for making me, may, now that Thou hast new-made me, yield Thee myself wholly again, and live henceforth no more unto myself, but always unto Thee, Who diedst for me; Who livest, &c.

AT VESPERS.

O LORD JESU, Who *at the evening hour* wouldst that Thy lifeless Body should be taken from the Cross, and be laid in Thy most holy Mother's arms, grant me never, while I live, to put from me my Cross, which in Thy goodness Thou mayest bestow on me; and when I die and am taken from it, make me worthy to be presented before Thee, and be received in the arms of Thy mercy[1]; Who livest, &c.

AT COMPLINE.

O LORD JESU, Who at the hour of *Compline* restedst in the grave, and wast mourned by Thy sad Mother and the other women, give us true tears to weep for Thy most holy Passion, and grant us never to do that which may crucify Thee afresh. Who livest.

[1] Altered.—ED.

CHAPTER IV.

ROSARIES AND EXERCISES, IN SUNDRY MEASURES, ON THE LIFE AND PASSION OF CHRIST.

Of the Meaning and Use of the following Rosary.

The trial of a Christian man is not his name but his life. The name implies a glorious profession; but of what avail is it to everlasting glory, unless the life be answerable to a name so holy?

The Life of CHRIST is our rule of living. Many there be who claim His Name, but think little of living worthily thereof: yet, strange to say, they promise themselves a share in His glory, Whose life and footsteps they neglect to follow. O how many (Christians in name) flatter themselves with this presumptuous hope, and forget, whether through ignorance or indolence, that a holy name should spur to a more holy life; that to be, not to be called *Christians*, should be our desire.

What must we then do? Look on the mirror of CHRIST's life: look on it, Christian, and, by it order thine own; and, since the straight rule tests both the crooked and the straight, behold in Him His wondrous beauty and His various virtues; in thyself thy deformities and sins: and yet shall these the sooner be washed out, as thou studiest more diligently His spotless mirror.

Let it be, therefore, ever before thine eyes; meditate on the Life of CHRIST day and night, so shalt thou learn to hate thy faults; so shalt thou love and long to imitate His virtues. For meditation imparts knowledge, enlightens the understanding, stirs the affections, and kindles the will. What is unknown cannot raise desire of itself, and so no wonder CHRIST has few who follow Him. How should man loathe to meditate on His holy life, and love to imitate it?

Touching the following Rosary; it sets forth briefly, for thee, who art a Christian, the whole life of CHRIST; yet it contains full material for pious meditation. The former part of each verse contains some mystery or event in the life and actions of CHRIST; in the latter some pious reflection is drawn forth from the first, and an earnest desire expressed for the special virtue there mentioned.

It contains five Decades, or divisions of ten verses.

1. *The Infancy and Youth* of our SAVIOUR, *down to His Baptism.*
2. *The Life of* CHRIST, *to His Passion.*
3. *The Passion of* CHRIST, *to His Crucifixion.*
4. *The Crucifixion and Death.*
5. *The events after His Death; then the Resurrection, Ascension, &c.*

This Rosary may be used

also with reference to the Holy Communion, whether in simply assisting at it, or in receiving. Both are pious remembrances of the LORD's *Passion;* and what better exercise can there be for them than the contemplation of these Mysteries?

And that the use of this Rosary may be the more profitable, whatever virtue of CHRIST you contemplate or read of, kindle forthwith within thy heart an affection answerable to it.

And various affections there are suited to this purpose, with which your meditation, which else might be profitless and barren, may, from time to time, be watered and refreshed. Such are the following:

1. *Suffering with* CHRIST *in pain, and joining with Him in gladness.* LORD, my soul grieves with Thee, Who sufferest so bitter and undeserved pains for me, miserable sinner, &c.

2. *Compunction and Contrition.* Woe is me, for I am a sinner: sorrow to me, the cause of so much woe to Thee. Can I think my soul of no account, which Thou hast so dearly bought? that soul, whose price is the Blood of CHRIST? Shall I go on miserably sinning, for whose sins the SON of GOD suffered pains so extreme?

3. *Hope and Joy.* It is good for me to hold me fast by GOD, and to put my trust in the LORD GOD. What is too much to hope from Thee, Who hast done and borne so much for me, my GOD, my only refuge?

4. *Praise and Thanksgiving.* What reward shall I give unto the LORD, for all the benefits that He hath done unto me? Bless the LORD, O my soul, and all that is within me, bless His holy Name.

5. *Imitation.* Thou hast left us an ensample, O LORD, and Thou wouldest that we should follow Thy steps. Grant what Thou commandest, and command what Thou willest.

6. *Wonder.* LORD, what art Thou, and what am I? Thou, in Thy Passion, art GOD and LORD, just and innocent: I, a poor slave, an earth-worm and a sinner; who merited the punishment borne (most wonderful!) by Thee.

7. *Love.* Sweet JESU, my Salvation and my Life: all Thy works, O LORD, tell me of Thy Love. Love drew Thee down from heaven

and confined Thee within the Virgin's womb: love nailed Thee to the Cross, and what shall separate me ever from Thy love? O let not life, nor death, nor any other creature.

In affections such as these, according to the subject, must the soul be exercised, and meditation on the Life and Passion of our Saviour be seasoned. The details will be supplied in the following Rosary, and more still will the unction of the Holy Ghost *intruct thee. But to beginners especially, let contrition and imitation be the main object of their affections. For this is the chief fruit of meditation on the Passion, to conceive therefrom, hatred for sin, and love for virtue. And what more profitable for the former than to reflect,* "What did it behove Christ to suffer to snatch us from our sins? *What more conducive to holy living than the thought,* "God became Man, that in our flesh, like unto us, and seen by our eyes, He might be our Example and Pattern of every virtue?"

Moreover, in this Rosary the chief virtues which are dwelt on are humility, obedience, meekness, patience, mercy, charity, *and the like. Strive to follow them, and kindle other such holy affections as appertain to them. Be of good cheer,* Christ *will be with thee; He that teaches thee by His Example, guides thee with the assistances of His grace, and shall finally, if thou follow Him, crown thee with eternal glory.*

ROSARY
OF OUR LORD JESUS CHRIST,

CONTAINING THE EVENTS OF HIS LIFE AND PASSION BRIEFLY AND ATTRACTIVELY NARRATED, AND SUPPLYING FULL MATERIAL AND AN EASY METHOD FOR MEDITATION.

Summe Pater.
Father, All-creating Mind!
Gracious Jesu, Saviour kind!
Quickening Spirit, with Both enshrin'd!
God, That rulest the universe!

Cleanse, good LORD, my lips and thought,
Ere for our Salvation wrought,
   I the mysteries rehearse.

JESU, Thou the Virgin's Seed,
Born to bruise the serpent's head,
   Hast a mother's yearnings known.
In Thy tender love abiding,
In Thy nurturing care confiding,
   Take me, SAVIOUR, for Thine own.

JESU, Thee Thy Saints attending,
With the choirs of angels blending,
   Hymn the world's great Judge and LORD.
Oh, to me who trembling raise,
'Neath their feet, a sinner's praise,
   LORD, a gracious ear afford.

I believe in God, &c.

FIRST DECADE.

JESU, for lost sinners' sake,
Our poor garb of flesh to take,
   Thou didst leave Thy throne of light.
By the power that Mystery gave us,
Quicken, mighty LORD, and save us,
   Earth's vile forms with Heaven's unite.

Our Father.

JESU, Thou a Virgin's breast
Hallowedst with Thy Presence blest,
   Through th' o'ershadowing SPIRIT's grace.
GOD of awe and purity,
Ere Thou deign to dwell in me,
   Cleanse me for Thy pure embrace.

O Saviour of the world, Who by Thy Cross and Precious Blood hast redeemed us, save us, and help us, we humbly beseech Thee, O Lord. Amen.

Jesu, Thee enshrin'd she bore,
When she sped the mountains o'er,
   To her cousin's lowly home,
Oh! mayst Thou, a Guest abiding,
In earth's veils Thy glory hiding,
   O'er my threshold frequent come.
         ✠ 𝕾𝖆𝖛𝖎𝖔𝖚𝖗 𝖔𝖋 𝖙𝖍𝖊 𝖜𝖔𝖗𝖑𝖉.

Jesu, Whose mysterious birth
Knew nor taint nor throe of earth,
   Born of Virgin Mother Thou;
Give me perfect charity,
Such a glowing love for Thee,
   As no earthly fear shall know.
         ✠ 𝕾𝖆𝖛𝖎𝖔𝖚𝖗 𝖔𝖋 𝖙𝖍𝖊 𝖜𝖔𝖗𝖑𝖉.

Jesu, Thou Who earth enfoldest,
In the world Thyself upholdest,
   Hast not where to lay Thy Head.
Wholesome check to boundless dreaming,
Humbling shock to man's esteeming,
   Thy poor weeds, and manger-bed!
         ✠ 𝕾𝖆𝖛𝖎𝖔𝖚𝖗 𝖔𝖋 𝖙𝖍𝖊 𝖜𝖔𝖗𝖑𝖉.

Jesu, shepherds run to meet Thee,
Angel hosts come down to greet Thee,
   With their joyous melody.
May I join that wondering throng,
Love and learn that ceaseless song,
   "Glory be to God on high."
         ✠ 𝕾𝖆𝖛𝖎𝖔𝖚𝖗 𝖔𝖋 𝖙𝖍𝖊 𝖜𝖔𝖗𝖑𝖉.

Jesu, God and Saviour dear,
Who the law's stern blade didst bear,
   In Thy sinless Infancy.
Grant me, Lord, with soul unbending,
Ne'er to spare or foot offending,
   Sinning hand, or wandering eye.
         ✠ 𝕾𝖆𝖛𝖎𝖔𝖚𝖗 𝖔𝖋 𝖙𝖍𝖊 𝖜𝖔𝖗𝖑𝖉.

Jesu, kings with gifts adore Thee,
King of kings, they bow before Thee,
    Prostrate on their face they fall:
For Thy boons of countless treasure,
Poor the best that I can measure,
    Lo! I give myself, my all.
        ✠ Saviour of the world.

Jesu, Thee, the Law fulfilling,
Parent hands, an offering willing
    Bear to Thine own altar's side:
Grant me a right heart, O Lord,
Every thought, and deed, and word,
    By Thy law of love to guide.
        ✠ Saviour of the world.

Jesu, when the murderer sought Thee,
Ere within his toils he brought Thee,
    Thou didst flee his deadly knife:
Keep me from whate'er might foil me,
Save me from whate'er might spoil me
    Of Thy Spirit's hallowing life.
        ✠ Saviour of the world.

Jesu, Whom Thy Mother's eye
Sought with tears, and found with joy
    In Thy temple's holy bound!
Blest, whoe'er can aye retain Thee,
Blest, who lost can yet regain Thee,
    Blest, whoe'er hath sought and found.
        ✠ Saviour of the world.

Hear, Creator, good and great!
Hear us, Saviour, mild and sweet!
Hear us, Holy Paraclete!
    God *Triune; my* God, *mine All!*
Saviour, *Who from sin hast freed me,*
In life's barren desert feed me,
Through death's darksome valley lead me,
    Homeward to my Father's *hall.*

SECOND DECADE.

Jesu, as the waters crown Thee,
And Thy Spirit lights upon Thee,
　　Thee Thy Father's words approve:
In Thy living fountain laved,
By Thy quickening Spirit saved,
　　May I know that Father's love.
　　　　　　　Our Father.

Jesu, Thy drear fasting ended,
With what holy might defended,
　　Satan's wiles Thou didst repel:
Oh! by no ill art confounded,
Strong in faith, with soul unwounded,
　　May I quench the darts of hell.
　　　　　　O Saviour of the world.

Jesu, at Thy piercing call,
Lo! the fishers leave their all,
　　Fishers hence of lost mankind:
Lord, whene'er in me Thou speakest,
Take the hand of him Thou seekest,
　　And his fetter'd step unbind.
　　　　　　O Saviour of the world.

Jesu, on whose Hand and Tongue
Famish'd crowds half-fainting hung,
　　By Thy Word creative fed:
Living Bread, my flesh preserving,
Angels' Food, my spirit nerving,
　　Give me, Lord, my daily bread.
　　　　　　O Saviour of the world.

Jesu, for Thy love all-healing,
Men restoring, fiends expelling,
　　What Thy meed?　Relentless scorn.

Give me, LORD, Thy gentle mind,
Generous deeds for words unkind,
   Love for envy to return.
        ✠ Saviour of the world.

JESU, who on Tabor's height,
Cloth'st Thee with Thy robe of light,
   Foretaste of Thy Presence blest.
Grant me, LORD, by grace prevailing,
Arms of light, and love unfailing,
   On Thy holy hill to rest.
        ✠ Saviour of the world.

JESU, Who, the bridegroom's guest,
Gavest wine, the last and best,
   At Thy Mother's gentle word:
Make me love each friend I see,
Thee in all, and all in Thee,
   More than all, my GOD and LORD.
        ✠ Saviour of the world.

JESU, LORD, a pilgrim weary,
O'er earth's waste, all dark and dreary,
   What a rugged lot was Thine!
Oh! for Thee, whate'er betide me,
Cold, or heat, or toil abide me,
   Thirst or hunger be it mine.
        ✠ Saviour of the world.

JESU, with what love deep-burning,
Ruin'd souls from sin returning,
   To Thy service Thou didst win!
Make me ere, with powerless zeal,
Others' wounds I spring to heal,
   With my own false heart begin.
        ✠ Saviour of the world.

JESU, o'er Thy chosen city
Drops Thy tear of tenderest pity,
   At the dreadful doom in store!

Oh! may those Thy tears of love
Me to tears of penance move,
   Bid me go, and sin no more!
          ✠ Saviour of the world.

JESU, lo, I see him weigh Thee,
Judas, waiting to betray Thee,
   Bartering GOD for earthly gain!
Grant me love that knows no measure,
Love for Thee, my only Treasure,
   Love that counts all others vain.
          ✠ Saviour of the world.

Hear, CREATOR, *good and great!*
Hear us, SAVIOUR, *mild and sweet!*
Hear us, HOLY PARACLETE!
   GOD *Triune; my* GOD, *mine all!*
SAVIOUR, *Who from sin hast freed me,*
In life's barren desert feed me,
Through death's darksome valley lead me,
   Homeward to my FATHER'S *hall.*

THIRD DECADE.

JESU, LORD and Master great,
Who didst wash Thy servants' feet,
   Stooping low to service mean:
Bend, O LORD, this mind unlowly,
Cleanse, O LORD, this heart unholy,
   Bow me, LORD, and make me clean.
          Our Father.

JESU, the true Paschal Food,
By Thyself on Thine bestow'd;
   Miracle of mightiest love!
Living Bread of Heaven, support me,
So no earthly chance may hurt me,
   World, nor flesh, nor Satan move.
          ✠ Saviour of the world.

JESU, in the garden bow'd,
Thou Thy will, all bathed in Blood,
    To Thy FATHER's didst resign:
Oh, that I my heart might offer,
Train'd t' obey, and school'd to suffer,
    Till my will be lost in Thine.
              O Saviour of the world.

JESU, when fierce wolves assail'd Thee,
When to death, meek LAMB, they haled Thee,
    'Twas Thy Love the Victim led:
Flames of love all hate consuming,
Love, my heart of hearts illuming,
    On its glowing altar shed.
              O Saviour of the world.

JESU, as the ruffians take Thee,
And Thou seest Thine own forsake Thee,
    LORD, with Thee who would not weep!
Grant from Thee no terror scare us,
Weal nor woe nor Satan tear us;
    At Thy side Thy servants keep.
              O Saviour of the world.

JESU, Thou in bonds appearest,
Silent all, Thy charge Thou hearest.
    Meekness' self, Thou standest, LORD!
From ill thought and sentence idle,
Rein my heart, my utterance bridle,
    Chasten every wish and word.
              O Saviour of the world.

JESU, thrice Thy friend denied Thee,
Then with bitter grief descried Thee,
    Melted by Thy piercing glance:
LORD, O might I ne'er deny,
Or 'mid floods of tears descry
    Thy returning Countenance.
              O Saviour of the world.

Jesu, with false judgment weigh'd,
In white robes, in sport, array'd!
    Thou true Judge, and Heav'n Thy Throne:
Let me never judge my brother,
Self-condemn'd, condemn none other,
    Stand or fall to Thee Alone.
        ✠ Saviour of the world.

Jesu, as the scourges scar Thee,
Spitting shames, and smitings mar Thee,
    And Thy spotless Form deface:
Bid me count what stripes abide me,
By Thy Stripes in mercy hide me
    From the tortures of that place!
        ✠ Saviour of the world.

Jesu, lo, with thorns they crown Thee,
As a King in mockery own Thee—
    King Thou art, Thy realm this ball!
O may I with reverence due,
Heartfelt praise, and service true,
    At Thy footstool ever fall.
        ✠ Saviour of the world.

Jesu, when to their fierce ban
Pilate cries, "Behold the Man,"
    Maddening crowds "Barabbas" crave.
King of sorrows, melt in me
What might aught prefer to Thee,
    Slay my King, a murderer save.
        ✠ Saviour of the world.

Hear, CREATOR, *good and great!*
Hear us, SAVIOUR, *mild and sweet!*
Hear us, HOLY PARACLETE!
    GOD *Triune; my* GOD, *mine All!*
SAVIOUR, *Who from sin hast freed me,*
In life's barren desert feed me,
Through death's darksome valley lead me,
    Homeward to my FATHER's *hall.*

FOURTH DECADE.

Jesu, now the hard Cross bearing,
Its huge weight Thy shoulders wearing,—
 Oh that I might follow Thee!
Take my daily cross and learn Thee,
Step by step the more discern Thee,
 Till that Tree's sweet fruit I see.
   Our Father.

Jesu, vest by vest laid bare,
To rude gaze and cruel stare
 Thou Thy virgin limbs dost yield:
Oh! may no foul fiend e'er strip me
Of the robe which Thine would keep me,
 Holy shame, our soul's bright shield.
   O Saviour of the world.

Jesu, on Thy Cross suspended,
Stretch'd each limb, each nerve distended,
 Strong, life-giving agony!
Aye may I my glory count
That dread Cross, that healing Fount,
 Glorying, Lord, in nought but Thee.
   O Saviour of the world.

Jesu, thrice with omen bright
In three tongues Thy Name they write,
 To all eyes Thy style is shown:
Jesu, Saviour, Nazarene!
Save us, for the sons of men
 No such saving name have known.
   O Saviour of the world.

Jesu, Lord, Who, as Thou bleedest,
For Thy cruel torturers pleadest,
 Lesson of all-conquering love!

Grant, by good o'er ill prevailing,
Love unfeign'd o'er hate unfailing,
 I my FATHER's child may prove.
    O Saviour of the world.

JESU, Fount of endless joy,
Who that mild forgiving eye
 On the contrite thief dost cast:
Give me, LORD, a broken heart,
So in Paradise a part
 I with Thee may have at last.
    O Saviour of the world.

JESU, Who Thy blessed Mother
And Thy friend, Thy more than brother,
 Each to other's care didst give:
May I learn, beneath their feet,
Mindful of their solace sweet,
 In this vale of tears to live.
    O Saviour of the world.

JESU, with that death-cry shaken,
"FATHER, why hast Thou forsaken?"—
 Strongest agony of all!
JESU, SAVIOUR, ne'er forsake me,
Lest the pains of Hell o'ertake me,
 And from Thee in death I fall.
    O Saviour of the world.

JESU, with what draught accurst
Do they slake Thy burning thirst,
 And in mockery pledge Thee, LORD!
Oh! of earth's soft sensual pleasure
Be that bitter draught the measure,
 Deep within this bosom stor'd.
    O Saviour of the world.

JESU, yea, "'Tis finishèd,"
By that Death sin's spell is dead,
 Thy Redeemer's crown is won.

Give me life, and love deep-yearning,
Aye Thy blest obedience learning,
   Till my work, Thy Will be done.
                    𝕺 𝕾𝖆𝖛𝖎𝖔𝖚𝖗 𝖔𝖋 𝖙𝖍𝖊 𝖜𝖔𝖗𝖑𝖉.

JESU, in Thy FATHER'S Breast
As Thou bidst Thy Spirit, rest,
   Day's veil'd eye bewails Thee fled.
LORD, may I at life's dark close
My freed soul in Thee repose:
   Cheer, true Light, my dying bed.
                    𝕺 𝕾𝖆𝖛𝖎𝖔𝖚𝖗 𝖔𝖋 𝖙𝖍𝖊 𝖜𝖔𝖗𝖑𝖉.

Hear, CREATOR, *good and great!*
Hear us, SAVIOUR, *mild and sweet!*
Hear us, HOLY PARACLETE!
   GOD *Triune; my* GOD, *mine All!*
SAVIOUR, *Who from sin hast freed me,*
In life's barren desert feed me,
Through death's darksome valley lead me,
   Homeward to my FATHER'S *hall.*

FIFTH DECADE.

JESU, by that Death of pain,
Guiltless for the guilty slain,
   Thou the guilty dost reprieve:
By Thy Death's strong life within us
To Thine own true Dying win us,
   From the death of deaths retrieve.
                    𝕺𝖚𝖗 𝕱𝖆𝖙𝖍𝖊𝖗.

JESU, from Thy piercèd side
Bursts Thy love's expanding tide,
   Earth's dry hearts embosoming:
Lo! Salvation's Fount is gushing;
What shall stay Thy lost ones rushing
   To embrace the healing spring?
                    𝕺 𝕾𝖆𝖛𝖎𝖔𝖚𝖗 𝖔𝖋 𝖙𝖍𝖊 𝖜𝖔𝖗𝖑𝖉.

Jesu, as Thy Mother's eye
On the sharp Cross watch'd Thee die,
   What a sword that bosom tried!
To that Cross, O Jesu, nail me,
Till all other love shall fail me,
   Save of Thee, the Crucified.
        ✠ Saviour of the world.

Jesu, with what tears they bathe Thee,
With what fragrant odours swathe Thee,
   Laid within Thy Tomb to rest:
In that deep repose, O, calm me,
Hide me, Saviour, and embalm me
   With Thy Spirit's unction blest.
        ✠ Saviour of the world.

Jesu, from their dismal region
Who hast freed th' imprison'd legion,—
   Death and Hell hast captive led:
Loose me from the sins that daunt me,
Save me from the fears that haunt me
   Of that realm so drear and dread.
        ✠ Saviour of the world.

Jesu, from Thy grave upraisèd,
Gladdening sight to hearts amazèd,
   Bidding fear and sorrow flee:
Grant, from sin's black sleep awaking,
From my soul earth's grave-clothes shaking,
   I may Thee in beauty see.
        ✠ Saviour of the world.

Jesu, Who Thy servants' talk
Joinest in their mournful walk,
   Knowing all, Thyself unknown:
Be Thou ever, Lord, beside me,
With Thine eye and counsel guide me,
   In the heart's deep converse shown.
        ✠ Saviour of the world.

Jesu, Thou, Thy triumph ended,
To the Heaven of Heavens ascended,
    Tak'st the Crown Thy pains have won!
Oh, that I Thyself may gain,
Cheer my course, my steps sustain,
    Till my earthly race be run.
        ✠ Saviour of the world.

Jesu, Who Thy Paraclete
Sending from Thy Holy Seat,
    Fill'st Thine own with Thy true grace:
By Thy Spirit of light and love,
Fill our hearts, our senses move,
    Fit us to behold Thy Face.
        ✠ Saviour of the world.

Jesu, Whom with glory crownèd,
Light of Light in light enthronèd,
    Angel-choirs and Saints adore:
Lord! from those Thy mansions bright,
Hearkening to their prayer of might,
    Watch and bless us evermore.
        ✠ Saviour of the world.

Jesu, Who our Judge art coming,
Saints rewarding, sinners dooming,
    Gracious Saviour, righteous Lord!
In Thy loving mercy chide me,
Ere I call the rocks to hide me,
    Outcast from Thy Face abhorr'd.
        ✠ Saviour of the world.

Hear, Creator, *good and great!*
Hear us, Saviour, *mild and sweet!*
Hear us, Holy Paraclete!
    God *Triune; my* God, *mine All!*
Saviour, *Who from sin hast freed me,*
In life's barren desert feed me,
Through death's darksome valley lead me,
    Homeward to my Father's *hall.*

AFFECTIONS OF THE DEVOUT SOUL

EXPRESSED IN RHYTHM
TO THE MEMBERS OF JESUS CHRIST CRUCIFIED.

FIRST DECADE.

SUNDAY.—TO THE FEET.

CHRIST, *of Saints and Angels* LORD!
This world's Light, in Heaven adored,
  Way and Truth and Life to all!
Peace and Health to every son,
Whom Thy dying Love hath won,
  Man of Sorrows, Thee I call.
         𝕺𝖚𝖗 𝕱𝖆𝖙𝖍𝖊𝖗.
    𝕺 𝕾𝖆𝖛𝖎𝖔𝖚𝖗 𝖔𝖋 𝖙𝖍𝖊 𝖜𝖔𝖗𝖑𝖉

JESU, Prince of Life and Power,
Death's own Doom, Salvation's Tower!
Oh, with Thee Thy sharp Cross bearing,
And Thy bitter death-cup sharing,
  Might I share Thy glory too!
Sin my trembling prayer would choke,
But that on that Cross I look,
And, at Thy stretch'd limbs scarce gazing,
Prostrate at the sight amazing,
  At Thy feet for mercy sue.

These blest Feet, so bruis'd, so bent,
With these nail-pierced gashes rent,
Ere I clasp, with awe-struck gladness,
All aghast, in tranced sadness,
  Shrinks my spirit at the thought.
LORD! for this vast charity,
Who shall duly thankful be!
Oh, the love ineffable,
Which, our ruin'd souls to heal,
  Such a remedy hath wrought!

Sweetest JESU, GOD of Might,
Thou, my Portion Infinite,
Having Thee, what have I not?
Gaining worlds, what have I got,
   LORD, without Thy love and power?
Oh that in Thy furrowed Feet,
Thine own Mercy's deep retreat,
When the day of wrath shall come,
I might run and find a home,
   Shelter'd from that blasting hour.

As before Thy Cross I lie,
And Thy tender Feet embrace,
JESU, LORD, hide not Thy face,
Cast on me that gentle eye,
   Which on prostrate Mary shone.
Oh, that from Thy Cross on high,
Thou wouldst turn that melting look,
Which Thy fallen Peter strook,—
Left him not to fall and die,
   Bade him rise, and weep alone.

Thee, and on Thy Cross I seek,
Nor shall fail if Thou shalt lead me,
By Thy Name, Blest JESU, aid me,
To Thine arms, Thy servant take,
   Breathless 'neath Thy wings protect.
By Thy sacred Feet, I pray,
Fellow-heirs with Thee, O, guide us,
Through the desert walk beside us,
Wandering feet, that find no way,
   In Thy paths of peace direct.

SECOND DECADE.

MONDAY.—TO THE KNEES.

CHRIST, *of Saints and Angels* LORD!
This world's Light, in Heaven adored,
   Way and Truth and Life to all!

Peace and Health to every son,
Whom Thy dying love hath won,
Man of Sorrows, Thee I call.

Our Father.
✠ **Saviour of the world.**

JESU, Fount of endless pleasure,
Sinners' Hope, and Life, and Treasure,
Spotless LAMB, True GOD of GOD,
How, like felon, on the wood,
   Thou Thy drooping knees dost bend!
Ah, how bare, how all forlorn,
Sport of what relentless scorn
Was our GOD-INCARNATE made,
Of His own free love betray'd,
   To these racks, this torturing end.

JESU, Who alone canst save us
From the thraldoms that enslave us,
GOD of Mercy! is it Thou,
Thus from Heaven to earth dost bow,
   Slave Thyself, sin's slaves to free?
Oh, Thou Majesty Divine,
Emptied thus to ransom Thine,
What for love so vast, so tender,
Shall my heart of hearts not render?
   What, for all that Blood I see?

Oh, what wondrous Love is there,
Thus to aid a world's despair!
LORD, of right shall earth adore Thee,
Heaven and Hell fall down before Thee,
   Every creature bow the knee.
Thou the frail from fall preservest,
Trembling knees 'tis Thou that nervest,
Thou the fall'n dost raise again,
Thou the fetter'd dost unchain;
   Heaven's steep way is smooth'd by Thee.

Strong Thy love, than death more strong,
Burning 'mid Death's whelming deeps;
By that love that never sleeps,
Save me when the billows throng,
   Snatch me from the yawning grave.
What shall such a wretch as I,
Sinner vile, with heart of stone,—
What, but live to Him alone,
Who not shrunk for me to die,
   This all-guilty soul to save!

Drawn by Thy pure love's sweet breeze,
As Thy fragrant steps I trace,
LORD! Who seest th' unequal race,
Lift and speed my feeble knees,
   Or with step beguiling stay.
All too poor the best I bring;
Limbs of death my soul oppress;
LORD! Thou know'st my nothingness;
Thou my laggard love canst wing,
   Thou Alone canst cleanse my way.

THIRD DECADE.

TUESDAY.—TO THE HANDS.

CHRIST, *of Saints and Angels* LORD!
This world's Light, in Heaven adored,
   Way and Truth and Life to all!
Peace and Health to every son,
Whom Thy dying Love hath won,
   Man of Sorrows, Thee I call.
                       Our Father.
              O Saviour of the world.

Gracious JESU, Shepherd good!
Ah, how faint from Sweat of Blood,
With the heavy Cross how worn
(Many a weary station borne)
   Bear those Hands Thy sinking breast!

Holy Hands, what have ye wrought,
Whence this bitter guerdon brought,
On the Tree's fell branches strung,
With the riving iron wrung,
  Ye that all the world have blest!

Hands! from whom, at either wound,
Run the trickling torrents round,
In your own sad purple dyed,
With the hard nails open'd wide,
  Oh, Salvation's wondrous cost!
Lord, on these, all straitly banded,
In unstraiten'd might expanded,
Fix'd I'll gaze in hour of need,
Nor on fruitless solace feed,
  In vain hope's long mazes lost.

Meetly all to Heaven upheld,
Heaven's own Hands with goodness fill'd!
Hands, whose touch could heal and save,
Ear and tongue, and eye-sight gave,
  Stretch'd to soothe each wounded soul!
Healer of the dead and dying,
On Thy hands, all health supplying,
I will rest my soul's despair,
Nor wilt Thou cast out my prayer,
  Heal me, and I shall be whole.

Lord, in such vast charity
Can I lose my share in Thee?—
From Thy Cross of strengthening balm
Pointing to Thy wreath of palm,
  Lead us on Thy conquering way.
Oh! so rudely rack'd for me,
Draw my every sense to Thee,
Let nor hand, nor head, nor heart
Ever from Thy Cross depart,
  With these Hands Thy servant stay.

Hands, That made and fashioned us,
And, when marr'd, remoulded thus!—
Jesu, for Thy gifts of might,
Wounds of life, and streams of light.
  What shall Thy poor creature yield?
In Thy cleansing Blood made Thine,
Lo, I yield whate'er is mine:
With Thy Staff, sweet Jesu, tend me,
With these fostering Hands defend me,
  And in every peril shield.

FOURTH DECADE.

WEDNESDAY.—TO THE SIDE.

CHRIST, *of Saints and Angels* LORD!
This world's Light, in Heaven ador'd,
  Way and Truth and Life to all!
Peace and Health to every son,
Whom Thy dying Love hath won,
  Man of Sorrows, Thee I call.

Our Father.
O Saviour of the world.

SAVIOUR, Whose all-pitying care
Loved to save, and yearn'd to spare,
Why thus hung with bleeding gashes,
Furrow'd o'er with harrowing lashes,
  On the smarting Cross to die!
Lo, my SAVIOUR's sacred Side,
That enwraps His Love's deep tide,
With the Blood and Water streaming,
With its melting brightness beaming
  O'er these hearts so dark and dry.

Lo, the Side that Thomas hailed
Ere his doubting faith had failed!
Lo, the open gate that leads
To my SAVIOUR's peaceful meads—
  Joyous gate to pastures green!

Here my breathless footsteps wending,
How, so oft, so sore offending,
Should I dare to lift my face,
Didst not Thou, the Fount of grace,
    Draw me to these heights serene?

Fount of Sweetness, never cloying,
The fell serpent's bane destroying!—
Ye that thirst, O, hither flying,
Drink of pleasures never dying,
    Drink of Life's exhaustless well.
Crimson Wound, Thy depths reveal,
Make my heart Thy secrets feel,
How should other thirst enthral me,
What to earth again recall me,
    Might I enter there and dwell?

Oh, how wondrous sweet to me,
JESU, every taste of Thee!
With Thy wondrous Goodness sated,
With Thy Love inebriated,
    Souls would burst their fleshly chain.
Lo, Thy Side all gently clasping,
And with reverent fervour grasping,
Shielded close beneath Thy wing,
Here I'll brave the dragon's sting,
    Here his fiery darts disdain.

Hide me in this healing Cave;
Shroud me in this quiet Grave;
Here shall all my sickness cease,
Here Thy servant rest in peace,
    Here the foe's fierce malice flee.
Let me, LORD, in death's dark hour,
Free from sin's dread guilt and power,
To Thy Side for ever joined,
There with happy souls be shrined,
    From the hunter hid in Thee.

FIFTH DECADE.

THURSDAY.—TO THE BREAST.

CHRIST, *of Saints and Angels* LORD !
This world's Light, in Heaven ador'd,
  Way and Truth and Life to all !
Peace and Health to every son,
Whom Thy dying Love hath won,
  Man of Sorrows, Thee I call.
          Our Father.
        O Saviour of the world.

Glory of the Heavens above,
Earth's true Light, my soul's true Love,
Knocking at Thy Breast I stand;
Life's dread Court, O LORD, expand,
  Let Thy Mercy ope the door.
Here in slave-like guise unknown,
Here is Goodness' royal Throne,
Here the Bliss that fills the Blest,
Here the downcast mourner's Rest,
  Here the Refuge of the poor.

JESU, may Thy Breast of fire
Wean from earth my soul's desire;
May its all enfolding flame
Every wayward wish reclaim;—
  Love's decaying embers light.
Give me, LORD, a breast that's clean,
Tender, cheerful and serene,
Strong and gentle, firm and kind,—
LORD, Thou knowest this fleshbound mind,
  How enchain'd its heavenward flight.

Breast, with heavenly dew distilling,
Earth with sweetest fragrance filling,
These our breasts of heavenly birth,
Soilèd o'er with things of earth,
  In Thy heavenly moisture steep.—

Of the FATHER Brightness Living,
Of the FATHER's Goodness giving,
On these breasts forlorn and poor
Pour of Thine o'erflowing store,
   Give us of that Ocean deep.

Breast of Sweetness infinite,
Give me of Thy strengthening Might,
So may I sin's fetters bursting,
And with love transcendent thirsting,
   Wing from earth my eagle view.—
Yea, 'tis Wisdom's deep abyss,
Whence flow'd forth those streams of bliss,
On the loved Disciple shining,
When upon this Breast reclining,
   He Its hidden mysteries drew.

Here is Goodness' inmost mine,
Here the Godhead's living Shrine,
Here Love weaves her threefold cord;
Of the Trinity adored.
   This the Seat, the glorious Rest.—
Oh, my GOD's most Holy Place,
Ark of Life and Light and Grace!—
LORD, from Whom all goodness flows,
Let us 'neath Thy Saints repose
   Gently on our SAVIOUR's Breast.

SIXTH DECADE.

FRIDAY.—TO THE HEART.

CHRIST, of Saints and Angels LORD!
This world's Light, in Heaven ador'd,
  Way und Truth and Life to all!
Peace and Health to every son,
Whom Thy dying Love hath won,
  Man of Sorrows, Thee I call.
             𝔒ur 𝔉ather.
          𝔒 𝔖aviour of the world.

Holy Heart, divinely Sweet,
Thee with gladsome heart I greet;
Thee with deep delight enfolding,
Thee with single eye beholding,
  All athirst for Heaven and Thee.
Oh, what love this Heart possess'd,
What a burning zeal oppress'd,
When upon Thine own, dear Lord,
Its full fount well-nigh outpour'd
  Thine unfathom'd Charity.

Death, dire Death, whose bitter raving,
Bloody thirst, and savage craving,
Even not Jesus' Self hath spared,
But with baleful dart hath dared
  This most gentle Heart to break!—
By that Death so meekly borne,
By That Heart so rudely torn,
Lord, my every wish and thought,
With Thine own in concert brought,
  To Thy Heart's deep music wake.

In this heart of hearts, dear Lord,
By Thine Own all-quickening Word,
Be Thy heavenly Love engrafted:—
Lord, be mine, from earth upwafted,
  Tranced in Thee in worlds above.
Whoso loves with soul sincere,
He hath ears these words to hear,
Knows how deep that love, how high,
Which for Whom we love can die,
  How than death more strong is Love.

'Tis the life the lover lives,
Knows no lets, true freedom gives;
What the Well-belov'd commands
Prompt essays with eager hands,
  Fears no peril, feels no pain.

Lord, my life's sole object be
With pure heart to follow Thee.
Oh, how true shall be my joy,
Oh, what bliss my praise employ,
  May my soul but Jesus gain!—

Open, Lord, Thy Heart's deep cell,
Thou, Who know'st where mine doth dwell,—
There, from Thee ere Hell can tear me,
World or flesh or fiend ensnare me,
  Shrine my heart, an offering free.
Panting for that Refuge blest,
Where this restless heart may rest,
Nought save Jesus would I know,
Nought desire of things below,
  Nothing love, dear Lord, but Thee.

SEVENTH DECADE.

SATURDAY.—TO THE HEAD.

Christ, *of Saints and Angels* Lord!
This world's Light, in Heaven ador'd,
  Way and Truth and Life to all!
Peace and Health to every son,
Whom Thy dying Love hath won,
  Man of Sorrows, Thee I call.
                  𝔒ur 𝔉ather.
        𝔒 𝔖abiour of the worlᵭ.

Ah, That Head with sharp thorns crown'd,
All adroop, with Bloodstreams drown'd,
With those living bruises scarr'd,
With that shameful spitting marr'd,
  Head, whose beams all Heaven do light!—
Jesu, full of Light and Grace,
Whom Thy foes so sore deface!
Veil'd in horrors how amazing,
On Whose wondrous Beauty gazing,
  Angels veil their raptured sight.

Gracious JESU, whither fled
All the glories of That Head!
Sun, of all Thy radiance shorn :—
How eclipsed, how all forlorn!
   All Thy Form and Beauty gone.
Sweetest JESU, for my sake
Who this guise of shame didst take,
Shine upon me through the cloud,
Show some token, LORD, for good,
   Bless me from Thy Mercy-throne.

Red Thine Eyes, all damp with death,
Blue Thy Lips, unset Thy Teeth,
Swoll'n Thy Cheek with sorest smiting,
Rent Thine Ears with insults biting,
   Which Thy burthened Heart might break.
FATHER, of Thy pardoning Grace,
Look on Thine Anointed's Face,
Oh, behold, with Face appeasèd,
Him in Whom Thou art well pleasèd,
   Save us for His Pity's sake.

JESU, Who, one Royal Head,
Heaven's vast hosts and earth's dost lead,
By that thorn-crown'd Head and scarr'd
Make me, LORD, a soldier hard,
   Of such Head a member meet.
Only by Thy Crown of pain,
I Thy Crown of bliss would gain:
Taught to love Thy bitter Tree,
Make me daily die with Thee,
   Trace through life Thy suffering Feet :

And when death's drear port is near,
Then my sheltering Rock appear :
In that last o'erwhelming hour,
Haste with Thine All-saving Power.
   With Thy stedfast anchor come.

Oh, when Thou shalt call me hence,
Jesu, rise, my soul's Defence,
Let Thy Mercy's bow surround me,
Not Thy Judgment's blaze confound me,
   Spare my deeds their righteous doom.

A RHYTHMICAL HYMN

IN PRAISE OF THE HOLY CROSS.

High toward Heaven the cross upraise ;—
Be the Cross our constant praise,
   Of the Cross, ye liegemen true.—
'Tis the Standard of our war,
Badge of our triumphal car,
   We by This the foe subdue.

Sweet the song, to Heaven 'tis rung,
Sweet the Wood, the royal Rood,
   Meet for sweetest melody.
Be our lips and lives in tune,
Where the lips and life are one,
   Sweet, how sweet, the harmony.

Sing the Cross, the Cross who bear;
Thro' the Cross who joy to share
   Life's high boon to man made free.
Then say all, say every one,
' Hail the world's Salvation,
   Hail, life-giving, healing Tree.'

Oh, how glorious, how divine,
Doth the saving Altar shine,
   In the LAMB's red Life-Blood dyed,—
Spotless LAMB, for sinners slain,
Who from sin's ingrained stain
   All creation purified.

Ladder bright to sinners given,
Step by which the Lord of Heaven
   All things to Himself doth bring.
In its form His mercy tracing
With outstretchèd Arms embracing
   Earth's four confines 'neath His wing.

By Its light what mysteries shine,
Veil'd in types Its power divine,
   Earnests of Its glories true.—
Wood, that made the waters sweet,
Wood, that 'mid the parching heat
   From the rock the waters drew.

For his house no life, no light,
Save whose hand on that dread night
   With the Cross his lintel seal'd.
He the sweeping death-blade turn'd,
He, nor son, nor servant mourn'd
   Shelter'd by this sevenfold shield.

E'en Sarepta's widow poor
Gathering sticks beside the door,
   Might the saving token hail.
How without faith's kindling wood
Nought avail'd her scanty food;
   How her cruse of oil must fail.

Thus in Scripture, in dim picture,
Lie conceal'd, in Christ reveal'd,
   All the boons the Cross hath won.
Kings bow down, and foes are flown.
By It led, 'neath Christ our Head,
   One hath bid his thousands gone.

To Its own the Cross is might,
To true warriors victory bright,
To the sick 'tis health and light :—
   This the powers of Hell restrains.

This to slaves true freedom gives,
Breathes new life through all that lives,
From the curse the world retrieves,
   Till o'er all Its glory reigns.

Fare thee well, triumphal Tree,
This lost world's Salvation be,
In the woods there's none like thee—
   Leaf, flower, bud, not one like thine.
Christian balm for Christian soul,
Save the sound, the sick make whole,
What surpasseth man's control
   Yieldeth to thy charm Divine.

As aloft the Cross we bear,
Hallower of the Cross, O, hear;—
Soldiers 'neath the Cross who fight,
Lead us to Thy crowns of light,
   To Thy Presence-chambers blest.
Who by sufferings wouldst subdue us,
Soften, LORD, those sufferings to us;
And when wrath's dread Day shall come
In Thy pity take us home,
   To Thine Own Eternal Rest.

A RHYTHM

REPRESENTING TO THE ETERNAL FATHER THE LIFE AND PASSION AND MERITS OF CHRIST.

Behold! O GOD our Defender: and look upon the Face of Thine Anointed.—Ps. lxxxiv. 9.

FIRST PART.

Remember, GOD of Might,
That Mercy Infinite,
Which to the world Thy SON Eternal gave!

Remember His own Love,
How from Thy Throne above
Himself an Exile came this exile world to save.

Remember that sweet Name,
CHRIST JESU!—How He came,
Thine own Co-equal Son in Servant's guise!
Remember, how, all mean,
In sinners' likeness seen,
Beneath the Law's stern knife the sinless SAVIOUR lies!

Remember, how array'd,
In the poor manger laid,
The Eastern Kings their sov'ran LORD adore.
Remember Symeon old,
Who to His Mother told
The sword and bitter cup his vision saw in store

Remember, how each day,
The Infant-GOD to slay,
Herod's dark wrath pursues His Childhood weak.
Remember, with what tears,
With what heart-rending fears
The SON so strangely dear the sorrowing parents seek.

Remember, FATHER kind,
With what a patient Mind
Hunger and thirst, and heat and cold He bears.
Remember, how, forlorn,
With weary wanderings worn,
The winds and rains He courts, how hardly fares.
How, livelong nights and days,
He teaches, heals, and prays,
And all our toils untired, and all our sorrows shares.

SECOND PART.

Remember, how their LORD
At that last Paschal board,
Washes, all lowly laid, His servants' feet!

Remember, with what Love,
His Mercy's might to prove,
He offers them Himself the Living Bread to eat.

Remember, with what woe,
What pains, which none may know,
All thrill'd He prays, in the dark garden bow'd!
Great GOD, remember, why,
Through that strong Agony,
His Pores dissolving weave a winding-sheet of Blood!

Remember, with what cries,
What whiles, what angry eyes,
The ruffian throng the meek-eyed LAMB surround.
Remember, with what bands
Those servants' ruthless hands,
Dragg'd like a felon forth, the LORD of Lords have bound.

Remember, where all torn
And bruised in bitter scorn
Thy Holy One on the hard earth they throw!
Remember where He stands,
All bound with blinding bands,
Whilst "Prophesy!" they cry, "Thou CHRIST, who dealt the blow?"

Remember, how bested,
That High and Holy Head,
Teeming with mercies, with sharp thorns is crown'd.
Remember, how all bared,
With stripes and spittle marr'd,
They throw the purple vest His Royal Limbs around.

Remember the rude spite,
That meetly robed in white
His Virgin Frame of gentlest Majesty!
Remember, how abused,
And falsely all accused,
Their GOD is yielded to His people's cry.

Remember that wild strife,
That asks Barabbas' life,
Th' unrighteous one released, the Righteous doom'd to die.

THIRD PART.

Remember, how low bow'd
He bears the Cross's load,
The world of its huge weight of sin to lighten!
Remember, how they pierce
With malice fell and fierce,
And on the racking Cross His innocent Members tighten.

Remember, how, a worm
And no man, yon frail Form,
All weak and worn, aloft in air is lifted.
Remember, in what pangs
Th' Unconquer'd Conqueror hangs,
The Blessed made a curse; the Rock of Ages rifted!

Remember, with what love,
Sent from Thy Heaven above,
Thy Son such base indignities endureth.
Remember with what woes,
What deep maternal throes,
His Mother at that sight her heart's full anguish poureth.

Remember that mild Face,
That Voice of pardoning grace,
In wondrous pity to the robber turning.
Remember, what curst draught
Those tenderest Lips had quaff'd,—
Sharp vinegar and gall to slake that thirst all-burning.

Remember that strong cry
Of death, Eli! Eli!
Which shuddering speaks Thine Own of Thee forsaken.
Remember, as in night
Expires the world's True Light,
The Sun's shock'd eye is closed, the Earth's deep centre
    shaken.

Remember, as the spear
Pierces that Heart so dear,
From the dark Wound the Blood and Water gushing.
Remember, how transfix'd,
With His her sorrows mix'd,
His Mother feels the sword through her cleft heart-strings rushing.

Remember, with what smart
Each sorrow-smitten heart
From the hard Cross His Holy Limbs unbindeth.
Remember, with what pain,
What tears, that scanty train
For the sad Burial His Blessed Body windeth.

Dread God, remember why
Thou didst so sorely try
Thine Holy One for us from Heaven descended.
Remember, from what height
Of Love, and Life, and Light,
To what a depth He came, with grief and shame attended!

Oh! what a Love was there
To draw Him down to bear
Sin's deadliest pains with Soul by sin unwounded.
Full truly in each one
His spotless Glory shone,
His Mercies numberless and Charity unbounded.

Oh! then in those bright Beams,
Those overflowing Streams
Of Charity wash me from sin's stains polluting;
Oh! grant through every heart
From Christ's deep Wounds may dart
His Rays of quickening Grace His seeds of goodness rooting.

TO THE SEVEN EFFUSIONS
OF THE MOST SACRED BLOOD OF JESUS CHRIST,
AGAINST THE SEVEN DEADLY SINS.

I. IN HIS CIRCUMCISION.—AGAINST LUST.

Jesu, Hail! Thy Blood Who pourest,
And the shame and pain endurest
   From Thy tender Infancy.
Oh, ere blasting sin can scathe us,
Heart, and tongue, and senses, swathe us
   In Thy Robe of purity.

II. IN HIS AGONY.—AGAINST PRIDE.

Jesu, Hail! what Blood-sweat weighs Thee,
Bow'd in prayer! what fears amaze Thee,
   For our sin's black burthen borne!
From high thoughts and vauntings wean us,
From the fall in mercy screen us,
   Ever join'd with pride and scorn.

III. IN HIS SCOURGING.—AGAINST ANGER.

Jesu, Hail! while scourges gore Thee,
And Thy Life-Blood trickles o'er Thee,
   All unmoved Thou standest fast.
Sweeten, Lord, Thy Cross unto us,
With Thy gentle scourge subdue us,
   Free from wrath's foul guilt at last.

IV. IN HIS CROWNING.—AGAINST GLUTTONY.

Jesu, Hail! with sharp thorns crown'd,
With Thy Robe of Blood around,
   In Thy royal Purple drest.
To Thy Heavenly Dainties call us,
Let nor flesh nor fiend enthral us,
   To the belly's curst behest.

V. IN THE STRIPPING OFF HIS GARMENTS.—AGAINST COVETOUSNESS.

Jesu, Hail! Lord, as they strip Thee,
Wound by Wound afresh unrip Thee,
   And Thy bleeding Limbs unwind.
Bared Thyself, Blest Jesu, bare us,
From the world's close thraldom tear us,
   And to Thy sole service bind.

VI. IN HIS CRUCIFIXION.—AGAINST SLOTH.

Jesu, Hail! Whose Limbs transfixèd
From Thy cup of woe full mixèd,
   Streams of Love unmingled pour.
Give us of that Love o'erflowing,
Kindling hearts and bosoms glowing
   Which dead sloth shall chill no more.

VII. IN THE PIERCING OF HIS HEART.—AGAINST ENVY.

Jesu, Hail! Whose Heart enlargèd,
With Thy heavenly Love o'erchargèd,
   Opens wide Thy Springs of Grace.
By those Springs our garments whiten,
Cleanse our hearts, our spirits brighten,
   Strangers to dark envy's face.

[SAINT AUGUSTINE.]

Look thou upon the wounds of Him Who hangeth; the Blood of Him Who dieth; the price paid by Him Who redeemeth Thee. His Head is bent to kiss; His Heart laid open to love; His Arms set wide to embrace; His Whole Body laid out to redeem. Think thou how great things are these; weigh them in the balance of thy heart, that He may be fixed Whole in thy heart, Who for thee was fixed Whole upon the Cross.

SALUTATIONS
TO THE FIVE WOUNDS OF CHRIST.

WITH A PETITION FOR THE CHIEF VIRTUES.

TO THE WOUND OF THE RIGHT FOOT.—FOR HUMILITY.

With the Blood of JESUS flowing,
  Hail, blest Wound of Life and Grace.
Grant me, in all goodness glowing
  Free from every sinful trace,
Lowly, true, with zeal deep-glowing
  Aye to love the lowest place.

THE WOUND OF THE LEFT FOOT.—FOR CHASTITY.

With divinest solace weeping,
  Hail, sweet Wound of deep delight;
In Thy cleansing torrent steeping
  This impure and fleshly sprite,
Till Thy chastened calmness reaping
  I with CHRIST may " walk in white."

TO THE WOUND OF THE RIGHT HAND.—FOR OBEDIENCE.

With the Blood of JESUS reeking,
  Hail, sweet wound of His Right Hand.
Give me holiest fervour, seeking
  Ever at Thy beck to stand;
Ever thinking, acting, speaking,
  At my LORD's most blest Command.

TO THE WOUND OF THE LEFT HAND.—FOR MEEKNESS.

With the Blood of JESUS streaming,
  Hail, pure Fount of gentle peace;
'Midst all sorrows brightly beaming;
  Bid each sullen murmur cease:
All who share Thy Love redeeming,
  Make my softened heart embrace.

TO THE WOUND OF THE HEART.—FOR CHARITY.

With acutest Anguish wounded,
  Hail, my Jesu's Heart most sweet.
Gladdened hearts with love unbounded
  Kindling from Thy deep retreat,
Where with living light surrounded,
  Love breathes out her quickening heat.

ON THE SEVEN WORDS UTTERED BY CHRIST ON THE CROSS.

FIRST WORD.

Jesu, Hail! Who, as Thou bleedest,
For Thy cruel murderers pleadest,
  "Father, spare, their sin forgive."
Give us hearts like Thine forgiving,
Tenderest words like Thine conceiving;
  Let no thought of vengeance live.

SECOND WORD.

Jesu, Hail! in Death Who savest,
Who the contrite robber gavest
  Earnest of Thy Blissful Face,
Grant our tears such pleading power,
Now and at our dying hour,
  As may win Thy pardoning Grace.

THIRD WORD.

Jesu, Hail! Thy Mother weeping,
To Thy lov'd Disciple's keeping,
  From Thy Cross Who dost commend;
With like tender love assure us,
With like constant care secure us,
  In all straits our lasting Friend.

FOURTH WORD.

Jesu, Hail! with deathcry shaken,
" Father, why hast Thou forsaken ?"
  In Thy last strong Agony.
Leave us not to fall in death,
Ever till our latest breath
  In all perils stay'd on Thee.

FIFTH WORD.

Jesu, Hail! Whose Word, " I thirst."
Mock Thy foes with draught accurst,
  Thou Who dost all needs supply.
Make us thirst for heavenly Treasures,
Earth's low joys and fleeting pleasures
  Passing with untempted eye.

SIXTH WORD.

Jesu, Hail! Who didst fulfil,
E'en to death Thy Father's Will,
  And to us the fruits dost give.
Lord, to Thee our first thoughts bending,
And in Thee our last works ending,
  In Thy pleasure let us live.

SEVENTH WORD.

Jesu, Hail! Thy Words Who closest,
And Thy Soul out-pour'd reposest
  Meekly in Thy Father's Breast;
By Thy Death's all-cleansing power,
O'er our lives Thy Graces shower,
  Let our ends in Thee be blest.

CHAPTER V.

VARIOUS COLLECTS ON THE PASSION OF OUR LORD.

A MOST DEVOUT COLLECT[1].

Ex prec. German. P. Canisii.

O JESU CHRIST, King of heaven and earth, our most sweet Saviour and Redeemer, I adore and bless Thee for so wonderfully, so lovingly redeeming both me and the whole world by Thy holy Cross. O how excellent, how precious, how prevailing a Victim hast Thou, upon the altar of the Cross, sacrificed for us! How didst Thou toil! how wast Thou straitened, till Thou hast completed the sacrifice Thou hadst begun! Satan of old seduced and ruined us by a tree; Thou, by a tree, hast now subdued the enemy: Thou hast mercifully redeemed us, Thou hast won for us everlasting salvation.

O precious Wood! O prevailing sign! O glorious mystery, worthy of all veneration! O peerless Tree, whence hung the Fruit of life!

Woe, Woe, most loving JESU, how wast Thou weighed down with weariness when all along that rough and steep ascent Thou carriedst Thy heavy Cross, even to Mount Calvary! With what pain and anguish were Thy most sacred Hands and Feet pierced with nails and fastened to the Cross! What did Thy tender Body suffer when stretched thereon, and all Thy limbs were out of joint, and all Thy sinews rent asunder, and all Thy bones were numbered! And why all this, but that Thou mightest do away the handwriting of the decree which was against us, and take it out of the way, fixing it to Thy Cross? That, with Thy sinless Blood, Thou mightest wash away our sins and rescind the sentence of damnation issued against us; and so making peace through the Blood of the Cross, mightest re-unite all things, whether they be things on earth, or things in heaven. (Col. i.)

Wherefore receive me too, O most sweet SAVIOUR, JESUS CHRIST, most faithful Shepherd of my Soul, receive me, Thy unworthy creature,

---

[1] To be said before a representation of CHRIST crucified. ORIG.

Thy poor wandering sheep. Open wide to me Thy Heart and Wounds; in them let me and all my miseries and sins be hidden and perfectly cleansed. Crucify in me my flesh with its affections and lusts: extinguish all pride and vanity, and root out all evil passions: renew a right spirit within me: kindle within me an earnest and effectual will for every good work, and so true a love for Thee Alone, so devout a worship and such unwearied service, that all other glorying may be far from me, save glorying in the Cross of my LORD JESUS CHRIST, by Whom the world is crucified unto me, and I unto the world. Thou hast said, When I am lifted up from the earth, I will draw all unto Me; draw *me*, O LORD, after Thee, that nothing may ever part me from Thee, Who wast lifted up upon the Cross for me, and camest not down therefrom till Thou hadst fully completed the work of my salvation. Amen.

SHORT AND FERVENT COLLECTS TO CHRIST SUFFERING.

O JESU CHRIST, my only SAVIOUR, Thy Death and most bitter Passion was for me; let it not be without its fruit and useless to me, miserable sinner. By all Thy shame, by Thy most agonizing Death and wounded Heart, give me Thy grace, now and in the hour of death. Amen.

II. O JESU CHRIST, SAVIOUR of the world, the Crucified, between Thy strict judgment and my wretched soul interpose Thy sorrows, Thy precious Blood and Death, and all Thy loving-kindness. Amen.

III. O good Shepherd, JESU CHRIST, Who dost cleanse and feed Thy sheep with Thine own precious Blood, may the plenteous outpouring of Thy most holy Blood be to me and to all poor sinners comfort and salvation. Amen.

IV. O innocent LAMB of GOD, Who by Thy Death and Crucifixion takest away the sins of the world; by Thy innocence, by Thy agonies, by Thy pangs and distress of soul upon the Cross, spare me in the awful day of judgment, and have pity on the living and the dead. Amen.

V. O SON, obedient to

God the Father! Who so promptly and cheerfully drankest Thy fearful Cup of Passion, and hadst gall and vinegar given Thee in Thy Thirst: by all Thy racking agonies and wounds make me gentle and patient and obedient to the Everlasting Father, even unto death. Amen.

VI. O Jesu, our High Priest, Who offeredst to God the Father a pure oblation, mighty to reconcile sinners unto God: by the infinite merits of Thy Life, Thy Passion and Death, make me die to the world and live to Thee Alone, and then, let Thy servant depart in peace. Amen.

VII. O Jesu of Nazareth, King of the Jews, by the victory and triumph won on the Cross against Thy enemies and ours, save me from mine. Guard from all peril my soul and body. Give Thy Church peace and concord, to the departed pardon and rest, to sinners repentance and forgiveness, grace and mercy to all. Amen.

BRIEF PRAYERS ON THE PASSION, BY ST. GREGORY.

1. O Lord Jesu Christ, I adore Thee hanging on the Cross and wearing on Thy Head the crown of thorns; I beseech Thee that Thy Cross may deliver me from the destroying angel. Amen.
Our Father. Glory be.

2. O Lord Jesu Christ, I adore Thee wounded on the Cross and given gall and vinegar to drink: I beseech Thee that Thy Wounds may be the medicine of my soul. Amen.
Our Father. Glory be.

3. O Lord Jesu Christ, I pray Thee by that bitterness of Thy Passion, which Thou sufferedst at the hour of death, and then above all when Thy most holy Soul passed forth from Thy blessed Body; pity my soul when it is departing out of my body, and bring it to everlasting life. Amen.
Our Father. Glory be.

4. O Lord Jesu Christ, I adore Thee laid in the sepulchre, embalmed with myrrh and spices: I beseech Thee that Thy Death may be my life. Amen.
Our Father. Glory be.

5. O Lord Jesu Christ, I adore Thee descending into hell and delivering thence Thy captives: I beseech

§ vi.] ON THE LIFE AND PASSION OF OUR LORD. 87

Thee, suffer me not to enter there. Amen.

Our FATHER. Glory be.

6. O LORD JESU CHRIST, I adore Thee rising from the dead, ascending into heaven, and sitting at the Right Hand of the FATHER: I beseech Thee that I may be found worthy to follow Thee thither and dwell in Thy Presence. Amen.

Our FATHER. Glory be.

7. O LORD JESU CHRIST, the Good Shepherd, guard Thou the just, justify sinners, have mercy on all the faithful, and be gracious to me, miserable, wretched sinner. Amen.

Our FATHER. Glory be.

PRAYER.

I beseech Thee, O LORD JESU CHRIST, let Thy Passion be my strength, whereby I may be fenced, protected, and defended: let Thy Wounds be my food and drink, whereby I may be fed, inebriated, and delighted: let the sprinkling of Thy Blood wash out all my sins: let Thy Death be to me endless glory. In these let me find my refreshment, exultation, health, longing, joy, gladness, and desire, both in soul and body, now and for ever. Amen.

ANOTHER PRAYER.

O LORD JESU CHRIST, SON of the living GOD, interpose Thy Passion, Cross, and Death, between Thy judgment and my soul, now and in the hour of my death.

Vouchsafe to give me grace and mercy, pardon to the living, rest to the dead, peace to Thy Church, and to all sinners life and everlasting glory: Who livest and reignest, &c.

MOST DEVOUT PRAYERS OF ST. BRIDGET ON THE PASSION OF CHRIST.

COLLECT I.

O JESU CHRIST, uncloying sweetness of them that love Thee, and thrilling joy far passing all that joys and all that heart desires, the Health and Lover of poor sinners, Who hast testified, by becoming Man for man, that Thy delight is to be with the sons of men; call to mind that drear foreboding and most inward sorrow, which, as the time (foreordained by Thy love, O GOD) of Thy health-giving Passion neared, made Thy human Soul exceeding heavy, even unto death.

Call to mind the sadness and the bitterness that filled Thy Soul, and whereof Thou spakest when at the last supper Thou gavest Thy disciples Thy Body and Thy Blood, washedst their feet and gently mingledst comfort with the announcement of Thy coming Passion.

Call to mind all the shuddering, the straitness, and the woe, borne in Thy tender Body before the Passion of Thy Cross, when after Thy threefold prayer and Bloody Sweat Thou wast betrayed by Thy disciple Judas, seized by the chosen people, charged by false witnesses, unjustly judged by three unrighteous judges, and (in the elect city, at the paschal season, and in the prime of manhood) wast condemned, although innocent, stripped of Thine own garments, and arrayed in strange apparel, wast buffeted and blindfold, wast rent with blows, bound to a pillar and scourged, crowned with thorns, smitten with a reed upon Thy Head, and assailed with numberless reproaches.

And when Thou callest to mind what Thou sufferedst before they nailed Thee to Thy Cross, grant me, I beseech Thee, O LORD GOD, before my death, true contrition; full confession, worthy satisfaction, and remission of all my sins. Amen.

Our FATHER. Glory be.

COLLECT II.

O JESU, Maker of the world, Whom no measure can reach nor bound contain, and Who containest the earth in a span, call to mind the anguish of Thy torment, when the Jews drove blunt nails through Thy most holy Hands into the Cross, and how they added agony on agony to Thy Wounds, when to fit Thy Body for their purpose and nail through Thy tender Feet, they wrenched Thee so upon the Cross's length and breadth, that all Thy limbs were out of joint.

I implore Thee by the memory of Thy Cross's hallowed and most bitter anguish, make me fear Thee, make me love Thee. Amen.

Our FATHER. Glory be.

COLLECT III.

O JESU, heavenly Physician, call to mind the languor, the deathliness, the woe, which, when raised aloft upon the Cross, Thou sufferedst in all Thy rended limbs: when all were wrenched asunder, and from the sole of the foot even unto the head there was no wholeness in Thee, and no sorrow could be found like unto Thy sorrow; and yet, wholly unmindful of all Thy griefs Thou prayedst the FATHER for Thine enemies, and saidst so lovingly, "FATHER, forgive them, for they know not what they do."

By this Thy mercy, by the memory of Thy sorrow, grant me that this remembrance of Thy most bitter Passion may be the full remission of all my sins. Amen.

Our FATHER. Glory be.

COLLECT IV.

O JESU, true Liberty of Angels, and Paradise of delights, call to mind that heaviness and shuddering of Thine, when Thy cruel enemies, like ravening lions, beset Thee, assailing Thee with cuffs and spitting, with their sharp nails and every pain they could invent, unheard before.

By these pains, by all the reproachful gibes, by the cruel tortures which Thy enemies, LORD JESU, put upon Thee, save me, I pray Thee, and set me free from my enemies I see around me: grant me, under the shadow of Thy wings, to come to perfect and everlasting safety. Amen.

Our FATHER. Glory be.

COLLECT V.

O JESU, Mirror of everlasting charity, call to mind that grief of Thine, when in the mirror of Thy deep serenity Thou beheldest the predestination of Thine Elect, whom the merits of Thine Agony should save, and the reprobation of the wicked, for their own demerits, damned; and by the depth of Thy compassion, whereby Thou feltest for us, lost and ruined sinners, and which Thou showedst on the Cross, in Thy saying to the robber, "To-day shalt thou be with me in Paradise;" I pray Thee, JESU, deal with me in mercy at the hour of my death. Amen.

Our FATHER. Glory be.

COLLECT VI.

O KING most lovely, and Loving One most dear, call

to mind that grief of Thine, when bare and pitiful Thou hangedst on the Cross, and all Thy friends and acquaintance set themselves against Thee; when Thou foundest none to comfort Thee, save only Thy dear Mother, who still stood by Thee in the bitterness of her soul, and whom Thou commendedst to Thy disciple, and saidst to her, "Woman, behold thy son!"

I pray Thee, most loving JESU, by that Sword of grief that then passed through her soul, have compassion with me in all my distresses and afflictions of soul or body, and give me comfort in the time of trouble and the hour of my death. Amen.

Our FATHER. Glory be.

COLLECT VII.

O JESU, unfailing Spring of love, Who from the lowest depth thereof saidst upon the Cross, "I thirst," even for man's salvation: Kindle the desires of our hearts for every perfect work: allay and staunch in us wholly the thirst of fleshly lust, and all the feverishness of this world's pleasures. Amen.

Our FATHER. Glory be.

COLLECT VIII.

O JESU, very Sweetness to the heart and soul, by the bitterness of the gall and vinegar which for us Thou tastedst, grant us, at the hour of our death, worthily to receive Thy Body and Blood, to the healing and refreshment of our souls. Amen.

Our FATHER. Glory be.

COLLECT IX.

O JESU, royal in Thy might and thrilling in Thy Presence in the soul, call to mind that sore distress and agony of Thine, when forlorn and desolate in the bitterness of death, and assailed by the Jews with gibes, Thou criedst with a loud Voice to Thy FATHER, "My GOD, My GOD, why hast Thou forsaken Me?" By this sore distress, forsake us not in our distresses, O LORD our GOD. Amen.

Our FATHER. Glory be.

COLLECT X.

O JESU, Alpha and Omega, everlasting Life and Strength, call to mind how from the sole of Thy Foot even to Thy Head, Thou didst drown

§ vi.] ON THE LIFE AND PASSION OF OUR LORD. 91

Thyself for us in the waters of Thy Passion.

By Thy Wounds, in their length and in their breadth, teach me, drowned though I am in sins, to keep Thy exceeding broad commandment, by perfect charity. Amen.

Our FATHER. Glory be.

COLLECT XI.

O JESU, unfathomed Depth of loving pity, by Thy Wounds in all their depth, which pierced even to Thy Heart and the marrow of Thy bones, raise me out again from the floods of my sins, and hide me in the opening of Thy Wounds, O LORD, from the presence of Thine anger, till it be passed by. Amen.

Our FATHER. Glory be.

COLLECT XII.

O JESU, Mirror of truth, Sign of unity and Bond of charity, call to mind the multitude of Thy uncounted wounds which covered Thee from the sole of Thy Foot even unto Thy Head; and how sore a grief Thy Virgin Flesh, red with Thy most holy Blood, endured for us! O loving JESU, what more couldest Thou have done than what Thou hast?

Write, with Thy most precious Blood, I pray Thee, LORD JESU, all Thy Wounds upon my heart; and in them let me read Thy grief and Death, and for ever give Thee thanks even to the end. Amen.

Our FATHER. Glory be.

COLLECT XIII.

O JESU, Almighty Lion, King Eternal and Invincible, call to mind that grief of Thine when Thy heart-strings brake, and all Thy strength gave way, and, bowing Thy Head, Thou saidst, "It is finished."

By this distress and anguish, pity me at my last end, when my course is finished, when my soul is sore amazed, and my spirit is in trouble. Amen.

Our FATHER. Glory be.

COLLECT XIV.

O JESU, Only-Begotten of the Most Highest FATHER, Brightness and Image of His Substance, call to mind that strong yearning effort when Thou criedst to the FATHER, "Into Thy Hands I commend

My Spirit;" when, with a torn Body, Thy heart-strings broke, and all the bowels of Thy love exposed for our redemption, with one mighty cry Thou gavest up the ghost. Amen.

By this most precious Death, I pray thee, King of Saints, give me strength to withstand flesh and blood, the world and the devil, that being dead to the world I may live to Thee; and in the last hour of my departure look on my wandering and banished soul that would return to Thee, and take it to Thyself. Amen.

Our Father. Glory be.

COLLECT XV.

O Jesu, true and faithful Vine, call to mind the overflowing outpoured streams of Blood, which, like the juice of the ripe grape, Thou sheddedst largely forth, when Thou troddest the wine-press on the Cross Alone, and from Thy Side, pierced by the soldier's lance, didst so pledge us in water and Blood, that no single drop remained within Thee, and Thou hangedst like a bundle of myrrh on high, and Thy Flesh was parched, and Thy moisture dried, and the marrow of Thy Bones was withered.

By this most bitter Passion and precious Blood-shedding, receive my soul, O loving Jesu, in my agony of death. Amen.

Our Father. Glory be.

CONCLUSION.

O Lord Jesu Christ, Son of the Living God, receive this my prayer, for the sake of that surpassing love whereby Thou sufferedst all the Wounds of Thy most holy Body, and have mercy upon me Thy servant; and to all sinners and all the faithful, as well the living as the dead, grant mercy and grace, remission of sins, and everlasting life. Amen.

PRAYER ON THE SEVERAL POINTS OF THE PASSION.

O God, Who for the redemption of the world, didst vouchsafe to be born, circumcised, rejected of the Jews, betrayed by the traitor Judas with a kiss, bound with cords, and led as an innocent lamb to the sacrifice; Who wast shamefully exposed in the presence of Annas, Caiaphas, Pilate, and Herod, accused by false witnesses, tormented with scourgings and reproaches, spit upon, crowned with thorns, buffeted, smitten with a reed, blindfolded, stripped, nailed to the Cross, lifted up on the Cross, numbered among thieves, made to drink vinegar and gall, and wounded with a spear; do Thou, O GOD, by these Thy most holy Pains, which I Thine unworthy servant call to mind, and by Thy holy Cross and Death, deliver me from the pains of hell, and vouchsafe to lead me whither Thou didst lead the thief who was crucified with Thee; Who livest and reignest with the FATHER and the HOLY GHOST for ever and ever. Amen.

A MOST EARNEST PRAYER BEFORE THE CROSS.

Most gracious and loving JESU, lo, I come to Thee for refuge; lo, I return to Thee All-loving; but I am covered with shame, yea, overtaken with confusion, when I look on these Thy Wounds and see Thy Crown of thorns, and remember that for my sake Thou sufferedst all these things. It is I, even I, who smote Thee with these cruel wounds; it is I, who pressed these thorns into Thy sacred Temples; even I, who nailed Thee to this Cross.

O who shall tell Thy love, who shall tell Thy mercy and Thy pity? It was I who sinned, and the punishment fell on Thee, and Thou hast paid the penalty of death for me. I was Thy enemy; by Thy Cross Thou makest me a son: I was a slave; by Thy Blood Thou claimes for me freedom.

O that Thou wouldest once light up the flame of Thy love within me, that I might wholly burn therewith; then will I, who owe Thee myself and all I have, cheerfully spend for Thee this my very life! Amen.

CHAPTER VI.
VARIOUS EXERCISES.
IN HONOUR OF THE FIVE WOUNDS AND THE SEVEN EFFUSIONS OF BLOOD, OF OUR LORD JESUS CHRIST.

TWO ROSARIES

OF OUR LORD JESUS CHRIST, WHICH MAY BE SAID EITHER IN MEMORY OF THE SHEDDINGS OF THE BLOOD OF CHRIST JESU, OR IN HONOUR OF HIS FIVE SACRED WOUNDS.

The first Rosary consists of seven decades, as follows:—
After the Apostles' Creed, I believe, &c., *say for each decade, first, the* LORD's *Prayer, and then, the following salutation ten times, varied only in each decade according to each special mystery of the shedding of* CHRIST's *Blood, in order.*

Hail most sweet LORD JESU CHRIST, full of grace, with Thee is mercy. Blessed is Thy most holy Life, Thy Passion, and Thy Death; and blessed is Thy Blood, which for us Thou sheddedst.

Add after each salutation,
In the 1st *Decade:* In Thy Circumcision.
In the 2nd, In Thy Agony.
In the 3rd, In Thy Scourging.
In the 4th, In Thy Crowning with thorns.
In the 5th, In the stripping off Thy garments.
In the 6th, In Thy Crucifixion.
In the 7th, In the opening of Thy Side.

This Rosary may be seasoned with many holy affections, aspirations, and resolves; each decade, for example, may be directed against one of the seven deadly sins, or, to obtain one of those principal graces of CHRIST, *which Canisius, Costerus, and others are constantly setting forth. Thus in the first decade we may pray for,*
1st, CHRIST's Humility.
In the 2nd, for His Meekness.
In the 3rd, for His Patience.

In the 4*th,* for His Obedience.
In the 5*th,* for His Kindness.
In the 6*th,* for His Charity.
In the 7*th,* for His Bounty.

And this may be done by adding in each salutation the appropriate title to our LORD's *Name* ;—1. Hail, most Humble LORD JESUS CHRIST; 2. Hail, Most Meek; 3. Most Patient; 4. Most Obedient; 5. Most Kind; 6. Most Loving; 7. Most Bountiful.

Again it may be said with reference to the seven gifts of the HOLY GHOST; *or, for the seven blessings contained in the* LORD's *Prayer.*

The other Rosary, which has reference to the five most sacred Wounds of CHRIST, *consists of five Decades. It is the same as the last, only at the end of each Salutation, after* Thou sheddedst, *is said,*

In the 1*st Decade,* From the Wound of Thy Right Foot.
In the 2*nd,* From the Wound of Thy Left Foot.
In the 3*rd,* From the Wound of Thy Right Hand.
In the 4*th,* From the Wound of Thy Left Hand.
In the 5*th,* From the Wound of Thy Heart.

Here, therefore, is an easy and most profitable means, and one most pleasing to GOD, *of daily calling to mind the Passion of our* LORD JESUS CHRIST, *the mysteries whereof are thus most readily brought to mind.*

SEVEN THANKSGIVINGS

FOR THE SEVEN EFFUSIONS OF OUR LORD'S BLOOD AGAINST THE SEVEN DEADLY SINS.

I.

O most humble LORD and Master, JESU CHRIST, Very GOD and Very Man, everlasting praise and thanksgiving be to Thee, for that in Thy tenderest age, on the eighth day of Thy mortal life, Thou vouchsafedst to shed Thy precious and innocent Blood for us, and be made by painful circumcision a true son of Abraham.

By this most holy shedding of Thy Blood, I beg of Thee the grace of humility, against all pride and this world's vanity.

Our FATHER. Hail most sweet LORD.

II.

O Thou, Whose love is like the pelican's for her little ones, JESU CHRIST, Very GOD and Very Man, everlasting praise and thanksgiving be to Thee, for that in the garden so sore wast Thou bested that Thou pouredst forth a Bloody Sweat, and, in full resignation to die for us, didst offer it to Thy FATHER.

By this most holy shedding of Thy Blood, I beg of Thee the grace of bountifulness, against all coveting and avarice.

Our FATHER. Hail most sweet LORD.

III.

O most chaste Spouse, JESU CHRIST, Very GOD and Very Man, everlasting praise and thankgiving be to Thee, for that in Pilate's judgment hall Thou didst suffer Thyself to be bound, and Thy virgin flesh to be, O how cruelly, scourged and mangled.

By this most holy shedding of Thy Blood, I pray Thee for the grace of chastity, against all luxuriousness and lust.

Our FATHER. Hail.

IV.

O most gentle Lamb, JESU CHRIST, Very GOD and Very Man, everlasting praise and thanksgiving be to Thee, for that Thou didst suffer Thy sacred Hand to be crowned with piercing thorns, which the blows of a hard reed drove still further in Thy Temples.

By this most holy shedding of Thy Blood, I pray Thee for the grace of meekness, against all wrath and desire of revenge.

Our FATHER. Hail.

V.

O most sweet and abstinent Guest, JESU CHRIST, Very GOD and Very Man, everlasting praise and thanksgiving be to Thee, for suffering Thy garments to be torn from off Thee, which both before and after the carrying of Thy Cross opened Thy Wounds again, and widened them most agonizingly.

By this most holy shedding of Thy Blood, I implore Thee for the grace of temperance and abstinence, against all greediness and gluttony.

Our FATHER. Hail.

VI.

O gracious and most faithful Samaritan, JESU CHRIST, Very GOD and Very Man, everlasting praise and thanksgiving be to Thee, for that of Thy burning love for us Thou didst suffer Thy Hands and Feet to be fastened to the Cross, and to be pierced through for our redemption.

By this most holy shedding of Thy Blood, I earnestly implore the grace of brotherly love, against all envy and ill-will.

Our FATHER. Hail.

VII.

O most zealous High Priest, JESU CHRIST, Very GOD and Very Man, everlasting praise and thanksgiving be to Thee, for that Thou didst suffer Thy sacred Side to be pierced, opened, and wounded with the spear.

By this most holy shedding of Thy Blood, I meekly pray Thee for the grace of holy zeal and fervour, against all weariness and irksomeness in Thy service and every exercise of piety.

Our FATHER. Hail.

ACT OF RESIGNATION,

WITH REFERENCE TO THE FIVE WOUNDS OF OUR SAVIOUR.

I.

O most gracious JESU, to the most sweet Wound of Thy Right Foot, from my heart of hearts, I offer all the pleasant and prosperous things which the kind counsel of Thy Providence may order for me; and myself along with them, I so unite to Thy holy Will, as to desire that I may never by any temptation be severed or rent away from it, to all eternity.

Our FATHER. Hail.

II.

O most gracious JESU, in the most sweet Wound of Thy Left Foot I hide all the troubles and adversities, distresses and disappointments, which, throughout my life, Thy Divine Providence may send, or may allow to come upon me: and uniting them with Thy most bitter dolours, this one thing I desire, that my light affliction, which is but for a moment, may work out for me an everlasting weight of glory in the heavens.

Our FATHER. Hail.

III.

O most gracious JESU, next in the most sweet Wound of Thy Right Hand, I lay up all the works which Thy grace shall enable me to do: and so entirely do I devote and consecrate them to Thy honour and glory, as to desire that no vain-glory may mar them, but that a full and plenteous reward may be laid up for me, and await me in the heavens.

Our FATHER. Hail.

IV.

O most gracious JESU, in the most sweet Wound of Thy Left Hand, I bury all my sins and wickednesses, with one entreaty, that Thou wouldest so efface them and blot them out by Thy ruddy Blood, which Thou sheddedst for us, that they accuse me not before Thy judgment seat, nor require from Thee, the righteous Judge, a sentence of damnation against me.

Our FATHER. Hail.

V.

O most gracious JESU, into that Wounded Heart of Thine, full of love, I resign my heart with all its attachments and affections: so steep it in Thy Divine love and draw it unto Thee, that it depart not henceforth one tittle from Thy commandments. Amen.

Our FATHER. Hail.

ANOTHER EXERCISE

ON THE FIVE WOUNDS.

I.

O most meek JESU, by the health-giving Wound of Thy Right Foot, forgive me all the evil thoughts wherewith I have offended Thee ; and by its infinite merits supply all that my neglect of holy thoughts has left deficient : so may I henceforth desire Thee alone, my sole chief Good, and seek and find Him Whom my soul loveth. Amen.

Our FATHER. Hail.

II.

O most sweet JESU, by the blessed Wound of Thy Left Foot, forgive me, I pray Thee, all that I have done amiss against Thy Divine good-pleasure, by evil imaginations or abuse of my outward senses: keep my thoughts in check henceforth by Thy holy fear, that so, becoming dead to the world and all created things, I may feel nothing and desire nothing, save Thee only, my God, crucified for me. Amen.

Our FATHER. Hail.

III.

O most sweet JESU, by the sacred Wound of Thy Right Hand, I most meekly pray Thee, forgive all my evil and sinful acts ; yea, and by its merits supply all that I have by guilty negligence, in whatever duty, left undone : and henceforth may I, by Thy grace, trade more profitably with the talents Thou hast given me. Amen.

Our FATHER. Hail.

IV.

O most Sweet JESU, by the Wound of Thy Left Hand, forgive my passionateness, my sudden angers and acts of impatience, into which I run so heedlessly and headlong, on the slightest provocation ; and from the rich stores of that heavenly Wound, deal out to me the balm of patience in all adversities, that I may be found worthy to inherit the land of the living which Thou hast promised to the meek. Amen.

Our FATHER. Hail.

V.

O most Sweet JESU, by the sacred Wound of Thy pierced Heart, graciously forgive all that my heart hath ever sinned, by perverse will or ill intention ; and so implant my frail heart in

Thine, O my God, that it may feel nothing, compass nothing, desire nothing, other than Thine Own; thus may it repose for ever, guided by Thine, and stedfastly persevere in all good, even to the end of life. Amen.

Our Father. Hail.

OBLATION

OF THE LORD'S PASSION, AND THE FIVE WOUNDS OF OUR SAVIOUR, TO GOD THE FATHER.

O most merciful Father, everlasting God, both for my sins and those of the whole world, I offer to Thee Thy well-beloved Son, hanging on the Cross. I offer to Thee His most sacred Wounds, which He received for our sake. I offer to Thee His Passion, woes, anguish, and misery, His Blood and Death in union with that burning love wherewith He offered Himself for us on the Altar of the Cross; giving myself up in union with Him to Thy Divine service; binding and pledging myself for ever to the praise and glory of Thy Divine Majesty. Amen.

I believe.

I.

O most merciful Father, the bleeding Wound and the painful toils borne by Thy well-beloved Son's Right Hand, I offer to Thee in atonement for all my rebellion and disobedience: most fervently praying that from Him Thou wilt infuse into me the spirit of perfect obedience, that I may as promptly follow the least sign of Thy good pleasure, as the shadow goes with the body, and henceforth love and seek and do Thy Will in all things. Amen.

Our Father. Hail.

II.

O most merciful Father, the Sacred painful Wound of Thy well-beloved Son's Left Hand and His profound humility, I offer Thee, in atonement for my pride and vain-glory, and all my sins that sprout from that rank root; devoutly praying Thee, by virtue of this Wound, utterly to pluck up and destroy in me all vanity and swelling thoughts, that knowing thoroughly my own vileness, I may, with true humility, in evil report, contempt and shame, serve Thee joyfully. Amen.

Our FATHER. Hail.

III.

O most merciful FATHER, the bleeding Wound, and the torturing anguish of Thy well-beloved SON's Right Foot and His most perfect patience, I offer Thee, in atonement for my cowardliness and impatience; praying Thee to give me the grace and virtue of Christian constancy and unwearied endurance, that so I may receive with thanksgiving whatever Thy Hand may send of calamity or distress in this life, may bear it patiently, overcome it manfully, and in every change and chance of life, may, with simple trust and resignation, cast myself and all I have into the arms of Thy good Providence. Amen.

Our FATHER. Hail.

IV.

O most merciful FATHER, the Sacred Wound of Thy well-beloved SON's Left Foot, and His most loving mercy, I offer Thee, in atonement for all my hardness, harshness, and envy: praying Thee to supply me, out of this Wound, as out of a most rich treasure-house of all virtues, with all feelings of kindness, love, compassion, and meekness, specially towards such as may have offended or injured me, that I may embrace them in need with the bowels of charity, be ever ready to give them help, and to support their weaknesses and failings with the spirit of gentleness. Amen.

Our FATHER. Hail.

V.

O most merciful FATHER, the ruddy Wound of Thy well-beloved SON's Blessed Heart and Side, and His most burning love wherewith He loved both Thee and man, I offer Thee, in atonement for all the wearisomeness, lukewarmness, and drowsiness in my services to Thee; most earnestly imploring Thee, out of this most over-flowing fount of grace to infuse into me such zeal for Thy honour and worship, that I may love Thee with my whole heart, and in all I do, hallow and bless from my soul Thy Holy Name; think of Thee Alone, desire Thee Alone, strive to please Thee Alone, and fear to displease Thee, and gladly and joyfully spend all my life only to Thy glory. Amen.

Our FATHER. Hail.

Receive, most merciful FATHER, this oblation of myself to the hallowed Wounds of JESUS CHRIST Thy SON, those divine remedies for our recovery, and monuments of Thy love: and out of them grant me grace, living and dying, safely and securely to lie hid under their shelter and protection, till finally, with all Thy Blessed, I may be worthy to contemplate them in the glory of Thy Majesty, and praise Thee for them for ever. Amen.

Our FATHER. Hail.

DEVOUT SALUTATIONS

OF OUR SAVIOUR'S WOUNDS.

I.

Hail, Wound of the Right Hand of my crucified LORD JESUS CHRIST, blessed above all, trickling with ruddy Blood for my salvation and that of all mankind: shield me, O LORD, and save me with Thy Right Hand, and let it smite my Satanic enemy, lest he say, I have prevailed against him, whom Thou redeemedst with Thy Blood. Let Thy Right Hand lead me marvellously, that all my thoughts, words, and deeds may ever be directed straight unto Thee as their aim and end. Grant me ever to carry my lamp burning and supplied with the oil of charity, that so I may be accounted worthy to be admitted with Thee to Thy heavenly marriage-feast, and, when Thou comest to judge the world, to be set at Thy Right Hand, and hear with Thine elect, Come, ye blessed of My FATHER, inherit the kingdom prepared for you from the foundation of the world. Amen.

Our FATHER. Hail.

II.

Hail, blissful Wound of the Left Hand of my LORD and SAVIOUR JESUS CHRIST, purple with most precious Blood. O LORD, with Thy mighty Hand and stretched-out Arm, bring to nought all the unjust, sinister, and perverse designs which my enemies intend against me. Quench the strength of them that hate me, and that take counsel against my soul. Defend me and stand by me in all my troubles and adversities; and from all evils past, present, or to come, graciously deliver me. Deliver me from the hand of them that persecute me, and that hate me without a cause. Say unto my soul, I am thy salvation; let them perish that are eager to destroy me; and let me, being delivered out of the hand of my enemies, serve Thee in holiness and righteousness all the days of my life. Amen.

Our FATHER. Hail.

III.

Hail, gracious Blood-besprinkled Wound of the Right Foot of my LORD JESUS CHRIST, the Spotless Lamb That taketh away the sins of the world. Make my feet, O LORD, as hart's feet, to run unwearied the way of Thy commandments, and to seek evermore whatsoever Thy Divine Will would have me do. Order my steps in Thy law, and in the works of Thy commandments, that I may go from strength to strength till I see the GOD of gods in Sion. Be Thy word a light to my feet and a lantern to my paths, that I may be to my neighbours also an example of light, and Thou, my GOD, mayest be glorified in all and above all, now, henceforth, and for ever. Amen.

Our FATHER. Hail.

IV.

Hail, venerable Wound, all wet with purple Blood, of the Left Foot of my LORD JESUS CHRIST: draw my feet, O LORD, out of the net that my enemies have laid about me: keep my soul from falling, that they make me not their prey. Let not the foot of pride be my portion, let me not be high-minded, or my looks be proud, nor let me exercise myself in great matters which are too high for me; but in simplicity of heart may I walk before Thee for ever. Lead me, O LORD, in the paths of righteousness; and teach me Thy ways, that I may at all times know what is pleasing in Thy sight, and gladly perform all that Thou commandest me. Amen.

Our FATHER. Hail.

v.

Hail, most health-bringing Wound of the Side and Heart of my LORD JESUS CHRIST, inflicted by the soldier's cruel spear, and running with a copious stream of Blood and water to wash away our sins: wound my heart, I beseech Thee, with the shaft of Thy love, that it may, in all things, and above all, worship, venerate, and honour Thee; and, for Thy sake, and Thine only, love the brotherhood, with a Christian brother's love. Cleanse my heart with that most pure Blood and healthful water, that, being cleansed from all spot of sin, I may be found worthy, O GOD my SAVIOUR, to behold Thee, Whom the pure in heart alone shall see, throughout eternity. Amen.

Our FATHER. Hail.

TO CHRIST,

To obtain devotion towards His most sacred Wounds.

i.

O JESU, sweetest Spouse of holy souls, kindle my heart with the fire of Thy Divine Love and of Thy healthful Wounds, that my whole heart may love Thee: visit me in mercy, and let Thy grace inebriate my soul; for my inmost heart burns for Thee, the Fount of Sweetness. O fire, that sweetly burnest, secretly enlightenest, mightily kindlest, take possession of my heart in all its breadth, with the remembrance of Thy most sacred

Wounds, that I may hunger and thirst only for Thee, Who sufferedst and was wounded for me; may sigh and pant for Thee; and burn with desire to behold Thy countenance melting with sweetness, sweeter than the honey. Amen.

Our FATHER. Hail.

II.

Pierce, O Lovely JESU, the marrow of my soul with the sweetly-penetrating arrow of Thy love, that my heart of hearts, wounded with love for Thee and for Thy wounds, may languish for Thee, and wholly melted into Thy love may lose its own substance, and pass forth all into Thee, and be inseparably joined to Thee. Amen.

Our FATHER. Hail.

III.

Wean my soul, O LORD, from all earthly creatures, that it may be free to give itself to Thee and to the Wounds which Thou receivedst for me: and as Thou art its rightful Owner and Master, dwell therein Alone.

May the remembrance of Thy sweet Death and Passion sink therein, and may that ineffable fragrance of Thy Love awake in me pure and heavenly aspirations and desires, that, as the hart desireth the water-brooks, my soul may long after Thee, O GOD. Amen.

Our FATHER. Hail.

IV.

Grant, LORD JESU, that I may be wholly kindled with burning devotion towards Thy awful Wounds, and repay Thy love with my entire heart: as Thou hast loved me, may I love Thee, O only Salvation of my soul; yea, I will love Thee all I can, for Thou hast first so loved me as to die for me, and by Thy Death and Wounds I will live in Thee. Amen.

Our FATHER. Hail.

V.

O most lovely JESU, most precious Spouse of Souls, marked with five special and conspicuous Wounds, like so many traces of Thy love; write on the table of my heart, print there indelibly, in characters which no forgetfulness may hide, the sweet affection for Thy Wounds: and, kindled with desire for Thee, may I burn in the fire of Thy Love, and be all absorbed in the ocean of Thy Goodness, till Thou take me up to contemplate for ever Thy Majesty and the glory of Thy most hallowed Wounds in heaven. Amen.

Our FATHER. Hail.

ANOTHER OBLATION

OF OUR LORD'S FIVE WOUNDS FOR THE EXPIATION OF SINS.

I.

I adore Thee, most merciful JESU, and give Thee thanks for all the injuries, persecutions, toils, and wearinesses sustained by Thee for me: and all these I deposit in the healthful Wound of Thy Right Foot, that Thou mayest present them to Thy Heavenly FATHER for my sins, in union with that Divine love of Thine, whereby Thou cheerfully barest them, and so much more, for our salvation. Amen.

Our FATHER. Hail.

II.

I adore Thee, most gracious JESU, and give Thee thanks for all the reproaches, gibes, derisions, and contempts, which Thou barest for our salvation: all these I offer into the healthful Wound of Thy Left Foot, that Thou mayest present them to Thy Heavenly FATHER for my sins, in union with that burning love whereby Thou barest all these pains for our salvation. Amen.

Our FATHER. Hail.

III.

I adore Thee, most pitiful JESU, and give Thee thanks for all the dolours, pains and torments, wounds and bruises, which Thou barest for love of me: all these I meekly offer into the Sacred Wound

of Thy Right Hand, that Thou mayest present them to Thy Heavenly FATHER for my sins, in union with that Divine charity of Thine, whereby Thou sufferedst all these things for our redemption. Amen.
Our FATHER. Hail.

IV.

I adore Thee, most gentle JESU, and give Thee thanks for all and every drop of Thy most precious Blood, shed in Thy most cruel Passion in my behalf; and I offer them all into the Wound of Thy Left Hand, that Thou mayest present them to Thy Heavenly FATHER for my sins, in union with that burning Love, whereby Thou pouredst forth that Blood for our salvation. Amen.
Our FATHER. Hail.

V.

I adore Thee, most patient JESU, and give Thee thanks for all the sobs and sighs and heavinesses of Thy Heart, for Thy Sweat and Tears, shed forth for us; and for Thy most bitter Death endured for me; and I offer them, all and each into the most hallowed Wound of Thy Blessed Heart and Side, that Thou mayest present them to Thy Heavenly FATHER for our sins, in union with that unfathomable Love of Thine, whereby Thou wentest through all this for man's salvation. Amen.
Our FATHER. Hail.

COLLECTS

FOR THE PROTECTION OF THE CHURCH FROM ALL EVILS AND CALAMITIES, BY THE MERITS AND VIRTUE OF THE WOUNDS OF CHRIST.

I.

O GOD, Who desirest not the death but the repentance of sinners, regard in mercy Thy people, who with a contrite heart seek refuge in Thy most sacred Wounds, and while they devoutly honour Them, ward off, in pity, war, famine, pestilence, and all the scourges of Thine indignation.

II.

O GOD, Who despisest not the sighing of the contrite, nor the desire of such as be sorrowful, assist our prayers, which we pour out in trouble to Thy sacred Wounds; receive them mercifully, and grant that whatsoever the subtlety of the devil or man worketh against us may be dispersed and brought to nought; that we, being hurt by no temptations, but delivered out of all trouble and distress, may give Thee thanks, O GOD, in Thy holy Church.

Forgive, O LORD, our sins, and out of Thy Sacred Wounds grant us the mercy that we pray for. Look upon our low estate, regard our tribulations, save us from our adversities, and hear us graciously to the full import of our supplication; keep us under the protection of Thy Wounds, that we may be shielded from all evil.

IV.

O most gracious GOD, Who rememberest not the iniquities of them that turn to Thee, but hearest their groans with pity, look upon the many temples, the many altars, the many holy places, once dedicated to Thy sacred Name, now profaned by the abominations of infidels and heretics; call to mind Thine heritage, bought at the cost of Thine awful Wounds and the shedding of Thy most precious Blood; visit with jealousy Thy vineyard, which the wild boar longeth to root up, and strengthen with Thy might its husbandmen against their madness who would lay it waste: give them the victory: and, after labouring here, give them at last Thy kingdom for a possession.

V.

O GOD, Who breakest the might of war, and dispersest with the power of Thy help the assailants of them that put their trust in Thee; send help to Thy faithful, who invoke the protection of Thy Almighty Wounds, that when

Thou hast crushed the fierceness of our foes, and brought to nought all their enmity, we may yield Thee never-ending thanksgiving and praise; Who livest and reignest with GOD the FATHER, in the unity of the Holy GHOST, GOD for ever and ever. Amen.

CHAPTER VII.

OF THE WORSHIP AND HONOUR OF THE MOST HOLY NAME OF JESUS.

Marvellous are the praises, great the privileges of this Name, more sweet than honey; and there is no true Christian man who will not embrace it with love and reverence. In this Name we pray for all we want, and we obtain it; "Whatsoever ye shall ask the FATHER in My Name, He will give it you." S. John xv.

But this honied Name is better praised by him whose words are honey: and thus speaks the holy Doctor:

JESUS is honey in the mouth, in the ear a honied strain, exultation in the heart; yea, and a balm no less. Doth any sorrow? Let JESUS come into his heart, and from its fulness the mouth will speak. Lo, let the light of that Name but gleam, the clouds are scattered and the sky is bright. Does any sin and meditate destruction in despair? Let him invoke the Name of Life, he breathes again and lives.

When hath ever hardness of heart, which so often broods upon the Christian, or slothful indolence, or irksome wearisomeness, resisted the presence of this healthful Name? What dried-up fount of tears has not gushed forth afresh, and still more plentifully, by invoking JESUS?

What like this checks the rage of anger, soothes the swelling of pride, heals the wound of envy, puts out the flame of lust, slakes the thirst of avarice, and allays all itching lust of shame.

When I name JESUS, I set before me One Who is meek and lowly of heart, kind, temperate, chaste, pitiful, the Pattern of all that is virtuous and holy; yea, Who is also

God Almighty; Who heals me by His example, and strengthens me by His help.

All this I hear, when I hear " Jesus." I take examples from Him as Man, help from the Mighty One ; *those are healthful aromatics ; this is that which combines them, and draws out their hidden strength* ; hereby I make up a confection, such as no physician's art can equal.

This, my soul, is thy electuary, laid up in the vessel of the Name of Jesus; and truly it is wholesome, and there is no sickness of thine which it cannot cure.

Be it, then, ever in thy bosom, ever in thy hand, and let all thy thoughts and acts be directed unto Jesus, &c. (Serm. 15 in Cant.)

A METHOD,

BOTH SWEET AND EASY, AT ONCE OF PRAYING ALWAYS, AND OF HONOURING THE MOST HOLY NAME OF JESUS.

Since we are bid by Christ *" always to pray and not to faint," and by the Apostle, "whatever we do, whether in word or deed, to do all in the Name of our Lord* Jesus Christ,*" the following is a compendious and easy way of praying always and withal of honouring* Jesus. *It consists of kindling aspirations, selected from the royal Prophet, such as may not only in every action readily raise the soul to* God, *but also instruct the soul in the certain means and rules towards its perfection.*

AN ASPIRATION FOR EVERY HOUR IN PRAISE OF THE MOST HOLY NAME OF JESUS.

Save me, O Lord, for Thy Name's sake, and avenge me in Thy strength.

And for the glory of Thy Name deliver us, O Lord, and be merciful unto our sins for Thy Name's sake.

Let them that know Thy Name put their trust in Thee ; for Thou, Lord, hast never failed them that seek Thee.

An offering of a free heart will I give Thee, and praise Thy Name, O Lord, because it is so comfortable.

Blessed be the Name of

the LORD, from this time forth for evermore.

AT RISING IN THE MORNING.

Lighten mine eyes, that I sleep not in death, lest mine enemy say, I have prevailed against him.

I laid me down and slept, and rose up again, for the LORD sustained me.

Have I not remembered Thee in my bed, and thought upon Thee when I was waking? for Thou hast been my Helper.

O that my ways were made so direct that I might keep Thy statutes!

I am Thy servant; O grant me understanding, and I shall live.

ON GOING FORTH FROM HOME.

I have had as great delight in the way of Thy testimonies as in all manner of riches.

Be Thou my strong Rock and my Castle, that Thou mayest save me.

Though I walk in the valley of the shadow of death, I will fear no evil; for Thou art with me.

Show me Thy ways, O LORD, and teach me Thy paths.

I have kept Thy commandments and testimonies, for all my ways are before Thee.

ON RETURNING HOME.

Be Thou my Judge, O LORD, for I have walked innocently; my trust hath been also in the LORD, therefore shall I not fall.

Be Thou my strong Rock, and House of defence, that Thou mayest save me.

When I said, My foot hath slipped, Thy mercy, O LORD, held me up.

Take from me the way of lying, and cause Thou me to make much of Thy law.

Let Thy loving Spirit lead me forth into the land of righteousness; quicken me, O LORD, for Thy Name's sake, and for Thy righteousness' sake bring my soul out of trouble.

ON ENTERING CHURCH.

As for me, I will come into Thine House, even upon the multitude of Thy mercy, and in Thy fear will I worship toward Thy holy temple.

Hear the voice of my prayer, O LORD, when I cry unto Thee, when I lift up my hands towards the mercy-seat of Thy holy temple.

As long as I live will I magnify Thee in this manner, and lift up my hands in Thy Name;

That I may see the loving kindnesses of the LORD, and visit His temple.

Like as the hart desireth the water-brooks, so longeth my soul after Thee, O GOD.

BEFORE PRAYER.

Let my supplication come before Thee; incline Thine ear unto my calling.

Hear my prayer, O LORD, and hide not Thyself from my petition; incline Thine Ear unto me and hear me.

As the eyes of servants look unto the hand of their masters, and as the eyes of a maiden unto the hand of her mistress; even so our eyes wait upon the LORD our GOD, until He have mercy upon us.

Hear my voice, O LORD, according unto Thy loving-kindness: quicken me, according as Thou art wont.

O stablish me according to Thy word, that I may live, and let me not be disappointed of my hope.

AFTER PRAYER.

Let my supplication come before Thee; quicken me according to Thy word.

Hear me, O LORD, for Thy mercy is great; and according to the multitude of Thy mercies look upon me.

According to Thy mercy, think Thou upon me, O LORD, for Thy goodness.

One thing have I desired of the LORD, which I will require, even that I may dwell in the house of the LORD all the days of my life.

My soul hath waited for His word; my soul hath put her trust in the LORD.

BEFORE SAYING THE HOURS.

Before the gods will I sing praise unto Thee: I will worship toward Thy holy temple, and praise Thy Name.

I will magnify Thee, O GOD my King, and I will praise Thy Name for ever and ever.

Seven times a day do I praise Thee, because of Thy righteous judgments.

Let the free-will offerings of my mouth please Thee, O LORD, and teach me Thy judgments.

Blessed be the Name of the LORD, from this time forth for evermore.

BEFORE THE HOLY EUCHARIST.

I will go into Thy house with burnt offerings, and pay Thee my vows, which I promised with my lips.

I will go unto the Altar of GOD, even unto the GOD of my joy and gladness.

Let Thy Priests be clothed with righteousness, and let Thy saints sing with joyfulness.

An offering of a free heart will I give Thee, and praise Thy Name, O LORD, because it is so comfortable.

My soul shall be satisfied, even as it were with marrow and fatness, when my mouth praiseth Thee with joyful lips.

AFTER THE HOLY EUCHARIST.

Lift up the light of Thy Countenance upon Thy servant, O LORD, and save me for Thy mercy's sake; let me not be confounded, for I have called upon Thee.

I have stretched forth my hands unto Thee; my soul gaspeth unto Thee, as a thirsty land.

My soul thirsteth for Thee, my flesh also longeth after Thee.

That Thy beloved may be delivered, save me with Thy right Hand, and hear me.

The sacrifice of GOD is a troubled spirit, a broken and contrite heart, O GOD, Thou wilt not despise.

INTERCESSION FOR OTHERS.

Give light to them that sit in darkness and the shadow of death, to guide our feet into the way of peace.

O LORD, arise, help us, and deliver us for Thy Name's sake.

Save Thy people, O LORD, and bless Thine inheritance, govern them and lift them up for ever.

That they may put their trust in GOD, and not to forget the works of GOD, but to keep His commandments.

O LORD, save Thy servants, that put their trust in Thee.

AT READING OR STUDY.

Give me understanding, O LORD, and I shall keep Thy law, yea, I shall keep it with my whole heart.

Deliver me, O LORD, from mine enemies, for I flee unto Thee to hide me; teach me to do the thing that pleaseth Thee, for Thou art my GOD.

I am Thy servant, O grant me understanding that I may know Thy testimonies.

Make me to understand the way of Thy Commandments, and so shall I talk of Thy wondrous works.

Holy and reverend is His Name; the fear of the LORD is the beginning of wisdom.

BEFORE ANY INTERVIEW OR CONVERSATION.

Give sentence with me, O LORD, and defend my cause against the ungodly people; O deliver me from the deceitful and wicked man.

O deliver me from the hand of the strange children, whose mouth talketh of vanity, and their right hand is a right hand of iniquity.

Make Thou Thy servant to delight in that which is good, that the proud do me no wrong.

Consider, O LORD, how I love Thy commandments; O quicken me according to Thy loving-kindness.

Save me, O LORD, for there is not one godly man left, and the faithful are minished from among the children of men.

AT DINNER OR SUPPER.

The eyes of all wait upon Thee, O LORD, and Thou givest them their meat in due season.

The poor shall eat and be satisfied; all they also that seek the LORD shall praise Him, your heart shall live for ever.

My soul thirsteth for Thee, my flesh also longeth after Thee.

That Thou mayest bring forth food out of the earth, and wine to gladden man's heart.

Whoso hath also a proud look and high stomach, I will not suffer him.

IN MEMORY OF THE LORD'S PASSION.

Into Thy hands I commend my spirit, for Thou hast redeemed me, O LORD GOD of truth.

Arise, O LORD, maintain Thine own cause; remember how the foolish man blasphemeth Thee daily.

We look for Thy lovingkindness, O LORD, in the midst of Thy temple.

Thou visitest the earth and blessest it; Thou makest it very plenteous.

Thou hast saved us from our persecutors, and put them to confusion that hate us.

IN ADVERSITY.

In Thee, O LORD, have I put my trust, let me never be put to confusion, but rid me and deliver me in Thy righteousness.

Bring my soul out of trouble, and of Thy goodness slay mine enemies.

According to the multitude of my sorrows that I had in my heart, Thy comforts have refreshed my soul.

Why standest Thou so far off, O LORD, and hidest Thy face in the needful time of trouble?

Though I walk in the midst of trouble, yet shalt Thou refresh me: Thou shalt stretch forth Thy hand upon the furiousness of my adversaries, and Thy right Hand shall save me.

IN TEMPTATION.

Bow down unto my soul and deliver it; deliver me because of mine enemies.

Bring forth the spear and stop the way against them that persecute me; say unto my soul, I am Thy salvation.

Though there rose up war against me, yet shall not my heart be afraid.

How long shall mine enemy triumph over me; consider and hear me, O LORD my GOD.

Keep me under the shadow of Thy wings, from the ungodly that trouble me.

ON UNDERTAKING ANY BUSINESS.

Bow down thine ear, O LORD, and hear me, for I am poor and in misery.

But my trust hath been in Thee, O LORD; I have said, Thou art my GOD; my times are in Thy Hands.

O quicken me after Thy loving-kindness, and so shall I keep the testimonies of Thy Mouth.

As the eyes of a maiden unto the hands of her mistress, even so our eyes wait upon the LORD our GOD, until He have mercy upon us.

IN THE EVENING, AT LYING DOWN.

Lighten mine eyes that I sleep not in death, lest mine enemy say, I have prevailed against him.

Be Thou my strong Rock and house of defence, that Thou mayest save me.

If I give mine eyes to sleep and my eyelids to slumber.

O let my soul live, and it shall praise Thee, and Thy judgments shall help me.

Under the shadow of Thy wings defend me from the wicked that afflict me.

AN ACT OF LOVE AND CONTRITION.

With my whole heart I love Thee, O LORD, my Strength; the LORD is my strong Rock and my defence: my fortress and deliverer.

I acknowledge my wickedness, and my sin is ever before me.

The sacrifice of God is a troubled spirit, a broken and a contrite heart, O GOD, Thou wilt not despise.

O that my ways were made so direct that I might keep Thy statutes.

O quicken me after Thy loving-kindness, and so shall I keep the testimonies of Thy mouth.

AN HOURLY ASPIRATION TO JESUS FOR A HAPPY DEATH.

Lighten mine eyes that I sleep not in death, lest mine enemy say, I have prevailed against him.

Be Thou my strong Rock and house of defence, that Thou mayest save me.

My soul is athirst for GOD, yea, even for the living GOD; when shall I come to appear before the Presence of GOD?

One thing have I desired of the LORD, which I will require, even that I may dwell in the house of the LORD all the days of my life.

Let Thy loving SPIRIT lead me forth into the land of righteousness; quicken me, O LORD, for Thy Name's sake, and for Thy righteousness' sake bring my soul out of trouble.

A MOST SWEET HYMN TO CHRIST JESUS.

OR THE JUBILATION OF THE LOVING SOUL.

FIRST DECADE.

Jesu, dulcis memoria.

Jesu, Who dost true joys impart,
   Sweet is Thy memory:
More sweet than honey to the heart,
   To know and feel Thee nigh.

There's nothing sweet in sweetest sound,
   In hearing nothing heard,
In sweetest thought nought sweet is found,
   As Jesus God and Lord.

Of penitents sole hope and stay;
   To wandering sinners kind;
To those that seek Thou art the way;
   But what to those that find?

Sweetness of heart, and living Fount,
   Of souls the light and fire,
All joys we know dost Thou surmount,
   And all that we desire.

No tongue of man hath power to tell,
   No written words can prove,
But he who loveth knoweth well
   What Jesus 'tis to love.

Thee would I seek upon my bed,
   In chamber of my breast,
In private and in public led,
   By anxious love possess'd.

I seek the tomb, wherein Thou art,
   With Mary in the morn,

Not with the eye, but with the heart,
  And sorrow's plaint forlorn.

There with my tears bedew Thy tomb,
  And fill with sighs the place;
There fall before Thee in the gloom,
  And Thy loved feet embrace.

There with love's tender offices,
  I to Thy feet would flee,
Nor shall my sighs and sorrows cease,
  Till I am fill'd with Thee,

Jesu, great King adorable,
  Of all Thy saints admired,
The sweetness which no words can tell,
  All and alone desired.

SECOND DECADE.

Mane nobiscum, Domine.

Stay with us, Lord, and lift Thy gracious light
Upon us; drive away the shades of night,
The darkness of our spirits else forlorn,
And with Thy sweetness fill the souls that mourn.

When Thou the heart dost visit, Light Divine,
The Truth before it doth unclouded shine,
Then vile esteem'd is this vain world below,
And charity within doth burn and glow.

More pleasant is Thy love than all beside;
True sweetness doth alone in that abide;
Thousand-fold more doth unto that belong
Than aught that we can speak with mortal tongue.

The Passion of His cross alone that love
And the outpouring of His Blood can prove,
By which Redemption from the penal rod
Is given us, and the vision of our God.

Seek ye to know Him; strive ye to attain;
Ask ye His love which none can ask in vain:
Your hearts e'en as ye seek shall in you burn,
While still the more ye seek the more ye learn.

His love with love return, it is His due;
The love He gave is all He asks of you;
After the odour of His ointments run,
Will as He wills and do as He hath done.

Jesu, great Author of all clemency,
The hope of all our joy is hid in Thee,
Of love and grace the fountain infinite,
In Whom Alone is found true heart's delight.

Jesu, good Lord, I pray Thee, let me prove
The full abundance of Thy pitying love;
Grant me, hereafter, in Thy Presence blest
Thy glory to behold, and in Thee rest.

Although I cannot speak Thee worthily,
Yet still I cannot silent be of Thee;
Love itself makes me venture without fear,
Since Thou Alone on earth to me art dear.

The sense of Thy dear love for ever kind
Is the refreshment of the weary mind;
Filling alone without satiety.
And giving hunger but to satisfy.

THIRD DEACDE.
Qui Te gustant esuriunt.

They who of Thee have tasted hunger more,
   And they who drink of Thee are thirsty still,
For nothing more they long for, nought implore
   But Jesus can Alone their bosom fill.

He whom Thy love makes glad as with new wine,
   He only knows what love of Thee can prove;

How blest is he who tastes those joys Divine!
   And there is nothing else that he can love.

Glory Angelical Thou JESUS art,
   Thou art upon the ear as pleasant song,
Thou art as Heavenly Manna to the heart,
   And marvellous as honey on the tongue.

A thousand times I seek Thee, longing sad:
   JESU, to my lone heart when wilt Thou come?
When shall Thy healing Presence make me glad,
   And I be satisfied, and find my home?

JESU, Thy love unchanged abideth still,
   While languor dwells with me and feeble pains;
Honey unceasing doth from Thee distil,
   And fruit of endless life with Thee remains.

JESU of all benignity the height,
   All pleasantness to me and joy of mind,
Incomprehended goodness infinite,
   May Thy great love to Thee my spirit bind.

'Tis good to me to love the LORD most High,
   For nothing else but Him to seek and strive,
And altogether to myself to die,
   That so I may have power in Him to live.

JESU, Thy love most pleasant is to me,
   Hope of the inmost soul for Thee that sighs,
Our penitential tears but seek for Thee,
   For Thee the deep heart longs with silent cries.

Wherever I may be, with pensive mind
   JESUS I seek, on Him my longings rest,
How joyful is my heart when Him I find,
   How happy am I when of Him possessed.

Then the embrace of Thy dear charities
   Surpasses chalices of honey sweet,

How blest is that communion, ere it flies,
 But ah, alas those joys how passing fleet!

FOURTH DECADE.

Jam quòd quæsivi video.

Now what I sought do I behold,
 What I desired, I hold;
The love of JESUS warms my soul,
 And fills my spirit whole.

Thus to the heart when CHRIST is dear,
 This flame burns bright and clear;
It never flags and never fails,
 But more and more prevails.

As from a font of fire it glows,
 With wondrous sweetness flows,
The savour of all true delight,
 And gladness infinite.

This love which is sent down from Heaven
 To heart of hearts is given;
The mind is kindled through and through,
 The spirit's bliss most true.

O beatific wondrous fire!
 O burning strong desire!
O sweet refreshing from above
 The SON of GOD to love.

JESU, the Virgin-Mother's flower,
 O love of sweetest power!
Thine be all praise and might Divine,
 The blessed kingdom Thine!

Come, King of gracious Majesty,
 Most glorious GOD Most High,

Let Thy true light our hearts illume,
  Thy long'd-for kingdom come.

More bright than sun in midday seat,
  Than balsam Thou more sweet,
Most sweet of things that sweetest are,
  Of loveliest things most fair.

Whose taste with true refreshment fills,
  Whose odour health distils,
In Whom my soul within me dies,
  In Thy true life to rise.

Be Thou, I pray, my joy and love,
  And my reward above;
My glory is Alone in Thee,
  Hope, Crown, and Victory.

FIFTH DECADE.

Tu mentis delectatio.

Thou art the mind's delight,
  Of love the consummation,
My glory, Thou, and might,
  Jesu, the world's salvation.

Return, dear Lord, below
  To Whom all power is given,
Who hast o'ercome the foe,
  And reignest now in Heaven.

Do Thou my footsteps lead,
  As Thou my heart hast taken,
By Thee Who art our Head.
  I shall not be forsaken.

Heaven's citizens to meet Him
  Lift up their shining portal,

Triumphant LORD they greet Him,
  Hail! Mighty King inmortal.

Great King of victory,
  King of might and glory,
All pardon is in Thee,
  Heaven of Heavens adore Thee!

Of pity living Well,
  True Light the Heavens o'erflowing,
The crowd of grief dispel,
  Thy glory's light bestowing.

The choirs celestial praise
  With endless hymns adoring:
Earth gladdens 'neath Thy rays,
  Our peace with God restoring.

Peace wherein CHRIST doth reign
  No sense of man e'er tasteth;
'Tis that my soul would gain,
  To that my spirit hasteth.

CHRIST with the FATHER One
  Hath ta'en His seat in Heaven;
My heart from me hath gone
  And unto Him is given.

We follow Him with love
  And hymns and adoration,
That we with Him above
  May sit in heavenly station.

THIRTY-THREE ASPIRATIONS

IN HONOUR OF THE YEARS OF THE LIFE OF OUR LORD JESUS CHRIST, COMMEMORATIVE OF HIS PRINCIPAL TITLES AND ATTRIBUTES,

ARRANGED FROM HOLY SCRIPTURE.

JESUS, VERY GOD.

O JESU, Very GOD of Very GOD; be unto me a strong Rock and house of defence, that Thou mayest save me.

O JESU, Word of the everlasting FATHER, Who spake unto us in these last days by His Son; O that I might hear what the LORD speaketh in me!

O JESU, Wisdom of the FATHER, grant me to seek and to relish the things that are above, that I may taste and see how gracious the LORD is.

JESUS, VERY MAN.

O JESU, First-Begotten among many brethren, make us joint-heirs with Thee in our FATHER's house.

O JESU, the Word made Flesh, Who being in the Form of GOD emptiedst Thyself, taking the form of a servant. Let me not feel it hard to be humbled for Thee.

O JESU, Son of Man, made in the likeness of man, and found in fashion as a man; make me by grace partaker of the Divine Nature.

JESUS, CREATOR.

O JESU, my CREATOR, create in me a new heart, and renew a right spirit within me.

O JESU, my Framer, remember that Thou hast made me of the clay. O may I be a vessel of honour and not of dishonour in Thy house.

O JESU, Author of my life; may my soul live to Thee; for to me to live is CHRIST, and to die is gain.

JESUS, OUR LORD.

O JESU, my LORD and my GOD, I am Thy servant, own Thou me and none beside Thee.

O JESU, my King; rule Thou me, and I shall lack nothing in the green pastures where Thou hast set me.

O Jesu, my FATHER, I am not worthy to be called Thy son, yet cast me not away from Thy Presence.

JESUS, TEACHER.

O Jesu, Who art a Teacher come from GOD to us, teach me goodness, discipline, and knowledge.

O Jesu, Instructor, Who didst begin to do and to teach; teach me to do Thy Will, that I may learn of Thee, for Thou art meek and lowly of heart.

O Jesu, Light of the world, the Way, the Truth, and the Life, lighten mine eyes, and lead me in the way of Thy commandments, for therein is my desire.

JESUS, SHEPHERD.

O Jesu, the good Shepherd, Who didst lay down Thy life for Thy sheep; lead me forth and feed me for Thy Name's sake.

O Jesu, Bread of Life, lo, my soul waiteth for Thee; send me not away fasting, lest I faint by the way.

O Jesu, Fountain of life: my soul thirsteth after Thee; O let me draw water with joy out of the wells of salvation.

JESUS, ADVOCATE.

O Jesu, our Advocate with GOD the FATHER; cause Him to turn away His anger from us.

O Jesu, Mediator between GOD and man; may Thy Blood cry not for vengeance upon us, but forgiveness.

O Jesu, SAVIOUR, Thou that camest to seek and to save that which was lost, save us.

JESUS, SPOUSE.

O Jesu, Husband of blood, espouse me to Thee in mercies and loving-kindnesses.

O Jesu Beloved, fairer than the sons of men; draw me after Thee with the cords of Thy love.

O Jesu, jealous for souls, Whose delight is to be with the sons of men; may I love Thee, and nothing but for Thee.

JESUS, PHYSICIAN.

O Jesu, Physician, Who by Thy stripes didst heal our sicknesses; heal my soul, for I have sinned against Thee.

O Jesu, innocent Lamb, led to slaughter, to take away

the sins of the world; take away *mine*, the chief of sinners.

O Jesu, good Samaritan, pour into my wounds the wine of penitence and the oil of loving-kindness.

JESUS, JUDGE.

O Jesu, Who shalt come to judge the quick and dead; enter not into judgment with Thy servant.

O Jesu, merciful Judge, Who camest not to destroy any; spare me and answer for me.

O Jesu, Judge of aweful majesty, set me with Thy sheep and Thine elect, nor let me be afraid for any evil tidings.

JESUS, GLORIFIED.

O Jesu, Lot of my inheritance, my Portion in the land of the living; restore me my inheritance.

O Jesu, my Glory, my Crown and exceeding great Reward; admit me to those good things which Thou hast prepared, Lord, for them that love Thee.

O Jesu, our Life, Health, and Resurrection; I desire to be dissolved and be with Thee. Nothing shall ever part me from Thee. It is a good thing for me to cleave to Thee. For what have I in heaven but Thee? and there is nothing upon earth that I desire in comparison of Thee.

PRAYER TO JESUS.

O good Jesu, most loving Jesu, most sweet Jesu, Jesu Son of the Virgin Mary, full of love and mercy: O sweet Jesu, have mercy upon me after Thy great goodness.

O most pitiful Jesu, I implore Thee by that precious Blood, which it was Thy will to shed for sinners, wash away my iniquities, and look Thou upon me in my misery and unworthiness, while I humbly beg forgiveness and invoke this Holy Name of Jesus.

O Name of Jesus, precious Name; O Name of Jesus, delightsome Name; O Name of Jesus, instrengthening Name. For what is Jesus, but Saviour? Wherefore, O Jesus, for Thy Holy Name's sake, be Jesus to me and save me; let not me be damned, whom Thou createdst out of nothing.

O good Jesu, let not my

iniquity be my ruin, whom Thy almighty goodness made. O sweet JESU, own what is Thine in me, and what is not Thine wipe away.

O most kindly JESU, pity me in the time of pity, lest Thou damn me in the time of judgment. What profit is there in my blood, when I go down to endless corruption? The dead praise not Thee, LORD JESU, neither they that go down into hell: O most loving JESU, O most beloved JESU, O most gentle JESU.

O JESU, JESU, JESU, make me one of the number of Thine elect; O JESU, SAVIOUR of them that believe in Thee; O JESU, solace of them that flee to Thee; O JESU, precious remission of all sins.

O JESU, SON of the Virgin Mary, pour into me grace, wisdom, charity, chastity, and humility, that I may perfectly love Thee, praise Thee, enjoy Thee, serve Thee, and glory in Thee; and so may all with me, that invoke Thy Name of JESUS. Amen.

COLLECT.

O GOD, Who hast made that most glorious Name of Thy SON, JESUS CHRIST our LORD, ineffably sweet and full of deepest love unto Thy faithful, and to evil spirits full of fearful terror and amazement; mercifully grant that all who devoutly venerate this Name of JESUS upon earth, may reap the sweetness of holy consolation in this life, and in the world to come, joyful exultation and endless bliss in heaven: through the same JESUS CHRIST our LORD.

AN ASPIRATION BEFORE ANY EMPLOYMENT.

O CHRIST JESU, in union with that love whereby Thou didst consummate the work of our Redemption in the midst of the earth, I offer to Thee this work of mine—, and all my actions, to the greater glory of Thy Name, and my neighbours' salvation, and my own.

END OF SECTION VI.

To Jesus,
The Good Shepherd,

WHO LAID DOWN HIS LIFE FOR HIS SHEEP,
THAT THROUGH DEATH HE MIGHT DESTROY HIM WHO HATH
THE POWER OF DEATH,

AND DELIVER US WHO, THROUGH FEAR OF DEATH,
WERE ALL OUR LIFE-TIME SUBJECT TO BONDAGE;
HIMSELF, AS MAN, OUR WAY WHEREIN IS NO DEATH;
HIMSELF, AS GOD, OUR HOME, IN WHOM IS TRUTH AND LIFE:

The Physician of our souls,

WHO HEALED US BY HIS OWN STRIPES,
AND GAVE HIMSELF AS A MEDICINE FOR OUR SICKNESS:

The Food of Immortality,

WHOM WHOSO EATETH HATH ETERNAL LIFE:

The Tree of Life,

WHOSE LEAVES ARE FOR THE HEALING OF THE NATIONS:

Protector of Penitents,
Intercessor for the Confessing,
Advocate, though Judge,

THE BEGINNING OF OUR STRENGTH,
THE END IN WHOM WE REST:

Sun of Righteousness,

WHO TURNEST THE SHADOW OF DEATH INTO THE MORNING,
SUFFER US NOT TO BE CAST INTO OUTER DARKNESS:

Fountain of Life,

IN WHOSE LIGHT WE SHALL SEE LIGHT,
FREE US FROM THE POWER OF THE SECOND DEATH:

Our Righteousness,
LET NOT OUR INIQUITIES PREVAIL AGAINST US:
Our Sanctification,
LET NOT THE ADVERSARY DEFILE THE DWELLING-PLACE
OF THY NAME:
Our Redemption,
WHO BY THE BLOOD OF THY COVENANT,
HAST FREED US FROM THE PIT;
LET NOT THE PIT SHUT HER MOUTH UPON US,
WHOM THOU HAST, AT SUCH PRICE, REDEEMED:
Our Salvation,
LET OUR EYES SEE THY SALVATION:
Good Master,
WHO, LOVING THINE OWN IN THE WORLD, DIDST LOVE THEM
TO THE END,
BE THOU OUR GUIDE UNTO DEATH, YEA, OVER DEATH:
The Resurrection and the Life,
WHO DIDST DIE AND RISE AGAIN AND REVIVE,
THAT THOU MIGHTEST BE LORD OF THE DEAD AND LIVING,
RISE ON US, IN US, THAT DYING IN THEE
WE MAY LIVE TO THEE:
Richness of the House of God,
LET ME SEE THY GOODNESS IN THE LAND OF THE LIVING:
LORD, WHAT IS MY HOPE?
TRULY, MY HOPE IS EVEN IN THEE.
O, LET ME NOT BE DISAPPOINTED OF MY HOPE!
BE WITH ME, LORD, WHEN I WALK THROUGH THE VALLEY
OF THE SHADOW OF DEATH:
Remember me, Lord, in Thy Kingdom.

PARADISE FOR THE CHRISTIAN SOUL.

PART VII.

ON THE CARE AND PREPARATION FOR DYING WELL AND HAPPILY.

CHAPTER I.

COLLOQUY BETWEEN CHRIST AND MAN ON THE MANNER OF DYING WELL AND HAPPILY.

§ 1. *An invitation to prepare for a pious death.*

"All flesh is grass, and all the goodliness thereof is as the flower of the field. The grass withereth, the flower fadeth."

CHRIST. Behold, O man, thy life upon earth; green grass to-day, to-morrow withering; a wind, a shadow that passeth quickly away; a smoke, a vapour that appeareth for a little: hear ye this, all ye people; ponder it with your ears, ye that dwell in the world: children of earth, sons of men, rich and poor, one with another; young men and maidens, old men and children, hear the words of My Mouth. One unchangeable decree of death holds you all: "It is appointed unto all men once to die, and after that the judgment." Ye must all, yea, sooner than ye think, appear before My judgment seat, to receive, every one, according as he hath done in his body, whether it be good or bad. And such as I find every man, when I summon him to appear, by death, M--

messenger, before Me, *so* I judge him.

Rejoice, then, O young man in thy youth, and let thy heart cheer thee in the days of thy youth, and walk n the ways of thy heart and in the sight of thine eyes; but know this, that for all these things God will bring thee into judgment. Haste, if thou be wise; set thine house in order betimes, for thou shalt die, and not live: trust not to thy strength or age. The young, the strong, the hale, yea, the poor and babes, die every day by chance or by some trifling cause: a glass or earthen vessel, though new made, is not the stronger; let it fall, and it is broken. Few men reach grey hairs, therefore expect them not.

Man. My God! Thou hast created man in Thine own Image; Thou hast crowned him with glory and honour, and set him over the works of Thine Hands, and wilt Thou thus suddenly bring me back to dust, and cut off like a weaver my life? Remember, Lord, how short my time is; wherefore hast Thou made all men for nought? Lo, we all die, and are as water spilt on the ground, which cannot be gathered up.

Christ. What man is he that liveth and shall not see death? and shall he deliver his soul from the hand of hell? But suppose I fill him with length of days; though a man live many years, and rejoice in them all, must he not even then call to mind the darkness to come, and the days of eternity, which shall make the past show like vanity? *That* shall have passed away like a shadow, like a ship that cleaveth the waves, that leaveth no trace behind. Happy they who remember that they are strangers and pilgrims upon earth, or, it may be, stewards and dispensers of their Lord's blessing, Who shall come at an hour when men think not, to take account with His servants.

Miserable they who, thinking of Me as gone into a far country to be long absent, revel in My goods, and think not of the time when I shall call them to give account of their stewardship. How is it that man, being by Me created in honour, hath no understanding, but is compared unto the beasts that perish, and like to them?

As though both perished alike, and man were no better than a brute! whereas I created him in My Image and My Likeness; yea, and when he was doomed to eternal death, with My own Blood I redeemed him, to be fellow-heir with Me in heaven! Why do they rush blindfold to death? why perish for ever, they whom I bought at so dear a cost; for whom I came that they might have life, and that they might have it more abundantly?

O how few take these things to heart, and deem it wisdom to meditate upon them! How many say, as though they had made a covenant with death and were at agreement with hell: "When the overflowing scourge of death passes by, it shall not come nigh us." They turn away their faces, not to look unto the end: there is no fear of GOD, no care of death before their eyes. So they spend their days in delights, and in a moment sink to hell.

MAN. What shall I do unto Thee, O Thou Preserver of men? Thy Hands have made and fashioned me wholly round about; and dost Thou so suddenly cast me down? Spare me, LORD; my days are nought. What profit is there in my blood, if I go down into the pit? Shall the dust give thanks unto Thee, or shall it declare Thy truth? Shall Thy loving kindness be showed in the grave, or Thy faithfulness in destruction? For in death no man remembereth Thee; and who shall give Thee thanks in the pit? Does it seem good to Thee thus to weigh me down, the work of Thy Hands? Shall my days be swifter than a post? shall they flee away and see no good? Shall they pass quicker than the weaver cuts his web, and be consumed without hope? O spare me a little, that I may recover my strength, before I go hence and be no more seen.

§ 2. *The art of dying well, necessary above all things.*

CHRIST. I made not death: but by envy of the devil, death entered into the world; for through him, by one man, sin entered into the world, and death by sin; for that all have sinned. And so it is appointed unto all men once to die. But this one consolation is left to thee; as in Adam all die, even so in Me shall all be made alive. If thou wouldest enjoy this My blessing, see that the second death have no power over thee; for the death of sinners is terrible. O whence is it that men forget how short life is, how insufficient to provide things really needful; above all, duly to prepare for death; and fritter it mostly away on vanities and emptinesses?

If all the years, days, hours, ages, that the world hath stood or shall stand, were thine alone; and with it all wisdom, skill, and energy; all science, wealth, connections, influence; all that earth has and men desire; were it not wise to turn them all to *this;* how to make *that* last moment happy which shall determine thy endless state, on which depends thy eternal bliss or misery?

MAN. When I consider all the works of men, and the toils wherein they labour in vain, I see that all is vanity and vexation of spirit, and that there is nothing abiding under the sun. Wherefore I was weary of my life, when I saw that all under the sun is evil, all vanity and vexation of spirit, so that in much wisdom is much grief; and he that increaseth knowledge, increaseth sorrow. O vanity of vanities! all is vanity.

CHRIST. Why, then, art thou so careful and troubled about many things? Why seekest to be over-wise? Why indulgest over-curiosity? Why exercisest thyself in matters which are too high for thee? Lo, one thing is needful, *To know how to die.* This is the only true art, the only science. Whoso knoweth this may lightly forego the rest; but all other knowledge shall little profit him, who knows not this. All else belongs to earth and life's short span; *this* to heaven and limitless eternity.

While then thou livest, learn to die; and beware, for there is but one accepted time, and if it pass, it may not be recalled. In other arts the errors of a first attempt may the next time be easily set right: one error here is fatal, and thenceforth penitence comes to late. The door of My Mercy will be shut: the hope of pardon shut out for ever. Where the tree falleth, northward or southward, there will it lie. He is truly wise, who often thinks on his last end, and strives to be in life such as he would be found in death. Who, then, is wise, and keepeth these things?

Verily it is great wisdom in a man to look into himself; to *know himself;* to know that he is made of a body from the dust, and of a spirit from heaven, whereof one will turn again by death to the earth, from which it came; the other will return to GOD Who gave it, and receive according to that he hath done in the body, whether it be good or bad.

Think on these things; give thyself wholly to them; dwell on them, O man, My creature. Recollect thy last end, and thou wilt never sin; nothing will so avail to make thee temperate in all things as the frequent meditation on death. For how shalt thou be high-minded or proud, who art but dust and ashes, and shalt ere long return to dust? How pamper thy flesh, for it soon will be food for worms? How give thy heart to riches, honours, vanities, from which perchance, this night, death, bitter to thy soul, will sever thee, shrinking and unprepared? Then whose shall those things be, which thou hast provided? O how cheap will he, who ever thinks he hath to die, count all these things? O that men would be wise, and understand, and ponder their last end!

MAN. LORD, I confess that man's days are few, and the number of his months is with Thee; Thou hast set him his bounds, which he shall not pass. I know that Thou wilt bring me to death, the house appointed to all living. And who am I, to answer Thee or plead in words with Thee? If I should answer, Thou, O LORD, art righteous; yet be not angry with Thy servant's prayer, O Lord; and one thing I will ask Thee: make me know my end and the number of my days, that I may know how long I have to live: how many are the days of Thy servant, for my appointed warfare upon earth, till my change come?

§ 3. *Timely preparation for death.*

CHRIST. It is not for thee, O man, to know the times and the seasons which the Father hath put in His own power. It is for thee to take heed, to watch, and be ready always. Thy day of death is hidden, that thou mayest watch every day; for any day may be thy death-day. It is for thee to redeem the time, to labour while it is day, for the night cometh when no man can work. It is for thee to give all diligence to make thy calling sure by holy works. Lo, now is the accepted time, now is the day of salvation. It is extreme folly to let the present pass, and look for days to come; wasting the present in the distractions of pleasures, vanities, and worldly cares.

Why wouldest thou know what is not good to know? Know of a surety that the uncertainty of death is a special proof of My Goodness and Loving-mercy. For were it certain, how many would excuse themselves and slumber in dangerous security, take far less heed to their salvation, and defer it to life's very end, and their deathbed? Is not this done commonly even now, though men cannot promise themselves a day, an hour, a moment? Alas! man knoweth not his end, and yet he careth not for it. And then, as fishes fall into the net, and birds are taken in the snare, man too is taken in the evil time, when he knew not it was nigh.

But thou, O man, remember now thy Creator in the days of thy youth, before the evil days come. O, it is good for a man to bear the LORD's yoke from his youth, for the last end of him that feareth GOD is happy, and in the days of his departure he shall be blessed.

See, then, that thou walk warily; not as a fool, but as wise. For what great folly, seeing that all eternity hangs upon this brief span of life, and that, at death, sentence is passed for all eternity, assigning thee for ever to misery or to glory: what greater folly than to take so little heed to this peril! to be eager in pursuit of all besides, and to give no thought to what alone deserves it!

Seeing there be many things that increase vanity, what is man the better? For who knoweth what is good for man in this life, the number of the days of his vain life, which he spendeth as a shadow?

O ye sons of men, how

long will ye be stiff-necked, and have such pleasure in vanity, and seek after leasing? Man walketh in a vain shadow, and disquieteth himself in vain. His years are drawn out as the spider's web, for, as with much toil she weaveth her web out of her own vitals, and then catcheth worthless flies, so men waste their years, and what is it they reap?

MAN. Lo, Thou hast made my days a span long, and mine age is even as nothing in respect of Thee; for a thousand years in Thy sight are but yesterday, which has passed away. Spare me, LORD, for my days are nought. Remember I am a stranger with Thee, and a sojourner as all my fathers were.

CHRIST. And, therefore, I exhort you, as strangers and pilgrims, abstain from fleshly lusts, which war against the soul. A pilgrim tarrieth not on the way, turns not out of the road to gather flowers and seek amusement, to dally and be idle: yea, rather, he presses forward in eager haste on the journey he has begun, longing for his home and those he loves. And when, from time to time, he seeks refreshment or repose, it is not of pleasure, but necessity, that he may journey on with new vigour and recruited strength.

Go, do thou likewise; redeem the time from these fleeting trifles, which are but vanity and vexation of spirit, and spend it upon that one thing needful—a happy death and blest eternity. Thou knowest not how long thy life is; whether thy Maker will call thee in a very little time: whatsoever then thy hand findeth to do, do it with all thy might, for the night cometh when no man can work. There is no working, no reasoning, no wisdom, or knowledge, in the grave, whither thou art hastening. What thou wilt then wish that thou hadst done, what, if left undone, will then cost thee bitterest tears, *do now*.

MAN. O LORD! Who art rich in mercy, I am straitened on every side; forsake me not. Stretch forth Thy Right Hand to the work of Thy Hands, and draw me out of the mire that I sink not. Lo, out of the deep do I cry unto Thee: daily I resolve to amend my life, and daily do I defer: it is still *to-morrow* and *to-morrow;* and what if that *to-morrow* shall never come? Lord Jesus! how long do I seek counsel in my heart? What profit is there in my blood, if I go down to the pit? Lighten mine eyes that I may never turn them from the sight of death, that I may see what threatens me, and that I sleep not in death; lest my enemy say, I have prevailed against him.

Christ. Didst thou but know how the memory of time mis-spent agonizes the dying man; couldst thou but see and hear the torments of the damned, their shrieks and wailings, (and all in vain), what wouldest thou not do? And this afflicts them most, that they once, by the easy labour of a few years, might have redeemed these torments, and yet they gave no thought to death; wasted in frivolities the time for providing oil in their vessels, and let slip the day of salvation and the occasion of good works. They spent their days, like so many still, in pleasure; and how soon they flew! And in an instant they went down to hell, and now are plagued without end. Happy thou, if thou profit by others' warnings!

Behold Dives, who fared sumptuously every day, now wailing in pain. Who of you would not once have preferred his lot to Lazarus', when one was full and the other famished? And who does not now call Lazarus blessed and Dives miserable? Here on earth, while one was receiving his good things, the other evil, thou understoodest not the real difference between them; rather, thou wast amazed and perplexed at the difference thou sawest: but hold thy peace till thou go into the Sanctuary of God, and understand the end of these men.

Man, Truly God is loving unto Israel, even unto such as are of a pure heart! Yea, and righteous art Thou, O Lord, and true is Thy Judgment. It is indeed true, (for why should I hide it from Thee, Who searchest my reins and my heart?) that often my feet were almost gone, my treadings had well nigh slipped, because I was grieved at the wicked; I did also see the ungodly in such prosperity. There is no fear of death before their eyes. But now will I sing of Thy Mercy and Judgment, O Lord, for in due time Thou renderest to every man according to his deeds.

CHRIST. Seeing, then, that their ends are so unlike, and that the choice between them is now given thee, how is it, that, while thou wishest to be blessed with Lazarus, thou choosest the life of Dives? Why pamper thy flesh with luxuries and softness? why spend so much, perchance, on favourite animals, that might feed the hungry and poor?

If by a special favour I restored the miserable Dives to life again, would he return, thinkest thou, to his former pleasures? Would he again go clothed in purple and fine linen, and fare sumptuously every day? Would he despise Lazarus lying at his gate? Yea, rather, he would do penance in sackcloth and ashes; nor let a moment pass without some thing done for his salvation. Yea, rather, he would choose to gather in one, and bear alone all the agonies and toils soever in the whole world, which thought could conceive, rather than return to that place of torment. How many hundred years has he been longing for but a drop of water to cool his tongue; and infinite millions of years to come shall he be still longing, and never obtain it!

What man shall hear these things and not fear, or fear and not repent? Who of you can dwell in that consuming fire? Who can dwell in everlasting burnings? Of all marvels that is the greatest, to believe in those everlasting torments prepared for sinners, and yet live so carelessly in sin; to go on living so boldly in a state wherein thou wouldest not dare to die; in death to expect a sentence for all eternity, and to take no more timely care for a happy death. Who hath so blinded your eyes, that ye will not look to the end? How very few of you there are, who try to live now as they would wish to be found at death, and appear before My Judgment-seat! Yet thou mayest be called to-morrow, to-day, this very hour!

Have I not in so many parables, and by so many warnings, yea, threats, taught you to watch, be careful, and be ready? Look at the numbers of every age, sex, condition, daily dying before your eyes: look at the many sudden accidents, the fevers, and various diseases! What do they cry but, Watch, be ready, set thine house in order, for thou shalt die?

Remember well, any one of these things may happen next to thee. To-day, to-day, hear the LORD's voice; harden not thine heart. Let the wicked forsake his ways, and the ungodly man his thoughts, and let him return unto Me, and I will have mercy upon him: now is the time of mercy; beware the time of punishment!

MAN. Thou art righteous, O LORD, but spare me, though I speak unwisely to my LORD, who am but dust and ashes. Dost thou then will the death of the sinner? Hast Thou not said, that Thou desirest it not? And, *as for the wickedness of the wicked, he shall not fall thereby in the day that he turneth from his wickedness?* and, again, *Whoso cometh unto Me, I will in no wise cast out?* What, then, if I come to Thee late, at even, or at the eleventh hour, wilt Thou reject me? What if I repent me of my sins in the act of dying, wilt Thou despise the broken and contrite heart?

CHRIST. What sayest thou? Truly thou speakest as one of the foolish ones, and turnest away thy heart to evil words, whilst thou wouldest persevere in sin, and yet excuse thyself. Wouldest thou give thy whole life to sin, and a moment only, the moment of death, to penitence? Is it repentance to cease from sinning, when the power of sinning is gone from thee? When thy sins forsake thee, rather than thou them? What reform is it to resolve to live better, when life is at an end? O self-deceiver, I have indeed promised pardon to the penitent, but not a morrow to the procrastinator.

But for thy warning learn that true penance stands in deploring and forsaking sin for My sake, and for love of Me; and, therefore, out of a hundred of such as delay repentance to their deathbed, scarce one is a true penitent. They sorrow for their own sakes, not for Mine; not for having offended Me, but for their own peril of damnation; and could they escape at once both this and death, they would return to their vomit and sin again. How then shall he be said to repent truly in death, who loves sin and fears not to commit it all his life long?

Surely I desire not the death of a sinner: I would not have thee despair, nor any sinner, while life lasts.

But I warn thee of thy peril, and would have thee shun it. For very many then perish; very few truly repent. And how darest thou presume, that thou too shalt be among those very few? O that thou couldst see all the obstacles to true penitence at death, and above all, at a sinner's death! First, there is the disease itself, oppressing the sick man; next, the consciousness of sin and its enormity, which then first appears in truer colours than ever before; his memory is loaded with remorse for bygone days, wasted in frivolities; and he looks forward with harrowing terror to the account, soon to be given, of all his words, deeds, and thoughts. On one side the devil subtly exaggerates his sins, and tempts him to despair; on the other, fear of his Judge and the horror of hell so overwhelm him, that his troubled conscience can only look for vengeance, and dwell only on My just Judgment, in wretched despair of pardon. For he sees his sins, and sees not My Mercy, which at that time the evil spirit does his best wholly to hide from him, or at least to under-rate.

What hope, what courage, thinkest thou, will then remain to the miserable man? He sees that he must now leave all that he held dear in life, and that from them he can look for no help, no comfort. Memory of sin terrifies: the coming account is at hand, and the irrevocable sentence astounds with horror. Flight or concealment is impossible; and what must it be to be obliged to appear? Does he look back upon his past life, its whole course seems but a moment's space: does he look forward to futurity, that is, to the infinite space of eternity, he has made shipwreck, and lost eternal bliss for the vanities of a moment; and what vanities! Amid this maze of thought, what room is there for aught that accompanies salvation? And so he oftentimes anticipates My judgment: yea, he damns himself, (for that he knew not the time of his visitation,) and goes desperate in the way of Cain, and says, with him, "My punishment is greater than I can bear.

MAN. Lord, I am sore bewildered, and my heart is disquieted within me; all my bones are troubled at the blast of Thy fearful words.

O how dreadful will it be to fall into the hands of the living God! Who shall endure the voice of Thy mighty thunder in that awful day? These are no vain words, spoken only to fray me; for who can tell how man dies so well as Thou? O, good Jesu! grant that I may come early before Thy Presence with confession, and repent at once, before my last day comes, lest trouble and distress oppress me in that hour.

Christ. Hear Me, therefore, and delay not. Why not say this moment, "Now have I begun?" To-day thou hearest My words, harden not then thine heart; defer not till to-morrow, for art thou sure of to-morrow? defer not till sickness, least of all, till death; for even sickness is but too ill-suited fitly to prepare for death: when the spirit fails, strength languishes; and so sorely is the mind often bestead with pain and want of ease, that it scarce can think of holy dying, far less give itself wholly to it.

How many does delirium, how many does wandering of mind, wholly unfit both for settling their worldly affairs and providing for the future! Thou knowest by experience how any sharp pain, toothache, or the like, diverts even the good and pious from heavenly things; for the mind is fixed upon the pain: what will it be in death?

With many words have I thus urged on thee, My son, not to defer the work of thy salvation, or provision for a holy death, till the hour of death. Why choose hazard, when security is offered? Why trust to chance in the matter, of all, the most weighty and perilous, thy eternal soul; while in all other things thou choosest so anxiously the safer side? I offer thee My Grace now: hereafter it may be, justice will oblige Me to withhold it. Is not this a mysterious chastisement, that the sinner who in life forgetteth Me, in death should forget himself? Canst thou presume to promise thyself My mercy in thy death, Whom thou so despisedst in thy life?

Consider this, O ye unwise among the people! O ye fools, when will ye understand? O that thou too knewest, in this thy day, the things that belong unto thy salvation and thy peace! O that thou wouldest not receive the time of My Grace and Love in vain! The time will come, perchance in the day that thou knowest not, and in an hour when thou art not aware, the time of My Justice: then, if thou have done well, thou shalt so receive; if ill, what wonder if I render thee according to thy deeds? Then shalt thou entreat in vain a respite till the morning, and cry to the LORD, with that wicked one, for mercy; for it shall not come. For how often have I called and thou refusedst; hast set at nought all My counsel, and wouldst none of My reproof? Well, then, may I also laugh at your calamity, and mock when your fear cometh: when your fear cometh as desolation and your destruction cometh as a whirlwind; when distress and anguish come upon you.

Thou chosest pleasure, the world, and the flesh, for masters in thy life; wilt thou repair to Me in the last moment of perplexity? Canst thou for very shame seek Me in thy need, Whom in prosperity thou despisedst? What if I then say to thee, 'Where now are thy gods wherein thou trustedst? Let them arise and help thee in thy need.' The sick man finds kind and ready care from the physician, whom in his health he treated well and kindly; but what could he expect if he had insulted and ill-used him? Dost thou not see daily how all that are at law on trifles of this world, take no rest, but are ever with their counsel and their lawyers, and their judges, with all that have influence with them, imploring their assistance and good-will? And does man still, in the only serious cause, that of eternal life and death, while it is yet before the Supreme Judge, stand idle and do nothing to secure it? What was it that shut out the foolish virgins from the Kingdom of Heaven? They slumbered, delayed, supplied not their vessels, or applied to the wise too late; and the Bridegroom said, *I know you not.* They only who were ready, entered with the Bridegroom to the marriage. Why dost not thou too watch? Understand this, ye that forget GOD, lest He pluck you away, and there be none to deliver you. He that hath ears to hear, let him hear; let him not cast these My words behind him, lest after his hardness and impenitent heart, he treasure up for himself wrath against the Day of Wrath and revelation of the righteous judgment of GOD. O that men would be wise and understand and look to their last end.

MAN. Woe for my blind and stony heart! Day after day I hear and still am idle, despite all my peril. Would that Thy Word, O LORD, Which is quick and powerful, and sharper than any two-edged sword, might pierce my heart, even to the dividing asunder of soul and spirit! That it might bring forth fruit in me, as it did in Thy Saints and Thine Elect, whose death was right dear in Thy Sight. Wherefore now they are inebriated with the richness of Thy House, and Thou givest them to drink of the flood of Thy pleasures. Blessed are they that dwell in Thy House, O LORD; they will be alway praising Thee. Blessed are the dead who die in the LORD. O may my soul die the death of the righteous, and my last end be like his.

They who suppose what is here said of a death-bed repentance too severe, should ¹ *St. Augustine, in Hom.* 41, *inter* 50; *and the De Pœnitent.* [ap. S. Aug. App. t. vi.] *as well as other writers on the Four Last Things.*

§ 4. *A good life the best security for a holy death.*

CHRIST. And why dost thou call them blessed? Surely because they passed through fire and water, and are now brought into a wealthy place, where there is no more death, or crying, or pain. For now they rest from their labours; and their works, which in this life they wrought, do follow them. Thou dost well in desiring their end. But thou wilt do better if thou live their life, that thou mayest die their death. Strive then to enter in at the strait gate, and as it is the violent who take heaven by force, be thou thus violent.

Balaam too, who loved the wages of ungodliness, desired the end of the righteous, but not his beginnings. The carnal too know, that dear unto Me is the death of the Saints, and the death of the wicked is terrible; and they would die like saints, but cannot bear their life. It is madness to live like Dives, and look for

Lazarus' end; to wish for a good death with a bad life. Do men gather grapes of thorns, or figs of thistles? Think not that the stream of pleasure here will bear thee on to pleasure there; a body taking its ease here, and there a soul at rest. Wilt thou die well? Thou must then live well, and, before dying, die to sin and pleasure. Yea, this alone is truly life, to die to the flesh and to the world, and live to God. Accustom thyself thus to death so long as thou livest; so shalt thou see it come and feel no fear.

And of this mystical death thou mayest form to thyself some image from what thou seest in natural death. No sooner does it seize hold of man than it takes away all sense of pleasure and all desire of it; it shuts the eyes, closes the ears, fixes the tongue in silence for ever, parts him from friends and kinsmen, puts out all longing for this world: inflict the like upon thyself, and be beforehand with thy enemy, and death will find it has no part in thee; thou wilt be conqueror to thy endless good.

MAN. What death, O LORD, is this thou biddest me die, and callest spiritual and self-inflicted?

CHRIST. Art thou yet without understanding, and knowest not that if thou live after the flesh, thou shalt die, but if, by the Spirit, thou do to death the deeds of the body, thou shalt live? Keep under thy body, and bring it into subjection; mortify thy members that are upon the earth. Put off the old man and his deeds; put on the new man; keep thy tongue from evil; turn away thine eyes, lest they behold vanity, &c. Love not the world, neither the things that are in the world; avoid those friends and companions with whom thou canst not have Me for a Friend, for such friends are indeed hurtful. Pass over injuries, render to no man evil for evil; be silent under reproaches, and as one in whose mouth are no reproofs. Submit thyself to thy superior's will, even as one dead, who resisteth not; thus lose thy life in this world to thy soul's health, and thou shalt keep it unto life eternal.

If thou be thus, thou shalt be counted dead upon earth, but thy life shall be hid with Me in GOD. Thou shalt not seem great and glorious before men; but all thy glory shall be within, in the testimony of a good conscience. Thou shalt walk as sorrowful, yet alway rejoicing; thou shalt possess, as possessing not; use the world as using it not. This is to die before thou diest.

In few words: flee from sin above all things, and thou needest not fear an evil death, for the sting of death is sin. Where is no sin, death cannot sting; that death cannot be evil, which closes a good life. Exercise thyself then unto godliness, and death will never come unprepared, for a holy, blameless life is a continual preparation. The righteous, if he be overtaken by death, shall find refreshment.

But, alas! how cruel is death to those who lived to the world and to its lusts. O how sharply does it sting them who are wise to do evil, and know not to do well. They who pass their days in pleasantness, then feel the misery that waits upon their end; the wine that was so sweet, now bites them like an adder, and spreads its poison like the asp.

MAN. LORD, I would desire to die to the world and the flesh, and live unto Thee, Who didst die for me: I would be ever prepared to die that I may live, yet now no longer I, but Thou in me, O JESU! I see, LORD, that nought, save holiness in life, can secure happiness in death. Still, O LORD, so it is, the terrors of death compass me round about, so that I shrink from it with horror; I fain would fly what I know I cannot fly.

And has it not been so with Thy Saints, O LORD; have not they too dreaded death? Yea, LORD, and Thyself: did not the horror of death seem to come over Thee, when in the garden Thy Soul was very heavy, and Thy Sweat, like drops of blood, fell to the earth? Thou saidst, My Soul is exceeding sorrowful, even unto death, and Thou prayedst that the cup might pass from Thee.

§ 5. *Remedies against the horror of death.*

CHRIST. Yes, I had taken your infirmities upon Me, that thou mightest see how much I suffered for you, and how truly I bare your sicknesses. Yet was it not so much the horror of death that was before My Eyes, as of sin which was to be destroyed by death. Notwithstanding, I so far allowed entrance to the fear of death also, as that thou mightest fear the less to die: for by virtue of My Death, death is to thee the end of sin and the door of life.

Consider now the many causes of the fear of death; sift them, and they will appear, groundless. It is not death that is evil, and therefore fearful; but an evil life, which is to be feared above all evil, because on it follow evils without end. The children of this world think the contrary; without fear they live in their sins, and yet they shrink from the extremest evil, death. So is it with fools that walk in darkness; they fear where no fear is; where there is fear, they walk securely; shadows fray them, true terrors they despise. What is the death they fear, but separation of soul and body? What is the death they fear not, but separation of the soul and GOD? It is less fearful that the body should perish than the soul.

But what, My son, so terrifies thee in death? The day of death is better than the day of birth. Believe Me; believe thine own experience. Man that is born of woman hath but a short time to live and is full of misery: for as the flower of the fields he cometh forth and is cut down; he fleeth like a shadow and never continueth in one stay. While he liveth, he walks in the midst of snares, the lust of the flesh, the lust of the eyes, and the pride of life; for these fill the world, which lieth in the evil one. Hence the law in his members warring against the law of his mind; heavy and wearisome the struggle; rare and difficult the victory.

And, therefore, have My friends ever borne with life, but been in love with death: hence their complaints, Woe is me, that I am constrained to dwell with Mesech; I am weary of my life; wretched man that I am! who shall deliver me from the body of this death? &c.

Man's life is a journey, a prison-house, an exile; and

he that flies from death, in fact desires to linger on in these. Strange, to be weary of a journey, and not wish it finished! to be shut up in a close and filthy prison, and not wish for freedom! to be far from home amid perils and enemies, and not to yearn for home! to be in exile, and not to prize deliverance! None should be loath to die but he who prefers misery to joy, exile to home, darkness to light, earth to heaven.

MAN. Truly our life upon earth is a warfare, O LORD; it is all one trial and continual strife. Woe is me that I am constrained to dwell so long amid the perils and snares of the world, the flesh, and Satan. What is long life but long vexation, evil felt or evil feared? Without are fightings, within are fears. The days of our pilgrimage are few and evil, and yet, in our blindness, we cling to life; we would put off death, which we cannot fly; and yet death is or ought to be to us the end of misery and sin, the gate of life, the entrance of our home, the enfolding of Thy Presence.

Wretched are we while we live; more wretched yet, that as we grow older we grow not better; we know not, yea rather we love our wretchedness. Open Thou mine eyes, that I may know where I am, viz. in exile, &c., and whither I should yearn, even towards my home: then I shall not fear to die; I shall desire to depart and be joined to Thee. For without Thee it cannot go well with me, it never can. O! when wilt Thou take me from this prison? when shall I be free from the body of this death?

CHRIST. Many are loath to die because they are full of this world's wealth, honours and delights; and, blessed are the people (say they) that are in such a case! O how bitter is death to him that is at ease in his possessions; whose ways go smoothly, and his food is pleasant. O fools and slow of heart! O men of little faith! Is it hard to quit earth's poor comforts, when heaven is before you, where is all good gathered in one, and perfect, where is the Chief Good? Eye hath not seen, nor ear heard, neither hath entered the heart of man, what good things I have prepared for them that love Me. I Myself will be their praise and glory, their heritage and pleasure, their exceeding great reward.

MAN. I believe verily to see the goodness of the LORD in the land of the living, where we shall be inebriated with the plenteousness of Thy house, and one day is better than a thousand. But why, alas! is my faith so frail, that heaven has no greater charms for me than a morsel of earth? Why longeth not my soul after Thee, O GOD, as the hart desireth the water-brooks? or the hireling his evening-rest? seeing that Thou, LORD, art my Portion in the land of the living: Thou art the Portion of my inheritance and of my cup, and Thou wilt maintain my lot. LORD, increase my faith, kindle my heart and my desire.

CHRIST. Consider, then, that death brings to the faithful far more than it takes away; to them it is not loss but gain. In place of a short and dying life, set full of miseries, they win a blest undying life, where sorrow is no more! For the fleeting goods of earth, they see the Goodness of the LORD in the land of the living! For the hollow pleasures of the flesh, they have to drink of the river of never-ending joy.

What ties thee then to earth? Is it a hard thing to leave friends, kinsfolk, and familiar friends? Think then whither thou art bound, to thy heavenly home, where there await thee choirs innumerable of those who love thee, Angels, Apostles, Martyrs, Virgins, and all My chosen ones! What pleasantness of earthly friendship can compare with the sight of these, and with their converse? Dost thou not feel this and long for fellowship with them? Forget then thy father's house; go forth from thy land and kinsfolk, for thy portion is in the land of the living: hast thou no wishes for the land flowing with milk and honey, and to be with Me in Paradise?

What! dost thou fear to go forth? My elect rejoiced when they received the sentence of death, and were soon to put off their tabernacle. Think of My "chosen vessel," how he desired to depart and be with Me, and counted death as gain.

MAN. True, Lord, but that was Paul. He had fought the good fight, he had kept the faith, he had finished his course; and thenceforth he knew there was laid up for him a crown of righteousness, with Thee, the Righteous Judge: he knew that nothing should separate him from Thee. But I am a sinner, and therefore fear to die: for the sinner's death is terrible: how should it not, when there is no hope of life? I fear to go forth; I tremble at the very harbour's mouth, lest there be none nigh to stand by me and to receive me. How shall I go forth without fear, unless Thou, Lord, keep my going out and coming in? Behold I should fall among thieves, and they would strip me and make a prey of me, if there be none by to redeem and to save me. I know that they are blessed who die in the Lord, (O how blessed!) but man knoweth not whether Thou love him or abhor him, and what portion awaiteth him in death; how shall he then not fear death, when it is so uncertain what will follow it?

CHRIST. Nay, fear not death then, but fear an evil life. Why flee what is inevitable, and live meanwhile in hazard? I would have thee work out thine own salvation in fear and trembling; strive to enter at the narrow gate and tread the way, which, though strait, leadeth to life. Wouldest thou fear death less? live in continual fear of God, and despise this life's pleasures in hope of those to come. Keep under thy body, as did Paul, and bring it to subjection. To him the world was crucified, and he unto the world; and how should he then not die gladly? Believe Me, he is not loath to die, who hath long since been dead to sin and to the world. What can death take from him who loves nothing in the world, and has his treasure in heaven?

It may surprise thee more, but to him even a sudden death has no terrors. Most men dread it exceedingly; and why? because it is evil? No! but because they are unprepared; too sorely entangled in sin and things of earth. But they who are prepared, find it no evil, yea rather a brief and easier passage from this world's evils to eternal good and endless rest.

O, with what peace and gladness he dies, for whom the world has no charms; how unshrinkingly he goes the way of all flesh, who hath been earnest to tread under foot its lusts. Death is no death to him, but peaceful sleep, that after toil and labour rests his weary limbs. It is written that they that love Me *die in the Lord*, that is, in all they did in life they looked to Me; in all they thought, I was their End; so, when they die, they attain to their last end, even Myself; they sink to sleep in Me and rest in peace: and now there is no more grief, neither crying nor any sorrow, for the former things are passed away. Well then is their death named peace.

Man's life on earth is warfare, a weary wrestling against the princes of darkness: when, therefore, My elect have followed Me, and fought manfully beneath My standard (Who by Dying have destroyed death and by My Resurrection have brought in life again,) they die in peace, since death puts an end to all their wars; in Me they enjoy peace and an eternal prize of victory. As for the ungodly, it is not so with them; they found their peace in sin and riches: they shall be troubled with horrible dismay, and wrestle with pains in hell for ever.

MAN. LORD, be it for me too to say, Now lettest Thou Thy servant depart in peace, for mine eyes have seen, and mine ears have heard Thy salutary words. Why should I fear to die, who am going to my Father? Why not joyfully abandon this tottering house of clay, knowing, as I do, that when our earthly house of this tabernacle is dissolved, we have a house of God, eternal in the heavens? When shall I be delivered from the body of this death? When shall I come to appear before the Presence of GOD? &c.

§ 6. *Recommendation of an early disposal of temporal goods.*

To secure thy death-bed against carefulness, it is well to set thine house in order, whilst thou art still in health. Let thy will be made, the claims of others satisfied, thy reckonings clear. Delay in these things to the hour of death may cost thee much both in thy property and thy soul.

At death there is the violence and pain of disease; or a cheating hope of life or wandering of mind; or a thousand things, all of which unhinge the mind. O how subtly does the devil persuade many, either from carelessness, or some superstitious prejudice against making a will in health, to delay the settlement of their temporal affairs till the world is passing from them and they ought to give their thoughts to heaven. And then the ill-timed carefulness draws their mind off from GOD and from their soul, and entangles it in worldly things: thus the last few precious hours, which should be given to a holy death, pass and are lost.

Let thy will be just, pious, and explicit; the seed of concord, not of litigation. Deal with thy property not as its owner, but as My steward. If thou forget Me Who gave thee all, thou art ungrateful to Me, and therefore cruel to thine own soul; and how shalt thou be good to others? Dispose of thy worldly goods that they lose thee not, yea that they win for thee, eternal life.

§ 7. *Recommendation of early almsgiving before death.*

MAN. Naked came I out of my mother's womb, and naked shall I return: I brought nothing into the world, and I shall take nothing out. What good shall it do me at the hour of death to possess gold and silver, yea, the whole world, and lose my soul? O that I might redeem my soul with riches! but my goods, O LORD, are nothing unto Thee; Thine is the silver, Thine the gold; Thine the world and all that therein is: what shall man give to GOD, Who hath and giveth all things?

CHRIST. Because this is so, therefore are the poor always with you, and what thou dost to one of the least of Mine, I reckon done to Me. The poor man's hand is My treasury; deposit what thou wilt there, and thou shalt find it again. But they who love riches shall sleep their sleep, and in their hands find nothing. Do good therefore to thy friend before thou die, and according to thy power distribute to the poor. Make the poor thy friends by the mammon of unrighteousness, that when thou failest, they may receive thee into everlasting habitations.

O blind and foolish avarice! Men lay up treasures and cannot tell for whom they gather them: whosoever be their heir, be he wise or foolish, he shall be master of their labours, wherein they toiled. Vanity of vanities! they go on toiling; their eye is not satisfied with riches, neither do they ask themselves, For whom do I thus labour and starve my soul? And then a stranger cometh and devours all the hoards, which they had denied the poor; and the miser reaps no profit from his riches; it is My righteous judgment; he beareth his own punishment, vexation and unprofitable craving; and then, at last, leaves his riches to aliens.

MAN. But suppose he were to make abundant alms after he is dead, to endow Churches, leave noble monuments, &c.

CHRIST. What else is this than for a man full to satiety to loath more food? What is it to give away what thou canst not take with thee, canst enjoy no longer; what, willingly or unwillingly, thou must leave? Almsgiving I love; but a single coin given in life, is better than a hundred bequeathed at death. I look not on the sum but on the will; but at death man and his wealth must needs part; necessity, not a loving will, makes him liberal now. Let not that common cheat delude you: give not by others' hands, but thine own.

Many and many have I known who every day despised the poor, or treated them harshly; and yet in their wills they have made provision for poor people after their death, nay, seemed to be concerned for such as should be poor, age after age. Think you that they really cared for the poor? that they loved works of charity for love of Me? I tell thee (for I know what is in man), that they who gloated over wealth, lived sparingly and harshly towards the poor, and grew liberal only on their death-beds, would not give even then, could they longer enjoy their wealth. And now when they can do no more, and know that their life has been despicable and mean, they make a last effort to blazon their names by a death-bed charity.

Miserable men! Who hath bewitched your eyes that ye see not, that of all vanities beneath the sun, this is the greatest? Ye cheat skilfully the eyes of men; think ye to mock My Eyes, which see, brighter than the sun, your inmost heart? Ye that have this world's good, if ye see your brethren have need, and shut up your bowels of compassion, how dwelleth the love of GOD in you?

If the misery, the nakedness, the famine of the poor which ye see with your own eyes, move you not, who will believe that ye are moved by the necessities of those whom ye shall never see? Does not actual present misery move more our eyes and senses than misery imagined? And are ye more sure of others' eyes and hands than of your own? Well were it for the poor, would the rich feed each the poor of their own day rather than those of posterity!

MAN. But, LORD, hast Thou not bidden us give alms of our abundance? Suppose then I were liberal to the poor in my life, and came to want myself? would this be prudent? I will give therefore when I have enough to spare: and when shall I know this, but at death?

CHRIST. Thinkest thou that He Who feeds the fowls of heaven, and giveth food to the cattle and to the young ravens that call upon Him, will forsake thee, if for love of Him thou feed Me in My members? O thou of little faith, wherefore dost thou doubt? This is fleshly and worldly prudence: but they that love GOD and trust in Him are bounteous to the poor, and yet have no misgivings for themselves. Have I not said, *Give and it shall be given unto you:* and, *He that giveth unto the poor, shall not lack. He that hath pity upon the poor, lendeth to the* LORD, *and what he giveth He will pay him again. He that soweth sparingly, shall reap also sparingly; but he that soweth bountifully shall reap also bountifully. He that ministereth seed to the sower shall both minister bread for your food and multiply your seed sown*, &c.? What fearest thou then, having such promises? If thou wert dealing with a Jew or a publican, thou wouldest trust his hand-writing; wilt thou not trust Mine in Holy Scripture? However, let a man look to his own necessities when he gives alms: I condemn not proper prudence, nor do I bid you give all away at once. Yet how very few there are, here one and there another, who measure what is needful for their condition in life by the rule of right reason, and not by the suggestions of the flesh! And blinded thus, they spend bountifully or lavishly on themselves and on superfluities; to the poor they are sparing, and have no means!

But be thou merciful after thy power; if thou have much, give plenteously; if little, do thy diligence gladly to give of that little. Whatsoever thou wouldest commit to others to do for thee, see thou do thyself. For if thou die and go to eternal punishment, (they are the words of a good and holy man[1]), what good will thy will with all its provisions, thy funeral solemnities, thy alms and offerings, do thee? Make these sacrifices while thou art still alive; so shalt thou not only be absolved from sin, but growing also in My grace, thou shalt not come to condemnation; so will I keep thee free from sin, that thou shalt persevere in holy works unto the end.

Do now, My beloved son, all thou canst: trust not to friends and relations, and delay not to think of thy salvation. Man will forget thee sooner than thou thinkest: make provision in time and be beforehand, rather than depend on others. If thou care not for thyself now, who will care for thee hereafter[m]?

Now thou art hale and strong, redeem thy sins with almsgiving[n]. To one walking in darkness, one torch carried in advance, gives more light than many behind. Give of thy substance while it is thine; when thou art dead, it will be another's and at his disposal: think not he will dis-

---

[1] Joannes Lanspergius.   [m] Thomas à Kempis, book i.   [n] Dan. iv.

pose of it exactly as thou desirest.

All that is of the world is left behind in the world; mercy alone will accompany the dead. If thou neglect it now, thy sins may go with thee instead, and they will take thee thither, whither no alms nor other help can follow after to bring thee back. But timely alms deliver from all sin and death, and keep the soul from entering into darkness, yea, make it find mercy and eternal life. Blessed, indeed, is he that considereth the poor and needy; the LORD shall deliver him in the time of trouble. Boldly and truly spake my servant Jerome, "I have never read of any that died ill, who practised cheerfully the works of mercy."

MAN. All that thou sayest is most true, O LORD, nor have I aught to answer: yet if the seeker of this world's gain should hear Thee, he would be much displeased and go away sorrowful, saying in his heart, This is a hard saying, who can bear it? like that rich young man whom (when he asked Thee how he should be perfect) Thou badest sell all he had, give to the poor, and follow Thee.

CHRIST. How hardly shall they that have riches enter into the kingdom of heaven. Woe to the rich who here receive their consolation and treat their brethren harshly. What is worse than love of money? For such an one will set even his own soul to sale. Wouldest thou be happy? go not after gold and riches, trust not in treasure. Few resist them; but be thou among these few. Lay up for thyself treasures in heaven, safe from moth and thief. Let others lay up treasure here, and call their lands after their own names: be it enough for thee that thy name be written in heaven. They that seek a name through the goods entrusted to them, like that of the great ones that are in the world in carnal pride, their memory perishes with terror. Not so with men of mercy: their righteousnesses are not forgotten; their name is blessed, and their alms are told of in every Church of the saints.

MAN. Incline my heart, O LORD, unto Thy testimonies, and not to covetousness.

Turn away mine eyes, lest they behold vanity: yea, teach me to see and know the utter vanity, the emptiest of all, of abounding for a little while and lacking for eternity, of seeking momentary fame and reaping perpetual confusion.

[Touching this subject, see St. Chrysost. Hom. 60 ad Popul. and 18 in Ep. ad Rom.; and especially St. Basil, Hom. 2 in Divites avaros; also Comm. in c. 14 Eccl. v. 13.]

§ 8. *Reconciliation necessary before death.*

CHRIST. Another excellent kind of mercy is very necessary for a happy death, besides abundant mercy to the poor; it consists in the perfect forgiveness of thine enemies. If man harbours wrath against man, how shall he seek peace with GOD? Wilt thou be extreme with thy offending brother, who hast wronged Me so infinitely more.

What if I summoned thee straightway to be judged, and searched out thy actions with candles, couldst thou endure it, or answer me one of a thousand? The mercy thou wilt then ask of Me, show thou now to thy fellow; for with the same measure shall it be measured to thee again. How wilt thou hope to find Me pitiful as thy Judge, if to thy fellow-servant thou show no pity?

Look then at both debts; thine to Me, and thy neighbour's debt to thee.

How great the difference! think of this, and thou wilt do by him as thou wouldest have Me do by thee. Forgive thy offending brother, and when thou prayest, thy sins shall be forgiven. But justice without mercy shall be on him that shows no mercy.

MAN. I confess, O LORD, in many things, daily, we all offend Thee: spare me, O LORD, and enter not into judgment with Thy servant, for in Thy sight shall no man living be justified. If Thou wilt be extreme to mark that is done amiss, who, O LORD, shall stand? Forgive me my debts, for cheerfully and heartily, for love of Thee, I forgive all my debtors. Indeed, when dying on the Cross, Thou Thyself taughtest me thus to die, for then Thou prayedst for Thine enemies and torturers, and while we too were yet Thine enemies, Thou willedst to die for us.

§ 9. *Repeated exhortation to provide for a holy death.*

CHRIST. Thus hast thou heard, O man, how to secure a holy and happy death. Lay hold on this instruction in good time, lest, if the LORD be angry, thou perish from the right way. What so much concerns thee as to die holily? As thou diest, thou wilt be blest or cursed to all eternity. To this end thou must live holily; and to obtain both for thee, both My Life and Death were given for thee. Thirty-three years and more was I seen on earth and dwelt with men, leaving thee an example, that thou shouldest follow My steps. My Soul was heavy, and the horror of death came upon Me so that My Sweat fell like blood, that thou shouldest not fear death. I suffered death itself to set thee free from the debt of eternal death by which thou wast bound. Look and see, O man, what thy God went through for thee; far more than it needed to create the world; for then GOD spake and it was done; He commanded, and it stood fast. But here My Words had gainsayers; My Actions, spies; My Pains had mockers; and My Death, revilers; and all this for thee. Behold, how I loved thee! How oughtest thou then to live, and how die, that so great a price of thy redemption may not have been in vain for thee, and all My labours frustrate!

MAN. LORD JESU, he deserves to die who will not live to Thee; very exceedingly shouldest Thou be loved by me, by Whom I live and have my being, now and for ever. What reward shall I give unto the LORD for all the benefits He hath done to me? Were all the lives of all the sons of Adam, all the days the world has stood, and all that man hath done or ever shall do, mine, what would it be to that Thou hast done for me? As the heaven is higher than the earth, so is Thy Life than our life, yet Thou didst lay it down for ours. When then I have given Thee all I can, what return is it? A star compared to the sun, a drop to a river, a pebble to a mountain, a grain of corn to the heap: finite to infinite. LORD, I have only two mites, my soul and body, or rather one, my will; and shall I not give up this to His Will, Who, being GOD so Great, hast presented one so little with such great and countless blessings of unbounded goodness; and with Thy Whole Self hast bought me wholly for Thyself?

The poor creature, then, that by Thy vouchsafement I am, O JESU, turn to Thyself; and of my miserable being take to Thee, I beseech Thee, the residue of my years. For the years that I have lived and lost, by living sinfully, give me, O LORD, a broken and contrite heart, such, as Thou wilt not despise. My days are gone down as a shadow, and have perished without fruit. I cannot recall them. May I remember them before Thee, and repent in the bitterness of my soul. And at last give me a happy death, that I may sing of the loving-kindness of the LORD for ever in the land of the living.

CHRIST. I bruise not the broken reed, nor quench the smoking flax. Only be thou faithful unto death. For I have no pleasure in the misery of them that die. Declare thy way unto the Lord and put thy trust in Him, and He will bring it to pass: without Him not a hair of thy head shall perish.

§ 10. *Perfect self-resignation to the will of God.*

MAN. LORD, I am certain of Thy unbounded love: I will therefore lay me down in peace and take my rest, neither in love with life nor in fear of death. My lot is in Thy Hands. I cast all my care, LORD, upon Thee, for Thou carest for me, and all the hairs of my head are numbered in Thy Sight. Thou hast set me my bounds which shall not be passed.

Thou art the LORD: do as seemeth good in Thine Eyes: who am I that I should say, What doest Thou? Shall the clay say to the potter, what doest thou? or the thing formed rebuke him that fashioned it? And are not we in Thy Hands as clay is in the potter's? Thy Will therefore shall be mine. If Thou wilt have me live, my heart is ready, O GOD; only increase Thy grace that I may serve Thee more faithfully: if Thou wilt have me die, my heart is ready, O God; only let my spirit be received in peace. Thou, O Christ, art life to me, and to die is gain. If longer life be given me, I will live to Thee, to Thy Honour and Glory. Wilt Thou that I shall die, death shall be my gain; for I shall follow and attain Thee Whom my soul seeketh and loveth. If then I walk in the midst of the valley of the shadow of death, I will fear no evil, for Thou art with me. Receive me according to Thy word (for Thou hast said, I desire not the death of a sinner), and I shall live, and let me not be disappointed of my hope. Only this one favour I beg of Thee, O Lord; whensoever Thou wilt have me die, to-day or to-morrow, in the midst of my years or in good old age, let me die in Thy favour. Lighten mine eyes that I sleep not in death, lest mine enemy say, I have prevailed against him. Into Thy Hands, O Lord, I commend my spirit, for Thou hast redeemed me, O Lord God of truth. Living or dying, Lord, I am Thine. In me Thy Will be done! and let me never be separated from Thee, O God, my God, my All!

Here hast thou, pious reader, the art of dying well, *treated with reference to that most needful preparation, a holy life. The more immediate preparation for death consists of acts and exercises of* Faith, Hope, Charity, &c., *and in the pious use of the Sacraments. Touching these see the Exercises that follow, and among others, those on the Lord's Prayer.*

EXERCISES FOR A GOOD AND HAPPY DEATH.

To the pious Reader.

This last Section contains various Prayers and Exercises for a happy death, suited to the healthy, the sick, and the dying, and needful for the first no less than for the other.

Remember that whatever will be of use to thee in sick-

ness and in death, it is safest to begin to practise while thou art in health. Whoso takes delight in exercises such as these in health, shall find most comfort in them in disease and death: he that loathes them in health, shall find no relish in them on his deathbed.

Read therefore and meditate upon them. Often imagine thyself a dying man, while thou art still in health, and do as you would do, or wish to have done, at the point of death. What in life you loved and gladly used, will come readily to mind in death; whereas remedies, to which, when things went well with thee, thou gavest no heed, will not readily occur to thee in time of need.

Exercises, contained in the Soliloquies of Thomas à Kempis, tending to diminish the love of life, and to kindle the desire of futurity, may be found, with other choice pieces of the same Author, in the "Christian Wayfarer[o]."

How a Christian should behave on the approach of sickness.

As soon as sickness comes upon thee, receive it as from

[o] Viator Christianus.

the Hand of GOD, and give Him thanks for dealing with thee as with a son. Offer thyself for greater trials still, and cast thyself wholly on His Divine Providence: rest not thy trust in physicians; remember what evil came of this to Asa.

Still call a physician to thee; above all, one for thy soul to whom thou mayest confess. Both, body and soul, need fitting remedies; and the soul more than the body, for its loss is far more fatal.

Even for the body's sake, see that the soul be sound. Its sicknesses, its sins, often affect the body; and GOD's Providence chastises us with afflicted limbs, and we grow ill because our hearts are evil. First, then, let us cure our souls, then will the other task be easier, or, (which should be no less desired) we shall bear our sicknesses with profit to our soul.

So taught the Great Physician, Who, when He healed the sick, looked to their soul's state before He cured their bodies.

Let us do likewise; and if we desire health of body, first heal our souls. But, wonder of wonders! Life eternal and life mortal are before us; the last has all our care, the for_ *mer scarcely any. Christian, if sickness overtake thee, first seek thee to God, and make Him thy Friend; then will He make the treatment of thy ailments restore thy body, or else thy ailments and thy death healthful to thy soul.*

CHAPTER II.

LITANIES FOR THE HEALTHY, THE SICK, AND DYING.

From Holy Scripture.

LORD, have mercy upon us.
CHRIST, have mercy upon us.
LORD, have mercy upon us.
O CHRIST, hear us.
O CHRIST, graciously hear us.
O GOD the FATHER of Heaven, have mercy upon us.
O GOD the SON, Redeemer of the world, have mercy upon us.
O GOD the HOLY GHOST, have mercy upon us.
HOLY TRINITY, ONE GOD, have mercy upon us.

Who didst form man after Thine own Image and Likeness [p],
Who didst breathe into his nostrils the breath of life [q],
Who didst plant the tree of life in the midst of Eden against the death of the body [r],
Who, after our first parents had incurred the sentence of death, didst oppose the Seed of the woman to the poison of the serpent [s],
Who, when the race of man was, through sin, subject to various miseries, to disease, and death, didst not leave them destitute of comfort and remedies [t],

} Have mercy upon us.

[p] Gen. i. [q] Ib. [r] Gen. ii. [s] Gen. iii. [t] Gen. iii. Job xiv.

Who, when all the first-born of Egypt were destroyed in one night, didst keep the Israelites unhurt [u],

Who didst cause Moses and Aaron, for the sin of unbelief, to die out of the promised land [v],

Who, when the people were bitten by fiery serpents, didst deliver them by the sight of the brazen serpent [w],

Who didst destroy by death more than fifty thousand of the men of Bethshemesh for looking curiously into the ark [x],

Who didst smite with three day's pestilence seventy thousand men of Israel, because of David's numbering the people [y],

Who, having compassion on the affliction of thy people, didst stay the destroying angel that he should not utterly destroy [z],

Who didst heal Naaman the Syrian of his leprosy by the hand of Elisha [a],

Who, at the prayers of Elijah the prophet, didst recall the dead child to life [b],

Who, when king Ahaziah enquired of an idol concerning his recovery, didst punish him with death [c],

Who, through Elijah the prophet, didst restore to life the son of the woman with whom he sojourned [d],

Who, by the bones of Elisha, didst recall a dead man to life [e],

Who didst cause Asa the king, trusting more in the physician than in God, to die before his time [f],

Who, when Hezekiah in his sickness prayed unto Thee with tears, didst deliver him from disease and death [g],

Who when Job, by Thy permission, was very sore afflicted of Satan, didst strengthen him with wonderful patience [h],

} Have mercy upon us.

[u] Exod. xii. [v] Num. xx. [w] Num. xxi. [x] 1 Sam. vi.
[y] 2 Sam. xxiv. [z] Ib. [a] 2 Kings v. [b] 1 Kings xvii.
[c] 2 Kings i. [d] 2 Kings iv. [e] Ib. xiii. [f] 2 Chron. xvi.
[g] Is. xxxviii. [h] Job i, &c.

Who dost chasten with pain upon the bed, and the bones of man with strong pain[i],

Who, to give an example of patience to after generations, didst prove Tobias with the plague of blindness[j],

Who hast provided physicians and numberless kinds of remedies for the need of men[k],

Who madest not death, neither hast pleasure in the destruction of the living[l],

Who wast sent to heal the broken-hearted, to preach deliverance to the captives, to comfort all that mourn[m];

Who, when Simeon, the just and devout old man, had seen the Messiah, didst let him depart out of this world in peace[n],

Who didst heal the son of the nobleman in Capernaum[o],

Who, didst make the man, who had had an infirmity thirty and eight years, whole with a word[p],

Who didst deliver the mother-in-law of Peter, held by a great fever[q],

Who didst do all things well, making both the deaf to hear and the dumb to speak[r],

Who didst live familiarly with publicans and sinners, saying, They that are whole need not a physician, but they that are sick[s],

Who didst cure the sick of the palsy, lying on a bed and let down through the roof[t],

Who didst heal the woman who had an issue of blood twelve years, and had suffered in vain many things from the physicians[u],

Who didst restore many that were blind to sight[v],

Who with a word alone didst cleanse many lepers from their leprosy[w],

} Have mercy upon us.

[i] Job xxxiii. [j] Tob. ii. [k] Eccl. xxxviii. [l] Wis. i.
[m] Is. lxi. [n] Luke ii. [o] John iv. [p] Ib. v.
[q] Luke iv. [r] Mark vii. [s] Matt. ix. [t] Ib. Luke v.
[u] Mark v. Luke viii. [v] Matt. ix. John ix, &c.
[w] Matt. viii. xi, &c.

§ vii.] A PREPARATION TO DIE WELL AND HAPPILY. 35

Who didst raise from the dead the daughter of Jairus, the chief ruler of the synagogue [x],
Who didst restore to perfect health the woman bowed down by a spirit of infirmity eighteen years [y],
Who didst deliver the lunatic sore vexed with a devil [z],
Who, in absence, didst cure the servant of the centurion who was sick [a],
Who didst give back unto his mother, a widow, her only son alive from the dead [b],
Who didst deliver the daughter of the Canaanitish woman, grievously vexed with a devil [c],
Who didst raise up Lazarus when he had lain four days in the grave [d],
Who didst heal all that were sick, those that were lunatic, and those that had the palsy and the dropsy, and all that were taken with divers diseases and torments [e],
Who being in an agony, sorrowful even unto death, didst shed forth as sweat great drops of Blood [f],
Who, when Thou didst pray that the Cup of Suffering and of Death might pass from Thee, didst submit Thine own unto Thy Father's Will [g],
Who, to the robber crucified with Thee, didst promise a portion in Thy Kingdom [h],
Who wast made for our sakes obedient unto God the Father, even unto Death, the Death of the Cross [i],
Who, in dying, didst commend Thy Spirit into the Hands of Thine everlasting Father [j],
Who, when Thou hadst cried with a loud voice, didst bow Thy Head and give up the ghost [k],
Who, through death, didst destroy him that had the power of death [l],
Who wast wounded for our transgressions, and bruised for our iniquities [m],

} Have mercy upon us.

[x] Luke viii. Matt. ix.   [y] Luke xiii.   [z] Matt. xvii.
[a] Ib. viii.   [b] Luke vii.   [c] Matt. xv.
[d] John xi.   [e] Mark iii. ix. Ib. i. Luke iv. xiv, &c.
[f] Luke xxii.   [g] Ib.   [h] Ib. xxiii.
[i] Phil. ii.   [j] Luke xxiii.   [k] John xix.   [l] Heb. ii.   [m] Is. liii.

Who didst Thyself take our infirmities, and bear our sicknesses [n],
Who wast wont to send pestilence and diseases as a punishment for sin [o],
Who dost ofttimes send diseases, not because of sin, but to show forth the glory of GOD [p],
Who dost chasten and correct those whom Thou dost love [q],
Who didst chasten ofttimes with diseases and untimely death, those who behaved irreverently towards Thy Holy Mysteries [r],
Who, by the shadow of Peter, didst deliver many from sickness [s],
Who, by handkerchiefs and aprons from the body of Paul, didst cure many sick [t],
Who, by the hands of Thy Apostles, didst give life to the dead, and various mercies of healing to the sick [u],
Who dost wipe away all tears from the eyes of Thine Elect [v],
O LORD, Who hast power of life and death [w],
O LORD, the Strength of our life [x],
FATHER of mercies and GOD of all comfort, Who comfortest us in all our tribulation [y],
The Faithful GOD, Who wilt not suffer us to be tempted above that we are able, but dost with the temptation make a way to escape, that we may be able to bear it [z],
Who makest sore and bindest up, Who woundest, and Thy Hands make whole [a],
Who wilt have all men to be saved, and to come to the knowledge of the truth [b],
Who killest and makest alive, bringest down to the grave and bringest up [c],
Who shalt come to judge the quick and the dead [d],

} Have mercy upon us.

[n] Is. liii. Matt. viii. [o] Deut. xxviii. Ezek. xxviii, &c.
[p] John ix. xi. [q] Heb. xii. [r] 1 Cor. xi. [s] Acts v. [t] Ib. xix.
[u] Ib. ix, &c. [v] Rev. vii. [w] Wis. xvi. [x] Ps. xxvii. [y] 2 Cor. i.
[z] 1 Cor. x. [a] Job v. [b] 1 Tim. ii. [c] 1 Sam. ii. [d] 2 Tim. iv.

§ vii.] A PREPARATION TO DIE WELL AND HAPPILY. 37

Be merciful, spare us, O LORD,
From all the pain of sickness,
From a sudden, unprepared, and evil death,
By the pain and torment of Thy Circumcision [e],
By the pain of death which encompassed Thee in the garden, when Thy Passion was at hand [f],
By the zeal of Thy love, whereby Thou didst bear our griefs, and carry our sorrows, and heal us with Thy stripes [g],
By the anguish of Thy Heart upon the Cross, when Thou didst cry aloud, that Thy FATHER had forsaken Thee [h],
By the sword of grief, wherewith the heart of Thy blessed Mother was pierced through Thy Passion [i],
} Deliver us, O LORD.

We sinners do beseech Thee to hear us.

That we may confess ourselves to be strangers and pilgrims upon the earth [k],
That, having here no continuing city, we may seek the more earnestly one to come [l],
That, among so many storms and perils of life, we may hasten to enter into that rest which we hope for in heaven [m],
That our light affliction, which is but for a moment, may work in us an eternal weight of glory [n],
That we may not despise the chastening of the LORD, nor faint when we are rebuked of Him [o],
That we may take cheerfully whatsoever shall be brought upon us, and be patient under suffering [p],
That, in all our diseases and afflictions, we may say nothing foolish against the LORD [q],
That, as we have received good of the Hand of the LORD, so we may with an equal mind endure evil [r],
} We beseech Thee to hear us,

[e] Luke ii.   [f] Ib. xxii.   [g] Is. liii.   [h] Matt. xxvii.
[i] Luke ii.   [k] Ps. xxxix.   [l] Heb. xiii.   [m] Ib. iv.
[n] 2 Cor. iv.   [o] Prov. iii. Heb. xii.   [p] Eccles ii.   [q] Job i.
[r] Ib. ii.

That, in the multitude of the sorrows that I have in my heart and in my body, Thy comforts may refresh my soul [s],

That, as the sufferings of CHRIST abound in us, so, through CHRIST, our consolation also may abound [t],

That we may always bear about in our body the Dying of JESUS CHRIST [u],

That looking unto JESUS, the Author and Finisher of our faith, Who for the joy that was set before Him endured the Cross, we may run with patience towards the prize that is set before us [v],

That CHRIST may be magnified in our body, whether by life or death [w],

That, as CHRIST hath suffered for us in in the flesh, we also may arm ourselves with the same mind [x],

That we may not slothfully waste this accepted time, this day of salvation [y],

That we may think over our past years before Thee in the bitterness of our soul [z],

That, being uncertain as to the coming of death and of the Judge, we may set our house in order betimes [a],

That, being delivered out of the hand of our enemies, we may serve Thee without fear, in holiness and righteousness all the days of our life [b],

That we may have a desire to depart and to be with CHRIST [c],

That Thou wouldest vouchsafe to make and smooth all our bed in our sickness [d],

That diseases and all evils of the body may work together for good to us who love GOD [e],

That, being healed of our sickness by Thy mercy, we may sin no more, lest a worse thing happen unto us [f],

⎫
⎬ We beseech Thee to hear us.
⎭

[s] Ps. xciv.   [t] 2 Cor. i.   [u] Ib. iv.   [v] Heb. xii.
[w] Phil. i.   [x] 1 Pet. iv.   [y] 2 Cor. vi.   [z] Is. xxxviii.
[a] Ib.   [b] Luke i.   [c] Phil. i.   [d] Ps. xli.
[e] Rom. viii.   [f] John v.

§ vii.] A PREPARATION TO DIE WELL AND HAPPILY.

That, taking to us the whole armour of GOD, we may be able to stand in the evil day, and quench the fiery darts of the wicked [g],

That, as in Adam we all die, even so in Christ we may all be made alive [h],

That, whether we live, we may live unto the LORD, and whether we die, we may die unto the Lord [i],

That neither life, nor death, nor any other creature may be able to separate us from CHRIST [k],

That to us to live may be CHRIST, and to die gain [l],

That, though I walk through the valley of the shadow of death, I may fear no evil, for Thou art with me [m],

That, in the last conflict, we may resist, strong in the faith, the roaring lion [n],

That we may die the death of the righteous, and that our last end may be like his [o],

That Thou wouldest lighten mine eyes, that I sleep not in death, lest mine enemy prevail against me [p],

That Thou wouldest deliver me from the body of this death [q],

That Thou wouldest bring my soul out of prison, that I may give thanks unto Thy Name [r],

That, when we are dying, Thou wouldest comfort us with the penitent thief, by Thy most sweet promise, and the expectation of Thy kingdom [s],

That Thou wouldest not enter into judgment with Thy servant, because in Thy sight shall no man living be justified [t],

That Thou wouldest not deal with us after our sins, nor reward us according to our iniquities [u],

That I may dwell in the house of the LORD all the days of my life [x],

That, when the earthly house of this tabernacle is dissolved, we may have a house not made with hands, eternal in the heavens [y],

} We beseech Thee to hear us.

[g] Eph. vi.   [h] 1 Cor. xv.   [i] Rom. xiv.   [k] Ib. viii.
[l] Phil. i.   [m] Ps. xxiii.   [n] 1 Pet. v.   [o] Num. xxiii.
[p] Ps. xiii. [q] Rom. vii.   [r] Ps. cxliii. [s] Luke xxiii.
[t] Ps. cxliii. [u] Ib. ciii.   [x] Ib. xxvii.   [y] 2 Cor. v.

O LAMB of GOD, Who takest away the sins of the world,
Have mercy upon us.
O LAMB of GOD, Who takest away the sins of the world,
Grant us Thy peace.
O CHRIST, hear us.
LORD, have mercy upon us.
CHRIST, have mercy upon us.
LORD, have mercy upon us.
Our FATHER.

Let us pray.

O GOD, Who by the patience of Thine Only Begotten, didst crush the pride of the ancient enemy, grant to us, we beseech Thee, worthily to commemorate those things which He suffered for us, and so, after His example, patiently to endure all adversity.

O GOD, Who in Thy great goodness didst make, and of Thy most tender mercy didst re-make the human race, Who, when man was cast down from eternal happiness by the malice of the devil, didst redeem him by the Precious Blood of Thine Only Begotten Son, quicken us Thy servants by the strength of Thy grace, and reach out Thy Life-giving Hand to us who are lying in the dust; fill us with joy of heart and gladness of spirit; drive far from us all the snares of the enemy, and send to us the messenger of health, the angel of peace, that he may raise us up from sorrow by Thy consolations, whereby we may obtain help at this present time, and in the time to come everlasting rewards.

O GOD, by Whose appointment the moments of our life pass away, receive the humble prayers of Thy servants who cry unto Thee, that we, being delivered from all sickness and adversity, may praise Thee with everlasting thanksgiving; through our LORD JESUS CHRIST Thy Son, Who liveth and reigneth with Thee and the Holy GHOST, One GOD, world without end. Amen.

COLLECT,

FOR OBTAINING THE SAME GIFT, WHICH IS THE ONLY THING NEEDFUL.

O LORD JESUS CHRIST, I beseech Thee, by that love through which Thou barest the burdens of all men, that Thou wouldest make me receive the burden of my sadness with gratitude from the Hand of Thy Providence and from the Will of Thy Fatherly Heart, and endure it, for Thy sake, as long as it shall please Thee, with the fullest resignation of myself, so Thou strengthen me by Thy grace, that I may never in little things offend Thee, nor depart in the least from Thy most holy Will.

[I would[a] that I could alone endure the afflictions of all and each of those who have suffered for Thee, that so I might make some slight return to Thine infinite love.] Yea, O most merciful JESU, so unite (I beseech Thee) my will with Thy most holy pleasure, that I may be unable to wish for any thing but what Thou willest.

CHAPTER III.

SEVEN STEPS TO A BLESSED DEATH; OR A DAILY EXERCISE ON THE LORD'S PRAYER FOR A HAPPY DEATH.

Our Father which art in Heaven.

O Everlasting FATHER of our LORD JESUS CHRIST, Thy Son by Nature, Thou art our FATHER by grace; for Thou didst create us in Thine own Image, and when we were, by sin, made children of wrath, Thou didst, by the Blood of Thy Son, adopt us to be children of grace, and heirs of everlasting life. And although heaven is the seat of Thy Majesty and of Thy Glory, yet dost Thou ever behold us, Thy children, upon earth,

[a] On this solemn prayer, see Preface to Part I.

and dost guide us with a Father's care, and love, and Providence.

I lift up mine eyes, O merciful FATHER, unto Thee, Who dwellest in the heavens, from whence cometh my help. My soul longeth after Thee, as the hart panteth after the waterbrooks. For Thou hast created us for Thyself, and our soul is disquieted until it turneth again unto its rest in Thee. Where my FATHER is, there is my home; there is my hope and my inheritance, and my portion in the land of the living. My heart sigheth after Thee; my soul hangeth upon Thee. O that Thy Right Hand would uphold me! For Thy loving kindness is better than the life itself. O when shall I be delivered from this banishment? when shall I be brought out of this prison, into which I have been sent, inveigled, and enticed from my native country? When shall I enter into my FATHER'S House, where there are many mansions? O when wilt Thou comfort me? When wilt Thou bring me out of the horrible pit, out of the mire and clay? When shall I come and appear before the presence of GOD my FATHER? When wilt Thou make me full of joy with Thy Countenance, that I may see, not through a glass darkly, but face to face? Blessed are they that dwell in Thy House, O LORD, they shall be always praising Thee! Behold, Thy ways are in my heart in this vale of tears, in the place where the disobedience of my first father hath placed me. Supported by Thy blessing, I shall go from strength to strength, until I see Thee the GOD of gods in Sion.

FIRST STEP.

LIVELY FAITH.

Hallowed be Thy Name,

First, by a true and lively Faith, because without faith it is impossible to please GOD; for he that cometh to Thee, O GOD, must believe that Thou art, and that Thou art a Rewarder of them that seek Thee. What, indeed, is our life upon the earth, but an approach and progress towards God, with the two feet of Faith and Hope? For quiet and rest in Him, and cleaving to Him, and His embrace and full fruition, which are the perfection of Charity, are reserved for our Heavenly Country. For then shalt Thou embrace Thy son, returning unto Thee out of a far country, and shalt put on him the best robe.

In the meanwhile, O Lord, I believe that THOU ART THAT THOU ART; that is, God most Mighty, Wise and Good above all, and that Thou shalt be Thyself the exceeding great Reward and Treasure of those that love Thee. I believe that my Redeemer liveth, and that at the last day I shall rise again out of the earth, and in my flesh shall see God my Saviour. In this faith, I desire to live and die. Supported by this faith, I shall stand steadfast and secure under every cross, tribulation, distress, disease, and even death itself; in adversity as in prosperity I will ever hallow and praise Thy Name; nothing doubting either Thy Divine Power or Thy Fatherly Love, whereby Thou art both able and willing to preserve me.

O Lord, strengthen and increase my faith for the Glory of Thy Name, because Thy Name is then best hallowed by us, when Thou art believed to be mighty in deed, true in word, and evermore faithful in promises. Wherefore Moses and Aaron were not suffered by Thee to enter into the promised Land, because they sanctified Thee not before the people, not believing Thee concerning bringing the water from the rock.

But the ready faith of Abraham is every where praised, who staggered not at Thy promise through unbelief, but was strong in faith, giving glory to God. For he straightway left his own country and his kindred, and came into the land which Thou didst show him, knowing that, whatsoever God hath promised, He is able also to perform.

I also believe verily to see the goodness of the Lord in the land of the living, when I shall have departed out of this world. Call me hence whensoever Thou wilt, but grant that, faith being my guide, I may follow cheerfully, firmly believing that Thou art mighty and good;

then shall Thy loving SPIRIT lead me forth into the land of uprightness, and Thou, for Thy Holy Name's sake, O LORD, wilt quicken me in Thy Righteousness.

SECOND STEP.

STEADFAST HOPE.

Thy Kingdom come,

Even the kingdom which is prepared for us from the foundation of the world; for Thou hast delivered us from the power of darkness, and hast translated us into the Kingdom of the SON of Thy love, that we may be fellow-heirs with Him according to the hope of Eternal Life. For if in this life only we have hope, we are of all men most miserable. The LORD is the Portion of my inheritance and of my cup; Thou art He that shall restore to me my heritage. Oh! when shall this be? for here we are only strangers and pilgrims, having no continuing city, but seeking one to come.

Meanwhile we rejoice in hope of the glory of the sons of GOD, and not only so, but we also joy in tribulation, knowing that tribulation worketh patience, and patience experience, and experience hope, and hope maketh not ashamed[a]. Doubtless we must, through much tribulation, enter into the Kingdom of GOD, but the hope of so great a reward is our comfort in all our labours. For the sufferings of this present time are not worthy to be compared with the glory which shall be revealed in us.

I will set Thee, therefore, O LORD, always before my face, for Thou art on my right hand, therefore shall I not be moved. Wherefore my heart shall be glad; moreover also my flesh shall rest in hope. In peace in Thee, the Self-same, shall I sleep and take my rest; for it is thou, LORD, only that makest me to dwell in safety, And now, LORD, what is my hope? truly, my hope is even in Thee. Oh! stablish me according to Thy word, that I may live, and let me not be

[a] Rom. v.

disappointed of my hope. In Thee, O LORD, have I put my trust; let me never be put to confusion; deliver me in Thy Righteousness.

THIRD STEP.

UNFEIGNED CHARITY.

Thy will be done in earth, as it is in heaven.

And what is Thy Will, O most loving FATHER, except that I should love Thee? Behold, Thou commandest that I should love Thee with all my heart and soul, with all my mind and strength; but grant Thou me that which Thou commandest, and command what Thou wilt. For Thou seest what hindrances of Thy will and obstacles of love we endure, whilst this corruptible body weigheth down the soul. I do indeed desire thus to love Thee, and I delight in Thy law after the inner man, but I find another law in my members warring against the law of my mind, so that the good that I will, I do not.

O, wretched man that I am! who shall deliver me from the body of this death? Thy Grace, through JESUS CHRIST our LORD. Grant, therefore, that I may not, by loving my life, lose it, but by a salutary hatred may preserve it unto life eternal.

But I hear also, that if any man love the world, or the things that are in the world, the love of GOD is not in him; let therefore, love as strong as death, yea, stronger than death, drive far from my heart this evil affection; that nothing, especially at my departure out of this world, may separate me from the love of GOD which is in CHRIST JESUS our LORD.

Let, therefore, the might of Thy love absorb me, that I may die to the world for the love of Thy Love, Who for the love of my love didst vouchsafe to die upon the Cross.

FOURTH STEP.

PARTAKING OF THE SACRAMENTS.

Give us this day our daily bread.

O GOD, Who hast fed me from my youth up until now, Oh! forsake me not in mine age, when my strength faileth me! For whilst we are journeying through this desert unto the Land of Promise, we have need of food for the soul no less than for the body, lest we faint by the way. For man liveth not by bread alone, but by every word that proceedeth out of Thy Mouth. Thy Word and Sacraments, therefore, are the food of the soul; but more especially that Bread of Angels, that true Manna from heaven, even the Body and Blood of our LORD JESUS CHRIST, as He Himself said, " My Flesh is meat indeed, and My Blood is drink indeed, Whereof if a man eat and drink, he shall never die."

O! grant unto me, LORD, that when I go the way of all flesh, and depart out of the desert of this world unto the everlasting Land of Promise, I may not lack refreshment by the way; above all, let that Heavenly Bread strengthen my heart; support my soul, I pray Thee, with Thy Body and Blood, that I may go in the strength of that Meat even unto the lofty mountain of Thy Glory, where thou shalt fill with the flour of wheat Thine elect, (whom on earth Thou didst feed with the bread of tears), and shalt satisfy them with the plenteousness of Thine House.

FIFTH STEP.

REMISSION OF SINS.

Forgive us our trespasses.

I know, O LORD, that nothing which is defiled can enter into the Kingdom of Heaven, neither dost Thou admit any one except he be reconciled unto Thee and to his neighbour. Alas! I am poor and in misery; unto Thee I owe infinite debts, and have nothing wherewith to pay or to satisfy Thee. What shall I do? Behold, with Thee, O LORD, there is mercy, and the redemption by Thy SON is plenteous. He came to pay our debts, and to save sinners, of whom I am chief. Enter not, I pray Thee, into judgment with Thy servant, for in Thy Sight shall no man living be justified, but look upon the Face of Christ.

I grieve from my inmost heart that I should ever have offended Thee, my GOD and my Chief Good. And, therefore, I heartily forgive all the offences of my neighbour against me, lest, perchance, I hope in vain for mercy from Thee my LORD, whilst I, Thy servant, retain anger against my fellow-servant. Forgive me, therefore, according to the promise of Thy SON, "Forgive, and ye shall be forgiven," and especially in that last hour when I shall appear before Thee, my Judge. Woe unto me if Thou shalt then be extreme to mark what I have done amiss! O let the hand-writing of ordinances which is against me, and all my sins be blotted out by the Blood of JESUS CHRIST, which was shed for us upon the Cross for the remission of sins.

SIXTH STEP.

VICTORY OVER TEMPTATION.

Lead us not into temptation.

For what is this our life but a temptation, and a continual conflict upon earth? We are engaged in a hard struggle with many and powerful enemies, whom we have no power to resist, except Thou, the LORD mighty in battle, dost fight for us and defend us.

O faithful GOD! suffer me not to be tempted above that I am able, but, with the temptation, make a way of escape, especially at the hour of my departure out of this world; for then the enemy is wont to attack more fiercely, lying in wait to bruise our heel.

, Be with me in that perilous struggle, and the moment of that last conflict on which all my eternity depends, together with the fruit of all the labours which Thy Son underwent, and the Blood which He poured out for me. Woe is me! if that price shall have been paid for me in vain. Strengthen me, lest I fall under the trial. Enlighten mine eyes that I sleep not in death, lest mine enemy say, I have prevailed against him. Grant unto me that, putting on the whole armour of God, I may be able to withstand in the evil day, and quench all the fiery darts of the wicked one; lest he snatch from me the crown of righteousness which is laid up for me. If Thou be for us, who shall be against us? Though I walk through the valley of the shadow of death, I will fear no evil, for Thou art with me. Though an host of men were laid against me, yet shall not my heart be afraid, and though there rose up war against me, yet will I put my trust in Thee.

SEVENTH STEP.

DELIVERANCE FROM EVERLASTING DEATH.

But deliver us from evil.

Many evils press upon us here, and compel us to flee to Thee, O God, to be delivered from them. The world that lieth in wickedness, Satan also, emphatically the Evil One, and numberless other evils, as punishment for sin. But there is no evil equal to the death of the soul, that miserable offspring of sin. For sin, when it is finished, bringeth forth death. The death of sinners is in truth the worst of evils, for to be separated from the Chief Good must be the evil of all evils. O that in that evil day the Lord would deliver me from that evil! For the dead praise not Thee, O God, neither all they that go down into hell. The living, the living, he shall praise Thee.

O Lord, deliver my soul; the Lord is righteous, yea, our God is merciful. Deliver my soul from death, mine eyes from tears, and my feet from falling, that I may sing a new song unto Thee, and offer to Thee the sacrifice of thanksgiving.

The LORD is my strength and my song, and is become my salvation.

The Right Hand of the LORD hath the pre-eminence, the Right Hand of the LORD hath upheld me.

I shall not die, but live, and declare the works of the LORD.

The LORD hath chastened and corrected me, but He hath not given me over unto death.

Thou hast broken my bonds in sunder; death is swallowed up in victory.

My soul is escaped as a bird out of the snare of the fowler. The snare is broken and I am delivered.

I will give thanks unto the LORD, for He is gracious, because His mercy endureth for ever. Amen. Amen.

CHAPTER IV.

EXERCISES TO BE USED DURING SICKNESS.

PRAYER

FOR PATIENCE IN DISEASES AND BODILY SUFFERINGS.

I will speak unto the LORD, who am but dust and ashes, a shadow that departeth, a vapour appearing for a little while: I will say, Remember, O LORD, what my frame is; remember that Thou hast made me as the clay, and shalt bring me to the dust again. Contend not with me, therefore, in thy strength; for what is my strength that I should endure; or what is my end that I should bear patiently? My strength is not the strength of stones, neither is my flesh of brass. Why, then, are the arrows of the LORD within me, whose poison shall drink up my spirit? wherefore do the terrors of GOD set themselves in array against me?

But what? shall I set my mouth in heaven, and speak

against the words of the Holy One? Should I not rather say, The Lord gave strength, health, &c., and the LORD hath taken them away. As it pleases the LORD, so is it done; blessed be the Name of the LORD. So I say, O LORD, and so I feel. Righteous art Thou, O LORD, and true is Thy judgment; and surely I have deserved greater things than these. If I were compelled myself to be the judge of my own deservings, I could take away nothing from this punishment which I am enduring.

Wherefore I acknowledge the Hand of a Father chastening in mercy, not the Right Hand of a Judge punishing in wrath. But this one thing I ask of Thee, most pitying FATHER, remember what this frail and feeble work of Thine Hands can bear without fainting? nothing, indeed, of itself, but all things in Thee, if strengthened by Thy Grace.

Wherefore grant me strength, that I may suffer and endure; patience alone I ask. This it is which is needful for me; LORD, give me this, and behold my heart is ready, O GOD, my heart is ready to receive whatsoever shall be laid upon me; so that it shall be even a consolation to me, that afflicting me with pain, Thou sparest not. Grant, O LORD, that in my patience I may possess my soul; and to that end may I often look upon the Face of CHRIST Thy SON, that as He hath suffered such terrible things in the Flesh, I may endeavour to be armed with the same mind. He was made obedient to Thee unto Death, the Death of the Cross. I have not yet resisted unto blood: yet I know how I am oppressed, when the pains of disease and the sorrows of death attack me.

Wherefore I commit my strength unto Thee. For Thou art my strength and my Refuge; Thou dost uphold my life. Examine me, O LORD, and prove me; try out with Thy fire my reins and my heart, that I may be found in some measure worthy of Thee; as gold which has been tried in the fire. I know, indeed, that the sufferings of this present time are not worthy to be compared with the glory which shall be revealed in us; but I also know, that as it behoved CHRIST to suffer and thus to enter into His Glory, so too the Christian, if he be not made like unto his Head, and pass through fire and water, shall not be brought out into a wealthy place. Behold, O LORD, now am I in the midst of the fire, and how long I shall be there, this is with Thee. Keep me in the mean while, Thou Who didst preserve unhurt the three children in the furnace at Babylon. Bring me forth safe like them, when it shall please Thee, that I also may bless Thee with all Thy creatures for ever, saying, "O all ye works of the LORD, bless ye the LORD, praise Him and magnify Him for ever," &c.

Another Exercise for Patience thou hast above, P. iv. c. 5, Exerc. 15.

ASPIRATIONS AND REFLECTIONS OF THE PIOUS SOUL, USEFUL IN SICKNESS AND ADVERSITY.

1. O Everlasting Wisdom! Who dost reach from one end to the other mightily[1], and dost sweetly order all things: Thou hast mightily smitten me with this disease and bodily evil; but do Thou order it sweetly to Thy glory and to my salvation, Who dost order all things by weight, and number, and measure.

2. O FATHER, from Whom is every good gift and every perfect gift, is not this my infirmity or affliction Thy gift also? Shall I attribute it to chance and fortune, not acknowledging Thy Providence? That be far from me. For I know that Thou dost govern all things; Thou, too, the same, dost also keep all our bones, so that not one of them shall be broken without Thee. Even the very hairs of our head are all numbered before Thee. My lot is in Thy Hands. Thou woundest and Thou healest, Thou killest and makest alive. Whether we live or whether we die, Thine are we, O LORD. Thy Will be done in all things. If we have received

[1] Wisd. viii. 1.

good at the Hand of the Lord, shall we not endure evil? which, indeed, will not be evil, if we receive it according to the purpose of the Lord, Who chasteneth us as His sons in discipline. Yea, those very evils work together for good to those that love God.

3. O Lord, I am Thy servant and the son of Thine handmaid; do with me whatsoever shall please Thee; and what am I, that I should withstand Thee? Who ever resisted Thee and was at peace? Behold, I am the clay, and Thou the Potter. Mould me and purify me, if it seem good unto Thee, in the furnace of affliction, that I may be made a vessel to honour.

O Physician! Who with a word dost cure all the diseases of the soul, and not less those of the body, when Thou knowest it to be expedient for the soul; heal me, O Lord, and I shall be healed in soul; save me, and I shall be saved in body also. I trust in Thee, and not in the physicians, or in any remedies. Those, indeed, I reject not, but unless Thou wilt raise up this ruinous house of my body, they all labour but in vain who build it.

Give Thou, therefore, strength to the remedies, if any are offered me, that they may have their due effect on me; or, at least, work in my soul patience; for that is the most sure and present remedy against all diseases and evils.

But behold! I acknowledge Thee to be in truth my Physician. The office of the physician is to expel the noxious humour from the bodies of the sick by some bitter potion or some severe remedy. This Thou art now doing, O heavenly Physician! by this affliction of my body. Severe, indeed, is the remedy, and distasteful, I confess it, to the flesh; but it is the unruly and disobedient patient that causes the physician to be cruel.

Doubtless I, too, (why should I deny it?) have often indulged the flesh and pampered it with dainties, and have contracted thereby many diseases of the soul. Thou judgest, perhaps, that these must be healed by the contrary remedies. Be it so, O Lord, let the flesh be delivered unto destruction that the spirit may be saved. The flesh in gladness led me into sin; grant that in affliction it may bring me back to pardon. Burn now, cut deep now, but spare me everlastingly.

PRAYER

TO CHRIST PRAYING IN THE GARDEN AT THE BEGINNING OF HIS PASSION.

For grace and comfort at the hour of death.

My Soul is sorrowful even unto death: and He went a little further and fell on His Face, and prayed, saying, O My Father, if it be possible, let this cup pass from Me: nevertheless, not as I will, but as Thou wilt. And being in an agony, He prayed more earnestly: and His Sweat was as it were great drops of blood falling down to the ground.

Ruler of Heaven and earth, JESUS CHRIST, the martyrs' strength, fortitude, and victory, by Whom they trample upon death, and rejoice in it as conquerors. Whence then this fear to Thee? Whence this anxious supplication? Whence this strange, unheard-of Bloody Sweat? Art Thou not offered because Thou willest? Is not this Thy Sacrifice, a wholly free-will offering to GOD the Father?

Who should not fear, O LORD, when Thou fearest, Whom all things fear? Who not fall down lifeless, when Thou fallest on Thy Face, to Whom all knees bow? Who not be amazed at sight of death, if Thou Who shalt be conqueror of death, so tremblest at its approach?

But blessed be Thou for ever, my JESU, that Thou vouchsafest to take on Thee these signs of weakness for the consolation of Thy weak members, lest, though the spirit be ready for suffering and for death, the weakness of the flesh should drive us to despair.

O, call to mind, O LORD, that vehement sorrow, that fearful horror, that terrible anguish which, on the very eve of Thy most bitter Passion entered in like overflowing waters unto Thy

Soul: and Thou didst fall to the earth and pray Thy Father that this cup might pass from Thee.

Call to mind that sore Agony, and that too cruel strife with death, and that most woeful night, which wrung from every pore in Thy whole frame a Sweat of Blood.

Remember, LORD, why Thou didst bear all this: even for us men and our salvation. And I too shall some time come to this hour; I shall come into this garden and have to strive with death. Woe is me; what will then become of me? I cannot stand without Thee; I must needs fail and be overcome, unless Thou be with me and fight for me, Thou that callest to Thee the weary and heavy-laden, to give them rest.

LORD, I too am ready to drink Thy cup; how should I a sinner refuse, when Thou, the spotless Lamb, hast first drunk of it? I dare not then deprecate it, but this I *do* pray, LORD, that Thou wouldest so temper it and its bitterness with the fountains of Thy grace and consolation, that I shrink not from it nor seek to shun it: if Thou strengthen me, I can by Thy grace do all things.

Yea, but how precious is the overflowing cup of Thy glory! O the richness of the house of .God, wherewith Thy chosen shall be inebriated! O torrent of pleasure, which Thou wilt give Thy friends to drink! What will not such hope and longing season, soothe, and sweeten! Of a truth that endless weight of glory makes light as air all the hardness and the weight of present tribulation.

But LORD, in all this, Thy Will, not mine, be done: I seek not an easy and gentle death; but such an one as Thou wilt, and knowest to be most to Thy glory and my salvation. I commit it wholly to Thy Will and Goodness. If Thy Divine Providence hath appointed me a hard struggle and sore straitness of death, Thy Will be done, my heart is ready, O GOD: only preserve and increase in me hope and faith in Thy Presence, Goodness, and Long-suffering; and forsake me not, O GOD my SAVIOUR, as Thy FATHER forsook not Thee; send to me also, I pray, Thy holy Angel to support and strengthen me by his consolations in that agony, and to drive far from me all the power of the enemy; and at last, O LORD, when the strife is over, give me joyful triumph, and may I win of Thee the Crown of life which Thou hast promised to them that love Thee, and that persevere unto the end. Amen.

CHAPTER V.

PROTESTATIONS TO BE FREQUENTLY MADE BY HIM THAT WOULD LIVE AND DIE CHRISTIANLY; SPECIALLY BEFORE DEATH.

I.

I protest that I most fully submit my will to the Will of GOD, and with entire readiness of soul accept this or any other cross, disease, yea, death itself at the hands of GOD's good Providence; and I confess that for my countless sins I deserve most worthily, not only this affliction, sickness, and death, but also all other and severer punishment, yea, Hell itself.

Wherefore also I receive this sickness and death in reverential memory of the most sacred Passion of our LORD JESUS CHRIST, and unite all the griefs, pains, and ills I suffer with those griefs and pains and most bitter agonies which He suffered in His Life, Passion, and Death; and I earnestly pray Him graciously to accept them in place of the punishments which my countless sins have, I confess, made due to me; that so they may avail to the remission of my misdeeds, of those especially which most vex my conscience, and which I now wish I had confessed more diligently, and undone by more diligent amends.

II.

I protest, that as I have ever lived in the true faith of the Catholic and Apostolic Church, and most firmly believed whatever she has believed, and put before me to be believed, and in particular, the Articles of the Apostles' Creed: so I desire to die in the same faith, and to that end say, I believe in GOD the FATHER Almighty, &c.; receiving every article in the sense wherein the Church, my holy Mother, has ever received them.

III.

I protest that I most humbly beg for pardon of all my sins committed against the Divine Majesty, my neighbour, and myself; in thought or word; by commission or omission, in keeping GOD's commandments or the precepts of the Church (or the obligations to which I have pledged myself); in the works of mercy, whether Spiritual or Corporeal; in abuse of the Sacraments, and neglect of watching over my senses: for all my sins, mortal or venial, secret, and merely suggested, I pray for pardon of my GOD, of His Infinite Goodness and Mercy, by the Merits of the Life, Passion, and Death of my LORD, His Son JESUS CHRIST, and by the prayers of the whole Church, visible or invisible, of the innumerable company of angels, and the Church of the firstborn, and the spirits of the just made perfect [1]. And most meekly I implore the Divine Goodness, out of His great treasure-house to supply my short-comings in confession, and, now at least, to bestow on me true and hearty contrition for all my sins.

IV.

I protest that I heartily forgive all that have ever offended or harmed me, and I pray of Thy Divine Majesty all the good for them that I desire for my own soul: moreover, I pray Thy pardon if I have given them occasion for offending me. And I pray Almighty GOD to give me a deep and lively feeling of forgivingness, that I may say truly and sincerely, Forgive me my debts, for I too forgive my debtors!

V.

I protest with my whole heart that I most humbly desire pardon from all whom I have in any way offended,

[1] Heb. xii.

knowingly or ignorantly, by bad example, by word or deed; and that I am most ready to give them satisfaction; and I earnestly pray to GOD, if I have hurt or defrauded any man, to bring it to my mind, and give me the sincere will, and the full means of repairing every injury before I die.

VI.

I protest that I am wholly unequal in thought, word, or deed, to the Divine Goodness, and that I can in no way answer to the infinite favours and benefits that Thou, my GOD, hast shown me, whether public or private, universal or particular, known to all or to myself alone: at Thy Feet, therefore, O my GOD, I thank Thee and bless Thee with all my soul.

I grieve, O GOD, for my exceeding want of thankfulness, and the poverty of my thanks; and I pray Thee to forgive them; may they be in some sort supplied by the praises and thanksgivings paid to Thee by the most blessed Virgin Thy Mother, by the holy Angels, specially my guardian angel, by all the Saints of the heavenly court. O that I had hearts and tongues as many as there are beings in the world, stars in heaven, leaves on trees, grains of sand on the sea-shore, that I might sing Thee praise in some way worthy of Thee. I take then as my own the prophet's words and say,

O all ye works of the LORD, bless ye the LORD, praise Him and magnify Him for ever.

Praise ye the LORD of heaven, praise Him in the height.

Bless the LORD, O my soul, and all that is within me, bless His holy Name.

Bless the LORD, O my soul, and forget not all His benefits.

I will alway give thanks unto the LORD, His praise shall ever be in my mouth.

And in like manner I give thanks to all who have bestowed on me any bodily or spiritual benefit; specially those who have instructed, rebuked, or admonished me, or who have given me an opportunity of doing any thing for my most sweet JESUS, by an act of charity.

VII.

I protest that my desire is to live and die, fortified by the Merits of the Passion, Death, and Blood of my SAVIOUR; and by the Prayers of all the whole Church; His Merits I present to GOD the FATHER for the remission of all my sins, and those prayers as a thanksgiving for all blessings received from the Divine Majesty.

VIII.

And may all the members in Christ's Church in heaven take part with me, and, by their effectual prayer, obtain for me, while I live, and chiefly at the hour of my death, true faith, sure hope, burning love, constant fortitude, deep humility, unconquered patience, and whatsoever graces else are needful for me in my life and at the point of death.

IX.

I protest that if, by GOD's permission, the wicked one assail me in life or at the time of death with any temptation, it is my will not to consent to it, directly or indirectly, by sign, or word, or deed: now, therefore, now, beforehand, I disclaim, abhor, and disavow whatever thoughts the evil spirit may suggest: it is my will to cleave to GOD Alone, my Maker, faithfully for ever: and I renounce again, henceforth and entirely, Satan and all his works and all his suggestions.

X.

Lastly, I commend my soul to GOD my Maker, Who created it from nothing: to CHRIST my SAVIOUR, Who redeemed it by His Blood and Death: and to the HOLY GHOST, Who sanctified it in Baptism to Himself. Into Thy Hands, O LORD, I commend my spirit: GOD be merciful to me a sinner.

And I protest that in the agony of death, when my tongue can speak no more, yet in soul I desire to be joined to GOD: and now, before it comes, I offer Him my agony, my pains, my sweats and sufferings, to be united with the Agony and Bloody Sweat, the Griefs and Passion of my most Sweet

SAVIOUR, JESUS CHRIST, for the remission of my sins and His eternal glory: and may the holy angels, who stand before Him, be with me at this point of death, and shield me with their faithful protection.

CHAPTER VI.

EXERCISE OR PROTESTATION OF A SICK AND DYING MAN, TO BE SAID AT THE HOLY SACRAMENT BEFORE RECEIVING IT ON THE EVE OF HIS DEPARTURE, OR TO BE READ BY ANOTHER IN HIS NAME.

Useful also for the sick or others at holy Communion.

FATHER of mercies, GOD of all comfort; behold, I Thy creature, made after Thy Image, and redeemed by the Blood of Thy Well-Beloved, appear before Thee my Creator; by Whom and for Whom I was created: by Whose Grace I have thus long lived; unto Whom, henceforth, so long as Thou seest good, I would wish to live; for Whom, and in Whom, I desire to die: I meekly adore Thee, Whom my soul desireth and strongly panteth for; to Thee I cry, Whom above all I love, O Thou my Rest, my Hope, my Love, my Longing, my heart's only Good.

Most loving FATHER, though I be the least of all Thy sons, yea, unworthy to be called Thy son, because I have not honoured Thee as my FATHER; yet I come with great confidence and cast myself into the Arms and Bosom of Thy most sweet Love and Mercy, grieving from my inmost soul, that I have ever forsaken Thee my GOD, the Fountain of all good; that I have gone aside from Thee, my most Sweet FATHER; and have forgotten Thee, Who, as though there were none else to care for, every moment rememberest me.

O that I had never offended Thee, my GOD, my all: at least accept this my burning desire and wish from my inmost heart; while it is still the time of pity, look Thou upon me and be merciful unto me; Thou knowest that I love Thee, or desire to love Thee, more than myself, more than all that claims or can claim my love. I know Whom I have believed, and that Thou art able to keep that I have committed to Thee: I know too that a broken and contrite heart, O GOD, Thou wilt not despise.

And I hope that Thou wilt never cast me from Thy Presence, Who dost so lovingly invite us to Thyself, *Come unto Me all that travail and are heavy-laden, and I will give you rest.* Behold, I come, O LORD; Thou that castest not out any that come to Thee, receive me according to Thy word, and I shall live, and let me not be disappointed of my hope. Bring my soul out of this prison, that I may give thanks unto Thy Name.

O blessed hour, when I shall be delivered from the body of this death; when I shall come to Thee and Thou wilt come and comfort me; when I shall no more see through a glass darkly, but see Thee face to face! when I shall lay aside this corruptible body that presseth down the soul, and praise Thee without hindrance! when Thou wilt let Thy servant depart in peace, to serve Thee wholly!

But before I go hence and be no more seen, I desire, in this vale of tears, at least to begin with all my soul to offer to Thy Divine Majesty the sacrifice of praise: that hereafter I may praise Thee for ever.

Wherefore I give Thee infinite thanks for vouchsafing to think of me with so great love from all eternity, for creating me in time after Thy Image, and, when the fulness of time was come, for redeeming me by the Blood of Thy Well-Beloved, sparing me so often when sinning, and calling me so often out of the darkness of sin into Thy marvellous light.

But what reward shall I give unto Thee, LORD JESU, for the labours of Thy Life and bitterness of thy Death, and for vouchsafing so often to feed me with Thy Flesh and Blood; what reward for all the benefits Thou hast done to me, my soul's beloved Spouse?

The deep of my nothingness and my misery calleth

the deep of Thy Goodness and Thy boundless Love, because of the noise of those five water-pipes, Thy Wounds: here lies all my hopeful trust; and for their sakes and the boundless ocean of Thy Love that flows from them, I come in confidence to Thee, wretched though I be, and poor and naked; for Thou art rich towards all, and my goods are nothing unto Thee. The cup of salvation which Thou givest me to drink, bitter though it be, I will take cheerfully at Thy Hand, and I will drink it with Thee, Who didst drain it first for me, when Thou didst so earnestly thirst for my salvation. I will call upon the Name of the LORD, and offer to Thee the sacrifice of thanksgiving.

O that in return for this I could embrace Thee with all the love of the heavenly company, Angels and Saints, and above all of Thy most holy Mother; and that, with the voices and affections of all these and all Thy creatures, I could praise and magnify Thy Name.

Accept, LORD, my heart as a burnt-sacrifice; I give it all to Thee: I give Thee mine eyes, to see Thee only and all besides in Thee: my ears, to hear Thy Word: my mouth, my lips and tongue, to be filled with Thy Glory and Praise all the day long: my hands, to stretch forth in prayer to Thee, or in alms to the poor, and to do Thy Will: my feet, to be led into the way of peace: all my members and bones, that they may say, LORD, who is like to Thee?

Bless the LORD, O my soul, and all that is within me, bless His holy Name: bless the LORD, O my soul, and forget not all His benefits. I now renounce all these earthly things, for I have all in Thee Alone: I renounce myself, for I am Thine, and I live, yet not I, but Thou, CHRIST JESU, livest in me: and I love Thee with all my heart, with all my mind, with all my soul, and all my strength.

Only set me near Thee, and it matters not who fights against me: and if, LORD, the soreness of disease, or the craft of the enemy ever seduce me to say or think other than I do now, such thoughts I now renounce and disavow, and I call Thee to witness, O my GOD, and all the company of heaven, that it is my will to live and die in the faith of the Catholic and Apostolic Church; that I trust in GOD Alone and my LORD JESUS CHRIST and His Merits: and I love Him above all things, with all my heart and all my soul, and I desire so to love Him till my last breath.

And if the subtlety of the enemy or the infirmity of the flesh, or the violence of disease, or distress of body, suggest any thought contrary to this my settled pious purpose, reckon it not, LORD, at Thy Judgment Seat; I utterly abhor, detest, and abjure it; and this my present purpose, which I am ready to seal with my blood, is my sole will and testament in the Day of Judgment; and for it and Thee, my GOD, I would die a thousand times, that I may live to Thee, to Whom all things live, and die to Thee, most sweet JESU, Who for love of me didst vouchsafe to die.

A PRAYER

TO JESUS CHRIST, THE SAVIOUR OF THE WORLD, AFTER RECEIVING THE HOLY EUCHARIST IN SICKNESS.

Useful also for others after the Communion.

Glory to Thee, O CHRIST, Who hast vouchsafed to visit and warm and receive my poor soul with Thy Sweetness. Now, LORD, lettest Thou Thy servant depart in peace according to Thy Word.

I hold Thee now, my Love and Sweetness, and will not let Thee go: gladly to the world, and all therein, I bid farewell; and now I come with joy, my GOD, to Thee.

Nothing now, O Good JESU, shall part me from Thee: I am joined to Thee, O CHRIST, I will live in Thee and die in Thee, and if Thou wilt, abide in Thee for ever. Now I live, yet not I, but CHRIST liveth in me.

I am weary of my life; I desire to depart and be with CHRIST; to me, to live is CHRIST, and to die is gain.

I will fear no evil as I walk in the region of the shadow of death, for Thou art with me: O LORD, as the hart desireth the water-brooks, so longeth my soul after Thee, O GOD; my soul is athirst for GOD, the living GOD; when shall I come to appear before the Presence of my God?

Bless me, most loving JESU, and let me now depart in peace, for I am Thine; and I will never let Thee depart for ever.

O that I were now strait joined to Thee in a blessed union for ever! O that I were wholly taken up, wholly absorbed and buried in Thee! O that my soul, resting sweetly in Thy Arms, were altogether taken up in Thee, and blissfully enjoyed Thee, her loving GOD!

What has the world any more to do with me, most loving JESU? Lo, there is nothing in heaven that I desire in comparison of Thee.

Into Thy Hands, Lord JESU, I commend my spirit. Receive me, my Love and Sweetness, that it may go well with me for ever, and that I may lay me down in peace in Thee, and gently take my rest.

PRAYERS

FOR A HAPPY DEATH, PROFITABLE FOR ALL; AND WHICH WITH SLIGHT ALTERATIONS MAY BE SAID BY THE FRIENDS OF THE DYING MAN AT HIS BED-SIDE.

PRAYER I.

O LORD JESU CHRIST, by Thine Agony and Thy most holy Prayer, offered on Mount Olivet for us, when Thy Sweat was like great drops of Blood falling to the ground, I implore Thee to offer those numberless drops of Bloody Sweat which, in Thy dreary horror, fell from Thee, and present them to GOD, the FATHER ALMIGHTY, against *my*[1] numberless iniquities; and deliver *me* in this hour of *my* death from all the pain and anguish which *I* fear lest by reason of *my* sins *I* deserve. Who with the same GOD the FATHER, and the HOLY GHOST.

Our FATHER.

O Blessed Saviour of the world, Who by Thy Cross and Precious Blood hast redeemed us, save *me* and help *me*, *I* humbly beseech Thee, O LORD. Amen.

---

[1] or "of this thy servant," if read for another.

PRAYER II.

O LORD JESU CHRIST, Who didst die for us upon the Cross, I implore Thee to vouchsafe to offer all the bitter Pangs of Thy dread Passion which Thou barest on the Cross for us miserable sinners, specially in that hour when Thy most Holy Soul parted from Thy most Holy Body, and present them to GOD the FATHER ALMIGHTY in behalf of *my* soul; O deliver *me* in this hour of *my* death from all the pangs and torments which I fear lest by reason of *my* sins *I* deserve. Who with the same GOD the FATHER, and the HOLY GHOST.

Our FATHER.
O Blessed SAVIOUR.

PRAYER III.

O LORD JESU CHRIST, Who by the mouth of Thy Prophet hast said, I have loved thee with everlasting love, and in loving kindness I have drawn thee; I implore Thee to offer that Thy same Love which brought Thee down from heaven to earth to go through all Thy most bitter Passion, and present it to GOD the FATHER ALMIGHTY in *my* soul's behalf; deliver *me* from all the pangs and torments which *I* fear, lest by reason of *my* sins *I* deserve, and save *my* soul in this hour of *my* departure. Open to *me*, O LORD, the gate of life, and give *me* joy with Thy Saints in glory. Who with the same GOD the FATHER and the HOLY GHOST.

Our FATHER.
O Blessed SAVIOUR.

PRAYER IV.

O LORD JESU CHRIST, Who hast redeemed us with Thy precious Blood, write with Thy Blood Thy most precious Wounds in *my* soul, that in them *I* may read both Thy woe, against the woe and torments which *I* fear lest for *my* sins *I* deserve; and Thy love, that I may be joined unto Thee with unconquerable love, and not be parted from Thee and Thine Elect for ever.

Give *me* a share, O LORD JESU CHRIST, in Thy most sacred Incarnation, Thy most Holy Life, Thy most bitter Passion, Thy most glorious Resurrection, Thy wondrous Ascension.

Give *me* a share, O LORD,

in Thy most Sacred Mysteries and Sacraments.

Give *me* a share, O LORD, in all the prayers and sacrifices offered in Thy holy Church.

Give *me* a share in all the blessings, graces, merits, and joys of Thine Elect, who have pleased Thee since the world was; and grant *me* with them all to be happy in Thy Sight for ever. Amen.

COMMENDATION

OF THE SOUL INTO THE HANDS OF OUR CREATOR.

Into Thy Hands, O LORD, I commend my spirit.

While I have still strength, O JESU, I commend my soul to Thee, that Thou mayest still keep it, when, though not as yet released from prison, I shall be unable to commend it. I' dread the time when I shall be still among the living and know it not. Many are the dying who still breathe and live, yet know not that they live. Who, then, shall receive this trembling spirit, as it feareth to pass, and yet passeth from its too loved prison, if Thou, my MAKER, shut it out?

O CHRIST most Suffering, call to mind that Thou, too, didst weep in that Agony, didst complain that Thou wast forsaken, didst commend Thy Spirit to the FATHER, criedst with a loud Voice, and gavest up the Ghost.

To Thee I now cry, my SAVIOUR; O take my spirit to Thyself, whensoever, wheresoever, and by whatever means it is parted from the body.

Call to mind, gracious JESU, how Thou stretchedst out Thine Hands upon the Cross, openedst Thy Bosom, and didst bow Thy Head. Lo, my soul, forsaken by all created things, seeks a shelter; it casts itself into Thy Arms, and throws itself upon Thy Breast: O receive it in its helplessness; drive it not thence, till God's Wrath be overpast. Here let it rest secure, here lie hid safe from the ministers of hell.

Into Thy hands, therefore, O LORD, I commend my spirit; yea, Thy spirit, for Thou didst make it and redeem it; Thine own creature, LORD, do not Thou despise.

CHAPTER VII.

OF VISITING THE SICK.

This most serious subject cannot here be fully spoken of. More may be found in the "Instructor for the Sick and Dying[a]."

Where so much as at the sick man's bed can Christian charity be shown? and most of all, when death is well nigh come, and the hazard is for all eternity? O perilous time: most perilous, if the dying man come to that conflict helpless and alone!

Away, then, with idle gazers: let pious men come near and help the dying brother in his sore strife, and guide him to a happy end by exhorting, comforting, praying.

Let most stress be laid on contrition, faith, hope, charity, and resignation: let the dying man be awakened to serious sorrow for his sins, to earnest and vigorous acts of faith, hope, and love to God *and man; to entire resignation and submission of himself to the Divine Will; to stedfast reliance on the Mercy of* God, *&c.*

[a] Pædagogus ægrotantium et agonizantium.

To this end many parts of the "Paradise" may be employed. But let the following remark be borne in mind.

In dealing with sick persons (and particularly if their pains are great, their head weak, or their reason wandering) do nothing hurriedly, nothing to overburthen them: give them time, and supply them gently, by degrees and at intervals, that they may make what they hear their own, and get profit from it. Oil poured in too largely and rapidly, does not feed but puts out the lamp: heavy rains flood and wash off the soil, while gentle showers sink into it, water, and fertilize it.

Be careful also to avoid wearying the patient with irrelevancies: let all you say or read be directly to the purpose.

Besides the present Section, suitable exercises for the sick are the following:

The Acts of Faith, Hope, and Charity in Part i.

Means of awaking Contrition (Part iii. § 9, p. 12);
Hope of Sinners in the Divine

Mercy (§ 10, p. 14); the Litanies of Penitents from Holy Scripture (p. 23); the Prayer of St. Bernard for remission of sins (p. 36); the LORD's Prayer adapted to Penitents (p. 39).

Act of compunction and hatred of sin (P. iv. c. 4.); Exercises of Faith, Hope, and Charity (ib. c. 5, § 1—3); of resignation (ib. § 9); of contempt for the world (§ 11); of patience (§ 15); of heroic devotion to GOD (ib. c. 6).

Much of Part vi. on the Passion of our LORD, especially the Colloquy between CHRIST and Man: the Litanies of the Passion: the Rhythmical Aspirations to the Suffering Members of CHRIST, and other Prayers on the LORD's Passion.

Much of the present Section, particularly from the Colloquy: the Litanies and LORD's Prayer adapted to the sick and dying; the Protestations, &c.

To all these may be added, Certain Select Sentences expressive of the Theological Virtues, most fitting at the approach of death.

FOR AN EXERCISE OF FAITH.

I believe in God the FATHER, Who hath created me in His Image, after His Likeness.

And in JESUS CHRIST my SAVIOUR, Who hath redeemed me with His Own Blood.

And in the HOLY GHOST, Who sanctified me in Baptism.

LORD, I believe; increase my faith.

I believe that my REDEEMER liveth, and that at the last day I shall rise from the earth, and that in my flesh I shall see GOD my SAVIOUR.

I believe that with GOD nothing is impossible.

I believe all that GOD's SON hath said: no word is truer than His Word of Truth.

I believe, LORD JESU, that Thou art CHRIST, SON of the living GOD, Who camest into this world not to destroy but to save us.

I believe all that the holy Catholic and Apostolic Church hath believed from the time of CHRIST and the Apostles till now, and all that she has proposed to my faith, and that the Rock and

Foundation of the Church is Jesus Christ, Who said, "Thou art Peter, and upon this Rock I will build My Church, and the gates of hell shall not prevail against it."

Here may be said the Apostles' Creed and after it,

In this faith I was born and baptized: in this I have lived, and by God's grace I will continue and die therein; may the Grace and Love of Jesus Christ my Saviour help and strengthen me against all temptation, &c.

Act of Faith, See Sect. i. p. 70.

FOR AN EXERCISE OF HOPE.

Numberless passages to this purpose may be found in the Psalms, Prophets, and Gospels; we will cull a few as they occur to memory: and be it remembered, that there is nothing so necessary for a dying man as a stedfast hope in God's mercy; of this, the ememy takes special pains to rob him.

The Lord is my Light and my Salvation; whom then shall I fear?

The Lord is the Strength of my life; of whom then shall I be afraid? *Ps.* xxvii.

Though I walk through the valley of the shadow of death, I will fear no evil, for Thou art with me. *Ps.* xxiii.

In Thee, O Lord, have I put my trust; let me never be put to confusion, deliver me in Thy righteousness. *Ps.* xxxi.

The Lord Himself is the Portion of mine inheritance, and of my cup; Thou shalt maintain my lot.

I have set God always before me; for He is on my right hand, therefore I shall not fall.

Wherefore my heart was glad, and my glory rejoiced; my flesh also shall rest in hope. *Ps.* xvi.

Let God arise, and let His enemies be scattered; let them also that hate Him flee before Him. Like as the smoke vanisheth, so shalt Thou drive them away; and like as wax melteth at the fire, so let the ungodly perish at the Presence of God. *Ps.* lxviii.

The Lord is nigh unto them that are of a contrite heart, and will save such as be of an humble spirit. *Ps.* xxxiv.

Why art thou so vexed, O my soul, and why art

thou so disquieted within me?

O put thy trust in God, for I will yet thank Him, Which is the Help of my countenance, and my God. *Ps.* xlii.

God so loved the world, that He gave His Only Begotten Son, that whosoever believeth in Him should not perish, but have everlasting life. For God sent not His Son into the world to condemn the world, but that the world through Him might be saved. *John* iii.

But if any man sin, we have an Advocate with the Father, Jesus Christ the righteous; and He is the Propitiation for our sins: and not for ours only, but also for the sins of the whole world. 1 *John* ii.

Verily, verily, I say unto you, he that heareth My Word, and believeth on Him that sent Me, hath everlasting life, and shall not come into condemnation; but is passed from death unto life. *John* v.

All that the Father giveth Me shall come to Me; and him that cometh to Me I will in no wise cast out. Verily, verily I say unto you, he that believeth on Me hath everlasting Life. *John* vi.

I am the Resurrection, and the Life: he that believeth in Me, though he were dead, yet shall he live: and whosoever liveth and believeth in me shall never die. *John* xi.

If God be for us, who can be against us? He that spared not His own Son, but delivered Him up for us all, how shall He not with Him also freely give us all things? Who shall lay any thing to the charge of God's elect? It is God that justifieth; who is he that condemneth? It is Christ that died, yea rather, that is risen again, Who is even at the Right Hand of God, Who also maketh intercession for us. *Rom.* viii.

None of us liveth to himself, and no man dieth to himself. For whether we live, we live unto the Lord; and whether we die, we die unto the Lord: whether we live therefore, or die, we are the Lord's. *Rom.* xiv.

For we know that if our earthly house of this tabernacle were dissolved, we have a building of God, an house not made with hands, eternal in the heavens. For in this we groan, earnestly desiring to be clothed upon with our house which is from heaven: if so be that being clothed we shall not be found naked. 2 *Cor.* v.

Now CHRIST shall be magnified in my body, whether it be by life or by death. For to me to live is CHRIST; and to die is gain. To be with CHRIST is far better. *Phil.* i.

Our conversation is in heaven; from whence also we look for the SAVIOUR, the LORD JESUS CHRIST: Who shall change our vile body, that it may be fashioned like unto His glorious Body. *Phil.* iii.

This is a faithful saying, and worthy of all acceptation, that CHRIST JESUS came into the world to save sinners; of whom I am chief. 1 *Tim.* i.

He that endureth unto the end shall be saved. *Matt.* xxiv.

Be thou faithful unto death, and I will give thee a crown of life. *Rev.* ii.

Let the wicked forsake his way, and the unrighteous man his thoughts; and let him return unto the LORD, and He will have mercy upon Him; and to our GOD, for He will abundantly pardon. For My thoughts are not your thoughts, neither are your ways My ways. For as the heavens are higher than the earth, so are My ways higher than your ways, and My thoughts than your thoughts. *Isa.* lv.

Have I any pleasure at all that the wicked should die, and not that he should return from his ways and live? Repent and turn yourselves from all your transgressions; and iniquity shall not be your ruin: for I have no pleasure in the death of him that dieth, wherefore turn yourselves, and live ye. *Ezek.* xviii.

As I live, saith the LORD GOD, I have no pleasure in the death of the wicked; but that the wicked turn from his way and live: turn ye from your evil ways; for why will ye die, O house of Israel? *Ezek.* xxxiii.

The LORD is full of compassion and mercy, long-suffering, and of great goodness. Yea, like as a father pitieth his own children, even so is the LORD merciful unto them that fear Him. For He knoweth whereof we are made, &c. *Ps.* ciii.

The LORD is loving unto every man, and His Mercy is over all His works.

The LORD upholdeth all such as fall, and lifteth up all those that are down. *Ps.* cxlv.

The Pharisees said unto the disciples of JESUS, Why eateth your Master with publicans and sinners? But when JESUS heard that, He said unto them, They that be whole need not a physician, but they that are sick. For I am not come to call the righteous, but sinners to repentance. *Matt.* ix.

Come unto Me, all ye that labour and are heavy laden, and I will give you rest. And ye shall find rest unto your souls. *Matt.* xi.

I am the good Shepherd, and I know My sheep; and am known of Mine. As the FATHER knoweth Me, even so know I the FATHER; and I lay down My life for My sheep. *John* x.

My sheep hear My voice, and I know them, and they follow Me: and I give unto them eternal life; and they shall never perish, neither shall any one pluck them out of My Hand. *John* x.

God commendeth His love toward us, in that, while we were yet sinners, CHRIST died for us. Much more then, being now justified by His Blood, we shall be saved from wrath through Him. For if, when we were enemies, we were reconciled to GOD by the Death of His SON, much more, being reconciled, we shall be saved by His Life. *Rom.* v.

For an Act of Hope, see Part i. p. 71.

FOR AN EXERCISE OF CHARITY.

I love Thee, O LORD my Strength: the LORD is my Might, and my Refuge, and my Deliverer. *Ps.* xviii.

It is good for me to hold me fast by GOD, and to put my trust in the LORD GOD.

For whom have I in heaven but Thee, and there is none upon earth that I desire in comparison of Thee?

My flesh and my heart faileth, but GOD is the Strength of my heart, and my Portion for ever. *Ps.* lxxiii.

Like as the hart desireth the water-brooks, so longeth my soul after Thee, O GOD.

My soul is athirst for GOD, yea, even for the living GOD; when shall I come to appear before the Presence of GOD? *Ps.* xlii.

Into Thy Hands, O LORD, I commend my spirit, for Thou hast redeemed me, O LORD, Thou GOD of truth. *Ps.* xxxi.

Who shall separate us from the love of CHRIST? shall tribulation, or distress, or persecution, or famine, or nakedness, or peril, or sword? Nay, in all these things we are more than conquerors, through Him that loved us. For I am persuaded, that neither death, nor life, nor angels, nor principalities, nor powers, nor things present, nor things to come, nor height, nor depth, nor any other creature, shall be able to separate us from the love of God, which is in CHRIST JESUS our LORD. *Rom.* viii.

For an Act of Charity, see Part i. p. 73.

For an Act of Resignation, see Part iv. c. 5. Exerc. 9.

FOR AN EXERCISE OF CONTRITION.

There are many passages to this effect in the Psalms, e. g. Have mercy upon me, O LORD, for I am weak; O LORD, heal me, for my bones are vexed. *Ps.* vi.

Who can tell how oft he offendeth? O cleanse Thou me from my secret faults, and keep Thy servant from presumptuous sins. *Ps.* xix.

O remember not the sins and offences of my youth.

For Thy Name's sake, O LORD, be merciful unto my sin, for it is great.

Look upon my adversity and misery: and forgive me all my sin. *Ps.* xxv.

LORD, Thou knowest all my desire; and my groaning is not hid from Thee. *Ps.* xxxviii.

Withdraw not Thou Thy Mercy from me, O LORD; let Thy Loving kindness and Thy Truth alway preserve me.

For innumerable troubles are come about me; my sins have taken such hold upon me, that I am not able to look up. *Ps.* xl.

Have mercy upon me, O GOD, after Thy great goodness. *Ps.* li., *and many other verses of the same Psalm.*

O remember not my old sins, but have mercy upon me, and that soon; for I am come to great misery.

Help me, O GOD of my

salvation, for the glory of Thy Name; O deliver me, and be merciful unto my sins, for Thy Name's sake. *Ps.* lxxix.

Shew us Thy Mercy, O LORD, and grant us Thy Salvation. *Ps.* lxxxv.

Enter not into judgment with Thy servant, O LORD; for in Thy Sight shall no man living be justified. *Ps.* cxliii.

Out of the deep have I called unto Thee, O LORD.

If Thou, LORD, shouldest be extreme to mark what is done amiss, O LORD, who shall stand? *Ps.* cxxx.

I omit other instances, as they are countless; but these may serve as a specimen.

CHAPTER VIII.

PRAYERS AND SENTENCES TO BE SAID BY THE BED-SIDE OF THE DYING.

Let the dying man or some others hold in his hand a cross or crucifix, and the following prayers be said.

I adore Thee, LORD JESU, and I bless Thee for the redemption of the world by Thy Holy Cross: SAVIOUR of the world, save me, Who by Thy Cross and Blood hast redeemed me. Draw me unto Thee, Good JESU, for Thou saidst, when I am lifted up, I will draw all things to Myself. Draw me and hold me fast, lest any snatch me from Thy Hand; and let nothing separate me and Thee for ever.

O most pitying JESU, by Thy precious Blood, Which Thou willest to shed for sinners, wash away my sins.

O Soul of CHRIST, sanctify me! O Blood of CHRIST, purify me! O Body of CHRIST, save me! Water from the Side of Christ, wash me! Passion of CHRIST, strengthen me! O Good JESU, hear me; hide me in Thy Wounds; O Good JESU, let me not be parted from Thee: in the hour of my death call me, bid me come to Thee, that I may praise Thee with Thy saints for ever.

O my Maker and my Saviour, CHRIST JESU, I give Thee myself, cast me not away; I come to Thee, drive me not from Thee.

Cast me not away from Thy Presence, and take not Thy Holy Spirit from me. Let not my iniquity destroy me, whom Thy Almighty Goodness brought into being.

Look on me with the eyes of Thy loving-kindness, O LORD JESU CHRIST, King Eternal, God-man, Crucified for man. Hear me, who rest my hope in Thee; pity me all full of sin and misery, Thou Whose Love shall flow on for ever. All hail, salutary Victim, offered for me and the whole race of man upon the Cross.

All hail, noble precious Blood gushing from my Crucified LORD JESUS' Wounds, and washing the sins of the whole world away. O remember Thy creature, O LORD, whom Thou hast redeemed with Thy Blood.

GOD forbid that I should glory save in the Cross of my LORD JESUS CHRIST, by Whom the world is crucified to me and I unto the world.

Lo, I see Thee, my most sweet SAVIOUR, hanging on the Cross, with stretched-out Arms, and Head bowed-down, as though longing to embrace us, and with most soothing voice persuasively inviting us all, "Come unto Me, all ye that travail and are heavy laden, and I will give you rest."

I come, LORD: do to me according to Thy Word and give me rest: I come weary and heavy-laden with my sins; O deal mercifully with Thy servant, Who hast borne our pains and sicknesses upon the Cross.

PRAYER

TO JESUS CHRIST, THE SAVIOUR OF THE WORLD.

O JESU, Fount of Love, show me Thy Love; I am a poor needy creature, help me in this my last necessity. O JESU, my Maker and Redeemer, set Thy Passion, Cross, and Death, betwixt Thy Judgment and my soul.

I give myself wholly unto Thee, cast me not away; I come to Thee, drive me not from Thee. Now LORD, deal mercifully with me, according to Thy Will, and bid my spirit be taken up in peace: Thou hast Redeemed me, O LORD GOD of truth; O may those soothing words sound in the ears of my soul, O LORD, JESU, "To-day shalt thou be with Me in Paradise."

Take me into those loving Arms, O crucified JESU, Whom I see stretched out for me upon the Cross, and on Whom I hang: take me into Thy loved embrace and draw to Thee my soul: take me, Good JESU, to Thy Mercy; O take my soul to peace. Amen.

Lighten mine eyes, O Good JESU, that I sleep not in death; lest mine enemy say, I have prevailed against him. *Ps.* xiii.

O LORD JESU CHRIST, SON of the Living GOD, set Thy Passion, Cross, and Death, betwixt Thy Judgment and my soul.

O Good JESU, remember not my old sins, but have mercy upon me and that soon, for I am come to great misery. *Ps.* lxxix.

O most sweet LORD JESU CHRIST, for the honour and virtue of Thy Blessed Passion, bid me be written in the number of Thine elect.

Enter not into judgment with Thy servant, most pitiful JESU, for in Thy Sight shall no man living be justified. *Ps.* cxliii.

One thing have I desired of the LORD which I will require, even that I may dwell in the House of the LORD all the days of my life.

Bring my soul out of prison, that I may give thanks unto Thy Name: lo, the righteous wait for me, till Thou recompense me.

O stablish me according to Thy Word, that I may live, and let me not be disappointed of my hope.

DEVOUT AND YEARNING STRIVINGS.

At the point of death.

O ever-living FATHER, I am that most unworthy servant, whom Thou so lovedst that Thou gavest for him Thy well-beloved SON. Deal mercifully with Thy servant now, lest that precious Blood be shed for me in vain. For what profit is there to me in my SAVIOUR's Blood, if I go down to hell?

O JESU, JESU, I am that lost sheep, for which Thou didst leave the ninety and nine in the wilderness, and seek so painfully, and set on Thy Shoulders to bring home again. Thou art the good Shepherd, Who layedst down Thy Life for Thy sheep. Let not that roaring lion, that goeth about seeking whom he may devour, snatch me and tear me: Save me from the lion's mouth, O LORD; &c.

O JESU, I am that poor traveller, who going down from Jerusalem, fell among thieves, and after many blows, was left half-dead. Thou art my Physician, and the good Samaritan Who wast moved with compassion for me, boundest up my wounds, yea, preparedst me a medicine from Thine own Wounds and Blood. Thou hast borne our sicknesses, and by Thy Stripes we are healed. Pity me, LORD, in this my last hour; O LORD, make haste to help, ere my soul die and perish for ever.

O JESU, I am that miserable sinner, accused of many crimes: Thou art my Advocate with the Father and the Propitiation of my sins. Thou desirest not the death of a sinner, but that he should live. Thou camest into the world to save sinners. Deal mercifully with me in this last hour of my life. Be my Mediator and Advocate with the Father. O good JESU, be gracious to me a sinner, &c. Into Thy Hands, O LORD, I commend my spirit, &c.

CHAPTER IX.

PRAYERS AND REMARKABLE SAYINGS OF SAINTS IN THEIR LAST HOUR.

Blessed Eloy, Bp. of Noyon, after embracing those around him with tears, and bidding them farewell, prayed for some time in secret, and then broke forth into these words:

LORD, now lettest Thou Thy servant depart in

peace according to Thy word. Remember, LORD, that Thou hast made me as the clay, and enter not into judgment with Thy servant, for in Thy Sight shall no man living be justified. Remember me, O CHRIST, Redeemer of the world, Who Alone art without sin; draw me from the death of this body, and translate me into Thy Kingdom. I know I deserve not to see Thee; but Thou knowest that my hope has ever been in Thy Mercy.

And now, O JESU, I will breathe out my last breath in confessing Thy Holy Name. Receive me according to Thy great Mercy, and let me not be disappointed of my hope. I am hastening, open me the gate of Life, and let not the princes of darkness come against me. Let Thy Hand bring me into the place of rest, yea, though it be into the last of those mansions, which Thou hast prepared for Thy servants that fear Thee.

At these words he breathed forth his spirit.

We have the following account from one present, of the solemn and golden words in which St. Bernard, Abbot of Clair-vaux (in the sickness which was supposed to be his last) baffled the enemy and accuser.

And when he seemed now to be at his last gasp, in a state of extacy he seemed to himself to be set before the Judgment-Seat of God. And Satan too was there to confront him, and assail him with heavy accusations: when he had come to an end, the man of GOD, *nothing terrified or troubled, answered thus:*

I confess I am not worthy: by my own merits I cannot win the kingdom of heaven. But my LORD Who has a double claim to it, one by inheritance from the FATHER, the other by the Merits of His Passion, foregoes the latter and makes it mine. I rest my claim therefore on His gift and I am not confounded. And with these words the enemy was baffled, &c. Lib. i. c. 12.

O glorious words and precious lesson for all dying men.

BLESSED LAURENCE JUSTINIANI, PATRIARCH OF VENICE, THUS PRAYED AT THE POINT OF DEATH.

As for my life, LORD, Thou knowest that when I consider it, I must account it rather bewilderment than life. Thou art my Life and my Salvation; O take me, Good JESU, with a humbled spirit and a contrite heart. Not in my righteousness, but in the multitude of Thy tender Mercies, I cast my supplication before Thy gracious Presence.

I am the lost sheep, and would return to Thee my Shepherd. Thy Voice I know, and not the voice of strangers. Bring me back, LORD, I beseech Thee, to Thy sheepfold. Canst Thou turn away from a poor bleating sheep, that seeks shelter in Thee? Hast not Thou said, "Come unto Me, all ye that travail and are heavy laden?" and, "He shall call upon me and I will hear him, yea, I am with him in trouble?"

Lo, I cry, yea my heart cries more than my tongue. Lo, trouble is hard at hand, and there is none to help: who can save and deliver, beside Thee, O Good JESU!

True, I could not aspire to the seats of the blessed spirits who gaze on and behold the most Holy Trinity; yet this Thy poor prostrate creature craveth a crumb from Thy delightsome Table. O that I deserved rather to be an abject at the threshold of the House of the LORD than to dwell in the tents of ungodliness! Vit. c. 11.

PRAYER OF ST. JEROME, TO BE SAID IN THE AGONY OF DEATH, OR TO BE READ TO THE DYING MAN.

O loving JESU, my Strength, my Refuge, my Helper, my Deliverer, in Whom I hope, in Whom I have believed, and Whom I have loved, O surpassing Sweetness, Tower of strength, my Hope from my youth up. Call me, Thou that guidest my life, and I will answer Thee. Be gracious to the work of Thine Hands, which Thou, that madest all, formedst from the clay, framedst of bones and sinews, and by Thy Dying hast quickened; stretch forth Thy Hand and save.

§ vii.] A PREPARATION TO DIE WELL AND HAPPILY. 79

It is a time for dust to go to dust, and the spirit to return to Thee, my SAVIOUR, Who didst send it forth. Open to it the gate of life, O LORD, for as a malefactor Thou hangedst for me on the Cross; receive me, O merciful GOD, according to the multiude of Thy Mercies. For when dying on the Cross, Thou didst receive the dying malefactor who sought to Thee. I am sick, my life is all destitute and weak, and I seek to Thee, O LORD, my Physican.

Heal me, LORD, and I shall be healed; and because I put my trust in Thee, I shall not be ashamed. In Thee have I put my trust, O LORD, let me never be confounded.

But who am I, most Loving LORD, to speak to Thee so boldly? A sinner and brought up in sin; a putrid carcase, a stinking vessel, and food of worms. Spare me, LORD. Is it a victory that Thou shouldest fight with me and overcome me? I am before Thee less than the stubble bfeore the wind. Forgive me my sins, and raise the beggar from the dunghill.

Arise and help me, LORD; arise and cast me not away for ever. Let my prayer enter into Thy Presence, O LORD, and stretch forth Thy Hand to save me. I am the man that went down from Jerusalem to Jericho, fell among thieves, was wounded and left half dead. O good Samaritan, have compassion on me. I have sinned grievously and done evil in Thy Sight: from the sole of my foot even to my head, there is no soundness in me.

Of a truth, hadst Thou not helped me by dying on the Cross, my soul had been only worthy to live in hell. But, loving JESU, Thou payedst that price for me also; for me Thou sheddedst Thy most precious Blood: O cast me not away from Thee. I am the stray sheep: seek me out, Good Shepherd, and set me in Thy sheep-fold, that Thou mayest be justified in Thy sayings, for Thou hast promised, that when the sinner sighs, he shall be saved. Lord, I grieve: I acknowledge my faults, and my sin is ever before me.

Of a truth I am not worthy to be called Thy son, for I have sinned against heaven and before Thee. But make me to hear of joy and gladness. Turn Thy Face from my sins, and put out all my misdeeds, according to Thy great Mercy. Cast me not away from Thy Presence; deal not with me according to my sins, neither reward me according to my wickedness: help me, O God my Saviour, and for the glory of Thy Name deliver me. O be gracious in Thy good pleasure, that I may dwell in Thy House all the days of my life, and praise Thee with them that dwell therein for ever.

A PRAYER

TO BE SAID BY THOSE FRIENDS PRESENT, FOR ONE, BREATHING HIS LAST.

O Jesu Christ, the Crucified, in union with that most burning love which constrained Thee, Who art the life of all living, to die upon the Cross; we knock at the secret chambers of Thy loving Heart, and pray Thee to forgive the sins of of our dear brother, Thy servant N.; supply his failings by Thy most holy Life, and the merit of Thy most bitter Agony; make him taste the exceeding multitude of Thy tender Mercies; prepare us all, as seems best to Thee, and especially this our brother N. whom Thou art now calling to Thee, and grant him with true patience, perfect resignation, free pardon of his sins, strong faith, stedfast hope and entire charity, made wholly perfect, peacefully and to Thy endless praise, into Thy most sweet Embrace and loving kiss to die away.

Ah! most sweet Redeemer, Jesus Christ, by those fearful words which Thou utteredst when dying on the Cross, exhausted by the Dolours of Thy Passion, "My God, My God, why hast Thou forsaken Me?" remove not from Thy servant, our brother N., the help of Thy tender Mercy, for lo, he can no longer call upon Thee: his strength is gone, and his spirit spent in this moment of last agony.

By the triumph of Thy Holy Cross, and by the infinite Merit of Thy Death and Passion, think Thou of him, thoughts of peace not of affliction, but of mercy and consolation. Deliver him from his hard straits, and with Thy most holy Hands, which Thou gavest to be pierced with nails for him and for us all upon the Cross, O Good JESU, most loving FATHER, snatch him from the torments due to him, and bring him safe to everlasting rest. Amen.

To this purport also are the prayers for a happy death, above, Ch. vi.

TO THE PIOUS READER.

Thus ends, pious reader, this PARADISE; *so use it, I pray thee, that it may smooth the way for thee to another, and when thou goest hence, mayest thou too be found worthy to hear :—*
To-day shall thou be with Me in PARADISE.

And with one heartfelt ejaculation to God, implore the same blessing for the Author and Translators, and all who have taken part herein; grant them this for charity: they ask no more.

SEQUENCE.

Day of wrath!—that aweful day,
Earth shall melt in fire away!
David and the sybil say.

The trembling, the agony,
When His coming shall be nigh,
Who shall all things judge and try!

When the trumpet's thrilling tone,
Through the tomb of ages gone,
Summons all before the Throne.

Death and Time shall stand aghast,
And Creation, at the blast,
Rise to answer for the past.

Then the volume shall be spread,
And the writing shall be read,
Which shall judge the quick and dead!

Then the Judge shall sit!—Oh! then,
All that's hid shall be made plain,
Unrequited nought remain.

What shall wretched I then plead?
Who for me shall intercede,
When the righteous scarce is freed?

King of dreadful Majesty,
Saving souls in mercy free,
Fount of Pity, save Thou me!

Bear me, LORD, in heart, I pray,
Object of Thy saving way,
Lest Thou lose me on that Day.

Weary, seeking me, wast Thou,
And for me in death didst bow—
Be Thy toils availing now!

Judge of justice, Thee I pray,
Grant me pardon while I may,
Ere that awful reckoning day.

O'er my crimes I guilty groan,
Blush to think what I have done,
Spare Thy suppliant, Holy One!

Thou didst set th' adultress free,—
Heard'st the thief upon the tree.—
Hope vouchsafing e'en to me.

Nought of Thee my prayers can claim,
Save in Thy free Mercy's Name,
Save me from the deathless flame!

With Thy sheep my place assign,
Separate from th' accursed line,
Set me on Thy Right with Thine.

When the lost, to silence driven,
To devouring flames are given,
Call me with the blest to Heaven!

Suppliant, fallen, now I bend,
My bruised heart to ashes rend,
Care Thou, LORD, for my last end!

Full of tears the day shall prove,
When, from ashes rising move

To the judgment, guilty men,—
Spare, Thou God of mercy, then!

LORD all-pitying, JESU blest!
Grant them Thine eternal rest.
Amen.

THE EPITAPH
OF A CHRISTIAN MAN,

EXPRESSIVE OF THE RULE OF LIFE.

𝕲𝖗𝖊𝖆𝖙 𝖎𝖘 𝕲𝖔𝖉 𝖆𝖓𝖉 𝕲𝖔𝖔𝖉.

Stay, Traveller;
For thee no less than me
HERE ENDS LIFE'S JOURNEY.
I once was born a man, and among men I moved;
Lo, now removed, I lie forgotten in this grave,
NAKED AND A NOTHING;
ASHES, DUST, THE FOOD OF WORMS.
I LIVED [N] YEARS, FEW, WEIGHED AGAINST ETERNITY;
And yet for this had I my race to run on the course of a fleeting life.
God gave me life in mercy, that I might learn to die,
AND LIFE ETERNAL WIN;
AND STILL HE GIVES IT THEE:
AND OF THAT LIFE, YEA EVERY MOMENT OF IT,
I was required by my Judge to give a strict account;
AND SO WILT THOU:
MY STATE WAS [N] AND MY DUTIES [N],
My honours were but onerous, irksome, and burdensome;
WOEFUL, THAT ANY STILL DO NOT PERCEIVE!
WONDERFUL, THAT ANY DO STILL PURSUE!

§ vii.] A PREPARATION TO DIE WELL AND HAPPILY.

Most rigid was the account required of my stewardship
BY THE GREAT MASTER OF THE FAMILY.
IF THOU ART WISE, TAKE WARNING FROM A FRIEND;
AND DAILY FOR THE LIKE THEE TOO PREPARE:
BE PRUDENT, AND FROM MY PERIL CAUTION LEARN,
AND IT SHALL BE WELL WITH THEE;
SCANTY WAS MY LOT IN THIS WORLD'S GOODS,
Enough, indeed, for life, enough for contentment,
FOR NEED, THOUGH NOT FOR GREEDINESS;
Yet of that scantling, even to the last farthing,
I HAD TO GIVE ACCOUNT.
ON EARTH BELOW, BE IT, MY MEANS WERE LESS,
(BELIEVE ME, I HAVE TRIED,)
THUS IS THE ROAD SURER MADE TO GREATER THINGS ABOVE.
Ye men of riches, ye lay up treasure, and know not for whom,
NOTHING BROUGHT I INTO THIS WORD.
NOTHING I CARRIED OUT:
That which I sent to Heaven before me by poor men's hands,
AND THAT ALONE I FOUND;
And ye too, when ye sleep your sleep, that only shall ye find.
LIVE YE GLADLY, FRIENDS, BUT SEE YE DIE NOT SADLY:
Gladsome once was I with you, now leaving you,
AND BY YOU LEFT,
I HAVE ENTERED ON ETERNITY ALONE.
WHAT YE ARE, I WAS: WHAT I AM, YE SHALL BE;
AND WHO KNOWS WHEN?
TO-MORROW, TO-DAY, THIS VERY HOUR!
BEAR IN MIND MY JUDGMENT, FOR SUCH WILL YOURS BE TOO.

O man, mere bubble, how short is time, how long Eternity!
MOMENTOUS MOMENT, WHEREON HANGS ETERNITY,
ETERNITY OF GLORY OR OF PAIN.
HOLINESS TO GLORY GUIDES, PLEASURE TO PAIN:
CHOOSE THEE OF THE TWAIN.
ONCE PERISH, 'TIS FOR ALL ETERNITY!
HEAR ME, HEAR ME BUT ONCE,
WHO LONG TO HAVE THEE WITH ME IN THE LAND OF LIFE,
ALONG WITH JESU,
In Whom Alone is Safety, and the Life of man that dieth:
Live to Him, Traveller, to Him die, and live for ever;
DIE FIRST TO SIN BEFORE THY DAY OF DEATH,
THAT IS THE HAPPIEST DEATH.
𝕭lessed are the dead that die in the Lord.

𝕮hanks be to 𝕲od.

www.ingramcontent.com/pod-product-compliance
Ingram Content Group UK Ltd.
Pitfield, Milton Keynes, MK11 3LW, UK
UKHW021337180725
6968UKWH00032B/356